Luke

ΠΑΙΔΕΙΑ paideia
COMMENTARIES ON THE NEW TESTAMENT

GENERAL EDITORS

Mikeal C. Parsons, Charles H. Talbert, and Bruce W. Longenecker

ADVISORY BOARD

†Paul J. Achtemeier
Loveday Alexander
C. Clifton Black
Susan R. Garrett
Francis J. Moloney

Luke

MIKEAL C. PARSONS

© 2015 by Mikeal C. Parsons

Published by Baker Academic
a division of Baker Publishing Group
PO Box 6287, Grand Rapids, MI 49516–6287
www.bakeracademic.com

Printed in the United States of America

All rights reserved. No part of this publication may be reproduced, stored in a retrieval system, or transmitted in any form or by any means—for example, electronic, photocopy, recording—without the prior written permission of the publisher. The only exception is brief quotations in printed reviews.

Library of Congress Cataloging-in-Publication Data
Parsons, Mikeal C. (Mikeal Carl), 1957–
   Luke / Mikeal C. Parsons.
      pages cm
   Includes bibliographical references and indexes.
   ISBN 978-0-8010-3190-8 (pbk. : alk. paper)
   1. Bible. Luke—Commentaries. I. Title.
BS2595.53.P37 2015
226.4′07—dc23
                                        2014042999

Translations from the Gospel of Luke (with occasional small adjustments) are from Martin M. Culy, Joshua J. Stigall, and Mikeal C. Parsons, *Luke: A Handbook on the Greek Text*, copyright © 2010 by Baylor University Press. Used by permission.

Unless otherwise indicated, all other Scripture quotations are from the New Revised Standard Version of the Bible, copyright © 1989, by the Division of Christian Education of the National Council of the Churches of Christ in the United States of America. Used by permission. All rights reserved.

Scripture quotations labeled ESV are from The Holy Bible, English Standard Version® (ESV®), copyright © 2001 by Crossway, a publishing ministry of Good News Publishers. Used by permission. All rights reserved. ESV Text Edition: 2007

Scripture quotations labeled KJV are from the King James Version of the Bible.

Scripture quotations labeled REB are from the Revised English Bible © 1989 Oxford University Press and Cambridge University Press.

Scripture quotations labeled RSV are from the Revised Standard Version of the Bible, copyright 1952 [2nd edition, 1971] by the Division of Christian Education of the National Council of the Churches of Christ in the United States of America. Used by permission. All rights reserved.

In keeping with biblical principles of creation stewardship, Baker Publishing Group advocates the responsible use of our natural resources. As a member of the Green Press Initiative, our company uses recycled paper when possible. The text paper of this book is composed in part of post-consumer waste.

15 16 17 18 19 20 21   7 6 5 4 3 2 1

For Heidi

Contents

List of Figures and Tables ix
Foreword xi
Preface xiii
Abbreviations xv

Introduction 3

Luke 1:1–4:13	**Part 1: Jesus's Origins and Training 21**
Luke 1:1–4	Preface 25
Luke 1:5–56	Annunciations: John and Jesus 33
Luke 1:57–2:52	Birth and Training: John and Jesus 44
Luke 3:1–4:13	Beginning Jesus's Public Ministry 62
Luke 4:14–9:50	**Part 2: Jesus's Mighty Words and Deeds in Galilee 77**
Luke 4:14–6:49	Jesus's Mission and Miracles and the Ingathering of His Followers 79
Luke 7:1–8:56	Jesus's Marvelous Words and Deeds 116
Luke 9:1–50	Jesus's Miracles and Mission and the Sending Out of His Followers 145
Luke 9:51–14:35	**Part 3: Jesus's Mighty Words and Deeds along the Way (Part 1) 163**
Luke 9:51–11:13	Beginning the Journey 167
Luke 11:14–13:9	Jesus in Dialogue 189
Luke 13:10–14:35	More Healings and Parables 216

Luke 15:1–19:44	**Part 4: Jesus's Mighty Words and Deeds along the Way (Part 2)** 233
Luke 15:1–32	The Character of God and the "Lost" Parables 235
Luke 16:1–17:10	The Use and Abuse of Wealth 244
Luke 17:11–18:30	Jesus's Teaching about the Kingdom 256
Luke 18:31–19:44	Drawing Near to Jerusalem 273
Luke 19:45–24:53	**Part 5: Jesus in Jerusalem: Teachings, Death, and Resurrection** 287
Luke 19:45–21:38	Jesus in and around the Temple 289
Luke 22:1–23:49	The Meaning and Manner of Jesus's Death 307
Luke 23:50–24:53	Jesus's Burial, Empty Tomb, and Postresurrection Appearances 343

Bibliography 359
Index of Subjects 385
Index of Modern Authors 395
Index of Scripture and Ancient Sources 401

Figures and Tables

Figures

1. Gabriel Speaking to Mary, from the Church of the Annunciation   37
2. Jacopo Pontormo, *Visitation*, SS. Annunziata   43
3. Caesar Augustus Primaporta   50
4. View toward Bethlehem from Herodium   51
5. Grotto Star Church of the Annunciation   52
6. Tiberius, Emperor of Rome from AD 14 to 37   64
7. The Jordan River   65
8. Judean Desert   70
9. Mount of Temptation   71
10. Important Cities in Galilee   78
11. Synagogue Ruins   80
12. Western Shore of the Sea of Galilee   86
13. Modern Village of Nain   121
14. Mosaic below the Altar of the Church at Heptapegon/Tabgha Commemorating the Multiplication of the Loaves and Fishes   148
15. Galilee and Judea in the Time of Jesus   165
16. Typical Roman Road   169
17. Ruins of Chorazin   174
18. Copper Coin of Nero from Sepphoris   202
19. Mosaic of a Hen Gathering Her Chicks in the Chapel of Dominus Flevit   224
20. Millstones from Capernaum   252
21. Dominus Flevit Church, Which Commemorates Jesus Weeping over Jerusalem   284
22. Palestinian Vineyard   293
23. Arch of Titus, Erected in Honor of Titus's Siege of Jerusalem   303

24. Grotto of Gethsemane, Traditional Site of Jesus's Prayer at Gethsemane 318
25. Traditional Site of Jesus's Burial 347

Tables

1. John the Baptist and Jesus Compared 23
2. Structure of Prologue 26
3. Comparing the Temptation Narratives 72
4. Conflict between God's Agents and God's People 72
5. List of Disciples in Synoptic Gospels and Acts 99
6. Progymnastic Topic of Double Encomium *Synkrisis*: Deeds 123
7. Shaping the Story of Jesus's First Followers 301
8. A Triptych of Favorable Acts and Attitudes toward Jesus 341

Foreword

Paideia: Commentaries on the New Testament is a series that sets out to comment on the final form of the New Testament text in a way that pays due attention both to the cultural, literary, and theological settings in which the text took form and to the interests of the contemporary readers to whom the commentaries are addressed. This series is aimed squarely at students—including MA students in religious and theological studies programs, seminarians, and upper-division undergraduates—who have theological interests in the biblical text. Thus, the didactic aim of the series is to enable students to understand each book of the New Testament as a literary whole rooted in a particular ancient setting and related to its context within the New Testament.

The name "Paideia" (Greek for "education") reflects (1) the instructional aim of the series—giving contemporary students a basic grounding in academic New Testament studies by guiding their engagement with New Testament texts; (2) the fact that the New Testament texts as literary unities are shaped by the educational categories and ideas (rhetorical, narratological, etc.) of their ancient writers and readers; and (3) the pedagogical aims of the texts themselves—their central aim being not simply to impart information but to form the theological convictions and moral habits of their readers.

Each commentary deals with the text in terms of larger rhetorical units; these are not verse-by-verse commentaries. This series thus stands within the stream of recent commentaries that attend to the final form of the text. Such reader-centered literary approaches are inherently more accessible to liberal arts students without extensive linguistic and historical-critical preparation than older exegetical approaches, but within the reader-centered world the sanest practitioners have paid careful attention to the extratext of the original readers, including not only these readers' knowledge of the geography, history, and other contextual elements reflected in the text but also their ability to respond correctly to the literary and rhetorical conventions used in the text. Paideia commentaries pay deliberate attention to this extratextual repertoire in order to highlight the ways in which the text is designed to persuade and move its readers. Each rhetorical unit is explored from three angles: (1) introductory matters; (2) tracing the train of thought or narrative or rhetorical flow of the argument; and (3) theological issues raised by the text that are of interest to the contemporary Christian. Thus, the primary focus remains on the text and not its historical context or its interpretation in the secondary literature.

Our authors represent a variety of confessional points of view: Protestant, Catholic, and Orthodox. What they share, beyond being New Testament scholars of national and international repute, is a commitment to reading the biblical text as theological documents within their ancient contexts. Working within the broad parameters described here, each author brings his or her own considerable exegetical talents and deep theological commitments to the task of laying bare the interpretation of Scripture for the faith and practice of God's people everywhere.

Mikeal C. Parsons
Charles H. Talbert
Bruce W. Longenecker

Preface

Paideia *Luke* represents my most recent stop in a lifelong journey with the Lukan writings. Luke's version of the gospel has been my favorite of the four since childhood. My first encounter with Luke in an academic context occurred over thirty years ago in my first semester of seminary in a Greek exegesis course on Luke taught by John Polhill in Louisville, Kentucky, in which we worked carefully through Luke's grammar with I. Howard Marshall's then recently published commentary as our primary guide. My professional career began with a published version of my dissertation, *The Departure of Jesus in Luke-Acts* (1987), followed by *Rethinking the Unity of Luke and Acts* (with Richard I. Pervo, 1993), *Body and Character in Luke and Acts* (2006, 2011) and *Luke: Storyteller, Interpreter, Evangelist* (2007, 2014). A trilogy of works on Luke and visual art, *Illuminating Luke* (2003, 2005, 2007), cowritten with my wife, Heidi Hornik, was sandwiched between two handbooks on the Greek text of Acts (with Martin Culy, 2003) and Luke (with Martin Culy and Joshua Stigall, 2010). Three edited volumes explored the interpretation of Acts in the works of three twentieth-century scholars, *Cadbury, Knox, and Talbert: North American Contributions to the Study of Acts* (with Joseph B. Tyson, 1992); the treatment of Acts among Baptist interpreters, *The Acts of the Apostles: Four Centuries of Baptist Interpretation* (with Beth Barr, Bill Leonard, and Doug Weaver, 2009); and the sea changes that occurred in Acts study in American and European scholarship since Vielhauer, *Paul and the Heritage of Israel: Luke's Narrative Claim upon Paul and Israel's Legacy* (with Daniel Marguerat, David Moessner, and Michael Wolter, 2012). Paideia *Luke* now joins its companion volume Paideia *Acts* (2008) and will be followed finally by *Acts through the Centuries* (with Heidi Hornik, forthcoming) in the Blackwell-Wiley Reception History Commentary Series.

These books represent various attempts to understand Luke and Acts in their originating contexts and their subsequent reception histories and, more importantly, to better know and love the God who is revealed by Luke's Jesus. As of now, I intend these two volumes, Paideia *Luke* and *Acts through the Centuries*, to be the last of my book-length contributions to the study of the Lukan writings, though, God willing, the journey will continue with occasional articles, classroom teaching, and dissertation supervision. It is time (some would say well past time!) to turn my attention and energies to other aspects of the New Testament.

Truth be told, I was not keen to write a commentary on Luke as part of my engagement with the Lukan writings. I felt that the commentary on Acts represented my best effort in that particular genre (and for my "take" on commentary writing that applies also to this volume, I point the reader to the preface of Paideia *Acts*). But our attempts to secure a commentator for Luke failed, and my coeditor, Charles Talbert, and Baker editor, James Ernest, prevailed upon me to accept the assignment. I am very grateful that they did! I also owe a debt of gratitude to the countless graduate students whose own research shaped my reading of Luke, and to Jon Carman and John Duncan who proofread the manuscript at various stages and helped prepare the indexes. I am particularly grateful to the administration and faculty of Baylor University for their continued support of my work. A better work environment I cannot imagine.

Nor can I imagine a more faithful companion in life than Heidi Hornik. Her life as a spouse, mother, daughter, sister, scholar, and teacher is marked by profound integrity. Our personal relationship over the years has been wonderfully rich and, along with our children, a source of deep and abiding joy. Professionally, we have joined together on numerous projects, none more rewarding than the work we have done together on the visual interpretation of Luke and Acts. I happily dedicate this volume to Heidi, the love of my life.

Mikeal C. Parsons
Department of Religion
Baylor University

Abbreviations

General

ca.	*circa*, approximately	no.	number
cf.	*confer*, compare	NT	New Testament
chap(s).	chapter(s)	OT	Old Testament
col(s).	column(s)	prol.	prologue
e.g.	*exempli gratia*, for example	Q	Quelle (hypothetical common source for Matthew and Luke)
Eng.	English		
esp.	especially	sg.	singular
frg(s).	fragment(s)	s.v.	*sub verbo*, under the word
hapax	*hapax legomenon*, term appearing only once	v(v).	verse(s)
		v.l.	*varia lectio*, variant reading
i.e.	*id est*, that is	vol(s).	volume(s)
lit.	literally	x	no. of times a form occurs

Bible Texts, Editions, and Versions

ASV	American Standard Version	NET	The NET Bible (New English Translation)
ESV	English Standard Version		
KJV	King James (Authorized) Version	NIV	New International Version
		NRSV	New Revised Standard Version
LXX	Septuagint, the Greek Bible	REB	Revised English Bible
MT	Masoretic Text, the Hebrew Bible	RSV	Revised Standard Version
NA[28]	Nestle-Aland: *Novum Testamentum Graece*. Edited by Barbara and Kurt Aland et al. 28th ed. Stuttgart: Deutsche Bibelgesellschaft, 2012.	UBS[4]	*The Greek New Testament*. Edited by Barbara and Kurt Aland et al. 4th rev. ed. Stuttgart: Deutsche Bibelgesellschaft/United Bible Societies, 1994.
NASB	New American Standard Bible		

Abbreviations

Ancient Corpora

Old Testament

Gen.	Genesis
Exod.	Exodus
Lev.	Leviticus
Num.	Numbers
Deut.	Deuteronomy
Josh.	Joshua
Judg.	Judges
Ruth	Ruth
1–2 Sam.	1–2 Samuel
1–2 Kings	1–2 Kings
1–2 Chron.	1–2 Chronicles
Ezra	Ezra
Neh.	Nehemiah
Esther	Esther
Job	Job
Ps(s).	Psalm(s)
Prov.	Proverbs
Eccles.	Ecclesiastes
Song	Song of Songs
Isa.	Isaiah
Jer.	Jeremiah
Lam.	Lamentations
Ezek.	Ezekiel
Dan.	Daniel
Hosea	Hosea
Joel	Joel
Amos	Amos
Obad.	Obadiah
Jon.	Jonah
Mic.	Micah
Nah.	Nahum
Hab.	Habakkuk
Zeph.	Zephaniah
Hag.	Haggai
Zech.	Zechariah
Mal.	Malachi

Deuterocanonical Books

1–2 Esd.	1–2 Esdras
1–4 Macc.	1–4 Maccabees
Sir.	Sirach/Ecclesiasticus
Sus.	Susanna
Tob.	Tobit
Wis.	Wisdom of Solomon

New Testament

Matt.	Matthew
Mark	Mark
Luke	Luke
John	John
Acts	Acts
Rom.	Romans
1–2 Cor.	1–2 Corinthians
Gal.	Galatians
Eph.	Ephesians
Phil.	Philippians
Col.	Colossians
1–2 Thess.	1–2 Thessalonians
1–2 Tim.	1–2 Timothy
Titus	Titus
Philem.	Philemon
Heb.	Hebrews
James	James
1–2 Pet.	1–2 Peter
1–3 John	1–3 John
Jude	Jude
Rev.	Revelation

Old Testament Pseudepigrapha

Apoc. El.	Apocalypse of Elijah
2 Bar.	2 Baruch (Syriac Apocalypse)
3 Bar.	3 Baruch (Greek Apocalypse)
1 En.	1 Enoch (Ethiopic Apocalypse)
2 En.	2 Enoch (Slavonic Apocalypse)
4 Ezra	4 Ezra
Jos. Asen.	Joseph and Aseneth
Jub.	Jubilees
L.A.B.	Liber antiquitatum biblicarum (Pseudo-Philo)
L.A.E.	Life of Adam and Eve
Let. Aris.	Letter of Aristeas
Odes Sol.	Odes of Solomon
Pss. Sol.	Psalms of Solomon
Sib. Or.	Sibylline Oracles

T. Ab.	Testament of Abraham	Midr. Ps.	Midrash on Psalms
T. Benj.	Testament of Benjamin	Miqw.	Miqwa'ot
T. Gad	Testament of Gad	Nid.	Niddah
T. Jud.	Testament of Judah	Pesaḥ.	Pesaḥim
T. Levi	Testament of Levi	Qidd.	Qiddušin
T. Mos.	Testament of Moses	Ruth Rab.	Ruth Rabbah
T. Naph.	Testament of Naphtali	Šabb.	Šabbat
T. Sol.	Testament of Solomon	Sanh.	Sanhedrin

Dead Sea Scrolls

Dead Sea Scrolls not listed here are cited by cave number followed by the letter Q (for Qumran) and the document number (e.g., 4Q175).

CD	Damascus Document
1QapGen[ar]	Genesis Apocryphon
1QM	Milḥamah (War Scroll)
1QpHab	Pesher Habakkuk
1QS	Serek Hayaḥad (Rule of the Community/Manual of Discipline)
1QSa	Rule of the Congregation
4QSam[a]	Samuel
11QMelch	Melchizedek
11QtgJob	Targum of Job

Targumic Texts

Tg. Song	Song of Songs Targum

Rabbinic Works

The letters prefixed to the names of Mishnaic tractates indicate the following sources: Mishnah (m.), Tosefta (t.), Babylonian Talmud (b.), and Jerusalem/Palestinian Talmud (y.).

'Abod. Zar.	'Abodah Zarah
'Abot R. Nat.	'Abot de Rabbi Nathan
B. Bat.	Baba Batra
B. Qam.	Baba Qamma
Ber.	Berakot
Esther Rab.	Esther Rabbah
Ketub.	Ketubbot
Lev. Rab.	Leviticus Rabbah

Šeb.	Šebi'it
Šeqal.	Šeqalim
Song Rab.	Song of Songs Rabbah
Soṭah	Soṭah
Sukkah	Sukkah
Ta'an.	Ta'anit
Tamid	Tamid
Ṭehar.	Ṭeharot
Yad.	Yadayim
Yoma	Yoma

Apostolic Fathers

Barn.	Barnabas
1–2 Clem.	1–2 Clement
Did.	Didache
Diogn.	Diognetus
Herm. Sim.	Shepherd of Hermas, Similitude
Ign. Magn.	Ignatius, To the Magnesians
Pol. Phil.	Polycarp, To the Philippians

New Testament Apocrypha and Pseudepigrapha

Acts Phil.	Acts of Philip
Acts Pil.	Acts of Pilate
Apos. Con.	Apostolic Constitutions and Canons
Gos. Pet.	Gospel of Peter
Gos. Thom.	Gospel of Thomas
Inf. Gos. Thom.	Infancy Gospel of Thomas
Prot. Jas.	Protevangelium of James

Ancient Authors

Aelius Aristides
Hier. log.   Hieroi logoi (Sacred Tales)

Aeschylus
Eum.   Eumenides

Abbreviations

AMBROSE
- Cain — *De Cain et Abel* (Cain and Abel)
- Exp. Luc. — *Expositio Evangelii secundum Lucam* (Exposition of the Gospel according to Luke)

APHTHONIUS
- Prog. — *Progymnasmata* (Preliminary Exercises)

APULEIUS
- Flor. — *Florida*
- Metam. — *Metamorphoses* (The Golden Ass)

ARCHILOCHUS
- Carm. — *Carmina*

ARISTOPHANES
- Lys. — *Lysistrata*

ARISTOTLE
- Eth. eud. — *Ethica eudemia* (Eudemian Ethics)
- Eth. nic. — *Ethica nichomachea* (Nichomachean Ethics)
- Hist. an. — *Historia animalium* (History of Animals)
- Rhet. — *Rhetorica* (Rhetoric)

ARRIAN
- Epict. diss. — *Epicteti dissertationes* (Discourses of Epictetus)

ATHENAEUS
- Deipn. — *Deipnosophistae* (Banquet of the Learned)

AUGUSTINE
- Civ. — *De civitate Dei* (The City of God)
- Cons. — *De consensu evangelistarum* (Harmony of the Gospels)
- Serm. — *Sermones* (Sermons)

CAELIUS AURELIANUS
- Tard. pass. — *Tardarum passionum* (On Chronic Diseases)

CELSUS
- Med. — *De medicina* (On Medicine)

CHARITON
- Chaer. — *De Chaerea et Callirhoe* (Chaereas and Callirhoe)

CICERO
- Amic. — *De amicitia* (On Friendship)
- De or. — *De oratore* (On the Orator)
- Div. — *De divinatione* (On Divination)
- Inv. — *De inventione rhetorica* (On Rhetorical Invention)
- Top. — *Topica* (Topics)

CLEMENT OF ALEXANDRIA
- Strom. — *Stromata* (Miscellanies)

CORPUS HIPPOCRATICUM
- M. sacr. — *De morbo sacro* (The Sacred Disease)

CYRIL OF ALEXANDRIA
- Comm. Luke — *Commentary on Luke*

CYRIL OF JERUSALEM
- Catech. — *Catechetical Lectures*

DEMETRIUS
- Eloc. — *De elocutione* (On Style)

DEMOSTHENES
- 1 Aristog. — *In Aristogitonem* (Against Aristogeiton)
- Or. — *Orationes* (Orations)

DIO CASSIUS
- Hist. Rom. — *Historia Romana* (Roman History)

DIO CHRYSOSTOM
- Charid. — *Charidemus* (Or. 30)
- Or. — *Orationes* (Orations)
- Ven. — *Venator* (Or. 7)

DIODORUS SICULUS
- Bibl. hist. — *Bibliotheca historica* (Library of History)

Diogenes Laertius
Vit. phil.   *Vitae philosophorum* (*Lives of the Philosophers*)

Dionysius of Halicarnassus
Ant. rom.   *Antiquitates romanae* (*Roman Antiquities*)
Thuc.   *De Thucydide* (*On Thucydides*)

Epictetus
Diatr.   *Diatribai* (*Dissertationes*)

Epiphanius
Pan.   *Panarion* (*Refutation of All Heresies*)

Euripides
Alc.   *Alcestis*
Hipp.   *Hippolytus*

Eusebius
Hist. eccl.   *Historia ecclesiastica* (*Ecclesiastical History*)

Galen
On Progn.   *On Prognosis*

Heliodorus
Aeth.   *Aethiopica*

Herodotus
Hist.   *Historiae* (*Histories*)

Hesiod
Op.   *Opera et dies* (*Works and Days*)

Hippolytus
Trad. ap.   *Traditio apostolica* (*The Apostolic Tradition*)

Homer
Il.   *Iliad*
Od.   *Odyssey*

Horace
Carm.   *Carmina* (*Odes*)
Ep.   *Epistulae* (*Epistles*)
Sat.   *Satirae* (*Satires*)

Irenaeus
Haer.   *Adversus haereses* (*Against Heresies*)

Isocrates
Nic.   *Nicocles*

Jerome
Comm. Isa.   *Commentariorum in Isaiam* (*Commentary on Isaiah*)
Epist.   *Epistulae* (*Letters*)
Tract. Ps.   *Tractatus in Psalmos* (*Tractate on Psalms*)
Vir. ill.   *De viris illustribus* (*On Illustrious Men*)

John Chrysostom
Hom. Gal.   *Homiliae in epistulam ad Galatas commentarius* (*Commentary on the Epistle to the Galatians*)
Hom. Matt.   *Homiliae in Matthaeum* (*Homilies on Matthew*)
Hom. Rom.   *Homiliae in epistulam ad Romanos* (*Homilies on the Epistle to the Romans*)

Josephus
Ag. Ap.   *Against Apion*
Ant.   *Antiquities of the Jews*
J.W.   *Jewish War*
Life   *The Life*

Justin Martyr
1 Apol.   *Apologia i* (*First Apology*)
2 Apol.   *Apologia ii* (*Second Apology*)
Dial.   *Dialogus cum Tryphone* (*Dialogue with Trypho*)

Juvenal
Sat.   *Satirae* (*Satires*)

Livy
Hist.   *Historiae* (*Histories*)

Longus
Daphn.   *Daphnis and Chloe*

Abbreviations

LUCIAN
- *Symp.* — Symposium

MELITO
- *Frag.* — Fragments

MENANDER
- *Dysk.* — Dyskolos

NICOLAUS
- *Prog.* — Progymnasmata (Preliminary Exercises)

ORIGEN
- *Cels.* — Contra Celsum (Against Celsus)
- *Comm. Jo.* — Commentarii in evangelium Joannis (Commentary on the Gospel of John)
- *Comm. Matt.* — Commentarium in evangelium Matthaei (Commentary on the Gospel of Matthew)
- *Fr. Luc.* — Fragmenta in Lucam (Fragments on Luke)
- *Hom. Jer.* — Homiliae in Jeremiam (Homilies on Jeremiah)
- *Hom. Luc.* — Homiliae in Lucam (Homilies on Luke)
- *Mart.* — Exhortatio ad martyrium (Exhortation to Martyrdom)

OVID
- *Metam.* — Metamorphoses

PAUSANIAS
- *Descr.* — Graeciae descriptio (Description of Greece)

PETRONIUS
- *Sat.* — Satyricon

PHILO
- *Abr.* — De Abrahamo (On the Life of Abraham)
- *Decal.* — De decalogo (On the Decalogue)
- *Flacc.* — In Flaccum (Against Flaccus)
- *Her.* — Quis rerum divinarum heres sit (Who Is the Heir?)
- *Legat.* — Legatio ad Gaium (On the Embassy to Gaius)
- *Mos.* — De vita Mosis (On the Life of Moses)
- *Sacr.* — De sacrificiis Abelis et Caini (On the Sacrifices of Cain and Abel)
- *Spec.* — De specialibus legibus (On the Special Laws)
- *Virt.* — De virtutibus (On the Virtues)

PHILOSTRATUS
- *Vit. Apoll.* — Vita Apollonii (Life of Apollonius of Tyana)
- *Vit. soph.* — Vitae sophistarum (Lives of the Sophists)

PHOTIUS
- *Lex.* — Lexicon

PLATO
- *Apol.* — Apologia (Apology of Socrates)
- *Euthyphr.* — Euthyphro
- *Gorg.* — Gorgias
- *Resp.* — Respublica (Republic)
- *Soph.* — Sophista (Sophist)

PLAUTUS
- *Mil. glor.* — Miles gloriosus (The Swaggering Soldier)

PLINY THE ELDER
- *Nat.* — Naturalis historia (Natural History)

PLUTARCH
- *Adul. amic.* — De adulatore et amico (How to Tell a Flatterer from a Friend)
- *Aem.* — Aemilius Paullus
- *Alc.* — Alcibiades
- *Apoph. Lac.* — Apophthegmata laconica (Sayings of the Spartans)
- *Cohib. ira* — De cohibenda ira (On the Control of Anger)
- *Cons. Apoll.* — Consolatio ad Apollonium (Letter of Condolence to Apollonius)

Cor.	Marcius Coriolanus	Ep.	Epistulae morales (Moral Letters)
Cupid. divit.	De cupiditate divitiarum (On the Love of Wealth)	Lucil.	Ad Lucilium (To Lucilius)
Curios.	De curiositate (On Being a Busybody)	Tro.	Troades (The Trojan Women)

SEXTUS EMPIRICUS

Eum.	Eumenes	Pyr.	Pyrrhoniae hypotyposes (Outlines of Pyrrhonism)
Fac.	De facie in orbe lunae (On the Face in the Moon)		
Lib. ed.	De liberis educandis (On the Education of Children)		

SOPHOCLES

		El.	Elektra
Luc.	Lucullus		
Rom.	Romulus		

STOBAEUS

Quaest. rom.	Quaestiones romanae et graecae (Roman and Greek Questions)	Flor.	Florilegium (Anthology)

STRABO

		Geogr.	Geographica (Geography)
Sept. sap. conv.	Septem Sapientium Convivium (Dinner of the Seven Wise Men)		

SUETONIUS

		Aug.	Divus Augustus (Divine Augustus)
Them.	Themistocles		
Tim.	Timolion	Gramm.	De grammaticis (On Grammarians)

POLEMO

Phys.	De physiognomia (On Physiognomy)	Vesp.	Vespasianus (Vespasian)

TACITUS

		Ann.	Annales (Annals)

POLLUX

Onom.	Onomasticon	Dial.	Dialogus de oratoribus (Dialogue on Oratory)

POLYBIUS

Hist.	Historiae (Histories)	Hist.	Historiae (Histories)

TERTULLIAN

PSEUDO-ARISTOTLE

		Idol.	De idololatria (Idolatry)
Physiog.	Physiognomonica (Physiognomics)	Marc.	Adversus Marcionem (Against Marcion)

PSEUDO-HERMOGENES (PS.-HERMOGENES)

Prog.	Progymnasmata (Preliminary Exercises)	Praescr.	De praescriptione haereticorum (Prescription against Heretics)

THEON

QUINTILIAN

		Prog.	Progymnasmata (Preliminary Exercises)
Decl.	Declamationes (Declamations)		
Inst.	Institutio oratoria (Institutes of Oratory)		

VARRO

		Ling.	De lingua latina (On the Latin Language)

SENECA

Ben.	De beneficiis (On Benefits)		
Brev. vit.	De brevitate vitae (On the Shortness of Life)		

VIRGIL

		Aen.	Aeneid
		Georg.	Georgica

Xenophon
Hell.	Hellenica
Mem.	Memorabilia

Xenophon of Ephesus
Anth.	An Ephesian Tale of Anthia and Habrocomes

Ancient Collections and Anonymous Works

Anon. Lat.	Anonymous Latin treatise *De physiognomonia*
Hom. Hym.	Homeric Hymns
Res gest. divi Aug.	Res gestae divi Augusti
Rh. Al.	Rhetorica ad Alexandrum
Rhet. Her.	Rhetorica ad Herennium

Series, Collections, and Reference Works

ANF	Alexander Roberts, James Donaldson, and A. Cleveland Coxe, eds. *The Ante-Nicene Fathers*. 10 vols. Buffalo: Christian Literature, 1885–97. Reprint, Peabody, MA: Hendrickson, 1994.
APOT	R. H. Charles, ed. *The Apocrypha and Pseudepigrapha of the Old Testament*. 2 vols. Oxford: Oxford University Press, 1913.
BDAG	W. Bauer, F. W. Danker, W. F. Arndt, and F. W. Gingrich. *A Greek-English Lexicon of the New Testament and Other Early Christian Literature*. 3rd ed. Chicago: University of Chicago Press, 2000.
BDF	*A Greek Grammar of the New Testament and Other Early Christian Literature*. Edited by F. Blass and A. Debrunner. Translated and revised by Robert W. Funk. Chicago: University of Chicago Press, 1961.
FC	Fathers of the Church: A New Translation. Washington, DC: Catholic University of America Press, 1947–.
IG	*Inscriptiones graecae*. Editio minor. Berlin: de Gruyter, 1924–.
I.Priene	F. H. von Gaertringen and C. J. Fredrich. *Die Inschriften von Priene*. Berlin: de Gruyter, 1968.
L&N	J. P. Louw and Eugene A. Nida. *Greek-English Lexicon of the New Testament: Based on Semantic Domains*. 2 vols. New York: United Bible Societies, 1988.
MM	J. H. Moulton and G. Milligan. *The Vocabulary of the Greek Testament*. 1930. Reprint, Peabody, MA: Hendrickson, 1997.
OTP	James H. Charlesworth, ed. *Old Testament Pseudepigrapha*. 2 vols. Garden City, NY: Doubleday, 1983–85.
PL	Patrologia latina [= Patrologiae cursus completus: Series latina]. Edited by J.-P. Migne. 221 vols. Paris, 1844–65 (with indexes).
SEG	Supplementum epigraphicum graecum
SIG	*Sylloge inscriptionum graecarum*. Edited by W. Dittenberger. 4 vols. 3rd ed. Leipzig: Hirzel, 1915–24.
Str-B	H. L. Strack and P. Billerbeck. *Kommentar zum Neuen Testament aus Talmud und Midrasch*. 6 vols. Munich: Beck, 1922–61.
TDNT	*Theological Dictionary of the New Testament*. Edited by Gerhard Kittel and Gerhard Friedrich. Translated by G. W. Bromiley. 10 vols. Grand Rapids: Eerdmans, 1964–76.

Luke

Introduction

The Gospel of Luke has certainly not suffered from any lack of scholarly attention over the past few decades. Commentaries continue to pour forth (Bock 1994–96; Fitzmyer 1981–85; Johnson 1991; Culpepper 1995; Green 1997; Talbert 1982, 2002; Vinson 2008; D. Garland 2011; Carroll 2012). This introduction aims to address topics necessary to orient the reader in using the commentary as a guide for interpreting Luke's Gospel. Some of these issues are typically associated with critical introductions (authorship, date, place, etc.); others are not. The focus of the introduction, as with the commentary, is on the text and its interpretation (for more on interpretation see Bovon 2002–13; Parsons 2008a, 7–11).

To orient the user of this commentary, it is helpful to speak of the now familiar relationship among author, text, and audience, adjusted here to account for the particular shape of composition and reception of ancient texts.

Model of Communication for Reading Ancient Literature

Author(s) → Scribe(s) → Text → Lector → Audience

The process of composing texts in antiquity often involved a scribe, whose participation in the process may have varied from that of being a kind of human "word processor" who simply wrote down everything dictated by the author to the role of coauthor of the document. The role(s) of the scribe has been rather fully explored in Pauline studies (O'Connor 1995). Most likely, if Luke did use a scribe it would have been for the purposes of writing down his dictation.

The other end of the model likewise represents a complicated situation. It is widely recognized in NT studies that early Christian literature would have been read to a congregation or gathering of Christians by one appointed to that task, usually referred to as the "reader" or "lector" (see Shiell 2004). The role of the reader was later institutionalized in the church in the form of the lector, a minor office in the church (see Tertullian, *Praescr.* 41; Hippolytus, *Trad. ap.* 1.12). We find references to "readers" and "public reading" in the various types of literature in the NT (Mark 13:14; 1 Tim. 4:13; Rev. 1:3; cf. Gamble 1995, 218–24). At the beginning of the Christian movement, then, those tapped for the task of public reading, whether of the Jewish Scriptures or of emerging Christian literature, would have been chosen on the basis of their gifts for public speaking. In addition to the reader being literate, this person's gifts would have included a strong voice and most likely some training in rhetoric. Among the rhetoricians, a strong voice was a natural gift. The reader of early Christian texts presumably had the "gift" of public speaking. The result of this idea being translated into the Christian thoughtworld was that effective public speaking was construed as evidence of a spiritual gift (*Apos. Con.* 8.22).

In the Roman period, training in rhetoric began in elementary school and continued, for those interested in pursuing a career in politics, through several advanced levels. We may assume that the first lectors or readers of early Christian literature were among those most highly trained in the practice of rhetoric. One bit of evidence for this point is found in Irenaeus, who claims that some heretics "do not know how to read Paul"; he gives as an example the need to clarify the use of *hyperbaton*, the transposition of words, in 2 Thess. 2:8 (*Haer.* 3.7.2). Irenaeus, at least, presumes that the "orthodox" reader will have enough rhetorical training to avoid some basic mistakes in delivery.

Relatively little attention is paid in this commentary to the actual "performance" of Luke's Gospel by the reader or lector, but the user of the commentary is well advised always to keep this fact in mind: the author of Luke expected his audience to experience the text aurally and communally (on the burgeoning field of "performance criticism," see Shiner 2003). For this reason, the commentary refers to "audience" or "authorial audience" (see Culy 2010) rather than "reader," not only in order to respect the role reserved for the "reader" or "lector" who "performs" the text by reading (or perhaps reciting) it aloud, but also to underscore the aural and communal context within which Luke expected his work to be experienced, and within which, in practice, it was. One imagines, then, a social context of early Christian worship in which the Third Gospel, as one among several early Christian texts, was read aloud as part of a Christian meeting, perhaps after a meal (following the pattern of the Hellenistic symposium), both for edification and for entertainment. The use of Luke as the textual basis for Christian proclamation did not arise until later.

The aim of this commentary, in keeping with the overall goals of the series in which it is published, is to read the final form of Luke's Gospel within the first-century historical, cultural, rhetorical, and theological contexts in which it was composed, as well as the first half of the first-century context, which it purports to recount. The focus here is on the earliest reception of the final form of Luke. The rubrics of author, text, and audience thus serve as helpful reminders of the importance of the first communication between author and audience in the form of a written text within its historical context. Exploring the author, in terms of issues of composition, and the audience, in terms of its reception and formation, allows the focus to remain on the text itself, not as an autonomous entity removed from its historical moorings but rather as a written communication between author and audience deeply embedded and implicated within its historical circumstances. The history of interpretation plays a role, in the sense that knowledge of it can give clues as to the important issues raised by the text, as they have been understood over the history of the reception of the Third Gospel within the Christian community. Contextualizing the text in this way also allows theological issues of interest to contemporary Christian communities to arise naturally out of the exegetical treatment.

Assessing the Traditions of Authorship

Over the centuries, numerous traditions have evolved around this somewhat shadowy evangelist: Luke is credited with writing not only his Gospel but the NT book of Acts as well (on the assessment of the literary relationship of Luke and Acts, see below). He was, according to tradition, a physician and a friend of Paul, and he is described as a gentile writing for a gentile audience. The textual evidence suggests that these stories are very early, dating to the first and second century. By the fourth century, these traditions were well enough established to be summarized by the historian Eusebius and the church father Jerome (see the sidebar, "The Infancy of Luke's Own Narrative").

The Gospel title—*Kata Loukan* ([The Gospel] according to Luke)—appears at the end of the oldest extant manuscript of the Gospel of Luke, a papyrus known as 𝔓^{75}, now in the Bodmer Library in Geneva. But this fragmentary manuscript dates only to about AD 175 to 225, or 100 to 125 years after the Gospel is thought to have been written. The title probably reflects the oldest tradition, linking an author named Luke to the writing of the Third Gospel. The reliability of this tradition, however, is uncertain. What else do we know about the author?

In the prologue to the Gospel the author seems to identify himself as a second-generation Christian relying on others' eyewitness testimonies (see comments on Luke 1:1–4). He cannot therefore be counted among the apostles. Furthermore, throughout the book of Acts, when describing Paul's activities the narrator occasionally shifts from the third- to the first-person plural "we" (Acts 16:10–17; 20:5–15; 21:1–18; 27:1–28:16). For example, of Paul's final trip to Jerusalem, he writes: "When we found a ship bound for Phoenicia, we went on board and set sail. We came in sight of Cyprus; and leaving it on our

> ### The Infancy of Luke's Own Narrative
>
> The biography of Luke developed early. By the early fourth century, Eusebius—the bishop of Caesarea and the father of church history—had identified most of the traditions that scholars puzzle over today. In his *Ecclesiastical History* (ca. 312–24), Eusebius wrote:
>
>> "Luke, being by birth one of the people of Antioch, by profession a physician, having been with Paul a good deal, and having associated intimately with the rest of the apostles, has left us examples of the art of curing souls that he obtained from them in two divinely inspired books—the Gospel, which he testifies that he wrote out even as they delivered to him who from the beginning were eyewitnesses and ministers of the word, all of whom [or "all of which facts"] he says he had followed even from the beginning, and the Acts of the Apostles, which he composed, receiving his information with his own eyes, no longer by hearsay." (*Hist. eccl.* 3.4, trans. Cadbury 1922a, 233–35)
>
> The church father Jerome (347–420) could add few details to Eusebius's account:
>
>> "The third [evangelist], Luke the physician, by birth a Syrian of Antioch, 'whose praise is in the gospel,' and himself a disciple of the apostle Paul, composed his book in the districts of Achaia and Boeotia, investigating some things from an earlier time, and, as he himself confesses in his preface, describing what he had heard rather than what he had seen." (*Comm. Matt.* preface, trans. Cadbury 1922a, 239)

left, we sailed to Syria and landed at Tyre, because the ship was to unload its cargo there. We looked up the disciples and stayed there for seven days. Through the Spirit they told Paul not to go into Jerusalem" (Acts 21:2–4). The church father Irenaeus was one of the first to interpret these "we" passages as evidence that Luke was a companion of Paul: "But that this Luke was inseparable from Paul and was his fellow-worker in the gospel he himself makes clear, not boasting of it, but compelled to do so by truth itself" (*Haer.* 3.14.1, trans. Cadbury 1922a, 213).

Modern scholars, however, are deeply divided regarding the significance of the "we" passages: Some argue that the first-person narration derives from diary material and demonstrates participation by the Gospel writer (or at least by the author of the diary material) (see Hemer 1989). Others argue that the author or a later editor is responsible for creating the first-person narration and that the "we" passages may not be used as evidence that the author was an inseparable or even sometime companion of Paul. Based on apparent tensions between the Lukan Paul and the Paul of the epistles, some have questioned whether the author of Acts knew Paul at all, much less was his traveling companion (see Vielhauer 1963 and the recent assessment of his work in Moessner et al. 2012). For example, Luke and Paul give conflicting accounts regarding the number and nature of Paul's visits to Jerusalem, and (except in Acts 20:28) the Lukan Paul never refers to the death of Jesus as a saving event—a central point in the Letters of Paul (Rom. 3:25; 1 Cor. 15:3; 2 Cor. 5:21; etc.). Still other scholars have argued that first-person narration was simply a common literary device in ancient sea-voyage literature and may not be used as evidence that the author was an eyewitness to the events narrated (Robbins 1978). None of these views has won a clear majority of support.

The name *Loukas* appears three times in letters attributed to Paul. This Luke, however, is never explicitly identified as the author of the Third Gospel. In a letter to Philemon, a Christian living in Colossae in Asia Minor, Paul lists a man named Luke as one of his "fellow workers" (Philem. 24); in an open letter to the Christian community of Colossae, the author sends greetings from "Luke, the beloved physician" (Col. 4:14). Finally, the author of the Pastoral Epistles, most likely one of Paul's followers who writes in Paul's voice, inserts these words in 2 Timothy: "Do your best to come to me soon, for Demas, in love with this present world, has deserted me and gone to Thessalonica; Crescens has gone to Galatia, Titus to Dalmatia. *Only Luke is with me.* Get Mark and bring him with you, for he is useful in my ministry" (2 Tim. 4:9–11; emphasis added). These scant references have augmented—or simply reflect—Luke's reputation as one of Paul's most faithful companions.

These references also lead us to the next assertion traditionally made about Luke: he was a physician, as is suggested by Col. 4:14. This too is repeated in the writings of Irenaeus and in the Muratorian Canon but has received mixed reviews in recent scholarship. Late in the nineteenth century, William K. Hobart searched the healing stories in Luke for what he believed were medical terms, such as "crippled," "pregnant," and "abscess," or ordinary words used in a "medical" sense. From this "internal evidence" Hobart (1882) concluded that Luke and Acts were written by the same person, and that the writer was a medical man. Henry Cadbury soon dismantled this argument by demonstrating that the terms on Hobart's lists occur in the Septuagint, Josephus, Plutarch, and Lucian, all nonmedical writers. Cadbury concluded, "The style of Luke bears no more evidence of medical training and interest than does the language of other writers who were not physicians" (1920, 50). In a tongue-in-cheek lexical note titled "Luke and the Horse-Doctors," Cadbury later (1933) showed that Luke's vocabulary shows a remarkable similarity with the corpus of writings of ancient veterinarians. His refutation was so effective that he virtually eliminated this special pleading to a so-called medical vocabulary (Fitzmyer 1981–85, 1:51–53). His students used to jest that Cadbury earned his doctorate by taking Luke's away. Cadbury (1920), however, remained agnostic regarding the identification of the author of the Third Gospel with Luke the physician.

The long-dominant view that Luke was a gentile has roots that reach back as far as the second century to an extrabiblical text, *Prologue to the Gospels*. This text, also known as the *Anti-Marcionite Prologue*, contained a description of Luke that Eusebius, among others, followed: "Luke was a Syrian of Antioch, by profession a physician, the disciple of the apostles, and later a follower of Paul" (trans. Fitzmyer 1981–85, 1:38; see Gutwenger 1946, 393–409).

The view that Luke was a gentile does not rest solely on the tradition that he was an Antiochene, however. Rather, some accept Col. 4:14 as identifying Luke as a gentile. In the preceding verses of this letter, the author lists a number of Jews who worked with Paul: "Aristarchus my fellow prisoner greets you, as does Mark the cousin of Barnabas, concerning whom you have received instructions—if he comes to you, welcome him. And Jesus who is called Justus greets you. *These are the only ones of the circumcision among my co-workers for the kingdom of God*, and they have been a comfort to me" (Col. 4:10–11; emphasis added). The author then goes on to list a handful of other workers who, many readers presume, must be not Jews but "Greeks." He includes "Luke, the beloved physician" in this latter list (Col. 4:14).

Recently, however, a small but vocal minority has raised the possibility that Luke was Jewish, or at least deeply interested in Judaism (see Jervell 1972; Tiede 1980). They assume that the Luke referred to in Colossians was either a "God-fearer" with deep Jewish interests or not the same person as the author of the Gospel. This view too has ancient roots. In the fourth century, Bishop Epiphanius of Cyprus suggested that Luke was one of the seventy disciples sent out by Jesus (Luke 10) and was thus presumably Jewish (Epiphanius, *Pan.* 51.110).

Some have assumed that if Luke was from such a well-known Greco-Roman city as Antioch, he must have been a gentile. However, Antioch did have a Jewish community: Josephus notes that the first Seleucid king, Seleucus Nicator (ca. 358–281 BC), who made Antioch his capital, granted the local Jews citizenship in gratitude for their having fought with the Greek armies. Thus, even the tradition that Luke was from Antioch, an "Antiochene," does not preclude his being Jewish (Josephus, *Ag. Ap.* 2.39). And according to John Chrysostom, who served as deacon of Antioch in the late fourth century AD, the city had several synagogues. The archaeological evidence of the Jewish community is limited, however, to a small stone fragment of a menorah and a lead curse tablet referring to the biblical God Yahweh. Furthermore, the narratives of Luke and Acts themselves have led scholars like David Tiede to conclude that "the polemics, scriptural arguments, and 'proofs' which are rehearsed in Luke-Acts are part of an intrafamily struggle [among Jews] that, in the wake of the destruction of the temple, is deteriorating into a fight over who is really the faithful 'Israel'" (Tiede 1980, 7).

Luke's literary artistry has long been recognized. The early church scholar Jerome (ca. 347–420) asserts that Luke's "language in the Gospel, as well as in the Acts of the Apostles, that is, in both volumes is more elegant, and smacks of secular eloquence" (*Comm. Isa.* 3.6, trans. Cadbury 1922a, 235–37). This view of Luke's literary prowess continued through the medieval and

Renaissance periods. In the thirteenth century, the writer Jacobus de Voragine (1229–98) praised Luke's writing as clear, pleasing, and touching: "His gospel is permeated by much truth, filled with much usefulness, adorned with much charm, and confirmed by many authorities" (*Golden Legend*, 2.251, trans. Ryan 1995). In ancient rhetorical traditions, clarity was often linked to vividness (appealing to the eye and not the ear; Quintilian, *Inst.* 8.3.62; *Rhet. Her.* 4.39.51). Perhaps Luke's vivid prose combined with his careful attention to Mary's story commended him as the obvious choice to be the sole portrayer of Mary's true likeness.

Physician, gentile or Jew, companion of Paul, writer of the Third Gospel and Acts—what one thinks about the identity of Luke rests in large part on one's assessment of these traditions. Did the early church have information about the identity of the author of Luke and Acts that is no longer available to us? Or did someone looking to identify the otherwise anonymous author simply deduce Luke's identity from the text of the NT?

Presumably the Gospel's prologue, where the author seems to identify himself as a second-generation Christian, excludes identifying the author as an apostle (and thus makes the choice of a "lesser" figure almost inevitable). The "we" sections in Acts seem to demand someone who was a companion of Paul, and Luke the beloved physician emerges as a likely—though, importantly, not the only—candidate.

However, we must consider the stability of the tradition that identifies Luke as the author (see Hengel 2000). Strictly speaking, the Third Gospel is an anonymous document, making no internal claims about its authorship. That all testimony agrees in identifying the author as a relatively obscure man named Luke is no trivial matter. Regardless of his identity, the author of Luke and Acts has left for us works that remain two of the most significant contributions by an early Christian to our understanding of the founder of Christianity and his first followers.

The Text of Luke and Issues of Intertextuality

Narrowly speaking, critical introductions to the "text" of Luke usually include discussions of the manuscript evidence and issues of textual criticism. While the term "text" is used here more broadly to speak of issues related to the work itself (rather than the author or audience), it is wise to begin with this more narrow understanding.

Occasionally, the commentary will treat textual variants as they might shed light on the meaning of a particular passage (e.g., see esp. the treatment of the notoriously difficult problems associated with Luke 22:43–44; for other textual issues in Luke see Culy, Parsons, and Stigall 2010), but the text of the Third Gospel does not have the same colorful textual history as does its sequel, the Acts of the Apostles (see below and Parsons 2008a, 11–15). For that reason and for the most part, I follow the text of NA[28]/UBS[4] in the commentary. There is one notable set of exceptions that occur mostly in Luke 24 and are part of a larger and fascinating chapter in the history of the text of the NT. Based on the work of Michael Martin (2005), who has revived the insights of B. F. Westcott and F. J. A. Hort (1881, 176), I follow the shorter text in seven places in Luke 24:

24:3: The word "Lord" is added before Jesus in "they did not find the body of Jesus."

24:5b: The sentence "He is not here; he has been raised" is added after the question "Why are you looking for the living among the dead?"

24:12: The entire verse is added: "Then Peter got up and ran to the tomb. When he bent over [to look inside], he saw the pieces of linen cloth lying there alone. Then he went home, amazed at what had happened."

24:36b: The clause "And he said to them, 'Peace be with you!'" is added at the end of the verse.

24:40: The entire verse is added: "When he had said this, he showed them his hands and feet."

24:51b: The clause "and he was brought up into heaven" is added at the end of the verse.

24:52: The phrase "after they had worshiped him" is added toward the beginning of the verse.

Luke, Acts, and the Other Gospels

There are also questions regarding the literary relationship between Luke and Acts that the widespread consensus that the author of Luke also wrote the Acts of the Apostles does not necessarily clarify (interest in the question of unity has reemerged since Parsons and Pervo 1993; see Rowe 2005, 2007; Johnson 2005; Bockmuehl 2005; Bird 2007; Spencer 2007). Each document has its own distinct reception history (see Gregory 2003, 300–301), a point that speaks against a precanonical "narrative" unity of the two documents. For example, the evidence of early Gospel collections fails to support an original unity (Parsons and Pervo 1993). The oldest copy of the fourfold Gospel, $\mathfrak{P}^{45}$ (ca. AD 200), also contains Acts but has the Gospels in the traditional order: Matthew, Mark, Luke, and John. Codex Bezae preserves the so-called Western order of the two apostles (Matthew and John), followed by the two "apostolic companions" (Luke and Mark). Here Luke and Acts could easily have been placed together, but Mark stands between Luke and Acts. Thus a great opportunity was missed to place Luke last in the order and alongside Acts, preserving both the tetraevangelium *and* the unity of Luke and Acts. The Cheltenham Canon (ca. 360) and the stichometry provided in Codex Claromontanus (seventh century) place Luke last among the Gospels, but Acts comes after the Pauline Epistles in the former and at the end of the NT books in the latter. 𝔓⁷⁴ (seventh century) puts Acts with the General Epistles (see Parsons and Pervo 1993, 22). The inescapable conclusion is that there is simply no manuscript evidence in which Luke and Acts ever appear side by side, ready for reading as one, continuous whole. Some have countered that the reception history does not necessarily reflect authorial intention, and in the example of Luke/Acts, most certainly does not (Johnson 2005). But is this necessarily the case?

That the textual history of Luke is distinct from that of Luke's other volume, the Acts of the Apostles, is not always fully appreciated in discussions of the relationship between Luke and Acts from the point of view of *intentio operis* (the intention of the work). Bruce Metzger has noted: "The text of the book of the Acts of the Apostles circulated in the early church in two quite distinct forms, commonly called the Alexandrian and the Western" (1994, 222). The same cannot be said about Luke's Gospel. Furthermore, while the Western tradition of Acts shares features with that of Luke (as well as of the other Gospels and the Pauline corpus), "there are variants of another kind, peculiar to the Western text of Acts" (1994, 233). These variants

> include many additions, long and short, of a substantive nature that reveal the hand of a reviser. . . . The reviser, who was obviously a meticulous and well-informed scholar, eliminated seams and gaps and added historical, biographical, and geographical details. Apparently, the reviser did his work at an early date, before the text of Acts had come to be generally regarded as a sacred text that must be preserved inviolate. (Metzger 1994, 233)

Regardless of how one accounts for the origins of these two textual traditions of Acts (Metzger 1994, 225–32), their existence provides further support for the conclusion that Acts has its own distinctive transmission history and points to a circulation of the text of Acts independent of the Third Gospel.

The little evidence that we do have, then, does *not* suggest that these two documents, Luke and Acts, were published together by Luke as one volume or even published at the same time, only later to be separated from each other with the emergence of the fourfold Gospel. Rather, the manuscript traditions suggest two distinct transmission histories, one for the Gospel and one for Acts. At the least, this implies that the two were published and disseminated separately and, quite probably, at different times. Furthermore, there is nothing in the Lukan prologue (1:1–4) that suggests that Luke already had Acts in mind when he wrote the Third Gospel (see Parsons 2007, 40–50). Thus, while reference will be made in the commentary to places in Acts that, in retrospect and after both documents were composed and circulated, enrich our reading of the Gospel, these points of contact are not based on the assumption that they were available to the authorial audience.

The prologue to the Third Gospel also suggests that Luke writes, in part, because previous attempts at Gospels have proven, in his opinion, unsuccessful in producing a rhetorically persuasive narrative (see Parsons 2007, 40–50). On the basis of Luke's reference to "many" other attempts to write accounts of Jesus's life, it seems that a plurality of Gospels was already a reality by the time the Third Gospel was written (probably in the 80s or early 90s). The number and content of these other "Gospels" is unknown; the "many" (even if hyperbolic) may have included "heretics" who "used traditional material in the interest of their own perverse propaganda" (Danker 1988, 24). In this sense, Luke may have been partially successful in replacing some of these previous "attempts," of which he is critical (and thus contributed to the loss of some early accounts that are no longer extant). Still, Luke probably did not think his version of the Jesus story would replace *all* other versions. And even if he did, by the time he published Acts, he would have known that this was not the case. His account of "the things accomplished" (Luke 1:1) had taken its place alongside other versions. Thus, when Luke wrote Acts he did so in the full knowledge that it would be read as a "sequel," not just to his Gospel, but to a plurality of narratives about Jesus, what would later be dubbed simply as "the gospel" (of which there emerged four authoritative versions, but still of ONE gospel). These Gospels (Luke and Mark and an indeterminate number of others) were already being read together in Christian worship by the time Acts was published (Parsons 2009).

From a plurality of Gospels would eventually emerge the notion of one Gospel in four versions, indirectly attested by the longer ending of Mark, which presumes a fourfold Gospel in the early second century (see Kelhoffer 2000). When canonizers/collectors placed Acts after the fourfold Gospel (whether in the "Eastern" or "Western" order), they were actually *fulfilling* the *intentio operis* that Luke be read primarily in relationship to the other Gospels. Later, Acts would be read as the sequel to "the Gospel," with Luke as the "first among equals," albeit in ways Luke could not perhaps have fully anticipated.

So the Third Gospel was originally read and heard as one version among several of the one story of Jesus. The relationship of Luke to those other versions is typically pursued along source-critical lines: which Gospel writer used which other texts? That question is typically answered from the point of view of composition. In this commentary (as with its companion, the Paideia commentary on Acts; see Parsons 2008a), I am attempting to understand the earliest reception of Luke by the "authorial audience" (see below) and so pose the question from a slightly different perspective (i.e., from the other end of the author/audience communication model): within what intertextual web did the authorial audience hear Luke's version of the story of Jesus? For purposes of the commentary, I am assuming that the early Christian audience was familiar with Mark and also with traditions found in common between Luke and Matthew. While from a compositional point of view, most scholars label as "Q" the ultimate source of this double tradition (though not all; e.g., consider the work of Farrer Hypothesis advocates, Mark Goodacre [2002], etc.), I analyze Luke from the point of view of its earliest reception and conclude that even if Luke was working with Q at a compositional level (a point about which I remain stubbornly agnostic), it is impossible finally to know if Luke's authorial audience had access to that double tradition material either through Matthew's Gospel or Q. It is reasonable, therefore, to ask how the authorial audience would have responded to Luke's version of the Jesus story, which at times presents a significantly different account of the same story. Here we are not interested in the minute alterations of single words or slight shifts in word order (the common stock of source and redaction criticism) but rather focus on those changes that the authorial audience, familiar with Matthew (or Q?) and Mark, would not have missed (which, of course, may at times include change of wording or word order). And we ask, what would be the rhetorical impact of such modifications on the authorial audience? Here, then, the issue is the way in which these previous texts are echoed and reconfigured in this new text. How did the authorial audience, familiar with Matthew and Mark, respond to Luke's version of the Jesus story? And how did the perceived genre of those Gospels affect the hearer's understanding?

Luke and Genre

Late nineteenth- and early twentieth-century scholarship on the Gospels recognized similarities between the canonical Gospels and ancient biographies and assumed they belonged to the same genre (Renan 1863; Votaw 1915). That view was soon overturned by the writings of Rudolf Bultmann, who mounted a forceful argument against this view and concluded that the canonical Gospels were *sui generis*, a genre unto themselves (1928, cols. 418–22). This opinion held sway in critical scholarship until the last quarter of the twentieth century. Earlier attempts (Shuler 1975, 1982; Talbert 1977) to classify the Gospels as ancient biographies had a mixed reception, but with the work of Richard Burridge (1992, 2004), the pendulum has seemingly swung back fully in the direction of Renan and Votaw. After a careful and exhaustive study of extant Greco-Roman biographies, and allowing for some minor differences, Burridge concludes that the canonical Gospels belong to the genre of ancient *bios* or biography. Ancient *bioi* focus on elucidating the "essence" of the individual who is the subject of the biography. What is the payoff in knowing the genre of the Gospels or, indeed, of any writing? Burridge elaborates: "To avoid the errors likely in simple application of a text to ourselves without regard for the setting and background of either, appreciation of genre is crucial as a major 'filter' through which the author 'encoded' his message, and through which we may 'decode' the same" (1992, 247). We may further classify the canonical Gospels in the subgenre of the encomiastic biography, whose purpose includes the praise of its subject around a cluster of topics. These topics are not required in every encomium (the progymnasmatists do not even agree on the list of topics), but they do recur with a remarkable frequency in ancient biography (e.g., Plutarch, *Parallel Lives*; Philostratus, *Life of Apollonius of Tyana*; Philo, *On the Life of Moses*; Josephus, *The Life*; cited by Martin 2008; see also Hock 1995, 15–20, on the *Protevangelium of James*).

These encomiastic features provide a convenient way of understanding the general flow of Luke's narrative. In line with the progymnastic conventions (Shuler 1990, 474–79; Martin 2008), Luke addresses the topics of Jesus's origins (1:26–31; 3:21–38; Aphthonius, *Prog.* 22R; Ps.-Hermogenes, *Prog.* 15; cf. Theon, *Prog.* 110); the marvelous occurrences associated with his birth (2:1–39; Ps.-Hermogenes, *Prog.* 15; Nicolaus, *Prog.* 51, 59–60); his nurture and training (2:40–52; 4:1–13; Ps.-Hermogenes, *Prog.* 16, 19; Nicolaus, *Prog.* 52; Theon, *Prog.* 110); his pursuits and deeds (4:14–21:38; Ps.-Hermogenes, *Prog.* 16, 19); the manner (and meaning) of his death (22:1–23:49; Ps.-Hermogenes, *Prog.* 16, 19; Aphthonius, *Prog.* 42); and events after his death (23:50–24:53; Ps.-Hermogenes, *Prog.* 16, 19). The proposed structure of Luke's Gospel in this commentary presumes, but does not conform exactly to, this basic list (see below).

Although they did not necessarily agree in every detail, the progymnastic theorists and authors of ancient *bios* literature did concur that after describing the national origin, birth, nurture, and upbringing of the significant person, one should turn attention to the subject's public accomplishments. According to Pseudo-Hermogenes, this involved an account of the subject's "profession, that is, what sort of life he led, a philosopher or a rhetor or a soldier? Most important are his deeds; for his deeds are part of his way of living. That is, having chosen a soldier's life, what sort of things did he accomplish in it?" (Ps.-Hermogenes, *Prog.* 16, trans. author). Thus, the deeds in an ancient *bios* were understood as both illustrating and fulfilling the subject's chosen profession and were necessary to give the "full range" of the subject's life (Burridge 2004; Martin 2008, 23–24). Certainly Luke agreed with this concern, as nearly two-thirds of the Third Gospel is devoted to an account of Jesus's public ministry (4:14–21:38).

For those treating philosophers or teachers (see Lucian, *Demonax*; Philostratus, *Life of Apollonius of Tyana*; Philo, *On the Life of Moses*), these deeds included the person's teaching (Burridge 2004, 202). Quintilian, for example, commented: "In some cases the more attractive course has proved to be to follow the successive stages of a man's life and the order of his actions; thus under his first years would come praise of his natural abilities, then of his education, then of the whole series of his works, that is to say his deeds and sayings" (*Inst.* 3.7.15, trans. Russell 2001; cf. Theon, *Prog.* 78). Thus, it comes as no surprise that Luke characterizes Jesus's greatness in terms both of his mighty words and of his mighty deeds (Luke 24:19; cf. Acts 1:1; 2:22–24), and in light of these comments about the structure and function of ancient *bioi*, this section of Luke that deals with Jesus's "pursuits and deeds" (4:14–19:44), that is, his public ministry, is the largest section in the Third Gospel and may aptly be further divided into two smaller units according to the locale of Jesus's public activities:

Jesus's Mighty Words and Deeds in Galilee (4:14–9:50)
Jesus's Mighty Words and Deeds along the Way (9:51–19:44)

In Luke's *bios* of Jesus, Jesus's mighty words and deeds substantiate the christological claims Luke is making for Jesus and his vocation (see Burridge 2004, 248–50, 288–94).

And what is that vocation? Jesus is God's Messiah (kingship was a typical *bios* topic; see Aphthonius, *Prog.* 41). Luke has already informed the audience of this in the announcement of Jesus's birth; he will be the "'Son of the Most High'; and the Lord God will give the throne of his ancestor David to him. He will reign over the house of Jacob forever, and his kingdom will have no end" (1:32–33). At his baptism, God declares that Jesus is the "beloved Son" (3:22). These two claims about Jesus—Davidic descent and divine sonship—are complementary, not competitive, titles (cf. Philo's complementary description of Moses as prophet, lawgiver, priest, and king in *On the Life of Moses*), and both point to Jesus's vocation as Messiah (see 4:41, in which the two titles are essentially presented as synonyms). Jesus's "messiahship is confirmed by both his Davidic descent and his sonship to God" (M. Strauss 1995, 92). Later, his role as eschatological prophet will serve to enrich this portrait of Jesus (24:19), and more immediately, the Lukan Jesus will reveal his messianic ministry as God's anointed one in Isaianic terms (4:14–30). Jesus's mighty words and deeds then must be viewed, in terms of the topics of an ancient *bios*, as an explication of Jesus's vocation as Messiah. Furthermore, these titles assigned to Jesus—whether Son, Messiah, or Prophet—are not static but rather accrue their meaning as the *bios* of Jesus unfolds in the Third Gospel.

The climax occurs in the Gospel's last section, which deals with the manner of Jesus's death (22:1–23:49; the account of the Last Supper is included here rather than with Jesus's pursuits and deeds, for reasons explained at that point in the commentary) and the events that follow his death, which revolve around the fact that the grave cannot hold him (23:50–24:53).

The Audience of Luke and Issues of Reception and Formation

Interest in the "reader(s)" or "audience" of biblical texts has soared in recent decades (see Fowler 1991; Powell 1990). Understanding the terminology of reader-oriented interpretations, however, is not always easy. This

> **Outline of Luke**
>
> **Jesus's origins and training (1:1–4:13)**
>   Preface (1:1–4)
>   Annunciations: John and Jesus (1:5–56)
>   Birth and training: John and Jesus (1:57–2:52)
>   Beginning Jesus's Public Ministry (3:1–4:13)
>
> **Jesus's mighty words and deeds in Galilee (4:14–9:50)**
>   Jesus's mission and miracles and the ingathering of his followers (4:14–6:49)
>   Jesus's marvelous words and deeds (7:1–8:56)
>   Jesus's miracles and mission and the sending out of his followers (9:1–50)
>
> **Jesus's mighty words and deeds along the way (part 1) (9:51–14:35)**
>   Beginning the journey (Luke 9:51–11:13)
>   Jesus in dialogue (11:14–13:9)
>   More healings and parables (13:10–14:35)
>
> **Jesus's mighty words and deeds along the way (part 2) (15:1–19:44)**
>   The character of God and the "lost" parables (15:1–32)
>   The use and abuse of wealth (16:1–17:10)
>   Jesus's teaching about the kingdom (17:11–18:30)
>   Drawing near to Jerusalem (18:31–19:44)
>
> **Jesus in Jerusalem: teachings, death, and resurrection (19:45–24:53)**
>   Jesus in and around the temple (19:45–21:38)
>   The meaning and manner of Jesus's death (22:1–23:49)
>   Jesus's burial, empty tomb, and postresurrection appearances (23:50–24:53)

commentary attempts to consider two kinds of readers or audiences: the constructed "authorial audience" and real, flesh-and-blood contemporary Christian communities, although the focus in the commentary proper is clearly on the former.

The Authorial Audience of Luke

This commentary is written from the perspective of the authorial audience, that is, the reception of the text by the audience that the author had in mind when he wrote his Gospel (see Rabinowitz 1987; Carter 1996; Talbert 1998, 2003; Parsons 2007). Presumably the authorial audience knew how to respond appropriately (if unconsciously) to the effects of persuasive rhetoric. Thus, the commentary attempts to understand the ways in which the rhetorical strategies, literary conventions, and cultural scripts in the final form of Luke were received by the authorial audience. The authorial audience is not a real, flesh-and-blood audience; it is, nonetheless, historically circumscribed.

The effort, then, is both historical and hermeneutical, and it is important to outline the parameters of that historical task. First, Luke's authorial audience is not to be mistaken for a specific second-century community; in other words, there was no "Lukan community" per se whose interests and needs we can tease from between the lines of Luke's Gospel (Johnson 1979). Rather, the Gospel of Luke was addressed to a general Christian audience, living in the Roman Empire at the turn of the second century (Bauckham 1998a). Thus, Luke is read in its historical context, but as Bauckham says, "That context is not the evangelist's community. It is the early Christian movement in the late first century" (1998a, 46). For this reason, attempts to locate the provenance of either the author or the audience have failed to create a critical consensus and, more telling, have proven mostly irrelevant for interpreting the text.

For purposes of the commentary, I assume that both Luke and the authorial audience of the Third Gospel were familiar with the cultural scripts and rhetorical conventions of the larger Greco-Roman world, scripts and conventions that were extant in specific documents that they may or may not have known. The audience is also familiar with the basic themes of the Jewish Scriptures, other Second Temple Jewish literature (or at least the prominent themes that those documents preserve and reflect), and other early Christian literature (at least Mark, double tradition material that they accessed through Matthew, and perhaps some other Christian literature).

The commentary focuses on how the authorial audience heard Luke within the web of other texts and contexts familiar to that audience. And we ask, what would be the rhetorical impact of such "intertextuality" on the authorial audience? Here, then, the issue is the way in which these cultural scripts and rhetorical conventions are echoed and reconfigured in this new text. This kind of intertextual exploration takes into account those rhetorical conventions, social scripts, and theological concepts reflected in those texts and with which the audience would likely have been familiar.

Luke also understood his task as having hermeneutical implications. Education, or *paideia*, in the ancient world (not unlike today in many quarters) "was based on the transmission of an established body of knowledge, about which there was wide consensus" (Cribiore 2001, 8). The transmission of traditional values resulted in the formation of the moral character of the students (or audience; Penner 2003). Theon of Alexandria, author of the earliest of the extant progymnasmata, confirms this point several times: "Surely the exercise . . . not only creates a certain faculty of speech but also good character [*ethos*], while we are being exercised in the moral sayings of the wise" (Theon, *Prog.* 60.18, trans. Kennedy 2003, 4; see also 71.6; 78.9). Thus, beyond acquiring facility in grammar and rhetoric, a fortunate by-product of the rhetorical exercises from the teacher's point of view was the shaping of moral habits that reflected the prevailing cultural values of the day.

At the same time that Luke acquired the ability to read and write through his rhetorical education, he also learned *ethos* argumentation, that is, how to shape the moral character of his audience and thus how to inculcate those values in the student/audience's moral vision. The moral vision propagated by the progymnasmatists was elitist, racist, and sexist. The ideal was the free, male Roman citizen against whom all others were deemed inferior (Gleason 1995). While Luke invokes the methods and categories of rhetorical argument, he often does so only to subvert or overturn them, a rhetorical move of *ethos* argumentation that he no doubt learned from the very teachers of grammar and rhetoric whose moral vision he so severely challenges (Parsons 2007). In its place, Luke offers a vision of God's family that is inclusive of Jew and gentile, rich and disenfranchised, male and female, slave and free, the physically whole and the physically disabled. Luke's use of rhetoric is aimed at forming the moral character and theological vision of the Christian community so that the followers may more faithfully imitate the founder, Jesus the Christ, whose story he tells (for a similar argument, see Bockmuehl 2006).

The Contemporary Christian Audience(s) of Luke

The contemporary Christian community is invited to participate in this vision, to adopt the point of view of the authorial audience Luke had in mind. Of course, such imitation of the authorial audience by a contemporary Christian community, removed by space and time, can only be approximate at best and may entail, from time to time, acknowledging contextual differences. For example, the contemporary Christian reader, living in a post-Holocaust context, must acknowledge the difficulty and difference in hearing Luke's story of the conflict between Jesus and his followers and other Jewish groups, as Luke intended it, as an intra-Jewish debate.

The "Theological Issues" section of the commentary draws on interpretive issues of interest to the contemporary Christian community, whose preunderstanding of Luke is shaped to varying degrees by these diverse liturgical and theological influences. Luke's own commitment to this formation of Christian character functions as the springboard for these reflections. Sometimes this section raises theological issues within the context of the larger Christian canon. At other times, the history of the interpretation of the text is brought to bear. As the meaning(s) of the text for the authorial audience comes into focus, the implications for the contemporary faith community become more transparent. This is not to suggest that the "Theological Issues" sections exhaust the possible topics for consideration; rather, they should be viewed as conversation starters and as attempts to extend Luke's spiritual formation of his audience into faithful disciples who can know more fully the truth of the matters in which they have been instructed.

Conclusion

To summarize: The author of the Third Gospel, who is traditionally known as Luke, also wrote what became known as the Acts of the Apostles as a sequel to a plurality of Gospels then currently in use, of which the Third Gospel (which "Luke" also wrote) stands as the "first among equals." The Third Gospel was written in the 80s (or 90s), followed some years later by Acts (within the first two decades of the second century, ca. AD 110). Little can be known for certain regarding the identity of the author of Luke; what is clear is that the text presents a distinct portrait of Jesus that takes its place alongside other versions of that story. In his composition of his Gospel, Luke demonstrated command of a number of rhetorical conventions and techniques, drew on various cultural and social scripts, and wrote his story of Jesus within the generic contours of ancient biography or *bios* (see Burridge 1992, 2004). The Third Gospel was written *not* for a specific "Lukan community" (Johnson 1979; Bauckham 1998a) but rather for a general audience of early Christians living in the ancient Mediterranean world. We cannot know—and fortunately for our purposes do not need to know—exactly where Luke was composed. It is difficult to distinguish when Luke's writing reflects things as they were when they happened, or things as they were in Luke's day at the time of his writing, or things as Luke hoped they would be. Luke's primary purpose in writing is to "school" his intended audience in the moral and theological implications of the Christian vision by telling the story of that movement's founder, Jesus of Nazareth. For contemporary Christians to adopt the point of view of the authorial audience (with the nuances necessary for a document set in circumstances nineteen hundred years ago) is to share in this vision; it is to be theologically formed by the perspectives of this part of the Christian canon.

PART 1

Luke 1:1–4:13

Jesus's Origins and Training

Under the influence of source and redactional analyses, many modern commentators have viewed the infancy narrative of Luke 1–2 as the first discrete unit of the Third Gospel (Plummer 1903; Laurentin 1957; Leaney 1961–62; Morris 1974; Fitzmyer 1981–85; Nolland 1989–93; Johnson 1991; Ernst 1993; Bock 1994–96; Culpepper 1995; Bovon 2002–13; but cf. Talbert 2002). From a redactional point of view, a clear demarcation emerges between Luke 1–2 (which contains material unique to Luke) and Luke 3 (which, like Mark, begins with the ministry of John and the baptism of Jesus). Based on the progymnastic topic lists conventional for ancient *bioi*, however, it is more likely that the authorial audience would have expected the opening segment to deal with matters related to Jesus's "prepublic" career and thus would have heard Luke 1:1–4:13, the material leading up to the beginning of Jesus's public ministry in Nazareth, as a coherent unit (see the introduction; Martin 2008). Furthermore, Luke employs the rhetorical device of *synkrisis*, or comparison, in his presentation of Jesus's origins and nurture/training. Specifically, he compares Jesus's origins and training with those of John the Baptist.

This Jesus/John comparison is especially concentrated on origins and nurture/training in this opening unit, 1:1–4:13 (see table 1), but does throughout

> ### *Synkrisis* in Luke
>
> In its simplest terms, *synkrisis* is "language setting the better or worse side by side" (Theon, *Prog.* 112, trans. Kennedy 2003, 52). Comparing two similarly noteworthy persons (or objects) for the purpose of praise is a *synkrisis* in a double encomium (see the introduction), which occurs, according to Nicolaus, when "the subjects under discussion are both equal to each other or that one is greater than the other" (Nicolaus, *Prog.* 60, trans. Kennedy 2003, 162; see Aphthonius, *Prog.* 31R–32R). In Luke 1:1–4:13, we have an example of a double encomium in which Luke praises both John the Baptist and Jesus but clearly prefers Jesus as John the Baptist's superior.

> ### Luke 1:1–4:13 in Context
>
> ▶ **Jesus's origins and training (1:1–4:13)**
>   **Preface (1:1–4)**
>   **Annunciations: John and Jesus (1:5–56)**
>   The annunciation of John's birth (1:5–25)
>   The annunciation of Jesus's birth (1:26–38)
>   The visitation (1:39–56)
>   **Birth and training: John and Jesus (1:57–2:52)**
>   John's birth and upbringing (1:57–80)
>   Jesus's birth and upbringing (2:1–52)
>   **Beginning Jesus's public ministry (3:1–4:13)**
>   John in the wilderness (3:1–20)
>   Jesus in the wilderness (3:21–4:13)
> **Jesus's mighty words and deeds in Galilee (4:14–9:50)**
> **Jesus's mighty words and deeds along the way (part 1) (9:51–14:35)**
> **Jesus's mighty words and deeds along the way (part 2) (15:1–19:44)**
> **Jesus in Jerusalem: teachings, death, and resurrection (19:45–24:53)**

the rest of the Gospel touch on the entire range of progymnastic topics, including John's pursuits and deeds (5:33–35; 7:18–33; 11:1; 16:16; 20:1–8), the manner of his death (9:7–9), and events after his death (9:7–20; see Martin 2008, 40).

Table 1. John the Baptist and Jesus Compared

Topic of *synkrisis*	John the Baptist	Jesus
Homeland	Judea (1:5a)	Galilee (1:26a)
City	Jerusalem (implied by father's status as "priest"; 1:5b)	Nazareth (1:26b), but born in Bethlehem (2:4)
Father	Zechariah (1:5b)	Joseph (1:27a), but conceived by the Holy Spirit as God's son (1:35; cf. 3:21–38)
Ancestors	Zechariah from the priestly order of Abijah (1:5b)	Joseph from the house of David (1:27b)
Mother	Zechariah's wife, a descendent of Aaron (1:5c); "Her name was Elizabeth" (1:5c)	"The name of the virgin was Mary" (1:27c)
Marvelous occurrences at birth	Zechariah's vision of an angel (1:11–12)	Mary's vision of an angel (1:28–29)
	angel's oracle to Zechariah concerning birth, name, and career (= preparer figure) of son (1:13–17)	angel's oracle to Mary concerning birth, name, and career (= Messiah) of son (1:30–37)
	Zechariah does not believe the oracle; he receives another oracle concerning his punishment for his unbelief (1:18–23)	Mary believes the oracle; she receives another oracle—from Elizabeth—blessing her and praising her for her belief (1:38–45)
	oracle's fulfillment celebrated by Elizabeth: the Lord "looks favorably upon her" (she conceives despite barrenness; 1:24–25)	oracle's fulfillment celebrated by Mary: the Lord "looks favorably upon her" (she conceives despite virginity; 1:46–56)
	oracle's fulfillment: Elizabeth bears a son (1:57)	oracle's fulfillment: Mary bears a son (2:1–7)
	neighbors/relatives told of birth (1:58)	shepherds told of birth (2:8–13) through visions (2:9, 13) and oracles (2:10–12, 14); given a "sign": "you will find a child wrapped in bands of cloth and lying in a manger" (2:12 NRSV)
		shepherd's witness, report marvelous events that occurred immediately after birth; amazement ensues (2:8–20)
		portentous distancing from Joseph: Jesus dedicated as firstborn to his "Father's house" (2:49), but not sacrificially redeemed by Joseph

Topic of synkrisis	John the Baptist	Jesus
		oracle's fulfillment: the child is named Jesus at his circumcision (2:21)
		Mary, hearing the shepherd's report, ponders marvelous events that occurred after Jesus's birth (2:19)
		three concluding oracles concerning the child Jesus (2:25–39)
Nurture and training	the child grows and becomes strong (1:80a)	the child grows and becomes strong (2:40–52)
	was in wilderness prior to beginning public career (1:80b)	was in wilderness prior to beginning public career (3:21–23; 4:1–13)

Note: Modified from Martin 2008, 39; see also O'Fearghail 1991, 16, 30.

The purpose of this *synkrisis* is to demonstrate the "superiority of Jesus" (O'Fearghail 1991, 35). The outline on page 22 takes into account the rhetorical topics of origins and nurture/training and the rhetorical vehicle of *synkrisis* through which those topics are conveyed.

Luke 1:1–4

Preface

Introductory Matters

The literature on Luke's preface is voluminous (see preeminently Alexander 1993; also Cadbury 1921, 1922b, 1922c; van Unnik 1973; Klein 1964; Du Plessis 1974; Callan 1985; Marshall 1993; Palmer 1993; and especially Moessner 1996, 1999a, 1999b, 2008). Unlike his canonical counterparts, Luke begins his Gospel with a self-conscious reflection on the task at hand. He does so in a well-crafted sentence that consists of forty-two Greek words. Luke's preface reflects the pattern of prefaces in ancient historiography (e.g., Dionysius of Halicarnassus, Polybius, Josephus), biography (e.g., Philo, *On the Life of Moses*), some novels (e.g., Lucian's satirical preface in *A True Story*), and scientific treatises (including some rhetorical handbooks; see Alexander 1993).

Tracing the Narrative Flow

1:1–4. Ancient prefaces tended to include certain elements, and Luke's opening sentence contains many of them. (1) There is a statement about the author's predecessors—Luke begins: **Many have attempted to compose a narrative** (1:1a)—often accompanied by critical remarks about their shortcomings (see comments below). (2) The work's subject matter is usually stated. So Luke describes **the events that have been**

> **Luke 1:1–4 in the Narrative Flow**
>
> **Jesus's origins and training (1:1–4:13)**
> ▶ Preface (1:1–4)

fulfilled among us (1:1b). It is impossible on the basis of the prologue itself to determine whether these "events" include those recorded in the Acts of the Apostles; on other grounds, however, it has been argued that Acts was written several decades later than Luke (see the introduction; Parsons 2008a, 16–17; 2009). (3) The writer's qualifications are given. Luke claims to be one **who has become thoroughly familiar with everything over a long period of time** (1:3a). (4) The plan or arrangement of the work is given. Luke claims to have given an **orderly account** (1:3b). (5) The purpose(s) for writing is given. Luke writes so that his reader **might know the certainty of the words you were taught** (1:4). (6) Sometimes the author's name is given. This element is missing in Luke. (7) Sometimes the addressee is named. In Luke, the addressee is the **most excellent Theophilus**, whose name means "friend of God" (1:3c; Talbert 1982, 7–10; Culpepper 1995, 39).

There has been much debate about the first component. Did Luke, like so many ancient writers, intend to criticize others who had written about Jesus? Further, if Luke did intend to refer to his predecessors' inadequacies, would the authorial audience have understood these criticisms? These questions require careful and nuanced examination of the prologue's structure.

Some have seen a two-part structure in the preface arranged in a protasis/apodosis pattern ("since" [vv. 1–2]; "then" [vv. 3–4]), with each part containing three corresponding elements. John Nolland, however, has argued that the "just as" (v. 2), rather than qualifying the writing activity of the "many," points to a comparison with what follows in verse 3. Further, the use of the word "passed on" (*paradidōmi*) may suggest the transmission of oral material rather than written narratives (see esp. Acts 16:4; also 1 Cor. 11:2, 23). Thus, verses 1 and 2 should be taken as parallel clauses, each with an independent relationship to verse 3 (Nolland 1989–93, 1:8; see table 2).

Table 2. Structure of Prologue

	Written sources (1:1)	**Oral traditions (1:2)**	**Luke's project (1:3)**
Clause	Since	just as	it seemed good
Who?	many	those who were, from the beginning, eyewitnesses who became servants of the message	to me as well
How?	have attempted to compose	handed to us	(as one) who has carefully investigated everything for a significant amount of time, to write ... for you
What?	a narrative	[the message/tradition]	an orderly account
Why?	the events that have been fulfilled among us		so that you might know the certainty of the words you were taught

In this construal, Luke is both continuous with and discontinuous from his predecessors. On the one hand, Luke shows his continuity with those previous attempts to narrate the Jesus story by beginning with a term, "since" or "inasmuch," that rightly suggests a causal relation between these earlier narratives and Luke's own narrative. Luke writes because others have written. The continuity is clear also in the phrase "it seemed good to me as well [*kamoi*]." Here Luke intends to stand in the tradition of those who had earlier narrated the matters that had been fulfilled. On the other hand, of course, Luke does write, and the very act of writing seems to imply some criticism of previous attempts. But how much criticism? This question takes us into the rhetorical flow of the argument itself (for much of what follows, see Parsons 2007, 40–50).

While there seems to be no criticism of those eyewitnesses who handed down the oral tradition (1:2), there is evidence of some dissatisfaction on Luke's part with his literary predecessors mentioned in 1:1 (see Klein 1964). We do not know the extent of the "many" (though it presumably included Mark; see the introduction). The use of this term and its cognates was a known rhetorical device employed in the beginning of narratives and speeches (e.g., Sir. prol. 1; Heb. 1:1; Acts 24:2, 10) and should not therefore be pressed to mean a large number. The term "attempt" (*epecheirēsan*; lit., "take into hand") is crucial for understanding Luke's attitude. The term is sometimes used in a neutral sense of "undertaken" (Polybius, *Hist.* 2.37.4), even in literary prefaces (Josephus, *Ag. Ap.* 1.13). Elsewhere, however, the term is used in a negative sense—that is, "they have attempted but did not succeed" (Josephus, *Life* 40; Herm. *Sim.* 92.6). More important, Luke will later use the term twice in Acts, and in both instances it is used in this negative sense: "He [Saul] was both speaking and debating against the Hellenists; but they were trying unsuccessfully to kill him" (Acts 9:29); "Now some of the itinerant Jewish exorcists also attempted unsuccessfully to invoke the name of the Lord Jesus over those who had evil spirits" (19:13). Luke's own use of the term, coupled with how prefaces typically contained a critique (implicit or explicit) of the writer's predecessors, leads to the conclusion that the use of the term in the preface would have been understood in its pejorative sense, "many have attempted unsuccessfully to write a narrative." For Luke, from a rhetorical perspective, these attempts failed *as rhetorical narratives* because either they lacked adequate coverage of the topics necessary for a *bios* (origins, birth, training and nurture, words and deeds, manner of death, and events after death; see the introduction) or they did not arrange the story in a rhetorically compelling way. To be sure, Luke would use the "many" as *sources* for his own narrative, even if they themselves did not reach the level of rhetorically complete and well-formed *narratives*.

Even though Mark has no doubt employed the *topoi* of his *bios* of Jesus to his own satisfaction, Luke was apparently dissatisfied with his effort. One of the problems Luke would have had with Mark's Gospel was that, in beginning with the public ministry of Jesus and omitting any reference to his birth, Mark presented an incomplete rhetorical narrative in terms of the "origins" and/ or "good birth" of Jesus. Missing from Mark is an account of Jesus's birth, and information regarding his place and family of origins and his nurture/ training are minimal (see Mark 1:9–13). All these elements are present in Luke 1–2 and are presented in what Luke claims to be a reliable way. Luke refers to **those who were, from the beginning, eyewitnesses who became servants of the message** (1:2). For the authorial audience familiar with the opening line of Mark, the use of the word "beginning" (*archē*) in Luke 1:2 would have had strong echoes with Mark 1:1, "The beginning [*archē*] of the good news of Jesus." While there is much scholarly discussion of the meaning of *archē* in Mark 1:1, many early readers of Mark interpreted it to refer to the beginning of Jesus's story with his baptism by John the Baptist, as seen in Augustine's observations: "Note that Mark mentions nothing of the nativity or infancy or youth of the Lord. He has made his Gospel *begin* directly with the preaching of John" (*Cons.* 2.6.18, trans. Oden and Hall 1998, 2; emphasis added).

Mark's Gospel begins with John's preaching and Jesus's baptism. Mark's beginning, while perhaps the place to start the "good news," is, for Luke, inappropriate for a rhetorically complete "narrative." Luke claims that he has received the message from those servants of the word who were eyewitnesses from the beginning. And for Luke, beginning properly included the story of Jesus's birth and his family. In fact, to be a complete narrative from a rhetorical perspective, Luke's story had to include these elements.

So who were these "eyewitnesses from the beginning"? Many have taken this phrase to refer to the tradition passed on by the apostles, and certainly the apostles would be included among these eyewitnesses. For Luke, however, these "eyewitnesses from the beginning"/ "servants" would also have included those who witnessed the events surrounding the birth of Jesus. Mary, Jesus's mother, and Simeon would surely count as eyewitnesses who became servants. In Luke 1:38, after Gabriel has revealed to Mary God's plan for her to bear the child Jesus, Mary responds: "I am the servant of the Lord! May it happen to me according to your word." Later in the Magnificat, she exclaims that God has looked upon the humble state of his *servant* (1:48). When Simeon, whom Luke describes as "righteous and devout, waiting for the consolation of Israel" (2:25), receives the Christ child in his arms, he praises God, saying, "Now you are dismissing your *servant* in peace, Lord, according to your word, for my eyes have seen your salvation" (2:29–30). The appeal to eyewitnesses/ servants from the beginning does not serve to ensure historical reliability (as some have claimed), but it does fit Luke's need to present a narrative that is, rhetorically speaking, complete. Further, if Luke's copy of Mark ended at 16:8, Luke might also have regarded this story as rhetorically incomplete in its ending, since it did not have the requisite account of events that occurred after the character's death (see Theon, *Prog.* 78, trans. Kennedy 2003; Ps.-Hermogenes, *Prog.* 16, 19, trans. Kennedy 2003).

Luke is likewise concerned with the presentation of events in the narrative. Luke claims to be "thoroughly familiar with everything" from the start (on this translation see Cadbury 1922b; 1922c; Moessner 2008); thus Luke is able to present not only a complete story but also a well-formed one that is rhetorically persuasive (Moessner 2008, 299). When read in light of the rhetorical exercises for story writing, this claim informs the audience that what is to follow is a properly executed narrative, not only complete in its coverage of the story of Jesus from start to finish, but ordered in such a way as to enhance understanding.

Luke claims to write in "an orderly fashion" (*kathexēs*; 1:3). What exactly does Luke mean by this term? Our first clue comes in Luke's use of the word elsewhere in his writings (Luke 8:1; Acts 3:24; 11:4; 18:23). Of those, surely the most significant is Luke's later use of the term in Acts 11:4. When the Jerusalem church heard about Peter's associations with gentiles, they sent an envoy to question him about these events. The narrator notes that Peter began to explain "in order" or "step by step" (*kathexēs*). The modern reader expecting the story to be told in chronological sequence will be surprised to hear that Peter begins by reversing the order of presentation of the visions: his own vision precedes that of Cornelius (cf. Acts 10, where Cornelius's vision is narrated first, followed by Peter's). But the word "in order" has little to do with chronological or linear order. Rather, Peter (and in a larger sense the narrator) is seeking to present the events in a manner that his audience will find convincing (Tannehill 1986–90, 2:144). For Luke, "in order" has to do with a rhetorically persuasive presentation. That was what Peter was attempting to do in Acts 11, and it is what Luke purports to do in his preface.

Presentation, of course, was an issue of concern to the rhetoricians. Theon writes: "Virtues of a narrative are three: clarity, conciseness, credibility. Best of all, if it is possible, the narrative should have all these virtues" (Theon, *Prog.* 79, trans. Kennedy 2003, 29). Clarity is an important (perhaps the most important) element of narrative, according to Theon, and one way clarity is achieved is through the "arrangement" (*taxis*) of the subject matter (Theon, *Prog.* 80, trans. Kennedy 2003). By order in the narrative, Theon does not imply any kind of strict historical or chronological order. Further, Theon distinguishes between unintentionally confusing the order of events, which he says one must guard against (Theon, *Prog.* 80), and intentionally rearranging the order, of which he approves (Theon, *Prog.* 86–87, trans. Kennedy 2003).

Not all later rhetorical treatises agreed with this practice of transposing the order, especially those associated with judicial speeches that may have revolved around preserving the exact sequence of events (e.g., *Rh. Al.* 30.1438a.28–31; *Rhet. Her.* 1.9.15). Quintilian, however, in support of this procedure, writes: "Neither do I agree with those who assert that the order of our *statement of facts* should always follow the actual order of events, but I have a preference for adopting the order which I consider most suitable" (*Inst.* 4.2.83, trans. Butler 1921; emphasis original).

By claiming that he will narrate his story "in an orderly fashion," Luke strongly hints that his literary predecessors, and certainly Mark, did not achieve the very important feature of "clarity" in their narratives (cf. the similar critique of Thucydides by Dionysius of Halicarnassus, *Thuc.* 9; cited in Moessner 2008, 294–95; also Theon, *Prog.* 80). Luke may have been the first to criticize Mark in this way, but he was certainly not the last. Papias wrote that Mark "wrote down accurately everything that he recalled of the Lord's words and deeds—but not in order. For he neither heard the Lord nor accompanied him; but later, as I indicated, he accompanied Peter, who used to adapt his teachings for the needs at hand, not arranging, as it were, an orderly composition" (*Fragments of Papias* 3.15, trans. Ehrman, 2003). Thus, it was possible to have a complete narrative in terms of content that was ineffective in its order of presentation. Luke, who like Mark "had neither heard the Lord nor accompanied him," was determined to write in an "orderly"—and rhetorically compelling—fashion.

For Luke, the "what" of his message, its content, was irreducibly shaped by and inextricably interwoven with the "how" of his message, that is, its rhetoric. It is as though, in contrast to his predecessors, Luke is saying to his audience: "If you want to gain a clearer understanding of the true significance of all of these events, then you must 'follow' the carefully arranged divisions and sequences of my . . . work" (Moessner 2008, 299). One notable example of how order of presentation affects the understanding of the narrative is the placement and expansion of the people-fishing saying of Mark 1:16–20, which, in Luke's version (5:1–11), is preceded by the healing of Peter's mother-in-law (Luke 4:38–39) in order to make the story more rhetorically credible, another virtue of a rhetorically well-formed narrative (see Parsons 2007, 24–25). Elsewhere in the commentary are detailed examples of changes Luke makes in the presentation of his narrative because Mark (for example) has, in his opinion, fallen short of the clarity, brevity, and plausibility that were rhetorically indispensable to the narrative (see Irenaeus's famous parable of the mosaic of the king in *Haer.* 1.8.1).

Finally, what is the goal of Luke's rhetorically persuasive presentation? That too is stated clearly in the preface: "so that you might know the certainty of the words you were taught" (1:4). The language here suggests that the audience in mind is primarily Christian and that the purpose of Luke's Gospel is one of instruction and assurance of "those events that have been fulfilled among us" (1:1). Here, for theological reasons, Luke departs from the rhetorical tradition that views narrative as explanation of "things that have happened or as though they have happened" (Theon, *Prog.* 78, trans. Kennedy 2003, 28). Luke's narrative, rather, is about matters that have been prophesied, whether by the Jewish Scriptures, living prophets, or heavenly messengers, and have now been fulfilled through the words and deeds of Jesus. "Certainty" is a standard rhetorical topic that has a persuasive appeal to the audience (see Aristotle, *Rhet.* 1.4.12; 1.5.3; *Rhet. Her.* 3.2.3). Though the persuasive quality of Luke's Gospel can be evaluated only after a close analysis of the whole Gospel, Luke's motive in writing includes an attempt to present these events that have been fulfilled and about which the audience has already been instructed in a rhetorically compelling order so that the authorial audience finds confirmation of the truthfulness of the narrative. Luke's narrative is thus both informational and transformational in character. By following closely this rhetorically complete and well-formed narrative, Theophilus will find his friendship with God deepened and enriched.

Theological Issues

Recently, much attention has been given to narrative beginnings, though there is no consensus regarding their significance (Said 1985; Rimmon-Kenan 2002; Parsons 1990). Luke's preface serves, as many have noted, as part of a frame that marks the boundaries of the work and separates it from the space of the real world that surrounds it. That the beginning of a narrative stands at the critical junction between the "real" world of the audience and the "symbolic" world of the text makes taking the audience into account unavoidable. A group of scholars, sometimes referred to as the Tel Aviv School (Meir Sternberg, Menakhem Perry, Shlomith Rimmon-Kenan), have explored the ways in which the order of a text affects the meaning appropriated by its reader. They have labeled the way the beginning of a text shapes its subsequent reading as the "primacy effect" (Sternberg 1978, 96).

Giving or withholding information can be used to create certain first impressions, and the primacy effect of those first expressions ensures that the audience will cling to those first thoughts as long as the narrative will possibly allow. Perry has observed: "There are cases in which meanings, constructed at the beginning of the text as a result of the distribution of information in the text-continuum, will remain stable until the reading is over simply because once constructed there is nothing in the sequel of the text to contradict or undermine them so as to cause their final rejection" (1979, 48). At times, though, hypotheses formed at the beginning of a text are subverted by later information. Thus, expectations have to be reexamined and sometimes revised (1979, 52).

What are the expectations that Luke creates with his preface? He suggests that, though he stands in continuity with his predecessors in his desire to narrate the story of Jesus, his will be a well-formed narrative, one that meets the expectations of a rhetorically complete story. Further, by promising to reassure his audience about the truthfulness of the matters in which they have already been instructed, he subjects his own storytelling prowess to the same prophecy-fulfillment schema that he uses to describe the contents of the story he narrates. He claims to have investigated everything carefully and completely and to have written "in order" so that the "friend of God" might be certain of the truth of previous teachings—a tall order indeed. Luke's preface is an invitation to the audience to suspend disbelief for the moment and enter and experience his world—a world filled with birth and death, with miracle and treachery, with song and parable, with conflict and resolution. Any reenactment of Luke's story, then, whether through preaching or teaching, ought to extend that invitation anew. Will Luke meet or disappoint the expectations his preface creates? Perhaps we shall know better when we reach the end.

> We shall not cease from exploration
> And the end of all our exploring
> Will be to arrive where we started
> And know the place for the first time. (T. S. Eliot, "Little Gidding")

Luke 1:5–56

Annunciations: John and Jesus

Introductory Matters

The *synkrisis* between Jesus and John the Baptist begins with the stories of their annunciations and births. Luke 1:5–56 is organized into three parts: the annunciation of the birth of John the Baptist (1:5–25), the annunciation of the birth of Jesus (1:26–38), and the visitation of Mary to Elizabeth (1:39–56).

Tracing the Narrative Flow

The Annunciation of the Birth of John the Baptist (1:5–25)

The annunciation of John's birth is in the form of a dream-vision narrative, which is usually constituted by the following parts: (1) scene-setting (1:5–10); (2) dream-vision terminology (1:11a); (3) dream-vision proper, which includes a commissioning/invitation (1:11b–20); (4) reaction/response, which can include an extended narrative demonstrating how the dream-vision is fulfilled (1:21–25; cf. Philostratus, *Vit. Apoll.* 4.34; Plutarch, *Luc.* 12.1; *Eum.* 6.4; J. Hanson 1980, 1400–1413; see also Dodson 2009; Parsons 2008a, 129, 144, 228, 317). Not all dream-visions contain all these elements, nor are they always in the same order (Dodson 2009, 59), but they do all seem to function as divine testimony to legitimate the event and/or character (cf. Cicero, *Top.* 20.76–77: "many things are revealed by visions . . . in order to win conviction" [trans. Hubbell, 1949]; Parsons 2008a, 43, 346). The audience familiar with this literary convention would recognize the annunciation to Zechariah (and later to Mary) as part of this larger dream-vision convention.

> **Luke 1:5–56 in the Narrative Flow**
>
> Jesus's origins and training (1:1–4:13)
>   Preface (1:1–4)
>   ▶ Annunciations: John and Jesus (1:5–56)
>   The annunciation of the birth of John the Baptist (1:5–25)
>   Scene-setting (1:5–10)
>   Dream-vision terminology (1:11a)
>   Dream-vision proper (1:11b–20)
>   Reaction/response (1:21–25)
>   The annunciation of the birth of Jesus (1:26–38)
>   Scene-setting (1:26–27)
>   Dream-vision terminology
>   Dream-vision proper (1:28–38a)
>   Reaction/response (1:38b)
>   The visitation of Mary to Elizabeth (1:39–56)

1:5–10. *Scene-setting.* In contrast to the stylized Greek prose of the preface (1:1–4), the style and substance of this opening scene in Luke's story takes a decidedly "Jewish" turn. The first words, *egeneto en tais hēmerais* (lit., "it happened in those days"), are a staple phrase in the LXX (e.g., Exod. 2:11; Judg. 19:1; cf. Judg. 13:2; Jdt. 1:1; Tob. 1:2; see also Marshall 1978, 51). Furthermore, like the Hebrew prophets ("in the days of King Uzziah of Judah," Amos 1:1; cf. Jer. 1:1–3), Luke begins his story with reference to a specific reign: **in the days of Herod, king of Judea** (1:5a). This allusion to Herod (who reigned in Judea 37–4 BC)—like the references to Caesar Augustus in 2:1 and to Tiberius Caesar, Pontius Pilate, and Herod in 3:1—serves to anchor the story within a particular historical epoch and suggests that these events will have political, as well as religious, implications.

One important constituent element of a dream-vision is identifying its recipient. Luke introduces **a particular priest named Zechariah from the priestly division of Abijah** (1:5b), along with his wife, who **was from the daughters of Aaron, and her name was Elizabeth** (1:5c). This couple, Luke reports, **were both righteous before God and lived in conformity with all the commands and decrees of the Lord** (1:6a); in other words, "as to righteousness under the law" (Phil. 3:6), they were **blameless** (Luke 1:6b). Like other characters in the Third Gospel who are described as "righteous," Zechariah and Elizabeth are depicted as models of Jewish piety (cf. Simeon, 2:25; Joseph of Arimathea, 23:50) but worthy imitators of Jesus himself, who will be pronounced "righteous" at his death (23:47) and later in Acts given the title "the Righteous One" (Acts 3:14; 7:52; 22:14). Despite their faithfulness, they have one significant, though not unprecedented, problem: **they had no children, because Elizabeth was barren, and both were now very old** (1:7).

Dream-visions often occur in a temple or cultic setting (1 Kings 3:1–5; *Jub.* 32.1–2; *T. Levi* 8.1–19; *2 Bar.* 34.1–43.3; Josephus, *Ant.* 11.326–28; Acts 22:17–22; and various Asclepian inscriptions [e.g., *IG* IV² 1, 513, 561]; see Parsons 2008a, 312). The emphasis on the Jewish character of these opening scenes in Luke continues with the description of the cultic setting within which the annunciation of John's birth takes place: **Now it happened while Zechariah was** performing his priestly duty before God, when his priestly division was on duty, according to the custom of the priestly office, he drew the lot of offering incense and thus entered the sanctuary of the Lord (1:8–9). Luke reflects (and presumes his audience to know) details regarding religious rituals associated with the Jewish temple. Even if the estimated number of 18,000 priests (750 priests times 24 priestly divisions, calculated on the basis of *Let. Aris.* 95; see Jeremias 1969, 200) is an exaggeration, that this was a once-in-a-lifetime event for Zechariah is suggested by the drawing of lots (cf. *m. Tamid* 5.4). The morning and evening offering of incense was mandated in Exod. 30:7–8 and was preparatory for the twice-daily sacrificial offering, known as the Tamid, or "the perpetual offering" (Bock 1994–96, 1:79; cf. Num. 28:1–10). As Dennis Hamm has observed, "it is safe to say that in the postexilic Jewish imagination, the regular Tamid service was the primary liturgy of the temple" (2003, 216; cf. Culpepper 1995, 46).

> **Inflection**
>
> Luke here employs "inflection" (*polyptoton* or *klisis*), in which the subject is inflected in all cases (Theon, *Prog.* 74–75, 85; Quintilian, *Inst.* 9.1.34). In a short space, the term "people" (*laos*) occurs in the genitive (1:10), accusative (1:17), and nominative cases (1:21). The inflection is completed in 1:68, in which the term is used in the dative case. The use of inflection to indicate subject is a Lukan convention (see Parsons 2008a, 71) and here places the annunciation of John's birth within a corporate context of salvation history.

The incense offering symbolized prayer (Ps. 141:2; Philo, *Her.* 199; cf. Marshall 1978, 54), so we are not surprised to find that **the whole crowd of people was praying outside at the hour of the incense offering** (1:10; cf. *Tg. Song* 4.16; cited by Marshall 1978, 54). The term "people" (*laos*) in Luke typically refers to the Jewish people and serves to highlight the significance of these events for the people of God (cf. Luke 2:32; 21:23; the term *laos* occurs 36x in Luke).

1:11a. *Dream-vision terminology.* **And there appeared to him an angel of the Lord.** The use of the word "appeared" (*ōphthē*) is typical of dream-visions and is used in Luke (24:34) and later in Acts of divine appearances (Acts 2:3; 7:2, 30, 35; 9:17; 13:31; 16:9; 26:16; but cf. Acts 7:26; Fitzmyer 1981–85, 1:324).

1:11b–20. *Dream-vision proper.* That the vision occurs on the **right side of the altar** (1:11b) should have suggested to Zechariah, and the authorial audience, that the "angel's visit was not ominous," since this was the "favored" side (Fitzmyer 1981–85, 1:325). Nonetheless, Zechariah's response is one of "acute emotional distress" (L&N 25.244; cf. Luke 24:38): **and Zechariah was very distressed when he saw the angel, and fear overwhelmed him** (1:12).

In the message of the dream-vision, the angel seeks to alleviate Zechariah's fear (**Do not be afraid, Zechariah;** 1:13a) by returning to the theme of prayer so prominent throughout this section (**your prayers have been**

> **Metonymy**
>
> Luke 1:17 uses the rhetorical figure of *metonymy*, "which draws from an object closely akin or associated an expression suggesting the object meant, but not called by its own name" (*Rhet. Her.* 4.32.43, trans. Caplan, 1954). Specifically, the author cites the following example: "'Italy cannot be vanquished in warfare nor Greece in studies'; for here instead of Greeks and Italians the lands that comprise them are designated" (*Rhet. Her.* 4.32.43, trans. Caplan, 1954). Here Luke uses "hearts" as a metonym for the "affections" or "commitments" of the fathers/ancestors.

heard) and promises Zechariah that his wife Elizabeth will give birth to a son for you (1:13b). He further predicts, **And you will name him John. And joy and exultation will be yours, and many will rejoice because of his birth** (1:13c–14). Typical of these accounts of the noble births and origins of heroes, the angel predicts John's future greatness: **For he will be great before the Lord** (1:15a). This greatness will be characterized by an ascetic lifestyle (**He will never drink wine or alcohol;** 1:15b), typical of a holy person of God (cf. Lev. 10:9; Num. 6:3; Judg. 13:4; 4QSam^a 1.3), and a Spirit-filled ministry (**and he will be filled with the Holy Spirit, while he is still in his mother's womb;** 1:15c), typical of a prophet of God (Jer. 1:5). Both these prophecies are fulfilled in Luke's narrative: John leaps within his mother (herself characterized as "filled with the Spirit") in recognition of the prenatal Jesus's presence (1:41), and Jesus claims that "John the Baptizer came neither eating bread nor drinking wine" (7:33).

John's ministry will be one of conversion: **he will turn many of the children of Israel to the Lord their God** (1:16; cf. 3:3–18). He will also function as a forerunner to the Messiah: **he will go ahead before him in the spirit and power of Elijah** (1:17a; cf. Mal. 3:1). According to Mal. 4:5–6, the prophet Elijah would come "before the great and terrible day of the Lord" in order to "turn the hearts of parents to their children and the hearts of children to their parents." Likewise, John the Baptist will **turn the hearts of the fathers to their children** (1:17b), but the parallel phrase that follows (**and the disobedient to the wisdom of the righteous**) suggests that the basic sense is that "as (hostile) fathers are turned to their children, so are faithless people turned to righteous thoughts" (Johnson 1991, 33; cf. Luke 7:35). The angel's message once again focuses on the role of God's people (on *laos*, see above) in this salvation drama. John the Baptist will **make ready for the Lord a people who have been prepared** (1:17c).

Often the message of a dream-vision is in the form of a dialogue between the messenger and recipient of the vision (e.g., Gen. 20:3–8; 31:10–13; 46:2–6). Such is also the case here. Zechariah's reaction comes in the form of a protest, a response typical of OT versions of the dream-vision (Gen. 18:12; Exod. 6:30; Judg. 6:15; 13:22): **And Zechariah said to the angel, "How will I know this? For I am an old man, and my wife is well along in years"** (1:18). This particular protest recalls for the reader the protest of another elderly man, Abraham, after he has

Tracing the Narrative Flow

Figure 1. Gabriel Speaking to Mary, from the Church of the Annunciation

been told in a dream-vision that he will become a father: "Then Abraham fell on his face and laughed, and said to himself, 'Can a child be born to a man who is a hundred years old? Can Sarah, who is ninety years old, bear a child?'" (Gen. 17:17). The messenger responds with a sign of the veracity of his message, in the form of a judgment: **The angel answered, "I am Gabriel, who stands before God, and I have been sent to speak to you and to tell this good news to you. You will be silent and not able to speak until the very day these things take place, because you did not believe my words, which will be fulfilled in their time!"** (1:19–20).

1:21–25. *Reaction/response.* The *response* feature of a dream-vision report can either "(1) note the immediate response of the dreamer-visionary or (2) provide an extended narrative of how the dream-vision was fulfilled" (Dodson 2009, 145). Luke chooses the latter:

> Now, the people were waiting for Zechariah and were wondering, as he was spending a long time in the temple. When he came out, he was not able to speak to them, and they realized that he had seen a vision in the temple. He was making signs to them and remained unable to speak. And when his days of service were completed, he went to his house. Some time later, Elizabeth his wife became pregnant, and she kept herself in seclusion for five months. (1:21–24)

All of Gabriel's predictions come true: Elizabeth becomes pregnant, Zechariah's prayers are heard and answered, and Zechariah is unable to speak (and

37

also presumably unable to complete the Tamid blessing over the people; cf. Sir. 50). While the form of Luke 1:5–25 is similar to the larger literary convention of the dream-vision in Greco-Roman literature, its function is peculiarly reminiscent of other and earlier barren couples in the Jewish Scriptures (Gen. 17–18; Judg. 13). As he did with Rachel ("God has taken away my reproach"; Gen. 30:22–23), God remembers Elizabeth, and she, like Hannah (1 Sam. 1:19–20), gives thanks: **This is what the Lord has done for me in the days in which he looked with favor on me and took away my shame among the people** (1:25).

Luke is more subtle in his echoes of the OT than Matthew, who uses an explicit quotation formula ("All this took place to fulfill what had been spoken to the Lord through the prophet") in order to connect the story of Jesus to Israel's story (Matt. 1:22–23; see also 2:15, 17–18, 23). Luke's technique is more like that of a palimpsest, a manuscript that has been washed and reused but in which the first text is, through proper knowledge and technique, still recoverable. And with the proper knowledge and technique, the audience not only can bring the other story to the surface; they also can, unlike the double-exposed photograph or palimpsest, make the primary story come more into focus: God continues his saving work with his people. And so the stage is set now for the coming of the One who not only will prove superior to John in every way but will also embody God's salvific activity.

The Annunciation of the Birth of Jesus (1:26–38)

Once again, the annunciation of Jesus's birth is in the form of a Greco-Roman dream-vision (Hanson 1980; Dodson 2009). The similarity in form between the two annunciation scenes serves the purposes of the *synkrisis* between John and Jesus (see below).

1:26–27. *Scene-setting.* **In the sixth month, the angel Gabriel was sent by God to a city in Galilee called Nazareth to a virgin who was engaged to a man named Joseph of the family line of David; and the name of the virgin was Mary.** The recipient of the vision, Mary, is identified, and a sketch of her character is provided: "a virgin who was engaged to a man named Joseph." In addition the dream-vision's locale, "a city in Galilee called Nazareth," and time, "in the sixth month" (of Elizabeth's pregnancy), are specified. These too are conventional elements of the dream-vision setting.

Dream-vision terminology. Interestingly, Luke uses no technical dream terminology (not even "appeared," as with Zechariah and the shepherds), but the scene-setting has stated that "the angel Gabriel was sent from God," which serves to tie this dream-vision closely to the preceding one.

1:28–38a. *Dream-vision proper.* The bulk of Mary's dream-vision is taken up with Gabriel's message, which includes dialogue with the recipient of this vision. Gabriel greets Mary: **Greetings, you who are highly favored; the Lord is with you** (1:28). The phrase "the Lord is with you" is found in an angel's message elsewhere only in Gideon's dream-vision recorded in Judg. 6. There the angel of the Lord greets Gideon with these words (the opening of which in the LXX agrees verbatim with Gabriel's words): "The LORD is with you, you mighty warrior" (Judg. 6:12). Mary knows her Scriptures and perhaps knows that this same greeting given to Gideon is followed by a divine message, which, in Gideon's case, involves an assignment.

Mary's puzzled pause over these words, **Now she was troubled because of what was said and began pondering what kind of greeting this might be** (1:29), encourages the audience to do the same. The pattern also encourages the audience to expect that like Moses and Gideon, Mary too will be given a task to do. What may surprise them (and us!) is the nature of the assignment: **And the angel said to her, "Do not be afraid, Mary, for you have found favor with God. You will become pregnant and give birth to a son; and you will name him Jesus! He will be great and will be called Son of the Most High; and the Lord God will give the throne of his ancestor David to him. He will reign over the house of Jacob forever, and his kingdom will have no end"** (1:30–33). Mary's objection, like those of Abraham, Moses, Gideon, and Zechariah before her, is by now expected. Gideon complains he is from the smallest tribe and the least in his own family. Abraham and Zechariah each plead advanced age. So, Mary too objects: **How will this be, since I am not sleeping with a man?** (1:34). Gabriel, of course, gives a sign to confirm the authenticity of the message: **The Holy Spirit will come upon you, and the power of the Most High will overshadow you. So then, the holy child who is born will be called the Son of God. Elizabeth, your relative—even she has conceived a son in her old age! Indeed, this is the sixth month for her who was called barren. For nothing is impossible for God** (1:35–37). For Mary, the convincing sign is that her relative Elizabeth, barren all those years, is now in her sixth month of pregnancy.

The obvious similarities between these two dream-visions underscore their comparative function in the larger *synkrisis* between John the Baptist and Jesus. It is revealed to Zechariah in a dream-vision that he is to become the father of John the Baptist, forerunner of the Messiah; likewise, it is revealed to Mary that she is to be mother of the Son of the Most High. But the redundancy of elements also highlights the differences between the two accounts. The account of Jesus's birth is parallel to John's birth, but, in this rhetorical *synkrisis*, Jesus's birth is superior in every way. John is to be born to aged parents who desperately want a child; Jesus is to be born to a young girl to whom the news comes as a total surprise. John is to be conceived by sexual intercourse; Jesus is to be conceived by the Holy Spirit overshadowing Mary, a virgin. Both will be great before the Lord, but John is "to make ready for the Lord a people who have been prepared"; John will later be called a "prophet of the Most High," but Jesus will be called "the Son of the Most High" and "will reign over the house of Jacob forever." This theme of John's annunciation, conception, birth, and commission as parallel but subordinate to Jesus continues throughout the rest of the birth narrative (compare 1:57–66, 80, with 2:15–27, 34–40).

As of old, God has revealed through a dream-vision to two of his people, an old priest and a young virgin, the task to which they are assigned. Another *synkrisis* is offered. For Zechariah, the commission is to father John, who will go before the Lord, making the people ready. For Mary, the assignment is to give birth to Jesus, to whom will be given the throne of his ancestor David. Both initially object, but ultimately Mary joins Zechariah and the band of witnesses who have gone before them and who have been faithful to the task given them: **And Mary said, "I am the servant of the Lord! May it happen to me according to your word"** (1:38a). This story has little room for sentimental musings about the first Christmas; rather, it demands that its hearers, then and now, discern their own commission, and despite whatever obvious shortcomings, commit themselves to its completion.

1:38b. *Reaction/response.* The dream-vision ends abruptly: **And the angel left her.** But, typical of Greco-Roman dream-visions, the response can be presented in "an extended narrative of how the dream-vision was fulfilled" (Dodson 2009, 145). And so the visitation of Mary to Elizabeth in the next scene provides the appropriate response to the dream-vision and continues the story of this holy child who "will be called Son of God!"

The Visitation of Mary to Elizabeth (1:39–56)

In the rhetorical flow of the Third Gospel, Luke 1:39–56 itself functions as a kind of bridge between the annunciations of John and Jesus (1:5–38) and the births and early lives of John and Jesus (1:57–2:52; Talbert 1982, 22). Luke 1:39–56 is composed of a narrative introduction (1:39–41), two hymns (1:42–45, 46–55), and a narrative conclusion (1:56).

1:39–41. Just as Mary is the object of attention in 1:26–38, so also is she the focus of 1:39–56 (Coleridge 1993, 76). The unit begins and ends by narrating Mary's arrival in and departure from the hill country (1:39, 56). In 1:39–41, Mary serves as the subject of all the verbs: Mary **quickly hurried off, entered Zechariah's house,** and **greeted Elizabeth** (1:39–40). Even when the subject changes to Elizabeth, Mary remains the focal point. At the sound of Mary's greeting, Elizabeth's baby **jumped in her womb** and **Elizabeth was filled with the Holy Spirit** (1:41). Mary is the subject of Elizabeth's speech (1:42–45), and then Mary is the speaker of the hymn in 1:46–55.

1:42–45. The first hymn by Elizabeth celebrates Mary as the "ideal believer" (Talbert 2002, 25–28). The absence of Mary's name from the canticle suggests that it is "not Mary in her own right who appears in the speech, but Mary in relation to God's plan" (Coleridge 1993, 85). Elizabeth's speech contains four oracles (Culpepper 1995, 54–55). The first declares that both Mary and her unborn child are **blessed** (1:42; cf. 11:27). The second oracle is in the form of a question (**Why has this happened to me?**), but contains in it a reference to **the mother of my Lord**, a thoroughly Christian confession (1:43). The third oracle gives Elizabeth's interpretation for why her baby moved in the womb:

the baby jumped for joy in my womb (1:44; "joy" is an important motif in the Lukan infancy narrative; cf. 1:14; 2:10). The last oracle is a beatitude on Mary and her faith and underscores her depiction as the ideal disciple (1:45).

1:46–55. If Elizabeth praises Mary in the first speech, Mary praises God in the second (1:46–55; Tannehill 1996, 53). In Luke 1:46, the rhetorical figure known as *synecdoche* is used. Unlike *metonymy* (see comments on 1:17 and the sidebar "Metonymy"), synecdoche specifically involves a part-whole relationship ("the whole is known from a small part"; *Rhet. Her.* 4.33.44, trans. Caplan, 1954). Here a part of the speaker, that is, **my soul**, is used to refer to the whole person (see Parsons 2008a, 167). Mary begins her speech with a present-tense verb, **magnifies** (1:46), as is common in reported speech, and it is conjoined with a parallel clause that uses an aorist verb (lit., "rejoiced"), providing perfective contrast (see Culy, Parsons, and Stigall 2010).

The canticle divides into two strophes: In the first, Mary declares what God has done for her, which serves as the rationale for her praise: **because he has looked upon the humble state of his servant. Indeed, from now on, all generations will consider me blessed, because the Mighty One has done great things for me! Holy is his name! From one generation to the next, his mercy extends to those who fear him!** (1:48–50). The second strophe (1:51–55) is concerned with God's activity in the larger society (Tannehill 1996, 54). The Magnificat is therefore not a direct response to Elizabeth's hymn of praise but rather a theological reflection on the work of God throughout the Lukan infancy narrative to this point. The six aorist tenses in 1:51–53 are translated as perfects and are understood to be proleptic, speaking of the future as already past (see Wallace 1996, 563): **He *has produced* strength with his arm; he *has scattered* those who are arrogant in the thinking of their heart. He *has brought down* the powerful from their thrones and *has lifted up* the lowly; he *has filled* the hungry with good things and *has sent* the rich away empty** (1:51–53).

There are important links between the two strophes; the Magnificat "clarifies the links between what God has done for one individual and what he will do for the structures of society at large" (Talbert 1982, 22). Mary speaks of her own "humble state" (1:48) and later talks of what God has done for the "lowly" in general (1:52). In the first strophe, God is the "Mighty One" (1:49); in the second, God brings down the "powerful" (1:52). In both parts God shows his "strength" (49, 51) and his "mercy" (50, 54). The most powerful language about the social reversal that God effects is found in a chiastic pattern in verses 52–53:

A   God has brought down the *powerful*;
   B   God has lifted up the *lowly*;
   B′ God has filled the *hungry*;
A′ God has sent the *rich* away empty.

These themes are repeated in Jesus's "messianic woes" recorded in Luke 6:20–26.

Mary's speech ends with reference to God, who has **come to the aid of Israel his servant, remembering mercy—just as he spoke to our ancestors—for Abraham and his descendants forever** (1:54–55; on the history of the translation difficulties associated with these verses, see Bock 1994–96, 1:159–60). Mary ends her speech with a reference to the Abrahamic covenant. The Abrahamic covenant is mentioned also in Zechariah's prophecy (1:73–75) and later in Peter's temple sermon in Acts 3:25 (see also Luke 3:8; 19:9; Acts 7:2–17; cf. Dahl 1966; Brawley 1995, 18–26) and plays a major role in Luke's understanding of the reconstituted people of God in light of his "remembering mercies" (see Parsons 2007, 81–82).

1:56. The scene concludes simply: **And Mary stayed with her for about three months and then returned to her home.**

Theological Issues

In the history of the interpretation of the visitation scene, Jacopo Pontormo's painting (ca. 1514–16) makes a distinctive, if not unique, contribution (see Hornik and Parsons 2003, 59–91). In Pontormo's version of *The Visitation* (see fig. 2), the sacrifice of Isaac depicted above the architecture suggests a parallel between the faith of Abraham and that of the Virgin Mary, united by the common sacrifice of their sons. Certainly, the Isaac/Christ parallels have been well-known since the patristic period (if not before; see Rom. 8:32; Heb. 11:17–18), but most of these parallels focus on the similarities between the (near) sacrifice of Isaac and the passion of Christ. Ambrose wrote: "Isaac is therefore a type of the suffering of Christ" (*Cain* 1.8, trans. author; see also Irenaeus, *Haer.* 4.5; Melito, *Frag.* 9, 10, 11, 15; Augustine, *Civ.* 16.32). Each was a "beloved son" offered as the consummate sacrifice by his father. Both sacrifices took place on a hill. The thorns of the bush that trapped the ram were the thorns of Christ's crown. The ram in the bush was Christ on the cross; Isaac was Christ in the Eucharist.

Pontormo (most likely on the advice of his patrons, the Servites) relocates the link between Isaac and Christ backward from the crucifixion to the scene of Mary's visitation. Furthermore, Pontormo draws our attention to a little-noted reference at the end of the Magnificat. There Mary says, "Because he [God] remembered mercy for Abraham and his seed forever" (1:55; cf. 1:73). Such a connection appears to be unprecedented in the history of interpretation, and Pontormo secures the linkage through several different strategies.

First, the two scenes are united by the cluster of complex gestures of the figures to the right of Mary and Elizabeth. The figure kneeling to the right of Elizabeth is presumably Joseph, who is turned toward the standing figure of Zechariah. With his right hand he points to the scene of Elizabeth and Mary, and with his left hand he points upward toward the sacrifice of Isaac.

Likewise, Zechariah points to the OT scene overhead, and a third female figure behind Joseph directs the viewer's attention toward Zechariah as well. That the viewer is to interpret these scenes in light of each other is made unmistakably clear by these characters in the lower part of the fresco. But what is the connection?

The answer is to be found in the tablets, held by two putti, or angels, that contain (now barely legible) inscriptions. The two flanking Latin inscriptions interpret the actions both of Abraham and Mary (NUM[INI] DEB[ET] EVM: "He [Abraham/Mary] owes him [Isaac/Jesus] to God") and of God (NEC VAN[E] IUR[AT]: "Nor does he swear [or promise] in vain"). Here in the context of the encounter between Mary and Elizabeth, Mary recalls the mercy that God had shown Abraham and his seed Isaac. That mercy was never more clearly revealed than in the near sacrifice of Isaac, when God spared Abraham's son Isaac because of Abraham's faithfulness. And in the most profound way, God's most beneficent act of grace is shown when he refuses to spare his own son in order that we might experience that mercy. There is another inscription in the center space between the two scenes: ANVE OPTIME DEUS: "Most Excellent God, look favorably." This involves the artist's audience in this drama of epiphany by articulating a prayer of petition: "Most Excellent God, look favorably" on us as well.

Figure 2. Jacopo Pontormo, *Visitation*, SS. Annunziata

Luke 1:57–2:52

Birth and Training: John and Jesus

Introductory Matters

According to Theon, an encomium that reveals the "greatness of virtuous actions and other good qualities belonging to a particular person" (*Prog.* 109, trans. Kennedy 2003, 50) will include, among other things, details of the person's "good birth," "education" or "training," and "goods of the body," such as "health, strength, beauty, and acuteness of sense" (*Prog.* 110, trans. Kennedy 2003, 50). Luke addresses all these issues in his encomiastic comparison of the birth and training of John (1:57–80) and Jesus (2:1–52).

Tracing the Narrative Flow

John's Birth and Upbringing (1:57–80)

The narrative of John's birth divides into two units: The first narrates events surrounding John's birth (1:57–66). The second (1:67–80) contains Zechariah's Benedictus, the second canticle, or song, in the infancy narrative.

John's birth (1:57–66). The first unit (1:57–66) can itself be subdivided into three parts: (a) the birth, circumcision, and naming of John (1:57–63); (b) events surrounding the restoration of Zechariah's speech (1:64–65); and (c) a brief question/answer regarding the destiny of the child, John (1:66).

1:57–63. Compared to the annunciation of John's birth, the narrative describing the birth is sparse: **Now the time came for Elizabeth to give birth, and she bore a son. Her neighbors and relatives heard that the Lord had lavished**

his mercy on her, and they rejoiced with her (1:57–58). The first and last details fulfill predictions made by Gabriel to Zechariah: Elizabeth gives birth to a son (1:57; cf. 1:13); the neighbors rejoice (1:58; cf. 1:14; see also Culpepper 1995, 58). In the center stands the "great mercy" that the neighbors and relatives hear that the Lord has shown Elizabeth. God's mercy has already been a central theme in Mary's Magnificat (1:50, 54) and will return in Zechariah's Benedictus (1:72, 78). In keeping with their earlier characterization as righteous before God and blameless with regard to the commandments (1:6), **on the eighth day they [Elizabeth and Zechariah] came to circumcise the child** (1:59a) in fulfillment of the law (see Gen. 17:12; Lev. 12:3).

> **Luke 1:57–2:52 in the Narrative Flow**
>
> Jesus's origins and training (1:1–4:13)
>   Preface (1:1–4)
>   Annunciations: John and Jesus (1:5–56)
> ▶ Birth and training: John and Jesus (1:57–2:52)
>   John's birth and upbringing (1:57–80)
>   John's birth (1:57–66)
>   Zechariah's Benedictus (1:67–80)
>   Jesus's birth and upbringing (2:1–52)
>   The birth of Jesus and the visitation of the shepherds (2:1–21)
>   The presentation of Jesus in the temple (2:22–39)
>   Jesus's nurture and training (Luke 2:40–52)

Naming the child takes much more narrative time than does the birth. The friends and relatives **began calling him Zechariah, after the name of his father** (1:59b). Elizabeth, aware of the prophecy made to Zechariah regarding the name, intervenes: **But his mother responded, "No! Instead, he will be called John"** (1:60). The crowd objects, **There is no one among your relatives who is called by that name** (1:61; even though the name was used during this time of priestly families—see 1 Macc. 2:1–2; Fitzmyer 1981–85, 1:381). Presumably, Zechariah is deaf as well as mute (1:22; on *kōphos* as both deaf and mute, see Hab. 2:18–19 LXX; 3 Macc. 4:16), so the crowd **motioned to his father to see what he would want him to be called** (1:62). Zechariah responds in dramatic fashion and confirms Elizabeth's choice: **So after asking for a writing tablet, he wrote, saying, "John is his name." And everyone was amazed** (1:63).

1:64–65. In encomia (and encomiastic biography), it was conventional to mention marvelous events that occurred in association with the birth of a hero. Pseudo-Hermogenes, for example, writes: "You will mention also any marvelous occurrences at birth, for example from dreams or signs or things like that" (Ps.-Hermogenes, *Prog.* 15, trans. Kennedy 2003, 82; see also Nicolaus, *Prog.* 51, 59–60). Thus, Luke reports that **immediately Zechariah's mouth was opened, and his tongue loosened, and he began speaking and praising God. And fear came upon all those living around them. All these matters were being discussed throughout the entire hill country of Judea** (1:64–65).

1:66. All who heard thought carefully about these things and wondered about the future greatness of this young child, **What then shall this child be?** (1:66a). The question is not purely rhetorical, for the narrator himself offers a brief, proleptic allusion to John's nurture and training (Theon, *Prog.* 110; Ps.-Hermogenes, *Prog.* 16, 19; Nicolaus, *Prog.* 52): **For the hand of the Lord was with him** (1:66b). The "hand of the Lord" was an expression used in the Jewish Scriptures to convey God's strength and protection (see LXX Exod. 13:3; 1 Chron. 4:10; Ps. 74:9 [75:8 Eng.]) and suggests that John's nurture and training had a divine as well as a human dimension (cf. 1:80). Even though the hand of the Lord was with John, he would not be spared from imprisonment and execution by Herod (3:20) any more than the young Jesus who had the "favor of God" upon him (2:40) would be excused from the way of Calvary (Fitzmyer 1981–85, 1:382).

Zechariah's Benedictus (1:67–80). This second unit (1:67–80) narrates Zechariah's Benedictus, which praises God for his mercy (1:67–75) and predicts the shape of John's future ministry (1:76–79). The section ends with a brief note regarding John's growth (1:80), the importance of which far exceeds its length.

1:67–75. In the first section of the speech (1:67–75), Zechariah focuses on God's merciful acts of deliverance: **Then Zechariah his father was filled with the Holy Spirit and prophesied: "Blessed be the Lord God of Israel, because he has shown his care and redeemed his people"** (1:67–68). The phrase "the Lord God of Israel" as a title for God occurs rarely in the LXX and deuterocanonical literature (Ezek. 4:13; 44:2; Mal. 2:16; 2 Macc. 9:5; *Odes Sol.* 9.68), and only here in the NT (in the LXX, "Lord God," *kyrios ho theos*, is the standard translation for YHWH; see Culy, Parsons, and Stigall 2010). Although the full realization of "redemption" (*lytrōsin*) will come only later, with the birth, life, and death of Jesus, Zechariah is attributing praise to God for already demonstrating his care for Israel and initiating their ultimate redemption by sending the forerunner of the Messiah.

Zechariah continues: **He has brought about a mighty deliverance for us** (lit., "he has raised up a horn of salvation for us"; 1:69a). The term "horn" is a common metaphor for strength (see, e.g., LXX 2 Sam. 22:3; Pss. 17:3 [18:2]; 88:18 [89:17]; 131:17 [132:17]; 148:14; Jer. 31:25 [48:25]). According to L&N 76.16, "the reference of the phrase *keras sōtērias* is to the role of the Messiah, and accordingly one may often best render this phrase as 'mighty Savior' or 'powerful Savior'" (see Marshall 1978, 91). Although **in the house of David, his servant** (1:69b), may suggest that a personal referent is in view, on the whole it seems best to give *sōtērias* its usual abstract sense, "salvation, deliverance," rather than "savior." Indeed, such a rendering fits better with what follows in 1:71.

The next section of Zechariah's speech (1:70–75) is grammatically complex, and its interpretation depends on clarifying its syntax. The parenthetical comment **just as he spoke through the mouth of his holy prophets from long ago**

(1:70) introduces an analogy between what precedes and what follows; that is, God's actions are in accord with what God said. This **salvation from our enemies and from the hand of all those who hate us** (1:71) is in apposition to the "mighty deliverance" specified in 1:69 (so Plummer 1903, 41; Marshall 1978, 91). Luke uses "hand" as a metonym for the "power" of the enemies (cf. *Rhet. Her.* 4.32.43). The speech continues: **thus showing mercy to our fathers and remembering his holy covenant** (1:72). Some have taken the infinitive clause—literally, "to do mercy with" (1:72)—as a purpose clause modifying "he brought a mighty deliverance" (e.g., "he . . . raised up a horn of salvation . . . to perform the mercy promised to our fathers" [1:69, 72 RSV]; see Plummer 1903, 41), but it is more likely an epex-

The "First" or the "Most Important" Census under Quirinius?

The word *prōtē*, usually translated "first" or "former," might in Luke 2:2 be understood as "the most prominent" or "significant" (BDAG). Luke certainly knows this usage (see Luke 15:22, which refers to the *stolēn tēn prōtēn*, "the special robe"; see also Luke 13:30; 19:47; later, Acts 13:50; 17:4; 25:2; 28:17). The resulting translation of this sense in the immediate Lukan context would be something like "this became a very important registration when Quirinius was governing Syria," in which the phrase would function as a narrative aside to Luke's audience, again a common literary device for Luke (see Sheeley 1992; see also Carlson 2004; Thorley 1979).

egetical infinitive, clarifying either 1:70 (i.e., "he raised a horn of salvation, . . . that is, he showed mercy to our ancestors") or 1:71 ("salvation from our enemies, that is, showing mercy to our ancestors"). Fitzmyer argues that these two options go together; since "salvation" is in apposition to "he brought a mighty deliverance," "so an infinitive that is epexegetical to 'salvation' is also epexegetical to 'mighty deliverance'" (1981–85, 1:384). This solution also makes sense of the next infinitive, "to remember," which is conjoined by *kai* with "to do mercy" and thus functions in the same manner (or conversely, it does *not* make sense to say that God raised up a horn of salvation in order to remember his covenant). One last clarifying comment places **the oath that he swore to Abraham our father** (1:73) in apposition to the "covenant," which, by implication, God continues to remember through the birth of this child, who "will go before the Lord" (1:76). And it is appropriate for Zechariah to recall God's oath to Abraham at the time of John's circumcision (1:59), the rite that commemorates that covenant and oath (Johnson 1991, 48).

The last part of the Benedictus introduces the content of that oath. God has sworn **to allow us, after being delivered from the hand of our enemies, to serve him without fear in holiness and righteousness before him all of our days** (1:74–75). In other words, Zechariah exclaims, God's oath is to enable us to serve him in response to our redemption/deliverance/salvation and to do so with holiness and righteousness, without fear and in perpetuity. The word "to serve" (*latreuein*) is often translated "to worship," but here "it refers to the total service one gives to God, not just to the worship or sacrificial service that a faithful Jew would render in the temple or synagogue" (Bock 1994–96, 1:186).

1:76–79. Zechariah then turns the focus of his speech to John the Baptist: **And you, child, will be called a prophet of the Most High** (1:76a). The verse begins with *kai sy de*. While the *de* marks this as a new development or shift in topic in the discourse (see Levinsohn 1987), the *kai* indicates that the prophecy about the child, John, is part of the overall action of God described in the first part of the speech (1:68–75). Like the first part of the canticle, 1:76–79 constitutes one sentence in the Greek. John's future role will be as a "prophet of the Most High," an exalted vocation yet one that is, in the extended Jesus/John *synkrisis* of Luke 1–4, subordinate to Jesus's destiny as the "Son of the Most High" (1:32). As God's prophet, John **will go before the Lord to prepare his ways** (1:76b; cf. Mal. 3:1; Isa. 40:3). In 1:76b, Zechariah alludes to Mal. 3:1 and Isa. 40:3 and to Luke 1:17, but he paraphrases those references by adding an explanatory note, amplifying what it means to "prepare the Lord's ways": **that is, to give the knowledge of salvation to his people *with respect to* the forgiveness of their sins** (1:77). This expansion through repetition reflects a well-known rhetorical exercise known as "paraphrase" (*paraphrasis*), in which a writer would "change the form of expression while keeping the thoughts" (Theon, *Prog.* 107P, trans. Kennedy 2003, 70). According to Theon, "all ancient writers seem to have used paraphrase in the best possible way, rephrasing not only their writings but those of each other" (*Prog.* 62, trans. Kennedy 2003, 6). Furthermore, there were four kinds of paraphrase: "variation in syntax, by addition, by subtraction and by substitution" (Theon, *Prog.* 107P–108P, trans. Kennedy 2003, 70). Here *paraphrasis* occurs by addition; "a 'prepared people' . . . is specified in terms of the 'forgiveness of sins'" (Johnson 1991, 46; on forgiveness of sins as providing the context or circumstance of salvation, see Luke 3:3; 4:18; 5:20–21, 23–24; 7:48–49; 11:4; 17:4; 23:34).

John's "ministry of preparation," Zechariah proclaims, is **on account of our God's merciful heart** (1:78a). The term *splanchna* (lit., "intestines") is most commonly used in its figurative senses in the NT; here it means "the psychological faculty of desire, intent, and feeling" (L&N 26.11; see Col. 3:12). The English "heart" is often used in an analogous fashion. This emphasis on God's mercy refers not only to the immediate context of God's deliverance (1:71) but also to the great mercy God has shown Elizabeth (1:58), and even earlier to the divine mercy to which Mary bears witness in the Magnificat (1:50, 54). But this mercy also points forward: **in the context of which [i.e., God's mercy] the Rising One from on high will visit us** (1:78b). Rhetorical ambiguity continues here as before, since the term translated "Rising One" (*anatolē*) has rich and varied Jewish symbolism. The term (and its verbal cognates) is used in the OT to refer to the divine light, which shines on God's people (LXX Isa. 58:10; Mal. 3:20), and may be understood to refer to God himself (Isa. 60:2; 2 Sam.

23:4). But the term *anatolē* is also used in the LXX to translate the Hebrew term *ṣemaḥ* ("shoot" or "branch") and is used in three texts that are clearly messianic ("I will raise up for David a righteous Branch"; Jer. 23:5; see also Zech. 3:8; 6:12). Both senses fit well with the imagery that immediately follows in Zechariah's speech (if the notion is of a preexistent messianic figure, the language is rather indirect): **in order to shine upon those sitting in darkness and the shadow of death, that is, to guide our feet in the way of peace** (1:79). Here again, as with the divine visitation of the Lord, which God chooses to make through the birth of Jesus, God illuminates from "on high" (cf. 24:49) those "sitting in darkness and the shadow of death" in the Dawn of Jesus. With this light of the Branch of David, the Way of Peace is illuminated.

This last reference to those "sitting in darkness and the shadow of death" suggests a certain universality: everyone must die. But God's response "remains deeply rooted in the ethos and symbolism of Judaism. . . . If Luke cannot show that 'the God of Israel visited and redeemed his people,' then the hope of the Gentiles is groundless" (Johnson 1991, 48).

With Mary's Magnificat, Zechariah's Benedictus shares a focus on God's merciful redemption. Mary, however, moves from her individual experience to speak of God's work in the social and political arena. Zechariah begins by recounting God's redemptive work in the house of his servant David and then proceeds to locate the role of John the Baptist (and the coming Messiah?) within this drama of salvation (see Johnson 1991, 48). God's liberating mercies are both social and political (so the Magnificat, 1:51–53) and personal and religious (see the Benedictus, 1:77–79).

1:80. This section ends quickly: **And the child grew and became strong in the Spirit, and he was in the wilderness until the day of his revealing to Israel** (1:80). John grew and became strong in the Spirit, and Luke leaves him in the desert until the time comes for him to begin his own public ministry. In the meantime, Luke turns his attention to the birth and nurture of Jesus.

Jesus's Birth and Upbringing (2:1–52)

This unit divides into three smaller segments: the birth of Jesus and the visitation of the shepherds (2:1–21); the presentation of Jesus in the temple (2:22–39); and Jesus's nurture and training (2:40–52).

The birth of Jesus and the visitation of the shepherds (2:1–21). This first unit has two parts: the census and report of Jesus's birth (2:1–7) and the annunciation and visitation of the shepherds (2:8–21).

2:1–7. This first section begins with a reference to an imperial census: **Now it happened in those days that a decree went out from Caesar Augustus for all the [Roman] world to be registered** (2:1). Locating the local events of Judea on the larger world map is typical of Luke in these early chapters (see 1:5; 3:1). Luke further specifies that **this census was the first while Quirinius was governing Syria** (2:2). The reference to the census is a notoriously difficult

Figure 3. Caesar Augustus Primaporta

crux interpretum, since there is no evidence of a registration of the whole Roman Empire under Augustus (Bock 1994–96, 1:202–4, 209; Fitzmyer 1981–85, 1:399–405).

However the historical issues are resolved, the theological significance is clear. By the time of Luke's Gospel, Augustan propaganda, which praised the peace Augustus had brought to the Roman Empire, was found throughout Roman literature (see Virgil's *Aeneid* and *Fourth Eclogue*) and art (see the *Augustus of Primaporta* [fig. 3] and *Ara Pacis Augustae*) and was no doubt familiar to Luke's authorial audience. In book 6 of Virgil's *Aeneid*, Aeneas visits the underworld and encounters his deceased father, Anchises, who prophesies about the coming of a "son of God," Caesar Augustus, through whom a great peace would be established.

The statue of Augustus that once stood at the entrance to Augustus's summer home at Primaporta likewise supports this Augustan propaganda (see fig. 3). Standing six feet and eight inches tall, the young Augustus poses in full armor, with hand raised in an oratorical gesture. On his breastplate is depicted Augustus's military victory over the Parthians in 39–38 BC, an event given cosmic significance here by the presence of gods and goddesses. The Cupid figure at his feet is a reminder that Augustus's family, the Julian clan, claimed to be descendants of the goddess Venus. The message is clear: Caesar, son of a god, has brought peace to the world.

This message was found throughout the Roman Empire. The Priene inscription boasts: "The birthday of the god [Augustus] has marked the beginning of the good news for the world" (trans. Brown 1977, 416). In Halicarnassus Augustus was called the "savior of the whole world." His birthday was even adopted as the first day of the New Year in parts of Asia Minor.

Luke challenges the conventional wisdom of this propaganda by setting the birth of the Messiah within the context of Augustus's edict (2:3–7a). This unit ends with the note that Mary and Joseph **laid him in a manger, because they did not have a place to stay** (2:7b). In the history of interpretation, this notice of "no room . . . in the inn" (KJV) has led into several exegetical cul-de-sacs.

Figure 4. View toward Bethlehem from Herodium

The phrase has been taken as a sign of Jesus's rejection by his own people (or as the author of the Fourth Gospel put it, "He came unto his own, and his own received him not"; John 1:11 KJV). Jerome's comments are typical in this regard: "The Lord is born on earth, and he does not have even a cell in which to be born, for there was no room for him in the inn. The entire human race had a place, and the Lord about to be born on earth had none. He found no room among men" (*Tract. Ps.* 44, trans. Ewald 1964, 331). This interpretation is based in part on a misunderstanding of the meaning of the term for "lodgings," *katalyma*, which is often translated as "inn," as though the reference were to a public inn with rooms for rent. Luke certainly knows a term for rented public accommodations; he uses it in the parable of the good Samaritan (*pandocheion*; 10:34). For Luke, the term used here, however, suggests a guest chamber in a private home (cf. Luke 22:11). In this scenario, while Mary and Joseph can find no space in the guest room of a private house (of a friend or relative of Joseph?), they are allowed to stay in the family room (into which the manger or feeding trough had been moved for the baby) or in the adjacent stable area (often hewn from stone, which may have given rise to the tradition that Jesus was born in a cave—so the patristic theologian Origen and the *Protevangelium of James*; see fig. 5). In either case, it would seem that Luke is highlighting the hospitality of the anonymous householder (friend or relative) and not condemning the inhospitality of an insensitive inn-keeper (Bailey 2008). Luke's point is that Jesus came to his own, and his own *did* receive him.

The emphasis on the humble environs of Jesus's birth is also firmly lodged in the tradition and, though not the primary focus of attention in Luke 2, is

Figure 5. Grotto Star Church of the Annunciation

not entirely without significance. The Venerable Bede captures that sense of the story when he writes:

> It should be noted that the sign given of the Savior's birth is not a child enfolded in Tyrian purple, but one wrapped with rough pieces of cloth. He is not to be found in an ornate golden bed, but in a manger. The meaning of this is that he did not merely take upon himself our lowly mortality, but for our sakes took upon himself the clothing of the poor. (*Exposition of the Gospel of Luke* 1, trans. Just 2003, 38–39)

Still we move too quickly from Bede's point to the view that Jesus was among the "poorest of the poor" (see Meier 1991–2009, 1:282). This is a hyperbole, and it certainly goes beyond Bede's point.

Both of these approaches (Jesus's rejection and/or lowly state) overshadow a more important, though often overlooked, detail in the report of the birth, that is, the place where the baby is placed—in a manger, or feeding trough. The stall, or manger, evokes the picture of Jesus, laying in a manger, as "food for the world." The theme of food and meals as one of the ways in which Jesus reveals his mission to others runs throughout Luke (see Luke 7; 11; 14; 22; 24; Karris 1985).

2:8–21. In the next section (2:8–21), Luke moves rather abruptly from the general notice of an Augustan decree to the Judean countryside. The story has the conventional elements of the dream-vision, which Luke has already used in the annunciations of John and Jesus (1:5–25, 26–38): scene-setting (2:8); dream-vision terminology (2:9); dream-vision proper, which includes a commissioning/invitation (2:10–14); and reaction/response, which can include an extended narrative demonstrating how the dream-vision is fulfilled (2:15–21). In this dream-vision (and unlike the earlier ones in Luke), more than one person has the same visionary experience at the same time (a rather common occurrence in ancient reports of dream-visions; e.g., Exod. 24:9–10; Luke 9:28–36; Pausanias, *Descr.* 38.13).

1. *Scene-setting* (2:8). Most modern readers are conditioned to hear this reference to shepherds **keeping watch during the night over their flock** as evoking a calm, pastoral scene. But the authorial audience would most likely have responded to this text in a much different way. Both the setting and the characters would alert the audience that God has chosen to disclose the birth of the Messiah in a dangerous place to a violence-prone group. Sparsely populated countrysides throughout the Roman Empire were havens for vagabonds and thieves (see the parable of the good Samaritan in Luke 10). Furthermore, while the image of the shepherd has a positive side and subsequently becomes a dominant image for Jesus and early church leaders, shepherds were often involved in conflict with settled villagers, conflict that usually escalated to violent activities.

2. *Dream-vision terminology* (2:9). As happened with Zechariah (1:12), the angel's appearance, accompanied by God's glory, evokes fear in the shepherds.

3. *Dream-vision proper* (2:10–14). Heard against the backdrop of the Augustan propaganda (see above), the angels' message is remarkable. It is Christ, not Caesar, who brings peace (2:14). Jesus's birthday, not Augustus's, divides the epochs of human history. The Savior, whose birth means **incredibly joyous news** (2:10), is born **Christ the Lord in the city of David** (2:11), not emperor

> **Shepherds: Irenic or Insurrectional?**
>
> Josephus reports that a certain Athrongaeus, a shepherd, aspired to Archelaus's throne:
>
> *"Now, too, a mere shepherd had the temerity to aspire to the throne. He was called Athrongaeus, and his sole recommendations, to raise such hopes, were vigor of body, a soul contemptuous of death, and four brothers resembling himself. To each of these he entrusted an armed band and employed them as generals and satraps for his raids, while he himself, like a king, handled matters of graver moment. It was now that he donned the diadem, his raiding expeditions continued long afterwards. Their principal object was to kill Romans and royalists, but no Jew, from whom they had anything to gain, escaped, if he fell into their hands." (J.W. 2.60–62, trans. Thackeray 1927)*
>
> Thus, far from a quaint little Christmas story, already the birth of the Messiah, according to Luke, has the power to lift up the lowly, the despised, and the violent (see 1:52).

> **"God's Favor"**
>
> Most scholars now agree that the phrase *anthrōpois eudokias* (2:14) reflects a common first-century Jewish way of expressing "those upon whom God's favor rests" (see, e.g., Plummer 1903, 58; Marshall 1978, 112; Fitzmyer 1981–85, 1:411–12; Bock 1994–96, 1:220). It should, therefore, not be read as a description of people who themselves show good will (a sense lodged into the English-speaking consciousness by the KJV translation). The variant reading with the nominative *eudokia* (ℵ² B² L Θ Ξ Ψ 𝔐 *al*) would place *eudokia* in apposition to *eirēnē*. The genitive reading *eudokias*, however, has stronger manuscript support (ℵ* A B* D W *pc*) and is preferred (see Culy, Parsons, and Stigall 2010).

in Rome. The notice of Jesus's birth is brief, yet the theological and political implications of Jesus's birth for Luke would be obvious to his audience.

4. *Reaction/response* (2:15–21). In the previous dream-visions to Zechariah and Mary, the reaction to the vision included an objection; that element is missing here. Even though the priest, Zechariah, and the mother-to-be of Jesus, Mary, initially resisted the divine message, these lowly shepherds resolve immediately to heed the command implicit in the angelic canticle to go to find this baby of whom the angels sing (2:12). Thus, these shepherds, whose vocation for the authorial audience at first conjures up an image of a despised and potentially violent group, by their actions align themselves with the more positive portrait of the good shepherd, an image already evoked by the mention of the city of *David*, who was, of course, himself a shepherd before becoming king. Thanks to these shepherds, not only the ox and the donkey recognize the "manger of their lord," but God's people, whom these shepherds now represent, have begun to know the manger of their Lord also. And Mary, as before (1:29), ponders the meaning of these things in her heart (2:19). The scene ends with the baby's circumcision and a reminder that the naming of the child, "Jesus," was in fulfillment of a previous dream-vision (2:21; cf. 1:31).

The presentation of Jesus in the temple (2:22–39). The passage divides into four units: the setting (2:22–24); the characterization and speech of Simeon (2:25–35); Anna's prophecy (2:36–38); and a conclusion (2:39).

2:22–24. In the setting, the ritual of the purification of the mother has been interwoven into the ritual dealing with the redemption of the firstborn in an ABB'A' pattern (Talbert 1982, 26):

A And when the days leading up to their purification were finished, according to the law of Moses (v. 22a)
   B they brought him up to Jerusalem to present him to the Lord (v. 22b)
   B' just as it is written in the Law of the Lord that "every male who opens the womb will be called holy to the Lord" (v. 23)
A' and in order to give a sacrifice according to what is said in the Law of the Lord: "a pair of doves or two young pigeons" (v. 24).

In this arrangement, the two middle lines deal with the dedication of the firstborn child (in a ritual described in Exod. 13), and the outer two lines deal with the ritual of the purification of mothers after childbirth (described in Lev. 12:1–8). The telescoping of these two events into one is Luke's way of focusing on the religious piety of Jesus's parents. This emphasis on the parents' piety is repeated in 2:27 and forms a transitional summary to the next scene (cf. 2:39). The combination of these two rituals into one event does not, however, detract from the view that, for Luke, the presentation of the child in the temple is clearly the main issue.

What is not clear is what the presentation is intended to convey. Some have argued that what lies behind the presentation account is the prescription in Jewish law that the firstborn child should be consecrated to the Lord (Exod. 13:2, 11–16) and redeemed, or bought back, at a price of five shekels (Num. 18:15–16) as a reminder of the exodus (Reicke 1978). Like Samuel, who at his birth was dedicated to God's service by his mother, Hannah (1 Sam. 1–2), Jesus is dedicated by Mary and Joseph to the Lord's service. That no mention of "ransom" money is made by the narrator is intentional. Jesus is left "unredeemed" in order that he may be fully dedicated to God's service, a point he later seems to understand better than his parents (see Luke 2:41–51; Talbert 1982, 36).

2:25–35. The second subunit consists of a rather detailed description of Simeon:

> Now there was a man in Jerusalem whose name was Simeon. This man was righteous and devout, waiting for the consolation of Israel; and the Holy Spirit was upon him! It had been revealed to him by the Holy Spirit that he would not die until he saw the Christ of the Lord. He came in the Spirit into the temple precincts; and as the parents brought the child Jesus in, in order that they might do in regard to him according to what is customary from the Law, he himself took him in his arms and blessed God. (2:25–28a)

Simeon was "righteous," "devout," and "waiting for the consolation of Israel." He had been the recipient of a divine revelation, "the Holy Spirit was upon him," and he "blessed God." The characterization of Simeon as a pious man of God is intended to undergird the authority of the speech.

The speech actually consists of two oracles. The first (2:29–32), known in subsequent church tradition as the Nunc Dimittis, is the fourth and last of the so-called canticles in the Lukan infancy narrative, the other three being the Magnificat (1:46–55), the Benedictus (1:67–79), and the Gloria in Excelsis (2:13–14):

> Now you are dismissing your servant in peace, Lord,
> according to your word,
> for my eyes have seen your salvation,

> which you prepared in front of all people,
> a light for a revelation of the Gentiles
> and glory of your people Israel. (2:29–32)

This oracle is directed toward God, is introduced with the theme of blessing or praise, and, using the language of Isaiah (esp. Isa. 40:5; 42:6; 46:13; 49:6; 52:9–10), celebrates the salvation God has brought through Jesus, providing a light to the gentiles and glory to Israel (cf. 1:79). Mary and Joseph **were amazed at the things that were being said about him** (2:33).

The second oracle (2:34–35) is directed toward Mary (2:34a): **This child is destined for the fall and rise of many in Israel and to be a sign to be spoken against—indeed, a sword will go through your very own soul—so that the thinking of many hearts might be revealed** (2:34b–35). It includes a general prediction that the child will be divisive and a specific prophecy that Mary's own soul will be pierced.

2:36–38. The third unit consists of a rather detailed description of Anna, emphasizing, as with Simeon, her piety: **Anna was a prophetess, a daughter of Phanuel, from the tribe of Asher. She was extremely old, since she had lived with her husband for seven years after their marriage, and she had been a widow for eighty-four years who did not leave the temple but worshiped with fasting and prayer night and day** (2:36–37). The phrase translated here "a widow for eighty-four years" is ambiguous in the Greek. It could either indicate that her widowhood had extended from the death of her husband until she was (now) eighty-four years old, or that she had been a widow for a span of eighty-four years, making her age somewhere around 105. This description is followed by a narrative summary of her speech (unlike in the case of Simeon, where the speech is actually given): **At that very moment, she approached them and began giving thanks to God and speaking about him to all who were waiting for the redemption of Jerusalem** (2:38). The pairing of male and female figures is common in Luke, and both share a common message regarding this child's role in the consolation/salvation/redemption of Israel.

2:39. And when they completed everything according to the law of the Lord, they returned into Galilee into their own city of Nazareth (2:39). The story ends by reiterating the piety of Joseph and Mary and recounting their return to Nazareth.

Jesus's nurture and training (2:40–52). The ancient rhetoricians insisted that nurture/training was an appropriate topic when discussing the life of a great person. After the circumstances of the birth of the specified person are narrated, Nicolaus, for example, advises that "we shall take up the circumstances of his upbringing, if we have something special to say about it that did not happen to others, as in the case of Achilles, (saying) that he was fed on the marrow of deer and taught by Cheiron and all the things told of him

> **The Piercing of Mary's Soul**
>
> Raymond Brown lists at least eight interpretations of the sword piercing Mary's soul:
>
> 1. The sword is a metaphor for Mary's doubt that scandalized her during Jesus's passion (so Origen, *Hom. Luc.* 17).
> 2. The sword refers to Mary's violent death (Epiphanius, *Pan.* 78.11).
> 3. The sword refers to the piercing of Mary's soul as she witnesses the piercing of Jesus on the cross with a lance.
> 4. The sword points to Mary's own rejection, much like her son's.
> 5. The piercing of the sword is caused by questions surrounding the legitimacy of Jesus's conception (see Matt. 1:18–19).
> 6. Mary's soul is pierced by the rejection of Jesus by his own people and the fall of Jerusalem.
> 7. The word of God is the sword that pierces Mary's heart (Ambrose, *Exp. Luc.* 2.61).
> 8. The sword evokes the "protevangelium" of Gen. 3:15 and refers to the enmity between the serpent and Eve and between his seed and her seed. That prophecy is now fulfilled in Mary, the "new Eve," and her offspring, Jesus. (1977, 462–63)
>
> Brown dismisses all of these interpretations as "implausible" and offers his own view that the sword consists of Mary "recognizing that the claims of Jesus's heavenly Father outrank any human attachments between him and his mother" (1977, 465). This reading is certainly plausible (cf. 2:48–50) but should not rule out pain caused by Jesus's death or by the conflict he caused in Israel.

in turn. After this, his activities in youth; for example, did he practice rhetoric or poetry or anything of the sort?" (Nicolaus, *Prog.* 52, trans. Kennedy 2003, 157; cf. Theon, *Prog.* 110; Ps.-Hermogenes, *Prog.* 16, 19; e.g., see Philo, *Mos.* 1.20–24; Samuel in Josephus, *Ant.* 5.348; Epicurus in Diogenes Laertius, *Vit. phil.* 10.14; cited by Talbert 2002, 39).

2:40. Luke begins and ends this section with general comments regarding Jesus's upbringing: **And so the child grew and became strong, becoming filled with wisdom, and the grace of God was upon him** (2:40; see also 2:52). This description is part of the *synkrisis* with John's upbringing ("And the child grew and became strong in the Spirit"; 1:80). Sandwiched between these two summary statements about Jesus's "divine" upbringing is a specific "snapshot" of Jesus's training/nurture in an episode that occurred when he was twelve. This episode has five parts: (1) the temporal setting (2:41–43a); (2) the loss of Jesus

(2:43b–45); (3) the finding of Jesus (2:46–48); (4) Jesus's pronouncement and his parents' response (2:49–50); and (5) Jesus's return to Nazareth (2:51–52).

2:41–43a. Initially the scene is set temporally, not spatially, highlighting the time of year and that this scene is still part of Jesus's precareer: **His parents went to Jerusalem year by year at the time of the feast of the Passover. When he was twelve years old, in the context of going up according to their custom relating to the feast, when they had finished their time (there), as they were returning . . .** (2:41–43a). The reference in 2:42 to Mary and Joseph obeying the "custom" of the feast keeps with the larger image of the characters in this story as pious and Torah-observant Jews (see also 1:6, 59; 2:21, 22–24, 25–27, 36–38). The spatial setting of Jerusalem (and the temple), which is presumed here, becomes increasingly important as the scene unfolds but at this point is subordinate to the temporal setting. Grammatically, the temporal setting for the pericope is located using a complex series of temporal constructions. The first one, "when he was twelve years old" (*hote egeneto etōn dōdeka*; 2:42), provides the broad temporal setting. This is then narrowed with two conjoined genitive absolute constructions—"they went up" (*anabainontōn autōn*; 2:42) and "completed the days [of the feast]" (*teleiōsantōn tas hēmeras*; 2:43)—that are followed by a fourth temporal construction: "as they were returning" (*en tō hypostrephein*; 2:43).

2:43b–45. All of these offline temporal elements serve to increasingly raise the question for the reader: what's going to happen? In the middle of verse 43, we finally find out: **the boy Jesus stayed in Jerusalem; and his parents were not aware of it. Now, since they thought that he was in their caravan, they went a day's journey and then began looking for him among their relatives and friends. When they did not find him, they returned to Jerusalem to search for him** (2:43b–45). These verses explain how Jesus, still a youth but on the threshold of manhood (cf. Josephus, *Ant.* 5.348, who dates the beginning of Samuel's career as a prophet in his twelfth year; Fitzmyer 1981–85, 1:440–41), came to be left behind in Jerusalem by his parents. The noun, *synodia*, translated here "caravan," is unique to the NT but used elsewhere to refer to a traveling party (e.g., Epictetus, *Diatr.* 4.1.91; Josephus, *J.W.* 2.587; Strabo, *Geogr.* 4.6.6); here it refers to a caravan of religious pilgrims (see Fitzmyer 1981–85, 1:441).

2:46–48. Eventually, they do find Jesus: **After three days they found him in the temple sitting in the midst of the teachers, listening to them, and asking them questions. Now, all those who heard him were astonished by his insight and answers. When his parents saw him, they were stunned; and his mother said to him, "Child, why did you act this way toward us? Your father and I were frantically searching for you"** (2:46–48). This report is what the authorial audience would expect to hear in terms of Jesus's remarkable upbringing and training: Jesus is found in the temple teaching the teachers (a similar point is made about Moses by Philo, *Mos.* 1.21, 27; cf. *Inf. Gos. Thom.* 14).

2:49–50. The "dramatic center of the story in Luke is not the teachers' praise of Jesus's wisdom . . . but Jesus's response to his parents" (Culpepper 1995, 76): **Then he said to them, "Why is it that you were searching for me? Did you not know that it is necessary for me to be in my father's house?" But they did not understand what he said to them** (2:49–50). The key here is found in Jesus's insistence that it is "necessary" (*dei*) for him to be in his father's house. In the larger Greco-Roman culture, actions that were done out of compulsion or necessity were regarded as the least praiseworthy kind of action (Theon, *Prog.* 111). Within the Jewish worldview, however, a worldview that is shaped by Israel's Scriptures (e.g., Lev. 4:1–2; 5:17) and that Jesus shares with his principle auditors, his parents and the temple teachers, the Creator God is in control of the affairs of the world, and one who submits totally to his plan is worthy of praise. Thus, even though his parents fail to comprehend, the authorial audience should not. Jesus's actions are to be commended, because they are done under compulsion of divine necessity (cf., e.g., Luke 2:49; 4:43; 9:22; 13:33; see also Parsons 2008a, 340). Obedience to God's will, for the Lukan Jesus, may not reduce its necessity, but it may, counterculturally, increase its praiseworthiness.

2:51–52. The scene ends on some familiar notes: **Then he went down with them [from Jerusalem] and came to Nazareth; and he was in submission to them. His mother kept all these things in her heart. And Jesus was progressing in wisdom and in maturity and in favor with God and humanity** (2:51–52). Jesus submits to the authority of his parents, evidenced by how he returns with them to Nazareth. Mary, once again, lodges these matters "in her heart" (cf. 2:19). While this scene certainly emphasizes the divine nature of Jesus's nurture and training (esp. 2:49), there is equal emphasis on Jesus's human nature and nurture. He is developing in wisdom and maturity (or stature; cf. 19:3); he is progressing in favor with God and humanity. "This is the type of language one uses for someone who develops both religiously and socially. . . . For Luke, Jesus grew and developed—in body, in mind, religiously, and socially" (Talbert 2002, 40). These references to Jesus's human and divine nurture and training ensure, from Luke's perspective, that this one is worthy of the accolades showered on him from his birth: "today a Savior has been born for you, who is Christ the Lord" (2:11).

Theological Issues

Whether Luke was familiar with the birth account (oral or written) preserved in Matthew is a fascinating, but perhaps ultimately unanswerable, question. But whether or not Luke knew these traditions, the modern reader of Luke 1–2 certainly reads them within the context of the Christian canon and, in particular, in light of the birth narrative preserved in Matt. 1–2. And it is worth pondering how that canonical context shapes our modern understanding of the story.

The contemporary reader of the Lukan infancy narrative cannot help being struck by the features shared in common between Matthew and Luke. Both stories set Jesus's birth during the reign of Herod the Great; both place the birth in Bethlehem, though both place Jesus's permanent address in Nazareth; both name Joseph and Mary as Jesus's parents; both claim Mary was a virgin at the time of her conception by the Holy Spirit; in both, a divine messenger gives directives about the naming of the child and refers to Jesus as "Savior."

Nonetheless, there are some significant differences a contemporary Christian audience will no doubt recognize. The following comments focus on a comparison of Matt. 2 with Luke 2, with an eye especially toward how an audience, familiar with the story of the magi's visitation and Herod's slaughter of the innocents, would understand Luke 2. The reader familiar with the Matthean infancy narrative knows already of the visit of the magi first to Herod and then to Jesus. The term "magi" could refer variously to (1) members of a Persian priestly class; (2) possessors of supernatural knowledge and power; (3) magicians; and (4) deceivers or seducers (G. Kittel, *TDNT* 4:356–59). While the question of how an audience would have understood these references to magi in Matthew can be debated (Powell 2001, 135–71), there is little doubt that the same terms in Luke's writings would have been understood to refer to the practice of magic, with negative connotations, a combination of meanings 3 and 4 above (see Acts 8:9, 11; 13:6, 8).

On the one hand, if the reader is aware that Luke used the "magician" to represent "all that is hostile to the purposes of God," then there is no surprise that it is shepherds, not magi, who make the first visitation to the infant Jesus (Garrett 1989, 103). While shepherds are not a uniformly positive group for Luke (see commentary above), at least they did not serve as foils to the Christian miracle workers as the "magicians" do in Acts. Thus shepherds make sense in the reader's reception of Luke's overall argument in ways that the magi do not. On the other hand, knowing Luke's disdain for magi may have forced the reader of canonical Scripture to seek some other meaning for the term in Matthew. Here we may have a clue to the early development of the tradition of viewing the magi as royalty or as wise men (on the magi as kings, see the cryptic comment in Tertullian, *Marc.* 3.13, and the fuller treatment in Augustine, "On the Lord's Epiphany," *Serm.* 200, trans. Hill 1993a, 83–85; on the magi as wise men, see the Venerable Bede, *In Matthaei Evangelium exposito* [PL 92:13–15]).

We may also ask about the rhetorical effect on the modern reader of Luke's lack of reference to the story of the massacre of the innocents. Here again, the reader will perceive that this story does not fit Luke's overall objectives. The story in Matthew serves to cast Herod in a thoroughly negative light as well as to underscore the parallels between Jesus and Moses with its echoes of Exod. 1–2. Luke, while not altogether sanguine about the Roman officials and appointees, is not interested in depicting them in absolutely negative terms either (see Tannehill 1986–90, 2:295–308). Nor will the reader see much development in Luke of the theme of Jesus as the "new Moses," at least not in the way that Matthew develops it.

In conclusion, the modern reader recognizes in Luke's story of Jesus's birth the remarkable similarities between the Lukan and Matthean accounts. At the same time, Luke's presentation contains distinctive material—for example, the canticles, the shepherds, and the annunciation, birth, and naming of John the Baptist—that would have underscored particular Lukan themes. Likewise the absence from Luke of the stories of the magi and the massacre of the innocents makes sense to the reader familiar with Luke's polemic against magic and his ambiguous characterization of Roman officials (developed especially in Acts). That same reader will no doubt have heard Matthew's version of Jesus's birth differently in light of this new story. Such intracanonical readings eventually, despite—if not through (perhaps especially through)—apparent conflicts and inconsistencies, give birth to a deeper understanding that God was in Christ reconciling the world.

Luke 3:1–4:13

Beginning Jesus's Public Ministry

Introductory Matters

Having described Jesus's origins and training in a *synkrisis* with John the Baptist (Luke 1–2), Luke returns to these topics in Luke 3:1–4:13. This unit divides into two scenes: John in the wilderness (3:1–20) and Jesus in the wilderness (3:21–4:13). The unit begins with a segment on John the Baptist (3:1–20); in this sense, the section continues the Jesus/John comparison that began in Luke 1–2. But there is one important difference. While the second (3:21–4:13) reiterates Jesus's prepublic origins and training, the material on John the Baptist describes his public ministry, a topic that typically follows origins and training (see, e.g., Ps.-Hermogenes, *Prog.* 15–16). Luke's point is subtle but significant. John's role in this story is secondary and supportive. His public ministry of forerunner, by its very nature, is subordinate to the story of Jesus. Thus, the inauguration of his public ministry most naturally finds it place in this story as a part of the reiteration of Jesus's prepublic origins and nurture. Here again is another example of Luke's concern for the placement and order of events to present a rhetorically compelling narrative (see comments on Luke 1:1–4).

Few dispute the historicity of the account of John's baptism of Jesus (Hartman 1997, 21; see also Beasley-Murray 1973; Erickson 1993; Aker 1988). Despite this widespread consensus, there are significant differences in the canonical accounts of Jesus's baptism, and a brief rehearsal of those differences will bring the distinctively Lukan features into bolder relief (Talbert 2002, 41–42).

In John, the Spirit's descent as a dove (presumably at the baptism) on Jesus identifies Jesus to John in order that John may disclose his identity to Israel

(John 1:31–34). The heavenly voice in Matthew seems to address the audience attending Jesus's baptism: "This is my beloved Son" (Matt. 3:17). Furthermore, Matthew contains an exchange between John and Jesus, unique among the canonical Gospels, that evidently anticipates later discussions as to why Jesus submitted to John's baptism of repentance, even though he, Jesus, was not a sinner: "John would have prevented him, saying, 'I need to be baptized by you, and do you come to me?' But Jesus answered him, 'Let it be so now, for thus it is fitting for us to fulfill all righteousness'" (Matt. 3:14–15 ESV). Mark's baptismal narrative is "an empowering of the Son of God for his battle with Satan and the demonic powers (Mark 3:22–27)" (Talbert 2002, 41). It is also the most personal of the accounts, since the voice from heaven addresses Jesus directly: "You are my beloved Son; with you I am well pleased" (Mark 1:11).

Luke's account agrees with Mark in making the heavenly voice a personal revelation ("*You* are my beloved son"; Luke 3:22) rather than a public declaration (cf. Matthew, "*This* is my beloved Son") and also in seeing the Spirit's descent as empowering Jesus in his struggle against Satan. But several elements are distinct to the Lukan account. First, there is the emphasis of the Holy Spirit descending on Jesus *in bodily form* as a dove (3:22; see Keck 1970–71). This corporeal emphasis is paralleled by the Pentecost scene in Acts, where the Spirit descends "like the rush of a mighty wind" and "like tongues of fire" (Acts 2:1–3). A second detail, unique to Luke, is the note that the Holy Spirit descends (after the baptism) while Jesus is praying. Of course, Jesus at prayer is a common theme throughout Luke (see 5:16; 6:12; 9:18, 28–29; 11:1; 22:32, 39–46; 23:46).

With regard to the historical value of the temptation narrative there is much less agreement. What tradition, if any, lies behind the canonical temptation accounts (Mark 1:12–13; Matt. 4:1–13; Luke 4:1–13)? Following Bultmann, a number of scholars have judged the accounts to be "the work of Christian scribes" (1968, 256; see also, e.g., Dibelius 1971). E. P. Sanders, on the contrary, has concluded: "It is reasonable to think that Jesus really did fast and pray before beginning his active ministry and that he was subject to temptation. The safest conclusion is that the synoptic gospels, especially Matthew

Luke 3:1–4:13 in the Narrative Flow

Jesus's origins and training (1:1–4:13)

  Preface (1:1–4)

  Annunciations: John and Jesus (1:5–56)

  Birth and training: John and Jesus (1:57–2:52)

  ▶ Beginning Jesus's public ministry (3:1–4:13)

    John in the wilderness (3:1–20)

      The setting of John the Baptist's ministry (3:1–6)

      John's message and the response(s) to it (3:7–17)

      John's arrest and imprisonment (3:18–20)

    Jesus in the wilderness (3:21–4:13)

      Jesus's baptism (3:21–22)

      Jesus's genealogy (3:23–38)

      Jesus's trial/temptation in the wilderness (4:1–13)

and Luke, are 'mythological' elaborations based on fact" (1993, 117; cf. Allison 1999, 213). Historical judgments notwithstanding, the interest here is in the literary presentation of the "essence" of Jesus—the sort of person he was and the sorts of things he did—that is, the essence of ancient *bioi*. It is to Luke's characterization of Jesus—through his origins and training, his baptism and temptation—that we now turn.

Tracing the Narrative Flow

John in the Wilderness (3:1–20)

The narrative of John the Baptist is composed of three segments: the setting of John the Baptist's ministry (3:1–6), John's message and the response(s) to it (3:7–17), and John's arrest and imprisonment (3:18–20).

3:1–6. *The setting of John the Baptist's ministry.* Once again (cf. 1:5), Luke roots John's prophetic ministry within the larger cultural context by detailing various political and religious leaders in power at the time of John's call: **In the fifteenth year of the reign of Tiberius Caesar, when Pontius Pilate was governor of Judea and Herod was tetrarch of Galilee, and when Philip his brother was tetrarch of the region of Iturea and Trachonitis and Lysanius was tetrarch of Abilene, in the time of the high priest Annas and Caiaphas . . .** (3:1–2a). These references defy specificity with regard to chronology, but they do underscore Luke's concern that the audience understand the universal implications of John's Isaianic vocation, namely, that "all persons should see the salvation of God" (3:6). Several of these figures will reappear later in the story either as important characters—Herod Antipas (3:19–20; 9:7, 9; 13:31; 23:7–8, 11–12, 15); Pilate (13:1; 23:1, 3, 4, 6, 11–13, 20, 24, 52)—or by reference—Caesar (20:22, 25; 23:2); high priest (22:50, 54). The mention of Annas, who served as high priest AD 6–15, reflects his continuing presence and power even after Caiaphas assumed the high priesthood (AD 18–36; see Green 1997, 169). After setting John's ministry in its broader political setting, Luke casts John's commissioning (cf. 1:80) within the mode of the Hebrew prophets: **the word of God came to John** (3:2b; cf. 1 Kings 18:1; Jer. 1:2; Ezek. 1:3; Hosea 1:1; Joel 1:1;

Figure 6. Tiberius, Emperor of Rome from AD 14 to 37

Tracing the Narrative Flow

Figure 7. The Jordan River

Jon. 1:1). The next two phrases echo earlier parts of the story; at this point in Luke, John is first and foremost not the "baptizer" (cf. Mark 1:4; Matt. 3:1; later Luke 7:20) but **the son of Zechariah** (cf. 1:5–25, 67–79), and the word of God comes to Zechariah's son in the wilderness, where the narrator left him at Luke 1:80a, "until the day of his commissioning before Israel" (1:80b).

Luke proceeds to describe John's "commissioning" in terms of his ministry and message: **And he went into the region around the Jordan, proclaiming a baptism of repentance for the forgiveness of sins** (3:3). The syntactic complexity of this construction flows from the fact that it includes three nouns (*baptisma, metanoias, aphesin*) that are verbal ideas. John is preaching that people should repent and be baptized so that their sins will be forgiven. This description of John's ministry once again echoes earlier prophecies (1:16–17, 77), as does the prophecy from Isaiah, which introduces an analogy with John's role as a harbinger of the one to come: **As it is written in the book of the words of Isaiah the prophet, "The voice of one who is shouting in the wilderness: 'Prepare the way of the Lord; make straight his paths. Every valley will be filled, and every mountain and hill leveled. The crooked paths will become straight, and the rough ways smooth. And all people will see the salvation of God'"** (3:4–6; cf. 1:17, 76; 7:27).

3:7–17. *John's message and the reponse(s) to it.* Next, Luke gives a summary of what John habitually preached: **So then, John was telling the crowds that were coming out to be baptized by him . . .** (3:7a, taking the imperfect *elegen* as reiterative; so Nolland 1989–93, 1:147). He begins his sermon with an invective: **Offspring of vipers!** (3:7b). In its cultural context, this insult evokes a number of negative connotations. In zoological physiognomy, which correlated human

65

moral behavior with physical characteristics of the animal kingdom, the serpent "is a cruel, harmful, insidious animal, terrible when it decides to be, quick to flee when afraid, gluttonous.... Such men are ... devoted to evil-doing" (*Anon. Lat.* 128, trans. André 1981, 137). In his oration against Aristogeiton, Demosthenes claims he "makes his way through the market-place like a snake [*echis*] ... on the look-out for someone on whom he can call down disaster or calumny or mischief of some sort, or whom he can terrify till he extorts money from him" (*1 Aristog.* 1.25.52, trans. Vince 1935; cf. 1.96; see Parsons 2011, 73–76). John then poses this rhetorical question, which expects no answer (Quintilian, *Inst.* 9.2.7; *Rhet. Her.* 4.15.22): **Who warned you to flee from the coming wrath?** (3:7b). The sense here seems to be: Who has shown you how to flee from the coming wrath merely by coming to be baptized? (Marshall 1978, 139).

John repeats his call to repentance: **Therefore, produce fruit worthy of repentance, and do not begin to say among yourselves, "We have a father—Abraham." For I tell you that God is able to raise up children for Abraham from these stones** (3:8). The Abrahamic covenant is particularly important for Luke's theology (Dahl 1966; Siker 1991; Green 1994; Brawley 1999). Abraham can be an ancestor with whom persons share a genetic descent or an archetype who functions typologically. Abraham as archetype is certainly the focus of Luke (Seim 2001). This is the distinction that John the Baptist is making in Luke 3:8. Bearing the fruits of repentance, and not some genetic descent, qualifies one as a child of Abraham. Thus, for Luke, to be a son or daughter of Abraham is to emulate the character and actions of Abraham the archetypal ancestor, and, for Luke, this promise is furthermore fulfilled in the eschatological community that is forming around the person of Jesus Christ. Failure to produce the fruits of repentance will result in judgment: **The ax, in fact, is already laid at the root of the trees. So, every tree that does not produce good fruit will be cut down and thrown into the fire** (3:9; cf. 13:6–9). But such failure will not deter the ingathering of this community, since God is able even from the stones to raise "children of Abraham." And later in the story God will do just that, pronouncing a "bent woman" (Luke 13) and a man "short in stature" (Luke 19) "daughter" and "son" of Abraham, respectively, not because of their genetic descent but because their actions of courage and hospitality imitate the archetypal behavior of Abraham (see Parsons 2011, 83).

The crowds respond in a typically Lukan fashion: **What, then, should we do?** (3:10; cf. Luke 3:12, 14; 10:25; 18:18; later, Acts 2:37; 16:30; 22:10). Specifically, what kind of fruit is this repentance supposed to bear? While the first part of John's speech (Luke 3:8–9) already would have been familiar to the authorial audience (through Matt. 3:8–9 or Q 3:8–9), his reply to this thrice-repeated question by the crowd (and others) is unique to the Third Gospel. The dialogue form used here is a conventional rhetorical device. Theon lists questions and dialogue as alternative ways to set out a narrative (*Prog.* 87). About dialogue he writes: "If we wish to use a dialogue form, we shall suppose some people talking with each other about what has been done, and one teaching, the other learning, about the occurrences" (*Prog.* 89, trans. Kennedy 2003, 37; cf. *Rhet. Her.* 4.52.65). Here John does the teaching, and the various groups who approach him do the learning.

The topic is the fruit appropriate to repentance, and John's social ethic is a particularly appropriate antidote for a group he has collectively described as "vipers." To the thrice-repeated question, John advises that, rather than leading a "gluttonous" lifestyle of excess, **The one who has two shirts should share with the one who does not have one, and the one who has food should do the same** (3:11). John advises tax collectors, whose toll-collecting practices often "called down disaster on others" (cf. Luke 19; Donahue 1971), **Do not collect any more than you are ordered to** (3:13). To those who use their position as soldiers to intimidate and extort their victims, John says, **Do not extort money from anyone or blackmail them; and be satisfied with your wages** (3:14). According to Josephus, soldiers extorting money from the residents of occupied territories was such a problem that Julius Caesar had to issue a decree forbidding that practice in the territories of the Jews (*Ant.* 14.204; cf. 14.392, 406; *J.W.* 1.288). John's summary of the fruits of repentance is noteworthy for what he does *not* say. John does not advise his audience to follow his example of withdrawing from society. Unlike the Qumran community, he does not lace his remarks with apocalyptic language of a coming judgment. Unlike the tradition of Hebrew prophets, he does not criticize the unjust social structures that lead to such abuses. Still, "the accusation that these ethics are bourgeois is terribly misplaced"; rather, John "calls for a radical generosity in which everything beyond subsistence necessities is vulnerable to the claim of need. Jesus asks for no more. He adds only the clarification that such generosity is not only for those of one's own group, but shows its true nature especially in being extended to the enemy (Luke 6:35–36)" (Nolland 1989–93, 1:149).

Clearly, John has impressed his listeners: **While the people were waiting and all of them were wondering in their hearts about John whether perhaps he might be the Christ . . .** (3:15). John's response promptly and decisively corrects their misperception: **John responded by saying to all of them, "I baptize you with water, but one more powerful than I is coming, the strap of whose sandals I am not qualified to untie. He will baptize you with the Holy Spirit and fire. His winnowing fork is in his hand to clean up his threshing floor and gather together the wheat into his storehouse; but he will burn the chaff in unquenchable fire"** (3:16–17). With these words, the Jesus/John *synkrisis* in the opening segment of Luke (1:5–4:13) comes to a climax, at least in terms of John's subordination to Jesus. For some rhetoricians, *synkrisis* could consist of an encomium/invective contrast in which "we blame one thing completely and praise the other" (Ps.-Hermogenes, *Prog.* 19, trans. Kennedy 2003, 84), and indeed some interpreters seem to read the Jesus/John comparison as an effort to put John in his place (see Wink 1968). But Luke's comparison most surely is one that seeks to compare two similarly noteworthy persons (or objects) for the purpose of praise; this technique is a *synkrisis* in a double encomium (see Aphthonius, *Prog.* 31R–32R). John's achievements are an important ingredient in the comparison Luke draws between the two in this double encomium; nonetheless, John (of whom Jesus would later say, "no one among those born of women is greater than John"; 7:28) is not worthy to untie the sandals of the One More Powerful Who Is Coming.

3:18–20. *John's arrest and imprisonment.* At this point, Luke pauses to flash forward to the point in the story in which John is imprisoned by Herod: **So, exhorting them to do many other things as well, John was proclaiming the good news to the people. But Herod the tetrarch, since he had been rebuked by John concerning Herodias, his brother's wife—and concerning *all* the horrible things Herod had done—added even this on top of everything else: he locked up John in prison** (3:18–20). John's rebuke of Herod was familiar to Luke's authorial audience, not only through the general convention of the prophet reproaching the king preserved in Israel's Scriptures (e.g., Nathan and David; Elijah and Ahab; see Darr 1998, 157–58), but also in the specific parallel found in Mark's Gospel. Mark records the incident this way: "For Herod himself had sent men who arrested John, bound him, and put him in prison on account of Herodias, his brother Philip's wife, because Herod had married her. For John had been telling Herod, 'It is not lawful for you to have your brother's wife'" (Mark 6:17–18). The charge leveled by John in Mark, and alluded to in Luke, was not only one of sexual impurity (cf. Lev. 18:16; 20:21) but also evidently against endogamy, marriage within one's extended family, a practice intended to preserve or advance the wealth, status, and power of a family. In a culture of limited goods, this practice had the devastating effect of keeping power in the hands of a very few (see comments on Luke 16:14–18). In this sexist system, women were possessions to be acquired. Herod's marriage to Herodias amounted to keeping his brother's wealth (including Herodias) in the family (see Josephus, *Ant.* 18.109–19). In Luke's paraphrase of Mark (Theon, *Prog.* 107P; see comments on Luke 1:77), the specific charge by John against Herod is compressed, but Luke expands John's rebuke to include "all the horrible things Herod had done," to which, Luke asserts, must now be added John's imprisonment (see Hoehner 1972, 110–71; Richardson 1996, 304–13).

Jesus in the Wilderness (3:21–4:13)

This next section recounts (again) Jesus's origins and education/training (3:21–4:13), with an account of Jesus's baptism (3:21–22), genealogy (3:23–38), and trial/temptation in the wilderness (4:1–13).

3:21–22. *Jesus's baptism.* The section begins with a brief notice regarding Jesus's baptism: **Now, it happened as all the people were baptized, when Jesus had also been baptized and was praying, heaven was opened, and the Holy Spirit descended upon him in bodily form like a dove, and a voice came from**

heaven: "You are my beloved Son; I am very pleased with you" (3:21–22). To understand the meaning of the baptism of Jesus in the Third Gospel, we must explore the significance of John's baptism as presented in Luke. In addition to the references to John's baptism found in Luke 3:1–20, the baptism of John will later be referenced in Acts, the sequel to Luke, on several occasions (Acts 1:5, 22; 10:37; 11:16–18; 13:24–25; 18:24–26; 19:1–7). The cumulative effect of these references is to underscore certain features of John's baptism: (1) it was a "repentance baptism," "in which cleansing and moral uprightness are tied together" (Green 1999, 163); (2) John's baptism held out "the promise of deliverance and restoration in the forgiveness of sins" (Green 1999, 165); and (3) John's baptismal ministry meant a redefinition of the people of God—the "children of Abraham" would now include all those who bore the "fruits worthy of repentance," a people that would include tax collectors and soldiers (Luke 3:8).

John's baptism, for Luke, was not *inherently* inadequate, as some have argued. Rather, in the Lukan writings it points in a christological direction. On the one hand, although Apollos knows only John's baptism, he is able to teach accurately concerning Jesus (Acts 18:24–28). The disciples of John (Acts 19:1–7), on the other hand, have an inadequate theology, since John's baptism has not been "realized through faith in Jesus and reception of the Spirit" (Green 1999, 169; see also Tannehill 1986–90, 2:233–34).

But why does Jesus submit to John's baptism? Jesus identifies with John's baptism by participating in it. The question, of course, is what is meant by this participation (on the various explanations, see Beasley-Murray 1973, 45–67). For Luke, at least, it seems Jesus came to fulfill his messianic vocation as a representative person in the kingdom of God who stands in solidarity with the sinners in need of deliverance (who have come to John for the baptism of repentance) and who represents the interests of God, the universal Sovereign (Beasley-Murray 1973, 57–58). The baptism of Jesus and the subsequent sending of the Spirit as confirmation of his vocation as Messiah provide the context within which to understand the temptations of Christ, where Jesus "faces, not the impossibility of his being a Messiah, but the possibilities of His way as Messiah; and the ways He declined were those which would have destroyed His solidarity with the people He had come to save" (Beasley-Murray 1973, 60). The baptismal narrative reflects several rhetorical strategies, all aimed at the same theological point. The omen (opening of heaven, voice from heaven, descent of the Spirit) provides divine confirmation of Jesus's identity (cf. Cicero, *Top.* 20.76–77) and is a rhetorical convention typical of *bios* literature to underscore the greatness of the protagonist. That the heavens opened and the Spirit descended in "bodily form like a dove" is ekphrastic language, intended to appeal to the eye and not just the ear (Theon, *Prog.* 118; *Rhet. Her.* 4.50.68), which was often used at key points in the plot of an ancient narrative (Luke 9:29–34; Acts 1:10–11; 2:1–5; see Krieger 1992, 7; Parsons 2008a, 38). These marvelous signs are also often associated with the birth of the hero

Figure 8. Judean Desert

(Ps.-Hermogenes, *Prog.* 15; Nicolaus, *Prog.* 51–52, 59–60), and while it may go too far to call Jesus's baptism a "second birth" (so Martin 2008, 37), nonetheless, the account does highlight Jesus's origins as God's "beloved Son" (3:22).

3:23–38. *Jesus's genealogy.* The emphasis on Jesus's origins continues with the genealogy of Jesus's ancestors. Unlike Matthew's genealogy (Matt. 1:1–17), which proceeds from Abraham to Jesus, using the formula "A was the father of B; B was the father of C," Luke traces Jesus's lineage back to Adam, using the formula "Z was the son of Y, the son of X." Luke's list is therefore predictably longer—some seventy-seven names compared to forty-one—but even in the range of time in which the two genealogies overlap (Abraham to Jesus), Luke's list is still longer (56 names in Luke, 41 in Matthew; Brown 1977, 84). There are, then, significant differences between the lists. "Matthew's intention" is "to show that Jesus is the Davidic Messiah, and Luke's intention" is "to show that Jesus is the Son of God" (Brown 1977, 85). To emphasize Jesus's origins as God's Son (see also 3:22), Luke characterizes **Adam** as **the son of God** (3:38b). The divine origins of the human race were, of course, firmly rooted in Israel's Scriptures ("let us make humankind in our image"; Gen. 1:26) but found also in some pagan philosophical traditions (Seneca, *Ep.* 44.1; Dio Chrysostom, *Charid.* 26). The theme will recur later, in Acts (17:26; see Parsons 2008a, 246–47). The reference here prepares the audience to hear Jesus's temptation narrative as "the undoing of Adam's sin" (Allison 1999, 196).

4:1–13. *Jesus's trial/temptation in the wilderness.* The temptation of Jesus stands at the end of the story of his prepublic career and on the threshold of his public ministry in Luke (Hester 1977; N. Taylor 2001; Brawley 1992; Paffenroth 1996; Kähler 1994; H. Humphrey 1991; Stegner 1990; Allison 1999; Tuckett 1992).

Figure 9. Mount of Temptation

The authorial audience would be familiar with both the brief notice of his trial in the wilderness in Mark 1:12–13 and a longer account (Matt./Q 4:1–13). Both of these fuller accounts mention that Jesus was in the desert for **forty days** (4:2), a period reminiscent of Israel's "forty" years of wandering in the desert. The content of the tests that Jesus not only endures but also passes, corresponds to the tests that Israel faced in the wilderness but failed. Jesus is tempted by his hunger, as was Israel (Exod. 16), but whereas Jesus rebukes the temptation with the words **A person must not live on bread alone** (4:4), the Israelites simply complained—first about the lack of bread (Exod. 16:3) and then about the lack of variety in their diet ("wherever we look there is nothing except this manna"; Num. 11:6). Jesus is also tempted to engage in idolatrous acts by worshiping Satan, but he rebukes Satan with the words **Worship the Lord your God and serve him alone** (Luke 4:8). Israel, however, succumbed to the temptation to commit idolatry and fashioned gold in the image of a calf and worshiped it (Exod. 32). Jesus is tempted to test God's faithfulness, as was Israel (Exod. 17). But whereas Jesus rebuts Satan with the words **Do not put the Lord your God to the test** (Luke 4:12), when Moses challenged the Israelites, "Why do you test the LORD?" the people continued to complain against Moses (Exod. 17:2–3). For both Matthew/Q and Luke, the specific content of the tests discloses that Jesus *is* Israel, God's son, who is called out of Egypt to complete Israel's exodus (see Luke 9:31). But Luke also casts this scene as a reversal of Adam's disobedience, in that sense filling out the allusions to Adam in Mark 1:12–13 (see Allison 1999, 196).

The order of the temptations may be just as important as their specific content. We have already seen the concern for rhetorical order that Luke shared with ancient rhetoricians (see comments on Luke 1:1–4). Communication theorists have coined the phrase "recency effect" to refer to the way hearers and readers respond to the last information given about a character or a plot (Perry 1979). Often we are able to remember only the last thing a person said or the last deed a character performed. How a story ends leaves a lasting impression on the hearer and shapes impressions of the story as a whole. The ending of a story, then, is critical to its overall message. This is true not only of the end of an entire story but also of the ways in which individual stories within a larger account are closed.

Recency effect plays a major role in understanding the function of the temptation narrative in both Matthew/Q and Luke. The two storytellers record the same three temptations, but in a different order. The scholarly consensus is that the order preserved in Matthew/Q was original (see Robinson, Hoffmann, and Kloppenborg 2000, 23–41; Tuckett 1992, 479). The first temptation is the same in both: Jesus is tempted to turn stones into bread. The order of the next two temptations, however, is reversed, as depicted in table 3.

Table 3. Comparing the Temptation Narratives

Luke		Matthew/Q	
Locale	Temptation	Locale	Temptation
1. desert	stones into bread	1. desert	stones into bread
2. "up"	worship devil	2. temple	throw self down
3. temple	throw self down	3. high mountain	worship devil

In Luke, the last temptation occurs on the **pinnacle of the temple** (Luke 4:9); in Matthew/Q the last temptation occurs on a "very high mountain" (Matt. 4:8/Q 4:5). According to the recency effect, and assuming Matthew/Q and Luke are competent storytellers, the last temptation of Christ in each account may be significant. This is certainly true for the Third Gospel (on the significance of mountains in Matthew, see Donaldson 1985).

In Luke's Gospel, the temple is the setting for several scenes, including the opening and closing scenes. In every case but the last, the temple is the location of a conflict between God's agents and God's people (Parsons 1987; see table 4).

Table 4. Conflict between God's Agents and God's People

Text	God's people	God's agent	Conflict
1:5–23	Zechariah	Gabriel	1:18–20
2:41–51	Jesus's parents	Jesus	2:48–50
19:45–48	religious leaders	Jesus	19:47

The opening scene (Luke 1:5–23) introduces the motif of conflict between the people of God and his agents. Zechariah—who, the narrator tells us, was "upright and devout, blamelessly observing all the commandments and ordinances of the Lord" (1:5–6)—is one of God's people. While Zechariah is in God's sanctuary (the temple), God's agent (an angel of the Lord; 1:11, 19) appears to him. The conflict begins in 1:18 when Zechariah doubts the angel's prophecy that he and Elizabeth will have a son. The angel rebukes Zechariah, revealing to him that he is none other than Gabriel, who was "sent to speak to you" (1:19). The conflict is resolved when Gabriel strikes Zechariah speechless until Elizabeth gives birth to John. This initial episode provides the type-scene for the other temple (and synagogue; see 4:16–30; 6:6–11; 13:10–17) encounters. The tension seems to intensify with each subsequent conflict and reaches a climax in the last temple conflict scene, where the tension is almost unbearable as God's people plot the death of God's agent (19:45–48).

How does the temptation narrative fit into this pattern? Since the last temptation occurs on the pinnacle of the temple, it both recalls the Zechariah episode and foreshadows the temple scene in Luke 19. Here God's agent, Jesus, is in direct conflict, not with God's people (as in Luke 1 and 19), but with God's adversary, Satan, on the pinnacle of God's house. The effect of this story is to set the other conflict scenes in a cosmic context and to make clear, at least from the narrator's point of view, that when God's people (Zechariah, the religious authorities) oppose God's agent (Gabriel, Jesus), they are choosing, perhaps unconsciously, to side with God's adversary, Satan.

The last temple scene in Luke depicts a resolution to the conflict. The Gospel concludes with the disciples returning to Jerusalem after the final departure of Jesus, where they "were continually in the temple praising God" (24:53). By the end of the Gospel, then, the disciples have become the pious people of God, and there is no conflict between the people of God and the agent of God in God's house. They are obediently, joyously, and continually praising God in the temple. In the Lukan temptation narrative, Jesus, God's beloved Son, is also obedient to God and in the climax of the story refuses to test God; his obedience is in sharp contrast to—indeed, reverses—the disobedience of God's first son, Adam (3:38). Thus **when he had carried out every temptation, the devil left him until [another] opportune time (4:13).**

Theological Issues

The temptation of Christ has proved fertile ground for subsequent Christian meditation (see Köppen 1961; Steiner 1962). François Bovon observes, "The history of the exegesis of Luke 4:1–13 is extraordinarily instructive because the life situations of the exegetes always influence their interpretation" (2002–13, 1:146).

Since Ambrose, there has been a persistent interpretation that connects the temptation narrative with an Adam typology, a point that is consonant with Luke's own emphasis (see above).

> It is fitting that it be recorded that the first Adam was cast out of Paradise into the desert, that you may observe how the second Adam returned from the desert to Paradise.... Adam brought death through the tree. Christ brought life through the cross. Adam, naked of spiritual things, covered himself with the foliage of a tree. Christ, naked of worldly things, did not desire the trappings of the body. Adam lived in the desert. Christ lived in the desert, for he knew where he could find the lost. With their error canceled, he could recall them to Paradise....
>
> So Jesus, full of the Holy Spirit, is led into the desert for a purpose, in order to challenge the devil. If he had not fought, he would not have conquered him for me. (Ambrose, *Exp. Luc.* 4.7.14, trans. Tomkinson 1998, 115–16, 119; cf. Origen, *Fr. Luc.* 96, FC 94:165–67)

A similar theme is found in Cyril of Alexandria: "Observe, I beg you, how the nature of man in Christ casts off the faults of Adam's gluttony. By eating we were conquered in Adam, by abstinence we conquered in Christ" (Cyril of Alexandria, *Comm. Luke*, homily 12, trans. Smith 1983, 88). And Ephrem the Syrian sees the Adam typology in the third temptation, set on the temple: "[Satan] set [Jesus] up on the pinnacle of the temple. Satan wanted him to suppose that he who was a man could become God, by means of the Godly house, just as Satan had once made Adam suppose that he could become God by means of that tree" (Ephrem the Syrian, *Commentary on Tatian's Diatessaron* 4.8B–C, trans. McCarthy 1993, 87–88).

Ambrose also includes Eve in his contrast between the first and last temptations: "Food had not persuaded Eve, nor had the forgetfulness of the commands deprived her. If she had been willing to worship the Lord alone, she would not have sought what was not due to her. So a remedy is given, which blunts the dart of ambition, so that we serve the Lord alone. Pious devotion lacks ambition" (Ambrose, *Exp. Luc.* 4.33–34, trans. Tomkinson 1998, 126–27).

Augustine's comments, including a brief Adamic allusion (in the form of the serpent), are typical of the early interpreters' christological focus, that is, their emphasis on the way in which the temptation narratives revealed the character of Christ:

> When the Lord had been tempted with this triple temptation—because in all the allurements of the world these three are to be found, either pleasure or curiosity or pride—what did the Evangelist say? After the devil had concluded every temptation—every kind, but of the alluring sort—there remained the other sort of temptation, by harsh and hard treatment, savage treatment, atrocious and ferocious treatment.... He departed from him in the form, that is, of the insidious serpent. He is going to come in the form of the roaring lion. The one

who will trample the lion and the cobra will conquer him. Satan will return. He will enter Judas and will make him betray his master. He will bring along the Jews, not flattering now, but raging. Taking possession of his own instruments, he will cry out with the tongues of all of them, "Crucify him, crucify him!" That Christ was the conqueror there, why should we be surprised? He was God almighty. (Augustine, *Serm.* 284.5, trans. Hill 1994, 91)

Not all early interpreters shared this christological focus. The Venerable Bede, for instance, saw in the temptation narratives a moral example for the faithful to follow:

Soon after he had been baptized he performed a fast of forty days by himself, and he taught and informed us by his example that, after we have received forgiveness of sins in baptism, we should devote ourselves to vigils, fasts, prayers, and other spiritually fruitful things, lest when we are sluggish and less vigilant the unclean spirit expelled from our heart by baptism may return, and finding us fruitless in spiritual riches, weigh us down with a sevenfold pestilence, and our last state would then be worse than the first. (Bede, *Homilies on the Gospels* 1.12, trans. Martin and Hurst 1990, 1:119–20)

Later, the magisterial reformer John Calvin would resist drawing any direct comparison between Jesus's temptations and ours, claiming, "Fasting brought Christ the distinction of divine glory" (Calvin 1972, 1:135). Bovon amplifies Calvin's logic: "Consequently, it would be mockery and detestable ridicule to imitate Christ. The temptation cannot be limited to gluttony, ambition, and avarice" (Bovon 2002–13, 1:146).

PART 2

Luke 4:14–9:50

Jesus's Mighty Words and Deeds in Galilee

Luke's account of Jesus's mighty words and deeds in Galilee (4:14–9:50) further divides into three units: Jesus's mission and miracles and the ingathering of his followers (4:14–6:49), Jesus's marvelous words and deeds (7:1–8:56), and Jesus's miracles and mission and the sending out of his followers (9:1–50).

Luke 4:14–9:50 in Context

Jesus's origins and training (1:1–4:13)

▶ **Jesus's mighty words and deeds in Galilee (4:14–9:50)**

    Jesus's mission and miracles and the ingathering of his followers (4:14–6:49)

    Jesus's marvelous words and deeds (7:1–8:56)

    Jesus's miracles and mission and the sending out of his followers (9:1–50)

Jesus's mighty words and deeds along the way (part 1) (9:51–14:35)

Jesus's mighty words and deeds along the way (part 2) (15:1–19:44)

Jesus in Jerusalem: teachings, death, and resurrection (19:45–24:53)

Luke 4:14–9:50

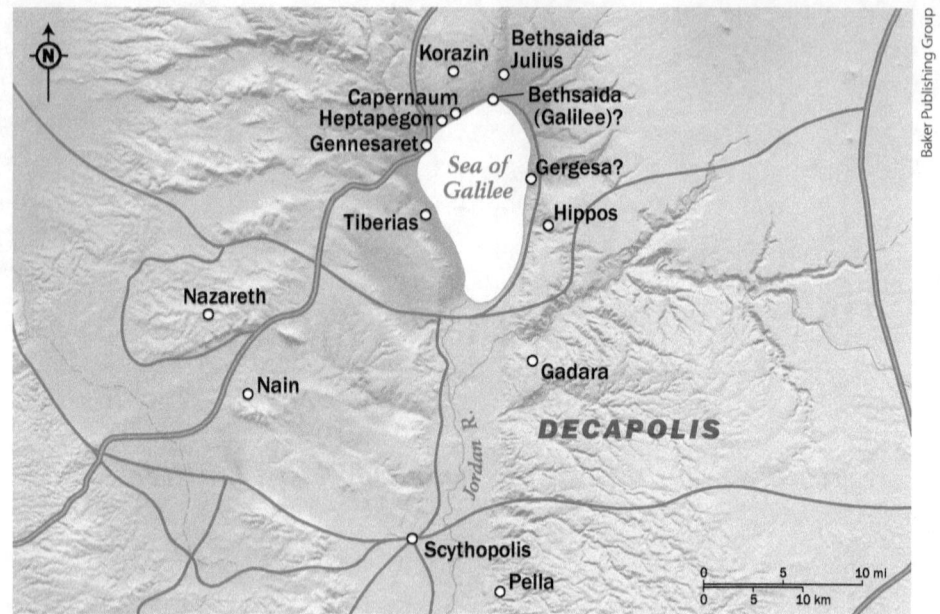

Figure 10. Important Cities in Galilee

Luke 4:14–6:49

Jesus's Mission and Miracles and the Ingathering of His Followers

Introductory Matters

The first unit of Jesus's words and deeds in Galilee (4:14–6:49) consists of pericopae that are interrelated in various ways, producing a richly textured beginning to Jesus's public ministry but not lending themselves to easy segmentation. The movement of the narrative is in three steps: proclaiming the good news in Galilee and Capernaum (4:14–44), Jesus's miraculous catch of fish and people (5:1–6:16), and Jesus's instructions to his followers in the Sermon on the Plain (6:17–49).

Tracing the Narrative Flow

Proclaiming the Good News in Galilee and Capernaum (4:14–44)

Luke 4:14–44 deals with Jesus proclaiming the "good news of the kingdom of God" through "marvelous words" in Nazareth in Galilee (4:16–30) and through "marvelous deeds" in Capernaum (4:31–43). The section is held together with two

---

Luke 4:14–6:49 in the Narrative Flow

Jesus's origins and training (1:1–4:13)

Jesus's mighty words and deeds in Galilee (4:14–9:50)

▶ Jesus's mission and miracles and the ingathering of his followers (4:14–6:49)

  Proclaiming the good news in Galilee and Capernaum (4:14–44)

  Jesus's miraculous catch of fish and people (5:1–6:16)

  The Sermon on the Plain (6:17–49)

Figure 11. Synagogue Ruins

summary statements about Jesus teaching in the synagogues (4:14–15; 4:44), which form an *inclusio* around 4:16–43; this structure of "summary + specific illustrations + summary" is used also in Luke 2:40–52 (Green 1997, 203). Luke 4:16–30 presents the teaching/preaching ministry of Jesus—his words—and 4:31–43 presents the healing/exorcism ministry of Jesus—his deeds.

4:14–30. Luke begins with a general description of Jesus's entry into public life after his wilderness testing and its positive reception: **Jesus returned in the power of the Spirit to Galilee. And news about him spread throughout the entire surrounding area. He was teaching them in their synagogues and being praised by everyone** (4:14–15). Luke 4:16–30 presents the inaugural sermon of Jesus in his hometown of Nazareth. The sermon not only introduces the Galilean section of Luke's Gospel (4:14–9:50); it is also the frontispiece to the entire Gospel. From it we learn about the character of Jesus's ministry from the lips of the Lukan Jesus himself. The passage is framed by double references to the movement of Jesus: in 4:16, **Jesus came to Nazareth where he had been brought up** and **entered the synagogue on the Sabbath day**; in 4:30, "after passing through the middle of the crowd, he went on his way." In between are two sections, 4:16b–22 and 4:23–29, each of which alternates between Jesus's speech and the crowd's reaction to it:

A Jesus's speech (4:16b–21)
  B crowd's reaction (4:22)
A′ Jesus's speech (4:23–27)
  B′ crowd's reaction (4:28–29)

The first unit, 4:16b–21, begins with Jesus's sermon in his hometown synagogue and includes a well-recognized chiastic structure (4:16b–20c):

A Jesus **stood up to read** (4:16b)
   B **the scroll of the prophet Isaiah was given to him** (4:17a)
      C **after unrolling the scroll** (4:17b)
         D **he found the place where it had been written** (4:17c)
            (and he read the Scripture) (4:18–19)
      C′ **After rolling up the scroll** (4:20a)
   B′ **he gave it back to the attendant** (4:20b)
A′ **and sat down** (4:20c)

In such a structure, the emphasis is on the middle item (4:18–19), which Luke uses to outline the shape of Jesus's ministry. The text is a paraphrase of Isa. 61:1–2 (see comments on Luke 1:77) with certain Lukan modifications:

> **The Spirit of the Lord is upon me,**
> **because he has anointed me.**
> **He has sent me to announce good news to the poor,**
> [Luke omits: to bind up the brokenhearted; cf. Isa. 61:1b]
> **to proclaim release to the prisoners,**
> **and gaining of sight to the blind,**
> **to set the oppressed free** [cf. Isa. 58:16]
> **to proclaim the favorable year of the Lord.** (4:18–19)

The authorial audience would have recognized the opening clause ("The Spirit of the Lord is upon me") as a reference to Jesus's baptism, where the Spirit descended upon Jesus in the form of a dove (3:22). Moreover, as we have noted, the reference to being "anointed" would have evoked the term "Messiah," or "Christ," both of which mean "anointed one." Thus, Jesus identifies himself through this scripture with the messianic expectations of his audience.

Jesus's first assignment is to "announce good news." The objects of this good news are the "humble" or "poor" (NRSV). While the term "poor" has primarily economic connotations, like the other designations ("captives," "blind," and "oppressed") it also carries a metaphorical meaning (cf. REB, "humble"). In Luke's writings, the poor are the economically disadvantaged (6:20–21; 7:22) *and* the spiritually impoverished (cf. 1:52–53, in which the hungry and humble are in contrast with the rich and proud). The captives are those who have been enslaved because they cannot pay their debts *and* those who are enslaved to sin (Luke 7:43). The blind are those who are physically *and* spiritually without sight (cf. Luke 7:21; 18:35). The oppressed are those who are subject to unwelcome forces of restraint *and* unwanted demons (cf. Luke 8:29).

The final phrase, "to proclaim the favorable year of the Lord," alludes to Lev. 25 and the Jubilee year legislation. The Jubilee year (the fiftieth year after seven intervals of seven years) was the "year of release" (see Lev. 25:10 LXX). Jesus's message in Luke 4 stands in sharp contrast with the note of vengeance that will accompany the Jubilee year in 11QMelch 13.

Here, then, in a nutshell at the beginning of Luke's Gospel is a précis of Jesus's public ministry as Messiah in Isaianic idiom. The rest of the story unfolds the ways in which Jesus preaches good news, proclaims new sight and forgiveness, and sends forth the oppressed in release. In Luke 4, Jesus declares that the "favorable year of the Lord" has already begun: **Today, he says, in your hearing this text has come true** (4:21). The emphasis is on the immediacy of the fulfillment; it has occurred "today" (on this word, see Luke 5:26; 19:5, 9; 23:43).

The audience's response is twofold. First, the narrator reports, **Everyone spoke well of him. They were amazed at the gracious words that were coming out of his mouth** (4:22a). Then they ask, **Isn't this man Joseph's son?** (4:22b). Often commentators take this question as a pejorative inquiry (perhaps because of the negative connotations found in the partial parallel to this story in Matt. 13:53–58 and Mark 6:1–6). By what authority could Joseph's son say such "gracious words"? In reality, both responses are positive. The question "Is not this Joseph's son?" should be taken as an example of "everyone" who "spoke well of him" (Luke 4:22a). From the point of view of the Nazareth crowd, being from their hometown entails certain social obligations. The "gracious words" that "were coming out of his mouth" were understood to refer primarily to his audience, members of his own village.

Jesus's first response/aphorism, **Physician, heal yourself** (4:23a), should be interpreted in light of the second, **Do as many things as we heard happened in Capernaum here in your hometown too!** (4:23b). Jesus understands full well that by referring to him as "Joseph's son," the crowd expects him to show preferential treatment to his own family and village. But he rejects their expectation: **I assure you, No prophet is acceptable in his hometown** (4:24; for other

---

Hearing Jesus's Nazareth Sermon within the World of Imperial Rome

"This [Augustus] is the Caesar who calmed the torrential storms on every side, who healed the pestilences common to Greeks and barbarians, pestilences which descending from the south and east coursed to the west and north sowing the seeds of calamity over the places and waters which lay between. This is he who not only loosed but broke the chains which had shackled and pressed so hard on the habitable world." (Philo, Legat. 145–49, trans. Colson 1962)

While the specific background for Luke's picture of the salvation brought by Jesus is Isa. 61:1–4 and Lev. 25:10, the list of saving benefits also resonates with the description of Caesar as savior. For Philo, "calming storms" and "healing" were metaphors for political storms and the ills of the body politic. For the NT such stories about Jesus often intend to portray actual events but are also symbolic of the salvation he brought (Boring, Berger, and Colpe 1995, no. 270).

versions of this saying, see Mark 6:4; Matt. 13:57; John 4:44). A prophet who, by the nature of his vocation, criticizes the unjust practices of his own people and is not ruled by the self-interests of his community is naturally displeasing to his own hometown or country. Jesus is such a prophet. His ministry of proclaiming good news to the poor is not limited to Israel's poor; he brings good news to *all* poor. His proclamation of release to the indentured and sight to the blind is not just for Israel's slaves or Israel's blind; he proclaims release and sight for *all* who are physically or spiritually enslaved or blind. He declares free *all* who are oppressed by soldier or spirit. This expansion beyond a provincial ethnocentrism, however, wins him no friends among his own people.

In Luke 4:25–27, Jesus cites two examples from Israel's Scriptures to prove his point: one about Elijah (1 Kings 17:1–24) and the other about Elisha (2 Kings 5:1–19). In recounting the two stories, Jesus emphasizes that the object of each prophet's miraculous ministry is a gentile. In Elijah's case, it is the poor widow at Zarephath in Sidon; with Elisha, it is Naaman the Syrian official. These stories make it clear that prophets of old did not limit their ministries to the "in-group." They, like Jesus, were no respecters of gender, class, or race.

The radical inclusiveness of Jesus's ministry shocks his audience: **everyone in the synagogue was filled with anger when they heard these things** (4:28). They have understood themselves to be the primary beneficiaries of Jesus's message. They can all relate to being poor, captive, blind, or oppressed. They are ready for deliverance, but they are not prepared to share it. When they hear that Jesus intends for his Jubilee ministry to extend to gentiles, they are "filled with anger" and fulfill Jesus's prophecy that "no prophet is acceptable in his hometown." Instead, **they got up and drove him out of the city, and then brought him to the ridge of the hill on which their city had been built in order to throw him off** (4:29), presumably in order to stone him. The crowd's intentions, however, are thwarted: **But after passing through the middle of the crowd, he went on his way** (4:30).

There is an abrupt shift between 4:29, in which Jesus has been pushed precariously to the edge of a cliff for the purpose of stoning, and 4:30, which states that Jesus passed "through the middle of the crowd" and "went on his way." The audience is left to fill this gap left in the story (on literary gaps in ancient and modern theory, see Maxwell 2010) and to ponder how Jesus managed this feat. Was he divinely transported, as Philip would later be in Acts 8:40? Did Jesus vanish and then reappear, as he did in his postresurrected state in Luke 24:31, 36? Did angels deliver him, as Satan had prophesied in the temptation narrative, guarding him from having his foot strike a stone (or vice versa; on this, see Longenecker 2012)? More fruitful than pondering the mechanics of the deliverance, however, are its theological purposes. Historically, the audience knows that Jesus died on a cross in Jerusalem and not by stoning in Nazareth. Luke makes clear the theological purpose for this historical fact. It was necessary for Jesus to die in Jerusalem. Why? Because Jesus the prophet, like other prophets before him, cannot "perish away from Jerusalem" (13:33; cf. 19:41). Further, the audience has just learned that Jesus has a vocation to fulfill: in Isaianic terms, he is called to preach good news to the poor, proclaim release to the prisoners, open the eyes of the blind, and free the oppressed (4:18). For these reasons he has been divinely delivered, whatever the mechanics. Of course, that does not mean that he will not eventually suffer at the "opportune time" (as others would also do, like Stephen, who is stoned for proclaiming a message very similar to Jesus's; see Acts 7).

On this day, Jesus escapes death on a hill in his hometown. His radical ministry of reaching out to those excluded because of race, gender, or economic and social status, however, eventually does lead to his execution on another hill, called Calvary, in the city of Jerusalem. This story should not be taken to mean that Israel, in Luke's view, is permanently rejected. Stories of positive Jewish response to Jesus's ministry are found throughout the Third Gospel (and later, Acts). But those who respond positively to Jesus's message recognize the inherent inclusiveness of his message. Those who do not hear that message of inclusion or who choose to reject it do not respond positively. "No prophet is acceptable in his hometown."

4:31–44. The Nazareth sermon, in which Jesus reveals in the words of Isaiah his messianic vocation to bring good news to everyone, is followed by three short scenes. Two stories of individual healings (4:31–37, 38–39) are followed by a summary statement about Jesus's public ministry and the extent/purpose of it (4:40–44). This section has parallels with Mark 1:21–39, though its placement (esp. that of 4:38–39) in relationship to 5:1–11 plays a significant role in the rhetorical argument of the Third Gospel. Further, the section is held together by chronological (4:31, 40, 42) and geographical references (4:31, 33, 38, 42; see Green 1997, 220). The most important link, however, is thematic. The descriptions of Jesus's mighty deeds toward those who are demon possessed and who suffer illness employ language ("rebuke"/"come out/leave") that demonstrates Jesus's messianic vocation is one of release for those held captive to demonic forces (4:18; Green 1997, 221).

The first story begins with Luke's report that Jesus **went down to Capernaum, a city in Galilee. He was teaching them on the Sabbath** (4:31). Although the context of the parallel account in Mark 1:21 points to Jesus's teaching in the synagogue on a particular day, the use of the imperfect periphrastic, "he was teaching" (*ēn didaskōn*), in 4:31 implies that Jesus was engaged in "an ongoing ministry of teaching" (Johnson 1991, 83; Fitzmyer 1981–85, 1:544). The response to Jesus, whether positive or negative, is an important element throughout this section, as it is here: **and they were amazed at his teaching, because he spoke with authority** (4:32; lit., "his word was with authority"; on the theological significance of Luke's use of *logos*, "word," cf. Luke 1:2; 5:1; 8:11; 11:28; Johnson 1991, 28).

Luke shifts from this brief reference to Jesus's words to focus now on a scene that will involve Jesus's miraculous actions. The scene begins with reference to **a man in the synagogue who had the spirit of an unclean demon**

(4:33a). This description stands in sharp contrast to the description of Jesus at the beginning of the unit as being "in the power of the Spirit" (4:14). The scene turns quickly to a confrontation between the Spirit and the diabolic: **and he shouted in a loud voice, "Ah! Why are you interfering with us, Jesus the Nazarene? Have you come to destroy us? I know who you are, the Holy One of God"** (4:33b–34). The form *ea* ("Ah!") could either be an exclamation of anger, displeasure, or dismay (e.g., NIV; Plummer 1903, 133; Fitzmyer 1981–85, 1:545) or an imperative form of *eaō* ("Leave us alone!"; e.g., NRSV; Green 1997, 223, argues that the latter reading is supported by the use of the verb *eia* in v. 41). The idiom "Why are you interfering with us?" (lit., "What to me and to you?") functions to highlight distance between the two referents (see Keener 2003, 506) and may here be translated, "What do we have to do with you?" "What do we have in common?" or "Leave us alone!" (BDAG 275, s.v. *egō*; see also 8:28). The translation above echoes the expression in the LXX (Josh. 22:24; Judg. 11:12; 2 Sam. 16:10; 19:22; 1 Kings 17:18; 2 Kings 3:13; see Marshall 1978, 193). The audience is familiar from Mark 1:24 with the title "Holy One of God"—unique here in Luke—and has also been prepared for the description by Luke 1:35 ("the holy [child] who is born will be called the Son of God") and 2:23 (quoting Exod. 13:2, "every male who opens the womb will be called holy to the Lord"; see Johnson 1991, 84).

Jesus releases the man from the demon's power: **Jesus rebuked him, saying, "Silence! Come out of him!" Then, after throwing him down into their midst, the demon came out of him without hurting him at all** (4:35). The term "rebuke," typical of exorcism stories (cf. 4:41; Zech. 3:2 LXX; Kee 1967–68; Fitzmyer 1981–85, 1:546), occurs in all three paragraphs and underscores again the struggle between God's Spirit-filled Holy One, Jesus, and diabolic forces (Talbert 2002, 61). Once again, the response to Jesus and his authority—this time, his authoritative actions—is highlighted: **They were all amazed and began talking with one another and saying, "What's going on here? He rebukes the unclean spirits with authority and power and they come out!" And news about him spread to every part of the surrounding region** (4:36–37).

In the second scene, Jesus moves from synagogue to house: **After leaving the synagogue, he entered the house of Simon. Now, Simon's mother-in-law was suffering from a high fever, and they asked him to help her** (4:38). The house and the sick mother-in-law belong to Simon, a character who has not yet been formally introduced in the narrative (a pattern later adopted in Acts for Philip [6:5; 8:5–40] and Saul/Paul [7:58; 9:1–31]; see Green 1997, 225). This brief notice plays an important role in Luke's presentation of the miraculous catch of fish in the next episode (see comments on 5:1–11). The healing itself sounds more like an exorcism ("rebuked/left"; cf. 4:35): **So, he stood over her and rebuked the fever; and it left her** (4:39a). Luke's description reflects the ancient view that "people who 'have a demon' and those who suffer from illness are both oppressed by diabolic forces and both in need of 'release'" (Green 1997, 221). Once again, the scene

Figure 12. Western Shore of the Sea of Galilee

ends by noting the response to Jesus, this time not of wonder and amazement but of hospitality. **She then immediately got up and began to serve them** (4:39b).

The third scene begins with a summary statement (4:40–41; cf. 5:15; 7:17; 8:1–3). The summary resonates with its counterpart in Mark (1:32–34): Jesus heals all those who come to him who have disease and demons. But once again the authorial audience notices two details missing from the Markan material that serve to highlight the focus of the Lukan account. Luke notes that the demons are crying out that Jesus is **the Son of God** (4:41a), and Luke paraphrases the end of Mark's scene by expansion: **But he rebuked them and would not allow them to speak, because they knew that he was the Christ** (4:41b). This entire unit, 4:14–44, is about Jesus's identity. Along with Mary (1:35) and Jesus (3:22), the demons recognize Jesus as "God's Son" who is the "Christ," an identification later made by Peter (Luke 9:20; cf. Johnson 1991, 84). In Luke's *bios*, Jesus's marvelous words (4:16–30) and deeds (4:31–43) are intended to reveal the essence of Jesus's character. His words reveal him to be the "anointed" one sent by God to proclaim "good news," an identity confirmed by the witness of Scripture (4:18); his deeds reveal him to be "God's Son," "the Christ," an identity confirmed by his demonic opponents.

Luke's concern about Jesus's identity continues in the final verses of this unit: **The next morning, he departed and went to a deserted place. The crowds, though, were looking for him. They came up to him and tried to prevent him from leaving them** (4:42). The crowds try to prevent Jesus from leaving because, unlike the demons, they do not understand his identity (4:34, 40–41); they can only marvel at his words and deeds (4:32, 37; see Green 1997, 221). And not knowing who he is prevents them from understanding his divinely ordained mission: **It is necessary for me to proclaim the kingdom of God to**

other cities, because I was sent for this reason (4:43; on the divine necessity of Jesus's mission, see comments on Luke 2:49–50). Jesus's proclamation of the "kingdom of God" involves both word and deed, and God's kingdom "refers both to God's saving activity and . . . to the community and practices that embody God's saving purpose" (Green 1997, 227).

The scene ends on what is a curious note, given that this section (4:14–9:50) purportedly focuses on Jesus's Galilean ministry: **So he preached [broadly] in the synagogues of Judea** (4:44). Elsewhere, Luke uses "Judea" to refer more broadly to the "country of the Jews" and not necessarily to the specific region of Palestine (cf. 1:5; 6:17; 7:17; 23:5). So here the unit ends by noting the reach of Jesus's influence "beyond the borders of Galilee" (Green 1997, 200; Fitzmyer 1981–85, 1:558).

Jesus's Miraculous Catch of Fish and People (5:1–6:16)

The miraculous catch of fish at the Sea of Galilee (5:1–11) is followed by two healing stories (5:12–16, 17–26). Jesus's prior wonder-working activities prepare for the account of Levi's call/commission (5:27–28); in that sense, the pattern of miracle as the foundation and rationale for the ensuing commission in Luke 4:31–5:11 is repeated here (see Talbert 2002, 64). The scene concludes with the religious authorities questioning Jesus and his disciples about his practices of "eating and drinking" in the context of Levi's banquet (5:29–39). The controversy continues with the debate about plucking grain (6:1–5) and healing (6:6–11) on the Sabbath and ends as it began, with Jesus choosing followers (6:12–16; cf. 5:10–11).

5:1–11. The story of the "miraculous catch of fish" (5:1–11), as it has come to be known, has a complicated tradition history; it is often viewed as a postresurrection story (cf. John 21:1–11) that has been retrojected into Jesus's public ministry (Bultmann 1968, 217–18; on the dis/similarities between the two accounts, see Brown 1966–70, 2:1090; Plummer 1903, 147). From the point of view of the authorial audience, familiar with Mark's account of the call of Simon, (Andrew), James, and John (Mark 1:16–20), more critical to understanding the function of the story in Luke's argument are the story's literary form and its placement within the larger context of the Third Gospel. We begin with placement.

Most scholars acknowledge that Luke has diverged from Mark's order of episodes in order to place the story of "the call of the disciples" in a different position in his Gospel (on the other six such transpositions, see Fitzmyer 1981–85, 1:71). Specifically, in Luke's account, the call and commission of Simon, James, and John occur after the healing of Simon's mother-in-law (4:38–39), whereas in Mark, the call of the disciples (including also Andrew, Simon's brother) occurs near the beginning of the story; Jesus has hardly begun his ministry when he sees two pairs of brothers fishing. He calls these presumably complete strangers, who inexplicably follow without hearing his teaching or witnessing his miraculous power. The rendering of the story sounds somewhat far-fetched, and perhaps Mark intends it so to emphasize the radical and uncompromising nature of Jesus's call to discipleship.

Luke's transposition of the story to follow the healing of Simon's mother-in-law, however, provides a context within which to make sense of the fishermen's response to Jesus's call to leave everything and follow him, prompting more than one scholar to label Luke's version a "psychologically plausible" setting for Simon's call (e.g., Bultmann 1968, 362–63; Grundmann 1966, 127; Fitzmyer 1981–85, 1:560; Culpepper 1995, 116).

In light of what we know of ancient compositional techniques, however, it may be more appropriate to view the Lukan transposition as an example of "rhetorical plausibility" (and another example of Luke's dissatisfaction with the rhetorical order of Mark; see comments on Luke 1:1–4; see also Parsons 2007, 24–25). Plausibility was a highly desired quality of ancient narrative (along with brevity and clarity; *Rhet. Her.* 1.8.14; Cicero, *Inv.* 20.28; *Top.* 26.97; Quintilian, *Inst.* 4.2). Theon observes that the narrative should reflect "subjects that are plausible and naturally follow from each another. One should briefly add the causes of things to the narration and say what is incredible in a believable way" (Theon, *Prog.* 84.19–24, trans. Kennedy 2003, 33). Luke makes changes in the story to tell the unbelievable in a believable way. Rhetorical plausibility is not exactly the same as historical veracity; rather, plausibility is a measure of whether characters respond in a manner appropriate to the virtues and vices expected by the audience. Among the healings that precede the call of Simon is the healing of Simon's mother-in-law. The audience is led to believe Simon knows of her miraculous recovery. This fact makes more understandable Simon's willingness to allow Jesus to board his boat and to teach from it. Simon, in Luke, is not welcoming a stranger on board but is acknowledging the holy man who has already healed a family member. Before commissioning him to be a "fisher of people," Jesus has already outlined his ministry in Luke 4:16–30, established a relationship with Simon through the healing of his mother-in law, and made a more modest request of Simon to cast his net for fish once more. Unlike the Markan Jesus with his abrupt command, the Lukan Jesus gradually leads Simon to an understanding and an acceptance of the nature of his call and commission.

Not only does the placement of the story in Luke's larger narrative shed light on its function but so also does its literary form. Luke 5:1–11 fits the pattern of an OT commissioning scene (Hubbard 1978, 190; Talbert 2002, 63), especially those in which "the commission is the final element" (Green 1997, 233; cf. Isa. 6:1–10). The pericope can be outlined in the following way (slightly modifying Green 1997, 233).

I. Introduction (5:1–3)
II. Encounter (5:4–7; cf. Isa. 6:1–4)
III. Reaction/protest (Luke 5:8–9; cf. Isa. 6:5)
IV. Commission (5:10; cf. Isa. 6:7–10)

The use of the commissioning form casts Jesus in the role of divine agent and Peter as divinely appointed prophet (who characteristically protests against the commission; cf. Isa. 6:5; Exod. 3–4; Judg. 6). Furthermore, the emphasis in this structure is clearly on Jesus's commission to Simon and the others to be **fishers of people** (5:10). This saying would have been recognized by the authorial audience as a *chreia*, that is, "a brief saying or action making a point, attributed to some specified person or something corresponding to a person" (Theon, *Prog.* 96, trans. Kennedy 2003, 15). The elaboration of *chreiae* was a basic building block of communication in rhetorical education. "We expand the chreia," Theon writes, "whenever we lengthen the question and answers in it, and the action or suffering, if any" (Theon, *Prog.* 103, trans. Kennedy 2003, 21). Later, Theon "elaborates" on the process of elaboration:

> Elaboration (*exergasia*) is language that adds what is lacking in thought or expression. What is "lacking" can be supplied by making clear what is obscure; by filling gaps in the language or content; by saying some things more strongly, or more believably, or more vividly, or more truly, or more wordily—each word repeating the same thing—or more legally, or more beautifully, or more appropriately, or more opportunely, or making the subject pleasanter, or by using a better arrangement or a style more ornate. (Theon, *Prog.* 110P, trans. Kennedy 2003, 71)

In addition to rendering the scene more rhetorically plausible through its placement in the narrative, Luke has also supplied what is "lacking" in his elaboration of the Markan *chreia* found in Mark 1:16–18. The image of "people-fishing" was ambivalent, sometimes containing negative connotations in the ancient world (see Wuellner 1967). The Jewish Scriptures frequently depict Israel as the target of their enemy's people-fishing activity, an activity often linked to divine judgment (Amos 4:2; Hab. 1:14–15; Jer. 16:16). In ancient philosophical thought, the image is used of duplicitous philosophers who seek to deceive others to their own ends (see Plato, *Soph.* 222A) or who are themselves caught on the hook baited with material wealth (Lucian, *The Fisherman*). By elaborating the Markan *chreia* to include the setting of the crowds gathering to hear Jesus proclaim "the word of God," Luke removes any potential misunderstanding related to the metaphor of people-fishing. The disciples are called and commissioned to participate in Jesus's people-fishing mission, and this mission, as Luke makes clear in Luke 4, is a mission of release and redemption, not one of deception and destruction. Its ultimate success is intimated and foreshadowed by the "great catch" that strains the nets (5:6). The mission of Jesus and his followers is confirmed and elaborated by the miraculous catch, and it leads to an elevation in the identity of Jesus from "master" to "Lord," not only for Simon (5:5, 8), but also for James and John, whom Simon has beckoned for help (5:7) and who join Simon in leaving everything and following Jesus (5:11), as well as the authorial audience, who in the process of hearing the story are also challenged to take up this mission.

5:12–16. The next scene (5:12–16) begins with a typical Lukan notice: **And it happened that while he was in one of the cities there was a man full of leprosy there!** (5:12a). The condition of leprosy is detailed in Lev. 13–14 and would have precluded the "unclean" person from the community until the disease was healed (Johnson 1991, 92). Like Simon (5:8), the leprous man **fell on his face** before Jesus; he then **begged him, saying, "Lord, if you want to, you are able to make me clean"** (5:12b). Defying social convention, Jesus **stretched out his hand and touched him, saying, "I do want to. Be clean!" And immediately, the leprosy left him. Then he commanded him to speak to no one, but instead, "Go and show yourself to the priest and make an offering concerning your cleansing just as Moses commanded, for a testimony to them"** (5:13–14). The adversative conjunction *alla* ("but instead") introduces a clause that runs counter to expectation: rather than doing the natural thing (spreading the news of his healing), the man is to do the necessary thing (follow the instructions in the law of Moses regarding being made clean from leprosy). To this point, the Lukan account is similar to the parallel account in Mark 1:40–45 (cf. also Matt. 8:1–4). The authorial audience, however, will notice several significant differences in detail in the way the scene ends.

In contrast to Mark's account (1:45), where it is the former leper who spreads the news despite Jesus's command, here the text simply indicates that the news spread: **Yet the news about him went on spreading even more, and many crowds were gathering to hear him and to be healed from their illnesses** (Luke 5:15). Seeing a contrast between Jesus's instructions to the former leper and the news spreading, then, flows from the parallel account rather than the present context. Also, the note that Jesus **was withdrawing into the wilderness and praying** (5:16) is distinctively Lukan (cf. 9:28; 11:1). The account that began with Jesus healing in one of the cities ends with him praying in the wilderness.

5:17–26. The following scene (5:17–26) begins with another general statement: **And it happened that on one of the days during that period of time he was teaching, and Pharisees and teachers of the law who had come from every village of Galilee and Judea and from Jerusalem were sitting there [listening]** (5:17a; contrast Mark's account, in which Jesus has returned home to Capernaum; Mark 2:1). The context quickly shifts from Jesus's teaching to healing: **And the power of the Lord was present for him to heal** (5:17b). His teaching and healing draw a considerable crowd, making access to Jesus very difficult: **And there were some men who were carrying a man on a cot who had been paralyzed! They were trying to carry him in and place him in front of Jesus. And when they could not find a way to bring him in because of the crowd, they went up on the roof and lowered him with his cot through the tiles into the midst of the crowd in front of Jesus** (5:18–19). The paralytic's friends are both persistent and resourceful. They remove the roof above him. In Mark the image is of the friends "digging" through the matting of reeds, branches, and dried mortar of what was probably a thatched hut, the kind found by archaeologists throughout ancient Capernaum. Luke contextualizes the story for his urban audience by reporting that the friends removed the "tiling" from the roof, evoking the image of a tiled, peristyle home more common among the Mediterranean city centers of late antiquity (McCown 1939; Fitzmyer 1981–85, 1:582).

Now the recognition of faith comes: **When he saw their faith . . .** (5:20a). Jesus sees what most others would not have seen. He sees *their* faith, the faith of these persistent friends, not, as one might expect, the paralytic's faith. Their persistence and sacrifice is not self-serving. Rather, it contributes to the healing of their friend. Jesus's response to this demonstration of faith is **Man, your sins have been forgiven** (5:20b). To the authorial audience, it would be most natural to equate the man's physical disability with some previous egregious sin. The OT and postbiblical Judaism give a variety of perspectives on physical suffering. Sometimes physical suffering was understood as divine punishment for sin (Pss. 37:1–2; 41:3–4; 107:17; Isa. 57:17). Sometimes the purpose of physical suffering was understood to serve as *paideia*, moral instruction, for the one stricken (Prov. 3:11–12; Wis. 3:4–6; 17:1; Sir. 2:5–6; *Pss. Sol.* 18.4–5). Sometimes the physical suffering of one was seen as beneficial to others (Gen. 50:15–21; Isa. 53:2–12; 2 Macc. 7:37–38). Early Christian writings reflect these same three views: suffering as divine punishment (John 5:14; 1 Cor. 11:30; James 5:16); suffering as moral instruction (Rom. 5:3–4; 1 Cor. 11:32; James 1:2–3); and suffering as beneficial for others (Mark 10:45; Gal. 1:3–4; Col. 1:24; see Talbert 1991).

Jesus's words in Luke 5 reflect the first perspective: the man's paralysis is somehow related to divine punishment for sin. A modern Western audience might find such a notion distasteful. Yet in "many traditional, non-Western societies, the domain of biological medicine is not differentiated from that of religion, politics, and broader social life, with the result that healing may include or require the resolution of spiritual and social disorder" (Green 1997, 241). And even in modern Western society, we now recognize the potential connection between unhealthy habits and disease: physical inactivity combined with overeating can lead to heart disease; smoking can contribute to cancer. Still, there is no explicit connection made about how the actions of this man in Luke 5 could have led to his paralysis. In the final analysis, however, it is in Jesus's pronouncement that the real healing takes place: God has released the man from the disease that had incapacitated him.

No sooner has Jesus pronounced the paralytic's sins forgiven than the religious authorities, lurking in the background until this point, bristle at his words—not at the equation of sin and suffering, but over the audacity of Jesus to claim the authority to forgive sins: **Then the scribes and the Pharisees began to argue, saying, "Who is this man who speaks blasphemies? Who but God alone is able to forgive sins?"** (5:21). In their ponderings, the religious leaders are actually reflecting another long-standing tradition: while the sacrificial system presumed that restitution and rituals could gain forgiveness for the sinful party (see Lev. 17:11), only God could forgive sins. The God of Israel declares: "I shall forgive their wrongdoing, and their sin I shall call to mind no more" (Jer. 31:34; cf. Isa. 33:22–24). The charge of blasphemy would not be difficult to establish, since the point of the story is that Jesus, as the anointed one of God, does indeed have the divine authority to forgive sins.

Luke presents these questions of the scribes and Pharisees as rhetorical, expecting no answer (Quintilian, *Inst.* 9.2.7; *Rhet. Her.* 4.15.22), so they (and the authorial audience) must be startled when Jesus responds to these inner musings with rhetorical questions of his own: **Recognizing what they were thinking, Jesus responded, "Why are you arguing in your hearts? What is easier, to say, 'Your sins have been forgiven,' or to say, 'Get up and walk'?"** (5:22–23). In the prophetic tradition, prophets were judged to be "true" or "false" (in part) on the basis of whether what they predicted actually came to pass. Therefore, it was easier to say, "your sins are forgiven," since such a statement was not open to human falsification. A declaration of healing, however, could be readily verified or falsified. Thus, Jesus, in typical Jewish fashion, reasons from the greater (harder) to the lesser (easier). If his opponents are able to verify the healing of the paralytic, then they must also accept his "lesser" (i.e., less verifiable) declaration of forgiveness: **"So in order that you may know that the Son of Man has power on the earth to forgive sins"**—he said to the paralytic—**"I say to you, Get up and, when you've picked up your bedding, go home"** (5:24).

Verification occurs instantly: **And immediately he stood up before them, picked up what he had been lying on, and left for his home glorifying God** (5:25). The story ends with the narrator's summary: **And amazement gripped everyone, and they began glorifying God, and they were filled with awe** (5:26a). If the reference to "everyone" here is taken seriously, then Jesus's detractors are apparently convinced of both words: Jesus, God's Messiah, has the power to heal illnesses and the authority to forgive sins— all because of four friends who, rather than sitting around trying to guess what sin had been committed to cause such an illness (like Job's friends), had the faith and persistence to bring the paralyzed man to one who could both heal and forgive. Luke's presentation of Jesus's marvelous deeds is reiterated by those gathered: **We have seen incredible things today!** (5:26b).

5:27–28. These two healing stories culminate in another call account, this time of Levi the tax collector: **After these things he went out and noticed a tax collector named Levi sitting at the tax booth and said to him, "Follow me." And he left everything behind, and he arose and followed him** (5:27–28; cf. 5:1–11). Once again, Luke's version is similar to the parallel account in Mark 2:13–17 (see also Matt. 9:9–13, in which the tax collector is identified as Matthew). The only notable change is the additional note that Levi "left everything behind," a phrase that echoes the response of Simon, James, and John (cf. Luke 5:11) and indicates through the disposition of possessions the radical nature of Jesus's call to discipleship (Johnson 1991, 97).

5:29–39. The reference to leaving everything behind obviously does not mean literally all his worldly possessions, since **Levi prepared a huge banquet for him at his house, and there was a large crowd of tax collectors and others who were dining with them** (5:29; the term banquet, *dochē*, is used also in 14:13). This is the first of several meal scenes in Luke followed by dialogue (7:36–50; 9:10–17; 10:38–42; 11:37–54; 14:1–24; 19:1–10; 22:14–38; 24:29–32, 41–43). Here the meal scene is the setting for conflict: **And the Pharisees and their scribes were complaining to his disciples** (5:30a). This scene also shares verbal similarities with Luke 15:2, in which the "Pharisees and scribes were complaining [*diegongyzon*; cf. *egongyzon* in 5:30] and saying, 'This man welcomes sinners and eats with them!'" In Luke 5:30, the complaint is leveled not only against Jesus but against his followers as well: **On what basis do you eat and drink with tax collectors and sinners?** (5:30b). The inclusion of the disciples in the complaint is missing from the parallel account in Mark 2:16 (see also Matt. 9:11). The inclusion here indicates the degree to which those, like Simon, James, John, and now Levi, have left everything to take up the mission of Jesus to proclaim "release" even to those who are captive to their own possessions. The coupling of tax collectors and sinners might seem odd on first hearing, although both are present at the banquet: Peter is a self-described "sinful man" (5:8), and Levi has invited fellow tax agents to his banquet (Johnson 1991, 99). Luke, however, has a broader application in mind for the description and repeatedly uses these terms in tandem "as a religious metaphor for those who display the proper spirit of contrition and repentance" (Neale 1991, 177; cf. 7:34; 15:1; 18:11; also 19:7).

Jesus responds with a *chreia*, and what precedes may be understood as an elaboration explaining the *chreia*, which in this context may be viewed as a defense of his followers' actions (Johnson 1991, 97): **Healthy people do not have need of a doctor, but those who are sick do. I have come not to call righteous people but to call sinners to repentance** (5:31–32). Jesus employs the language of conventional Hellenistic moral teaching (the philosopher = the doctor; vice = sickness; virtue = health; cf. Dio Chrysostom, *Or.* 32.14–30; Epictetus, *Diatr.* 3.23, 30; cited by Johnson 1991, 97); here "Jesus is doctor, sickness is sin, and health is righteousness" (Johnson 1991, 97). The authorial audience will note that Luke has added the phrase "to repentance" to Mark's account (2:17), underscoring another major theme in Luke's Gospel (the term "repentance" occurs at Luke 3:3, 8; 15:7; 24:47; and, later, in Acts 5:31; 11:18; 13:24; 19:4; 20:21; 26:20; see Nave 2002).

Unlike the parallel account in Mark, which suggests a scene change ("Now John's disciples and the Pharisees were fasting; and people came and said to him, 'Why do John's disciples and the disciples of the Pharisees fast?'"; Mark

2:18), Luke continues the table talk of the banquet scene: **Then they said to him, "John's disciples fast frequently and offer prayers, as the disciples of the Pharisees also do; but the ones belonging to you eat and drink [all the time]"** (5:33). The "they said" (*hoi de eipan*), however, need not refer to the Pharisees (which makes awkward the third-person reference to the Pharisees in the direct speech), since in a banquet scene others may be expected to join in the discourse (Green 1997, 248). Continuity in the scene does not demand continuity of speaker. Jesus responds by defending his followers' actions: **Surely, you are not able to make the wedding guests fast while the bridegroom is with them?** (5:34). Fasting was the "deliberate, temporary abstention from food for religious reasons" (Muddiman 1992, 2:773). The issue, for Jesus, is not *whether* to fast but *when* to fast (Tiede 1988, 129). Luke clearly does not reject fasting as a religious ritual; both Jesus and his followers fast (see Luke 4:1–2; later, Acts 13:2; 14:23; 27:9). In addition to the Day of Atonement, the national day of fasting, a variety of occasions were recommended in the OT as appropriate for individual fasting: penance (1 Sam. 7:6); mourning (2 Sam. 1:12; 3:35–38; 12:16); and in conjunction with prayer (Tob. 12:8; see Culpepper 1995, 130). Fasting was also depicted as an appropriate activity in preparation for a divine visitation (Exod. 34:28; Dan. 9:3; Luke 2:37; Acts 13:2). It is this practice of fasting, as an expression of eschatological hope, that Jesus rejects *at this time*. While the term "bridegroom" may not have been a messianic title (see Fitzmyer 1981–85, 1:599), the image of the wedding celebration does draw on traditional eschatological symbolism for divine visitation (Isa. 54:5–6; 62:4–5; Jer. 2:2; 16:9; Hosea 2:16–23; see Green 1997, 249; Johnson 1991, 97–98). The repeated emphasis on the immediacy of God's divine visitation ("Today this scripture is fulfilled"; Luke 4:21; cf. 1:78; 2:36–37) nullifies the present need to fast as an expression of eschatological hope. Jesus, the bridegroom, is here; the eschatological wedding has begun; it is the time "for feasting, not fasting!" (Green 1997, 249). Is it ever appropriate to fast? Yes, according to Jesus. The authorial audience will not miss the allusion to Jesus's death in the language of the forced removal of the bridegroom from the scene: **The days will come, though, when the bridegroom is taken away from them. Then, in those days, they will fast** (5:35).

Jesus ends this discussion with a "parabolic commentary" (Green 1997, 249), which contains a series of analogies intended to surprise the audience (Eriksson 2005, 63–64).

> And so he told them an illustration: "No one after tearing a patch from a new garment puts it on an old garment! Otherwise, he will both tear the new one and the piece from the new one will not fit the old one. And no one puts new wine into old wineskins. Otherwise, the new wine will burst the wineskins, it will spill out, and the wineskins will be ruined. Instead, new wine, which must be put in something, is put into fresh wineskins. And no one drinking old wine wants new. For he says, 'The old is better.'" (5:36–39)

The premise of all three analogies is that the new and the old are utterly incompatible and that to try to mix them is absurdly foolish. What is debated is what are the referents of "old" and "new." Jesus's views represent the "old" or "ancient" way, and the Pharisees' views are, in reality, "new" and innovative. This is true not only of the immediate context of fasting but also with regard to Jesus's teachings in general. Luke 5:39, then, draws on conventional Greek and Jewish wisdom and continues the argument in a straightforward way: "the 'old' (Jesus's way) is better" (Green 1997, 250; for a different interpretation of the basic point "the old is better," see Eriksson 2005).

This interpretation is to be preferred over the more traditional reading (where "old" = Pharisaic teachings and "new" = Jesus's teachings) for four reasons.

1. In the immediate context and by appealing to the traditional eschatological imagery of divine visitation as wedding celebration, Jesus is appealing to, and justifying the practices of his followers by, Israel's Scriptures and tradition. In the two scenes that follow, Jesus also will appeal to Jewish Scripture and tradition in his continuing controversies with the religious authorities (see Luke 6:1–5, 6–11). In each case, Jesus is arguing that his teaching and practice, even though they may appear to be radically different, are true to what is authentic in Jewish ancestral religion.
2. In Luke's larger narrative argument to this point, he uses the birth narratives, the genealogy, the temptation narrative, and the Nazareth sermon to show that "Jesus is doing nothing more than bringing to fruition the ancient purpose of God" (Green 1997, 250). He will later continue this argument in Acts when he counters the criticism that Jesus and his disciples are "changing the customs of Moses" (6:13–14). Jesus and his followers are not changing the ancestral practices; they are clarifying and thereby fulfilling them (see Parsons 2008a, 94–102; Balch 1995).
3. The traditional interpretation ("old" = inferior Judaism; "new" = superior Christianity), firmly rooted in Christian exegetical tradition since patristic times—which claims that Jesus's novel teaching, preserved in Christianity, cannot be held by the "old" garment or wineskin of Judaism—is an anachronistic reading of the text, presuming that the conflict between Christianity and Judaism as discrete religious expressions extends back into the time of Luke (or Jesus). To the contrary, in the Third Gospel and later in Acts, Luke consistently depicts the struggle between Jesus's followers and other Jews as an intra-Jewish struggle over identity and who most authentically embodies true heirs of Israel (see Parsons 2008a, 161–63).
4. This struggle for Jewish self-identity must be viewed within the larger cultural preference for that which was "old." It was axiomatic in Luke's day to prefer the ancient over the innovative (see *Res gestae divi Augusti*;

Cicero, *Div.* 2.75; cited by Esler 1987, 214–15). It would have been strange to the authorial audience's ears to hear the "new" in terms of innovative religious teachings and practices to be preferred to the "old" ancestral traditions and patterns (on the possible preference for "old" garments and wineskins, see Eriksson 2005, 65–67). Rather, "Jesus interprets his behaviors, which are questionable and innovative to some onlookers, as manifestations of God's ancient purpose coming to fruition, while the concerns of the Pharisees are rejected not only as innovative but also as quite inconsistent with God's program" (Green 1997, 250; cf. Forbes 2000, 330). Further, Luke demonstrates that the "old" way of Jesus is "better" in the next two stories (6:1–5, 6–11). In his conflict with the religious authorities, Jesus appeals to the Scriptures and the tradition of Jewish ancestral religion in order to argue for the appropriateness of his or his disciples' actions.

6:1–5. This first story begins innocently enough: **One Sabbath day Jesus was passing through grain fields** (6:1a). The trouble starts when the audience learns that **his disciples were plucking and eating the heads of grain, after rubbing the husks off with their hands** (6:1b). **Some of the Pharisees,** appearing literally out of nowhere, **said, "Why are you doing what is not permitted on the Sabbath?"** (6:2), evidently a reference to the various prohibitions against harvesting grain on the Sabbath (see Exod. 34:21; *Jub.* 2.29–30; *m. Šabb.* 7.2).

While it is true that it is the disciples' behavior and not Jesus's that is under scrutiny here, Jesus, as their leader, is nonetheless implicated by the accusation, since in ancient thought the master is responsible for the behavior of the disciples (so Seneca, "He who does not forbid sin when in control, commands it," *Tro.* 290, author's trans.). So Jesus offers a defense on behalf of his followers.

Jesus responds by citing a scriptural precedent (drawing, with some variation, on 1 Sam. 21:1–6): **Have you not even read what David did when he and those with him were hungry? How he went into the house of God, and took the sacred bread and ate it, and then gave it to those with him—bread that no one may eat except the priests alone?** (6:3–4). Clearly here was a case where the urgency of human need, in this case hunger, took precedence over strict Sabbath observance. In his appeal, Jesus draws on a well-established tradition, grounded in the Jewish Scriptures (see Exod. 23:12; Deut. 5:14), that understands the law to have a humanitarian intent (a view whose adherents no doubt included some Pharisees), which challenges another stream of Jewish tradition that is more legalistic (and "novel"? cf. 5:33–39). This view of the law's humanitarian function continues in postbiblical Judaism. For example, in the *Mekilta* on Exod. 31:14 we read: "The Sabbath is handed over to you, not you to it" (trans. J. Marcus 2000–2009, 1:245; see also 1 Macc. 2:39–41; 2 Macc. 5:19; *b. Yoma* 85b; *t. Ber.* 3.7). It would therefore be a mistake, one that is unfortunately common in Christian proclamation, to characterize this story as pitting a Christian view of the humanitarian intent of the law (represented here by Jesus's words) over against a Jewish legalistic understanding of the law (represented here by the Pharisees).

Jesus concludes the story with these words (reducing Mark's enthymeme to a simple *chreia*; see Parsons 2005, 57–60): **The Son of Man is Lord of the Sabbath** (6:5). Certainly this passage then affirms that meeting human need takes priority over strict observance of religious ritual, and this assertion is grounded in the Jewish Scriptures of Jesus's ancestral religion. But this story is *not* therefore to be taken as exclusively or even primarily a celebration of human freedom over tradition, for Luke goes beyond the law's humanitarian intent to speak of Jesus's authority over the Sabbath. If strict Sabbath observance can be set aside for David in the urgent circumstance of fleeing for his life, how much more can such rigid observance be abrogated for Jesus, who is, after all, David's Lord (see Luke 20:41–44, esp. 44a)? The Messiah was to be Davidic both in lineage and in likeness. And that this Son of Man figure is none other than Jesus the Davidic Messiah has already been established in Luke 5:23–24. Whatever the background of the Son of Man in Luke (cf. Dan. 7), the immediate context makes it clear that here in Luke 6:5 Jesus is claiming for himself authority over the Sabbath and its observance.

6:6–11. Following the parallel account in Mark 2:1–3:6, Luke 6:6–11 is the last of five conflict stories between Jesus and the religious leaders, and so reflects a conflict that has escalated in intensity as it culminates in the religious authorities' discussion about what "they might do to Jesus" (6:11). Once again the setting is on a Sabbath: **Now it happened on another Sabbath that he entered into the synagogue and was teaching** (6:6a). The plot thickens with the notice that **a man was there whose right hand was withered** (6:6b). Contra Mark 3:1, Luke "adds that it was the man's right hand, the hand normally used for work, gesturing, and greeting. Since one performed chores of bodily hygiene with one's left hand, that hand was not to be presented in public. The man had lost the use of his good hand, presumably forcing him to use his left hand in public, thereby adding shame to his physical disability" (Culpepper 1995, 134). Luke reports that **the scribes and the Pharisees were watching him closely to see if he continued to heal on the Sabbath, in order to find an accusation against him** (6:7). Jesus **knew what they were thinking. So he said to the man who had the withered hand, "Get up and stand among us"** (6:8a). Through *hyperbaton* (the transposition of the natural word order; see Quintilian, *Inst.* 8.6.62–67), Luke highlights the condition of the man's hand (Greek: *tō andri tō xēran echonti tēn cheira*; lit., "the man, *the withered* having the hand"; cf. Mark 3:3, which has the more "natural" order, *tō anthrōpō tō tēn xēran cheira echonti*). To Mark's parallel account, Luke also adds the note that the man **got up and stood there** (6:8b). Both changes contribute to the focus on the man and his healing, and, concomitantly, to the characterization of Jesus as a Sabbath healer.

> ### He Heals or He Will Heal?
>
> Many scribes ($\mathfrak{P}^4$ B Θ $f^{1,13}$ al.) use the future *therapeusei* ("he will heal" on the Sabbath) in Luke 6:7 rather than the present *therapeuei* (translated here, "if he continued to heal" on the Sabbath) (ℵ A D L W Ψ 565 pc). The present tense conveys imperfective aspect and points to Jesus's custom. The future tense, however, points to future time and conveys perfective aspect (Wallace 1996, 566; Campbell 2007, 159) or is aspectually vague (Porter 1989, 438). It conveys expectation regarding something that does not yet exist (Porter 1989, 439), and although it does not convey uncertainty on its own (Campbell 2007, 156), its semantic makeup does make the future tense a natural choice in constructions where uncertainty is in view (cf. 1:18; Matt. 26:33). More important, the future tense would focus on the single event rather than Jesus's habit. The choice, then, is between the present reading, which is concerned with the question "Does he heal on the Sabbath?" and the future reading, which addresses the question "Will he heal on the Sabbath?" If the future tense is followed, the verse would be translated "(to see) if he would heal..." The authorial audience, familiar with the future tense of Mark 3:2, will recognize that Luke is subtly shifting the focus on Jesus's habitual Sabbath healings. The future tense in the manuscript tradition, then, arises through harmonization to Mark's account and destroys the intent of Luke's rhetoric (cf. ℵ and W, which harmonize Mark with the present tense in Luke and also have the effect of distorting Luke's argument; see also Culy, Parsons, and Stigall 2010).

With the man standing before them, Jesus asks a rhetorical question (*Rhet. Her.* 4.15.22) to reinforce his argument: **I ask you, is it in fact lawful to do good on the Sabbath or to do evil, to save a life or to destroy it?** (6:9). The alternatives he poses (doing good or evil; saving a life or destroying it) admit only a positive answer (Marshall 1978, 234). His argument is also grounded in biblical precedence (Isa. 56:2 lauds the one who "keeps the Sabbath" by refraining "from doing any evil"; cf. Isa. 1:11–17; Deut. 5:12–15; see also Danker 1988, 133), once again underscoring that it is Jesus and not his opponents who is preserving what is old and therefore preferred in Jewish Scripture and tradition (later rabbinic tradition puts it this way: "And whenever there is doubt whether life is in danger, this overrides the Sabbath"; *m. Yoma* 8.6). Further, Jesus's comments return conceptually to the previous story's argument (human need takes precedence over the Sabbath; Luke 6:3–4) and aphorism ("The Son of Man is Lord of the Sabbath"; Luke 6:5).

Rhetorical questions expect no answer, and Jesus receives none. Rather, **after looking around at all of them he said to him, "Hold out your hand." And he did, and his hand was restored** to normal condition (6:10). The authorial audience recognizes that Luke has omitted Mark's report concerning the responses of the religious leaders and Jesus ("*But they were silent.* And he looked around at them with *anger, grieved at their hardness of heart,* and said to the man . . ."; Mark 3:4b–5a ESV). Not only does this have the effect of economy of style (see Theon, *Prog.* 83), but it also continues the emphasis on the Sabbath healing and Jesus as Sabbath healer who has authority over the Sabbath. The conclusion to the story serves also as the conclusion to this series of conflict scenes (Luke 5:17–6:11) and a foreshadowing of more conflict to come over Jesus's identity and authority (cf. 13:1–9; 14:1–6; note that here, contra Mark 3:5–6, it is the religious authorities, and not Jesus, who are filled with anger [*anoias*; lit., "mindless rage"]): **Then they were filled with fury and began discussing with one another what they might do to Jesus (6:11).**

6:12–16. This section (5:1–6:16) ends as it began, with Jesus calling disciples (6:12–16; cf. 5:10–11). First, however, as was his custom, the Lukan Jesus prays: **Now it happened in those days that he went away to a mountain to pray, and he spent the night praying to God** (6:12; cf. 3:21; 5:16; 9:18, 28–29; 11:1; 22:41, 44–45; 23:46). Next follows the choosing of the Twelve: **When morning came, he called to his disciples [to come to him], and after choosing twelve from among them, whom he also named apostles . . .** (6:13). Luke paraphrases Mark's account by indicating that the Twelve are chosen from among a larger group of disciples and by naming them "apostles" (though not the "twelve apostles"; cf. Matt. 10:1–2). Their commission (cf. Mark 3:14) is deferred until Luke 9:1. The number echoes the twelve tribes of Israel (cf. Luke 22:28–30) and continues Luke's design to view Jesus's ministry in light of the larger story of God's involvement with Israel. The names of the Twelve (6:14–16) differ slightly in the tradition, as table 5 demonstrates (see Culpepper 1995, 138).

Table 5. List of Disciples in Synoptic Gospels and Acts

Luke 6:14–16	Acts 1:13	Mark 3:16–19	Matt. 10:2–4
Simon, whom he also called Peter	Peter	Simon whom he surnamed Peter	Simon, who is called Peter
Andrew, his brother	John	James the son of Zebedee	Andrew, his brother
James	James	John, the brother of James, whom he surnamed Boanerges, that is, sons of thunder	James the son of Zebedee
John	Andrew	Andrew	John his brother
Philip	Philip	Philip	Philip
Bartholomew	Thomas	Bartholomew	Bartholomew
Matthew	Bartholomew	Matthew	Thomas

Luke 6:14–16	Acts 1:13	Mark 3:16–19	Matt. 10:2–4
Thomas	Matthew	Thomas	Matthew the tax collector
James the son of Alphaeus	James the son of Alphaeus	James the son of Alphaeus	James the son of Alphaeus
Simon who is called the Zealot	Simon the Zealot	Thaddaeus	Thaddaeus
Judas (son) of James	Judas the son of James	Simon the Cananaean	Simon the Cananaean
and Judas Iscariot, who became a traitor		Judas Iscariot, who betrayed him	Judas Iscariot, who betrayed him

While the list of names in Luke has the same content as Acts 1:13, the order is slightly different (Peter, John, and James are listed first, presumably because they are the only ones to receive any attention in Acts beyond the list; see Parsons 2008a, 30). The list of apostles is a "bridge" passage (Topel 2001, 49; Beutler 1991, 231–33), serving both as an *inclusio* for the previous section (with the call of disciples in 5:10–11) and also as the introduction for the next unit, the Sermon on the Plain (Luke 6:17–49).

The Sermon on the Plain (6:17–49)

The authorial audience recognized that Luke's version of Jesus's sermon shares content, and in many instances also sequence, with its parallel material (whether Matthew or Q); nonetheless, there is distinctive Lukan material (modifying Topel 2001, 57; Lambrecht 1985, 36–37; Talbert 2006):

Luke 6:20–23	beatitudes	Matt. 5:2–12/Q 6:20–23
Luke 6:24–26	woes	—/—
Luke 6:27–28	love of enemies	Matt. 5:43–44/Q 6:27–28
Luke 6:29–30	nonretaliation	Matt. 5:39–40, 42/Q 6:29, 30
Luke 6:31	Golden Rule	Matt. 7:12/Q 6:31
Luke 6:32	Christian retribution	Matt. 5:46/Q 6:32
Luke 6:33	doing good to others	—/—
Luke 6:34	loans	—/Q 6:34
Luke 6:35a–b	love of enemies (repeated)	—/—
Luke 6:35c–d	sons of the most high	Matt. 5:45/Q 6:35c–d (between Q 6:27–28 and 6:29)
Luke 6:36	imitation of the father	Matt. 5:45, 48/Q 6:36
Luke 6:37a, 38b	on not judging	Matt. 7:1, 2b/Q 6:37–38

Luke 6:37b–38a	on forgiving, giving	—/—
Luke 6:39	blind leader	Matt. 15:14/Q 6:39
Luke 6:40	master/disciple	Matt. 10:24/Q 6:40
Luke 6:41–42	splinter/beam	Matt. 7:3–5/Q 6:41–42
Luke 6:43–44	trees and fruit	Matt. 7:16–17/Q 6:43–44
Luke 6:45	good person	Matt. 12:34–35/Q 6:45
Luke 6:46–49	exhortation/housebuilders	Matt. 7:21, 24–27/Q 6:46–49

Further, there is a distinctively Lukan shape to the sermon. Following the sermon's setting (6:17–19), Luke has shaped this material into three sections, 6:20–26, 27–38, 39–49, each delineated with a rhetorical marker: "Then after making careful eye contact with his disciples, he turned and said" (6:20a); "to you who are listening I say" (6:27a); and "Then he told them an illustration" (6:39a). Through attention to the distinctively Lukan content and the arrangement, the Lukan perspective on Jesus's teaching may be detected (Talbert 2002, 71–72). That shape and content also contribute to our understanding of the sermon's function. Its function is less about giving specific instructions to Jesus's followers regarding ethical decision making and more about the character of God and God's Messiah, Jesus; that is, the sermon has both a theological and a christological focus.

6:17–19. The section begins with reference to Jesus and the Twelve: **after coming down *with them*, he stood on a level place** (6:17a). Jesus is met on the plain by **a large crowd of his disciples and a large number of the people from all of Judea and Jerusalem and the seacoast of Tyre and Sidon** (6:17b). Luke frames his narrative with an initial reference to Jesus looking on "his disciples" (6:20) and a concluding note that "all the people" listened, thus highlighting the "mixed character" of the auditors (Topel 2001, 57). The "people" reappear here in 6:17 for the first time since Luke 3:21 (Culpepper 1995, 142). All of them **had come to hear him and to be healed from their diseases** (6:18a), to experience both his mighty deeds and his marvelous words, and they are not disappointed: **And those troubled by unclean spirits were being healed. The entire crowd was trying to touch him, because power was coming out of him and healing everyone** (6:18b–19). The manifestation of his power is not confined to his healing ministry, however; power flows from him through his mighty words as well.

6:20–26. We see the theological character of the Sermon on the Plain in this first section. Luke has paraphrased the parallel material (whether Matt. 5:2–12 or Q 6:20–23) by adding the corresponding "woes" section (6:24–26) to the beatitudes (6:20–23). The four beatitudes in strophe one (6:20–23) are balanced by the four woes in strophe two (6:24–26); the content of each woe is the negative mirror image of the corresponding beatitude (Topel 2001, 59). The last saying in each strophe is considerably longer and is composed of a beatitude or makarism (a saying introduced with "blessed"), a "when" (*hotan*) clause, stating certain causal factors, and a reason (introduced by "for") for those actions, rooted in the past treatment of Israel's prophets (Nolland 1989–93, 1:284–85; Topel 2001, 59).

Beatitudes were common in Jewish wisdom literature (e.g., Pss. 1:1; 41:1; Prov. 14:21; Sir. 31:8; cf. 4Q525); their function was "platitudinous, expressing common wisdom in which those who are near to God already share divine favors and prosperity" (Topel 2001, 63). Jewish apocalyptic literature expands the makarism to include hope for eschatological deliverance rooted in Yahweh (Dan. 12:12; cf. *Pss. Sol.* 17.50; Tob. 13:14; see also Nolland 1989–93, 1:280, for other texts). Here the Lukan Jesus reflects the eschatological function of the beatitude, which focuses not on the "painful reality of the present" but on "an awareness of the ultimate outcome of history" (Talbert 2002, 73). "Under the strain of expressing the Reign of God," the beatitude "has been transformed from a platitudinous to a paradoxical expression" (Topel 2001, 67). This paradoxical expression is generally typical of Jesus's makarisms elsewhere in Luke's Gospel (1:45; 7:23; 10:23; 11:27–28; 12:37–38, 43; 14:14, 15; 23:29). Each beatitude contributes to unpacking Jesus's understanding of God's kingdom and God's justice that undergirds it.

Jesus begins, **Blessed are the poor, for the kingdom of God is yours** (6:20). While the reference to the "poor" here does not exclude understanding the term in spiritual terms (see comments on 4:18–19), in Luke, the term, echoing its usage in the OT, most frequently refers to the victims of social and economic oppression (see, e.g., 14:13, 21; 16:20, 22; 21:2, 3). To these poor belongs the kingdom of God, which in Luke is both a present reality as well as a future one (11:20; 16:16; 17:21) and the locus for Jesus's ministry of deliverance through his words—good news to the poor—and deeds—healings and exorcisms (cf. 4:43).

Jesus's second beatitude is really an intensification of the first: **Blessed are those who are hungry now, for you will be satisfied** (6:21a). Once again, spiritual hunger is not excluded from the purview (see 1:51–53 and above; see also Matt. 5:6), but the emphasis is on physical hunger (4:2; 6:3; 15:14; 16:20–21), which in its most extreme experience—starvation—is itself a "direr form of poverty" (Topel 2001, 98). Conversely, Jesus pronounces that those starving will be "stuffed." The passive voice suggests divine activity (cf. Isa. 49:9–10; 65:13; Ezek. 34:29; Ps. 17:14) and gives no little hint of the eschatological banquet. But the kingdom's banquet is a present reality as well, as demonstrated by Jesus's earlier statement regarding the appropriateness of celebrating while the bridegroom is present and later his feeding ("stuffing") of the five thousand (9:10–17, esp. v. 17).

Blessed are those who weep now, for you will laugh (6:21b). The authorial audience, familiar with the parallel material (whether Q 6:21 or Matt. 5:4), will notice that Luke has changed this makarism from "Blessed are those who mourn, for they shall be comforted" (cf. Isa. 61:2). Tears turned to joy "in personal deliverance, in restoration from the exile, and in the apocalyptic new creation (Isa. 35:10; 60:20; 61:3; 65:17–25; Jer. 31:13; Job 30:25; Pss. 126:1–6; 137:1)"; the specific transformation of weeping into laughter occurs in Ps. 126:1–6; Eccles. 3:4 (Topel 2001, 101–2). "Weeping" is a favorite Lukan term; eleven of its twenty-five occurrences in the Gospels are in Luke. It is used in a variety of ways in the Third Gospel: crying or wailing at a loved one's death (7:13, 32; 8:52; 23:28); lamenting sin (7:38; 22:62); and weeping at the impending destruction of Jerusalem (19:41; 23:28). In this context, it would appear that the wailing includes both those in need of Jubilee liberation—the destitute and starving whose pain is too deep for silence—and also those who weep with them (Topel 2001, 102). As Paul puts it in his exposition of the sermon: "weep with those who weep" (Rom. 12:15). The verb for "laughing" occurs only here and in 6:25 in the NT, but it appears with some frequency in the OT. In many of those instances, the laughter is derisive (e.g., Jer. 20:7–8; Lam. 3:14; Ps. 52:6; Job 8:21; 22:19; the noun *gelōs* occurs in James 4:9 in such a scornful context; see Topel 2001, 103). In other places, however, it expresses the intense emotion of the joy associated with Israel's return to Zion ("our mouth was filled with laughter"; Ps. 126:2 RSV; cf. Eccles. 3:4, "a time to wail and a time to laugh"). In Luke, the "laughter" of those who have been weeping is associated with the good news of deliverance inaugurated in the words and deeds of Jesus and is related to the larger theme of joy and rejoicing, which marks the life of the believer, who will rejoice over Jesus's coming (Luke 1:14; 2:10), his teaching (8:13), and his resurrection (24:41, 52), as well as the incorporation of those who were previously lost into the kingdom (15:6, 7, 9, 10, 32). Even persecution and insult can be the occasion for the believer's rejoicing (see 6:23 below).

The last beatitude is the longest and most grammatically complex: **Blessed are you whenever people hate you, and whenever they exclude you and insult and malign your name as evil on account of the Son of Man** (6:22). This makarism recalls the persecution and ostracism experienced by those who follow God's ways (Pss. 18:17; 25:19; 35:19; Isa. 66:5) and anticipates Jesus's prediction that his followers will suffer hate and persecution for his sake (21:12–17). The idiom "they malign your name as evil" (lit., "they throw out your name as evil") may be a synecdoche for "you" (so NET; see *Rhet. Her.* 4.33.44, and comments on Luke 1:46; see also James 2:7). In any case, the exclusion of the believers need not be understood as a formal synagogue expulsion (Nolland 1989–93, 1:285), but it does reflect "total rejection" (Bock 1994–96, 1:579). It is not the persecution per se that serves as the basis for the blessedness but rather the identification of the persecuted

Jesus, "Poorest of the Poor"?

To suggest that Luke, in his characterization of Jesus, numbers him among the "poor" is not to claim that the historical Jesus was the "poorest of the poor," as is often asserted, both in scholarly and popular circles. This is a hyperbolic overstatement that goes beyond what little evidence we have. John Meier has a helpful description of socioeconomic conditions in first-century Galilee and Judea:

"Many people fell into a vague middle group (not our American 'middle class'), including business people and craftsmen in cities, towns, and villages, as well as freehold farmers with fair-sized plots of land. In speaking of this middle group, we must not be deluded into thinking that belonging to this group meant the economic security known to middle-class Americans today. Small farmers in particular led a precarious existence, sometimes at subsistence level, subject as they were to the vagaries of weather, market prices, inflation, grasping rulers, wars, and heavy taxes (both civil and religious). Further down the ladder were day laborers, hired servants, traveling craftsmen, and dispossessed farmers forced into banditry. . . . At the bottom of the ladder stood the slaves, the worst lot falling to slaves engaged in agricultural labor on large estates—though this was not the most common pattern for Galilean agriculture.

"On this rough scale, Jesus the woodworker in Nazareth would have ranked somewhere at the lower end of the vague middle, perhaps equivalent—if we may use a hazy analogy—to a blue-collar worker in lower-middle-class America. He was indeed in one sense poor, and a comfortable, middle-class urban American would find living conditions in ancient Nazareth appalling. But Jesus was probably no poorer or less respectable than almost anyone else in Nazareth, or for that matter in most of Galilee. His was not the grinding, degrading poverty of the day laborer or the rural slave." (Meier 1991–2009, 1:282)

Still, while Luke's portrayal of Jesus does not qualify for the socioeconomic description of "poorest of the poor," it is important to note that much of the evidence for Jesus's "lower-middle-class" status rests on material not found in Luke (e.g., Jesus's or Joseph's occupation as a woodworker [cf. Mark 6:3; Matt. 13:55]; Jesus as homeowner [Mark 2:1]). Further, there is no evidence in Luke that he holds to the distinction known in the Hellenistic period between the destitute poor, beggars (*ptōchos*), and the working poor (*penēs*). But the fact, as Meier notes, that Jesus was no poorer than anyone else in Nazareth means among other things that Luke's literary characterization of Jesus as poor does, in fact, resonate with the historical evidence.

---

with the Son of Man. This identification is the basis for celebration (see comments on 6:21b), and once again the paradoxical nature of the eschatological blessing in the face of present reality is drawn sharply: **Rejoice on** that day, and leap for joy, because your reward in heaven is great! (6:23a). Finally, the Lukan Jesus reminds his followers of the historical precedence for this rejection: **For their ancestors did the same things to the prophets** (6:23b). Opposition to the prophets in Israel's Scriptures was tantamount to willful and sinful opposition to God himself (Topel 2001, 112–13). The disciples' persecution identifies them with this prophetic tradition, but it also specifically identifies them with the words and deeds of Jesus and his accompanying rejection.

In the Third Gospel, Jesus embodies each of the beatitudes in a kind of portrait of the persecuted.

1. Jesus not only came to preach good news to the poor (4:18; 7:22), to feast with the poor (14:13, 21; cf. 16:20, 22), to seek restitution for the poor (19:8), and to commend the poor (21:2–3); in the Third Gospel, Jesus is himself also poor, dependent on others for food (8:1–3) and shelter (9:58; contra Mark 2:1), a lifestyle his disciples are expected to imitate (9:1–5; 10:1–2). In other words, Luke depicts Jesus living the life of the poor one who preaches good news to the poor (6:20). To them—and him—belongs the kingdom of God (22:30; 23:43; cf. 10:9, 11; 11:20; 16:16; 17:21).
2. Although Jesus is accused of gluttony (7:34; something of a false accusation, given that Jesus is actually rarely depicted as eating at those meals; see Karris 1985), Luke also depicts Jesus as experiencing severe hunger in the temptation narrative (4:2). Even after his resurrection, he appears before the disciples and asks if they have anything to eat (24:41). And as Lord of the eschatological banquet, Jesus too will fill and be filled (13:29; 22:16, 30).
3. Jesus weeps over Jerusalem (19:41), yet he calls his followers to rejoice (10:20) and rejoices himself "in the Holy Spirit" (10:21–22).
4. Finally, of course, Luke not only records Jesus's predictions of his suffering (9:22; 17:25) but he also recounts instances of Jesus being despised, reviled, and persecuted both during his public ministry (4:29; 5:21; 6:11; etc.) and in his passion (22:54, 63–64; 23:35–38, 39). Yet through these sufferings, Jesus is able to enter his glory (24:26).

Thus the auditors of the Sermon on the Plain (and the authorial audience as well) are given a model to imitate in terms of their character formation. The sermon is not about individual decision making but about altering one's "dispositions, and intentions" (Talbert 2006, 119). There is, in other words, a christological focus to the sermon.

But the beatitudes do more than give a snapshot characterization of Jesus in the Third Gospel. They address the theme of God's justice. This is seen most clearly in Luke's expansion of the beatitudes to include their corresponding woes:

> On the other hand, woe to you who are rich, because you are receiving your comfort!
> Woe to you, you who are filled now, because you will be hungry!
> Woe to you, you who laugh now, because you will mourn and weep! (6:24–25).

These woes not only are the mirror reversal of the beatitudes, but they also recall Jesus's inaugural sermon (Luke 4), and more important, Mary's Magnificat, in which the image of the "great reversal" of God's justice is presented in strikingly similar language (1:51–53). Mary and Jesus assume that those on the bottom are there not out of their own fault but as the result of oppressive injustice. This vision of God's justice, therefore, requires a social reversal: the low are raised up, and the high and mighty, who have pushed the lowly down, are themselves brought down (or made hungry or made to mourn). Only then is God's justice possible. In Luke's Gospel, Jesus is God's agent of transforming justice, which is why at the climax of the Gospel, the centurion does not pronounce Jesus the "Son of God" but rather claims, "Surely this man was just [*dikaios*]" (Luke 23:47). The woes end with an expanded warning against flattery (the reversal of the beatitude in 6:22–23; on flattery, see Plutarch, *Adul. amic.* 56; Parsons 2008a, 324–25): **Woe to you when all people speak well about you** (6:26a). Once again, Jesus reminds his followers of their shared experience with prophets who tailored their message to receive the people's praise: **For their ancestors did the same things to the false prophets** (6:26b).

6:27–38. The next section of the sermon is composed of four subsections; the first three (6:27b–31, 32–34, 35–36) form a ring structure, and the last (6:37–38) is a hinge unit preparing the audience for the third and final unit of the sermon (6:39–49). Syntactically, the ring structure may be set out as follows (modifying Topel 2001, 130–31):

> A Two strophes of imperatives (four present plural imperatives, 6:27–28; three indirect objects followed by singular imperatives, 6:29–30; a plural imperative with a causal complement, explaining the preceding imperatives, 6:31)
> > B Three rhetorical questions (*Rhet. Her.* 4.15.22) in the form of first- or third-class conditions, followed by an example denoting the commonplace of the action (6:32–34).
> A′ Three second-person plural imperatives (using the same verbs as 6:32–34) used syntactically in a way that echoes 6:27–30 (6:35a), followed by two future verbs and another second-person plural imperative (6:35b–36a), which gives the underlying principle of the whole passage: imitate the compassion of God.

> ### Wolterstorff on God's Justice in Luke
>
> *"Metaphors common in present-day discourse about society are those of the* margin *and the* outside. *We speak of people as outsiders and as living on the margins. . . .*
>
> *"[Old Testament] writers worked instead with the image of up and down; some are at the top of the social hierarchy, some are at the bottom. Those at the bottom are usually not there because it is their fault. They are there because they are downtrodden. Those at the top 'trample the heads of the poor into the dust of the earth' (Amos 2:7).*
>
> *"When* center *and* circumference *are one's basic metaphors, the undoing of injustice will be described as* including *the outsiders. When* up *and* down *are one's basic metaphors, the undoing of injustice will be described as lifting up those at the bottom. The poor do not have to be included within the social order; they have always been there, usually indispensable to its functioning (Ps. 113:7). . . .*
>
> *"All this is also true of the New Testament. But a striking feature of the New Testament writings, and of Jesus's preaching as they report it, is the frequency with which the up-and-down metaphor common in the writings of the Old Testament is employed to say something that the Old Testament writers at most hint at. The rectification of injustice requires not only lifting up the low ones but casting down the high ones. The coming of justice requires social inversion. . . .*
>
> *"For the coming of justice it is not sufficient to raise up the ones at the bottom, leaving everything else the same. Something must also happen to those at the top; they must be cast down. Justice for the downtrodden requires casting down the ones who tread them down. The coming of justice can be a painful experience.*
>
> *"But what exactly does this lifting up and casting down come to? . . . Jesus did not mean, literally, that justice requires that beggars become kings and kings become beggars. The beggars would soon start acting like kings. . . . The coming of justice requires the humbling of those who exalt themselves. The arrogant must be cured of their arrogance; the rich and powerful must be cured of their attachment to wealth and power. Only then is justice for all possible."* (Wolterstorff 2008, 109, 123, 124)

Luke 6:37–38 serves as a hinge passage, providing examples of this compassion, using the now familiar linguistic form of the second-person plural imperative but conceptually introducing new ideas that will be picked up on in the next section, 6:39–49.

The Lukan Jesus signals a new section in his speech with this verbal marker: **Contrary to what you might think, to you who are listening I say . . .** (6:27a). Those "who are listening" presumably includes the Twelve (6:12–16) and other disciples (6:17) as well as the "crowd of people" from the surrounding environs who came to hear and to be healed (6:17b). The first imperative is deceptively simple: **Love your enemies** (6:27b; cf. Matt. 5:44/Q 6:27). Within Israel's Scriptures, one finds commands to love one's neighbor (Lev. 19:18) or the alien in the land (Deut. 10:19/Lev. 19:34), and there are commands to deal justly with the enemy's property (Exod. 23:4–5; cf. Deut. 22:1–4). By implication, these laws transform the enemy into neighbor and "provide some foundation for Jesus' teaching" (Topel 2001, 136). But there is no explicit OT command to love one's enemy (nor, conversely, is there any explicit command to hate one's enemy; cf. Piper 1979, 28–41). These ideas, however, are not entirely missing from postbiblical Judaism (on hating the "sons of darkness," see 1QS 1.2–10); there were numerous efforts in Second Temple Judaism to widen the scope of Lev. 19:18 to include one's enemies (Philo, *Spec.* 3.155; *Let. Aris.* 207; *T. Benj.* 4.1–5.4 [a theme perhaps enhanced by later Christian editing?]; see Ruzer 2002).

In the *Testament of Benjamin*, a second-century BC Jewish document, we read:

> A good man . . . shows mercy to all, even though they are sinners. And, though they devise evil against him, he overcomes evil by doing good. . . . If anyone does violence to a holy person, he repents because the holy person is merciful to his reviler and holds his peace. If anyone betrays a righteous person, the righteous person prays. (*T. Benj.* 4.1–5.4, trans. Topel 2001, 136)

In the *Testament of Benjamin* the righteous person shows mercy to the enemy and refuses to retaliate in violence in response to acts of violence, but what does it mean "to love one's enemy" in the Gospel of Luke? In the immediate context of Luke 6, the verb "love" suggests a commitment to beneficent action based on personal attachment or esteem. Thus, in the next chapter the centurion "loves" (i.e., holds in high esteem) the Jewish people and builds a synagogue for them (Luke 7:5; cf. 7:42, 45). The "enemies" in view here include, but are not limited to, the personal enemies of the disciples. Rather, echoing the immediate context, in which disciples are persecuted on account of the Son of Man (6:22), the "enemies" extend to include all those who are actively opposing God or God's people (cf. 1:71, 74; 19:43; 20:43).

The next three imperatives flow from the first and add additional material to the parallel material (whether Matt. 5:43–44 or Q 6:27–28): **do good to those who hate you; bless those who curse you; pray for those who mistreat you** (6:27b–28). There is a progression in hostility from attitude ("hate") to word ("curse") to action ("mistreat") (Grundmann 1966, 147). Jesus's proposed responses become more spiritualized ("do good," "bless," "pray") as the persecutors' actions become more aggressive (Topel 2001, 143). The language of "doing good" moves us into the realm of ancient benefaction, which is taken up squarely in the next section. Here as there, the benefaction assumes no reciprocity. Later in Acts Jesus will be depicted as a benefactor who is "doing good" (Acts 10:38). Blessing those who curse you echoes those whose names are "maligned as evil on account of the Son of Man" (Luke 6:22). It is a dominical tradition that plays an important role for Paul: "Bless those who persecute you; bless and do not curse them" (Rom. 12:14). The notion of praying for those who are mistreating is later echoed in Stephen's prayer (Acts 7:60) and is preserved in an agraphon attributed to Jesus that finds its way eventually into canonical Luke (see the sidebar "The Question of Luke 23:34a" at Luke 23:33–43).

Each imperative in 6:29–30 is preceded by an indirect object (6:29a, 30a) or prepositional phrase (6:29b, 30b), and in these verses the second person shifts from plural to singular, an individualization that perhaps adds to the concreteness of the examples: **To the one who strikes you on the cheek offer the other one as well; and from the one who takes away your cloak do not withhold your tunic either. Give to everyone who asks you for something, and do not demand repayment from the one who takes what is yours** (6:29–30). The theme throughout is nonretaliation. Being struck on the cheek added insult to injury in both ancient Jewish (1 Esd. 4:30) and Greek (Plato, *Gorg.* 486C, 508C–D) thought. Jesus's command is to resist retaliation and "remain vulnerable to the insult again" (Bock 1994–96, 1:592). In contrast to the parallel material (Matt. 5:40 or Q 6:29), in the next imperative Luke apparently reverses the order of "disrobement" (outer coat, then inner garment) and, more important, shifts the setting from the courtroom ("to the person wanting to take you to court and get your shirt, turn over to him also the coat as well"; Matt. 5:40 or Q 6:29) perhaps to the scene of a crime, specifically a robbery (Plummer 1903, 185; Bock 1994–96, 1:593), or perhaps to the mistreatment by enemies of the Christian community as an ostracized minority, a mistreatment that meets with the "tacit approval of the wider community" (Nolland 1989–93, 1:296). The Lukan version continues to hold currency into the second century and beyond (cf. *Did.* 1.4; Justin Martyr, *1 Apol.* 16.1).

With the next imperative, Jesus moves from a negative command ("do not withhold") to an audaciously positive one: "give to everyone who asks for something." Whether or not the reference is specifically to almsgiving, the point is "a genuine readiness to meet needs without reference to prejudices" (Bock 1994–96, 1:594). Such unlimited philanthropy could, of course, lead to abject poverty (so Lucian's *Timon the Misanthrope*) and resulted in the *Didache*'s instruction that givers must be prudent (*Did.* 1.5–6)—little wonder one commentator labeled this imperative "the most outrageous and difficult command of the whole Sermon" (Topel 2001, 153). The final imperative ("do not demand repayment from the one who takes what is yours") continues the argument for not seeking retribution or retaliation (and reinforces the view that the earlier example suggests a garment surrendered under the threat, or as a result, of force).

Despite the vivid details of each of these examples, it would be a mistake to view any of these commands as "a rule of behavior that should be followed mechanistically"; rather, the "specificity is intended to shock the hearers with an extreme command, at striking variance with the way people usually behave in such a situation, . . . and to reflect on the whole pattern of behavior that dominates life" (Talbert 2002, 76). Jesus illustrates this general principle with the so-called Golden Rule: **And just as you want people to treat you, treat them likewise** (6:31). This moral maxim is joined to what precedes it by the connective *kai* ("and"). The Golden Rule is not unique to Jesus's teaching (cf. Homer, *Od.* 5.188–89; Isocrates, *Nic.* 49.1; Seneca, *Ben.* 2.1.1; Tob. 4:15; 2 *En.* 61.1; *T. Naph.* 1; *Let. Aris.* 207; *b. Šabb.* 31a; cited by Talbert 2002, 76; Bock 1994–96, 1:596). The motive is wholly altruistic: we are to treat others as we wish to be treated but without the expectation (or illusion) that the other person will be obligated to reciprocate that benevolence (Topel 2001, 156–57). This altruistic motive stands in contrast to the reciprocity embedded in the benefaction system that was widespread in the ancient Mediterranean world in the sense that one acts in a particular way to entice or evoke a similar response from another. The *Rhetoric to Alexander* is typical in this regard: "Everyone gives presents in the hope of receiving some repayment or as a recompense for prior benefits" (1446b.36–38, author's trans.). This view of reciprocity is explicitly rejected by Jesus as the motivational basis for the love of the enemy:

> If you love those who love you, what credit is that to you? For even sinners love those who love them. Indeed, if you happen to do good to those who do good to you, what credit is that to you? Even sinners do the same. And if you happen to lend to someone from whom you hope to get something back, what credit is that to you? Even sinners lend to sinners in order to receive equivalent benefits in return. (6:32–34)

Throughout this section, the benefaction system is clearly in focus. In a passage unique to the Third Gospel (i.e., missing from both Matthew and Q), the Lukan Jesus refers to "doing good" and "credit"; both terms were part of the semantic domain of benefaction (cf. also the change from "reward" to "credit" in 6:32, 34).

He then repeats the command to love one's enemies as part of a triad that corresponds to the preceding three questions, all based on the general principle espoused in 6:31 ("as you want people to treat you, treat them likewise"): **Instead, love your enemies, do good [to all], and lend expecting nothing** (6:35a). This doublet is missing from the parallel material (Matthew or Q) and drives home the point of the sermon thus far in no uncertain terms: love, do good, and lend, without the expectation of reciprocation. The rejection of reciprocity does not mean the total absence of reward for the one who follows Jesus's instruction; the reward, however, is eschatological: **Then your reward will be**

great (6:35b; cf. 6:23, in which the verbatim phrase is expanded: "your reward *in heaven* will be great"). Jesus then specifies this eschatological reward: **you will be children of the Most High** (6:35c). The "Most High" is a synonym for God in Luke (1:32, 35, 76; 8:28; cf. its LXX usage for Yahweh, e.g., Gen. 14:18; Deut. 32:8; also used of Zeus, Pausanias, *Descr.* 9.8.5), and the phrase "children of the Most High" echoes Sir. 4:10 (see also Ps. 82:6, and for similar language in the NT, cf. Rom. 8:14–15; Gal. 4:5–6; John 1:12–13). The reference in Sirach is instructive: "Be like a father to the orphan, and a husband to their mother; you will then be like a son of the Most High" (4:10). Care for widows and orphans in this life suggests that, while the reward is eschatological, the reference to "children of the Most High" has a clear present reality and application. This seems the implication of Jesus's argument as well: **because he [God] is kind to the ungrateful and the wicked. Be merciful just as your Father is merciful** (6:35d–36). This call to imitate God's compassion confirms that being the children of the Most High entails loving enemies, doing good to those who hate you, and lending expecting nothing in return; it is, in other words, a call to be like God—merciful and kind to the ungrateful and the wicked, who are unlikely to reciprocate such kindness and mercy. The reward, rather, is to be found in the very imitation of God's altruistic love and mercy. The *imitatio Dei* provides the theological foundation for transforming the believer's perceptions, disposition, and intentions—thus forming the follower's character and orientation in a way consistent with the character and orientation of God the Father.

Structurally, Luke 6:37–38 is the conclusion to what precedes in 6:27–36, with four second-person plural imperatives. Two prohibitions ("do not judge," "do not condemn") are followed by two positive commands ("forgive," "give"), with the last having an expanded explanation (6:37–38a). Thematically, however, the verses anticipate the theme of "not judging" developed in the concluding unit, especially in the three parabolic examples of 6:39–42. Thus, the passage serves as narrative glue holding the two units together (for examples of this technique in Acts, see Parsons 2008a, 48).

The first prohibition, **Do not judge, and you will certainly not be judged** (6:37a), should be heard in light of the second, **do not condemn, and you will certainly not be condemned** (6:37b); that is, Jesus is forbidding not all forms of human evaluation (cf. 6:41–42) but rather condemnatory judgment (Marshall 1978, 265; Bock 1994–96, 1:605). The second prohibition intensifies the first, perhaps prohibiting condemnation in a more formal, judicial sense (Topel 2001, 183). What is the result of avoiding such condemnation? While it is possible that the promise of not being judged/condemned could refer to a near-future action of a fellow human who does not condemn because he or she has not been condemned (Betz 1995, 616), the use of the theological passive and the immediate context (in which human reciprocity is explicitly rejected as an appropriate motive for action) suggest an eschatological context in which divine judgment will be withheld from those who avoid unjust condemnation.

The same logic occurs in the next two imperatives: **Forgive, and you will be forgiven. Give, and it will be given to you** (6:37c–38a). The first of these commands follows a natural progression of the previous prohibitions "from not judging someone on the basis of some evidence, to not condemning where the evidence is more certain and public, to pardoning where the debt or personal offense is established" (Topel 2001, 184). The result is also more positive—not simply the avoidance of judgment but the reward of divine forgiveness. The last imperative shifts the context from a quasi-juridical one back to the more general theme of generosity. Standing as the climax of the four imperatives, it reiterates the teaching of the Golden Rule. Jesus then gives an extended and vivid description of the reward for this generosity, unique to Luke: **they will pour a good measure that has been pressed down, has been shaken together, and is overflowing into the fold of your garment** (6:38b). Given the various prohibitions in the ancient world against defrauding the buyer of grain (Deut. 25:13–16; Lev. 19:35–36), the process described here is remarkable. The seller presses and shakes the grain to remove any air pockets and to insure a "good measure"; then the grain is heaped (without leveling) into the fold of the buyer's garment, which serves as a pocket or basket (Couroyer 1970, 369–70). All the descriptions point beyond "just practice" to the extravagance of the act. The use of the third-person active plural ("they will pour"; lit. "they will give") is driven in part by the reference to vendors measuring grain, but, like its third-person passive counterpart ("it will be given"; 6:38a; cf. 6:38c), it also points to divine activity (cf. Luke 12:20, 48; 16:9; 23:31; Rehkopf 1959, 99; Marshall 1978, 267). Thus will God respond to those who follow his practice of gracious generosity: **For with the very same measure you measure, it will be measured to you in return** (6:38c). The proverb, or some approximation of it, was known not only in Jewish literature ("With what measure a man metes it shall be measured to him again"; *m. Soṭah* 1.7, trans. Danby 1933) and early Christian literature (Matt. 7:2; Mark 4:24 [though both with very different functions]; Pol. *Phil.* 2.3; *1 Clem.* 13.2) but in pagan literature as well (Hesiod, *Op.* 349–51; see Betz 1995, 619). The maxim here, despite the repeated use of the terms for "measure," is not limited to the immediate context of the "good measure" (6:38) but rather reflects the entirety of Jesus's teaching on generosity throughout the sermon. Nor is it a return to the reciprocity system that governed most human social interaction in antiquity; rather, Jesus reiterates his call to his disciples to imitate God's unlimited generosity, in the hope of an unlimited divine reward in the eschaton (Topel 2001, 187).

6:39–49. The previous two verses, 6:37–38, segue into the next pericope (6:39–42), which is the first unit of the sermon's final section. The new unit is signaled with a Lukan editorial comment: **Then he told them an illustration** (lit., "parable"; 6:39a; cf. 4:23; 5:36). The singular *parabolē* probably refers to all three examples that follow. First, Jesus asks, **Surely a blind person cannot lead another blind person, can he? Won't they both fall into a pit?** (6:39b). The Greek negative particle *mēti* in the first question signals a negative answer, "No, a blind person cannot lead another," while the negative particle *ouchi* in the second expects a positive answer, "Yes, they will both fall into a pit" (Culy, Parsons, and Stigall 2010). Jesus uses the well-known proverb of the futility of the blind leading the blind (Plato, *Resp.* 8.554b; Philo, *Virt.* 7; cf. Matt. 15:14; *Gos. Thom.* 34) to make the point that unless the disciples' perceptions are transformed and reoriented in the ways described by Jesus in his sermon, they will remain spiritually blind and will be unable to lead others in this new way of life (Marshall 1978, 269). Rather, "the blind leading the blind is a walk to disaster" (Bock 1994–96, 1:611). Jesus's second illustration makes a similar point: **A disciple is not superior to his or her teacher; but everyone who is fully trained will be like the teacher** (6:40; cf. Matt. 10:24a; John 13:16; 15:20a). In some Greek philosophical traditions, teachers could expect students' knowledge to exceed their own (see Betz 1995, 623n293), but here the expectation is that the student's understanding of the teaching in its full-orbed expression of ethics and doctrine cannot exceed the teacher's understanding of the tradition. Specifically, in the relationship between Jesus and his disciples, "the impossibility of surpassing the teacher lies in the authority of Jesus as *the* teacher" (Topel 2001, 190). This point is made clear by Luke's addition of *katērtismenos* (translated here "fully trained") to the parallel material (Matt. 10:24a/Q 6:40). The verb means something like "to make someone completely adequate or sufficient for something" (L&N 75.5) or "to restore to a former condition" (BDAG 526). The emphasis is on the formation of the disciples' moral imagination. The disciple whose character is well formed and restored to its "right order" with the help of Jesus the teacher will be like *the* teacher (Topel 2001, 192). This idea of the disciple being restored to a former good state resonates well with Jesus's next example (cf. Matt. 7:3–5/Q 6:41–42; *Gos. Thom.* 26):

> So, why do you see the speck that is in your brother's or sister's eye, but you do not notice the beam that is in your own eye? How are you able to say to your brother or sister, "Please let me remove the speck that is in your eye," when you yourself do not see the beam of wood in your own eye? Hypocrite! First remove the beam of wood from your own eye, and then you will see clearly to remove the speck that is in your brother's or sister's eye. (6:41–42)

Jesus poses a pair of rhetorical questions designed to bring together the imagery of the first two illustrations. The disciple who is not morally "restored" to "good order" is unable to see, and this spiritual blindness extends both inwardly to the beam in one's own eye and outwardly to the speck in the other's eye, which is obstructed by the larger beam. Jesus labels this follower a "hypocrite," a derogatory term reserved elsewhere in Luke for those who lack sincerity in their religious beliefs and/or practices (cf. 12:1, 56; 13:15). Rather, the pupil is to attend to his or her own faults (cf. Epictetus, *Diatr.* 3.22.9–15), and the beam is to be removed; that is, the disciple's moral condition and imagination is to be reordered and reoriented through the adoption and embodiment of Jesus's teaching. Then the disciple will be in a position to remove the speck from the brother's or sister's eye and thus guide the spiritually blind into a new way of "seeing" (e.g., perceptions, dispositions, and intentions; cf. 6:35d–36), a "seeing" formed by none other than Jesus the Teacher, who remains the focus of this part of the sermon no less than he was at its beginning (see comments on 6:20–26; Topel 2001, 199).

Throughout the Sermon on the Plain, the conviction that "character precedes action" has been prominent (Johnson 1991, 114). That conviction is highlighted in Jesus's next maxim, regarding good trees producing good fruit and its application (cf. Matt. 7:16–17/Q 6:43–45):

> A tree that produces bad fruit is not good; nor, on the other hand, is a tree bad that produces good fruit. For each tree is known by its own fruit. For people do not gather figs from thorn bushes, nor do they pick grapes from a prickly shrub. The good person brings out something good from the good storehouse of the heart, while the evil person brings out something evil from the evil [storehouse of the heart]. For the mouth conveys what the heart is full of. (6:43–45)

From the example of the good and bad fruit, Jesus concludes that there is an integral and intimate connection between who a person is and what a person does, between the inner moral character and the outward expression of that character. Jesus's intent in the Sermon on the Plain is to reshape the habits of the heart in the conviction that action follows being.

Like the connection between being and doing, the connection between what one says (and hears) and what one does must also be intact, a point Jesus makes in the conclusion to his sermon:

> Why do you call me "Lord, Lord," but do not do what I say? I will show you what everyone who comes to me and hears my words and does them is like: This one is like a person who builds a house, who dug deep and set the foundation on the rock. When a flood came, the river struck against that house but was not able to shake it, because it had been built well. But the one who hears my words and does not do them is like a person who built a house on the earth without a foundation, against which the river struck; and immediately it collapsed and was completely destroyed. (6:46–49)

The Lukan Jesus concludes his sermon with imagery of the Two Ways (Ps. 1; *Did.* 1–6; *Barn.* 18–21). There is the way of the wise one, who hears and does Jesus's words and emulates his deeds. The wise person builds a house on a rock foundation that can withstand the floods. But there is also the way of the foolish one, whose house is built without foundation and immediately collapses when the river rises. Luke has contemporized the parallel material, which sets the scene in a typically agrarian setting in which the wise person's house built on rock withstands the heavy rains and winds of a violent storm while the house built on sand by the foolish person does not (Matt. 7:26–27 or Q 6:46–49; cf. Ezek. 13:10–16; 'Abot R. Nat. 24). In both scenarios, Jesus urges the disciples to reorient their way of being, seeing, and doing in the world. "When the whole self responds totally to the one Lord, the result is an indissoluble union between confession and walk" (Talbert 2002, 79).

Theological Issues

"Because I could" was former president Bill Clinton's answer, in an interview about his biography *My Life*, to the question of why he engaged in actions that violated his marriage vows and ultimately risked damaging his presidential legacy. While perhaps an extreme example of the devastating fusion of seemingly unlimited freedom with apparently unlimited power, the response "because I could" draws on the ideals of individual freedom and rights deeply imbedded in our collective, cultural psyche. We often do something simply because we can—because, like Mount Everest, it's there.

The appropriate response to the story in Luke 6:1–5 by the follower of Jesus, then and now, is not to insist on the right and freedom to do something "because I could" but rather to submit oneself wholly to the lordship of Christ. We are not called to be Lord of the Sabbath; that role is reserved exclusively for Christ. Rather, in the words of Paul, we are "servants for Jesus's sake" (2 Cor. 4:5–12 RSV). Of course, not everyone will be impressed by Luke's christological reinterpretation of the Sabbath and its demands on Jesus's followers, a point proven by the religious leaders in the very next story, another controversy about Sabbath observance (Luke 6:6–11). In Jesus's day, the breaking of the Sabbath was an acknowledgment by his disciples of Jesus's lordship over the Sabbath—and over them. In our contemporary context, however, the disciples of Jesus may best honor Jesus's lordship over the Sabbath—and over us—by, among other things, observing the Sabbath as a day of corporate worship and rest. After all, "the Son of Man is Lord of the Sabbath!"

Luke 7:1–8:56

Jesus's Marvelous Words and Deeds

Introductory Matters

This second section consists of two units, Luke 7:1–50 and 8:1–56. Luke 7 characterizes the "compassionate ministry of Jesus" (Green 1997, 26) through the cultural lens of benefaction (Danker 1982, 403–6), and Luke 8 proclaims "the kingdom of God" (8:1–3) through Jesus's wondrous words (8:4–21) and his mighty acts (8:22–56).

Tracing the Narrative Flow

The Beneficent Ministry of Jesus (Luke 7:1–50)

Luke 7:1–50 contains four scenes: the healing of a centurion's slave (7:1–10), the raising of a widow's son (7:11–17), Jesus and John the Baptist redux (7:18–35), and the anointing of Jesus in Simon's house (7:36–50).

7:1–10. *The healing of a centurion's slave.* Structurally, after a brief introduction, the story proper is framed with the chiasm of 7:2–3 and 7:10:

    A A centurion's slave is terminally ill (7:2)
        B The centurion sends a delegation (7:3)
        B′ The delegation returns to the centurion's house (7:10a)
    A′ The slave is in good health (7:10b; Green 1997, 283).

The scene begins by transitioning from Jesus's Sermon on the Plain: **When Jesus had finished saying all of this as the people listened, he went into Capernaum** (7:1; cf. Matt. 7:28a; 8:5a/Q 7:1). The reference to Capernaum reminds the audience of Jesus's previous healing activities there (Luke 4:23, 31–37, 38–39, 40–41) and explains how the centurion would have known about Jesus. The audience is left to ponder whether the synagogue in which Jesus had earlier healed (4:33–37) might be the same one that the centurion built (7:4–5). Rather, the narrator reports that **a slave of a particular centurion was sick and was about to die—one who was important to him. When he heard about Jesus, he sent Jewish elders to him to ask him to come and heal his servant** (7:2–3).

The authorial audience would already be familiar with the story of the healing of a centurion's slave (Matt. 8:5–13 or Q 7:1, 3, 6b–9; cf. John 4:46b–54). Luke's version of the story, however, invokes Israel's Scriptures (the story of Naaman in 2 Kings 5) and the Greco-Roman benefaction system to draw out the theological and political implications of the healing.

First, the story shares certain features with the story of Elisha and Naaman in 2 Kings 5, a story that has already figured prominently in Jesus's Nazareth sermon as an example of God's mercy extending beyond the Jews to the gentiles (Luke 4:27). The two stories share several common elements (Gowler 2003, 104–5; see also Green 1997, 284):

1. Both the centurion ("worthy"; Luke 7:4) and Naaman ("great man," in "high favor," and "a mighty warrior"; 2 Kings 5:1–2) are highly regarded gentile officers.
2. Jews (elders in the case of the centurion; a Jewish girl in the case of Naaman) intercede on behalf of the officer in the process of healing (Luke 7:3–5; 2 Kings 5:2–3).
3. Neither supplicant meets the healer (Luke 7:6–9; 2 Kings 5:5–10).
4. Both healings take place at a distance (Luke 7:10; 2 Kings 5:14).

> **Luke 7:1–8:56 in the Narrative Flow**
>
> Jesus's origins and training (1:1–4:13)
>
> Jesus's mighty words and deeds in Galilee (4:14–9:50)
>
>   Jesus's mission and miracles and the ingathering of his followers (4:14–6:49)
>
> ▶ Jesus's marvelous words and deeds (7:1–8:56)
>
>   The beneficent ministry of Jesus (Luke 7:1–50)
>
>   The healing of a centurion's slave (7:1–10)
>
>   The raising of a widow's son (7:11–17)
>
>   Jesus and John the Baptist redux (7:18–35)
>
>   The anointing of Jesus in Simon's house (7:36–50)
>
>   Jesus's wondrous teachings and miraculous acts (8:1–56)
>
>   Jesus on mission (8:1–3)
>
>   Jesus's wondrous teachings (8:4–21)
>
>   Underscoring Jesus's authority (8:22–56)

> ### The Centurion and His Slave
>
> The semantic range of "important" (*entimos*; 7:2) and the context leave the question open whether the slave was "valuable" to (so, e.g., BDAG 340.2) or "respected" by (so, e.g., Marshall 1978, 279) the centurion. While there is "no socio-historical reason to doubt that, as an urban slave in the home of a wealthy master (cf. v. 6b), this dying man might have enjoyed friendship with the centurion" (Green 1997, 286), I have sought to maintain the ambiguity in the translation (see Culy, Parsons, and Stigall 2010). Despite this semantic ambiguity, it is unlikely that Luke intends through the use of the word to indicate a sexual dimension (some form of pederasty) in the relationship between the centurion and his slave (Danker 1988, 158; contra Hanks 2000, 195; Gray-Fow 1986). The only other occurrence of *entimos* in Luke(/Acts) is Luke 14:8, a context totally devoid of any hint of sexual intimacy or even emotional attachment. The relationship presumed here is more likely akin to the household slave who is commended by his master in Jesus's parable in Luke 16.

By invoking the precedent of Scripture, and shaped by the previous use of the Naaman story in Luke 4, Luke claims through the story of the healing of the centurion's slave that God's mercies have burst beyond traditional religious and ethnic boundaries (see also the story of Cornelius the centurion, which functions in much the same way, in Acts 10–11).

On another level, the story invokes the larger Greco-Roman pattern of imperial benefaction only to challenge it, in at least one important aspect. The story is replete with the language and concepts of benefaction (which are missing from the parallel story in Matthew/Q). The delegation of Jewish elders **who came to Jesus earnestly urged him, saying, "The one for whom you would do this is worthy. For he loves our nation and has himself built a synagogue for us." So Jesus went along with them** (7:4–6a). Whether an officer in the Roman army or serving Herod Antipas in some capacity (on the historical issues, see Fitzmyer 1981–85, 1:651), the centurion of Luke 7 ultimately is an agent of Roman imperial benefaction (since Antipas himself is but a puppet of Rome; see Gowler 2003, 111; on the historical role of centurions in Roman Galilee and Palestine, see Goodman 1983, 141–44; Isaac 1990, 101–60). The centurion serves as a benefactor to the Jews of Capernaum, building for them a synagogue ("Erection of public works is typical of a benefactor's activity"; Danker 1982, 415n59; see also, e.g., Danker 1982, document 20). Presumably the centurion has paid for the construction from his own resources, which ultimately derived from his service in the Roman army (see Dobson 1974, 393–96; Safrai 1999). In return, the Jews reciprocate the centurion's benefaction by acknowledging his love for the Jewish nation and by praising him as "worthy" (another typical honorific title bestowed on benefactors; see Danker 1982, 429n12; *I.Priene* 6.26–27).

The Emperor as Healer

There were a number of stories in antiquity of a ruler's healing power. Such power "would be explained as one sign of the king's divine empowerment from heaven for his authoritative role on earth" (Cotter 1999, 39). Tacitus's story about Vespasian is illustrative:

> "One of the common people of Alexandria, well known for his loss of sight, threw himself before Vespasian's knees, praying him with groans to cure his blindness, being so directed by the god Serapis, whom this most superstitious of nations worships before all others; and he besought the emperor to deign to moisten his cheeks and eyes with his spittle. Another, whose hand was useless, prompted by the same god, begged Caesar to step and trample on it. Vespasian at first ridiculed these appeals and treated them with scorn; then, when the men persisted, he began at one moment to fear the discredit of failure, at another to be inspired with hopes of success by the appeals of the suppliants and the flattery of his courtiers.... Such perhaps was the wish of the gods, and it might be that the emperor had been chosen for this divine service; in any case, if a cure were obtained, the glory would be Caesar's, but in the event of failure, ridicule would fall only on the poor supplicants. So Vespasian, believing that his good fortune was capable of anything and that nothing was any longer incredible, with a smiling countenance, and amid intense excitement on the part of the bystanders, did as he was asked to do. The hand was instantly restored to use, and the day again shone for the blind man. Both facts are told by eyewitnesses even now when falsehood brings no reward." (Tacitus, *Hist.* 4.81, trans. Moore and Jackson 1931, cited by Cotter 1999, 40–41)

Given the cultural framework of imperial benefaction, it is startling that the centurion/benefactor should turn to Jesus and his God to provide healing for his servant, for within the imperial benefaction system it was assumed that the emperor himself was capable of such healing acts (Tacitus, *Hist.* 4.81; cited by Cotter 1999, 40–41; see the sidebar "The Emperor as Healer"; see also Suetonius, *Vesp.* 7.2; Dio Cassius, *Hist. Rom.* 65.8). Rather than turn to the emperor, however, the centurion turns to Jesus, the healing agent of Israel's God. In this regard, the centurion breaks from the Roman benefaction system in a way that the delegation of Jewish elders is unwilling to follow.

The centurion acknowledges the authority of Jesus, while confessing his own unworthiness (contrary to the testimony of the Jewish elders):

> Now, when he had already nearly reached the house, the centurion sent friends to say to him, "Lord, do not trouble yourself, for I am not qualified that you should enter my house. That is why I did not consider myself worthy to come to you. Instead, merely say the word, and my servant will be healed. For I too am a man placed under authority, who has soldiers under me; and I say to this

one, 'Go!' and he goes, and to another, 'Come!' and he comes, and to my servant, 'Do this!' and he does it." (7:6b–8)

The authority to send delegations (*hoi paragenomenoi*, 7:4) of Jews or "friends" (*philous*, 7:6; on the use of "friends" as subordinates in benefactor/client relationships, see Balch and Osiek 1997, 48–54) is characteristic of a benefactor (Danker 1982, 379n107 and document 16), as is the confession of humility ("I do not consider myself worthy to come to you"; Danker 1982, 351–52). Both details contribute to the centurion's reliability as a witness to Jesus's authority.

The humbled centurion foreshadows Jesus's later pronouncement that those "who humble themselves will be exalted" (14:11; 18:14; see Gowler 2003, 115), and accordingly, Jesus approves of the centurion's point of view, expressed through others: **When Jesus heard these things, he was very impressed by him, and he turned and said to the crowd that was following him, "I tell you, I have not found such faith in Israel!"** (7:9). Jesus contrasts the gentile centurion's behavior with that of those in the nation of Israel, including presumably the crowd gathered around him. By turning to Jesus and his God for help, the centurion does not regard Jesus as one of his clients but recognizes Jesus's superiority to the benefaction system in which he is embedded. He has (through his "friends") addressed Jesus as "Lord," confessed his own unworthiness, and expressed his confidence that Jesus can heal his slave with the utterance of a word (Could the emperor replicate this "healing from a distance"?). In other words, this is a "story of not one but two benefactors" (Danker 1982, 406). Thus, it is now Jesus's turn to be "amazed" (*ethaumasen*, a term previously applied to the crowd's response to Jesus's miracles; cf. 4:22). It is a gentile, and not the Jewish elders, who has recognized Jesus's authority to dispense God's blessings. The centurion may be the first non-Jew whose faith is commended by Jesus in the Third Gospel, but he will not

> **Human Testimony**
>
> Cicero says that human testimony is a reliable witness to another's character if the witness himself is reliable:
>
> > "In the case of a man, it is the opinion of his virtue which is most important. For opinion regards as virtuous not only those who really are virtuous, but also those who seem to be. [Not only] men endowed with genius, industry and learning and those whose life has been consistent and of approved goodness ... [and] those who have been honoured by the people with public office and are busy with matters of state, but also about orators, philosophers, poets, and historians. Their sayings and writings are often used as authority to win conviction." (Cicero, *Top.* 20.78, trans. Hubbell 1949)
>
> Thus, the centurion's testimony joins previous examples of divine testimony (see comments on Luke 1:5–25) to bear witness to Jesus's authority as God's agent.

Figure 13. Modern Village of Nain

be the last (cf. the Samaritan leper in 17:11–19). Nor will Jews be excluded from future commendation for their faith (7:36–50; 8:43–48; 18:35–43). In the end, though, the story points to the supreme benefaction of Israel's God, preferred even, or perhaps especially, in comparison to imperial benefaction (an added dimension that might account for Jesus's commendation of the centurion, even though he has already commended the faith of the paralytic's friends in Luke 5): "In the world of Luke-Acts, God is the ultimate patron and benefactor (e.g., 1:46–55, 68–79), whose resources are graciously given and mediated through Jesus" (Gowler 2003, 114). The scene ends on a satisfying note: **And when those who had been sent returned to the house they found the servant healthy** (7:10). It is left to the audience to imagine how the centurion's relationships might have been transformed as a result of this encounter with Jesus from a distance.

7:11–17. *The raising of a widow's son.* The scene shifts locations, and Jesus encounters a funeral in progress: **Later, Jesus went to a city called Nain, and his disciples and a large crowd were accompanying him. When he came near to the city gate, a dead person was being carried out—the only son of his mother; and she was a widow! A large crowd from the city was with her** (7:11–12). Jesus pities the grieving mother: **When he saw her, the Lord had compassion for her and said to her, "Don't cry." And he went up to the bier and touched it. Then those who were carrying it stopped, and he said, "Young man, I tell you, get up!" Then the dead man sat up and began to speak** (7:13–15a).

The story of the raising of the widow of Nain's son is the first of two resuscitations in the Third Gospel (cf. Luke 8:40–42, 49–56; see also Acts 9:36–43; 20:7–12). This account also foreshadows Jesus's pronouncement to John the Baptist's disciples later in this same chapter: "Go and tell John what you have seen and heard: the blind are able to see, the lame walk, lepers are cleansed, the deaf hear, *the dead are raised*, and the poor hear the good news proclaimed" (7:22; see Fitzmyer 1981–85, 1:656). Like the previous episode (7:1–10; cf. 2 Kings 5), this story also recalls an OT story to which Jesus already alluded in his Nazareth sermon (4:26), in this case the story of Elijah and the widow at Zarephath (1 Kings 17). In addition to conceptual parallels (both Elijah and Jesus enter a town and meet a widow at a gate, Luke 7:11–12/1 Kings 17:10; both restore to life the widow's son, Luke 7:14–15/1 Kings 17:22), there is a verbatim parallel with 1 Kings 17:23 LXX: Jesus **gave him to his mother** (7:15b). This intertextual echo signals that the widow's restoration to the community is equally in view with the restoration of her son to life (Green 1997, 289–90). As a widow in a patriarchal culture who has lost her "only son" (7:12), she has lost her sole means of support. Through the resuscitation, Jesus acts as the compassionate benefactor of the widow (Price 1997, 85; on the benefaction theme, see comments on 7:1–10, above). The focus on the widow is also a distinctive feature of this account when compared with similar resuscitation stories from the larger Greco-Roman environment (e.g., Diodorus Siculus, *Bibl. hist.* 1.25.6, 27; 1.27.3–4; Celsus, *Med.* 2.6.16–18; Apuleius, *Flor.* 19; cited by Cotter 1999, 33–34, 45–47).

The focus of the pericope in Luke 7, however, is not exclusively on the widow. By means of the rhetorical device of *synkrisis*, or comparison, Luke argues for the superiority of Jesus over the prophet Elijah (contra, e.g., Fitzmyer 1981–85, 1:213–15, who argues that Luke casts Jesus as an *Elias redivivus* figure). Indeed, the contrast between Elijah's and Jesus's actions is striking. Elijah engages in ritual speech, beseeching God's help, and in ritual action, stretching himself over the boy three times (1 Kings 17:19–21). Ultimately God responds to the prophet's intercession, and the boy is resuscitated. Jesus, however, does not offer supplication to God but utters a command to the boy ("Young man, I tell you, get up!" 7:14). Nor does Jesus have to engage in any ritual act. Jesus's words alone are powerful enough to accomplish the task (Tiede 1988, 153). Jesus is a great prophet, even greater than Elijah (see Culpepper 1995, 158).

This point is made forcefully in the conclusion to the story: **So, fear gripped everyone, and they were glorifying God and saying, "A great prophet has risen up among us!"** (7:16a). Like Elijah of old, Jesus has come to the aid of a grieving widow, but Jesus's actions are superior to those of Elijah and warrant the further acclamation of the disciples and crowds: **God has come to help his people!** (7:16b). The use of the word *epeskepsato* (translated here "has come to help") recalls Zechariah's speech (1:68). Through Jesus, God himself has come to the aid of his people. The crowd's confession is the climax in this portrayal of Jesus, but this high Christology has already been suggested in several details of the story. For the first time, the narrator refers to Jesus as "the Lord" in 7:13 (Rowe 2006, 118; Culpepper 1995, 158). Furthermore, the Lord "had compassion" on the widow. This word, *esplanchnisthē*, in Luke is an attribute of the character of God (Schürmann 1982, 403). Thus, there is "implicit unity to the action of Jesus and the God of Israel at the point of the power of their compassion" (Rowe 2006, 121). **And this report concerning him**, namely, that God has acted in Jesus, the prophet greater than Elijah, **spread throughout the whole of Judea and all the surrounding region** (7:17).

Jesus and John the Baptist redux (7:18–35). In this next section, Luke returns to the *synkrisis* between John the Baptist and Jesus. Here "deeds" are the progymnastic topic for comparison (see Ps.-Hermogenes, *Prog.* 16). As before, this is a double encomium *synkrisis* in which both John and Jesus are praised, but Jesus is clearly depicted as superior (on double encomia, see Nicolaus, *Prog.* 60; see also Aphthonius, *Prog.* 31R–32R), and it is Jesus's identity that Luke seeks to clarify.

Table 6. Progymnastic Topic of Double Encomium *Synkrisis*: Deeds

John	Jesus
John prepares Jesus's way (7:24–27)	Jesus gives sight to blind, makes lame walk, cleanses lepers, gives hearing to deaf, raises dead, gives good news to poor (7:21–23)
"no one among those born of women is greater than John" (7:28a)	"but the one who is least in the kingdom of God is greater than he" (7:28b)
"For John the Baptizer came neither eating bread nor drinking wine" (7:33)	"The Son of Man has come eating and drinking" (7:34)

Note: Adapted from Martin 2008, 40.

This unit consists of two parts (7:18–23, 24–35), marked by the movement of John's disciples.

7:18–23. The section begins with a report to John by his disciples: **John's disciples informed him about all these things** (7:18a). John's response is prompt, if ambiguous, both in terms of John's reason for asking the question and the identity of the expected figure (Culpepper 1995, 160): **So John summoned two of his disciples and sent them to the Lord to ask, "Are you the Coming One, or should we expect another?"** (7:18b–19). Why does John pose the question? The psychological frame of mind of the historical John the Baptist is beyond access, but the narrative does contain clues in terms of the literary character's motive. The immediate context of "all these things" is primarily Jesus's benefaction to the centurion and his slave and the raising of the widow's son, both activities that "differ substantially and strikingly . . . from John's expectations of the coming one who would bring judgment" (Green 1997, 295). Jesus's benevolent ministry (both the immediate activities of Luke 7, as well as the overall character of his words and deeds to this point) does not fit the description of the fiery reformer of whom John spoke in 3:17. Thus, he is seeking confirmation of Jesus's identity. The second issue raised by John's question is whether the "Coming One" to whom he refers is an Elijah-like figure (Fitzmyer 1981–85, 1:664) or the Messiah (Green 1997, 295–97). The larger narrative suggests that this Coming One is, in fact, a messianic figure. Already, Jesus has been portrayed not as *Elijah redivivus* but as a figure greater than Elijah (see 7:11–17). Later the identification of the Coming One with a kingly, messianic figure is made explicit by the disciples at the triumphal entry (19:38). The following description of Jesus's ministry is in Isaianic terms of messianic activities; thus, ironically, even if "John expects Jesus to be Elijah, he is mistaken—the Gospel has already assigned that role to John himself" (Culpepper 1995, 160).

The importance of the question is seen in the fact that Luke has John's disciples repeat it verbatim (a point made all the more important in that the repeated question is missing in the parallel material; see Matt. 11:1–5/Q 7:18–19, 22–23): **When they reached him, the men said, "John the Baptizer sent us to you to ask, 'Are you the Coming One, or should we expect another?'"** (7:20). Jesus's response actually begins with the narrative summary in the next verse: **At that very time he healed many from diseases, afflictions, and unclean spirits, and he graciously gave sight to many blind people** (7:21). Once again, the authorial audience, familiar with the parallel material (Matt. 11:4–5 or Q 7:18–19, 22–23) will recognize that Luke has added this material to his version of the account. Its importance is further underscored by the phrase "at that very time." This and similar phrases are used elsewhere in Luke to signal important moments in the narrative (2:38; 10:21; 12:12; 13:31; 20:19; 22:53; 24:33; see Green 1997, 296). Jesus complements his response through deeds with one of words: **Then, he responded and said to them, "Go and tell John what you have seen and heard: the blind are able to see, the lame walk, lepers are cleansed, the deaf hear, the dead are raised, and the poor hear the good news proclaimed"** (7:22). In a "symphony of Isaianic echoes," Jesus's words draw heavily on Isa. 29:18–19, 35–36; 42:18; 43:8; 61:1 (Green 1997, 297). Of these activities, it is only the restoration of sight that Jesus has failed to perform by this point in the story (though he will do that also in 18:35–43), opening the possibility that he does this too in a metaphorical sense by opening the "eyes" of John's disciples to the nature of his ministry and commanding them to tell John not only what they have heard but also what they have now seen (7:22; see Green 1997, 296–97; on Luke's metaphorical use of sight and blindness, see Hartsock 2008). In any case, this "festival of salvation" (Schürrmann 1982, 410–11) is not limited to physical expression, though from Luke's perspective such literal fulfillment certainly validates his portrayal of Jesus. Proclaiming the good news to the poor holds the last place in Jesus's list, indicating its importance (cf. Luke 4:18, in which it holds the correspondingly important first place). Further, Jesus's recent activity in healing the centurion's slave and restoring the widow's son illustrates that "'the poor' include but are not limited to those who are without material resources" (Green 1997, 297). The economically vulnerable widow has her means of support restored to her; the centurion, though presumably wealthy enough to build a synagogue, is nevertheless a gentile outsider who receives Jesus's help (Green 1997, 297).

Jesus concludes his words with a makarism: **Blessed is whoever does not stumble because of me** (7:23). The beatitude continues the focus on Jesus's identity but now includes an allusion to those who may (like John?) be "scandalized" (*skandalisthē*) by "preconceived ideas" about Jesus and the nature of his words and deeds (Marshall 1978, 292); it also recalls Simeon's prediction that Jesus would be the "rise and fall" of many in Israel (Green 1997, 297).

> **"Messianic Apocalypse" at Qumran**
>
> The similarities between Luke 7 and 4Q521 are striking:
>
>> "⁵For the Lord will observe the devout, and call the just by name, ⁶and upon the poor he will place his spirit, and the faithful he will renew with his strength. ⁷For he will honour the devout upon the throne of eternal royalty, ⁸freeing prisoners, giving sight to the blind, straightening out the twisted.... ¹²for he will heal the badly wounded and will make the dead live, he will proclaim good news to the meek ¹³give lavishly [to the need]y, lead the exiled and enrich the hungry ¹⁴[...] and all [...]" (4Q521 2.2.6–14, trans. García Martínez 1996)
>
> Jesus, in his ministry of physical healing and restoration, fulfilled not only Isaianic expectations but, more generally, messianic expectations as they existed in pluriform Second Temple Judaism (see Novakovic 2007; Kvalbein 1998).

7:24–35. John's disciples depart, but interest in John the Baptist does not end (Green 1997, 297): **When the messengers from John had left, he began to speak to the crowds about John** (7:24a). Three times Jesus asks his audience what they went out to see with regard to John the Baptist: **What did you go out into the desert to observe? A reed shaken by the wind? What, in that case, did you go out to see? A man dressed in delicate clothes? People in expensive clothes and living in luxury are found in palaces!** (7:24b–25). These questions presume that Jesus knows of the crowds who have rushed to hear the preaching of John the Baptist (cf. 3:1–9). The first two answers to the question "What did you go out to see?" are ludicrous. Taken literally, one would no more make the effort to journey to the desert to watch proverbial reeds blowing in the wind than they would expect to see someone dressed in fine array. Taken figuratively, the resolute John is nothing like a reed blowing in the wind, which in proverbial contexts expressed a tender, not an uncompromising, disposition: "Humans should strive to be tender like a reed, not hard like the cedar" (*b. Ta'an.* 20a, cited by T. Manson 1949, 68; cf. Marshall 1978, 294; 1 Kings 14:15). And although Luke does not mention John's hairy garment in the Third Gospel, he will expect his audience to know it from the account in Mark 1:6, and the contrast between the ascetic John's dress and the fine clothes of the indulgent who live in palaces is sharp indeed and points toward the authentic identity of John.

The third time Jesus raises the question, however, his suggested answer begins to ring true, though it is still inadequate (Marshall 1978, 294): **What, then, did you go out to see? A prophet?** (7:26a). Jesus confirms that John is a prophet but suggests that he is even more: **Yes, I tell you, and more than a prophet** (7:26b). Jesus then clarifies John's identity by paraphrasing Exod. 23:20 and Mal. 3:1: **This is the one about whom it is written, "I am sending my messenger ahead of you, who will prepare your way before you!"** (7:27; cf. 1:17, 76; 3:4). Jesus has shifted the pronoun in Mal. 3:1 from "before me" to "before you [sg.]" (cf. Exod. 23:20). Here the singular "you" is collective and suggests that John's activity as described here has an ecclesial rather than christological function: he is getting the "people" ready (see Culy, Parsons, and Stigall 2010). This section ends with a brief encomium of John: **I tell you, no one among those born of women is greater than John** (7:28a). Given the double encomium *synkrisis* that runs throughout this first part of the Third Gospel, this high praise of John serves to undergird the implicit *synkrisis*: John is greater than any other human, but Jesus is greater still. And not only Jesus, **but the one who is least in the kingdom of God is greater than he** (7:28b; cf. *Gos. Thom.* 46). Even greater than John—who is more than a prophet, who prepares the people for the Lord's way, who is the greatest of those born of women—is the least of the members of God's kingdom, for "presence in the kingdom changes and elevates everyone who shares in it" (Bock 1994–96, 1:676).

Luke then interrupts Jesus's discourse with a narrative aside (Sheeley 1992, 114–15), material that is not found in the parallel accounts (cf. Matt. 11:7–30/Q 7:24–30): **(And when all the people heard, including the tax collectors, they acknowledged that God is just, because they had been baptized with John's baptism. The Pharisees and lawyers, on the other hand, rejected God's will for themselves, because they had not been baptized by him)** (7:29–30). Just as Jesus was set for the "fall and rise of many in Israel" (2:34), so also John's ministry, focalized here on his baptism of repentance, separates those (the people, including tax collectors) who have been baptized with John's baptism and who acknowledge God's justice (lit., "justified God") from those (Pharisees and lawyers) who reject "God's will" because they have rejected John's baptism and remain resolutely unrepentant (Green 1997, 300). The categories here—acknowledging God's justice and rejecting God's will—are absolute;

the people populating those categories are not (Green 1997, 302). That is to say, not every crowd affirms God's justice (22:47), nor do all Pharisees and scribes reject God's will (13:31; 23:50–53).

Without notice, the story shifts from the narrator's aside back to Jesus's discourse. This part of the discourse is composed of a question (7:31), a parable (7:32), its application (7:33–34), and a concluding aphorism (7:35). He asks: **With what, then, shall I compare the people of this generation? And what are they like?** (7:31). References to "this generation" elsewhere in Luke are either neutral (11:50; 21:32) or negative (11:29; see also 17:25, echoing Deut. 32:5, 20; Judg. 2:10; Pss. 78:8; 95:10; Jer. 7:29). Here the "people of this generation" are compared to complaining children: **They are like children sitting in the marketplace and calling out to one another who say, "We played the flute for you, and you did not dance; we sang a dirge, and you did not weep"** (7:32). In this "parable of the brats" (Bock 1994–96, 1:680), the children complain that their compatriots refuse to conform to the music that they are playing; they do not dance to the wedding music or weep at the sound of a funeral dirge. They are "at fault for not listening to them" (Bock 1994–96, 1:681).

And who are those who refuse these dictates of another's script or score? Jesus makes this plain in his application of the parable: **For John the Baptizer came neither eating bread nor drinking wine, and you say, "He has a demon!" The Son of Man has come eating and drinking, and you say, "The man is a glutton and a drunk, a friend of tax collectors and sinners!"** (7:33–34). Neither of God's messengers conforms to the conventional protocols; they refuse to "play the games" of "this generation" and are "branded as deviants, beyond the boundaries of acceptable social discourse, people not to be taken seriously" (Green 1997, 303). Ironically, they are rejected for faithfulness to ministries to which they believe God has called them. And who constitutes "this generation"? They are those who "do not wish to enter the game unless it is played according to their rules. This generation is like children who will play only if they can make the rules" (Bock 1994–96, 1:682). This interpretation fits the larger context of Jesus's argument. Those who rejected God's plan for themselves (7:30) are those who have also rejected John and Jesus. Those who "justified God" (7:29), we learn from Jesus's closing aphorism, are Wisdom's children: **But Wisdom is vindicated by all of her children** (7:35). Wisdom here is a personified Wisdom, or better, "simply a way of speaking of God and, by extension, of the purpose of God" (Green 1997, 304). First among Wisdom's children are John and Jesus, who in their differing ways fulfill the plan of God, but God's children include all those who defend and vindicate God's redeeming purposes.

7:36–50. *The anointing of Jesus in Simon's house.* The next episode continues several of the themes introduced in Luke 7:18–35. Once again we have one of the people, a "sinner," in this case an anonymous woman, whose tears of repentance and devotion are an act acknowledging that "God is just" (7:29), and a Pharisee, in this case Simon, who has refused John's baptism of repentance and has "rejected God's will" for himself (7:30; Kilgallen 1985, 678; on the connections between 7:18–35 and 7:36–50, see Talbert 2002, 88). Further, Jesus's identity is also front and center in the story. Like John the Baptist, Jesus is a prophet (cf. 7:16) and "more than a prophet" (cf. 7:26, 39), and he is a "friend of sinners" (7:34, 37; cf. 5:30).

This anointing story has a number of similarities with (and differences from) the story of Jesus's anointing found in Mark 14:3–9//Matt. 26:6–13//John 12:1–8 (for a detailed comparison, see Johnson 1991, 129; Fitzmyer 1981–85, 1:684–85; Bock 1994–96, 1:689–91), and the authorial audience would have heard Luke's version in conjunction with the one(s) with which they were already familiar (at least the Markan account).

Luke first sets the scene: **One of the Pharisees invited him to eat with him, and he entered the house of the Pharisee and reclined to eat** (7:36). The story is part of a recurrent "type-scene"; that is, it shares common features—setting, cast of characters, and/or key phrases—with several other stories. In this case, the type-scene is one in which Jesus dines in the house of a Pharisee (11:37–54; 14:1–24; see Tannehill 1986–90, 1:170–72). In each case, a conflict arises in which "Jesus criticizes the views and behavior of the Pharisee(s)" (Tannehill 1986–90, 1:171). In these scenes, "the Pharisees tend to collect negative values, thus becoming the representatives of those things which the narrator wants readers to avoid" (Tannehill 1986–90, 1:171). As we shall see, however, the response of Simon the Pharisee to Jesus's teaching is not narrated; thus, the possibility is left open that Simon (and the authorial audience who might identify with Simon's disdain for these "sinners") might finally accept Jesus's critique, repent, and accept God's will for himself (Tannehill 1994; see also comments on 7:29–30, above). The categories of "sinner" and "Pharisee" are absolute; the response of the individual characters, however, need not be stereotypical.

A third character enters the scene: **There was a woman who was in that city, a sinner! And when she learned that he was having a meal in the house of the Pharisee, she brought an alabaster jar of aromatic ointment, stood behind him at his feet, weeping, and began to moisten his feet with her tears. She was wiping them dry with her own hair, kissing his feet, and anointing them with the aromatic ointment** (7:37–38). From the patristic interpreters (e.g., Origen, *Comm. Matt.* 4; though cf. Tertullian, *Marc.* 4.18) to modern commentators (e.g., Green 1997, 309–10; Culpepper 1995, 169), the woman has been identified as a prostitute. Some translate the opening phrase as "a sinner in the city," interpreting the phrase as the ancient equivalent of the modern-day idioms "street walker" or "public woman" (Corley 1993, 124); however, the word order ("a woman in the [that] city, a sinner") resists this rendering, and no primary sources have yet been offered to corroborate this interpretation (Hornsby 1998, 93). Others point out that a woman at an otherwise all-male banquet suggests she has been provided by the host to offer entertainment, including that of a sexual or erotic nature (Corley 1989, 490), but this woman is obviously not there at Simon's invitation, and whatever other elements this Pharisaic meal shares with the Greco-Roman symposium, it would not seem to include the provision of prostitutes for after-dinner entertainment. For others this identification has been confirmed by the gesture of the woman wiping Jesus's feet with her loosened hair (Plummer 1903, 210–11; Orchard 1937; Witherington 1984, 54–55).

The evidence for how prostitutes wore their hair in antiquity, however, is scant and mixed (unbound, see Plautus, *Mil. glor.* 790–93; bound in public, see Athenaeus, *Deipn.* 13.590; cited by Cosgrove 2005, 680). Further, Luke knows the word for "prostitute" (15:30) and could have used it here had he wanted to specify the nature of her sinfulness (Mullen 2004, 112). Thus, we should be cautious in making this identification, especially since the nature of the woman's sinfulness is left unstated in Luke 7 (as is the nature of Peter's sinfulness in 5:8), and the gesture of unbound hair may evoke a variety of images for the authorial audience (for what follows, see Cosgrove 2005). Certainly a woman's unbound hair could have sexual connotations. Poseidon is attracted to Medusa's long hair and rapes her; Athena punishes her by changing her hair into a tangle of snakes (Ovid, *Metam.* 4.794–803; for other examples of the seductive nature of unbound hair in antiquity, see Herm. *Sim.* 9.9.6; 15.1–3; Euripides, *Hipp.* 198–202; Apuleius, *Metam.* 2.17). But this is not the only image that a woman's unbound hair would evoke in an ancient audience. In some texts, unbound hair is a sign that a Roman or Greek girl is unmarried (*Hom. Hym.* 2.176–78; Heliodorus, *Aeth.* 3.4; Xenophon of Ephesus, *Anth.* 1.2; cited by Cosgrove 2005, 681). In some descriptions of nymphs or female warriors, unbound hair signifies a kind of fierceness or wildness that defies cultural convention (Longus, *Daphn.* 1.4; 2.23; Aristophanes, *Lys.* 1308–13; Ovid, *Metam.* 1.477; Heliodorus, *Aeth.* 1.2). Thus, it was generally considered shameful for a married woman to make a public appearance with unbound hair (Varro, *Ling.* 7.44). One exception to this general rule, however, was grieving rituals in which it was acceptable for a woman, regardless of age or marital status, to "let down her hair in public without risking censure" (Cosgrove 2005, 683). Examples abound in antiquity of mourning women unbinding their hair as part of the grieving ritual (Xenophon of Ephesus, *Anth.* 3.5; Virgil, *Aen.* 3.65; *Passion of Perpetua* 20; for other examples, see Cosgrove 2005, 683–84).

Given the wide range of understandings that unbound hair might elicit among an ancient audience, it is best to attend to the immediate contours of the text as well as its larger cultural context in order to understand how the authorial audience would have been expected to hear this text. In this regard, one other interpretation is significant. The image of a woman's unbound hair (or the unbinding of it) could also be understood in tandem with other gestures as an act of devotion or veneration of a deity. In a fascinating passage at the end of the Greek novel *Chaereas and Callirhoe*, the heroine Callirhoe visits the temple of Aphrodite to give thanks for her reunion with her husband: "Callirhoe went to Aphrodite's temple before entering her house. She put her hands on the goddess's feet, placed her face on them, let down her hair, and kissed them. 'Thank you, Aphrodite!' she said" (Chariton, *Chaer.* 8.8.15, trans. Reardon 1989, 124; for other, more formally ritualistic examples of women worshiping in a "natural state" of "purity in spirit," i.e., shoeless and with unbound hair, and perhaps without jewelry or makeup, see *SIG* vol. 2, no. 736; Petronius, *Sat.* 45; cited by Cosgrove 2005, 680).

The woman's actions in Luke 7 parallel those of Callirhoe and other women who demonstrate veneration for a deity. Jesus is the object of her devotion and thanksgiving. The additional element of tears (which she wipes away with her unbound hair) suggests tears of remembered repentance and thanksgiving for forgiveness (but clearly forgiveness is the primary theme here). The fact that she has brought an alabaster jar of aromatic ointment with which to anoint him suggests a premeditated act of thanksgiving and devotion for a previous encounter with Jesus that Luke has left unnarrated—a gap for the audience to fill. Thus, the importance of the woman's identification as a "sinner" lies not in the specific nature of her sin (she could have been a notorious debtor [cf. 7:41–42] or a female merchant [like Lydia in Acts] in fine perfumes who overcharged for her wares) but in her status as a "sinner," which, for Luke, indicates those persons who recognize their need for repentance and who respond positively to Jesus's ministry (over against the category of religious authorities, who refuse God's plan for themselves; cf. 7:30; Neale 1991, 191).

That nothing untoward should be perceived in the woman's actions is unwittingly confirmed by Simon's statement: **When the Pharisee who had invited him saw this, he said to himself, "This man, if he were a prophet, would have known who and what kind of person the woman is who is touching him, that she is a sinner"** (7:39). From the Pharisee's perspective, there is nothing in her appearance or gestures that would indicate impropriety in her actions or that she was a sinner; this fact was previously known to Simon, since they were from the same city. Nonetheless, even if Jesus was unaware of her reputation as a sinner, this is something Jesus should have known if he possessed the clairvoyance of a prophet (Cosgrove 2005, 689). For Simon, the character flaw belongs to Jesus and not just the woman!

Jesus immediately and ironically demonstrates that he is "a prophet . . . and more than a prophet" (7:26) by employing his prophetic clairvoyance to respond to what Simon has uttered only to himself. **Then Jesus responded and said to him, "Simon, I have something to say to you"** (7:40a). Startled, Simon shows deference to Jesus by addressing him as "Teacher" (cf. the use of the term for Jesus elsewhere at 8:49; 9:38; 10:25; 11:45; 12:13; 18:18; 19:39; 20:21, 28, 39; 21:7; 22:11), reminding the audience that he is, after all, the guest of honor at this party: **And he said, "Teacher, speak"** (7:40b). Jesus responds with a brief parable, whose application to the current situation Jesus will clarify momentarily: **Two people were in debt to a certain moneylender; the one owed five hundred denarii, and the other fifty. Since they did not have the means to pay, he cancelled both debts** (7:41–42a). The amounts of the debts are equal to two months' wages versus nearly two years' wages (Bock 1994–96, 1:699), though it is the difference in the amount of money owed that is significant. If the two debtors in the story correspond to Simon (who owes little) and the woman (who owes much), then the creditor is Jesus, who forgives the debts in behalf of God, a fact recognized later by those at table with him (see 7:49). Jesus poses the relevant question: **Which of them, then, will love him more?** (7:42b). Simon's response is a reluctant acknowledgment of the obvious answer: **I suppose the one for whom the greater debt was cancelled** (7:43a).

Jesus responds first by affirming Simon's answer: **He said to him, "You have judged correctly"** (7:43b). Jesus continues, however, by contrasting the woman's gestures of love and devotion toward him with Simon's lack of attention:

> Then he turned toward the woman and said to Simon, "Do you see this woman? I came into *your* house, and you did not give me water for my feet. But *this woman* moistened my feet with her tears and wiped them with her hair! You did not give me a kiss; but *this woman*, from the moment I came in, did not stop kissing my feet! You did not anoint my head with oil; but *this woman* anointed my feet with aromatic ointment!" (7:44–46)

In a nutshell, the woman has performed gestures that meet or exceed the cultural expectations of conventional hospitality; Simon has not (see Arterbury 2005, 138–39). Jesus then pointedly draws the conclusion to his own parable: **On account of which I tell you, her many sins are forgiven, since she loved much** (7:47a). The syntax of this sentence has long bothered interpreters. Some have taken the *hoti* clause as causal in the sense that her actions of extravagant devotion have led to the forgiveness of her sins (Heil 1999, 50), but this is in conflict with the preceding parable and the overall flow of the story. It is better to take the *hoti* clause as a result clause (Bailey 1980, 18) or, perhaps better, as a causal clause in a deductive sense. Thus, "Luke will have regarded the woman's love as the consequence, not the cause of her forgiveness" (Marshall 1978, 306).

The story concludes with Jesus addressing the woman directly: **Then he said to her, "Your sins have been forgiven"** (7:48). This is a public pronouncement of a previously established fact. Finally, **those reclining with him at the meal began to say among themselves, "Who is this who even forgives sins?"** (7:49), recognizing that Jesus is the creditor able to cancel the debt of sin. The story concludes with Jesus's pronouncement to the woman: **Your faith has saved you. Go in peace** (7:50; cf. 8:12, 48; 17:19; 18:42). This is a story that begins and ends *in medias res*. We are not told of a previous encounter between the

> **"Since She Loved Much"**
>
> The conjunction *hoti* introduces a causal clause, though there is much debate as to what the clause in Luke 7:47 means. The *hoti* clause indicates the cause of logical deduction, "tracing known evidence back to what must be its cause" (Just 1996–97, 1:324). In the statement "There is fire because there is smoke," the smoke is the cause of the deduction that there is fire, even though the smoke is the result and not the cause of the fire. So in Luke 7:47 the woman's gestures of love and devotion are the "*cause* or *reason for deducing that she must have been forgiven much*. But the actual cause of her great love is something else, something that must have happened *first*" (Just 1996–97, 1:324; original emphasis), in this case a previous encounter between Jesus and the woman left unnarrated by Luke (see also Nolland 1989–93, 1:358). Jesus then publicly pronounces (7:48) what has been previously established in much the same way that the woman's gestures demonstrate the prior reality of her repentance/forgiveness (for similar instances of the evidential use of the *hoti* clause in this kind of deductive logic, see John 9:16; 1 Cor. 10:17; Homer, *Il.* 16.34–35; cf. Culy, Parsons, and Stigall 2010, 251–52).

woman and Jesus that results in her lavish expression of adoration and veneration. Neither are we told how Simon, who at best has "loved little," will respond to Jesus's actions and words: "Jesus has carefully led him toward a judgment about the woman that is different from his initial one. The scene leaves Simon poised on the threshold of decision. He may finally accept Jesus's teaching, or he may not. Simon is more than a negative stereotype. It is quite possible to view him as an open character who might change" (Tannehill 1996, 137). Both gaps, at beginning and end, create space for the authorial audience to enter the story, either as a sinner in need of forgiveness or a self-righteous religionist, also in need of forgiveness.

Jesus's Wondrous Teachings and Miraculous Acts (8:1–56)

The next unit is composed of a summary statement about Jesus and his followers on mission (8:1–3), his wondrous teachings (8:4–21), and his miraculous acts (8:22–56).

8:1–3. *Jesus on mission.* Luke transitions to the next unit via a summary statement describing Jesus's preaching mission: **Some time afterward it happened that he was traveling from city to city and village to village, preaching and proclaiming the kingdom of God** (8:1a). This summary statement is the third in Luke (cf. 4:14, 44) and echoes the previous description of Jesus preaching and proclaiming the "kingdom of God to other cities" (4:43). At this point the Twelve reappear in the narrative (cf. 6:12–16), along with the first specific mention of female followers: **and the Twelve were with him, as were certain**

women who had been healed from evil spirits and illnesses, including **Mary who was called Magdalene, from whom seven demons had gone out; Joanna the wife of Chuza, the steward of Herod; and Susanna** (8:1b–3a). The three named women share in common the fact that they, like the Twelve, are "with" Jesus; they also have been the recipients of Jesus's healing ministry (cf. the healing of Simon's mother-in-law, 4:38–39), although none of these particular healings is narrated in the preceding narrative. Nothing more is known about the exorcism of Mary Magdalene's demons other than the number of them, seven. This number suggests a particularly difficult case of demon possession (cf. 11:24–26) and implies that she has been both "totally possessed and subsequently completely healed" (de Boer 2002, 149). Nothing is said regarding the ailment of Joanna, although we do learn that she is connected through her marriage to the administration of Herod Antipas (cf. 3:1). This identification is two-edged; through her husband's status, Joanna would be a woman of some socioeconomic standing, but that standing would be compromised by association with Herod, the puppet tetrarch who is negatively characterized in Luke's Gospel (see 13:31). Joanna demonstrates that "the gospel has penetrated Herod's own establishment" (Danker 1988, 101), but the link with Herod also casts her in a suspicious light, not unlike the tax collector Levi (see 5:27–32). We know nothing further about the third woman, Susanna.

The summary ends by making mention of **many other women who were serving them from their own resources** (8:3b). It is unclear whether the three named women serve as a subset of these other unnamed women (and thus also contribute to the support of Jesus and the Twelve out of their resources), but it is unlikely that Luke intends to suggest that all these women, named and unnamed, have previously been sick or demon possessed. And while it is true that "serving" (*diakoneō*) in Luke typically refers to serving food or waiting table, it would be a mistake to view this reference as limiting these women disciples' role to traditional domestic service (de Boer 2002, 143). First, in Luke neither are women limited to traditional domestic activity (e.g., Mary in 10:38–42), nor is the role of "serving" limited to women. The disciples serve the crowds in the story of the feeding of the five thousand (9:14–15), and Peter and John make preparations for the Passover meal (22:7–13). Furthermore, Jesus identifies "serving" as a hallmark both of his own ministry and of that of his followers (22:24–27). Thus, these women are depicted as fulfilling the role of disciples through their service. Support of Jesus and the disciples through their resources need not suggest that the women were wealthy; rather, it suggests that they have put what resources they have at the disposal of Jesus and his mission (cf. the widow and her mite in 21:1–4). Finally, the whole of Luke's narrative suggests that these women remain faithful followers, even though they are not specified again until near the end of the story, when we learn that "the women who had followed him from Galilee" (23:49) observed the events of the crucifixion. Further, the women who "remembered" Jesus's predictions of his passion and resurrection (24:8 recalling 9:22; 13:33) include Mary Magdalene, Joanna, and the "other women," suggesting that they have been included in the circle of disciples privy to Jesus's teaching on these matters.

Jesus's wondrous teachings (8:4–21). The next section has three parts: the parable of the sower (or soils) and its interpretation (8:4–15), Jesus's teaching about what is hidden and revealed (8:16–18), and his family's response (8:19–21).

8:4–15. The section begins with a crowd assembling to hear Jesus: **Now, as a large crowd was coming together, and those from city after city were coming to him, he spoke through a parable** (8:4). The Greek of the parable's opening, *exēlthen ho speirōn tou speirai ton sporon autou*, uses alliteration (Demetrius, *Eloc.* 25; here words begin with sigma, an ess sound) that is pleasing to the ear and inviting to the audience (and also evident in the translation): **A sower went out to sow his seed** (8:5a). The parable continues: **and as this one sowed, some fell along the path and was trampled underfoot, and the birds of the air ate it up. Other seed fell on rocky soil, and when it grew up, it dried up, because it did not have moisture. Other seed fell among thorns, and when they grew up with it, the thorn plants choked it. And still other seed fell on good soil, and when it grew up, it produced fruit one hundredfold** (8:5b–8a). The successive phrases that begin 8:6–8 employ the rhetorical figure of *epanaphora* (or *repetitio*; see *Rhet. Her.* 4.13.19), in which the same words (here *kai heteron katepesen* or *kai heteron epesen*; lit., "and another [part] fell") are used for emphasis (also in Mark 4). Interpreters have debated the agrarian sequence of planting before plowing in ancient Palestine (implied by *Jub.* 11.11; cf. *t. Ber.* 7.2; *b. Šabb.* 73b), which might explain the apparent wastefulness of the process (Jeremias 1972, 11–12 [originally published in German in 1958]; challenged by White 1964 and countered by Payne 1978–79). The sower intends to plow under all those scattered seeds, although some waste from broadcast planting is unavoidable (Culpepper 1995, 177). The surprising result is that the seed "produced fruit one hundredfold" (8:8a; see also McIver 1994). The point is a difficult one, as Jesus's admonition implies: **As he was saying these things, he was shouting, "The one who has ears to hear, let that one hear!"** (8:8b). So the disciples must request a private tutorial: **Now, his disciples were asking him what this parable might mean** (8:9).

Before commenting on the parable specifically, Jesus makes a general observation about his parabolic teaching: **To you has been given the privilege to know the mysteries about the kingdom of God, but to the rest [I speak] in parables, so that "although they see they might not see, and although they hear they might not understand"** (8:10). Luke's version softens Jesus's response by omitting the phrase "so that they may not turn again and be forgiven" (Mark 4:12). The translation here is intended to preserve the ambiguity of the *hina* clause, which may be taken as either result or purpose (Fitzmyer 1981–85, 1:708–9; Bovon 2002–13, 1:312). Jesus alludes to Isa. 6:9 LXX, which reflects the same grammatical ambiguity. In the immediate context (see 8:16–18, below), it seems that the Lukan Jesus is claiming that although his parables are given for the purpose of revealing the mysteries of the kingdom, they can nonetheless have the *effect* of separating those who see and understand from those who are spiritually oblivious to the sights and sounds around them.

Jesus then proceeds to interpret the parable for the disciples so that they may respond positively when it comes to understanding the "mysteries about the kingdom of God." The interpretation of the parable is something of a template for responses to Jesus and his message in the Third Gospel (for a similar reading, see Culpepper 1995, 178–79): **This is what the parable means: The seed is the word of God** (8:11). In the context of Luke's Gospel, the parable's interpretation can be viewed as a way to categorize the various responses by characters in the Third Gospel to Jesus, who is spreading the "word of God": **The ones [that fell] along the path are the ones who heard [the word]. Then the devil comes and takes away the word from their hearts, so that they might not believe and be saved** (8:12). Judas, of course, is the prime example of one whom the "devil," or Satan, entered and deprived of Jesus's word (22:3). The religious leaders too are those whose hearts harbor what is an abomination in God's sight (16:15). Even those in the clutches of evil are not beyond hope, however. Satan wishes to sift Peter too, but Jesus prays that he might turn and strengthen his fellow believers (22:31), which ultimately he will do (see Acts 1).

The ones [that fell] on the rocky soil, according to Jesus, **are those who receive the word with joy when they hear it. But these have no roots, these who believe for a while, but in a time of trial fall away** (8:13). Trial does come, of course, for the disciples when Jesus is arrested in the vicinity of the Mount of Olives (22:40, 46), and while Luke does not describe their failure as starkly as does Mark ("they all forsook him, and fled," Mark 14:50 RSV), the disciples are not prepared for what will happen and resort to violence (Luke 22:49–51). In particular, Peter (*petros*), rocky soil (*petra*) that he is, denies Jesus three times in the courtyard of the high priest (22:54–62), his protests notwithstanding (22:33).

The seed that falls among thorns reflects yet a third response to Jesus's message: **That which fell among thorns—these are the ones who hear [the word], and as they go their way, they are choked by the anxieties, wealth, and pleasures of life; and their fruit does not mature** (8:14). Martha is so anxious that she cannot join Mary in attending to Jesus's teachings (10:38–42). Jesus encourages his followers not to be burdened by what they say before the authorities (12:11) or what they will eat or wear (12:22), since they cannot change anything with worry (12:25; see Culpepper 1995, 179). The excuses offered by the guests in Jesus's parable of the big dinner certainly indicate their interest in the word has been choked out by wealth and the pleasures of life (14:15–24). Later, Jesus will warn his disciples that they should not be weighed down with the "cares [*merimnais*] of everyday life . . . so that that day [of judgment] will not come upon you suddenly, like a trap" (21:34b–35a).

Likewise, those like the rich ruler are vulnerable to having their fruit wither because they are overly concerned for their possessions (18:18–25; cf. 12:16; 16:1, 19–31; 21:1). The prodigal son, at least according to the elder brother, has wasted his "living" (*bios*) on loose living (15:30). Many things in the world can extinguish the fire of interest in Jesus's message about the kingdom (cf. 17:27). But in all these cases, there is the possibility of turning again, at least in Luke's version. The rich ruler is sad but does not leave (contra Mark 10:22). The prodigal son comes to himself and returns to a loving father. At least some of those hearing Jesus's warning of the impending judgment remain faithful amid the chaos, keeping their heads while those about them are losing theirs.

Still, in the parable it is the last, "good soil" that is held up as a model of discipleship: **And that which [fell] on good soil—these are the ones who, after hearing the word with a truly good heart, hold to it firmly and bear fruit with endurance** (8:15). Who hears the word with a truly good heart and holds to it firmly (cf. 6:45; 21:19)? Surely the "minor characters" in Luke (as in Mark) who respond in persistent and obedient faith qualify as examples of good soil: the friends of the paralytic who persist in getting their friend to Jesus (5:17–20); the demoniac who declares all that Jesus has done for him (8:26–39); the woman with the hemorrhage and the synagogue ruler who both persist in approaching Jesus (8:40–56); the blind beggar who begs for healing (18:35–43); Zacchaeus, who repays his debts fourfold (19:1–10); the poor widow who gives her all (21:1–4). All of these produce fruit in surprising abundance (on the minor characters' function in Mark, see Rhoads and Michie 1982, 135). But in Luke, perhaps the best example of those who represent the "good soil" is Jesus's mother, Mary. Mary ponders in her heart the words spoken to her (2:19) and treasures in her heart all that happens (2:51). She will appear later in this episode and will represent those who are Jesus's family both by blood relations and by hearing and doing the word of God (8:19; cf. Acts 1:12–14).

8:16–18. Jesus now employs two proverbial sayings or maxims (*Rhet. Her.* 4.17.24) to reinforce his point. These two sayings in 8:16–17 recur in 11:33 and 12:2, respectively (with slight variations and for different purposes). Here they continue the image of Jesus as agent. Jesus was the one "sowing the word"; he is now the one who lets the word shine forth like a lamp: **No one, after lighting a lamp, hides it in a container or puts it under a bed. Instead, this one puts it on a lampstand so that those who enter may see the light** (8:16). Just as Jesus sows in order to reap (and not for the purpose of having the seed trampled underfoot or choked out by thorns), so Jesus lights a lamp in order to give light and not in order to hide it. Anyone who enters the house may benefit from the light of the lamp; Jesus gives the word as light—indeed, he is a light intended for "revelation to the Gentiles" and "for glory to the people of Israel" (2:32). His second maxim makes the same point: **Indeed, there is no hidden thing that will not become visible, nor a secret thing that will not certainly be made known and come into the open** (8:17). Jesus's teachings are not intended as secret knowledge for a privileged few but are intended to be made known to all who will hear. Jesus admonishes his audience, which has already been invited to hear the word and produce fruit a hundredfold: **Pay attention, then, to how you listen** (8:18a). Failure to listen risks great loss: **For whoever has, to them will be given; and whoever does not have, even that which they appear to have will be taken from them** (8:18b; cf. 19:26).

8:19–21. As Jesus is speaking, his family approaches: **Now, his mother and brothers came to him but were not able to get near him because of the crowd. So it was reported to him, "Your mother and your brothers are standing outside, wanting to see you"** (8:19–20). Luke here omits the negative reference to Jesus's family thinking that he is out of his mind (cf. Mark 3:20–21). The result is to make Jesus's family the primary example of those who hear and do the word of God as Jesus commands: **He responded and said to them, "My mother and my brothers—these are the ones who hear the word of God and do it"** (8:21; contrary to Mark, where Jesus's family of flesh stands over against his family of faith; see Culpepper 1995, 181). This interpretation reinforces the earlier point that Mary is the ideal example of the one who, like the good soil, hears the word with a good heart and bears fruit in endurance.

Jesus's miraculous acts (8:22–56). What follows consists of three stories that underscore Jesus's authority over the sea (chaos) (8:22–25), the demonic (8:26–39), and disease and death (8:40–56).

8:22–25. The authorial audience will recognize that the first scene, in which Jesus is portrayed as Lord over the sea (8:22–25), continues to follow Mark's sequence (Mark 4:35–41; see also Matt. 8:23–27), although Luke's account is shorter (94 words compared to Mark's 118; see Culpepper 1995, 184), indicating Luke's concern for brevity in description (see Theon, *Prog.* 83.15–19; comments on Luke 1:1–4). The episode occurs at an unspecified time (contrast Mark 4:35): **Now it happened on one of those days that both he and his disciples got into a boat** (8:22a). Jesus suggests to his disciples that they cross over to the other side of the Sea of Galilee (here called a "lake" by Luke; cf. 5:1): **and he said to them, "Let's go to the opposite side of the lake." So they set out** (8:22b). With an economical use of words (cf. *Rhet. Her.* 4.54.68), Luke notes that **as they sailed, Jesus fell asleep** (8:23a). The detail of Jesus asleep in the boat is an important element in Luke's portrayal of Jesus exercising his divine sovereignty over the forces of evil and chaos.

The authorial audience, familiar with stories of sudden storms on the Sea of Galilee (see Fitzmyer 1981–85, 1:729), would not be surprised at what happens next: **And a wind storm came down on the lake** (8:23b). The storm in Luke 8 is no small event; it is a violent and sudden squall: **the boat immediately began to fill with water, and they were being swamped with water and were in danger** (8:23c). The disciples, some of whom are seasoned fishermen, immediately turn to Jesus for help: **So they went and woke him, saying, "Master, master, we're about to die!"** (8:24a).

Jesus initially ignores the disciples, dealing rather with the immediate crisis: **Then he woke up and rebuked the wind and the rough water; and they ceased, and it was calm** (8:24b). The language of Jesus "rebuking" the wind and water is reminiscent of an exorcism story and highlights the nature of the miracle. Jesus is not simply manipulating the elements into a more favorable weather pattern; he is engaging demonic powers and demonstrating his authority over them. Here the narrator picks up on a common theme in antiquity, especially in Jewish literature, that the sea is to be equated with chaos and evil. From the beginning, when the spirit of God hovered over the unformed and unfilled waters (Gen. 1:2), "creation" was understood as bringing order to chaos (cf. Pss. 74:12–14; 89:8–10). Apocalyptic texts, both Jewish and Christian, speak of a future world in which the watery chaos has been finally defeated, variously depicted by the monsters of the sea being devoured at the messianic banquet (*2 Bar.* 29.4; cf. 2 Esd. 6:49–52) or by a simple assertion that "there was no longer any sea" (Rev. 21:1). So Jesus's calming of the sea has both christological and eschatological implications. Jesus has authority over the watery chaos, an authority typically associated with God or those like Antiochus IV Epiphanes, who erroneously thought "in his superhuman arrogance that he could command the waves of the sea" (2 Macc. 9:8; see Nolland 1989–93, 1:398–99). Jesus's calming of the sea is a demonstration of his divine power and a foreshadowing of the world to come.

> **"Master, Master!"**
>
> In 8:24a, Luke employs the rhetorical figure of *epanadiplosis*, "the repetition of an important word for emphasis" (BDF §493.1; see Quintilian, *Inst.* 9.3.28–29). This figure is closely related to the rhetorical figure of reduplication (*conduplicatio*), which "is the repetition of one or more words for the purpose of amplification or appeal to pity" (*Rhet. Her.* 4.28.38, trans. Caplan 1954). Here the disciples, out of desperation, repeat Jesus's title, "Master, Master!" (cf. Luke 10:41; Matt. 25:11; Acts 9:4).

Jesus then turns his attention to the disciples and asks: **Where is your faith?** (8:25a). This question puts the disciples in a bad light. Even though they have heard his teaching, they still do not grasp the significance of his miracles. They lack faith in Jesus, a point confirmed by their closing question: **And they were afraid and amazed, saying to one another, "Who can this man be, since he even rebukes the winds and the water and they obey him?"** (8:25b). Those who have been called to be his disciples are now revealed to be clueless regarding the true identity of Jesus. He is sovereign over wind and sea; he is Lord over evil and chaos.

8:26–39. The authorial audience will recognize that the story of the Gerasene demoniac in Luke 8:26–39 follows the general flow of the story as recorded in Mark 5:1–20, with some subtle differences. Luke begins: **So they sailed down to the region of the Gerasenes, which is opposite Galilee. And a certain**

man from the city who had demons met Jesus, who had just stepped ashore (8:26–27a). Like Mark (5:1–2a), Luke implies that Jesus has set sail across the Sea of Galilee with his disciples in tow. But when they reach the other shore, only Jesus disembarks. Jesus is met by a demon-possessed man, about whom Luke notes: **For a long time he had not worn clothes and had not been living in a house but rather in the tombs** (8:27b). The demoniac confronts Jesus: **Now, when he saw Jesus, he screamed and fell before him, and he said in a loud voice, "Why are you interfering with us, Jesus, Son of the Most High God? I beg you, do not torment me!"** (8:28). The exclamation fulfills Gabriel's prediction to Mary that Jesus would be called "Son of the Most High" (1:32).

The demoniac, however, invokes the name in a defensive maneuver aimed at deflecting Jesus's intent to heal the man. In a brief flashback, Luke (following Mark) recounts that Jesus **had commanded the unclean spirit to come out of the man** (Luke 8:29a), and at this point, for dramatic effect, Luke adds a parenthetical aside (cf. Mark 5:3–5): (**For on many occasions it had seized him, and he had been bound with chains and shackles and kept under guard. But he would break the restraints and be driven by the demon into the uninhabited areas**) (Luke 8:29b). He is physically violent and destructive, socially alienated, and ritually unclean (living as he is, among the tombs; see 8:27). Jesus then questions him: **What is your name?** (8:30a), to which the demoniac replies: **"Legion"—because many demons had entered him** (8:30b). There is an ironic reversal of the one and the many. "Jesus, Son of the Most High God" (8:28) began a journey with many followers, the destination of which was an encounter with a man possessed by an unclean spirit. But at the dramatic climax of the encounter, the "many" who were ostensibly on the side of the good have been reduced to one, Jesus, and the one representative of evil, the demoniac, turns out to be a man with "many" demons. The Legion of demons **began begging him not to command them to depart into the abyss** (8:31). The authorial audience, familiar with Mark's version, will note that in Luke's account the demons beg not to be cast into the "abyss" rather than not to be banned from that country (cf. Mark 5:10). The word "abyss" (*abyssos*) is used in the LXX to refer to the "watery

Sleeping Jesus

Sleep in the OT is a symbol of divine inactivity that prompts the community of faith to summon Yahweh God to awake and express his divine sovereignty:

> "Awake, awake! Arm of the
> Lord, *put on strength;*
> *awake as you did in days of*
> *old, in ages long past.*
> ... *Was it not you who dried*
> *up the sea,*
> *the waters of the great abyss,*
> *and made the ocean depths*
> *a path for the redeemed?"*
> (Isa. 51:9, 10 REB)

Jesus's sleeping, then, is no less an indication of his divine power than is his calming of the storm.

deep," which in OT cosmology is the symbol of chaos (Gen. 1:2) or the abode of evil spirits (cf. *Jub.* 5.6; *1 En.* 10.4–6; 18.11–16; Rev. 20:3). Instead, the demons bargain with Jesus to be allowed to enter a herd of swine feeding on an adjacent hillside: **Now, a herd of quite a few pigs was there, grazing on the hill; and the demons begged him to allow them to enter them; and he allowed them** (Luke 8:32). This aspect of the story would have been humorous to an authorial audience who was either Jewish or familiar with Jewish dietary law (a familiarity that early gentile Christians presumably possessed). And the anti-Roman jab of associating the "Legion" (a Roman military term) with pigs would not have been missed either.

The unclean swine are an appropriate refuge for the unclean spirits. Jesus grants their request, and **the demons came out from the man and entered the pigs; and the herd rushed down the steep bank into the lake and drowned** (8:33). The demons end up in the watery abyss after all, a place over which Jesus has just demonstrated his authority. The disciples, presumably still in their boats, have an uncomfortably close view of this demonstration, as the pigs plunge over the cliff into the water. These two seemingly unrelated stories, the stilling of the storm and the healing of the Gerasene demoniac, underscore the same reality (see also Ps. 65:7: "You calm the seas and their raging waves, and the tumult of the nations" [REB]). Jesus has ultimate authority over evil, whether that evil manifests itself in nature or in the life of an individual. By the end of these stories, the audience is hopefully much better prepared to answer the pressing question, "Who can this man be?" (see 8:25).

Luke then reports the reaction of the bystanders: **When the herders saw what had happened, they ran away and told the news in the city and countryside. Then [people from the area] went out to see what had happened. They came to Jesus and found the man from whom the demons had come out clothed and in his right mind, sitting at Jesus's feet, and they were afraid** (8:34–35). Rather than rejoice at the sight of the demon-possessed man now healed and in his "right mind," they are afraid. And when they learn the details of his healing, they put their fear into action, by asking Jesus to leave: **Those who had seen what had happened told them how the man who had been demon possessed had been made well. Then the whole crowd from the surrounding region of the Gerasenes asked him to leave them because they were seized with great fear** (8:36–37a). Jesus complies without so much as a word: **So he got into the boat and returned** to the other side of the lake (8:37b).

The scene ends with one more encounter between Jesus and the formerly demon-possessed man: **Now, [before he left] the man from whom the demons had come out was begging to be with him; but Jesus sent him away, saying, "Return to your home, and tell how much God has done for you." So he went throughout the whole city proclaiming how much Jesus had done for him** (8:38–39). Jesus leaves the man to return home to testify to the wondrous deeds of God.

8:40–56. In the stories of Jairus's daughter and a woman's faith (8:40–56), Luke (following Mark) employs a rhetorical technique known as intercalation, a "sandwich" structure in which one story is enveloped, or sandwiched, inside another. The rhetorical effect is to suggest that the two seemingly unrelated stories are best understood when read in light of each other. The story about Jairus and his daughter begins with this report: **As Jesus was returning, a crowd welcomed him, for everyone was waiting for him. And a man whose name was Jairus came—this man was a ruler of the synagogue—and after falling at Jesus's feet he began pleading with him to come to his house! For he had an only daughter, about twelve years of age, and she was dying** (8:40–42a). Jairus, a leader in the community—a ruler of the local synagogue—pleads with Jesus to heal his only daughter, who is dying. Luke foregrounds a detail given only later in Mark's version of the account, namely, that she is twelve years old. This reference to "twelve years" appears to function as a lexical link between the two stories (for this is the length of the hemorrhaging woman's illness as well). Twelve years prior, the woman with the hemorrhage became ill and began her descent down the path of disease and affliction toward death. At the same time, a little girl was born to Jairus and his wife and began the journey of life. Twelve years later, both are at the point of destruction when Jesus crosses their paths. His life-giving power restores the woman with the hemorrhage from physical illness and rescues the little girl from the clutches of death. Without comment, Jesus goes with Jairus and is jostled by the crowd: **Now, as he was going along, the crowds were nearly smothering him** (8:42b).

The authorial audience soon learns that this daughter is not the only one dying. **There was a woman, suffering from a discharge of blood for twelve years, who [although she had spent her whole livelihood on doctors] was unable to be cured by anyone** (8:43). The nature of the woman's illness is not detailed, but presumably the authorial audience would recall Levitical restrictions: "And if a woman have an issue of her blood many days out of the time of her separation, or if it run beyond the time of her separation, all the days of the issue of her uncleanness shall be as the days of her separation: she *shall be* unclean" (Lev. 15:26 KJV). A close reading of Lev. 15 suggests that this restriction refers to what in later rabbinic law was the category of impurity known as *zaba*, that is, a woman "who has a discharge ('oozes') outside of, or in addition to, her regular period" (S. Cohen 1991, 274). In the case of an "*irregularly bleeding woman*, Leviticus 15 assumes only the '*simple*' contamination of the objects on which she sits and lies" (Weissenrieder 2003, 238–39) and does not indicate the contamination of people. A "close reading of Leviticus 15 indicates that Jesus was not risking contamination being touched by the hemorrhaging woman" (Weissenrieder 2003, 239–40), nor presumably does she put others at risk of contamination (to invoke later rabbinic texts in support of this view is anachronistic; see S. Cohen 1991, 275–79). Thus, the story of the woman with the flow of blood, even if Lev. 15 is in the background, "does not give any indication that the woman's condition put any person (including Jesus) at risk of contamination or that she suffered any degree of isolation as a result of her affliction" (S. Cohen 1991, 279), the *communis opinio* of modern commentators notwithstanding.

The focus of the passage, then, is on the miraculous restoration of the woman's health and not on Jesus's rewriting of Jewish purity codes. In the Greco-Roman world, the female body was described as more porous than the male and more prone to "leakage" (Galen, *On Progn.* 3.15; 618K). Excessive fluid was therefore associated with disease and illness; underlying this judgment of the Hippocratics and others is a value judgment: "firm and compact is good/loose and spongy is bad" (Dean-Jones 1994, 115). Further, "post-Hippokratic female physiology continues to view woman as a creature of excess" (Hanson 1990, 333). Luke, then, presents a woman in paradox. She is a woman with an "excess" of blood over a long period of time, indicating an incurable disease of unknown origins; at the same time, she is a woman of abject scarcity, having "spent her whole livelihood on doctors" (8:43; on the textual problem, see Metzger 1994, 121).

In this state of desperation, the woman **approached him from behind and touched the edge of his garment** (8:44a). The purpose of the woman's touch is to highlight Jesus's extraordinary power (cf. 5:13; 8:46; Acts 5:15; 19:12), not to portray a violation of purity law (Weissenrieder 2003, 249; contra Bovon 2002–13, 1:338). The woman's strategy is effective: **and immediately her bleeding stopped** (8:44b).

The woman's action does not go undetected. Jesus asks: **Who is the one who touched me?** (8:45a). In the confusion, Peter responds: **And while everyone was denying it, Peter said, "Master, the crowds are pressing in on you and crowding against you"** (8:45b). But the woman is not the only one to perceive what has happened in and through her body: **Jesus replied, "Someone touched me, for I recognized power going out of me." When the woman saw that she had not escaped notice, she came trembling, and she fell before him and announced in the presence of all the people the precise reason why she had touched him and how she had been immediately cured** (8:46–47). Jesus's power is at the root of her trembling. She already knows of his power to heal, because she knows what has happened to her; she fears perhaps what he will do with that power now that she is discovered. Nonetheless, she turns fully to Jesus with her emotion, her knowledge, her obeisance, and her speech. Jesus does not condemn her but confirms her physical restoration, addressing her in the language of intimate kinship: **Then he said to her, "Daughter, your faith has delivered you. Go in peace"** (8:48). The reference to her "faith" makes it clear that it is not the magical properties of his clothing that heal her but rather her act of faith in reaching out to him and in standing up to be identified. That faith has made her well. The Greek word for "delivered" here (*sōzō*) is also the word translated "save." Her faith has made her physically whole as well as placing her in a right relationship with God.

The scene then abruptly shifts back to the first story. With Jesus's comforting words addressed to this "daughter of faith" still ringing in his ears, Jairus is confronted by messengers from his household who report rather coldly: **While he was still speaking, someone came from the house of the ruler of the synagogue and said, "Your daughter has died. Do not trouble the teacher any longer"** (8:49). The delay caused by Jesus's interaction with the woman with the hemorrhage has had catastrophic consequences for Jairus's daughter. Before Jairus can respond, Jesus gently reassures this powerful synagogue ruler: **When Jesus heard this, however, he responded to Jairus, "Do not be afraid; only believe, and she will be saved"** (8:50). Taking with him only the inner core of the disciples, closing ranks, Jesus proceeds to Jairus's house: **Then, when he came to the home, he did not allow anyone to enter with him except Peter, John, James, and the father and mother of the child** (8:51).

They arrive at a scene of much commotion: **Now, everyone was crying and mourning for her. Then he said, "Do not cry; for she is not dead but asleep"** (8:52). The mourners' remorse is not very deep (they may have been professional mourners rather than family members or friends; see *m. Ketub.* 4.4)," because their tears quickly turn to jeers: **But they proceeded to laugh at him, because they knew that she was dead** (8:53). Unlike the authorial audience,

---

The "Edge" of the Garment

Luke adds to the story of the hemorrhaging woman a detail not found in Mark 5 (though perhaps drawn from Mark 6:56) that the woman touched the "edge" or "fringe" (*kraspedon*) of Jesus's garment (Luke 8:44). Many commentators (e.g., Luz 2001–7, 2:42; Bovon 2002–13, 1:338) claim that this detail, which reflects the prescription of Num. 15:38–40, portrays Jesus as a "pious Jew." Dale Allison has "recovered" an interesting ancient interpretation that reads the reference to the "fringe" of the garment in light of Mal. 4:2 (3:20 LXX): "to those who fear his name, the sun of righteousness rises having healing in his wings [*pteryxin*]." Pseudo-Epiphanius cites Mal. 4:2 in support of the view that "the fringe of his [Jesus's] garment would heal" (*Testimony Book* 7.30, cited by Allison 2008, 138). Photius, a ninth-century lexicographer, gives further explanation for Pseudo-Epiphanius's interpretation: "'For,' it says, 'the sun of righteousness will arise upon you who fear my name, and healing will be in his wings.' The sun of righteousness is the Lord of good things, and the wings [*pterygas*] are the tassels [*kraspeda*] of his garments" (Photius, *Lex.* 271, cited by Allison 2008, 140). Allison concludes with this tantalizing suggestion: "we undeniably have here an old exegetical tradition; and given our fragmentary knowledge, a first-century origin for it is really no less plausible than a second- or third-century genesis. Maybe indeed it is as old as the story it belongs to" (2008, 146). Whether or not Mal. 4:2 lies in the background, the reference to healing from the very fringe of Jesus's garment highlights the pervasive power of his healing.

these mourners have not witnessed the calming of a violent storm or the restoration of a violent demoniac. Jesus ignores them: **he took hold of her hand and called to her, saying, "Child, get up." And her spirit returned, and she immediately got up** (8:54–55a). Jesus attends to her physical needs: **Then he gave orders for something to eat to be given to her** (8:55b). The scene is intimate and poignant. Immediately the little girl gets up and walks around, much to the amazement of those who have been privileged to witness this event: **Her parents were amazed** (8:56a). Nonetheless, Jesus **instructed them to tell no one what had happened** (8:56b). Though not as pronounced as the Markan "messianic secret" (see Mark 5:43), the episode ends with Jesus instructing the girl's parents to say nothing about what they have witnessed.

Theological Issues

Until this point in Luke's Gospel, the audience has been led to expect many individual episodes to end with an aphorism by Jesus—a memorable, pithy saying that summarizes the lesson to be learned from the story. Thus, in the story of the paralytic (5:17–26) Jesus says, "the Son of Man has power on the earth to forgive sins" (5:24); at the conclusion of the call of Levi (5:27–32), Jesus says, "I have come not to call righteous people but sinners to repentance" (5:32). At the end of the story of the disciples' plucking heads of grain (6:1–5), Jesus says, "The Son of Man is Lord of the Sabbath" (6:5). At the conclusion of the story of the Gerasene demoniac (8:26–39), which immediately precedes the story of Jairus's daughter, Jesus says, "Return to your home, and tell how much God has done for you" (8:39). The story of Jairus's daughter ends on a rather different note: Jesus "gave orders for something to eat to be given to her" (8:55). No clever aphorism here, simply a command that the girl's needs not be left unmet. Certainly, the mention of food confirms that the girl is really alive and not a phantom or ghost, but more important, Jesus's attention to detail is consistent with the compassion he displays throughout both stories in Luke 8. He commends the woman with the hemorrhage, "Daughter, your faith has delivered you," when he could very well have condemned her actions. He reassures Jairus when members of his own household callously report that Jairus's daughter is dead. These actions contribute no less than his words to Luke's characterization of Jesus.

Luke 9:1–50

Jesus's Miracles and Mission and the Sending Out of His Followers

Introductory Matters

Luke 9:1–50 is a crucial turning point in the overall narration of the Third Gospel. Not only does it represent the "culmination of . . . Jesus's Galilean tour" (Bock 1994–96, 1:810), Luke 9:1–50 also "provides a preview of the journey that follows in 9:51–19:44" (Moessner 1989, 46). The chapter focuses both on Jesus's identity (as prophet and Messiah) and on the disciples' response to Jesus (both positive and negative; O'Toole 1987). The chapter divides into five scenes: the mission of the Twelve, Herod's perplexity, and the feeding of the five thousand (9:1–17); Peter and Jesus on Jesus's identity and vocation (9:18–27); the transfiguration of Jesus (9:28–36); the healing of the boy with an unclean spirit (9:37–43a); and intensifying the misunderstandings regarding Jesus's identity and vocation (9:43b–50). The climax of Luke 9:1–50, as many have recognized, is the transfiguration scene (see Moessner 1989, 69–70).

Tracing the Narrative Flow

The Mission of the Twelve, Herod's Perplexity, and the Feeding of the Five Thousand (9:1–17)

This unit is composed of three scenes: the mission of the Twelve (9:1–6), Herod's perplexity over Jesus's identity (9:7–9), and the feeding of the five thousand (9:10–17).

> **Luke 9:1-50 in the Narrative Flow**
>
> **Jesus's origins and training (1:1-4:13)**
>
> **Jesus's mighty words and deeds in Galilee (4:14-9:50)**
>
> Jesus's mission and miracles and the ingathering of his followers (4:14-6:49)
>
> Jesus's marvelous words and deeds (7:1-8:56)
>
> ▶Jesus's miracles and mission and the sending out of his followers (9:1-50)
>
> The mission of the Twelve, Herod's perplexity, and the feeding of the five thousand (9:1-17)
>
> The mission of the Twelve (Luke 9:1-6)
>
> Herod's perplexity over Jesus's identity (9:7-9)
>
> The feeding of the five thousand (9:10-17)
>
> Peter and Jesus on Jesus's identity and vocation (Luke 9:18-27)
>
> The transfiguration of Jesus (9:28-36)
>
> The healing of the boy with an unclean spirit (9:37-43a)
>
> Intensifying the misunderstandings regarding Jesus's identity and vocation (9:43b-50)

9:1–6. *The mission of the Twelve.* Jesus's power and authority, characteristic of his activity in general (4:36; 5:17; 6:19; 8:46; see Johnson 1991, 145), are extended to the disciples (9:1–6). Luke 9:1 is similar to, but not identical with, Mark 6:7: **Jesus called the Twelve together and gave them power and authority over all demons and to cure diseases** (9:1). Luke extends the mission even further: **and he sent them to proclaim the kingdom of God and to heal [the sick]** (9:2). Now the "apostles" (*apostoloi*; lit., "sent ones"), as they are called in Luke 6:13 and 9:10, are "sent" (*apostellō*) to continue Jesus's Isaianic ministry of teaching and healing (cf. Luke 4:18). Jesus gives them specific instructions regarding what they should (or should not) take with them on this assignment: **He said to them, "Take nothing on the journey—no staff, nor travel bag, nor bread, nor money, nor two tunics [each]"** (9:3). The Lukan Jesus uses the rhetorical figure of *epanaphora* (the same word, here "nor," *mēte*, beginning a series of phrases; see *Rhet. Her.* 4.13.19), but the grammar is difficult. Most likely the phrase "no staff, nor travel bag, nor bread, nor money, nor two tunics" is "one lengthy epexegetical infinitival clause" intended to specify what is *not* to be taken on the journey (see Culy, Parsons, and Stigall 2010, 294). But it is hard to be more specific than that. Does the staff refer to a walking stick or a club used to ward off potential robbers? Is the bag a beggar's bag or a traveler's knapsack? Are the tunics to be imagined as worn at the same time or as a second tunic? What can we say regarding Jesus's prohibitions? Perhaps nothing more than that the lack of provisions signals the "urgency of their mission" as well as the apostles' "complete dependence on God's provision for their needs" (Culpepper 1995, 194). Further, Luke understands that God will provide through the hospitality of those to whom the apostles proclaim the kingdom of God.

That (in)hospitality is the primary context of this passage is clear from Jesus's next words: **And whatever house you happen to enter, stay there until you leave the area. And as for all those who do not welcome you, when you**

Tracing the Narrative Flow

leave that city shake the dust from your feet as a testimony to them (9:4–5). The vocabulary Jesus uses ("enter," "welcome," "stay") represents some of the "most common semantic markers" for "the custom of hospitality" (Arterbury 2005, 140). The apostles may expect to receive God's provision through the hospitality of those who are recipients of their message. Failure to provide this hospitality invites judgment against them. Furthermore, the practice of hospitality explains the gesture of "shaking dust from the feet" as testimony to them (see "Theological Issues" at the end of this chapter). Rather than this action being reminiscent of the practice of Pharisees who, on returning to Judea from gentile areas, would shake the dust from their feet out of fear of impurity (so Plummer 1903, 240; and Str-B 1:571), the gesture here is surely not meant as an effort at self-purification on the part of the apostles. Rather, if rejected the apostles were "supposed to wipe the very dust off their feet that should have been washed off if their potential hosts had taken the appropriate actions [of hospitality] and made sure the travelers' feet were washed" (Arterbury 2005, 140). The mission of the Twelve here is a "dress rehearsal" (so Nolland 1989–93, 1:428) not only for the mission of the seventy(-two) soon to follow in 10:1–12 but also for the "post-Pentecost role" of Jesus's followers foretold by Jesus (24:48–49) and narrated in Acts (esp. 13:48–52). The scene concludes with the Twelve obeying Jesus's instructions: **Then they went out and traveled from village to village, proclaiming the good news and healing everywhere** (9:6).

9:7–9. *Herod's perplexity over Jesus's identity*. The apostles' preaching and healing activities do not escape the notice of Herod: **Now, Herod the tetrarch heard about everything that had happened** (9:7a). Reports about the disciples' activities quickly shift to questions regarding the identity of the one who sent them: **and he was quite perplexed because it was being said by some that John had risen from the dead, by some that Elijah had appeared, and by others that some ancient prophet had risen** (9:7b–8). These

---

The Identity of Jesus in Luke

Herod's question in 9:9 stands in a series of questions regarding Jesus's identity that have been posed by characters in the narrative:

Scribes and Pharisees: "Who is this man who speaks blasphemies?" (5:21)

John the Baptist: "Are you the Coming One, or should we expect another?" (7:19)

Those reclining at table in Simon's house: "Who is this who even forgives sins?" (7:49)

Disciples: "Who can this man be, since he even rebukes the winds and the water and they obey him?" (8:25)

These questions focus the audience's attention on Jesus, even when the speculations are not accurate. "The questions are even more powerful than the lofty titles attributed to Jesus because the answer to the questions is not exhausted by the titles" (Culpepper 1995, 194).

Figure 14. Mosaic below the Altar of the Church at Heptapegon/Tabgha Commemorating the Multiplication of the Loaves and Fishes

"popular" views of Jesus's identity resurface in 9:18 and have some basis in what has already taken place in the Gospel (Johnson 1991, 146). Earlier Luke remarks that the people have wondered if John "might be the Christ" (3:15). Jesus's words (4:26) and actions (7:11–16) have recalled the ministry of Elijah, and as a result of the resuscitation of the widow's son the people have declared, "A great prophet has risen up" (7:16). Herod is not portrayed as jumping to conclusions about Jesus's identity (contrast Mark 6:16; cf. Matt. 14:12) but is rather "perplexed" or "confused" (9:7): **Then Herod said, "I beheaded John! So, who is this person about whom I am hearing such things?"** (9:9a).

The scene ends with the note that Herod **was trying to see him** (9:9b). Eventually, it is revealed that Herod is seeking not just to see him but also to kill him (13:31). When they finally do meet, Herod is forced to "see" that Jesus is innocent (23:15; see Culpepper 1995, 194).

9:10–17. *The feeding of the five thousand.* The feeding of the five thousand is the only miracle to occur in all four Gospels (Matt. 14:13–21; Mark 6:32–44; Luke 9:10–17; John 6:1–15). Therefore, it is an important window into the nature of Jesus's ministry. Each story has its own particular nuances and emphases. In Luke, the story shows continuity between Jesus's ministry and the mission of the apostles; anticipates, through the rhetorical device of a *chreia* of action, Jesus's eschatologically oriented banqueting with his followers at the Last Supper (Luke 22) and a postresurrection meal in Emmaus (Luke 24); and highlights Jesus's role as prophet by echoing OT stories of miraculous provision.

When the apostles returned, they described to him everything they had done (9:10a). The apostles return to report to Jesus on their mission. What they have done includes proclaiming the kingdom of God and healing (9:1, 6), thus identifying with and extending Jesus's own mission (4:18, 43–44; 6:20; 8:1–3; see Heil 1999, 56). Jesus then withdraws with his disciples, perhaps for further instruction (cf. 8:9–10; 10:23) or prayer (cf. 5:16), but certainly to escape the crowd: **And he took them along and withdrew privately to a city called Bethsaida**, a city in the tetrarchy of Philip (9:10b). This effort to be alone with his disciples is not successful, however: **But when the crowd learned about it, they followed him** (9:11a). Despite this intrusion, Jesus offers them hospitality: **After welcoming them he began speaking to them about the kingdom of God, and those who needed healing he proceeded to heal** (9:11b). Jesus now resumes his ministry of preaching and healing, thus bringing the mission of the apostles full circle. The day wanes, and the disciples worry about what to do with the crowds after sunset: **Now, the day began to draw to a close. So the Twelve came and said to him, "Send the crowd away so that they can go into the surrounding villages and countryside and rest and find provisions, because we are in an isolated place here"** (9:12). Evidently, the disciples, who were instructed to seek hospitality on their preaching and healing mission (9:1–5), do not think they have the resources necessary to reciprocate such hospitality, because they are in an "isolated place." Jesus, however, refuses to allow them to shirk their responsibility as hosts to his guests: **But he said to them, "You give them something to eat"** (9:13a). They persist in their resistance: **Then they said, "We do not have more than five loaves and two fish—unless perhaps we go and buy food for all these people?"** (9:13b). Luke moves the summary statement regarding the number of people fed from the end of the story in Mark 6:44 (cf. Matt. 14:21) to this point in the narrative, providing further justification to the disciples' objection: **there were about five thousand men there** (9:14a; Matt. 14:21 specifies that the number does not include women and children). Jesus ignores their protest and gives further instruction: **Then he said to his disciples, "Seat them in groups, about fifty apiece"** (9:14b). Finally, the disciples comply: **And they did so and seated everyone** (9:15). Jesus then engages in action that will become very familiar to the authorial audience and, indeed, to Christians across the centuries: **He took the five loaves and two fish, looked up toward heaven, and blessed them. Then he broke them and began giving them to the disciples to give to the crowd** (9:16). Jesus's gestures qualify for what the ancient rhetoricians called a *"chreia* of action." While most *chreiae* were associated with pithy and memorable sayings of a famous person, Theon and other ancient rhetoricians define a *chreia* as "a concise statement *or action*, which is attributed with aptness to some specified character" (Theon, *Prog.* 96, trans. Kennedy 2003, 15, emphasis added; see also Ps.-Hermogenes, *Prog.* 6–8; Nicolaus, *Prog.* 17–24). *Chreiae*, then, can be brief descriptions of some characteristic action attributed to a specific person and appropriate to the situation at hand. Jesus's performative gestures of taking, blessing, breaking, and giving are certainly actions closely associated with him in the NT. Besides the tradition of the miraculous feeding in all four

> ### *Chreiae* of Action
>
> There are numerous examples of *chreiae* of action, which writers used to demonstrate something of the "essence" of the person they were describing:
>
> > "When somebody declared that there is no such thing as motion, he [Diogenes] got up and walked about." (Diogenes Laertius, *Vit. phil.* 6.39, trans. Hicks 1925b, 41)
>
> > "Pythagoras the philosopher, having been asked how long is the life of men, going up onto the roof, peeped out briefly, by this making clear that life was short." (Theon, *Prog.* 99, trans. Kennedy 2003, 17)
>
> One of the progymnastic exercises involved elaborating a *chreia* (whether a saying or action) by expansion, comment, and/or contradiction. For later rhetoricians, these elaborations became formulaic and included eight components: (1) praise; (2) paraphrase of the *chreia*; (3) rationale; (4) statement of the contrary; (5) analogy; (6) example; (7) judgment/authority; and (8) exhortation/conclusion (Ps.-Hermogenes, *Prog.* 7–8). While there is no reason to expect prose writers (like Luke) to follow this formula mechanistically, one sees in Luke 9:10–17: the rationale for the *chreia* of action (the day is ending, and the crowds have nothing to eat), a statement of the contrary (the disciples initially oppose Jesus's proposal to provide hospitality), analogy (echoes of OT miraculous provision—see below), and authority (Jesus's authority comes from God, as indicated by his lifting his eyes toward heaven).

Gospels, the apostle Paul, quoting a received tradition (1 Cor. 11:23), refers to Jesus taking bread, blessing it, and breaking it at the Last Supper (1 Cor. 11:23–24). These gestures are also found in the Synoptic accounts of the subsequent feeding of the four thousand (Matt. 15:36; Mark 8:6; absent in Luke) and the Last Supper (Matt. 26:26; Mark 14:22; Luke 22:19) and, significant for Luke, in the supper at Emmaus, in which once again Jesus "took bread and blessed it. Then, after breaking it, he began giving it to them" (24:30). This *chreia* of action is appropriate to the character of Jesus, especially in Luke, in which Jesus is depicted as "going to, coming from, or at a meal" (Karris 1985) and is himself depicted as "food for the world" (cf. comments on Luke 2:7b). In Luke, this *chreia* of action serves to link these three scenes (feeding of the five thousand, Last Supper, supper at Emmaus): "The feeding of the five thousand is the climax of Jesus's Galilean ministry, just as the Last Supper is the climax of his Jerusalem ministry, and the meal at Emmaus is the climax of his post-resurrection appearances" (Just 1993, 156–57).

The scene ends with a deceptively simple statement regarding the aftermath of the feeding: **They ate, and everyone was satisfied. Then the food that was too much for them was collected—twelve baskets of scraps** (9:17). The authorial

> **Intertextual Echoes in the Feeding of the Five Thousand**
>
> The echoes of the OT in the feeding of the five thousand are very strong, especially the story of Elisha in 2 Kings 2:1–8:29. Reginald Fuller (1974, 406) has called the story of Elisha a "literary prototype" for the NT feeding stories and has cataloged the following features shared by both:
>
> 1. food is brought to the men of God;
> 2. the amount of food is specified;
> 3. an objection is raised that the quantity provided is inadequate;
> 4. the men of God ignore the objection and command that the food be distributed;
> 5. the crowd eats, and there is food left over.
>
> Once again, the similarities in the stories are used to draw comparisons and to argue implicitly for the superiority of Jesus's provision (see also Luke 7:15 on the *synkrisis* between Jesus and Elijah).

audience, familiar with Scripture stories of miraculous provision, will surely recall what God did through Moses in providing manna in the wilderness (Exod. 16; Num. 11) and through Elisha, who fed one hundred men with barley loaves and grain (2 Kings 4:42–44). Through *synkrisis*, or comparison, Jesus the "prophet like Moses" is a prophet "greater than Elisha," having fed more people, with an abundance of leftovers (Marshall 1978, 357).

Peter and Jesus on Jesus's Identity and Vocation (9:18–27)

9:18–27. The authorial audience, familiar with Mark, would also have recognized that Luke has passed from the feeding of the five thousand (found in Mark 6:30–44) to Peter's confession (Mark 8:27–30). The omission of Mark 6:45–8:26 (known subsequently to source critics as the "great omission"; see Hawkins 1911, 61) has the effect of focusing Luke 9:18–27 on the question of Jesus's identity, first raised by Herod at the beginning of the chapter (9:7–9). Furthermore, in the parallel accounts in Mark (8:27–30) and Matthew (16:13–20), the location of Peter's confession is specified as Caesarea Philippi; in Luke, the narrator reports that the setting is not spatial but temporal; it is a time of prayer. In Luke's Gospel, when *egeneto* ("it happened") is followed by a temporal setting ("while he was praying"), it links thematically with the preceding episode; in this case the feeding of the five thousand supplies "the general background for the following conversation" (Levinsohn 2000, 179): **And it happened that while he was praying privately, the disciples were with him** (9:18a). Jesus at prayer is a common theme in the account of his public ministry (3:21; 5:16; 6:12; 11:1) as well as his passion (22:40–41, 44, 46; 23:46) and will also be the setting for the transfiguration, in the next episode (9:28–36; see Talbert 2002, 108). Luke apparently sees no tension in reporting that Jesus is praying privately (or "alone") in the presence of his disciples, since "in the cultural context of Luke's gospel, to be 'alone' was to be away from the people who were not part of your inner circle of family, friends, or in this case disciples" (Culy, Parsons, and Stigall 2010, 307). So in this prayerful setting, Jesus poses a question to his followers: **So he asked them, "Who do the crowds say that I am?"** (9:18b). The disciples' response echoes the general assessment of Jesus expressed by "some" earlier: **They responded and said, "John the Baptizer; others [say] Elijah, and others that some ancient prophet has risen"** (9:19). The last part of the statement ("some ancient prophet has risen") is in verbatim agreement with 9:8b and underscores that the identity of Jesus is, indeed, the focus of attention at this point. Jesus brushes aside the rumors of the day regarding his identity: **he said to them, "But you, who do you say that I am?"** (9:20a). The adversative particle *de* combines with the fronted emphatic personal pronoun "you" to focus attention on the disciples' response in contrast to the views circulating about Jesus (see Culy, Parsons, and Stigall 2010, 308). In light of what Jesus has just done in feeding the five thousand, how does the disciples' view of him differ from that of the crowds?

Luke then reports that **Peter responded and said, "The Christ of God"** (9:20b). To this point in the narrative, angels have heralded the birth of Jesus as "Christ the Lord" (2:11). The narrator has revealed that Simeon was promised to see the Lord's Christ before he died, a promise fulfilled when he holds the infant Jesus in the temple (2:26–35, esp. v. 26). The crowds who came to be baptized by John the Baptist have speculated that John is the Christ (3:15). Jesus himself has proclaimed that he has been "anointed" (*echrisen*) by the Spirit of the Lord (4:18). Even the demons have recognized Jesus as the Christ (4:41). But Peter is the first follower, indeed the first human, to identify Jesus as "the Christ of God." Having witnessed Jesus's words and deeds—proclaiming the kingdom of God and performing miracles (most recently the miraculous provision of food for the five thousand)—Peter acknowledges that Jesus is God's anointed one, a confession he will later repeat and expand when he proclaims the good news in Cornelius's house (Acts 10:38). Peter's confession functions differently in the various Gospels, canonical and apocryphal. "The confession of Peter turns out to be no longer a climactic point in the gospel-story, as it is in Mark 8, nor is it a church-founding episode, as it is in Matthew 16 (with the addition of vv. 16b–19). Rather the scene functions as one of the important answers given in this chapter to Herod's question" (Fitzmyer 1981–85, 1:771).

Jesus responds to this confession by ordering the disciples to keep quiet and by issuing the first of his passion predictions: **Then he strongly commanded them to tell this to no one and said, "It is necessary for the Son of Man to suffer many things, and to be rejected by the elders and chief priests** and scribes, and to be killed, and on the third day to be raised" (9:21–22). In the Lukan context, this passion prediction represents Jesus's own response to Herod's question, "Who is this?" Jesus's response moves beyond understanding his role in purely prophetic terms, as the crowds have done (9:19), or even in traditional messianic terms, as the disciples, represented by Peter, have done (9:20; see Culpepper 1995, 200). The title "Son of Man" (cf. Dan. 7:13) "occurs only in the mouth of Jesus and is self-referential. It is used in three contexts: Jesus's present ministry (5:24; 6:5; 7:34; 9:56, 58; 19:10), the suffering of the Messiah (9:22, 26, 44; 18:31; 22:22, 48; 24:7), and the future role of judging (11:30; 12:8, 10, 40; 17:22, 24, 26, 30; 18:8; 21:27, 36; 22:69)" (Johnson 1991, 94). Jesus articulates to his disciples for the first time that he must suffer, be rejected, be killed, and be raised (Talbert 2002, 108).

In a series of five discipleship sayings, Jesus then makes clear that the fate of his followers is inextricably bound up with his destiny: **Then he proceeded to say to everyone, "If anyone wants to become my follower, let them deny themselves, take up their cross daily, and follow me"** (9:23). This invitation to discipleship is extended to everyone and involves self-denial, loyalty, and participating daily in Christ's self-sacrifice on the cross: **For those who want to save their lives will lose them; and whoever loses their life for my sake, such a person will save it** (9:24). This second statement expresses a paradox through the use of the rhetorical figure of *commutatio* (reciprocal change), which is when two discrepant thoughts are so expressed by transposition that the latter follows from the former although contradictory to it—for example, "you must eat to live, not live to eat" and "I do not write poems because I cannot write the sort I wish, and I do not wish to write the sort I can" (*Rhet. Her.* 4.28.39, trans. Caplan 1954).

The paradox of salvation is that only in losing oneself can one's life be saved. The saying may find its background on the battlefield, in which the general exhorts the soldiers that the one who seeks to save his life by deserting will be the first to die, while paradoxically, the one who enters into the fray, giving no thought to preserving his life, is most likely to preserve it (Culpepper 1995, 202; Fitzmyer 1981–85, 1:786; Bauer 1963). In this light, the saying may relate particularly to martyrdom, but it is an apt description of the self-denial that is to characterize the life of the believer.

The rhetorical figure changes from *commutatio* to the rhetorical question (asking a question to reinforce the argument; see *Rhet. Her.* 4.15.22) in the next saying: **Indeed, what good will it do if a person gains the whole world and loses the self or suffers a loss?** (9:25). This saying resonates with Jesus's fundamental teaching elsewhere in the Third Gospel regarding one's attitude and disposition toward material possessions (see 12:15), and the message is clear: financial gains mean nothing if one loses one's soul in the process.

The fourth saying is a warning: **For whoever is ashamed of me and my words, the Son of Man will be ashamed of that one when he comes in his** glory and the glory of the Father and the holy angels (9:26). By shifting the possessive pronoun "his" (*autou*) so that it modifies "glory" and not "Father" (cf. Mark 8:38), Luke has subtly prepared the audience for the transfiguration scene, which follows next and in which Jesus will indeed come "in his glory."

The section ends with this final and enigmatic saying of Jesus: **I tell you for certain, there are some of those standing here who will certainly not experience death until they see the kingdom of God** (9:27). Strictly speaking, this saying is a kingdom saying and not a discipleship saying (Culpepper 1995, 203), but what does it mean? Perhaps the Lukan Jesus implies that those standing there who have witnessed his teaching about the kingdom of God and his healing ministry have seen the kingdom of God. This kind of realized eschatology finds support later in Jesus's claim in 11:20. Perhaps Jesus refers to his transfiguration, in which Peter, John, and James see Jesus's glory and thus experience a "preview" of the coming kingdom and an inauguration of "the guarantee of a day when Jesus will fully manifest his power on earth" (Bock 1994–96, 1:859). Perhaps Jesus is referring to the time after his resurrection, when the disciples will finally comprehend the "mysteries about the kingdom of God" (8:10) and understand fully that the Christ must "suffer these very things and then enter into his glory" (24:26). All of these ultimately point to a future coming of the kingdom, so that finally "the saying preserves a futurist eschatological saying of Jesus, and not one that has to be understood [solely] in terms of realized eschatology" (Fitzmyer 1981–85, 1:790).

The Transfiguration of Jesus (9:28–36)

9:28–36. The transfiguration is in the form of a dream-vision (see comments on Luke 1:5–25; Matthew explicitly refers to the transfiguration as a "vision," *horama*, 17:9; see also Dodson 2009, 175–85): scene-setting (9:28), dream-vision proper (9:29–31, 34–36a), and reaction/response (9:32–33, 36b). Luke first sets the scene with a temporal note: **Now it happened about eight days after these words . . .** (9:28a). Matthew and Mark agree in noting that the transfiguration occurred "six days later" (Matt. 17:1//Mark 9:2). "These words" have to do with the disciples taking up their crosses and following Jesus. Thus, there is an intimate connection between the suffering Jesus and his followers will endure and the glory revealed in the transfiguration. Luke continues the scene-setting by noting that Jesus **took Peter and John and James and went up on a mountain to pray** (9:28b). Matthew and Mark say that Jesus led Peter, James, and John up a mountain to be apart from the rest; the scene-setting of prayer is unique to Luke (and is the second such prayer scene in this chapter; cf. 9:18).

The dream-vision proper occurs in two parts with two corresponding reactions. In the first part of the dream-vision, Luke reports: **And it happened that while he was praying the appearance of his face became different and his clothes became gleaming white** (9:29). The description of Jesus's changing countenance and transformed garments uses the rhetorical device of oracular

> ### "Behold, Two Men"
>
> The phrase "all of a sudden two men" (lit., "behold, two men") occurs verbatim in two other places in Luke/Acts. First, in Luke's account of the empty tomb, we read, "While they [the women] were perplexed about this, *behold, two men* stood by them in dazzling apparel" (Luke 24:4 ESV). Again, in the account of the ascension in Acts, we read: "And while they [the disciples] were gazing into heaven as he went, *behold, two men* stood by them in white robes" (Acts 1:10 ESV). While it is not necessary to identify these two men in the later accounts as Moses and Elijah, the verbal link between the three passages in Luke is striking. At the three moments in the Lukan narratives where the divine status of Jesus is most obvious—the transfiguration, the resurrection, and the ascension—two men appear to discuss the significance of the event. In the empty tomb and ascension accounts the two men speak of the event's meaning in direct discourse. The empty tomb is a reminder of Jesus's words that on the third day he would rise (Luke 24:6–7). The ascension is a foreshadowing of the way in which Jesus will return at the parousia (Acts 1:11). The transfiguration points to the way in which Jesus will embody Israel's hope for deliverance from bondage (see this section and Wright 1996).

demonstration (*Rhet. Her.* 4.55.68), or *ekphrasis*, "to bring what is portrayed clearly before the eyes" (Theon, *Prog.* 118, trans. Kennedy 2003, 45; see Humphrey 2007, 141) and to mark the event as a dream-vision narrative. Luke then reports that Jesus is joined by two figures: **And all of a sudden two men were talking with him, who were Moses and Elijah** (9:30).

All three Synoptics report that Jesus is joined by Moses and Elijah (Matt. 17:3//Mark 9:4). While it is unusual for the deceased to appear in dream-visions in Jewish literature (see the exception of the deceased high priest, Onias, and Jeremiah, who appear to Nicanor; 2 Macc. 15:12–16), it is fairly common in Greco-Roman literature (e.g., Homer, *Il.* 23; Sophocles, *El.* 410–25; Aeschylus, *Eum.* 94–104; Virgil, *Aen.* 1.341–72; 2.254–60; 5.705–39; see Dodson 2009, 178; Flannery-Dailey 2004, 373). Luke draws heavily on the Jewish Scriptures to narrate the transfiguration, and the parallels between Jesus and Moses are especially highlighted:

1. Jesus takes three disciples up the mountain; Moses goes with three named persons (and 70 others) up the mountain (Exod. 24:1, 9).
2. Jesus is transfigured, and his face shines and his clothes became dazzling white; Moses's skin shines when he comes down from the mountain (Exod. 34:29).
3. God's voice is heard from an overshadowing cloud; God's voice is heard from an overshadowing cloud (Exod. 24:15–18).

Moses, however, is not the only one to appear with Jesus at his transfiguration; Elijah is there as well. Both are eschatological figures and are associated with the end times. "A prophet like Moses" was expected to arise and liberate Israel (see Deut. 18:15). Before "the great and terrible day of the Lord" (Mal. 4:5), Elijah would appear (Mal. 4:6). With the appearance of Elijah and Moses, the transfiguration is a foreshadowing of the end time; the kingdom of God is at hand, and Jesus will reign supreme. But the connection to "these words" in 9:28 reminds the audience that Jesus's glory is inseparable from his suffering; there is no easy triumphalism here.

Luke is distinctive among the accounts in reporting the content of their discussion: **who after appearing in glory began talking about his departure, which he was about to fulfill in Jerusalem** (9:31). The Greek word for "departure" here, *exodos*, connotes again the story of Moses, in this case as deliverer of the Israelite slaves from Egyptian bondage. This word, standing near the beginning of the travel narrative and as a summary of it, encourages the authorial audience to read the travel narrative as the story of Jesus, "the prophet like Moses" (cf. Acts 3:22; 7:37), who embarks on another "exodus," this time to deliver all people from the bondage of sin. The verbal link of "behold, two men" (see the sidebar) combines with the narrator's second description of Jesus's journey to Jerusalem as the "time for him to be taken up" (9:51) to suggest that this journey is not completed until the ascension in Acts 1. Jesus's exodus includes the entire death/resurrection/ascension transit, and only then can repentance and forgiveness of sins be preached to all nations (cf. 24:47).

The first reaction/response is recorded in 9:32: **Now, Peter and those with him were extremely sleepy, but when they were fully awake, they saw his glory and two men standing with him.** The authorial audience familiar with the rest of Luke's story may hear in the reference to Peter, James, and John being "extremely sleepy" an echo of their inability to watch and pray during Jesus's ordeal in Gethsemane (22:39–46; see Humphrey 2007, 143–44). Peter suggests building a monument to commemorate the event: **And it happened that as they were leaving him, Peter said to Jesus, "Master, it is good for us to be here. Let us make three shelters, one for you and one for Moses and one for Elijah," not knowing what he was saying** (9:33). Peter's impulse to build three shelters is puzzling but may be understandable in light of contemporary Jewish interpretation of Ps. 43 (Basser 1998). In the midrash on Ps. 43, Moses and Elijah appear with the "chosen one" of Isa. 4:1 (identified in the Aramaic targum on Isaiah as the Messiah). In Ps. 43:3 the psalmist pleads with God: "Send out your light and your truth." The midrash replies that God has already sent Moses and Aaron (citing Ps. 105:26) and promises now to send Elijah and the "chosen one" (quoting Mal. 4:5 and Isa. 42:1, respectively). Thus, the midrashist insists, "this is the interpretation of the words of Ps. 43:3: 'Send "your Light" [i.e., Elijah] and "your Truth" [i.e., the "chosen one," the Messiah] . . . they will bring me to your holy mountain and to your tents'" (*Midr. Ps.* 43, cited by Basser 1998, 35; see the sidebar). If these later Jewish writings preserve traditions that date back to the first century (so Basser 1998, 35), then they would explain Peter's impulse to pitch tents for these three eschatological figures. If, from Luke's perspective, this eschatological preview of Jesus's divinity has occurred in the "middle of time," then it is premature and therefore inappropriate to erect three "tents of meeting" at this time—hence the judgment that Peter does not know what he is saying.

While Peter is speaking, the dream-vision continues: **Now, while he was saying these things, a cloud came and began to engulf them; and they became afraid as they entered the cloud** (9:34). The two references to the cloud combine with two references to Jesus's "glory" to suggest an allusion to the presence of God's "glory" in a pillar of cloud (Exod. 24:15–18; cf. 13:20–21). Jesus's splendor, echoing God's own glory, is striking and partially justifies Peter's response, however misguided it ultimately is.

> **Midrash on Psalm 43**
>
> "Psalm 43:2 states: 'Why do I go about mourning, under the oppression of the enemy?' [Has not God saved me in the past and does he not tell me now]—Did I not send you redemption (in Egypt), as it is said: 'Please send Moses, his servant, Aaron whom he chose' [Ps. 105:26]. Please send us another two as their counterparts, as the next verse in Psalm 43:3 says: 'Send "your Light" and "your Truth"; they will lead me.' God informed them: I will send you salvation again. And so Scripture says, 'Behold I will send you Elijah the Prophet' [Mal. 3:23]. So now one has been named. The second one is 'Yea my servant, I shall take hold of him, my chosen one [in whom I delight]' [Isa. 42:1]. This is the interpretation of the words of Ps. 43:3: 'Send "your Light" and "your Truth"; they will lead me; they will bring me to your holy mountain and to your tents.'"
> (Midr. Ps. 43, cited by Basser 1998, 35)

At this point, the dream-vision continues, now with an added auditory component: **Then there was a voice from the cloud that said, "This is my chosen Son. Listen to him." As the voice spoke, Jesus was found alone** (9:35–36a). "At the Transfiguration, God's voice confirms Jesus' Sonship as the final answer to the Christological debates in Jesus' Galilean ministry" (Lee 2009, 108). The divine voice gives the ultimate response to the question posed by Herod, "Who is this?" He is God's Chosen (cf. Isa. 42:1; on divine testimony, see comments on Luke 1:5–25; compare 3:22 and Matthew and Mark's accounts, in which Jesus is called God's "beloved Son"). The second response to this second vision is much more subdued: **They were silent, and at that time they told nothing of what they had seen to anyone** (9:36b).

The Healing of the Boy with an Unclean Spirit (9:37–43a)

9:37–43a. The next scene, Luke 9:37–43a, generally follows the Markan order (cf. Mark 9:11–29), but there are significant omissions in Luke's account in the beginning, middle, and end. At the beginning of the episode Luke omits the discussion with the disciples regarding the role of Elijah (cf. Mark 9:11–13), and at the end, the disciples' question as to why they could not cast out the demon (cf. Mark 9:28–29). The first omission unites more closely the transfiguration scene with the current passage, and the last omission contributes to the understanding of the Lukan account as a healing rather than an exorcism (see below). Together, both omissions have the effect of focusing the scene more clearly on Jesus and his authority. Luke begins: **Now, it happened on the next day that when they had come down from the mountain a large crowd met him. And a man from the crowd shouted out, saying, "Teacher, I beg you to take a look at my son, since he is my only son!"** (9:37–38). Culpepper has observed, "On the mountaintop, God affirmed his Son; now a troubled father asks for help for his only son" (1995, 208). The man pleads with Jesus: **A spirit seizes him, and he suddenly cries out. It throws him into convulsions with foaming at the mouth. It hardly ever leaves him and severely harms him!** (9:39). Many modern interpreters (see, e.g., Fitzmyer 1981–85, 1:808) see in this description a parallel to the modern description of epilepsy, under the assumption that there is a "consistent understanding of this illness, which has simply been expanded upon through our modern scientific knowledge" (Weissenrieder 2003, 267). According to ancient medicine, however, "there are two types of epilepsy. One appears to be like a deep sleep; the other racks the body with various convulsions" (Caelius Aurelianus, *Tard. pass.* 1.4.61, cited by Weissenrieder 2003, 274). The symptoms of the second kind of epilepsy included dramatic movements of the body ("He strikes out with his feet when the air in the limbs is cut off and cannot be forced outward due to the phlegm"; Corpus Hippocraticum, *M. sacr.* 7.12, cited by Weissenrieder 2003, 275n228) and foam emitted from the mouth ("The foam that is emitted from the mouth comes from the lungs"; Corpus Hippocraticum, *M. sacr.* 7.10, cited by Weissenrieder 2003, 275n225). Luke's description of the boy's condition most closely reflects this second kind of "epileptic phenomena," and this explains why Luke omits the second, longer description of the child's paralysis in Mark 9:21–27, which combines features of both types. Luke "limits himself to the features of a seizure caused by phlegm" (Weissenrieder 2003, 282), but this does not preclude seeing demonic forces at work in this illness (see below).

The father continues: **I begged your disciples to cast it out, but they were not able to** (9:40). The man reports that while Jesus and his inner circle were atop the mountain, the rest of his followers were unable to assist in his son's travail. Jesus's exasperation is indicated by the use of exclamatory "O" (BDF §146.2) and is aimed at his ineffective disciples (contra Marshall 1978, 391): **Jesus responded and said, "O faithless and crooked generation! How long must I be with you and put up with you? Bring your son here"** (9:41). While he is speaking, the child experiences another seizure: **Now, while he was still coming, the demon knocked him to the ground** (9:42a). The differentiation between the two types of epileptic phenomena now gives way to Luke's understanding of the demonic as the source of the illness. This understanding allows Luke to accentuate the authority of Jesus over the demon: **Then Jesus rebuked the unclean spirit** (9:42b). Still, it is noteworthy that Luke's description of this scene is more appropriate to a healing story than to an exorcism (which features prominently in both Mark 9:25–26 and Matt. 17:18): **Jesus healed the child and gave him back to his father** (9:42c). The scene ends on a note of amazement: **And everyone was amazed at the greatness of God** (9:43a).

Intensifying the Misunderstandings regarding Jesus's Identity and Vocation (9:43b–50)

9:43b–50. Luke transitions from these expressions of amazement to Jesus's pronouncement of his impending betrayal: **While everyone was marveling at everything he was doing, he said to his disciples, "Listen carefully to these words, for the Son of Man is about to be handed over into the hands of the people"** (9:43b–44). Jesus introduces his prediction of betrayal with an appeal for his disciples to listen carefully (lit., "You put these words into your ears!"). Despite his plea, however, the disciples do not understand: **But they were just not grasping what he had said. Indeed, it had been hidden from them so that they did not comprehend it** (9:45a). The focus of attention in the preceding scenes has been on Jesus's identity, culminating with God's exhortation, "This is my chosen Son. Listen to him." The disciples are unable to move from this divine affirmation of Jesus's identity to Jesus's own words regarding his fate to be turned over to hostile hands. Their ignorance (expressed three different ways, "not grasping," "hidden from them," "did not comprehend") is exacerbated by the fact that **they were afraid to ask him about what he had said** (9:45b).

Their response seems disconnected and inappropriate: **Now, a dispute arose among them, namely, who might be the greatest of them** (9:46). Jesus gives a powerful response to this debate about who is the greatest: **So Jesus, knowing what they were thinking, took a child and stood the child beside him. And he said to them, "Whoever welcomes this child in my name welcomes me"** (9:47–48b). Jesus takes a child and places the child "beside him" (rather than "in their midst," as Mark 9:36 and Matt. 18:2 state). Over against the disciples' efforts to achieve honor and greatness, Jesus invites them to redirect their thoughts and actions to receive the child with hospitality. The child represents both the vulnerable in society *and* Jesus himself. "If one desires to honor Jesus, and God, one will do so precisely by extending gracious hospitality—to the young child. By honoring a child, Jesus's own envoy, one honors Jesus, and in honoring Jesus one honors God" (Carroll 2008, 189). This act of hospitality toward the marginalized is yet another way that Jesus calls his followers to fulfill the demands of the "great reversal" (see comments on Luke 6:24–25; see also 1:51–53). Jesus comments further: **whoever welcomes me welcomes the one who sent me** (9:48b). Here Jesus echoes the Jewish principle of "shaliach," that is, "a man's agent is like himself" (*m. Ber.* 5.5, cited by Culpepper 1995, 211; see Marshall 1978, 397). Thus, Jesus is God's agent: whoever welcomes Jesus welcomes God. And this child beside Jesus is Jesus's agent, which completes the reversal of values: **For the one who is least among all of you, this one is truly great** (9:48c).

Again, the disciples, represented by John, respond in a way that seems disconnected from what Jesus has just said: **John responded and said, "Master, we saw someone casting out demons in your name, and we stopped him because he does not follow with us"** (9:49). Jesus reprimands them, **Do not stop such people**, and reminds them, **for the one who is not against us is for us** (9:50).

> **Luke 9:47–48 as a Mixed *Chreia***
>
> A "mixed *chreia*" consists of both an action and a saying. Aphthonius cites the following as an example: "When Diogenes saw an undisciplined youth he struck his pedagogue, saying, 'Why do you teach him such things?'" (Aphthonius, *Prog.* 23, trans. Kennedy 2003, 97). Nicolaus offers another example of a mixed *chreia*: "When a Laconian was asked where the walls of Sparta were, holding up his spear, he said, 'Here'" (Nicolaus, *Prog.* 20, trans. Kennedy 2003, 141). So too Jesus combines an action, placing a child beside him, with a saying, "Whoever welcomes this child welcomes me," to instruct the disciples regarding true greatness.

Theological Issues

Luke's world, of course, knows the importance of embodied faith, of developing Christian identity in the midst of the journey's sufferings, of bearing witness to the redemptive suffering of the Messiah wherever one goes. For Luke, places can be pivotal in shaping identity. In Ferrol Sams's *When All the World Was Young*, a novel set during World War II, Sams's protagonist, Porter Osborne Jr., is a native of Georgia and is affectionately known as "Sambo." He is stationed for boot camp at Camp Grant near Chicago and is away from his beloved South for the first time in his life. When he finds himself in the lobby of a Chicago hotel named for a Yankee general (Sherman), it is more than his Southern heart can take:

> Perching on the edge of an easy chair, he [Porter] removed one of his shoes, tapped it deliberately against his palm, and deposited a small mound of red dirt on an ivory-colored portion of the plush and patterned carpet. Replacing his shoe, he carefully twisted his foot and ground the Brewton County soil into the fabric, noting with satisfaction the resultant smudge. The Army could force him to go to Camp Grant, but if he of his own free will was going to roam Sheridan and Stanton Avenues and compromise his heritage by chatting in the Hotel Sherman, then he would leave a mark of defiance. He knew from multiple wash days on the farm how difficult it would be to remove that mark. (Sams 1991, 197)

Porter's identity is profoundly shaped by a place, and that place goes with him literally everywhere he goes. Luke would have affirmed the sense of place that Porter feels. But in Luke's world, place can only be a starting point, for no place is perfect, and certainly in this particular case of the South, the flaws need not be rehearsed in detail: "Yet the Most High certainly does not live in something made by human hands" (Acts 7:48).

Within Luke's world, we find another such "earthy" image. It is the reference to the disciples' shaking the dust from their feet. The phrase occurs three times in Luke and Acts. Most of us, because of our reading of the last two references, would view this sign as basically negative, as a sign of judgment, and in Luke 10 and Acts 13, the connotations are indeed quite negative. But the first use of the metaphor, in Luke 9, is wonderfully polyvalent. The NRSV understands the shaking of the dust negatively, as "a testimony against them" (9:5). Several commentators, pointing to parallel constructions (Acts 14:3 and 2 Thess. 1:10), offer a more neutral translation, as is done here, as "a testimony to them." To be sure, on the one hand, if the recipients of the sign continue to reject, then the witness will have a negative effect. But, on the other hand, the witness could have a positive impact. This gesture of testimony is much like the child Jesus, who, in Simeon's prophecy, "is destined for the fall and rise of many" (Luke 2:34). They are marking the territory, leaving traces of the gospel as unnoticeable as the dust on our feet, and as permanent as that same good earth—Sambo, after all, was right—dirt, whether the rich red clay of Georgia or the sandy soil of the Middle East or the limestone-laden field dirt of central Texas. It is an earthy image, but could we expect anything else from Luke?

This is the essence of Luke's symbolic world. Those of us who dare allow ourselves to be oriented by it will find that we are profoundly shaped by where we are and where we have been, but we are not enslaved to those places. And, for those of us who are followers of Jesus, we have the opportunity—the vocation—to deposit the collective witness of all those persons and places who have shaped our own identity in those places that desperately need to receive it—so that the dust may lie as a witness to them, waiting for the sweet breath of God to quicken it once more.

PART 3

Luke 9:51–14:35

*Jesus's Mighty Words and Deeds
along the Way (Part 1)*

The central section of Luke's Gospel, 9:51–19:44, is set within the framework of a journey narrative. But the way of Jesus is expressive not just of his physical arrival in Jerusalem or of his progress toward his passion. At the outset, the journey is described as Jesus's *analēmpsis*, literally his "taking up" (9:51). This "taking up" refers to the entire complex of events that forms Jesus's transit to the Father: his passion, death, burial, resurrection, and ascension/exaltation. Jesus's journeying along the way is also depicted in Luke as an "exodus." In the transfiguration scene in Luke 9:28–36, only Luke among the Synoptic Gospels reports that Jesus, Moses, and Elijah were speaking of Jesus's "departure," or "exodus" (*exodos*), "which he was about to fulfill in Jerusalem" (9:31). So the journey to Jerusalem is a new exodus, by which Jesus forges a redemptive path to the glory of the Father. The way of Jesus becomes paradigmatic for Jesus's followers: "The didactic material given in the context of a journey fits Luke's conception of the life of faith as a pilgrimage, always on the move" (Talbert 1982, 113).

The focus in this part of Jesus's *bios* is on his words and not so much his deeds. Much of this didactic material in the Lukan journey narrative is in the form of parables: twenty-five or so parables are found within Luke 9–19. Three themes are highlighted in the travel parables. First is the issue of life eternal. Luke apparently inherited a parable collection in which the parable of the good Samaritan held first place. The first parable retains that position in its placement in the final form of Luke (cf. Parsons 2007, 112–23). In this first parable of the travel narrative, Jesus's interlocutor, a lawyer, asks, "Teacher, what must I do to inherit eternal life?" (10:25). Near the end of the travel narrative, a rich ruler asks the very same question (18:18). Jesus responds in ways appropriate to the specific context, but in neither case, that of the rich man in Luke 18 (contrary to Mark) or the lawyer in Luke 10, does Luke record their response. The open-endedness of these two stories means the potential for repentance—for transformation, for life eternal—is still held out as a possibility.

> **Luke 9:51–14:35 in Context**
>
> Jesus's origins and training (1:1–4:13)
>
> Jesus's mighty words and deeds in Galilee (4:14–9:50)
>
> ▶ Jesus's mighty words and deeds along the way (part 1) (9:51–14:35)
>
>   Beginning the journey (Luke 9:51–11:13)
>
>   Jesus in dialogue (11:14–13:9)
>
>   More healings and parables (13:10–14:35)
>
> Jesus's mighty words and deeds along the way (part 2) (15:1–19:44)
>
> Jesus in Jerusalem: teachings, death, and resurrection (19:45–24:53)

Second, there is the theme of reversal. In addition to this bookend question ("What must I do . . . ?"), the travel narrative is also linked from the center to the end. The most significant element of the ring composition of the pre-Lukan parables collection is its center. Luke 14:7–11, the parable of the choice at the table, retains its place of prominence in canonical Luke by its location at the heart of the parables in the travel narrative (12 parables come before it, 12 after it). This parable contains the saying "Because all who exalt themselves will be humbled, and all who humble themselves will be exalted" (14:11). This statement is repeated verbatim in Luke near the end of the travel narrative in the parable of the Pharisee and the tax collector (18:14), which was the last parable in the pre-Lukan parable collection. This theme of reversal is the overarching theme of the Lukan travel narrative. Jesus's journey is filled with unexpected twists and turns. Along the way, outsiders can become insiders, and insiders can become outsiders. Along the way, the exalted can be humbled, and the humble exalted. Indeed, this theme of reversal is an important overall motif in the Gospel of Luke (see, e.g., 1:53–55; 6:20–26; 7:34; 9:24; 24:46). It is a point that would have been well understood by a first-century Mediterranean audience, for whom stories of the reversals of fortune were commonplace (e.g., Plutarch, *Cons. Apoll.* 116–17; see York 1991, 164–81). The Lukan Jesus, of course, credits God, not Tyche/Fortuna, with this power to effect reversals in human affairs, but the authorial audience would have been familiar with this emphasis.

Third, the parables are not focused entirely on the human situation of seeking and finding redemption or reversal; many of these parables have a theocentric emphasis, focusing squarely on the character of God. Indeed, much of Jesus's teaching in the travel narrative may be viewed as theodicy, defending the nature and character of God in the face of human and natural evil (esp. Luke 13 and 18). For convenience's sake, the commentary on the journey narrative has been divided into two parts: "Jesus's Mighty Words and Deeds along the Way (Part 1)": 9:51–14:35; and "Jesus's Mighty Words and Deeds along the Way (Part 2)": 15:1–19:44. This will allow for part 1 (9:51–14:35) to climax with a focus on the central section of the journey narrative (chap. 14) and for the second part (15:1–19:44) to take up the justly famous and distinctively Lukan parables of the lost sheep, lost coin, lost sons (and loving father), unjust steward, rich man and Lazarus, unjust judge, and the Pharisee and tax collector. Part 1 consists of three units: 9:51–11:13; 11:14–13:9; and 13:10–14:35.

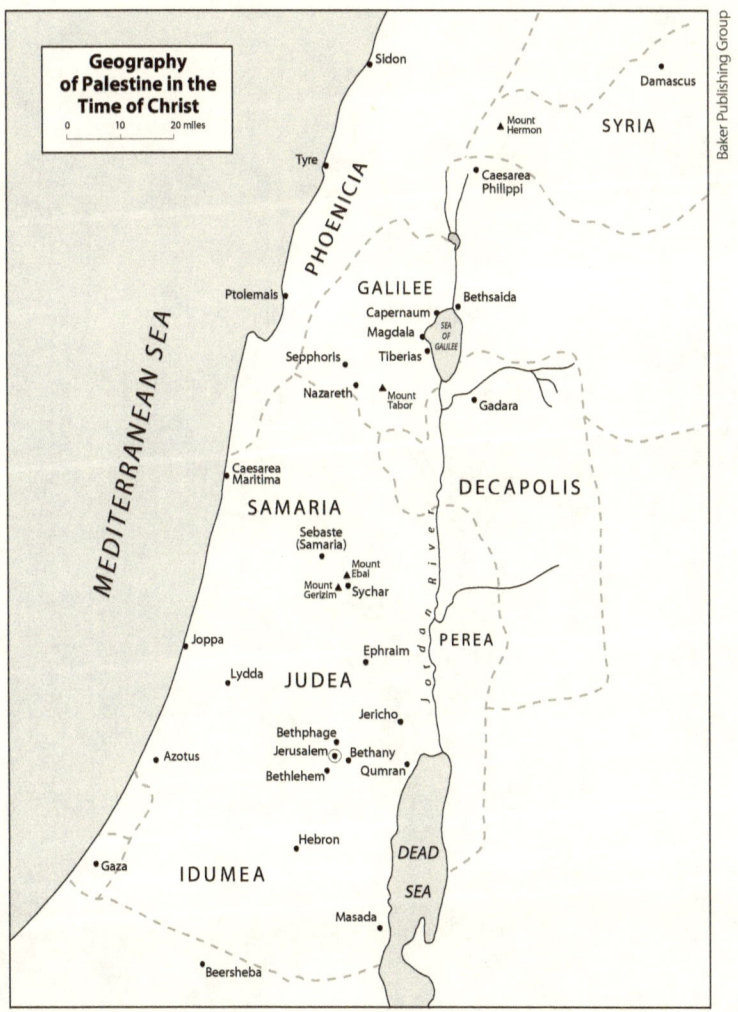

Figure 15. Galilee and Judea in the Time of Jesus

Luke 9:51–11:13

Beginning the Journey

Introductory Matters

The first unit of the travel narrative, 9:51–11:13 consists of three scenes: the demands of the journey (9:51–62), the mission of the seventy(-two) and its aftermath (10:1–24), and loving God and loving neighbor (10:25–11:13).

Tracing the Narrative Flow

The Demands of the Journey (9:51–62)

9:51–62. The travel narrative begins with a notice of Jesus's resolve to go to Jerusalem and his inhospitable reception by a Samaritan village. Luke sets the stage: **Now it happened that as the time was drawing near for him to be taken up, he firmly resolved to go to Jerusalem** (9:51). The notice that "the time was drawing near" (lit., "as the days were being fulfilled") elsewhere in Luke/Acts suggests a fulfillment of prophecy (e.g., the phrase in Acts 2:1 indicating that Pentecost is fulfilling Jesus's prediction in Luke 24:49) and sets the journey within the divine plan (Green 1997, 403). But what is drawing near? Luke indicates that it is the time for Jesus "to be taken up" (*analēmpseōs*). Certainly this term parallels the discussion of Jesus's departure (*exodos*), which Jesus, Moses, and Elijah discussed at the transfiguration (9:31). The departure encompasses the events, including his passion, leading to his final departure from the disciples. Jesus is "firmly resolved to go to Jerusalem," where these events will be fulfilled. The Greek is literally "he set his face" (*autos to prosōpon estērisen*), which reflects a Hebraism (cf. Ezek. 21:2; C. A. Evans 1987) that suggests a "fixedness of

> **Luke 9:51–11:13 in the Narrative Flow**
>
> Jesus's origins and training (1:1–4:13)
>
> Jesus's mighty words and deeds in Galilee (4:14–9:50)
>
> Jesus's mighty words and deeds along the way (part 1) (9:51–14:35)
>
> ▶ Beginning the journey (9:51–11:13)
>
>   The demands of the journey (9:51–62)
>
>   The mission of the seventy(-two) and its aftermath (10:1–24)
>
>   Loving God and loving neighbor (10:25–11:13)
>
>   The parable of the good Samaritan (10:25–37)
>
>   Mary and Martha (10:38–42)
>
>   The Lord's Prayer (11:1–4)
>
>   The parable of the friend at midnight (11:5–13)

purpose" (Plummer 1903, 263; cited by D. Garland 2011, 413).

The journey to Jerusalem has a less than auspicious beginning. Luke narrates: **He sent messengers ahead of him, and they went and entered a Samaritan village to prepare for him. But the people there did not welcome him, because he was set on going to Jerusalem** (9:52–53). Given the animosity between Jews and Samaritans, it is not surprising that the Samaritans refuse to show hospitality to the traveling prophet, Jesus, and his followers (Arterbury 2005, 141–42). The disciples James and John offer an immediate remedy that they believe has scriptural warrant: **Lord, do you want us to tell fire to come down from heaven and wipe them out?** (9:53b). They are perhaps echoing Elijah's summoning heavenly fire to consume some soldiers (2 Kings 1:9–12), as surmised by some scribes who added "as Elijah did" at the end of verse 54 (A C D W; sans $\mathfrak{P}^{75}$). Jesus's response is no less decisive: **But he turned and rebuked them. Then they went to another village** (9:55–56; for a similar rebuke of a disciple's violence [both proposed and actual], see *Acts Phil.* 26–27). Jesus's rebuke of the disciples' proposed violence resonates with other Second Temple Jewish texts, which likewise offer critiques of those passages that depict prophets and even Abraham as calling for the destruction of "sinners" (see, e.g., *T. Ab.* 10; other texts cited by Allison 2002). The judgment on the disciples' prejudice against these Samaritans will come into sharper focus very soon when Jesus tells the parable of a "good" Samaritan, who is held up as the model of hospitality and philanthropy (see Luke 10:25–37; also 17:11–19).

What follows is a series of three *chreiae*. Recall that a *chreia* is "a brief saying or action making a point, attributed to some specified person" (Theon, *Prog.* 96, trans. Kennedy 2003, 15). These are "apocritic *chreiae*" (see Theon, *Prog.* 98), which are embedded *chreiae* spoken in response to another's statement. The first two *chreiae* are familiar to the authorial audience, which would recognize them from other versions (Matt 8:18–22/Q 9:57–60):

> As they were going along the road, someone said to him, "I will follow you wherever you go!" And Jesus said to him, "Foxes have dens, and birds of the

sky have nests, but the Son of Man does not have a place where he can lay his head." Then he said to another, "Follow me." But he replied, "[Lord,] first allow me to go bury my father." Then he said to him, "Let the dead bury their own dead; but you, when you have left, proclaim the kingdom of God." (9:57–60)

In Luke's version, by eliminating the reference to Jesus as "Teacher" (Matt. 8:19), the statements that elicit the *chreia* begin with a form of *akoloutheō* ("I will follow"; "follow me"), which introduces the theme of discipleship. To follow Jesus, the "Son of Man," who—unlike "foxes" and "birds of the sky"—has no place to lay his head, is to embark on a journey that may involve alienation; indeed, it already has in the preceding rejection by a Samaritan village (9:51–56). Further, the call to follow Jesus on the journey of "proclaiming the kingdom of God" is a call to radical commitment, whether the dead who are left to bury the dead are understood literally as referring to those who deal with corpses (e.g., grave diggers) or metaphorically as referring to those who are spiritually dead and who refuse to take up this challenge (see Bockmuehl 1998, 557). In this regard, the call to follow Jesus is a call to participate in a prophetic drama that, like Jeremiah's or Ezekiel's refusal to mourn the dead, underscores the crisis at hand (Jer. 16:5–9; Ezek. 24:16–24; cited by Bockmuehl 1998, 564).

The third statement, a responsive *chreia*, is unique to Luke. Notice first that this third would-be disciple combines elements from the first two: **I will**

Figure 16. Typical Roman Road

follow you (cf. v. 57) **Lord, but first allow me** (cf. v. 59) **to say good-bye to those in my household** (9:61). Missing in this excuse is any sense of urgency ("I will follow you wherever you go!"; "first allow me to go bury my father"); rather, the request is simply to return home to say good-bye to family (as Elisha did; see 1 Kings 19:19–21). Jesus's response functions to provide a rationale for why the would-be disciple must leave the dead and cannot return to his family: **But Jesus said to him, "Nobody who has put his or her hand to the plow and looks back is fit for the kingdom of God"** (9:62). Luke has elaborated the *chreiae* "let the dead bury the dead" and "(you) preach the kingdom" into the form of an enthymeme (a syllogism with a missing premise; see Theon, *Prog.* 99) by adding one of the missing premises. The logic of the Lukan Jesus can be reconstructed as follows (slightly modified from Mack and Robbins 1989, 80):

> First premise: No one who puts his or her hand to the plow and looks back is fit for the kingdom of God.
> (Missing) second premise: You wish to be fit for the kingdom of God.
> Conclusion: Therefore, leave the dead to bury the dead, and go, proclaim the kingdom of God.

Furthermore, the new *chreia* is a gnomic saying in form (Theon, *Prog.* 99), that is, it attributes to Jesus a saying that would have been rather well-known in the ancient Mediterranean world. For example, in Hesiod's *Works and Days*, a plowman is described as one "who attends to his work and drives a straight furrow and no longer gapes after his comrades, but keeps his mind on his work" (1.443, cited by Mack and Robbins 1989, 80; see also Pliny the Elder, *Nat.* 18.19.49). In other words, to look back from the plow (whether to family living or dead) was to risk cutting a crooked or shallow furrow and thus ruining the work altogether. There is no place for looking back or even trying to look in two directions at once (being "two-faced"); rather, would-be disciples must be single-minded in purpose, setting their faces, like Jesus, on the task at hand.

The Mission of the Seventy(-Two) and Its Aftermath (10:1–24)

The audience of Luke 10:1–24 will hear both intra- and intertextual echoes. Within Luke, the passage is tied closely to what immediately precedes (9:57–62), parallels the mission of the Twelve (9:1–5; cf. 22:35), recalls the ministry of John the Baptist (7:28), and foreshadows the gentile mission (24:47). Various aspects of the passage also have close parallels with Synoptic and other traditions (Matt 9:37–38; 10:7–16/Q 10:2–12; John 4:35; *Gos. Thom.* 14b, 73). Reference will be made to these various intertexts in the interpretation that follows.

10:1–12. The introductory phrase, **After these things** (10:1a), ties this episode to what immediately precedes, and thus the passage functions as an application of the conditions for discipleship set out in 9:57–62. The mission of the seventy(-two) also repeats on a grander scale the mission of the Twelve in 9:1–6. In Luke 9:1 Jesus "called the Twelve together (*synkalesamenos*); in this scene **the Lord publicly commissioned [*anedeixen*] seventy[-two] others** (10:1b; on the textual issue of whether the number is 70 or 72, see Omanson 2006, 127–28). Why the difference? The term occurs elsewhere in Luke only in its cognate noun form (*anadeixis*) at 1:80 and indicates the "public recognition of an appointed official" (BDAG 62). The reference there anticipates the public presentation of John the Baptist to Israel as he begins his ministry. Like John the Baptist, who was sent "before the face" (*pro prosōpou*) of Jesus (7:27), so Jesus **sent them before him [*pro prosōpou*] in groups of two to every city and place where he himself was about to go** (10:1c). Thus, the seventy(-two) are "publicly commissioned" to continue the forerunner role of John the Baptist (cf. 16:16). They go out "in groups of two," which anticipates the missionary pattern of Acts (Peter/John, 8:14; Barnabas/Saul, 13:2; Barnabas/Mark, 15:39; Paul/Silas, 15:40; Priscilla/Aquila, 18:2).

There are hints also in the text and its context that the mission of the seventy(-two) not only continues the forerunner ministry of John the Baptist but also is expanded to anticipate the mission to the gentiles (see Luke 24:47). First, there is the reference to the seventy(-two) who are commissioned. Regardless of whether the number is "seventy" or "seventy-two," Luke seems to be alluding to the (gentile) Table of Nations traditions in Genesis 10. Thus the commissioning of the seventy(-two) "foreshadows the mission of the church to the nations" (Culpepper 1995, 219). Second, this reading gains further traction when we note that the reference in Matthew that limits the mission to Israel ("Go nowhere among the Gentiles, . . . but go rather to the lost sheep of the house of Israel"; 10:5–6) is missing in the parallel passage in Luke (Talbert 2002, 122).

Luke explains the rationale for the mission: **He had been saying to them, "The harvest is plentiful, but the workers are few"** (10:2a). The first part of the statement is a *chreia* that occurs elsewhere in various forms (see John 4:35; *Gos. Thom.* 73); references to the "harvest" in the Jewish Scriptures allude both to eschatological judgment (Joel 3:13; Mic. 4:11–13) and to preservation (Hosea 6:11). Both aspects are present (cf. 10:7–8), though the emphasis here is on the ingathering of God's people and the lack of workers to assist in this task (Bock 1994–96, 2:995). The disciples, then, are to ask ("beseech"; "pray") **the Lord of the harvest to send out workers into his harvest** (10:2b). The "Lord of the harvest" clearly refers to God, but in the immediate and larger contexts in which Jesus is also referred to as *kyrios* (here at 10:2 and, e.g., 7:13, 19; 10:39, 41), the audience will conclude that

Jesus, who sends out the seventy(-two), is also "Lord of the harvest" (Rowe 2006, 134; D. Garland 2011, 425).

Jesus then instructs them regarding the danger of their assignment: **Go! I am sending you like lambs surrounded by wolves** (10:3). To the ancients, "the wolf is a rapacious animal, irascible, deceitful, bold, violent" and "men of this type are crafty, impious, blood-thirsty, quick to anger, vicious to the extent that they refuse what is given or offered them, but steal what is not given" (*Anon. Lat.* 126, trans. André 1981, 136–37; see also Polemo, *Phys.* 172; Arrian, *Epict. diss.* 1.3.7). Of course, the imagery of lambs and wolves also echoes Isaiah ("the wolf will lie down with the lamb"; 11:6; 65:25; cf. *Tanḥuma Toledot* 5; Str-B 1:574; cited by Bock 1994–96, 2:996), though that eschatological vision seems not quite fulfilled in Jesus's warnings (cf. *2 Clem.* 5.2–4). The authorial audience would know that the dangers inherent in the mission include the very ones to whom the disciples are being sent.

Rather than equipping the disciples for "Holy War" against infidels, Jesus "de-equips" them of the requisite travel paraphernalia: **Do not carry a wallet, a travel bag, or sandals; and greet no one along the way** (10:4; cf. 9:3). The absence of standard traveling equipment indicates the total dependence of the disciples on the Sender (Danker 1988, 214). The instruction to "greet no one along the way" is a time-saving measure and underscores the urgency of the mission (many commentators remark about the "time-consuming" nature of "oriental greetings," which might involve hugs, kisses, and the exchange of news; see Bock 1994–96, 2:997; Marshall 1978, 418). The message echoes 9:57–62: be single-minded in purpose, and do not be distracted.

Jesus gives further instruction regarding the disciples' behavior when entering a house: **Into whatever house you enter, first say, "Peace to this house!" And if peaceful people happen to be there, your peace will remain on them. If that is not the case, it will return to you** (10:5–6). The command to greet householders with "peace" is not only adopting common Jewish practice (Judg. 6:23; 19:20), but it characterizes the message of Jesus's good news (Acts 10:36), fulfills the promise expressed in the infancy narrative (Luke 1:79; 2:14, 29), anticipates the greeting issued by the resurrected Christ to the disciples (Luke 24:36), and thus expresses a robust eschatological hope (Bosold 1978, 84–85). The pronouncement of peace will find fulfillment if within the house there is a "peaceful person" (lit., a "son of peace"). While this specific phrase is not found elsewhere, it was an "idiom that felt at home in both Hebrew and Greek" (Danker 1960–61, 94). In both cases, to be a "son" (or child) of X is to be characterized by or inclined toward that attribute. Thus, Absalom's command to his servants to "be sons of power" (*hyioi dynameōs*) is equivalent to being a person who is strong or valiant (2 Sam. 13:28 LXX). Similar expressions are found in Greek literature and inscriptions (e.g., "son of fortune" = lucky; see also examples cited by MM

649; Danker 1960–61, 94). Analagous constructions are also found elsewhere in Luke (16:8; 20:36) and in the NT (Matt. 23:15; John 17:12; Eph. 2:3; see Bock 1994–96, 2:998). What does the idiom mean here? Jesus, "when he asked his disciples to go out to gather the sons of peace, was sending them out to identify with those in Galilee who were bent on pursuing peace" (Klassen 1981, 487). With such as these, peace will reside. If there is no one worthy of peace (as Matt. 10:13 puts it), Jesus warns, the peace will return to the sender.

Jesus gives further instructions: **Stay in that same house, eating and drinking what they provide; for the worker is worthy of a wage. Do not move from house to house. And whatever city you enter and they welcome you, eat what is placed before you** (10:7–8). The social context is hospitality. The command to eat and drink what is provided is standard etiquette for a guest in a hospitality context (see *T. Ab.* 4.7, 10; Arterbury 2005, 143); such activity is an act of table fellowship and "seals the acceptance of the gospel by the household" (Marshall 1978, 421). Furthermore, Jesus's followers are not to beg for money (as Cynics and others did); their wage is hospitality and shelter. Nor are they to move from house to house, becoming a "parasite at large with no fixed stable" (Horace, *Ep.* 1.15.28; cf. Sir. 29:23–24; cited by D. Garland 2011, 427). Beyond guest etiquette required in hospitality, the second reference to "eat what is placed before you" may allude also to setting aside strict food laws for the sake of sharing the good news, especially if the mission of the seventy(-two) is intended to foreshadow the mission to the gentiles (cf. Acts 10–11; Gal. 2). Furthermore, when the followers find a hospitable reception, they are to **heal those who are sick there, and say to them, "The kingdom of God has come near to you"** (10:9). Emulating Jesus, his followers are to respond to these acts of hospitality in deed (heal the sick) and word (preach the kingdom).

Jesus also prepares the seventy(-two) for times when the response to them is one of rejection rather than reception: **And whatever city you enter and they do not welcome you, go out into its streets and say, "Even the dust that stuck to us from your city on our feet we shake off against you. But know this: The kingdom of God has come near." I tell you, in those days it will be more tolerable for Sodom than for that city** (10:10–12). Jesus has replaced the knee-jerk vigilante vengeance of James and John (9:54) with a powerful, prophetic gesture (Danker 1988, 215). The shaking of the dust from their feet is an appropriate symbolic act toward those who have not acted hospitably, for if they had been proper hosts (who washed the feet of their guests), there would be no dust to shake (see Arterbury 2005, 143). Regardless of their response, the kingdom has still come near, and the eschatological judgment against them will potentially be more severe than that experienced by Sodom, whose wickedness was proverbial (Gen. 13:13; Isa. 3:9; Ezek. 16:48, 56, Jer. 23:14) and whose great sin was inhospitality

(Gen. 19:1–23; Jude 7; 2 Pet. 2:6; Rom. 9:29; see Johnson 1991, 168). Reference to Sodom also provides a transition to the second part of Jesus's discourse (10:13–24).

10:13–16. The reference to Sodom moves Jesus to engage in "an aside or soliloquy" (10:13–16) that is not "an integral part of the instructions to the disciples" (Fitzmyer 1981–85, 2:850) but rather is "heavily rhetorical and comparative" (Bock 1994–96, 2:1003). The section is composed of two parts, a three-membered structure and a two-membered structure. The three-membered unit consists of a woe + the basis for judgment + the consequences of the judgment (Nolland 1989–93, 2:549). Jesus begins his litany with repeated woes: **Woe to you, Chorazin; woe to you, Bethsaida!** (10:13a). The repeti-

Figure 17. Ruins of Chorazin

tion of "woe" reflects the rhetorical device of *anaphora* (in which a number of clauses begin with the same word; Quintilian, *Inst.* 9.3.30; see also *Rhet. Her.* 4.13.19). The interjection "woe" does not represent a curse but rather introduces "an expression of pity for those who stand under divine judgment" (Marshall 1978, 255). Why are Chorazin and Bethsaida the objects of Jesus's pity? Jesus gives the basis for his judgment in the form of a second-class, contrary-to-fact condition (presuming that the event, e.g., miracles, did not occur in Tyre and Sidon): **Because if the miracles that happened in you had occurred in Tyre and Sidon, they would have repented long ago, sitting in sackcloth and ashes** (10:13b). Bethsaida, of course, is in the vicinity of Jesus's healings and the feeding of the five thousand (9:10–17). Apart from the parallel passage in Matt. 11:21, Chorazin is unattested elsewhere in the OT or NT; presumably it was also located in the Galilee region, though efforts to locate it definitely have failed (see fig. 17; see Fitzmyer 1981–85, 2:853). Linked with Bethsaida, the mention of Chorazin provides symmetry with the traditional pairing of Tyre and Sidon. Those paired Phoenician cities were well-known for their reputations of sinfulness and oppression in the Jewish Scriptures (Isa. 23; Jer. 25:22; Joel 3:4–8; Amos 1:9–10) and for their enmity with the Jews (see Zech. 9:3; Josephus, *Ag. Ap.* 1.70). Nevertheless, in the third component of the woe, Jesus employs *synkrisis* (comparison) in the form of a double invective (see Aphthonius, *Prog.* 31R) to show that the severity of the judgment against Bethsaida and Chorazin will be worse than for the notorious cities of Tyre and Sidon: **It will, in fact, be more tolerable for Tyre and Sidon at the judgment than for you** (10:14).

The second part of the soliloquy has two parts, a question (expecting a negative answer) followed by a prediction of the opposite (Nolland 1989–93, 2:549): **And you, Capernaum, will you really be elevated to heaven? No! You will go down to Hades!** (10:15). In Luke's narrative, Capernaum is also the site of Jesus's wondrous deeds (4:23, 31–37; 7:1–10) yet evidently has fared no better than the other two cities in terms of its response to Jesus. "Hades" (cf. 16:23) is the Greek place of the dead and the equivalent of the Hebrew "Sheol" (cf. LXX Gen. 37:35; Ps. 6:5; cited by Johnson 1991, 168). The language is reminiscent of Isaiah, in which the haughty Babylonian king says, "I will ascend to heaven" (Isa. 14:13), to which Yahweh responds, "But you are brought down to Sheol, to the depths of the Pit" (Isa. 14:15 RSV). Jesus ends the section with a pronouncement, by returning to the mission of the seventy(-two). The first part of the pronouncement clarifies that this harsh denunciation of the Galilean cities of Chorazin, Bethsaida, and Capernaum contains hidden within it a subtle invitation to the gentiles, especially if we take seriously Jesus's earlier judgment that had Tyre and Sidon been afforded the same opportunity of witnessing Jesus's miracle-working ministry, they would have repented: **The one who listens to you, listens to me** (10:16a). The second part of the pronouncement, however, focuses on the emphasis on rejection and judgment that holds a central place in this invective: **the one who rejects you, rejects me. Moreover, the one who rejects me rejects the one who sent me** (10:16b). Taken together, the saying returns to the topic of the mission of the seventy(-two) and clarifies that to reject the disciples is to reject Jesus and, ultimately, even God who sent him.

10:17–24. The next unit (10:17–24) is woven around another apocritic *chreia* (see Theon, *Prog.* 98; see above), in which Jesus responds to a statement by his disciples (10:17) with the report of a vision in the form of a *chreia*—an "elaborated *chreia*," which preserves a memorable, if mysterious, saying of Jesus (10:18). The *chreia* is elaborated to illuminate its meaning along the lines laid out in the *Progymnasmata* (brief praise, anecdote, rationale, contrast, comparison, example, citation of authority, conclusion; see Ps.-Hermogenes, *Prog.* 7–8; Aphthonius, *Prog.* 8), although there is no reason to expect that in practice such elaboration would follow the form and content strictly. The elaborated *chreia* in Luke contains the following elements:

Introduction ("Lord")	10:17
Chreia ("I watched Satan falling")	10:18
Rationale ("I have given you the authority")	10:19
Opposite ("However, do not rejoice")	10:20
Example ("He was overjoyed in the Holy Spirit")	10:21
Authority ("Everything has been given")	10:22
Conclusion ("Blessed are the eyes")	10:23–24

Note: Modified from Humphrey 2007, 105.

The first section (10:17–20) has no parallels in the Synoptic tradition (though see Mark 16:18; Luke 10:19). The unit begins with the disciples' return. Their joy recalls the joy associated with God's anticipated action in the annunciation (Luke 1:14; 2:10) and foreshadows the disciples' joy following the resurrection (24:52; see Culpepper 1995, 223): **The seventy[-two] returned with joy, saying, "Lord, even the demons are subject to us in your name"** (10:17). Although the introduction is missing any *explicit* praise of Jesus (typical of an elaborated *chreia*), it does include *implicit* encomiastic language: Jesus is referred to as "Lord," strengthening the identification of Jesus (with God) as "Lord of the harvest" (10:2), and the power of Jesus's name is acknowledged (10:17b; cf. Acts 3:6; 4:10, 17–18, 30; 5:40; 9:27). The commission of the seventy(-two) contains no explicit command to perform exorcisms (10:1–2), but the authorial audience could easily accommodate the subjection of demons under the general command to heal as part of the proclamation of the kingdom of God (cf. 9:1; 4:40–41).

Jesus responds with a verbal *chreia*: **Then he said to them, "I watched Satan falling from heaven like lightning"** (10:18). The nature of the *chreia* is much debated (for much of what follows, see Gathercole 2003, 145–58). Some take it as a metaphorical description, that is, a "symbolic way of summing up the effects of the disciples' mission" (Fitzmyer 1981–85, 2:860; see also Marshall 1978, 429). Others see it as a "prophetic vision" but disagree on the timing and the content of the vision. Some view it as a vision of the primeval fall of Satan (see *L.A.E.* 11–14; *2 En.* 29.3–6) witnessed by the preexistent Christ (a view common among patristic writers [e.g., Jerome, *Comm. Isa.* 73] and followed by some commentators [e.g., G. Kittel, *TDNT* 4:130n220]). Others see it as a vision of Satan's fall witnessed by Jesus at some point in his earthly ministry (whether temptation [Geldenhuys 1951] or baptism [J. Marcus 1995]). Still others see Satan's fall as an event associated with the mission of the seventy(-two) (Danker 1988, 217; Bock 1994–96, 2:1007). Most likely, Jesus is reporting a vision of the eschatological future (such as one finds in Amos 8:1–3; Jer. 1:13–19; Ezek. 2:9–10; see Nolland 1989–93, 2:454) that has been foreshadowed by the mission of the seventy(-two). In the OT, Satan plays the role of God's (and humanity's) adversary in the heavenly council (Job 1:6–12; 2:1–7; Zech 3:1–2), and the fall of Satan reflects the apocalyptic texts of Second Temple Judaism (*Sib. Or.* 3.796–807; 11QMelch 12–13; *1 En.* 83.4) and early Christianity (John 12:27–33; Col. 2:15; Rev. 12:7–10; 20:3–10; Rom. 16:20) in which Satan and the powers of darkness are defeated by God in an end-time cosmic battle (Garrett 1989, 51–53). Quite possibly the Lukan Jesus saw in the fall of the Babylonian king (Isa. 14:11–15 and allusion in Luke 10:15) a connection to the fall of Satan: the fall of earthly powers and principalities foreshadows the downfall of Satan and his minions (cf. Acts 12). In his vision, Jesus's mission is tied to God's "coming triumph over the rule of Satan" (Nolland 1989–93, 2:564).

The *chreia* is followed by its rationale: the mission of the seventy(-two) is a harbinger of the cosmic battle between God and Satan, not because of the disciples' own power, but because Christ has empowered them: **I have given you the authority to walk on snakes and scorpions, and over all the power of the Enemy** (10:19a). Through Christ the disciples have the authority to tread on "snakes and scorpions," which are well-known symbols for the sources of evil (Gen. 3:14; Num. 21:6–9; Sir. 21:2; Pss. 58:4; 140:3). The two are paired in Deut. 8:15 as a vivid reminder of the dangerous wasteland through which God led his people (see also Luke 11:11–12). The reference to "walk on" may echo Ps. 90:13 LXX: "you shall tread on the asp" (author's trans.); the identification of the combination of the snake and scorpion as a symbol of evil gains further traction in the *Testament of Levi*'s rewriting of the same Psalm: "And Beliar shall be bound by him [God] and he [God] shall give *power to his children to tread upon the evil spirits*" (*T. Levi* 18.12, APOT 2:315, my emphasis). That the downfall of Satan is anticipated by, but not ultimately fulfilled in, the mission of the seventy(-two) is underscored by the use of the future tense at the end of the rationale: **and nothing will by any means harm you!** (10:19b). Through the complex of events that leads to Jesus's exaltation in Luke, Satan will be defeated decisively. In some Christian apocalyptic texts, however, Satan's fall may also hint at some temporary period in which he wreaks havoc (Rev. 12:7–12; among Jewish texts, see possibly *T. Sol.* 20.17). Jesus also hints at this eschatological havoc in Luke 21:12–27 and reassures his followers that "not even a hair on your head will be destroyed" (21:18; see Gathercole 2003, 159). Jesus's words here also provide assurance that this victory over Satan will happen—indeed, has already begun to happen—and the reference to Satan's fall (Luke 10:18) anticipates an event destined to occur when Jesus is raised to God's right hand.

The elaboration of the *chreia* continues with a statement of contrast intended to clarify what the disciples should rejoice over (and what they should not): **However, do not rejoice in this, that the spirits are subject to you, but rejoice that your names have been written in heaven** (10:20). It is clear from what precedes that the disciples have no reason to rejoice over how the spirits are subject to them, since their dominion over the spirits is due exclusively to the authority of the Lord, who has sent them. Rather, they should rejoice because their names have been written in the "heavenly registry" (Fitzmyer 1981–85, 2:860; see also Nolland 1989–93, 2:566). In the face of impending eschatological woes, they should take consolation that the source of their joy is their status in heaven, which they owe to God, and not their success over the spirits (D. Garland 2011, 429).

Next in the elaborated *chreia*, the Lukan Jesus provides an example of how and why the disciples should rejoice: **At that very time he was overjoyed in the Holy Spirit and said, "I acknowledge to you, Father, Lord of heaven and earth, that you concealed these things from the wise and intelligent and revealed them to little children"** (10:21a). Jesus is "overjoyed" in the Spirit and offers a prayer of thanksgiving to God, who is "Father" and "Lord of heaven and earth," who has chosen, in his sovereignty, to reveal "these things" (Satan's fall and the ultimate protection of God's people) not to the wise and intelligent but to "little children" (*nēpiois*; lit., "babies"; cf. Matt. 21:16). Clearly, the disciples' source of joy is not in their own abilities and power to perform miracles but in the fact that they, as "babes," are the beneficiaries of God's revelation to them (cf. LXX Pss. 18:8; 114:6; 118:13). The disciples and Jesus are not the only ones who rejoice that this insight into God's sovereign character has been revealed to them: **Yes, Father, because doing it this way was pleasing to you** (10:21b).

In a further elaboration, Jesus turns from praising God as Father and Lord to discussing his own authority and the source of it: **Everything has been given to me by my Father; and no one knows who the Son is except the Father, and who the Father is except the Son and the one to whom the Son wishes to reveal him** (10:22). This intimate relational language is unusual for Luke (and the Synoptics; however, see Luke 20:41–44; 22:69–70) and more typical of the Fourth Gospel (see John 3:35; 7:29; 10:14–15; 13:3; 17:2, 25; Bock 1994–96, 2:1011, calls this verse a "bolt out of the Johannine blue"). The high Christology reflected here "grants to the Son the authority to dispense the authority of the Father" (Culpepper 1995, 225).

The conclusion to the elaborated *chreia* begins with a beatitude: **Then he turned to the disciples and said privately, "Blessed are the eyes that see what you are seeing"** (10:23). Jesus places emphasis on eyewitness, a theme found at the beginning and end of Luke's narrative (1:2; 24:31, 48). Jesus underscores the privileged place the disciples have in seeing and hearing this revelation from God through the Son by claiming, **For I tell you, many prophets and kings wanted to see what you are seeing and did not see it, and to hear what you are hearing and did not hear it** (10:24).

Loving God and Loving Neighbor (10:25–11:13)

The question posed and the answer given in Luke 10:25–28 governs the final form of Luke 10:29–11:13. To gain eternal life, one must love the Lord, and one must love the neighbor. The parables and stories that immediately follow in Luke 10 and 11 illustrate these points.

The pattern is a simple chiasm:

A On loving neighbors (parable of the good Samaritan, Luke 10:29–37)—example, Samaritan as Christ figure
  B On loving the Lord (Mary and Martha, Luke 10:38–42); example, Mary
  B' On loving the Lord (the Lord's Prayer, Luke 11:1–4); example, Jesus
A' On loving neighbors/friends (the parable of the friend at midnight, Luke 11:5–13); example, friend seeking bread

Far from a loosely connected collection of sayings and stories, as some have argued, this section is intricately woven together. The lawyer's question and answer is followed by a section that sandwiches two parables around two scenes, which themselves present a narrative scene and a brief discourse. Furthermore, the stories chiastically provide examples of loving the Lord and loving the neighbor.

10:25–37. *The parable of the good Samaritan.* In the Lukan context, the parable of the good Samaritan is prompted by a dialogue between Jesus and a lawyer. **A certain lawyer stood up to test him, saying, "Teacher, what must I do to inherit eternal life?"** (10:25). This question is repeated verbatim near the end of the travel narrative on the lips of the rich ruler (18:18). Here Jesus responds with his own questions. **He said to him, "What has been written in the Law? How do you read it?"** (10:26). This rhetorical device of asking rhetorical questions in an adversarial context is known as *hypophora* (*Rhet. Her.* 4.23.33–24.34), in which the questions are used to guide the discussion toward a particular line of reasoning. The lawyer takes the bait by quoting from the Law (Deut. 6:5; Lev. 19:18) as Jesus has directed him: **He responded and said, "Love the Lord your God with all your heart, with all your soul, with all your strength, and with all your mind; and love your neighbor as yourself"** (10:27). The response is in the form of a rhetorical *exemplum*, that is, the citation as authoritative of something done or said in the past (*Rhet. Her.* 4.49). Jesus affirms his answer, noting that observing these commandments will lead to the life the lawyer seeks: **Then he said to him, "You have answered correctly. Do this, and you will live"** (10:28). But now the lawyer has a question of his own: **But he, since he wanted to justify himself, said to Jesus, "Who is my neighbor?"** (10:29). Questions of the "who" and "how" of justification will recur later in the parable of the Pharisee and the tax collector (see comments on Luke 18:9–14). Jesus responds to the question, not with another question, but with the story of the good Samaritan (Schneider 1977, 1:247):

> In response Jesus said, "A man was going down from Jerusalem to Jericho and stumbled upon some robbers, who, after they had both stripped him and subjected him to a beating, went away and left him half-dead. Now, by chance a priest was going down [from Jerusalem] on that road; and when he saw him he passed by on the other side of the road. Likewise, a Levite, when he came upon that place and saw him, also passed by on the other side. But a Samaritan who was traveling on a trip came across him, and when he saw him he felt compassion for him. He went to him and bandaged his wounds, pouring oil and wine on them. Then he put him on his own mount, brought him to an inn, and took care of him. On the next day, he took out two denarii and gave them to the innkeeper and said, 'Take care of him, and whatever you spend in addition, I, on my return journey, will repay you.'" (10:30–35)

The parable draws on both Jewish and Greco-Roman conventions to make its point. Within the Jewish halakhic context of the parable, there is the question as to which Mosaic rule should prevail—the need for the priest to avoid corpse defilement or the obligation (for any Israelite) to assist a fellow Israelite in dire need of help. The commandment to love neighbor must always prevail (Bauckham 1998b).

The meaning of the parable in a larger Greco-Roman context is illuminated by relating the Samaritan's act of compassion with the virtue of philanthropy as practiced in the ancient world and as it would have been understood by an ancient audience. Of course, that such virtuous philanthropy is exhibited by a Samaritan and not the pious Jewish layperson would have come as a surprise to the lawyer listening to the story in Luke (and no doubt to Jesus's Jewish audience; see Nolland 1989–93, 2:598).

What more can be said regarding the parable within its Lukan framework? Even though modern scholarship has been generally negative toward a christological reading (C. A. Evans 1990, 178, states flatly: "The Samaritan is not Jesus"), it is worth revisiting the argument. The term *esplanchnisthē* ("he felt compassion") occurs three times in all of Luke; in the other two instances, only God's agent, Jesus (7:13), and a figure for God, the father of the prodigal (15:20), show compassion. In other words, "showing compassion" in the Lukan narrative is a divine prerogative and a divine action (Menken 1988, 111). Here is our first clue in the text of Luke that the good Samaritan, when he shows compassion on the man in the ditch, is functioning figuratively as God's agent.

This interpretation gains momentum when one considers the Lukan frame within which the parable is set. At the conclusion of the parable, Jesus asks, **Which of these three seems to you to have been a neighbor of the one who fell into the hands of the robbers?** (10:36). The lawyer responds by saying, **The one who had mercy on him** (10:37a). This comment is usually understood to show the lawyer's reluctance to even utter the word "Samaritan" (on the animosity between Jews and Samaritans, see Josephus, *Ant.* 9.29; *m. Qidd.* 4.3; John 4:8–9; Luke 9:54). Although this claim may be true, the response also has the effect of creating an interpretive gloss on the Samaritan's action. The Samaritan's act of compassion is construed by the lawyer as the dynamic equivalent of "showing mercy." This interpretation is evidently accepted by Jesus and the narrator, since neither corrects or contradicts the lawyer. This interpretation would seem crucial for getting at Luke's understanding of the Samaritan's action, and through that action to the Samaritan's identity. As with "compassion," virtually every instance of "mercy" in Luke is associated with acts of God or God's agent, Jesus (1:47–50, 54, 72, 78; 17:13; 18:38–39; the only exception is when Father Abraham refuses to show the rich man "mercy" [16:24], an exception that ultimately proves the rule that in Luke's Gospel only God and Jesus show mercy). Within the immediate context of Luke's Gospel, the good Samaritan, who shows compassion and has mercy, functions as a "Christ" figure who ultimately acts as God's agent (cf. Origen, *Hom. Luc.* 34.9).

The story ends with Jesus admonishing the lawyer, **Go and do likewise yourself!** (10:37b), causing many interpreters to label the parable as an "example story" (Tucker 1998). Certainly this is an important aspect of the parable within its Lukan context, but to label the parable of the good Samaritan an "example story," as though the story were itself devoid of a christological or theological referent, is to miss a significant point of the parable. The parable, in its narrative context, does *not* primarily focus on the perspective of the man in the ditch (contra Funk 1974). Rather, Jesus's admonition to the lawyer demands that the primary perspective be that of the good Samaritan, whose example the lawyer is admonished to follow. The example is here enlivened in that the example of the good Samaritan's compassion and mercy is, as the text of Luke affirms, the example of none other than God and God's agent, Jesus. Thus, we have in its literary context a call by Jesus to imitate the compassionate Samaritan and in so doing to imitate the compassion of Jesus. Ethical admonition is grounded in a christological basis.

For the Lukan Jesus to depict himself as a compassionate Samaritan has profound implications. In the immediate context of Luke 9–10, it is to identify with the group on whom James and John have just offered to call down consuming fire from heaven (9:51–56), an act certainly understandable to those familiar with Jewish/Samaritan hostilities. Such scandalous identification is not unknown to Luke's Jesus; rather, it fits in with the generally acknowledged pattern of reversal in Luke's Gospel, where the world is turned upside down (see the introduction to Part 3: Luke 9:51–14:35). Furthermore, the radical claims of the parable of the good Samaritan are not avoided when one excludes Jesus as the referent of the parable, since Jesus calls the lawyer to "act like a Samaritan." Why should Jesus, a Jew, expect something of a Jewish lawyer that he is not prepared to expect of himself? It is in the very offense of the image of the Samaritan as a Christ figure that the parable has its evocative power in its fullest sense. (We should note also that the "Samaritan" receives assistance in his care for the wounded man from an innkeeper, also a despised person in antiquity [see Longenecker 2009].)

10:38–42. *Mary and Martha.* The design and structure of Luke's story about Jesus's visit in the home of Mary and Martha is straightforward, and it is told in a linear fashion (Arterbury 2005, 144).

> Martha extends hospitality to Jesus (10:38).
>
> Mary listens to Jesus's teachings (10:39).
>
> Martha attends to the duties of hospitality (10:40a).
>
> Martha complains that Mary has neglected the duties of hospitality (10:40b).
>
> Martha asks Jesus to instruct Mary to help her (10:40c).
>
> Jesus responds that Mary has chosen the better activity (10:41–42).

Within the larger travel narrative, such stories as this revolve around the act of traveling (Culpepper 1995, 231) and feature elements that are representative of the ancient Mediterranean custom of either hospitality or inhospitality.

The passage begins on this note: **Now, as they went along, he entered a particular village, and a woman named Martha welcomed him** (10:38). The language and setting of the scene are reminiscent of the customs of ancient hospitality, which were generally understood, in the ancient world, to refer to kindness shown to strangers (Arterbury 2005). Luke has a particular interest in issues of hospitality (Luke 7:36–46; 10:38–40; 19:1–9; see also Acts 9:43–11:3; 21:3–6, 7, 8–16; 28:6–10, 13–14). Often, as in our text here, the host initiates hospitality (Luke 7:36; 10:38; Acts 10:22, 23; 28:7).

While Martha has fulfilled the typical expectations associated with a host, it is her sister, Mary, for whom Jesus reserves his highest praise. The contrast between the sisters' actions is striking: **She had a sister named Mary, who had taken a seat at the feet of the Lord and was listening to him speak. Martha, though, was distracted by all that needed to be done** (10:39–40a). Martha busies herself with the details of serving, while Mary chooses to sit at the Lord's feet and listen to what he is saying. Apparently exasperated, Martha confronts Jesus about her sister's actions: **Lord, doesn't it concern you that my sister left me to serve alone? So, speak to her in order that she might help me** (10:40b–c). Rather surprisingly, Jesus replies, **Martha, Martha, you are worried and troubled about many things, but only one thing is necessary. Mary, in fact, has made the right choice, and it will not be taken from her** (10:41–42). In this light, it is difficult to imagine that the authorial audience would understand Jesus's praise of Mary to be an implicit criticism of Martha's hospitality (a point underscored by the repetition of Martha's name, an example of *conduplicatio*, a rhetorical device used to indicate compassion or pity; *Rhet. Her.* 4.28.38). Of course, Jesus has the capacity to level such criticism, as we see in the story of Simon the Pharisee, who fails to follow proper hospitality protocols (Luke 7:36–50).

The passage turns on the meaning of the "one thing" (on the textual problem, see Fee 1981). The "one thing" in Jesus's logic is the "right choice," which Mary has chosen. And what is that? According to Jesus, hearing the word of God's messenger is the one thing needed, not providing for his physical needs (Fitzmyer 1981–85, 2:892; see also Luke 8:15, 21). Thus, however important hospitality is in Luke as a social context for the spread of the Christian message, it is even more important to have followers who attend to Jesus's message (Arterbury 2005, 144). The saying is less a condemnation of Martha's frenzied activity and more a commendation of Mary's posture as a disciple.

11:1–4. *The Lord's Prayer.* Responding to a certain disciple who has asked how one should pray, the Lukan Jesus gives the disciples what has been called the "model prayer":

> Now it happened while he was praying in a certain place that when he had finished, one of his disciples said to him, "Lord, teach us to pray, just as John taught his disciples." So he said to them, "When you pray, say, 'Father, may your name be treated as holy; may your kingdom come. Give us the food we need day by day; and forgive us our sins, for we ourselves also forgive everyone who sins against us. And do not bring us into trial.'" (11:1–4)

The prayer begins with the requests "Father, may your name be treated as holy" and "may your kingdom come" and ends with the petition "do not bring us into trial [*peirasmos*]." The first request points forward to 11:13, where the Lukan Jesus assures his disciples that God will give the "Holy Spirit to those who ask." The presence of the Holy Spirit in Luke/Acts is the evidence that the kingdom of God has come (Luke 1:34–35; Acts 1:4–8; Talbert 1982, 131). Moreover, the presence of the kingdom carries an eschatological connotation implying a deliverance from *peirasmos* (Luke 22:28). In Luke, *peirasmos* is characterized by opposition that often results in suffering (8:13; 22:28; Acts 20:19).

11:5–13. *The parable of the friend at midnight.* In the parable of the friend at midnight that follows (11:5–8), the reverberations of the parable's friendship *topos* form an interlinking network with its immediate Lukan context (11:1–13) as well as with the overall plot of Luke's narrative. Luke has signaled the parable's friendship *topos* in order to address an issue of God's character by showing how God is a reliable friend who will remain loyal to the obligations of friendship reciprocity:

> Then he said to them, "Suppose one of you has a friend and goes to him at midnight and says to him, 'Friend, please lend me three loaves of bread, because my friend who is traveling has stopped at my home, and I do not have anything to put before him.' And he responds from inside his house and says, 'Don't

bother me! The door has already been closed and my children are in bed with me; I am not able to get up and give you something.'" (11:5–7)

Only a rude person would ignore the presence of his friend by staying in bed (see the sidebar "The Inattentive Patron"). Such a scenario, however, warrants further consideration of the analogy between the sleeping friend who will answer (11:8) and God who will answer (11:9–13). How is the sleeping friend similar to and/or dissimilar from the God whose character Luke is describing through the parable?

The predicament of the friend who sleeps when his petitioning friend has a need is an image that is similar to the problem of a god who seemingly sleeps in spite of human injustice and suffering. References to a sleeping god appear in both Greek and Jewish literature. Homer's *Iliad*, for example, narrates an account in which Zeus "went to his couch, where of old he was wont to take his rest, when sweet sleep came upon him" (1.611, trans. Murray 1924). The analogy of a sleeping god in reference to a god who is inactive in spite of human suffering, however, is much more explicit in Ps. 44:23–24: "Rouse yourself! Why do you sleep, O Lord? Awake, do not cast us off forever! Why do you hide your face? Why do you forget our affliction and oppression? . . . Rise up, come to our help" (see also Ps. 78:65). A similar reference appears in postbiblical Judaism in reference to the Levites who, before the reign of Hyrcanus, would cry daily, "Awake, why sleepest Thou, O Lord?" (*b. Soṭah* 48a, trans. A. Cohen 1936).

Aesop's Fable of the Wayfarers and the Bear

The fable of the wayfarers and the bear appropriately illustrates how the violation of friendship reciprocity is a legitimate reason to terminate the friendship.

> "Two friends were walking on the same street. When a bear appeared before them, the first one had time to climb a tree and hide there, while the other, being close to being caught by the bear, fell to the ground and pretended to be dead. As the bear moved her snout close to him and smelt him, he held his breath; for it is said that this animal does not touch the dead. When the bear left, the one who was on the tree asked him what the bear told him in his ear. And he answered 'not to travel from now on together with the kind of friend who does not assist in time of danger.'" (cited in Zafiropoulos 2001, 90)

As the conclusion of this fable implies, only a disloyal friend will refuse to help his or her friend when placed in a situation of immediate danger or hardship (Sir. 6:7, 14–17). In both of these relationships (i.e., the friendship between the sleeper and the petitioner in Luke's parable, and that between the petitioner and the traveler in Aesop's fable) the continuation of the friendship between each pair of characters is at stake.

An accusation of the inactivity of God, especially within the context of the parable's friendship *topos*, would have serious consequences for the friendship between God and Luke's audience. One of the only reasons for dissolving a friendship in the ancient world was due to the activity or *inactivity* of an unreliable and disloyal friend who violated the obligations of friendship reciprocity (see Xenophon, *Hell.* 2.3.43). Similar concerns of friendship loyalty are emphatically interwoven throughout Aesop's fables (see Beavis 1990).

The parable concludes with Jesus stating that even if friendship will not motivate the sleeping neighbor to action, at least the friend's "shamelessness" will: **I tell you, even if he will not get up and give him anything because he is his friend, at least because of his shamelessness he will get up and give him as much as he needs** (11:8). This is now the fourth time Jesus has used the word "friend" (*philos*) in the parable (twice in the accusative, once in the vocative, and once in the nominative; on the significance of inflection, see Theon, *Prog.* 74.24–75.8; 85.29–31; Quintilian, *Inst.* 9.1.34; see also the sidebar "Inflection" at Luke 1:10). His words assume familiarity with the social custom of friendship and suggest that friendship insinuates certain obligations between friends, even if the sleeping neighbor fails to keep his end of the bargain.

Friendship language was often used to describe the relationship between two individuals of unequal status, such as a patron and client. Using "friendship" to describe the relationship between the petitioner and the sleeper of the parable does not assume that these two characters are of equal status. Given that the petitioner automatically knows who will have bread available and thus goes to him to make a request, the parable likely depicts the situation of a client going to his patron for the needed sustenance. The duty of a patron demanded that bread be given to a petitioning client.

If the audience of the parable does indeed understand the sleeper as a patron and the petitioner as a client, then the comparison between the sleeper who answers (11:8) and the God who will answer (11:9–13) is much more explicit. This connection between the sleeping patron and God would have been especially clear to Luke's audience if its members conceived of God as a patron figure, an analogy widely attested in the ancient world. For example, prosperity

> **The Inattentive Patron**
>
> According to Seneca the Younger, only rude patrons would ignore a request from their clients:
>
> *"How many patrons are there who drive away their clients by staying in bed when they call, or ignoring their presence, or being rude? ... How many, still hungover and half-asleep from last night's drinking, will yawn disdainfully at men who have interrupted their own sleep in order to wait upon his awaking, and will mumble a greeting through half-open lips, and will need to be reminded a thousand times of the client's name?"* (Brev. vit. 14.4, trans. Shelton 1998, 14–15)

and good luck are benefits bestowed by the gods (Pliny the Elder, *Nat.* 12.1; Quintilian, *Decl.* 268; Seneca, *Lucil.* 8.3), and the gods deserve gratitude in return (Seneca, *Lucil.* 119.16; Tacitus, *Ann.* 11.15; see Malina 1988).

What does Luke's presentation of the parable communicate about the friendship between God and Luke's audience? In its immediate context, the parable serves an illustrative purpose by providing an example that complements a larger section (11:1–13) addressing the issue of prayer. Such a usage of the parable is analogous to a practice given in the preliminary rhetorical exercises of Pseudo-Hermogenes, which notes that one of the uses of the Greek fable is to give an example of the issue at hand (*Prog.* 4). This rhetorical practice calls for students to place "the statement explaining the moral" of the fable at either the beginning or the end of the fable (*Prog.* 4, trans. Kennedy 2003, 75).

Similarly, Luke provides commentary for understanding the moral of the parable in the subsequent verses:

> I also tell you, ask, and it will be given to you; seek, and you will find; knock, and it will be opened for you. For everyone who asks receives, and the one who seeks finds, and for the one who knocks it will be opened. Which father among you will a son ask for a fish, and instead of a fish he will give him a snake? Or the son will ask for an egg, will he give him a scorpion? If, then, you who are evil know to give good gifts to your children, how much more will the Father from heaven give the Holy Spirit to those who ask him? (11:9–13)

The image of the sleeping friend in the parable stands in parallel to the image of the father who knows how to give good gifts to his children (11:11–13). In both of these images, Luke uses an argument from the lesser to the greater (Aristotle, *Rhet.* 2.23.4; see Nolland 1989–93, 2:629) to show how, if one can expect a friend and a father to answer his or her requests, that much more one should expect God, the divine friend and father, to answer the requests of those who pray with "shamelessness" (11:8; on the meaning of *anaideia*, see Snodgrass 1997) during times of trial.

Theological Issues

Three social customs from antiquity are featured conceptually and semantically in Luke 10:25–11:13: philanthropy, hospitality, and friendship.

1. The ancients recognized *philanthropy* as a virtue (Demosthenes, *Or.* 19.225; Plato, *Euthyphr.* 3d; Plutarch, *Aem.* 39; Iamblichus quoted in Stobaeus, *Flor.* 4.5.76; cited in Barrett 1994–98, 2:1183). According to Diogenes Laertius, Plato cataloged philanthropy into three categories. In addition to (a) offering greetings or (b) hosting dinners, philanthropy was also expressed (c) through offering benefactions, especially in times

of trouble ("one is given to assisting everyone in distress"; see *Vit. phil.* 3.98, trans. Hicks 1925a). Philanthropic characters figure prominently in ancient literature (see Longus, *Daphn.* 1.3.1–20; Chariton, *Chaer.* 2.5.4), as do, conversely, misanthropic figures (see Menander, *Dysk.* 726.427–28; Dio Chrysostom, *Ven.* 7.56–58). Philanthropy in Luke 10 falls into the category of assisting those in distress (see also Acts 27:3; Hock 1998, 132–37). The good Samaritan has compassion on the man in the ditch and engages in philanthropic acts by binding his wounds and paying for his convalescence.

2. In the story of Mary and Martha we find the social custom of *hospitality* on display (10:38–42). The constant social context in ancient hospitality scenes appears to be travel. Hospitality was a highly valued and presumably widely practiced custom among pagans, Jews, and Christians. Hosts were expected to provide food, shelter, amenities, and protection to these traveling strangers, who sometimes turned out to be gods incognito (Ovid, *Metam.* 8.626–724). In Greek culture, Zeus was celebrated as the god of hospitality (Homer, *Od.* 9.266–71; Heliodorus, *Aeth.* 2.22.2), and the practice of hospitality (among other things) separated high Greek civilization from the "barbarians." Often these hospitality scenes ended with the host bestowing gifts on the guest (e.g., Homer, *Od.* 1.311–18; Chariton, *Chaer.* 5.97; Longus, *Daphn.* 3.9; 4.6; Dio Chrysostom, *Ven.* 7.21–22, 45, 57–58; Virgil, *Aen.* 8.152–69). Jewish examples of hospitality also abound (e.g., Gen. 18:1–16; see also Gen. 19:1–23; 24:10–61; 43:16–34; Exod. 2:15–22; Josh. 2:1–22; Judg. 4:17–22; see Arterbury 2005, 55–86). Luke makes reference to hospitality in his Gospel (e.g., 7:36–50; 9:51–56; 10:38–42; 19:1–10) and in Acts (9:11; 16:11–15; 17:5–7; 18:2–3; 21:7–16; 28:7–10). Successful ancient hospitality often precipitated the formation of permanent friendship (see Hock 1998, 132–37), and Luke was also well aware of the cultural protocols and expectations associated with hospitality in antiquity (see Parsons 2007, 54–61).

3. The social custom of *friendship* underlies the parable of the friend at midnight (11:5–8). In Greco-Roman society there was no better or more noble possession than private, genuine friendship (Plutarch, *Adul. amic.* 49F). Cicero considered friendship to be the most valuable gift, with the exception of wisdom, that the gods had granted to humankind (*Amic.* 6.20). One of the key components of genuine friendship was commonality. True friends did not cling to their possessions as their own private property. Rather, friends shared everything, tangibly demonstrating their affection for and commitment to one another. The expression "Friends have all things in common" dates back at least to the time of Aristotle (*Eth. nic.* 9.8.2; see also Plutarch, *Adul. amic.* 65A). In the Greco-Roman world, "friendship" was a very broad idea that covered

"largely utilitarian relations of self-interest and advancement as well as those bonds which spring from family ties or social relations of true affection and commonality of character" (Fiore 1997, 73). Greco-Roman friendships tended to be based on the concept of reciprocity, which was expressed by such things as gift giving, loyalty, honor, and political support (Garnsey and Saller 1987, 154; Stambaugh and Balch 1986, 63–64). Friends were expected both to provide help during times of need and to publicly acknowledge any help they had received from other friends.

In the ancient world, the protocols of these cultural conventions often overlap. Philanthropy involved a moral obligation to accept "a limited number of responsibilities toward an unlimited number of people" (Hock 1998, 137). The language of philanthropy is frequently used in specific contexts of assisting the "other" in duress (victims of brigands or shipwreck or prisoners). Friendship, however, "calls for an unlimited number of responsibilities to a limited number of people" (Hock 1998, 137; see also Chariton, *Chaer.* 3.5). Luke uses philanthropy to describe acts of kindness by an outsider (a Samaritan) toward an insider (Israelite) under duress (Luke 10:25–37; cf. Acts 27:3a; 28:2) and friendship to describe obligations of those in community with one another (Luke 11:5–8; cf. Acts 27:3b; 2:44).

Hospitality in Luke 10:38–42 occurs in a context in which one person has traveled to another geographic region, and, unlike philanthropy, it focuses on a household scene (cf. Luke 7; Acts 10). Thus, hospitality can overlap with both philanthropy and friendship. This Lukan social ethic provides a solid foundation for Christian habits and practices both within the community (we have unlimited responsibilities to fellow believers) and with the world (we are called to provide Christian philanthropy to those unlike us in nationality, faith, or ethnicity and assistance to those in immediate crisis). Christians are called to extend hospitality both as hosts and guests, and to fellow believers and nonbelievers alike. Such hospitality calls for personal and intimate engagement in a way that an insipid value such as "tolerance" does not. We are called *not* simply to tolerate or endure those not like us (see Conyers 2001); rather, the ancient Christian virtues of philanthropy and especially hospitality demand that we engage and interact with the Other, whether we are guest or host, and Christian friendship obligates us to practices that are mutually beneficial to the whole community, even when we may not always be in complete agreement with our Christian friends. Philanthropy, hospitality, and friendship are three Christian virtues well worth our consideration and cultivation as we attempt to practice the "one necessary thing" (see Luke 10:42).

Luke 11:14–13:9

Jesus in Dialogue

Introductory Matters

The next unit, 11:14–13:9, contains three sections: 11:14–36, 11:37–54, and 12:1–13:9. The first section (11:14–36) contains a familiar pattern (cf. 5:17–26; 7:36–50): Jesus's action (11:14) elicits objections by his opponents (11:15–16), which is followed by Jesus's response to each objection respectively (11:17–26, 29–36; see Talbert 1982, 141); sandwiched between are two contrasting beatitudes (11:27–28). The second section, Luke 11:37–54, is set in the home of a Pharisee, where Jesus has gone to dine (cf. 7:36–50; 14:16–24; see also Tannehill 1996, 197). Jesus engages in an invective of six woes, three against Pharisees paralleled by three more against lawyers (cf. Luke 6:20–26; Matt. 23). The final unit, Luke 12:1–13:9 consists of six units of Jesus's teaching: a dialogue between Jesus and his disciples (12:1–12), an elaborated *chreia* on the topic of greed (12:13–34), a discourse on the impending eschatological judgment (12:35–48), a discussion of the purpose of Jesus's ministry (12:49–53), instructions to the crowds (12:54–59), and the parable of the barren fig tree (13:1–9).

> **Luke 11:14–13:9 in the Narrative Flow**
>
> Jesus's origins and training (1:1–4:13)
> Jesus's mighty words and deeds in Galilee (4:14–9:50)
> Jesus's mighty words and deeds along the way (part 1) (9:51–14:35)
>   Beginning the journey (Luke 9:51–11:13)
> ▶ Jesus in dialogue (11:14–13:9)
>   Jesus's exorcism and resulting teaching (11:14–36)
>   Jesus in the home of a Pharisee (11:37–54)
>   Continuing conversations (12:1–13:9)

Tracing the Narrative Flow

Jesus's Exorcism and Resulting Teaching (11:14–36)

11:14–16. Luke 11:14–36 begins with Jesus exorcising a demon: **Later, he was in the process of casting out a mute demon. Now it happened that when the demon had come out the mute man spoke** (11:14a). This is the first recorded miracle of Jesus healing a mute, but it does recall the beginning of the Gospel, in which Zechariah is struck mute (*kōphos*) until John the Baptist is born (1:22). It is the kind of miracle expected of a prophet/messiah (cf. 7:22, which refers to the closely related miracle of healing the deaf; i.e., the same Greek word *kōphos* refers to being deaf and/or mute). Jesus's actions provoke an immediate positive—**and the crowds were amazed** (11:14b)—and a twofold negative response (11:15–16).

The first objection is in the form of an accusation: **Then some of them said, "He casts out demons by Beelzebul, the ruler of the demons!"** (11:15). By the first century, Beelzebul ("Baal, the Prince," a variant of Beelzebub) was the semantic equivalent of Satan (Culpepper 1995, 241; on the variant spellings and meanings of Beelzebul, see Fitzmyer 1981–85, 2:920). The charge, then, is that Jesus is an "agent" of Satan, casting out demons by Beelzebul (contrast Mark 3:22, where Jesus is depicted as being demon possessed—he "has Beelzebul"). The second objection is in the form of a test: **Others, in order to test him, were seeking a sign from heaven from him** (11:16). The use of the word "test" recalls the "testing" of Jesus in the desert by the devil (4:2). Despite witnessing the exorcism, they seek a sign; only those opposed to Jesus seek a sign from him (e.g., Herod in 23:8). And the last "sign" seen, ironically, was "Satan falling from heaven" because of the submission of demons to Jesus's followers (10:17–18; see Johnson 1991, 182).

11:17–26. Jesus responds to the first charge, that he is an agent of Satan, by challenging their logic (Culpepper 1995, 241–42): **Then, since he knew their thoughts, he said to them, "Every kingdom that is divided against itself is wiped out, and a house divided against a house falls. Furthermore, if Satan is also divided against himself, how will his kingdom stand? For you are saying that I cast out demons by Beelzebul"** (11:17–18). Demons are aligned with Satan. Since his ministry of healing and exorcism is an assault on Satan, how can Jesus also be an agent of Satan? Satan would then be divided against himself, like one household against another, and his kingdom would fall. Jesus then poses a rhetorical question (see *Rhet. Her.* 4.15.22) to demonstrate the inconsistency of their argument: **If, however, I am casting out demons by Beelzebul, by whom do your sons cast them out?** (11:19a). "Son" is being used in the sense of "adherent" or "pupil" (1 Pet. 5:13; Heb. 12:5; Marshall 1978, 474). Other Jewish exorcists were known in antiquity (cf. Acts 19:13–14). Abram was credited with driving an evil spirit from Pharaoh's household (1QapGen^{ar} 20.29). Josephus reports that a fellow Jew, Eleazar, "freed people seized by demons" (*Ant.* 8.2.5.46, cited by Fitzmyer 1981–85, 2:921). If Jesus's exorcism labels him as an agent of Satan, then under whose power do these (otherwise anonymous) Jewish exorcists act? Jesus continues: **For this reason, they will be your judges** (11:19b). The inability of Jesus's opponents to label their own exorcists as Satan's allies means those same Jewish exorcists stand in judgment over the inconsistency of their argument.

Finally, far from identifying Jesus as an agent of Satan, his exorcism ministry identifies him as an agent of God: **But if I cast out demons by the finger of God, then the kingdom of God has come upon you** (11:20). Jesus casts out demons not by Beelzebul but by the "finger of God" (cf. Matt. 12:28, which has "spirit of God"). This metonymic expression, which "expresses the ease with which Jesus has expelled the demon," recalls Exod. 8:19, in which Pharaoh's magicians, unable to reproduce Aaron's miracle of producing gnats from dust, credit Aaron's action to the "finger of God" (Woods 2001, 61–100; cf. Exod. 31:18; Ps. 8:3). Jesus's actions, then, cast him in the role of God's agent, announcing the inbreaking of the rule of God.

Jesus's opponents in Luke 11:14–20 stand in contrast to Jesus's followers in Luke 11:1–13 (Johnson 1991, 183). The disciples seek the Holy Spirit from heaven; the opponents futilely seek a sign. Jesus's followers are to pray that they might be delivered from testing (11:4); the opponents put Jesus to the test (11:16). Jesus's followers ask for forgiveness (11:4); his opponents accuse Jesus of the sin of satanic collusion. The two passages demand ultimately that the audience recognize Jesus either as a minion of Satan's rule or as the harbinger of the coming kingdom of God.

Jesus next employs an allegory to drive home his point: **Whenever a strong man protects his own palace fully armed, his possessions are safe; but when one who is stronger than he comes and conquers him, he takes away his armor in which he had placed his confidence and distributes his plunder** (11:21–22). Luke's version is more elaborate than the parallel stories found in Mark 3:27 and Matt. 12:29–30, and the details are significant. Luke describes the strong man as "fully armed" in "armor in which he had placed his confidence." These militaristic references to armor and plunder suggest a battle between kingdoms of cosmic proportion, a view reinforced if the term *aulē* (often translated "house," perhaps influenced by the use of *oikia* in both Matthew and Mark) carries the connotation of "palace" (so BDAG 150) or "castle" (Culpepper 1995, 242). Furthermore, Luke specifies the strong man's opponent as one "stronger." The "stronger one" seems to function as a quasi-technical title for Jesus (the "Stronger One") and recalls John the Baptist's prophecy of the "Stronger One" who would come after him and whose sandals he was not worthy to untie (3:16). Through his exorcisms, Jesus, the "Stronger One" who is empowered by God, defeats the "Strong Man," Satan, and as a victorious warrior, plunders Satan's possessions (Fitzmyer 1981–85, 2:922; D. Garland 2011, 483). Jesus then offers a more restrictive form of an aphorism first found in Luke 9:50 ("the one who is not against us is for us") and unique among the Synoptics here: **The one who is not with me is against me, and the one who does not gather with me scatters** (11:23). In this context, the one who is not with Jesus is with Satan and rather than participating in Jesus's ministry of reconciliation and restoration joins with the dark forces, whose aim is to scatter and divide (Marshall 1978, 479).

Jesus follows the allegory with a parable: **When an unclean spirit leaves a person, it goes through a parched region seeking rest. And when it does not find it, [then] it says, "I will return to my house that I left." After it goes back, it finds it swept clean and in order. Then it goes and takes along seven other spirits more evil than itself, and after entering the person they live there; and the final condition of that person is worse than the first** (11:24–26). It is not enough, Jesus says, to vacate the premises of "dark forces"; rather, one must "fill his or her life with the kingdom of God (v. 20) and obedience to the Word of God (v. 28)" (Culpepper 1995, 242). Otherwise, the demonic will return to its original location and take possession with sevenfold devastating results. The reference to the seven evil spirits may represent a counterpart to the seven angels of presence (Tob. 12:15) or may suggest by the number seven that the demon possession is utterly complete.

11:27–28. A voice from the crowd interrupts the action: **Now it happened that as he was saying these things a woman from the crowd raised her voice and said to him, "Blessed is the womb that carried you and the breasts that you nursed from"** (11:27; cf. *Gos. Thom.* 79; see also the sidebar "Luke and the *Gospel of Thomas*" at Luke 23:26–32). Such beatitudes praising an offspring by extolling the parents and caregivers were common in the ancient world (cf. Prov. 23:24–25). For example, Eumolpus cries out: "How blessed is the mother who bore such a one as you" (Petronius, *Sat.* 94.1, cited by Danker 1988, 234–35; see also Tacitus, *Dial.* 28–29; *Inf. Gos. Thom.* 7.5–8; 17.3; *Prot. Jas.* 5.10; 6.10; 19.16). And Ovid writes:

> Blessed are those
> Who call you son. Blessed is the one
> Who boasts your brother, and she who calls
> Herself a sister. Blessed is the nurse
> Who tendered you her breasts.
> (*Metam.* 4.320–24,
> cited by Danker 1988, 234–35)

Jesus deflects this flattery with a beatitude of his own: **But he said, "On the contrary, blessed are those who hear the word of God and are careful to obey it"** (11:28). This makarism recalls Jesus's earlier saying in 8:21: "My mother and my brothers—these are the ones who hear the word of God and do it." Flattery was such a commonplace in antiquity that Plutarch penned an essay titled *How to Tell a Flatterer from a Friend*, in which he warned against being seduced by false praise: "And is not almost any king called an Apollo if he can hum a tune, and a Dionysus if he gets drunk, and a Heracles if he can wrestle? And is he not delighted, and thus led on into all kinds of disgrace by the flattery? For this reason we must be especially on our guard against the flatterer in the matter of his praises" (*Adul. amic.* 56–67, trans. Babbitt 1927). Jesus is more concerned with obedience to God than with any kind of praise that may come his way.

11:29–36. Next, Jesus addresses the objections of those who were "seeking a sign from heaven from him" (11:16; cf. Mark 8:11–12; Matt. 12:38–42): **As the crowds were increasingly gathering, he began to say, "This generation is a wicked generation! It seeks a sign, but a sign will not be given to it except the sign of Jonah"** (11:29). The emphasis on this "generation" and the "sign" it seeks is seen in the use of the rhetorical device of transplacement (*traductio*), in which certain words are repeated ("generation" [2x]; "sign" [3x]; *Rhet. Her.* 4.14.21; Quintilian, *Inst.* 9.3.70–74). The Synoptic tradition preserves a variety of responses to the request for a sign from Jesus. In Luke's version, Jonah and his preaching are compared to Jesus and his preaching (see Landes 1996; Hooker 1997, 18): **For just as Jonah was a sign for the Ninevites, so also the Son of Man will be for this generation** (11:30). The comparison reinforces Jesus's admonition to hear and obey God's word (11:28). "The Ninevites, who heeded the preaching of Jonah, reformed their lives; they will then rise and point an accuser's finger at this 'evil generation' in the day of judgment" (Fitzmyer 1981–85, 2:933). Thus, the Lukan Jesus points to Jonah as a sign of the current generation's need for repentance (T. Manson 1949, 90–91; see also Fitzmyer 1981–85, 2:930).

This interpretation is reinforced by the subsequent examples Jesus cites: **The Queen of the South will rise at the judgment with the people of this generation and will condemn them, because she came from the ends of the earth to hear the wisdom of Solomon, and something greater than Solomon**

> **Parched Regions**
>
> Jesus's reference to the evil spirit going through "parched" or "waterless" regions (11:24) is puzzling. On the one hand, it could be that in popular thinking such waterless places were haunted by demons (cf. Lev. 16:10; Isa. 34:13–14). The author of 2 Peter describes apostates as "waterless springs" for whom "the nether gloom of darkness has been reserved" (2 Pet. 2:17 RSV). On the other hand, it could be that "the point is perhaps not the dryness but the absence of men from such desert regions, so that the demon cannot find anywhere to rest" (Marshall 1978, 479). Luke Johnson has pointed to the humorous element of derelict spirits taking up residence again in the same person: "One must choose between kingdoms. It is the empty tenement that invites squatters" (1991, 184; see also Emmrich 2000).

is here! The people of Nineveh will come back to life with this generation at the judgment and will condemn it, because they repented at the preaching of Jonah, and something greater than Jonah is here! (11:31–32). In an encomium/invective *synkrisis*, Jesus praises the Queen of Sheba and the Ninevites in order to condemn this "wicked generation." Jesus appeals first to the story of the Queen of Sheba, who visits King Solomon to experience for herself his wisdom; convinced, she bestows her blessing on him (1 Kings 10:1–13; see also 2 Chron. 9:1–12). At the judgment, she will rise and condemn "this generation" (Jesus's contemporaries), because she has heard and believed Solomon's wisdom, while "this generation" has refused to hear "something greater than Solomon." Likewise, the Ninevites who repented at the preaching of Jonah will condemn "this generation" at the judgment because they have heard and rejected "something greater than Jonah." This generation stands condemned because they have not obeyed God's word, even though it has been proclaimed to them by Jesus, who is "greater than either a prophet (Jonah) or a king (Solomon)" (Culpepper 1995, 243; cf. 7:18–35).

Further sayings of Jesus are joined to these warnings against Jesus's detractors; the sayings are held together by "the idea of light and its effects or influence" (Fitzmyer 1981–85, 2:938):

> No one lights a lamp and then puts it in a hidden place [or under a bushel]. Instead, people put it on a lampstand in order that those who enter may benefit from the light. Your eye is the lamp of your body. When your eye is healthy, your whole body is also full of light; but when it is sick, your body is also in the dark. Watch out, then, that the light that is in you is not darkness. So then, if your whole body is full of light, not having any part in the dark, it will be completely full of light, like when a lamp shines its light on you. (11:33–36)

In Luke 11:34–36 (//Matt. 6:22–23), Jesus speaks of the relationship of the eye to the whole body.

The eye is central in physiognomic thinking (see Parsons 2007, 2011). According to pseudo-Aristotle, "The most favorable part for examination is the region around the eyes, forehead, head and face" (*Physiog.* 814b.3–4, trans. Hett 1936). Pseudo-Aristotle follows his own advice, citing the eyes as a distinguishing mark of various character types eighteen times in his treatise (*Physiog.* 807b.1, 7, 19, 23, 29, 35; 808a.1, 3, 8, 9, 12, 16, 28, 30, 34; 808b.6; 812b.8; 813a.21). The anonymous author of the Latin treatise asserts: "now we discuss the eyes where the sum total of all physiognomy is situated" (*Anon. Lat.* 20, trans. André 1981, 66; cf. 142; see also Cicero, *De or.* 3.221–23).

The connection between the eyes and the inner character is attested in Jewish literature as well. Persons with "good eyes" were morally sound: "[The person with] a good eye will be blessed, for he shared his bread with the poor" (Prov. 22:9 author's trans.). Sirach claims: "He is hard who has an evil eye, who turns his back on need and looks the other way. The evil eye is not satisfied with its share; greedy injustice shrivels the soul. Someone with an evil eye begrudges bread and keeps a bare table" (Sir. 14:8–10 author's trans.). In Christian literature, we find this connection was expressed through a linking of "eyes" and "heart": Eph. 1:18 speaks of the "eyes of your heart" (see also *1 Clem.* 36.2).

In Luke 11:34–36, the ethical admonition is to focus on the inner character (11:35). The physical and moral implications of "the eye is the lamp of the body" would have been front and center all the time (contra Allison 1987, 76–77). These verses tie in with the previous ones to make the same point: "This generation, which would have recognized Solomon's wisdom and responded to Jonah's preaching of judgment, does not accept Jesus because its 'eye' is evil.... The controversy concludes, therefore, with the insistence that the light Jesus gives to all who enter should fill the whole body" (Culpepper 1995, 244; see also Garrett 1991, 96).

Jesus in the Home of a Pharisee (11:37–54)

11:37–54. The next section (11:37–54) is in the form of a type-scene of a meal in the home of a Pharisee (Tannehill 1996, 197). The passage unfolds thusly (Talbert 1982, 147–48):

- A. The invitation (11:37)
- B. The Pharisee's objection (11:38)
- C. Jesus's response (11:39–44)
    1. A reply with no woe (11:39–41)
    2. The first woe (11:42)
    3. The second woe (11:43)
    4. The third woe (11:44)
- D. The lawyer's objection (11:45)
- E. Jesus's response (11:46–52)
    1. The first woe (11:46)
    2. The second woe (11:47–51)
    3. The third woe (11:52)
- F. The resulting plot to trap Jesus (11:53–54)

The story begins with an invitation to dine (cf. 7:36; 14:1): **Now, as he spoke, a Pharisee asked him to eat with him. So he went in and sat down to eat** (11:37). Immediately a controversy arises about Jesus's lax purity practice: **Then, the Pharisee, when he saw it, was shocked that he did not wash first before the meal** (11:38; cf. 7:39; 14:2–3). The ceremonial washing of hands was well grounded in Jewish Scripture and tradition (see Gen. 18:4; Judg. 19:21; Mark 7:1–9; Josephus, *J.W.* 2.8.5.129; cited by Fitzmyer 1981–85, 2:947), although the biblical mandate applied only to priests (Exod. 30:19–21; 40:12). The Pharisees had "extended this tradition to all persons, not just priests, and as a preparation for eating all food, not just holy offerings" (D. Garland 2011, 493, citing *m. Yad.* 1.1: "[To render the hands clean] a quarter-log [of water] must be poured over the hands [to suffice] for one person"). Jesus gives a sharp response (though without the introductory "woe"): **So the Lord said to him, "As it is, you Pharisees clean the outside of the cup and the dish, but the inside of you is full of violent greed and wickedness"** (11:39; cf. Matt. 23:25; *Gos. Thom.* 89.1). The logic is that if the inside of the cup (or person) is unclean, then the whole cup (or person) is unclean; thus it is futile to care for outer appearances while neglecting the inside. This kind of rebuke of hypocrisy was not uncommon in Second Temple Judaism: "[these 'godless' persons] represent themselves as being righteous, but [. . .] will (in fact) arouse their inner wrath, for they will be deceitful men, pleasing only themselves, false in every way imaginable, (such as) loving feasts at any hour of the day—devouring, gluttonous" (*T. Mos.* 7, *OTP* 1:930). "Jesus' words are therefore a strong rebuke, tantamount to classifying some Pharisees with the very publicans and sinners they despised" (Danker 1988, 239).

Jesus then employs the rhetorical figure of *exclamatio*: **Foolish men!** (11:40a). Such an expression is a stock feature of Hellenistic diatribe (Epictetus, *Diatr.* 3.22.85; 4.10.23; cited by Johnson 1991, 189) and links the "foolish" Pharisees with the "godless" (cf. Luke 12:20; Ps. 14:1; Prov. 6:12; see also Danker 1988, 240; D. Garland 2011, 490; Donald 1963). Jesus continues with a rhetorical question (*interrogatio*), which functions to reinforce the argument (on both, see *Rhet. Her.* 4.15.22): **Didn't the one who made the outside also make the inside?** (11:40b; cf. *Gos. Thom.* 89.2). The "Maker" is identified elsewhere by Luke as God (Acts 1:24; 15:8). God is Lord of both outer actions and inner attitudes, and God knows the human heart (cf. 16:15). Jesus advises one way in which the inside can also be cleansed: **Nevertheless, make the things inside of you your alms, and all things will be clean for you!** (11:41). The outward appearance of piety (e.g., washing the hands) must be replaced by the genuinely pious act of almsgiving (cf. Acts 10:2). Their cup is full of their wickedness and greed. This view echoes Isaiah's indictment: "It is you who have devoured the vineyard; the spoil of the poor is in your houses" (Isa. 3:14 ESV). Therefore, only by giving away the spoils of their greed may they be cleansed of their inner "violent greed and wickedness" (C. Hays 2010, 121; on the efficacy of almsgiving, see Tob. 4:7–12; *b. Sukkah* 49b; Johnson 1991, 189).

Next, Jesus launches into the first of three woes against the Pharisees: **Instead, woe to you Pharisees, because you tithe mint and rue and everything you grow, but you bypass justice and love for God!** (11:42a; cf. Matt. 23:23). Jesus specifies two herbs, mint and rue ("an evergreen aromatic plant used for seasoning"; L&N 3.22), before broadening the reference to "everything you grow," which could denote "any one of the smaller plants cultivated in a garden" (L&N 3.29). The reference to "rue" may indicate Jesus's hyperbole, since rue is "specifically exempt from being tithed according to *m. Šeb.* 9.1 and 'mint' is never mentioned in rabbinic literature" (D. Garland 2011, 494;

see also Fitzmyer 1981–85, 2:948). These Pharisees' "excessive scrupulosity" (Nolland 1989–93, 2:670) causes them to neglect what really matters: "justice and love for God." Those two activities echo Mic. 6:8 ("do justice") and recall Jesus's summary of the law ("love the Lord") in Luke 10:27. "Neither loving God nor doing justice can be limited to ten per cent but requires all one's heart, soul, strength, and mind" (D. Garland 2011, 495). **It was necessary to do these things and not avoid the others** (11:42b). Jesus does not dismiss the commitment to render a portion of one's possessions back to God, but the one cannot replace the other.

The next woe chastises the religious leaders for self-aggrandizement: **Woe to you Pharisees, because you love the best seats in the synagogues and being greeted in the marketplaces!** (11:43; cf. Matt. 23:5–7). The charge here is similar to the one Jesus will level several times later in the narrative (Luke 14:7–11; 16:14–15; 20:46–47). But such criticism of "social climbers" was common in antiquity (see Dio Chrysostom, *Or.* 32.30; Danker 1988, 241; Talbert 1982, 152). In the third woe, Jesus employs a simile (the rhetorical figure *imago*; *Rhet. Her.* 4.49.62), comparing the Pharisees to unmarked graves: **Woe to you, because you are like the unmarked graves, and the people who walk over them do not know it!** (11:44). Similes imply a certain resemblance between the entities compared and can be used in either an encomium or an invective for praise or censure; in this case, it is part of a *synkrisis* intended to criticize the consequences of the Pharisees' actions. According to Israel's Scriptures, coming into contact with a grave rendered a person unclean for a week's period (Num. 19:16; D. Garland 2011, 495). Persons could be unknowingly contaminated by the attitudes and actions of the Pharisees, because their hypocrisy, like "secret graves," aimed at "deliberate concealment" (Johnson 1991, 190; Matt. 23:27–28 makes the charge of hypocrisy more transparent). However deceptive they are to others, they do not fool God! It is important to note that in this invective Jesus is condemning a lack of "best practices" among certain Pharisees; it is "not a condemnation of Pharisaism as a system" (T. Manson 1949, 99). Such critique could have been, and often was, made within Pharisaic Judaism itself (Danker 1988, 240).

One of Jesus's listeners complains: **Then, one of the lawyers responded and said to him, "Teacher, by saying these things you are insulting us as well"** (11:45). Jesus wastes no time in expanding his invective, lodging three woes against the interpreters of the law: **So he said, "Woe to you lawyers as well, because you load people with burdens that are hard to bear, but you yourselves won't even touch those burdens with one of your fingers!"** (11:46; cf. Matt 23:4). The first woe parallels the woe against the Pharisees; lawyers have "minute legalistic interpretations of Mosaic law" (Fitzmyer 1981–85, 2:945), which have the effect of placing a burden on people that is hard to bear. Jesus here uses the rhetorical figure of *traductio*, in which the same or similar words (here forms of the stem *phort-*) are repeated for emphasis (Quintilian, *Inst.* 9.3.70–74). By the "finger of God" (Luke 11:20), Jesus will cast out demons, but the lawyers will not "lift a finger to help" to relieve the burden they have created (on the idiom, see Culy, Parsons, and Stigall 2010, 405; Danker 1988, 241).

Honoring the dead with proper burial was widely praised in antiquity (see Sophocles's *Antigone*). But Jesus turns this practice against the lawyers: **Woe to you, because you build the tombs of the prophets! Your ancestors are the ones who killed them! So then, you are witnesses, and you approve of what your ancestors did, because they killed them, but you build their tombs!** (11:47–48; cf. Matt. 23:29–32). By approving of and participating in the persecution of the prophets, the act of "building tombs" for the prophets, rather than being viewed as an act of piety, aligns the lawyers with the enemies of the prophets (cf. Acts 7:52). Metaphorically, Jesus may be referring to the role of scholars of the law as "builders" of Torah interpretation (*m. Miqw.* 9.6; *b. Šabb.* 114a). It is easy to give the impression of honoring the dead by building monuments in their memory, but in reality the interpretations that the lawyers "build" place them in opposition to Israel's prophetic tradition, past and present (D. Garland 2011, 496). This point becomes more clear in Jesus's next statement (cf. Matt. 23:34–36):

> For this reason, in fact, the wisdom of God said, "I will send them prophets and apostles, and they will kill and persecute some of them," with the result that the blood of all the prophets, which was poured out from the foundation of the world, will be exacted from this generation, from the blood of Abel until the blood of Zechariah, who died between the altar and the temple. Yes, I tell you, it will be exacted from this generation! (11:49–51)

While some view the reference to the "wisdom of God" as the title of a book, more likely the phrase reflects the rhetorical figure of *autonomasia*, in which a word or epithet is substituted for a proper name (Quintilian, *Inst.* 8.6.29–30). As a possible epithet, the phrase here has the same "sapiential cast" of 11:31 (cf. 7:35) and may have Jesus himself as its referent (on Jesus as God's wisdom, see 1 Cor. 1:24, 30; 2:7; Col. 2:3; Fitzmyer 1981–85, 2:950). The opponents of the prophets have been shedding their blood since the foundation of the world, from Abel, the first person murdered in the Bible (Gen. 4; cf. Heb. 11:4; 12:24; 1 John 3:12; *T. Benj.* 7.5) to Zechariah, the last person murdered in the Bible (2 Chron. 24:20–22; assuming Jesus's Bible roughly followed the sequence of the MT; see Fitzmyer 1981–85, 2:951). There are a number of parallels between Abel and Zechariah, beyond the fact that they represent the first and last murders in Israel's Scriptures (Allison 2000, 85–87). Zechariah was stoned to death, and, in postbiblical tradition, Abel was also killed by a stone (*Jub.* 4.31; see Allison 2000, 85–87). Furthermore, Abel's blood cries out to God (Gen. 4:10; cf. *1 En.* 22.5–7; *L.A.B.* 16.2–3), and Zechariah also cries out as he dies ("May Yahweh see and avenge"; 2 Chron. 24:22). Presumably both are viewed, at least by the Lukan Jesus, as "prophets" or at least as standing within the prophetic tradition (cf. Luke 13:34). By the end of the narrative, Jesus's blood will join the blood of all the martyrs from Abel to Zechariah to bear witness against this generation.

Jesus concludes with the sixth and final woe: **Woe to you lawyers, because you take away the key to knowledge. You yourselves do not enter, and you hinder those who are entering** (11:52; cf. *Gos. Thom.* 39.1–2). Jesus later levels a similar charge against his disciples when he instructs them not to "hinder" the children from coming to him since no one can "enter" God's kingdom without first becoming like a child (18:16). That incident suggests a connection between knowledge of the Scriptures and entrance into the kingdom. Instead of "opening" the Scriptures for the people (cf. Luke 24:32), the interpreters of the law have locked knowledge of them away "in regulations and obscurities" (Tiede 1988, 255). Rather than assisting their entrance into the kingdom, they have hindered those who would enter (cf. Matt. 23:13, where the "kingdom of heaven" is explictly that which people are hindered from entering).

The scene concludes on an ominous note: **And when he had left there, the scribes and the Pharisees began to be very hostile and to lecture him about many things, lying in wait for him to catch him in what he said** (11:53–54). The idea here seems to be that the scribes' and Pharisees' aggressive lecturing of Jesus on many topics was designed to elicit responses that would expose problems in his teachings (Culy, Parsons, and Stigall 2010, 409). This kind of polemic was common among members of rival schools, whether intra-Jewish (e.g., *T. Mos.* 7; see comments on 11:39, above) or Greco-Roman (e.g., Dio Chrysostom, *Or.* 32, 33, 38; Johnson 1991, 192). The passage "is not intended as a history lesson about the evils of Jesus' first-century foes but as a warning to Christian leaders not to commit the same sins or they will face the same condemnation" (D. Garland 2011, 498–99). On the narrative level, the story ends on an ominous note with Jesus's adversaries "lying in wait to catch him."

> ### *Epanaphora* as a Rhetorical Device
>
> In Luke 11:52, for the sixth time Jesus pronounces a "woe" (*ouai*; see 11:42, 43, 44, 46, 47, 52). The pathos of Jesus's words is intensified by Luke's use of the rhetorical figure *epanaphora*, in which "one and the same word forms successive beginnings ... as follows: 'Scipio razed Numantia, Scipio destroyed Carthage, Scipio brought peace, Scipio saved the state!'" (*Rhet. Her.* 4.13.19, trans. Caplan 1954). *Epanaphora* "has not only much charm, but also impressiveness and vigour in the highest degree" (*Rhet. Her.* 4.13.19, trans. Caplan 1954). The author continues: "There inheres in the repetition an elegance which the ear can distinguish more easily than words can explain" (*Rhet. Her.* 4.14.21, trans. Caplan 1954).

Continuing Conversations (12:1–13:9)

The final unit in the section, 12:1–13:9, subdivides into a series of dialogues between Jesus and the disciples and Jesus and the crowds.

12:1–12. Luke transitions from Jesus's condemnation of his adversaries (11:37–54): **Meanwhile, after thousands of people had gathered, so that they were trampling one another . . .** (12:1a). The use of *en hois* (preposition plus dative relative) is a temporal expression, translated here "meanwhile," and ties the unit closely to what precedes (see also Acts 26:12; Culy 1989, 72–73). The use of hyperbole, "thousands of people" (lit., "myriads of a crowd"; cf. Acts 21:20) trampling one another to be near Jesus, creates an atmosphere that is "electric" (Johnson 1991, 196). In this context, Jesus addresses his disciples: **he began to say to his disciples first, "Guard yourselves from the leaven of the Pharisees, which is hypocrisy"** (12:1b). The adverbial accusative "first" could modify the verb "guard" (e.g., "above all, guard yourselves"; so Johnson 1991, 193), but given Jesus's alternating address to the disciples and the crowd, it more probably modifies *legein* ("to say"; so Marshall 1978, 511; see Culy, Parsons, and Stigall 2010, 410). Leaven, or sourdough, was fermented and was a necessary element in the production of bread in the ancient world (Danker 1988, 244); it could, however, easily become tainted and spoil the rest of the bread (in modern idiom, it might be better likened to a virus; see D. Garland 2011, 503). The pervasive corrupting force of leaven was well-known among Jewish, Christian, and pagan writers (see Amos 4:4–5; Ign. *Magn.* 10.2; Plutarch, *Quaest. rom.* 109). The phrase "leaven of the Pharisees" occurs in all three Synoptics (cf. Matt. 16:5–6; Mark 8:15), but only Luke identifies the leaven as "hypocrisy" (see Fitzmyer 1981–85, 2:953). Although Luke does not label the Pharisees as "hypocrites" elsewhere in his Gospel (as Matthew does in chap. 23; cf. Mark 7:6), the connotation of concealing corruption under outward piety is consistent with Jesus's condemnation of the Pharisees in 11:44, where he compares them to "unmarked graves," in which "they do not come across on the surface as that which they really are" (Fitzmyer 1981–85, 2:954).

This theme continues in Jesus's next remarks: **Nothing has been concealed that will not be revealed, and nothing is secret that will not be made known; because whatever you have said in the darkness will be heard in the light, and that which you have whispered in inner rooms will be proclaimed from the rooftops** (12:2–3). The Lukan Jesus employs a combination of rhetorical figures in these verses. Antithesis (or *contentio*), according to one ancient writer, "is built upon contraries" (e.g., "When there is need for you to be silent, you are uproarious; when you should speak, you grow mute. Present, you wish to be absent; absent you are eager to return"; *Rhet. Her.* 4.15.21, trans. Caplan 1954) and uses these contrasting words or thoughts in succession in order to give "impressiveness and distinction" (*Rhet. Her.* 4.15.21, trans. Caplan 1954; see also Quintilian, *Inst.* 9.3.81–86). Jesus contrasts concealed/revealed, secret/made known, darkness/light, and whispered in inner rooms/proclaimed from rooftops (cf. 8:16–17; 11:34–36). These verses also reflect pleonasm, a rhetorical figure of thought that repeats the same thought in different words (Quintilian, *Inst.* 9.3.45–46; see also *Rhet. Her.* 4.42.54; Reich 2011, 53). These figures drive home the point for the hearers that Jesus's followers "must not share the hypocrisy of which he accused the Pharisees" (Tannehill 1996, 201), because in the face of trials and tribulations each person's true character will be disclosed (Culpepper 1995, 252).

The implied context of persecution is made clear in Jesus's next words: **I tell you, my friends, do not shy away from those who kill the body and afterward cannot do anything more. I will show you whom to fear: fear the one who, after killing, has authority to throw you into Gehenna. Yes, I tell you, fear this one!** (12:4–5). For the only time in the Gospel of Luke, Jesus calls his disciples "friends" (see "Theological Issues" for 9:51–11:13; cf. John 15:13–15) and advises them not to shy away from those who can kill only the body. Ancient philosophers made similar diagnoses, arguing that fear, especially the fear of death, creates cowards (e.g., Aristotle, *Eth. nic.* 3.6; Seneca, *Ep.* 4; cited by Johnson 1991, 196). Epictetus counseled that one should fear the loss of reason, not death (*Diatr.* 3.10.12–20). Jesus's remedy is grounded in his Jewish worldview: fear the one who has authority over one's body *and* one's ultimate existence, namely, God. Only God has the power to cast one into Gehenna (a name based on the Valley of Hinnom outside Jerusalem; it was long known as the earlier site of child sacrifice and as a constantly burning garbage heap [see Jer. 7:29–34], and later it was a metaphor for a fiery place of punishment [2 Esd. (*4 Ezra*) 7:36; *Sib. Or.* 1.100–103; 2.283–312]). This sentiment closely echoes that found in 4 Maccabees: "Let us not fear him who thinks he is killing us, for great is the struggle of the soul and the danger of external torment lying before those who transgress the commandment of God" (4 Macc. 13:14–15). This view also has affinities with the view of some Greco-Roman traditions. Epictetus gives this example of an imagined response of a subject to a ruler who threatens imprisonment: "You don't actually think, do you, that God would permit me, one of God's sons, to be enslaved? Of my dead body you are, of course, the master; so go ahead and take it" (*Diatr.* 1.19.8–9, cited by Danker 1988, 245).

Jesus then uses a "lesser to greater" (*a minori ad maius*) argument (see also 12:24–28, below) to reassure his audience that God is not only all-powerful but also endlessly protective: **Are not five sparrows sold for two assaria? And not one of them has been forgotten before God. Contrary to what you might think, even the hairs of your head have all been numbered! Do not be afraid. You are more valuable than many sparrows** (12:6–7). God does not forget the sparrows, whose limited market value made them a favored source of protein among the poor (Fitzmyer 1981–85, 2:960). How much more valuable are those created in God's image than many sparrows? God even knows the number of hairs on each head (cf. Luke 21:18). Jesus urges his followers to replace fear in the form of anxiety in the face of the hostilities of one's human adversaries with fear in the form of religious awe of God, who is all-powerful and endlessly compassionate (see Johnson 1991, 196).

Jesus's final words in this unit presume two courtroom settings; the first is eschatological: **I tell you, everyone who acknowledges me before people, the Son of Man will also acknowledge him before God's angels; but the one who denies me before people will be denied before God's angels** (12:8–9). The unit begins with the same words as the previous pericope (12:4), "I tell you," and continues the theme of the need to publicly confess allegiance to Jesus in this world in order that the Son of Man will claim his followers in the judgment to come before God's council of angels. The next saying has been the subject of much debate over the centuries: **And everyone who says a word against the Son of Man will be forgiven, but the one who blasphemes against the Holy Spirit will not be forgiven** (12:10). What is the difference between speaking against the Son of Man and blaspheming against the Holy Spirit? Why can

The Roman Assarion

Figure 18. Copper Coin of Nero from Sepphoris

To make his point that God cares for his creation, Jesus uses the illustration that God does not forget the sparrow, which had little market value in the Roman economy: five sparrows could be bought for two assaria (12:6; cf. the Matthean Jesus, whose calculations differ slightly, stating that two sparrows can be bought for one assarion; Matt. 10:29). Under Tiberius and Caligula, the remaining mints in the western half of the empire closed, and coins, classified now as "Roman imperial coinage," were supplied by the imperial mints in Rome and Lugdunum (Lyons, France). Many cities in the Roman East, however, continued to mint local coinage ("Roman provincial coinage") until the end of the third century AD, when reforms forced the closure of civic mints.

The assarion (Latin, *as*) was the smallest denomination in the coinage of ancient Rome. One assarion was typically worth 1/16 of a denarius, although its buying power could vary across the empire. Other common denominations included the dupondius (1/8 denarius, or two assaria) and the sestertius (1/4 denarius, or four assaria and the unit of account). The smallest coin in use in first-century Judea was the lepton (called a quadrantes [*kodrantēs*] in Matt. 5:26), which was valued at 1/4 of an assarion (Fitzmyer 1981–85, 2:1003; cf. Luke 12:59; 21:2, below). At the time of Tiberius, regular soldiers demanded a pay increase from two and one-half sestertii to one denarius a day (Tacitus, *Ann.* 1.17, 26). To use the relatively inexpensive sparrow as an example of God's concern forcefully underscores Jesus's point of God's provision for his followers.

one be forgiven and the other cannot? Denying the Son of Man may reflect a momentary lapse of judgment while under intense pressure, which anticipates Peter's denial of and subsequent forgiveness by Jesus (22:54; 24:34; consider also the example of Paul in Acts). In contrast, unforgiveable blasphemy is characterized by the persistent and obdurate rejection of the work of the Spirit by those who are found to be fighting against God (*theomachoi*; cf. Acts 5:39; e.g., Ananias and Sapphira, who have sinned against the Holy Spirit [Acts 5:4, 9], or Judas, who is full of Satan [Luke 22:3] and not the Holy Spirit [11:13] and who finally descends to his "own place" [Acts 1:25]).

The second trial scene is grounded in the here and now: **When they bring you before the synagogues and rulers and authorities, do not worry how or what you will say in defense or about what you will tell them. For the Holy Spirit will teach you at that very time what you must say** (12:11–12). The situation foretold by Jesus, of course, finds its fulfillment in Acts. Jesus's followers must demonstrate their ultimate dependence on God by relying on the Holy Spirit to teach them what to say in their defense.

12:13–34. The next subunit, 12:13–34, deals with "greed," a familiar topic in the ancient world (Sir. 11:18–19; *T. Jud.* 18–19; Dio Chrysostom, *Or.* 17; Plutarch, *Cupid. divit.*; see Malherbe 1996). Jesus argues that greed produces an insatiable and anxious obsession with the superfluities of wealth. The Lukan Jesus makes his argument through the rhetorical convention of an elaborated *chreia* (Stegman 2007, 332; see also comments on Luke 10:17–24, above). According to Pseudo-Hermogenes (*Prog.* 7–8), an elaborated *chreia* consists of eight steps: (1) a note of praise for the speaker; (2) the *chreia* or saying itself; (3) the rationale or explanation of the *chreia*; (4) a statement of the contrary; (5) a statement from analogy; (6) a statement from example (usually of a well-known historical figure); (7) a statement by an authority figure; and (8) a closing exhortation (*Rhet. Her.* 4.43.56; Stegman 2007, 333).

Luke does not follow these steps slavishly, but the rhetorical convention of the elaborated *chreia* does illuminate the ways in which the Lukan Jesus points out the damaging effects of greed and offers an antidote to those suffering from it. The unit can be outlined as follows (modifying Stegman 2007, 329):

12:13–14 setting and a brief *encomium* of speaker (Jesus addressed as "Teacher")

12:15a *responsive chreia* ("Watch out for and keep away from all greed")

12:15b *rationale* ("because/for even when someone has more than he or she needs that person's life does not consist of his belongings")

12:16–21 *statement of the contrary* (parable of the rich fool)

12:22–23 teaching on anxiety

12:24–27a *statements from analogy* (ravens and lilies)

12:27b–28 *example* of Solomon

12:29–30a (negative) *example* of gentiles
12:30b–32 *testimony* of an authority
12:33–34 *closing exhortations* (12:33) with *rationale* (12:34)

Only one of these elements, the teaching on anxiety, does not fit the features of an elaborated *chreia*, and the cumulative effect of these elements taken together is to make what ancient rhetoricians labelled a "complete argument" regarding the dangers of greediness.

The setting is a dispute regarding inheritance between brothers: **Someone from the crowd said to him, "Teacher, tell my brother to divide the inheritance with me"** (12:13). Mosaic law did address issues of inheritance, of which the firstborn son was allocated a double portion (Deut. 21:15–17; cf. Num. 27:1–11; 36:7–9; this was also a topic of interest in postbiblical Judaism—cf. *m. B. Bat.* 8–9 and the parable of the prodigal in Luke 15, esp. 15:12). But such disputes were not limited to the Jewish context; in the Greco-Roman agrarian economy "wealth was far more likely to be inherited than earned, making disputes about inheritance far more frequent and important" (Hock 2003, 183). Nor was it unusual for those involved in inheritance disputes to appeal to third parties, such as philosophers or religious leaders, for arbitration (e.g., Polemo in Philostratus, *Vit. soph.* 532; Philetas in Longus, *Daphn.* 2.15.1; cited by Hock 2003, 183). Thus Jesus is addressed with the honorific title "Teacher" (which contributes to the overall positive picture of Jesus in this encomiastic *bios*) and then is requested (demanded?) to adjudicate the debate. The nature of the debate was not considered important by Luke (Fitzmyer 1981–85, 2:969). Jesus's response is sharp: **But he said to him, "Man, who appointed me judge or arbitrator over you?"** (12:14). The vocative "man" is a "rebuking term, implying aloofness" (Fitzmyer 1981–85, 2:969; cf. Luke 22:58, 60). The rhetorical question implies that Jesus rejects the request; he has more important things to accomplish than to judge or arbitrate in a domestic dispute over inheritance.

But Jesus does use the occasion to offer his thoughts on the topic of greed. **Then he said to them, "Watch out for and keep away from all greed"** (12:15a). This is a variation of a "responsive *chreia*," which, according to Theon, is a *chreia* that gives "a cause for the answer to a question" that "apart from the answer to the question, include[s] some cause or advice" (Theon, *Prog.* 98, trans. Kennedy 2003, 16). Jesus warns "them" (the disputants, the disciples, and the crowd) to watch out for greed; next, he gives the rationale for his *chreia*: **for even when someone has more than he or she needs that person's life does not consist of his or her belongings** (12:15b). Jesus's saying resonates with other discussions of greed (or covetousness). Plutarch observes this about those who wasted their living on superfluous luxuries: "For his ailment is not poverty, but insatiability and avarice, arising from the presence in him of a false and unreflecting judgment; and unless someone removes this, like a tapeworm, from his mind, he will never cease to 'need' superfluities—that is, to want what he does not need" (*Cupid. divit.* 524D, cited by Malherbe 1996, 126).

Jesus then further elaborates on the *chreia* by giving a statement to the contrary in the form of a parable: **Then he told them a parable, saying, "A certain rich man's farm produced a good harvest"** (12:16). The parables of the rich fool and the rich man and Lazarus both begin with the verbal parallel "a certain rich man" (*anthrōpos tis plousios*; 12:16; 16:19—found elsewhere only in the parable of the unjust steward, 16:1). The rich fool and the rich man of Luke 16:19–31 parallel each other not only in that they are rich but also in that each seems unconcerned with anyone except himself. As Blomberg notes: "The rich fool ignores God; the rich man ignores Lazarus. Both die; no other parables of Jesus relate the death of one of their characters. Both parables continue by recounting the tragic consequences of the rich men's deaths" (Blomberg 1990, 241). The land brings forth an abundant yield, but of course, it is God who is the source and agent of the harvest (Ps. 24:1), a fact the rich farmer does not acknowledge.

Rather than seeking God's counsel through prayer regarding how to handle his good fortune (cf. Ps. 112), the farmer soliloquizes: **So he began thinking to himself and saying, "What should I do, since I do not have a place where I can store my crops?"** (12:17). The inner dialogue discloses his "true values and motivations" (Sellew 1992, 252), and the use of first-person singulars hints that his answer is already in his question: **Then he said, "Here is what I will do: I will tear down my barns and build bigger ones. I will store all the grain and my goods there"** (12:18). The man's response violates authentic Jewish piety, which expects that the rich will use their surplus to benefit those in need of relief (see Tob. 4:16). Then the man will be able to put up his feet and rest: **and I will say to myself, "You have many good things that have been stockpiled for many years to come. Relax! Eat! Drink! Be happy!"** (12:19). His self-satisfaction is inscribed in these acts of "carefree, luxurious, even dissipated living" (Fitzmyer 1981–85, 2:973; cf. Eccles. 8:15; Euripides, *Alc.* 788–89). The farmer has given in to his greed and refuses to recognize any responsibility to bring relief to those less fortunate.

He has calculated his possessions carefully, but not wisely, and there is another reckoning to come: **But God said to him, "Fool! This night your life will be demanded from you. Then that which you have prepared, whose will it be?"** (12:20). So God suddenly appears and pronounces the man a "fool"; in the background is Ps. 13:1 LXX: "The fool says in his heart, 'There is no God'" (RSV). Certainly this farmer has been acting as a "functional atheist." Failure to acknowledge God also means failure to acknowledge the one who is the source and owner of life and the fragility and unpredictability of life. Suddenly, with the knowledge that his life is at an end, all of his premeditated calculations regarding his possessions do indeed seem foolish.

Jesus steps back into the picture and hammers home the parable's point that a person's life does not consist of possessions: **So shall it be for the one who stores things up for oneself and is not rich toward God** (12:21). By now it is clear that becoming rich toward God involves the opposite of storing things up for oneself; being rich toward God means sharing one's riches with others. Only then can covetousness be healed.

Jesus next addresses the anxieties that (over)concern with the materiality/physicality of life can cause: **Then he said to his disciples, "Because of this I tell you, do not worry, with regard to life, about what you will eat, nor with regard to the body, about what you will wear"** (12:22). Here Jesus has moved from the superfluities of wealth to the necessities of subsistence: food and clothing. But even these necessities, like the superfluities, do not define life. Jesus clarifies his claim by making a "greater to lesser" argument: **For life is more than food, and the body more than clothing** (12:23). Neither the life we live nor the bodies we occupy can be circumscribed or totally defined by the materiality necessary to sustain them. The Lukan Jesus continues the *chreia* elaboration by making statements from analogy, again in the form of a lesser-to-greater argument: **Consider the ravens: they neither sow nor harvest; they do not have a storeroom or a barn, and God provides food for them. You are much more valuable than birds!** (12:24). God cares for the ravens (cf. Ps. 147:9; Job 38:41), considered unclean by Jewish law (Lev. 11:15; Deut. 14:14) and mostly despised in antiquity (see Pliny the Elder, *Nat.* 35.7.23; Fitzmyer 1981–85, 2:978). How much more, then, does God care for humans, the crowning act

---

Riches and the Unpredictability of Life

Both Jewish and Greco-Roman sources comment on the futility of hoarding possessions in the face of a fragile existence. Seneca writes:

"How stupid to plan out the years that lie ahead when you are not even master of tomorrow. What madness to start out with long-term hopes, thinking, 'I'll buy and sell and build. I'll lend money and take back more, and I'll gain positions of honor. And when I'm too old and tired, I'll retire.' Believe me when I tell you everything is unsure, even for the most fortunate." (*Ep.* 101.4, cited by D. Garland 2011, 513)

A similar note is struck by the author of *1 Enoch*:

"Woe to you who acquire silver and gold, but not in righteousness, and say, 'we have become very rich and have possessions and have acquired everything that we desired. Now let us do what we have planned, for we have gathered silver and filled our storehouses, and as many as water are the husbandmen of our houses.' Like water your life will flow away." (*1 En.* 97.8–9, cited by D. Garland 2011, 516)

of God's creative work? Jesus then celebrates human grandeur; God's children are entitled to God's provision of the basic requirements of subsistence. At the same time, Jesus gives a reminder of human finitude: **Who among you is able to add a cubit to your height by worrying? If, then, you are not able to do such a minor thing, why do you worry about the other things?** (12:25–26). Humans cannot control even the size of their own bodies, much less the cosmos in which they live. Their creatureliness means an utter dependence on God for all provisions. This is the human predicament; the insatiable drive to acquire possessions rests in part on the denial of inherent human self-worth and value and in part on the denial of human finitude (Dillon 1991, 621–22). Anxiety proves no remedy to either.

Jesus gives a second analogy from nature and the example of an authority figure from the past: **Consider the lilies, how they grow. They neither work nor spin. But I tell you, not even Solomon in all his glory was clothed like one of them** (12:27). Solomon's possessions (including his servants' clothing) were proverbial; they completely bedazzled the Queen of Sheba (1 Kings 10:4–5). Yet these were nothing compared to the lilies, who do not even have to work or spin for their clothes. By combining the traditionally female activity of providing clothing (spinning; 12:27) with the traditionally male activity of producing food (sowing, harvesting, and storing; 12:24), Jesus has encompassed the labors "of the human race at large" (Dillon 1991, 619). Jesus then offers another lesser-to-greater argument: **Now, if God clothes the grass in this way, which is in the field today and tomorrow is thrown into an oven, how much more will he clothe you, you of little faith!** (12:28). To make the point more forcefully, Jesus changes "lilies" to "grass," which is both transitory (cf. Isa. 40:6–8) and more mundane. God cares for the grass underfoot; how much more will he care for those created in his image?

Next, Jesus provides a negative example by appealing to the behavior of the "nations," or gentiles, thus encompassing ethnic identity as he has gender: **So do not pursue what you will eat and what you will drink, and do not be unsettled. For all the nations of the world pursue these things** (12:29–30a). Those who "pursue these things" ("eating and drinking" is a metonymy for material security; see Green 1997, 494) are restricted to those who are "of the world" (Danker 1988, 251). Once again, Jesus exhorts his hearers not to be "unsettled" or anxious like these worldly gentiles.

The typical *chreia* elaboration expects testimony from an authoritative figure (Aphthonius, *Prog.* 24–25). Here Jesus appeals neither to Israel's Scriptures nor a figure from Israel's past, but rather he provides witness to the teaching regarding greed on the basis of his own authority as one possessing intimate knowledge of God and God's knowledge (Stegman 2007, 349): **Your Father knows that you need them. Instead, pursue his kingdom, and these things will be provided for you. Do not be afraid, little flock, because your Father was pleased to give the kingdom to you** (12:30b–32). Jesus claims to know that God the father-shepherd knows the needs of his flock and that God is "pleased" to give them the kingdom. The ultimate authority is God, and Jesus, as one with privileged knowledge of God's will, is depicted as God's agent (Stegman 2007, 349–50).

The section ends with Jesus's exhortations (see Ps.-Hermogenes, *Prog.* 8): **Sell your possessions, and give to the needy** (12:33a; cf. Acts 2:42–47; 4:32–35). Generosity is the best antidote for greed, according to Jesus, so he exhorts his followers to engage in almsgiving, a practice valued not only by Jews (see comments on 11:41, above) but also in the larger Greco-Roman world (Philostratus [*Vit. soph.* 2.1] attributes these words to Herodes Atticus: "Right use of wealth means giving to the needy so that their need might end," cited by Danker 1982, 375). Jesus also instructs them on where to store their true treasure: **Make for yourselves purses that do not get old, an inexhaustible treasure in heaven, where a thief cannot come near it nor a moth destroy it** (12:33b; cf. Matt. 6:19–20; *Gos. Thom.* 76). The best safeguard to anxiety over material possessions is to store one's true treasure (membership in God's kingdom) in heaven, where it is not subject to theft. These exhortations are followed by a rationale in the form of a maxim, which "sums it all up" (Fitzmyer 1981–85, 2:982): **For where your treasure is, there your heart will be also** (12:34; cf. Matt. 6:21). The sense here seems to be "follow the trail of the use of money and it will lead you to the heart" (Nolland 1989–93, 2:695; for similar sentiments in pagan philosophy, see Epictetus, *Diatr.* 2.22.19; Sextus Empiricus, *Pyr.* 1.136).

12:35–48. In light of the uncertainty of the timing of the eschaton, in the next unit, 12:35–48, Jesus continues his focus on the impending eschatological judgment (already anticipated by his references to "Gehenna," 12:5; being acknowledged in judgment before "God's angels," 12:9; and storing up "treasure in heaven," 12:33). Jesus begins by employing two well-known images to appeal to his followers to be in a state of "perpetual preparation" (Talbert 1982, 159–60): **Be properly dressed, and have your lamps lit** (12:35). Being "properly dressed" (lit., "let your loins be girded") evokes the figure of a person adjusting ankle-length robes by gathering them up around the waist and loins (Fitzmyer 1981–85, 2:987), and it alludes to the state of readiness required for the Israelites during the first Passover in Egypt (Exod 12:11). The image is used repeatedly in Israel's Scriptures, as well as Second Temple Jewish and early Christian texts, to indicate a posture of preparedness, literally or figuratively (1 Kings 18:46; Job 38:3; see also 2 Kings 4:29; 9:1; Jer. 1:17; Nah. 2:1; 2 Macc. 10:25; 11QtgJob 30.1; 1QM 15.14; Philo, *Sacr.* 63; Eph. 6:14; 1 Pet. 1:13; Pol. *Phil.* 2.1). The lit lamp indicates "watchfulness" (Fitzmyer 1981–85, 2:988; cf. Exod. 27:20; Lev. 24:2; Matt. 25:1). The *Didache* combines these images to make a similar point: "Watch for your life's sake. Let not your lamps be quenched, nor your loins unloosed; but be ready, for you know not the hour in which our Lord will come" (16.1, *ANF* 7:382).

Jesus next employs parabolic language and the figures of the master and slave to continue his plea for readiness. He explores the eschatological context from three perspectives (see Fitzmyer 1981–85, 2:985): (1) the watchful servants awaiting the return of an absent master (12:36–38); (2) the watchful master (12:39–40); and (3) the duties of the manager-slave in charge of the other slaves in the absence of the master (12:41–46).

1. Jesus begins by comparing his followers to servants awaiting their master's return:

> Indeed, you are like people who are waiting for their master, when he returns from the wedding feast, so that when he comes and knocks they might open the door for him immediately. Blessed are those slaves whom the master finds keeping watch when he comes. I assure you, he will dress himself and seat them at the table, and he will come and serve them! And if he should come at the second or third watch and find them doing this, blessed are those people. (12:36–38)

Within the Lukan context, the authorial audience can easily hear allusions in this image to the parousia, and perhaps its delay (2 Pet. 3:3–4, 8–10). The term *kyrios* has a primary meaning here of "master," "but it could easily be understood to refer to Jesus" (Marshall 1978, 535). The watchful servants are ready to open the door for their master (cf. Rev. 3:20), and they will be blessed when they are found keeping watch (Luke 12:37; the eleventh makarism in Luke; see Johnson 1991, 203). The master will reward them by reversing his normal behavior and seating and serving his servants (cf. Luke 17:7–10; Horace, *Sat.* 2.6.107–9; Marshall 1978, 535). The action of the master as servant anticipates Jesus's self-description at the Last Supper (22:27; cf. John 13:1–17) and alludes to the eschatological banquet at which Jesus's followers will feast (13:29; 22:28–30; see Culpepper 1995, 263). If they keep watch late into the night, again they will be called "blessed" (12:38; twelfth makarism).

2. Jesus next turns to the perspective of the watchful master: **But know this: if the master of the house had known at what hour the thief would come, he would not have allowed his house to be broken into!** (12:39). The image of the thief in the night is a common one in early Christian texts, appearing often in the context of the uncertainty of the timing of the parousia (in addition to the parallel tradition in Matt. 24:43, see 1 Thess. 5:2; 2 Pet. 3:10; Rev. 3:3, 16:15; *Gos. Thom.* 21). Here the householder is compared not to Jesus, but to the actions of his audience: **You also must be prepared, because the Son of Man will come at a particular time you do not expect** (12:40). Jesus here makes explicit the eschatological import of his message.

3. Jesus next shifts to the point of view of the manager-slave. First, Peter interrupts to pose a question: **Lord, are you telling this parable to us or to everyone?** (12:41). Peter wonders if Jesus's teaching, which has been alternating back and forth between the disciples and the crowds, is limited to the disciples. The question, unique to the Third Gospel, informs Jesus's response, even though it may seem on the surface that Jesus ignores the query: **The Lord said,**

"Who, then, is the faithful, wise steward, whom the master will put in charge over his servants to give them their allotted food at the proper time?" (12:42). In this context, the "steward" is the slave who oversees the other household slaves (cf. Luke 16:1–8). Jesus points to the responsibilities of the "faithful, wise" manager-slave toward fellow slaves; the authorial audience will naturally make the connection between the steward and their leaders, like Peter (Culpepper 1995, 263; Danker 1988, 254). The distribution of food is singled out as a responsibility of the one in charge (cf. Acts 6:1). Jesus continues: **Blessed is that servant whom the master finds doing his work when he comes. I tell you for certain, he will put him in charge of all his possessions!** (12:43–44). The servant who is wise and faithful in dealing with the others will be blessed by the Master and rewarded with additional responsibilities, but the disobedient steward will suffer a "fate fit for the faithless" (Fitzmyer 1981–85, 2:990): **But if that slave should say in his heart, "My master is taking a long time to come," and should begin to beat the male and female servants, and to eat and drink and become drunk . . .** (12:45). Now the authorial audience understands that the Lukan Jesus is criticizing those in leadership who become lax in their duties as the expectations for an imminent parousia begin to fade ("My master is taking a long time to come"; cf. 2 Pet. 3:4). These leaders cannot be faithful to the master while abusing fellow slaves (cf. Luke 16:1–8; Johnson 1991, 206). To "eat and drink" recalls the selfish actions of the rich fool in 12:19, and becoming drunk is evidence of those who are ill-prepared for the Lord's return (21:34; cf. 1 Thess. 5:6–7).

The Lord's return is certain even though the "day" and "hour" remain unknown (cf. Mark 13:32; Rev. 3:3), and punishment for failed leadership is inevitable and severe: **the master of that servant will arrive on a day when he is not expecting him and at an hour that he does not anticipate, and he will cut him in two and will assign him a place with the unfaithful** (12:46). Some reject the view that the punishment "cut in two" should be taken literally (Johnson 1991, 205), asserting that it is a figure of speech like "I'll tan your hide" (Marshall 1978, 543). Of course, the reference is within parabolic material, and there is no reason to think that such a punishment was meted out in "reality" in this particular situation. It is doubtful, however, that Jesus's audience, who participated in the narrative world created by the story, took the punishment as a figure of speech. Such brutal executions, while perhaps not common, were nevertheless not unknown in the ancient world (Homer, *Od.* 18.339; Herodotus, *Hist.* 2.139; Sus. 55; *3 Bar.* 16; Heb. 11:37), and this was a punishment that perfectly fit the crime and corresponded to "the double life that he [the manager] would be leading" (Fitzmyer 1981–85, 2:986). The punishment may also allude to Jer. 34:18–19, in which the consequences for breaking covenant with God entail having the transgressors cut in two, like the animal originally used to "cut the covenant." The place of the "unfaithful" to which the disobedient leader is assigned is an eschatological destiny

(Nolland 1989–93, 2:704; Tannehill 1996, 212) and need not push toward a figurative rendering of the punishment (cf. Judas, who "burst in the middle" and went to his own "place" of punishment; Acts 1:18, 25).

Furthermore, there is a "gradation of punishment" (Talbert 1982, 160), using the rhetorical figure of antithesis (Quintilian, *Inst.* 9.3.81–86; *Rhet. Her.* 4.15.21; see above): **That servant who knew the desire of his master and did not prepare or act in accord with his desire will be beaten with many blows; but the one who did not know [his master's will], although he did things worthy of blows, will be beaten with few blows** (12:47–48a). Tyrannical abuse of authority is punished by death; deliberate neglect by the servant results in a severe beating. Unintended neglect leads to a "light" beating. Again, there is no indication that this kind of discipline was actually practiced among early Christians, but these sayings do reflect the common assumption in Jewish tradition that there was a difference in punishment expected for deliberate sin versus that committed in ignorance (Num. 15:27–30; 1QS 5.12; CD 8.8; 10.3; Fitzmyer 1981–85, 2:992; cf. Epictetus, *Diatr.* 1.26.6–7, who also argues that moral considerations need to take into account actions done in ignorance). Jesus offers this apt summary: **Regarding all to whom much is given, much will be required of them; and to those to whom much is entrusted, much more will be asked of them** (12:48b). Jesus's words here are consistent with the view that leaders have greater responsibility for their actions: "For the lowliest may be pardoned in mercy, but the mighty will be mightily tested" (Wis. 6:6).

12:49–53. Jesus next turns to the purpose and effects of his ministry: **I have come to cast fire on the earth, and how I wish it had already been kindled! I have a baptism with which to be baptized, and how distressed I am until it is completed. Do you think that I came to bring about peace on earth? No, I tell you, but rather division!** (12:49–51; on the translation of 12:49b, see Culy, Parsons, and Stigall 2010, 442). Jesus issues three pronouncements regarding his mission: "I have come to cast fire" (cf. *Gos. Thom.* 10, 82); "I have a baptism" (cf. Mark 10:38); and "I came to bring . . . division" (cf. Luke 2:34–35). While some have seen in Jesus's claim to cast fire on the earth a foreshadowing of the gift of the Spirit at Pentecost (with the concomitant sign of fire; Acts 2; see Talbert 1982, 160–61), the immediate context of conflict and judgment and the larger argument of the Third Gospel demand that the imagery of fire be associated with eschatological judgment (Luke 3:9, 17; 17:29; see Marshall 1978, 547; D. Garland 2011, 530). This fire, however, is only properly a sign of divine judgment (3:9, 17) and not human revenge or retaliation (cf. 9:54).

The Lukan Jesus does not specify the nature of his baptism, although the authorial audience, familiar with Mark (10:38), will infer that he is referring to his suffering and death, or in Lukan idiom, his being "taken up" in death/resurrection/exaltation (Luke 9:51); he is distressed until the mission in Jerusalem, toward which he set his face at the beginning of this journey, is completed. The most startling revelation here is that Jesus claims to have come not "to bring about peace on earth" but "rather division." The angelic chorus proclaiming "peace on earth" (2:14) seems far away now (as does 1:17); much closer seems Simeon's prophecy that the child Jesus was "to be a sign to be spoken against" (2:34). Rome's peace was "false and only preserved the existing order" (D. Garland 2011, 531); Jesus's peace would come at a cost, because "the call for decision is a call for 'division'" (Ellis 1974, 182). Conflict precedes real peace; division marks the beginning of authentic reconciliation (Culpepper 1995, 266).

These divisions would begin with the basic social unit, the family: **For from now on there will be five in one house who are divided, three against two and two against three. Father will be divided against son and son against father, mother against daughter and daughter against mother, mother-in-law against her daughter-in-law and daughter-in-law against mother-in-law** (12:52–53). These divisions echo the divisions of Mic. 7:6 ("for the son treats the father with contempt, the daughter rises up against her mother, the daughter-in-law against her mother-in-law; your enemies are members of your own household"; cf. *Jub.* 23.19; *1 En.* 100.2) and presume a family unit of "five in one house": father, mother, daughter, son, and son's wife (Marshall 1978, 549). Jesus's own family members were the first to suffer from this divisiveness: Simeon predicted that because of this child a sword would pierce Mary's soul (2:35; cf. 2:48–50; 8:19–21).

12:54–59. Jesus turns his attention to the crowds again: **Then he also proceeded to say to the crowds, "When you see a cloud rising in the west, immediately you say, 'A rainstorm is coming'; and it does. And when you see a south wind blowing, you say, 'There will be a scorching heat,' and there is"** (12:54–55). The "weather-wise" Palestinian farmers were able to read the meteorological signs, since their livelihood depended on it. Clouds from the west, from the direction of the Mediterranean Sea, foretold of impending rain; the prognosis of southerly and southwesterly winds, from the direction of the desert, was scorching heat (Culpepper 1995, 266; cf., however, Bovon 2002–13, 2:40–43, who argues that Luke has adapted the weather signs to fit his own situation, which Bovon thinks is Greece). Jesus criticizes their lack of "religious sensitiveness" by way of contrast with their prowess in "meteorological sensitiveness" (T. Manson 1949, 121): **Hypocrites! You know how to interpret the appearance of the earth and sky; so how is it that you do not know how to interpret this present time?** (12:56). Again the argument is from lesser to greater: they are hypocrites (cf. 12:1) because they are able to discern weather patterns but they are missing the more important signs of the time (cf. *Gos. Thom.* 91).

Jesus next asks a rhetorical question (see *Rhet. Her.* 4.15.22): **And why do you not also judge for yourselves what is right?** (12:57). Their inability to judge what is "right" (*dikaion*) will be tragically revealed later in the story when it takes an outsider, a Roman centurion, to recognize and confess at Jesus's death that "surely this man was righteous [*dikaios*]!" (23:47). Jesus then ends this section, as he did 12:1–12, with an appeal to a juridical setting: **As you are going to appear before an official with your accuser, make an effort to settle the matter with him on the way, so that he will not drag you before the judge, and the judge hand you over to the bailiff, and the bailiff throw you in prison. I tell you, you will certainly not leave there until you repay the very last penny** (12:58–59). The case seems to be that of a debtor being dragged to court (Marshall 1978, 551; Nolland 1989–93, 2:714). Jesus urges his auditors to discern the urgency of the times and settle all accounts lest they be left in a hopeless situation with no way out (Culpepper 1995, 268).

13:1–9. Some from within the crowd press Jesus with a question based on a current event: **Now, at that very time some were present who told him about the Galileans whose blood Pilate had mixed with their sacrifices** (13:1). No other ancient source corroborates this event, but Josephus confirms that Jews experienced similar acts of violence under Pilate's rule (see *Ant.* 18.55–59, 60–62, 86–87; *J.W.* 2.169–77). The reference likely is to some Galilean pilgrims who had come to Jerusalem and were slaughtered while making sacrifices at a Jewish festival, perhaps Passover (Fitzmyer 1981–85, 2:1006). Maybe the crowd was looking for a political indictment of Pilate from Jesus (cf. 13:31); if so, they were sorely disappointed (Tannehill 1996, 216). Jesus makes clear the issue is not simply political (Just 1996–97, 2:533) and exposes its theological roots: **He responded and said to them, "Do you think that these Galileans were worse sinners than all the other Galileans because they suffered these things? No, I tell you!"** (13:2–3a). Jesus reveals that underlying the crowd's question was the widespread assumption that calamity is produced by sin (cf. Job 4:7; John 9:2), and he emphatically refutes the notion that there is a direct correlation between tragedy and sinfulness. He then issues a call to repent: **But if you do not repent, you will all likewise perish!** (13:3b). The repentance envisaged here, in light of the immediate context of 12:1–59, involves a turning away from sin (specifically the anxiety over material possessions and perhaps even the view that so easily correlates sin and suffering) but also a turning toward Jesus's message of the inbreaking of God's kingdom (Johnson 1991, 213). That "all" who do not repent will "perish" (e.g., experience "eschatological perdition"; Just 1996–97, 2:531; cf. Luke 4:34; 6:9; 9:24–25) refutes the idea that there is any kind of "privileged exemption" for the apparent righteous (Danker 1988, 260). While Jesus has deflected the invitation to offer political commentary on Pilate's policies by tracing the issue back to the problem of divine justice (Tiede 1988, 246), political aspects are not altogether missing. Jesus's call to repentence had "eschatological and political ramifications"; it was a call for Israel to abandon its nationalistic violence and revolutionary zeal (D. Garland 2011, 542).

If the crowd has brought up the example of human suffering that is the result of intentional human evil, Jesus does them one better by using an example of accidental death, for which there is no apparent guilt to assign (contra Marshall 1978, 554, who suggests Pilate may have had something to do with the tower's faulty construction and ultimate collapse): **Or those eighteen on whom the tower in Siloam fell and killed them, do you think that they were worse offenders than all the people who inhabit Jerusalem?** (13:4). The tower was presumably associated with the reservoir that supplied water to Jerusalem (John 9:7, 11), though there is no mention of its construction (or collapse) in ancient sources; it was apparently "an incident too trifling to figure in a history book" (Marshall 1978, 554). The Lukan Jesus changes "sinners" to "offenders" (lit., "debtors"), a term that refers to "one who commits sin and thus incurs a moral debt" (L&N 88.300; see Culy, Parsons, and Stigall 2010, 451). Jesus's response is the same: **No, I tell you! But if you do not repent, you will all perish as well** (13:5). As with acts of human evil, "natural calamities afford no proof that those who suffer in them are any worse sinners than anybody else" (Marshall 1978, 554). By including both Galileans and Judeans, the "all" of Jesus's warning becomes more prodding to the ears of his listeners.

Jesus then tells a parable to further illustrate his point:

> Then he proceeded to tell this parable: "A certain man had a fig tree planted in his vineyard, and he came looking for fruit on it but did not find any. So he said to the gardener, 'It has been three years since I first came looking for fruit on this fig tree and didn't find any! So, cut it down! Why should it even use up the soil?' He responded and said to him, 'Sir, leave it alone again this year until I have loosened the soil around it and added fertilizer, and it might bear fruit in the future. But if not, you can cut it down.'" (13:6–9)

Jesus explores the other side of his argument in a parable. Rather than pointing to the urgency of a tragedy, Jesus presents the story of a fig tree that, even though it has a choice spot in the vineyard, has failed to produce fruit for three years. Rather than allow the tree to continue to "use up the soil," its owner understandably orders it cut down (cf. John the Baptist's imagery of the ax laid at the root of the tree in Luke 3:9). But the gardener intervenes and asks for one more season to care for the tree; if it does not produce fruit then, it can be cut down. The fig tree is a "symbol of the human being whose life is marked by unproductivity" (Fitzmyer 1981–85, 2:1105), and the absence of God's judgment is not to be taken as a sign of one's righteousness; it is a "sign of God's mercy, not his approval" (Talbert 1982, 161; cf. Acts 14:15–17; Rom. 2:4–5; 2 Pet. 3:9–10).

Theological Issues

The motif of a barren fig tree that faces destruction is found elsewhere in the Synoptic tradition (Mark 11:13–14, 20–21; Matt 21:18–19) and was not unknown in ancient Near Eastern literature. A particularly striking story of an unproductive tree is found in the late Armenian version of the story of Ahiqar:

> And I spake to Nathan thus: Son, thou has been to me like a palm-tree which has grown with roots on the bank of the river. When the fruit ripened, it fell into the river. The lord of the tree came to cut it down, and the tree said: Leave me in the place, that in the next year I may bear fruit. The lord of the tree said: Up to this day hast thou been useless to me, in the future thou wilt not become useful. (*Ahiqar* 8.25, cited by Culpepper 1995, 271)

Those familiar with this story, or some version like it, would have been surprised that the possibility for the tree to produce is left open in Jesus's parable. But the opportunity to produce is not based on the tree's "merits," nor is the invitation open-ended, for "there may be a wideness to God's mercy, but there is a limit to God's patience" (D. Garland 2011, 534).

It is also tempting to allegorize the parable of the barren fig tree within the larger context of Luke's narrative and with a christological focus. The fig tree represents those who have refused to respond to the ministry of Jesus the gardener, who in his compassion offers to tend the tree one more year when God, the owner of the vineyard, arrives to pronounce judgment. There are, of course, problems with this kind of allegory that seeks a referent for every detail. Luke shows no knowledge of a three-year ministry of Jesus (this "fact" is inferred from the Gospel of John). And what does one do with the reference to adding "fertilizer" (lit., "manure") to the tree? Nonetheless, it would seem difficult for the authorial audience not to hear some christological overtones in the context of Luke's Gospel, in which Jesus is another Galilean on the way to Jerusalem to have his blood shed by Pilate while he prays.

Luke 13:10–14:35

More Healings and Parables

Introductory Matters

The final unit of this section consists of five scenes: 13:10–17; 13:18–35; 14:1–14; 14:15–24; and 14:25–35. This section focuses again on Jesus's words and deeds: his healings (the bent woman and the man with dropsy) and his teaching on topics that range from the eschatological banquet to the cost of discipleship.

Tracing the Narrative Flow

The Bent Woman (13:10–17)

The story of the bent woman reveals "Luke's considerable literary skill" (O'Toole 1992). The passage is a diptych composed of two panels, with verses 11–13 paralleling 14–17 (O'Toole 1992; on the relationship of the pericope to the larger context, see Green 1989; Seim 1994, 39–57):

> First Panel (13:11–13)
>   1. Bent woman gets Jesus's attention (13:11)
>   2. Jesus calls the woman and cures her (13:12–13a)
>   3. Twofold results of Jesus's actions (13:13b)
>   a. Immediately, she is made straight
>   b. And she praises God
> Second Panel (13:14–17)
>   1. Ruler of synagogue's words get Jesus's attention (13:14)

2. Jesus reacts to the ruler's words (13:15–16)
3. Twofold results of Jesus's words (13:17)
   a. Jesus's adversaries are put to shame
   b. All the people rejoice

> **Luke 13:10–14:35 in the Narrative Flow**
>
> Jesus's origins and training (1:1–4:13)
> Jesus's mighty words and deeds in Galilee (4:14–9:50)
> Jesus's mighty words and deeds along the way (part 1) (9:51–14:35)
>   Beginning the journey (Luke 9:51–11:13)
>   Jesus in dialogue (11:14–13:9)
>   ▶ More healings and parables (13:10–14:35)
>   The bent woman (13:10–17)
>   On the kingdom and tyrants (13:18–35)
>   The thirst for status (14:1–14)
>   The parable of the big dinner (14:15–24)
>   More sayings along the way (14:25–35)

13:10–13. The story begins with Jesus in the synagogue: **Now, he was teaching in one of the synagogues on the Sabbath, and there was a woman there who had had a spirit that caused an illness for eighteen years! She was bent over and unable to stand up completely straight** (13:10–11). Attempts to give a modern medical diagnosis of the woman's condition (*ankylosing spondylitis* according to Wilkinson 1980, 74) are largely irrelevant to Luke's purposes. More important, given the interest in the "physiognomic consciousness" in the Greco-Roman world, would be Luke's attempt to link the woman's physical condition with her inner moral characteristics (see Parsons 2011). Luke couples the physical description of the woman in Luke 13 as having a physical condition of being "doubled over" and "unable to stand up straight" with the comment that she has a spirit that has caused an illness (*pneuma echousa astheneias*; lit., "having a spirit of weakness"), making a connection between the physical and spiritual in physiognomic terms.

Reference is made to the physical characteristic of the "bent" or "crooked" back in the physiognomic tractates. In pseudo-Aristotle's *Physiognomics*, we read: "Those whose back is very large and strong are of strong character; witness the male. Those which have a narrow, weak back are feeble; witness the female" (810b.10–12, trans. Hett 1936; cf. 810b.25–32; Polemo, *Phys.* 11). According to physiognomic traditions, then, the bent woman's problem is best understood as a "moral" problem. Her bent back is the result of a "feeble" character, if not an "evil disposition" (Ps.-Aristotle, *Phys.* 809a, trans. Hett 1936). This characterization sheds light on Luke's description of the woman as having a "spirit of weakness," which, according to the physiognomic handbooks, is a characteristically feminine problem.

In this thinking, women are weaker in moral character than men and are therefore more prone to bent backs. The woman's crooked stature would have been understood to indicate, as pseudo-Aristotle suggests, an "evil disposition," and it would have been apparent to the Lukan Jesus that this was a physical manifestation of a satanic possession, the bonds of which Jesus has decided to break. This explanation also clarifies Jesus's comments before he heals the woman: **So when Jesus saw her, he called out and said to her, "Woman, you have been released from your illness!" Then he placed his hands on her, and immediately she was straightened and began glorifying God** (13:12–13). The language of "release" suggests some kind of demonic bondage (see also 13:16). Here Luke is giving a distinctively Jewish explanation for the evil disposition: it was caused by Satan.

13:14–17. Luke does not let this misogynist characterization of women as "feeble" and of "evil disposition" go unchallenged. The story continues: **But the ruler of the synagogue, who was indignant because Jesus had healed on the Sabbath, responded and proceeded to say to the crowd, "There are six days on which one ought to work. So then, come and be healed on them, and not on the Sabbath day." The Lord responded to him and said, "Hypocrites! Does not each of you on the Sabbath untie his ox or donkey from its stall and, after leading it out, give it water?"** (13:14–15). Interpreters have long queried why these specific animals are chosen for comparison with the bent woman. Aside from the fact that they are domestic animals and thus provide a way for Jesus to show that his opponents care more for livestock than for a fellow human, is there any other point of contact? The zoological method of the physiognomic handbooks sheds some light here as well. The ox (or cattle) and ass are repeatedly singled out in pseudo-Aristotle for physical traits that indicate some mar in character for humans who resemble those traits. We may cite several examples. "Those that have thick extremities to the nostrils are lazy; witness cattle" (*Physiog.* 6.811a.28–29, trans. Hett 1936; see also 6.811b.5–6, where cattle are depicted as lazy again). In the next sentence we read that "those with thin faces are careful, with fleshiness are cowardly, witness *donkeys* and deer" (6.811b.6–7, trans. Hett 1936, emphasis mine). Of particular interest is a passage in which donkeys and cattle share a negative trait: "Those with large faces are sluggish: witness *donkeys and cattle*" (6.811b.9–10, trans. Hett 1936, emphasis mine). Elsewhere donkeys are depicted as stupid, because of their bulging eyes (6.811b.25–26); insensitive, because of their round faces (6.811b.31–32) or small heads (6.812a.7–8); and insolent, because of their braying voices (6.813a.31–32). Similarly, cattle are singled out as sluggish, because of their large eyes (6.811b.21–22) or their large faces (6.811b.30–31), and despondent, because their voices begin deep and end high pitched (6.813a.32–34). To the audience familiar with these characterizations, the message of the Lukan Jesus is clear. Not only are Jesus's opponents more willing to aid an animal than a woman, but they are also more willing to aid those animals who symbolize negative traits such as cowardice, sluggishness, stupidity, laziness, or insolence than to help a daughter of Abraham whose status is masked, *not* reflected, by her physical condition.

Jesus's response to his detractors continues: **So shouldn't this woman, who is a daughter of Abraham whom Satan has bound for eighteen years, be set free from this bondage on the Sabbath day?** (13:16). When he is challenged by the synagogue ruler for healing on the Sabbath, Jesus declares that the woman *is* a "daughter of Abraham," and here is another clue to Luke's strategy of introducing physiognomic concerns in order to subvert them (see Grundmann 1966, 280). Strictly speaking, not only is the phrase "daughter of Abraham" unique in the NT, it also does not occur in any Jewish literature prior to, or contemporary with, Luke (Jervell 1984, 148). A similar, but not verbatim, phrase, however, does occur in several passages in 4 Maccabees (14:20; 15:28; 17:6; 18:20), a Hellenistic Jewish document (first century BC–first century AD) that is echoed in the writings of Paul and Hebrews (O'Toole 1992, 96–97; Seim 1994, 44–49). In each of these passages, Abrahamic categories are applied to the same woman, the courageous mother of the seven sons, whom she encourages to accept martyrdom rather than violate food laws. After watching all seven of her sons die a cruel death, she herself is martyred (Young 1991, 72).

The woman in 4 Maccabees is "the daughter of Abraham's strength" (4 Macc. 15:28 author's trans.). She recalls the "strength" of Abraham, both in her role as mother willing to sacrifice her sons and ultimately also in her role as martyr willing to lay down her own life in order that both she and her sons remain faithful to their religious faith. According to physiognomic tradition, the contrast between the apparent "moral weakness" of the bent woman and the "moral strength" of the Maccabean mother could not be starker. Thus, by having Jesus refer to the bent woman as a "daughter of Abraham," Luke is doing much more than making a bland reference to the fact that she was a "Jewess" (Jervell 1984, 148). Rather, he echoes a tradition with which much of his audience would have been familiar—the tradition of the Jewish mother who courageously sacrificed both sons and self for her faith and thereby brought honor to the strength of Abraham, founder of her faith. The bent woman, moreover, has *always* been a "daughter of Abraham" (note the present participle). Thus Jesus acknowledges that the woman *is* a daughter of Abraham, not that she has now become one as a result of her healing. Her status as daughter of Abraham is "one of the premises of the healing, not a consequence of it" (Seim 1994, 48).

Luke is able to critique the pervading physiognomic consciousness that would have presumed to know the woman's inner moral condition by her outward appearance. Though her appearance might have prompted those around her to value cowardly, sluggish, or lazy animals above her, this woman, according to Jesus, is—indeed, always has been—a daughter of Abraham, like the Maccabean mother. Her strong moral character has been hidden by her current physical condition, and in unveiling that strength by loosing the satanic bonds, Jesus at the same time exposes the limitations of the physiognomic thinking. Thus the narrator ends the pericope with this evaluative comment: **As he said these things, all those who were opposing him were put to shame, and the whole crowd was rejoicing at the wonderful things that were being done by him** (13:17).

On the Kingdom and Tyrants (13:18–35)

13:18–35. The narrator turns from Jesus's deeds back to his words, in which Jesus compares the kingdom of God to a mustard seed and leaven by way of simile (*imago*; see *Rhet. Her.* 4.49.62): **Then he proceeded to say, "What is the kingdom of God like, and to what shall I compare it? It is like a mustard seed that a person took and tossed into a garden, and it grew and became a tree, and the birds of the air nested in its branches"** (13:18–19). In the parallel traditions, Mark (4:30–32) and Matthew (13:31–32; see also *Gos. Thom.* 20) draw an explicit contrast between the tiny mustard seed and the very large shrub into which it grows; in Luke, the emphasis is on growth and development (Fitzmyer 1981–85, 2:1016)—a seed grows into a tree. The contrast between small and large is not entirely missing, however (and is reinforced by the reference to the leaven; see below); the tree is large enough to support "the birds of the air" in its branches. Luke has several other interesting variations. Mark

A Christological Interpretation of "Eighteen"?

The formula of Luke 13:16, ten and eight (*deka kai oktō*), is reminiscent of the noncanonical text of *Barnabas*, a late first- or second-century Christian text. In *Barn.* 9.7–9, the author explains that the number 318 (= *tau iōta ēta*, since Greek letters functioned as numerals), which occurs at Gen. 14:14, has hidden meaning. About eighteen, he writes: "As for the 'ten and eight,' the I [*iōta*] is ten and the H [*ēta*] is eight; thus you have 'Jesus.' And because the cross, which is shaped like the T [*tau*], was destined to convey grace, it mentions also the 'three hundred.' So he reveals Jesus in the two letters, and the cross in the other one" (*Barn.* 9.8, trans. Holmes 2007, 409; cf. Clement of Alexandria, *Strom.* 9). Luke, like other early Christian writers, saw the christological value of the number eighteen. For Luke, eighteen was the appropriate length of time for the woman's illness, for Christ himself is hidden in the number. Read properly, the reference to "eighteen" would have served as a rhetorical marker that the woman's time of illness had reached its fullness. The very length of the bent woman's illness, eighteen years, is the sacred name of Jesus. Despite the nature and length of her illness, or perhaps because of it (!), this woman is revealed by Jesus to be a daughter of Abraham, one who is not a woman of weak character or evil disposition, but rather a woman of courage, who, as the length of her illness reminds us, is reclaimed by Christ. Thus, she takes her rightful place within the family of God as a "daughter of Abraham."

says that the seed is "sown upon the ground" (4:31). Matthew refers to a man who took the seed and "sowed in his field" (13:31). Luke refers to the seed being "tossed" (*ebalen*) rather than "sowed" (*espeiren*). Is Luke portraying a less-than-intentional act (cf. Luke 8:4–8)? Further, the Lukan Jesus refers to a "garden" (cf. "cultivated soil" in *Gos. Thom.* 20) rather than Mark's nondescript "ground" (or even Matthew's "field"). This reference could be to parallel the saying with the one that follows: both occur in "domestic" space (Nolland 1989–93, 2:728) but should not, contrary to patristic tradition, be allegorized as referring to the "garden" of Eden (the LXX uses a different word for that, *paradeisos*; see Gen. 2:8 LXX; Luke 23:43). Underlying the parable is an allusion to Ezekiel, in which God also plants a tree and provides nesting in its branches for "winged creatures of every kind" (17:22). That tree, however, is a "noble cedar" (17:23) and not a mustard bush. From the modest beginnings of Jesus's ministry will come God's rule. "The lesson of the parable stresses the organic unity between Jesus's present ministry in Israel and a future form of the kingdom of God" (Fitzmyer 1981–85, 2:1016; see also Dahl 1952, 141–66).

Jesus makes a second comparison: **Again he said, "To what shall I compare the kingdom of God? It is like leaven that a woman took and worked into three measures of wheat until the whole was completely leavened"** (13:20–21; cf. Matt. 13:33; *Gos. Thom.* 96). The second comparison is based on the positive properties of leaven (Danker 1988, 263; on its negative properties, see comments on Luke 12:1b). Even hidden (rather than "mixed"), the leaven is able to fulfill its function as an agent of change and the "three measures of wheat" (i.e., fifty pounds) were "completely leavened." Again, the emphasis is on the unlikely growth from small to large. "Who can calculate what great things have come from these small beginnings? So what is the kingdom of God like? A mustard seed. Leaven" (Culpepper 1995, 276).

Jesus's journey continues: **Now, he was traveling from city to city and village to village, teaching and journeying toward Jerusalem** (13:22). This is the first of several travel notices (see also 17:11; 19:28) since the travel narrative began in 9:51 (Just 1996–97, 2:547). Its purpose is not to locate Jesus in some particular space or time but to keep the audience's attention on the overall journey framework and on Jesus's vocation of teaching and his intended destination, Jerusalem (Johnson 1991, 216). Once again, someone from the crowd addresses him (see also 9:57; 10:25; 11:15, 27, 45; 12:13, 41; 13:1): **And someone said to him, "Lord, will those who are saved truly be only a few?"** (13:23a). The question about who and how many would populate the world to come was much debated in the Judaism of Jesus's day, and different answers were given. The author of 2 Esdras (*4 Ezra*) writes: "The Most High made this world for the sake of many, but the world to come for the sake of only a few ... many have been created but only a few shall be saved" (2 Esd. [*4 Ezra*] 8:1–3, cited by Vinson 2008, 465). The Mishnah, on the contrary, claims, "All Israelites have a share in the world to come," although it then goes on to qualify that statement by excluding those who deny the resurrection or that the law has divine origins, or who pronounce the Holy Name (*m. Sanh.* 10.1, trans. Danby 1933; see Bock 1994–96, 2:1234; see also 1QS 5.7–11; CD-B 19.33b–35; Luke 18:26; Acts 15; Vinson 2008, 466). In Luke's context, the question may have been prompted by the nature of Jesus's recent teaching: a mustard plant provides a haven for only a few birds; three measures of dough will feed only a small crowd (13:18–21; D. Garland 2011, 557).

> **"Will Those Who Are Saved *Truly* Be Only a Few?"**
>
> Although it has often been argued that *ei* introduces direct questions, under the influence of Hebrew (Fitzmyer 1981–85, 2:1024), Caragounis (2006, 208–16) conclusively demonstrates that *ei* was being confused with *ē*, which was pronounced in the same way, during this period (cf. Heb. 6:14). Caragounis concludes by arguing that as the adverb *ē* was dying out during this period, writers were at times using the homonym *ei* as a substitute (2006, 216). Where *ei* is used in this manner, then, one should likely read the text as if the adverb were being used. Thus, rather than introducing a direct question, *ei* (= *ē*) serves as a "confirmatory" adverb with the sense of something like "certainly," "really," "truly," or "actually," or simply to add rhetorical force to a direct question (see the translation of Luke 13:23a; see also 6:9; 22:49; Culy, Parsons, and Stigall 2010, 187–88).

Jesus, however, refuses to engage in theoretical speculations regarding specific numbers saved but rather chooses to turn the conversation toward what is required of those who would follow his path of discipleship (Carroll 2012, 290). He responded: **Strive to enter through the narrow door, for I tell you, many will try to enter and will not be able** (13:24). Jesus uses the image of entering through a "narrow door," to indicate the arduous nature of discipleship: it is a struggle, not a stroll (Manson 1949, 125). The use of the rhetorical figure of *hyperbaton* (Quintilian, *Inst.* 8.6.62–67), in which the natural word order is transposed (here the words "I tell you" are interposed between the subject, "many," and the verb, "will try"), emphasizes the result that many will not be able to enter. The image then shifts from a narrow to a locked door: **From the time when the householder gets up and locks the door, and you begin to stand outside and knock on the door, saying, "Lord, open for us"** . . . (13:25a). The word describing the action of the householder, "get up," is the same word (*egeirō*) used earlier to refer to Jesus's resurrection (9:22). Could the householder's "rising" allude to the time of judgment following the resurrection (Johnson 1991, 216)? There is a time when those who stand outside and knock will be heard and served (11:10), but there is also a knocking that occurs after the time of salvation, and "no amount of knocking will avail" (Vinson 2008, 467). The picture of the audience standing and knocking at the door of the "Lord" reverses the image of Rev. 3:20. The householder **will in fact respond and say** to you, "I don't know where you come from" (13:25b). One cannot simply rely on inherited religious association or collective ethnic identity to secure entrance (Danker 1988, 264; cf. Luke 3:8).

Jesus anticipates his audience's response: **Then you will begin to say, "We ate and drank in your presence, and you taught in our streets"** (13:26). They protest that they ate and drank with the Lord, an act suggesting intimate communion and interaction, but that will not prove to be enough. Teaching in the streets may allude to the peripatetic nature of Jesus's ministry, but it may also imply some criticism. Perhaps the reason he teaches "in the streets" is because they did not welcome him into their homes (10:10–11; see Vinson 2008, 467). The protest elicits only a repeated rebuke: **And he will certainly say to you, "I don't know where you come from"** (13:27a). It is not that the householder does not know their geographical origins; he cannot discern their spiritual roots (D. Garland 2011, 558). The rebuke ends by quoting a slightly modified version of Ps. 6:9 LXX: **Go away from me, all you evildoers!** (13:27b). The Lukan Jesus has replaced "workers of lawlessness" (Matt. 7:23) with "evildoers" (lit., "workers of injustice"). Listening to Jesus's teachings and enjoying table fellowship with him must lead to deeds of justice. "One must not only hear Jesus's teaching, one must do it" (Carroll 2012, 290; cf. Luke 6:46–49; 8:11–15; 19:21).

The harsh warning continues: **There will be weeping and gnashing of teeth when you see Abraham, Isaac, and Jacob, and all the prophets in the kingdom of God, but yourselves being thrown out!** (13:28). The image is of those who are excluded viewing from the outside those who have gained entry into the kingdom of God. The patriarchal triumvirate (cf. 4 Macc. 7:19; 13:17) are joined in Luke's version by "all the prophets," recalling Jesus's teaching in 6:23. The image of "weeping and gnashing of teeth" is a familiar combination associated with those cast into eschatological "outer darkness" in Matthew (8:12; 13:42, 50; 22:13; 24:51; 25:30), but it is found only here in Luke (Johnson 1991, 217). The emotion expressed by the weeping is accompanied by the gnashing of teeth, which expresses rage (Prov. 19:12; Sir. 51:3), suggesting not soul-searching repentance but self-righteous indignation at the master (Marshall 1978, 567). The judgment, depicted as a shut door, is an "anti-hospitality event" against those who have stubbornly and unrepentantly refused to extend hospitality (Vinson 2008, 463).

Finally, Jesus settles on the image of the eschatological banquet to describe the kingdom of God (cf. Isa. 25:6): **And people will come from east and west and from north and south, and they will take their places at the feast in the kingdom of God** (13:29). In Luke's Gospel, the banquet has been anticipated by the feeding of the five thousand (9:12–17), and it will be figured symbolically in 14:15–24 and ritually enacted in 22:14–30 (see Johnson 1991, 217). Those coming from the four corners of the earth need not be exclusively gentiles, since there was an expected end-time ingathering of the lost tribes of Israel (Isa.

43:5–6; see D. Garland 2011, 558). Nor does the Lukan Jesus mean to suggest that none of his Jewish contemporaries have succeeded in their struggle to enter the narrow door, but the image certainly now includes gentiles among the eschatological people of God (Fitzmyer 1981–85, 2:1023). The pericope ends with a proverbial saying: **Indeed, there are last ones who will be first, and first ones who will be last!** (13:30). The saying generally refers to the great reversal of status that will accompany the eschaton—the lowly will be exalted, and the high and mighty will be brought down (1:53–55; 6:20–26; 9:24; see the introduction to Part 3: Luke 9:51–14:35). In its immediate context, the saying may also function to place Jew ("first") and gentile ("last") on equal footing when it comes to the opportunity to struggle through the narrow door before it closes (see Marshall 1978, 568).

The story now turns to an encounter with some religious authorities: **At that very hour, some Pharisees came to him, saying, "Get away from here quickly, because Herod wants to kill you"** (13:31). Although the Pharisees are antagonists in the narrative, the authorial audience has no reason to doubt the veracity of their claim that Herod wants to put Jesus to death; after all, Herod was more than capable of evil things (3:19). Jesus's resolve to fulfill his vocation is unswerving: **He said to them, "Go and tell that fox, 'I am casting out**

Figure 19. Mosaic of a Hen Gathering Her Chicks in the Chapel of Dominus Flevit

demons and performing healings today and tomorrow, and on the third day I will be finished! Nevertheless, it is necessary for me to continue traveling today, tomorrow, and on the following day, because it is not possible for a prophet to die outside Jerusalem'" (13:32–33). Why call Herod a fox? Polemo comments:

"The fox is wily, deceitful, coy, evasive, rapacious, shrewd" (*Phys.* 174, cited by Malina and Neyrey 1996, 125). Pseudo-Aristotle remarks rather briefly that, in contrast to lions, who are "brave," foxes, because they are "reddish," are of "bad character" (*Physiog.* 812a.17, trans. Hett 1936; cf. Aristotle, *Hist. an.* 1.1.488b.20). This judgment is confirmed in Israel's Scriptures (LXX Ezek. 13:4–5; Song 2:15a) and throughout ancient Mediterranean literature, where foxes are depicted in a mostly negative manner (Arrian, *Epict. diss.* 1.3.7–9; for more, see Parsons 2011, 58).

The primary understanding of the image of "Herod the fox" must be sought within the developing characterization of Herod within the Lukan narrative. It is Herod's foxlike trait of destructiveness that is most likely in the mind of the Lukan audience, a metaphor that is continued in Jesus's next statement about Jerusalem, which begins with the rhetorical figure of reduplication (*conduplicatio*; see *Rhet. Her.* 4.28.38), in which a word is repeated to create a sense of pity or pathos: **Jerusalem, Jerusalem, which kills the prophets and stones those sent to it, how often I wanted to gather together your children just like a hen gathers together her own brood under her wings, and you were not willing!** (13:34). The image is of a hen defending her chicks against an unnamed predator. Given the proximity of the description of Herod, the audience would easily identify that predator as a fox. Jesus would have assumed the seemingly futile role of a protective mother hen defending the children of Jerusalem (had they only been willing) from Herod's destructive and rapacious nature (Darr 1998, 182–83). But that door too has been shut: **Your house is abandoned! I tell you, you will certainly not see me again until [(the time) comes when] you say, "Blessed is the one coming in the name of the Lord!"** (13:35). That day is not far off (19:38) and provides the occasion when Jesus will once again lament the fate of Jerusalem (19:41–44).

The Thirst for Status (14:1–14)

In the next episode (14:1–14), Jesus's action (14:1–6) is intimately connected with his words (14:7–14).

14:1–6. First, Jesus heals a man with dropsy: **And it happened that as he entered the house of one of the leaders of the Pharisees on a Sabbath day to eat some food, they were watching him closely. And a certain man, right in front of him, was sick with dropsy. Jesus responded and spoke to the lawyers and Pharisees, saying, "Is it lawful to heal on the Sabbath, or not?" But they were silent. So, taking hold of the man, he healed him and sent him away** (14:1–4). For many commentators, the illness of the man with dropsy is incidental to the plot, which is an opportunity for the Pharisees to tempt Jesus to heal on the Sabbath. In that view, the man could just as easily have been stricken with leprosy or blindness, but that is to underestimate the function of references to the disease in ancient literature. Dropsy was an ailment usually associated with the severe retention of water (known today as edema), which leads to bloating, weight gain, renal failure, and, more often than not in antiquity, death. In antiquity, dropsy was employed as a favorite metaphor for the vice of avarice (Braun 1995, 30–42). Though popular with the Cynics, this metaphor was not confined to their circles. Polybius writes, "in the case of dropsy the thirst of the sufferer never ceases and is never allayed by the administration of liquids from without, unless we cure the morbid condition of the body itself, so it is impossible to satiate the greed for gain, unless we correct by reasoning the vice inherent in the soul" (Polybius, *Hist.* 13.2.2, trans. Paton 1925). Thus, the dropsical man "appears to be there . . . as a hapless literary figure whose brief cameo role is to be a physical, visual representation of an ethos of craving desire" (Braun 1995, 14, 41).

Jesus then poses a rhetorical question (see *Rhet. Her.* 4.15.22): **"Which of you has a son or ox that falls into a pit and will not immediately pull him out on the Sabbath day?" And they were not able to respond to these things** (14:5–6). Part of the issue, of course, focuses once again on Sabbath restrictions, and Jesus, drawing on Jewish Scripture and tradition, understands the law to have a humanitarian intent (see comments on Luke 6:3–4). Certainly, this saying of Jesus affirms the claim that meeting human need takes priority over strict observance of religious ritual. The views expressed represent distinct humanitarian and legalistic streams within ancient Judaism itself.

14:7–14. The authorial audience would naturally hear the scene that follows against the backdrop of dropsy as a metaphor for the insatiable desire for status and honor: **Then he proceeded to tell a parable to the ones who had been invited, because he had observed how they were choosing the places of honor** (14:7). Their impulsive choosing of places of honor at the table causes Jesus to instruct the guests regarding seating etiquette:

> When you are invited by someone to a wedding, do not sit down in the place of honor, in case someone more important than you has been invited by him, and he who invited you and that person will come and say to you, "Give your place to this person." And then, humiliated, you will be stuck with the least important place. Instead, when you are invited, go and sit down to eat in the least important place, so that when the one who has invited you comes he will say to you, "Friend, move up to a better place." Then you will have glory before everyone dining with you. (14:8–10)

The "craving desire" for status is forcefully represented by the dinner guests in the Pharisee's home and in Jesus's teaching. The social context is that of a big dinner where only the elite are invited. The guests crave to be the best of the best. They are, as it were, drowning in their own insatiable thirst for wealth and status. Jesus admonishes them and then proclaims: **Because all who exalt themselves will be humbled, and all who humble themselves will be exalted** (14:11). Herein is epitomized the theme of reversal in Luke's travel narrative, a theme prevalent in the ancient world (see the introduction to

Part 3: Luke 9:51–14:35) and so important to the Lukan Jesus that he will repeat it near the end of his journey to Jerusalem (18:14). The man with the dropsy represents the unquenchable desires of the dinner guests; his healing represents the possibility for the transformation of their desires from seeking self-exaltation to a life of humility.

Finally, Jesus has a word for his host:

> Then he also proceeded to say to the one who had invited him, "Whenever you prepare a meal, whether an early meal or a late meal, do not invite your friends or your siblings or your relatives or your rich neighbors, lest they invite you in return and that be your reward. But whenever you prepare a banquet, invite the poor, crippled, lame, and blind; and you will be blessed, because they do not have the ability to repay you." (14:12–14a)

Jesus returns to the theme of the inclusivity of the eschatological banquet. He instructs the host, rather than to be bound by the vicious cycle of reciprocity, to invite those who are on the margins of society—the poor, crippled, lame, and blind—in the need of most assistance, material and spiritual (Roth 1997). These do not have the ability to repay the debt incurred by such an invitation, but Jesus claims: **it will be repaid to you at the resurrection of the just** (14:14b). Such acts of benevolence will prevent the host (and others) from being sent away on the charge of being a worker of injustice (cf. 13:27).

The Parable of the Big Dinner (14:15–24)

14:15–24. Jesus's words prompt a response from his audience: **Now, when one of those dining with him heard these things, he said to him, "Blessed is the one who eats a meal in the kingdom of God"** (14:15). The guest's beatitude echoes Jesus's words in 14:14 but diverts attention away from the "poor, crippled, lame, and blind." The guest's beatitude presumes that they will be included in God's banquet (D. Garland 2011, 585). References to the eschatological banquet frame the parable that Jesus relates: **Then he said to him, "A certain man was preparing a special meal and had invited many people. So he sent his slave at the time of the meal to say to those who had been invited, 'Come, because it is now ready'"** (14:16–17). Double invitations were common in antiquity among the elite (e.g., Plutarch, *Sept. sap. conv.* 147E; Apuleius, *Metam.* 3.12; Esther 5:8), and acceptance of the first invitation was binding, since there was no way to preserve leftovers (D. Garland 2011, 586).

The initial invitation is followed by a second one that announces the meal is ready. This invitation is simply like ringing the dinner bell; no rejections are expected. But something goes very wrong for the host in the story Jesus tells: **But they all, without exception, began to make excuses** (14:18a). The phrase translated "without exception" (*apo mias*; lit., "from one [voice]") suggests a "coordinated act of ostracism" (Tannehill 1996, 234; see also Rohrbaugh 1991,

142–43) in which the guests decided to boycott the banquet in order to shame the host (Braun 1995, 106–31). The three excuses, therefore, are pretenses and not legitimate reasons for the guests' absence from the banquet (Culpepper 1995, 289): **The first one said to him, "I just bought a field and need to go out and see it. I ask you, please consider me excused." And another said, "I just bought five pairs of oxen and am going to examine them. I ask you, please consider me excused." And another said, "I just got married, and because of this I am not able to come"** (14:18b–20). The first guest, who has just bought a field, appeals to the "necessity" of examining it. But why wait to examine it until after it has been purchased? The second guest does not even appeal to necessity but simply states he is on his way to examine the five pairs of oxen he has purchased. Five pairs of oxen could work one hundred acres of land, and the number indicates that the guest (like the host) is a person of means (Green 1997, 560). At least these first two guests request to be excused from the meal. The third guest has just married and states simply that he is "not able to come." He does not state why his recent marriage prevents him from attending the feast. Does he, like the first two guests, need to "examine" his recent investment (on the potential humor of the parable, see Longenecker 2008, 186–87)? Nor does he request to be excused, which adds more insult to the rejection. With the first two guests there is a presumed, if fabricated, sense of urgency (indicated by the addition of "just" to the translation), but are we to assume that this guest married between the first and second invitations? The host has become a "social pariah" (Vinson 2008, 489).

The host is understandably irritated by this turn of events: **When the slave returned, he told his master these things. Then the householder became angry and said to his slave, "Go out quickly into the streets and alleys of the city, and bring the poor and crippled and blind and lame here"** (14:21). In his anger, the host commands the servant to bring in the "poor and crippled and blind and lame," that is, those who are in no socioeconomic position to reciprocate the invitation (cf. 14:13–14) yet who are the focus of Jesus's healing and teaching ministry (7:22). The host's response is a rejection of the prevailing system of reciprocity. The slave returns and reports: **Master, what you commanded has been done, and there is still room** (14:22). This really is a "big dinner"—so big, in fact, that the revised guest list still does not fill the house. **So the master said to the slave, "Go out into the roads and paths, and force people to come in, so that my house might be full"** (14:23). The master now sends the slave into the roads and paths to bring in those from outcast groups (beggars, prostitutes) who are banned to live outside the city walls and are excluded from social interaction with the urban elites (Rohrbaugh 1991, 144–45). They are to be compelled to attend, not by physical force or violence, but by words of assurance that they will not be obligated to repay this social debt (D. Garland 2011, 591). The section ends with these words: **For I tell you, none of those men who were invited will taste my meal!** (14:24). The opening phrase, "for

I tell you," are words characteristic of the Lukan Jesus (10:24; 22:16, 18, 37) and suggest that it is Jesus and not the host of the story who is now speaking. This view is supported in that the "you" addressed is plural in Greek (*hymin*, not the expected *soi* if the host were addressing the servant). Jesus brings the story back to the present circumstance, reminding the dinner guests gathered in the Pharisee's house that the "meal in the kingdom of God" (14:15) is actually Jesus's banquet (cf. Rev. 19:9) and that those who refuse his invitation will have no place there. Rather, Jesus's eschatological banquet will include those routinely marginalized by society (Isa. 35:5–6).

More Sayings along the Way (14:25–35)

14:25–35. The scene shifts from the table back to the road: **Now, large crowds were going along with him** (14:25a). Jesus's words are addressed to any in the crowd who might consider becoming his disciple: **And he turned and said to them, "If anyone comes to me and does not hate his own father and mother and wife and children and brothers and sisters, and even his own life, he cannot be my disciple"** (14:25b–26). This is one of several "anti-family" sayings in Luke (8:19–21; 9:52–69; 12:51–53; 18:29; 21:16; see Tannehill 1996, 255). Jesus uses a Semitic hyperbole (cf. Gen. 29:30–31; Deut. 21:15–17; Judg. 14:6) to insist that disciples "must put Jesus so strongly in the center of their thinking that they will appear to others as despisers or haters of their closest relatives" (Danker 1988, 272; cf. 16:13). The list of family members is extensive, including more than those invited to the Pharisee's dinner (14:12; see Johnson 1991, 230) or than the list in the parallel passage, Matt. 10:37, and includes even the would-be disciple's "own life" (*psychē*; cf. John 12:25). The saying reflects the reality of many first-century disciples, whose choice to follow Jesus inevitably alienated families (cf. Luke 18:28–29). There was no casual devotion to Jesus, no Christendom, in the first century (Bock 1994–96, 2:1285). Jesus continues: **Whoever does not carry his or her own cross and follow me cannot be my disciple** (14:27). This saying echoes the similarly worded saying in 9:23–24 (there one is told to "take up" rather than "bear" the cross). The audience would have heard this saying literally, as crucifixion was an ever-present reality: "Every criminal condemned to death bears his cross on his back" (Plutarch, *Sera* 554A–B, trans. De Lacy and Einarson 1959). The reference to "his or her own cross" makes the pain of persecution very personal (Johnson 1991, 229).

Jesus then poses two rhetorical questions (see *Rhet. Her.* 4.15.22) to demonstrate the necessity of weighing the costs of commitment: **Who among you, when wanting to build a tower, does not first, after sitting down, calculate the cost, to see if he has enough for completing it? [A person does this] so that everyone watching never begins to ridicule him, saying, "This man began to build and was not able to finish!" because he has laid the foundation and is unable to complete it** (14:28–30). Watchtowers were constructed not only to guard cities but also to safeguard the vineyards or homes of private citizens, although even those could be substantive enough to require a foundation. One must first plan whether there are funds sufficient to complete the project, in order to avoid public humiliation ("This man . . . was not able to finish!"). Of course, choosing to follow Jesus could itself lead to a different kind of public humiliation, as it does for Jesus ("He saved others! Let him save himself!" 23:35). One can, however, choose the basis for such public mockery. The second illustration escalates the danger from that of public humiliation to military defeat or even death: **Or what king, when going out to meet another king in battle, will not first sit down and carefully consider if he is able with ten thousand men to face the one coming against him with twenty thousand? Otherwise, while he is still far away, by sending a representative he requests terms for peace** (14:31–32). The military example is proverbial. Juvenal warns that once the soldier's helmet is on, it is too late to withdraw from the fight (*Sat.* 1.169–70; cited by Danker 1988, 273). Philo applies the image to Virtue personified: "Virtue's nature is most peaceable, and she is careful, so they say, to test her own strength before the conflict, so that if she is able to contend to the end she may take the field; but if she finds her strength too weak, she may shrink from entering the contest at all" (*Abr.* 105, trans. Colson 1935). The king who is outnumbered may ask for the "terms for peace" (cf. 19:42) in order to avoid unnecessary bloodshed. But those terms may be very harsh (selling troops as slaves; heavy financial tariffs; see Vinson 2008, 494).

Just as Jesus has set his face for Jerusalem and is prepared to complete his exodus, which includes his death, so too must the disciple count the cost: **In this manner, then, every one of you who does not give up all your possessions cannot be my disciple** (14:33). As elsewhere such singular commitment to Christ includes one's material possessions (6:30; 12:33–34; 18:18–30). Demand for such radical obedience was not unique to the followers of Jesus, however. Epictetus writes about the unswerving loyalty demanded of the philosopher:

> Do you imagine that you can keep on doing the things you are doing and still claim to be a philosopher? Do you actually think you can dine and drink as you do now, or continue to be given to anger and irritability? No, you must be alert, work hard, get the better of certain desires, leave those who are close to you, be despised by a mere slave, be ridiculed by all those who meet you, take second place in everything, including office, honor and the courts. . . . That is to say, you must labor to develop your inner self or work on things outside it. Do you want to be an expert or an amateur in matters philosophical? (*Diatr.* 3.15.10–13, cited by Danker 1988, 273; cf. Xenophon, *Mem.* 1.2.49–55)

Jesus next turns to the very common element of salt to issue a warning to those who are disciples (Culpepper 1995, 293): **So then, salt is good, but if in fact salt loses its flavor, how will it be made salty again? It is fit neither for the soil nor for the manure pile. People just throw it away!** (14:34–35a). Sodium chloride (NaCl), of course, cannot lose its properties, but much of the salt in ancient Judea was a complex mixture of compounds taken from the Dead Sea. If the salt crystals dissolved, the remaining residue was useless, fit for nothing (on Palestinian salt, see Marshall 1978, 596; D. Garland 2011, 603–4). Of course, the Lukan Jesus is here concerned with commitment, not chemistry. Jesus concludes: **Those who have ears to hear, let them hear!** (14:35b; cf. 8:8).

Theological Issues

"The cross is laid on every Christian. It begins with the call to abandon the attachments of this world. . . . When Christ calls a [hu]man, he bids him come and die" (Bonhoeffer 1948, 73). Thus German theologian and martyr Dietrich Bonhoeffer captures the stark demands made by the gospel. This radical obedience and absolute allegiance to Jesus may sound harsh and impossible to most contemporary Christians in the West. And yet the history of the church is filled with those who have heard this call and responded with utter abandonment. Martyrs like Polycarp and Perpetua laid down their lives, refusing the plea of family and friends to renounce their faith. Saints like Francis rejected worldly comforts for a life of Christian discipline. This is our history and our calling too. But we are prone to lose the edge of our commitment; we are vulnerable to let other distractions erode our allegiance to Christ. Fred Craddock (1990, 183) has put it well: "Just as salt can lose its savor, so can an initial commitment, however sincere, fade in the course of time. . . . Under pressures both open and subtle, pressures all of us know, salt does not decide to become pepper; it just gradually loses its savor. The process can be so gradual, in fact, that no one really notices. Well, almost nobody." Those with ears to hear, let them hear.

PART 4

Luke 15:1–19:44

Jesus's Mighty Words and Deeds along the Way (Part 2)

Part 2 of the travel narrative begins with the three famous "lost" parables of Luke 15:1–32. That section is followed by Luke 16:1–17:10, which deals with the themes of the use and abuse of wealth and the demands of discipleship. Luke 17:11–18:30 parallels the following unit, 18:31–19:44. Both sections are marked by healing/conversion stories and Jesus's teaching regarding the kingdom of God and the (in)appropriate human responses to its demands (for more details, see "Introductory Matters" for Luke 17:11–18:30).

Luke 15:1–19:44 in Context

Jesus's origins and training (1:1–4:13)
Jesus's mighty words and deeds in Galilee (4:14–9:50)
Jesus's mighty words and deeds along the way (part 1) (9:51–14:35)
▶ **Jesus's mighty words and deeds along the way (part 2) (15:1–19:44)**
  The character of God and the "lost" parables (15:1–32)
  The use and abuse of wealth (16:1–17:10)
  Jesus's teaching about the kingdom (17:11–18:30)
  Drawing near to Jerusalem (18:31–19:44)
Jesus in Jerusalem: teachings, death, and resurrection (19:45–24:53)

Luke 15:1–32

The Character of God and the "Lost" Parables

Introductory Matters

This unit consists of what are traditionally known as the "lost" parables: the lost sheep (15:1–7), the lost coin (15:8–10), and the lost sons (15:11–32). As the interpretation below will show, it may be more helpful to think about the parables in terms of what they reveal about the character of God: God is like a shepherd seeking a lost sheep (15:1–7), God is like a female householder seeking a lost coin (15:8–10), and God is like a father seeking lost sons (15:11–32). Two of the images, God as shepherd and God as father, are traditional imagery for God in the Jewish Scriptures and tradition. The other, God as a female householder, introduces a surprising (though not unprecedented) way of imagining God's interaction with the created order.

> **Luke 15:1–32 in the Narrative Flow**
>
> Jesus's origins and training (1:1–4:13)
>
> Jesus's mighty words and deeds in Galilee (4:14–9:50)
>
> Jesus's mighty words and deeds along the way (part 1) (9:51–14:35)
>
> Jesus's mighty words and deeds along the way (part 2) (15:1–19:44)
>
> ▶The character of God and the "lost" parables (15:1–32)
>
> > The shepherd and the lost sheep (15:1–7)
> >
> > The female householder and the lost coin (15:8–10)
> >
> > The father and the lost sons (15:11–32)

Tracing the Narrative Flow

The Shepherd and the Lost Sheep (15:1–7)

15:1–7. The section begins with the Pharisees again complaining about Jesus's actions: **Now all the tax collectors and sinners were drawing near to hear him; and both the Pharisees and scribes were complaining, saying, "This man welcomes sinners and eats with them!"** (15:1–2). Jesus does not respond to their criticism directly but rather tells the parable of the shepherds and the lost sheep (15:3–6). Jesus casts the hearers in the role of a shepherd. The image itself is not univocally positive. Certainly the image of God as Good Shepherd was imbedded in the Scriptures and imagination of Israel (cf. Ps. 23), but there was plenty of evidence of bad and neglectful shepherds (Ezek. 34:2b–6). What shepherd would leave ninety-nine sheep unattended to retrieve one stray sheep? This conundrum may have produced the version of the parable found in the *Gospel of Thomas*, which explains that the shepherd sought the one lost sheep because it was the "largest" and, on finding it, pronounced, "I love you more than the ninety-nine" (*Gos. Thom.* 107, trans. Meyer 2007). Here in Luke, however, the actions of the shepherd are intended to reflect the extravagant love of the Divine, echoing God's words to Israel (Ezek. 34:11–16).

In the parable, the shepherd is not the only one who is happy that the lost sheep has been recovered. The shepherd invites his community to rejoice with him: **Then, after going home, he calls together his friends and neighbors and says to them, "Rejoice with me, because I have found my sheep that I had lost!"** (15:6). In the Lukan version, the lost sheep stands for the sinner who repents: **I tell you, in the same way there will be more joy in heaven over one sinner who repents than over ninety-nine righteous people who do not need repentance** (15:7). Of course, the point of the parable in Luke's version is to defend Jesus's habit, recorded at the beginning of the chapter, of associating with "tax collectors and sinners" (15:1).

The joy of finding the lost sheep is compounded by how its recovery restores the flock to its original and full number of one hundred. This would not be lost on an ancient audience, steeped in the significance of numerology (see Bovon 2001; Parsons 2008b). Both literary writings and archaeological artifacts provide ample evidence that counting with one's fingers was a commonplace in the ancient world, especially during Roman times (Williams and Williams 1995). Quintilian considered the ability to count accurately on one's fingers (*flexio digitorum*) an indispensable skill for the educated orator (*Inst.* 1.10.35).

In finger counting in antiquity, calculations up to ninety-nine were done on the left hand, and triple-digit (and above) calculations were done on the right hand (i.e., "The number one hundred is transferred from the left hand to the right"; Joannes Cassianus, *Collationes* 24.26.7, cited by Williams and Williams 1995, 598; Bovon 2001, 284). In a world that valued right-handedness, recognition of the superiority of counting on the right hand is hardly surprising.

Juvenal, for example, commends Nestor: "Happy certainly [is Nestor] who has postponed death for so many generations and now counts his years on his right hand" (*Sat.* 10.248–49, cited by Bovon 2001, 284; cf. Williams and Williams 1995, 588, 600). In economic terms, counting on the right hand also had certain implications: "He holds his left hand on his left thigh, he computes a sum with the fingers of the right [thus implying a large amount of money]" (Plautus, *Mil. glor.* 203–4, cited by Williams and Williams 1995, 602).

Among early Christian writers, reference to counting on the right hand took on theological significance. Augustine observes: "What is pertinent to ninety-nine? They are on the left hand, not on the right hand. For ninety-nine is counted on the left hand: add one, it is transferred to the right hand" (*Serm.* 175.1, cited by Williams and Williams 1995, 597; see also Cassiodorus's comments on the symbolic significance of the "one hundredth" psalm in *Expositio in Psalmum 100 Conclusio*). The return of the lost sheep affects the ninety-nine to whom it is returned. The original number of "one hundred" is now restored, and the community, whose destiny is inextricably tied to the return of the one, can continue to enjoy the benefits of being on the "right side."

The Female Householder and the Lost Coin (15:8–10)

15:8–10. Jesus tells a second parable, about a female householder and a lost coin (15:8–10). **Or, what woman who has ten drachmas, if she should lose one, will not light a lamp, sweep the house, and search carefully until she actually finds it? And after she finds (it) she calls her friends and neighbors together and says, "Rejoice with me, because I found the drachma that I had lost." In the same way, I tell you, there is joy in the presence of the angels of God over one sinner who repents.** The parable of the lost coin stands in contrast to the first parable in several ways. First, the expansive space presumed in the shepherd's search contrasts with the intensive search in a small domestic space by the housewife. Further, the protagonist of the first parable is a male, and of the second, a female. Jesus here uses female imagery in reference to the activity of God and his own role as God's agent. In the parable of the lost coin, the image of a woman searching for her lost drachma is sandwiched between the parables of the lost sheep and the loving father. Thus two traditional images for God—God is like a loving father, and God is like a good shepherd (also used of God's agent, Jesus; see John 10)—are juxtaposed with this radical image: God is like a female householder. This theological—or more properly, christological—interpretation is found in the writings of Cyril of Alexandria (*Comm. Luke*, homily 106, trans. Smith 1983): "That we then who had fallen, and, so to speak, been lost, have been found by Christ, and transformed by holiness and righteousness into his image. . . . For we were found, as I said, by the wisdom of God the Father, Which is the Son." Cyril plays on the identification of Jesus as the "wisdom" (grammatically feminine in Greek, *sophia*) of God (1 Cor. 1:24; cf. comments on Luke 7:35; 11:49), and his interpretation

The Symbolism of the Lost Coin in Jewish Parabolic Tradition

Rabbi Phineas ben Jair (late second-century figure) tells this parable, preserved in the *Song of Songs Rabbah*:

> "If a man loses a sela' or an obol [a small coin] in his house, he lights lamp after lamp, wick after wick, till he finds it. Now does it not stand to reason: if for these things which are only ephemeral and of this world a man will light so many lamps and light till he finds where they are hidden, for the words of the Torah which are the life both of this world and of the next world, ought you not to search as for hidden treasures?" (*Song Rab.* 1.1.9, trans. Simon 1983)

Here a man goes to extraordinary lengths (lighting wick after wick) to find a coin, which is only an "ephemeral" thing. Both Rabbi Phineas (explicitly) and Jesus (implicitly) use the conventional lesser-to-greater argument ("how much more") to propose that the search for the lost coin is analagous to something much more important (Blomberg 1990, 61). In the case of Rabbi Phineas, the search for the coin symbolizes the much more important search for the "hidden treasure" in the words of Torah, which are the "life both of this world and of the next." For Jesus, the search and its resultant celebration point to the search for and celebration of the lost sinner now found.

---

preserves the parable's proposition, startling in its original context, that the divine activity of recovering the lost can be reflected in the ordinary activity of a woman looking for a lost coin. This interpretation eventually gives way to what becomes the dominant view of the exegetical tradition, represented by Ambrose, where the woman represents the church: "Who are these three, the father, the shepherd, the woman? Who if not God the Father, Christ, and the Church? . . . the Church seeks . . . the Church searches out like a mother" (*Exp. Luc.* 7.207–8, author's trans.; on the history of interpretation of this passage, see Bovon 2002–2013, 2:414–16).

The Father and the Lost Sons (15:11–32)

15:11–24. The last of Jesus's three parables in this chapter is the so-called parable of the prodigal son (15:11–32). The story is well-known and much beloved. It falls into two parts. The first deals with a father and his younger son (15:11–24).

> Then he said, "A man had two sons, and the younger of them said to the father, 'Father, give me the share of the property that is due me.' So he divided the property for them. A few days later, the younger son gathered up everything and set out for a distant country. There he squandered his wealth by living recklessly.
> Now, when he had spent everything, there was a terrible famine throughout that country, and he began to go without. So he went and took a job with one

of the citizens of that country, and the man sent him into his fields to feed pigs. He longed to fill up on (even) the carob pods that the pigs were eating, but no one was giving him (anything).

Now, when he came to his senses, he thought, How many of my father's hired hands have an abundance of food? And I am here dying of hunger! I will head back to my father and say to him, "Father, I have sinned against heaven and in your view. I am no longer worthy to be called your son. (Please) make me like one of your hired hands." So he headed off to his father, but while he was still a long way off, his father saw him and was filled with compassion. He ran and embraced him and kissed him. Then the son said to him, "Father, I have sinned against heaven and in your view. I am no longer worthy to be called your son." But the father said to his slaves, "Quick, bring out a robe—the best one—and put it on him! Put a ring on his finger and sandals on his feet. Bring the fattened calf. Kill it and let's eat it and celebrate, because this son of mine was dead and has come back to life! He was lost and has been found!" So they began to celebrate.

How are we to understand the story? *Klisis*, inflecting the main subject or topic, was one of the first exercises taught to beginning students of elementary rhetoric and provided a transition from the study of grammar to the study of rhetoric, since the exercise focused on the rhetorical function of inflection (Nicolaus, *Prog.* 18–19; see also the sidebar "Inflection" at Luke 1:10). Such inflection provides an interpretive clue to the parable's significance. Quintilian (*Inst.* 9.3.37; cf. 9.1.34) comments briefly on the use of inflection as a rhetorical device (see *Rhet. Her.* 4.22.30–31; Theon, *Prog.* 74.24–35; see also 101.10–103.2):

> At times the cases and genders of the words repeated may be varied, as in "Great is the goal of speaking, and great the task, etc."; a similar instance is found in Rutilius, but in a long period. I therefore merely cite the beginnings of the clauses. Pater hic tuus? Patrem nunc appellas? Patris tui filius es? [Is this your father? Do you still call him father? Are you your father's son?] This figure may also be effected solely by change of cases, a proceeding which the Greeks call *poluptōton*. (trans. Butler 1922)

What Theon calls *klisis*, Quintilian refers to as *polyptōton*, but the phenomenon is the same. Inflection was more than just an ornamental figure of style designed to please the aesthetical tastes of the audience. In fact, Quintilian includes inflection in his discussion of figures of thought, a "class of figure, which does not merely depend on the form of the language for its effect, but lends both charm and force to the thought as well" (*Inst.* 9.3.28, trans. Butler 1922). The function of inflection was for emphasis (*Inst.* 9.3.67) and to attract the audience's attention to the subject under discussion (*Inst.* 9.3.27).

Any student of elementary rhetoric, then, would have been accustomed to inflecting the main topic or subject of a *chreia*, fable, or narrative, and presumably an ancient audience would have been able to identify the main subject by hearing the topic inflected in the various cases of the Greek noun.

Does the grammar of inflection help us to understand better how the authorial audience may have heard this parable? The term "son" occurs eight times in Luke 15:11–32; once in the accusative case (and plural, 15:11) and seven times in the nominative singular, in reference to the prodigal (15:13, 19, 21 [2x], 24, 25, 30). We might reasonably expect that the subject of a parable or story would occur most frequently in the nominative case; however, if we take seriously the role of grammatical inflection in the educational system of late antiquity, then we might not be surprised to learn that not only does the word "father" occur twelve times in the parable, but it also appears in all five cases at least once, and in four cases, including the vocative (a rarity in Luke) at least twice: nominative (15:20, 22, 27, 28), genitive (15:17), dative (15:12, 29), accusative (15:18, 20), and vocative (15:12, 18, 21).

Thus, when hearing Luke 15, an ancient audience, conditioned (even unconsciously) on "hearing" a word inflected to identify that term as the subject of the story at hand, would have naturally understood that the subject of the parable was the father and his love. Of course, Luke does not use inflection to mark the subject of every parable or story. Quintilian rightly warns that these figures are effective only "if the figures are not excessive in number nor all of the same type or combined or closely packed, since economy in their use, no less than variety, will prevent the hearer from being surfeited" (*Inst.* 9.3.27, trans. Butler 1922).

Nor should we view the use of inflection as a particularly elegant rhetorical device. Remember, it was one of the first exercises practiced by the beginning student of rhetoric, who quickly passed on to more challenging exercises. Quintilian recognizes that inflection and other figures like it "derive something of their charm from their very resemblance to blemishes, just as a trace of bitterness in food will sometimes tickle the palate" (*Inst.* 9.3.27, trans. Butler 1922). But its "ordinary" nature might argue for its effectiveness as a rhetorical device in signaling the importance of the inflected term for the understanding of the narrative in which it is couched. The emphasis in this part of the parable is on the lavish love of the father.

15:25–32. The father has another son who demands his attention. This is the second half to the story of the father's love (15:25–32).

> Now, the older son was out in the field (during this time). After he had come (in from the field), he approached the house and heard music and dancing. And when he had summoned one of the servants, he began asking what could possibly be happening. So he said to him, "Your brother has come, and your father has killed the fattened calf because he got him back safe and sound." Then (the older son) was angry and was not willing to go in. So his father came out and urged him (to come in). But he responded and said to his father, "I have slaved for you all these years and I have never ignored your orders, and you have never given me (even) a goat so that I could celebrate with my friends! But when this son of yours, who threw away your property with whores, came (home) you

killed the fattened calf for him!" (The father) said to him, "Son, you are always with me, and everything I have is yours. But we *had* to celebrate and rejoice, because this brother of yours was dead and has (now) been made alive! He had been lost and (now) has been found!"

The elder brother is dismayed to return home and find that the father has killed the fattened calf for his long-lost brother (15:29–30). Many commentators have been influenced on this point by the "neglected firstborn" theme in their reading of the parable (see the sidebar). This theme was certainly significant in postbiblical Judaism. In the midrash to Ps. 9 is the following story: "R. Berechiah said in the name of R. Jonathan: . . . The verse means therefore that God has set love of little children in their father's hearts. For example, there was a king who had two sons, one grown up, the other a little one. The grown-up one was scrubbed clean, and the little one was covered with dirt, but the king loved the little one more than he loved the grown-up one" (*Midr. Ps.* 9, cited by Scott 1989, 123–24).

Attending to the literary details of the parable, however, demonstrates that the "rejected elder son" theme is actually not perpetuated by the parable but

---

The Neglected Firstborn in the Bible

The literary critic Northrop Frye points out that the passing over of the firstborn son recurs frequently in the Torah:

> "The firstborn son of Adam, Cain, is sent into exile, and the line of descent goes through Seth.... Abraham is told to reject his son Ishmael because a younger son (Isaac) is to be born to him. Isaac's eldest son Esau loses his birthright to Jacob through some rather dubious maneuvers on Jacob's part, some of them backed by his mother. Jacob's eldest son Reuben loses his inheritance for the reason given in Genesis 49:4. Joseph's younger son Ephraim takes precedence over the elder Manasseh (and Joseph himself lives to see fulfilled his dream that his parents and older brothers will bow down to worship him). The same theme is extended, though not essentially changed, in the story of the founding of the monarchy, where the first chosen king, Saul, is rejected and his line passed over in favor of David, who is practically his adopted son (I Samuel 18:2)." (1982, 180–81)

For Frye,

> "the theme of the passed-over firstborn seems to have something to do with the insufficiency of the human desire for continuity which underlies the custom of passing the inheritance on to the eldest son.... Hence the deliberate choice of a younger son represents a divine intervention in human affairs, a vertical descent into the continuity that breaks its pattern, but gives human life a new dimension by doing so." (1982, 182; see also Brueggemann 1982, 62)

subverted by it (see Scott 1989, 122–25). To be sure, the fact that the elder brother is in the field (15:25) is a spatial metaphor indicating distance from the father and perhaps failure. The brother's indignation at the father's treatment of the returning prodigal also places him in a bad light and sets up the audience to expect the performance of another "scrubbed clean" older son being rejected in favor of the younger. But the parable takes a surprising turn: the father does not reject the elder brother as the "rejected elder son" theme would demand. There is no "I loved Jacob, but Esau I hated" (Mal. 1:2–3 ASV; see also Rom. 9:13) note here. Rather, the father reassures the elder son, everything I have is yours (Luke 15:31c). Nor is the elder brother banished or exiled: Son, you are always with me (15:31b). The parable subverts the "rejected elder son" theme that demands that one be chosen and the other rejected. Both are chosen.

Both sons have sinned; yet both sons are rewarded: "The younger son violates the moral code and gets a feast; the elder rejects the father but gets all. The father is interested neither in morality nor in inheritance. He is concerned with the unity of his sons" (Scott 1989, 125). The father abandons his honorable role as patriarch and shamelessly embraces both sons. In the parable, Jesus rejects any apocalyptic notion of some group's being rejected at the expense of another.

Although a subversion of the "rejected elder son" theme might be the meaning of the parable when interpreted apart from its narrative context, its Lukan framework seems to force the audience to identify the elder brother with the grumbling Pharisees, who are judged and banished. In other words, in the original setting in which Jesus told this parable it is possible to imagine that the parable had the sort of impact described above, namely, a reversal of the "rejected elder son" theme and an emphasis on the extravagant if not excessive compassion of the father. But in Luke's framing of the story, readers are invited, perhaps even compelled, to identify the elder brother with the Pharisees of 15:1–2.

The question is whether the religious leaders, or at least individual members of that group, are depicted as being *absolutely* rejected on the primary level of Luke's Gospel. Is the elder brother, like the Pharisees he represents, banished from the party forever? Or does the elder brother stand, like the Pharisees, at the crossroads where he, like they, must make a decision about whether to join the feast? The story is an open-ended one. The story ends with the father's invitation "to make merry and be glad" ringing in the elder brother's ears. And the elder brother stands at the threshold, confronted with the choice of whether to join the banquet.

Theological Issues

The open-endedness of the parable of the father's love in Luke 15 points to the openness of the narrator to the individual religious leaders who, as a group, are opposed to Jesus. Despite some sharply negative comments directed at the leaders as a group, as Robert Tannehill notes, "in some cases the possibility of change . . . is clearly left open" (Tannehill 1986–90, 1:178). This openness is clear in the parable of the good Samaritan (Luke 10:25–37) and the story of the rich ruler (Luke 18; contra the parallels in Mark 10:22 and Matt. 19:22, in which the ruler goes away sadly). In both cases, the stories end without reporting the response of Jesus's interlocutors. We do not know if the lawyer imitated the example of the good Samaritan. We do not know if the rich ruler sold everything to follow Jesus and claim his heavenly treasure. The open-endedness of the stories leaves open the possibility for change.

Joseph Fitzmyer (1981–85, 2:1092) has remarked: "We never learn—and one misses the point to ask—about the subsequent reaction of the elder son (Did he yield to his father's persuasion? Did he go in and greet his younger brother? Did he join in the feasting?)." While it is impossible to know the elder brother's response, to ask that question is hardly to miss the point. To ask how the elder brother responds is exactly one of the major points of the parable. What will he do? What will we do?

Luke 16:1–17:10

The Use and Abuse of Wealth

Introductory Matters

Luke 16:1–17:10 deals with the themes of the use and abuse of wealth and the demands of discipleship. The sense unit is tied more closely together than often is recognized. The parable of the "dishonest" steward elicits a response of scoffing from the Pharisees (16:1–13); furthermore, 16:14–18 makes two points that are then picked up by the second parable in the chapter, the rich man and Lazarus.

1. Luke 16:14–15 reveals that what is prized by humans—"the outer appearances"—is an abomination in the sight of God. Luke 16:19–25 demonstrates that wealth is no sign of one's righteousness, nor is poverty proof of one's evil. So God's opposition to the self-sufficient who are insensitive to the needs of the poor is evident in the fate of the rich man.
2. Luke 16:16–17 demonstrates (a) the universality of the kingdom and (b) the continuing validity of the law. In Luke 16:27–31, Lazarus's inclusion demonstrates the inclusiveness of the kingdom. Furthermore, the law is still in force, especially with regard to care for the poor: "they have Moses and the prophets, let them hear" (16:31 RSV). It is this *disregard* for Moses and the prophets, not the invalidity of their authority, that is at the root of the problem described in the parable. Finally, the teaching section of 17:1–10 presents in didactic form some of the points made by the parables.

Tracing the Narrative Flow

The Prudent Use of Wealth by an "Unrighteous" Manager (16:1–13)

16:1–8a. The parable of the unrighteous manager has proved resistant to facile interpretation over the centuries. "The seeming incongruity of a story that praises a scoundrel has been an embarrassment to the Church at least since Julian the Apostate used the parable to assert the inferiority of the Christian faith and its founder" (Bailey 1976, 86). The parable begins with the dismissal of the steward: **Then he also proceeded to say to his disciples, "A certain man was wealthy, and he had a manager. This manager was accused of squandering his resources. So he called him to come and said to him, 'What is this I am hearing about you? Give an account of your management. For you can no longer serve as my manager'"** (16:1–2). In order to understand the nature of the dismissal, we must first ponder the relationship of the master to the steward. Many commentators assume we have here an employer/employee relationship, in which the employer has fired the untrustworthy employee, but in the ancient world, the term "manager" (*oikonomos*) more often than not referred to a domestic slave who had been placed in charge of his master's household or estate (Beavis 1992, 45). If the steward here is a slave, then this parable is one of nine Synoptic parables in which servants or slaves figure prominently (Crossan 1974, 17–32).

Assuming the ancient audience would have recognized a master/slave relationship as the parable's context, we may infer that the master has decided to demote the slave to outside labor or expel him from the premises altogether. But what is the master's motive? Again, we are faced with two alternatives. Most commentators assume that the master acts on reliable information and justifiably dismisses the steward. But it is more probable that the ancient audience would have imagined the manager has been falsely accused and that the master has summarily dismissed him without a proper hearing. Several features internal to the text suggest this reading. First, the master is described as "wealthy." Throughout the Gospel of Luke, the rich are understood

---

Luke 16:1–17:10 in the Narrative Flow

Jesus's origins and training (1:1–4:13)

Jesus's mighty words and deeds in Galilee (4:14–9:50)

Jesus's mighty words and deeds along the way (part 1) (9:51–14:35)

Jesus's mighty words and deeds along the way (part 2) (15:1–19:44)

   The character of God and the "lost" parables (15:1–32)

▶ The use and abuse of wealth (16:1–17:10)

     The prudent use of wealth by an "unrighteous" manager (16:1–13)

     On the lovers of money and the Law and the Prophets (16:14–18)

     The inequity of wealth and poverty in this life (16:19–31)

     Forgiveness, faith, and duty (17:1–10)

negatively. Remember, Jesus includes the rich in the list of woes in chapter 6: "Woe to you who are rich, for you have already received your consolation" (6:24; cf. 12:16–21; 14:12; 16:1–13, 19–31; 18:25; 21:1–4). The audience (regardless of their own socioeconomic status) would be inclined immediately to side against the rich man (Scott 1989, 187).

Second, the accusers are anonymous and have made their accusation "offstage," raising questions as to their credibility. Finally, there is no indication in the text that the rich master has made any attempts to verify the veracity of

Aesop, Falsely Accused Trickster

Aesop is falsely accused by his fellow slaves of having stolen some figs. At this point in the story, Aesop is unable to speak.

> "At the appointed hour the master came from his bath and dinner with his mouth all set for figs. He said, 'Agathopous, give me the figs.' The master, seeing that he was cheated for all his pains and learning that Aesop had eaten the figs, said, 'Somebody call Aesop.' He was called, and when he came, the master said to him, 'You scoundrel, do you have so little respect for me that you go to the storeroom and eat the figs that were set aside for me?' Aesop heard but couldn't talk because of the impediment in his speech, and seeing his accusers face-to-face, and knowing he would get a beating, he threw himself at his master's knees and begged him to wait a bit. When the master acceded, he took a pitcher that he saw at hand and by gestures asked for some warm water. Then, putting a basin before him, he drank the water, put his fingers into the throat, retched, and threw up the water he had drunk. He hadn't eaten a thing. Then having proved his point through his resourcefulness, he asked that his fellow slaves do the same thing so that they might find out who had eaten the figs. The master was pleased with this idea and ordered the others to drink and vomit. The other slaves said to themselves: 'What shall we do, Hermas? Let's drink and not put our fingers down our throat but only in our cheek.' But as soon as they drank the warm water, the figs, now mixed with bile, rose up, and they no sooner removed their fingers than out came the figs. The master said, 'Look how you've lied against a man who can't speak. Strip them.' They got their beating and learned a good lesson to the effect that when you scheme up trouble for someone else, the first thing you know, you are bringing the trouble on yourself." (*Life of Aesop* 3, cited by Beavis 1992, 46)

Here Aesop, falsely accused of eating his master's figs, is able both to outsmart his master and to vindicate himself by exposing the lies of his fellow slaves. In the Synoptic tradition, relations between masters and slaves are often hostile (cf. the parables of the wicked tenants, talents/pounds, and laborers in the vineyard), and the Aesop material "amply illustrates the motif of harsh, foolish, or vain masters who are quick to punish slaves for real or imagined faults" (Beavis 1992, 48).

their claims. Presumably strictly on the basis of hearsay the master dismisses the manager before he submits his records for review. Therefore, this story fits nicely into the larger category of "slave as trickster" stories that circulated widely in the Greco-Roman world (see the sidebar). In these stories, a slave, most often falsely accused by his or her master, resorts to cunning and trickery in order to be vindicated and outsmart the master.

The manager is quick to act:

> Then the manager said to himself, "What should I do, since my master is taking my manager position away from me? I'm not strong enough to dig; I'm ashamed to beg. I know what I'll do so that when I'm removed from the management position people will welcome me into their homes!" So, after he had summoned his master's debtors one by one, he proceeded to say to the first one: "How much do you owe my master?" He replied, "One hundred baths of oil." So he said to him, "Take your bill and quickly sit down and write fifty." Then he said to another, "You! How much do you owe?" He replied, "One hundred cors of wheat." He said to him, "Take your bill and write eighty!" (16:3–7)

The size of the debtors' indebtedness indicates that the rich master was engaged in a commercial business (see Bock 1994–96, 2:1331). The manager's actions can be interpreted in one of two ways:

1. His action is not dishonest at all. Either he is foregoing his own commission on the deal (so using what is properly his own quite legitimately and to good effect) or he is canceling out that part of the debt that is interest on the loan, thus bringing his master into line with the OT prohibitions on the charging of interest (Lev. 25:36). It is doubtful, however, that the steward's own commission would be included in the statement of the amount owed to the master.
2. More probably, the manager's action effectively puts the master into a corner: the relieved debtors will be so full of gratitude and praise for the master for his unexpected generosity that either the master has to risk great bitterness by disowning the steward's action, or he is forced, whatever he really feels privately, to praise the steward for his action: **Then the master commended the crooked manager because he had acted shrewdly** (16:8a). In this sense, the story is again part of the larger stock of slave-as-trickster stories (as in the *Life of Aesop*), in which the shrewd slave outwits the master. These stories found their way into Jewish tradition as well (see Culpepper 1995, 310).

16:8b–13. The parable is followed by a series of interpretations (16:8b–13). The relation of the parable proper (16:1–8a) to the material that immediately follows (16:8b–13) has long vexed interpreters. C. H. Dodd (1961, 17) called verses 8–13 "notes for three separate sermons on the parable as text." Joseph

Fitzmyer (1981–85, 2:1105) concludes that the applications of the parable found in verses 8–9, 10–12, and 13 "undoubtedly stem from different settings."

The perspective of the *Progymnasmata*, however, provides an alternative angle on the interpretation. Theon devotes an entire chapter to the "fable," and his definition of the fable as "a fictitious story giving an image of truth" (Theon, *Prog.* 72, trans. Kennedy 2003, 23) sounds like a typical, rough-and-ready definition many would use to describe Jesus's parables. Theon later notes, "There can be several conclusions (*epilogoi*) for one fable when we take a start from the contents of the fable" (Theon, *Prog.* 75, trans. Kennedy 2003, 26). Thus, if Luke and his audience were accustomed to a fable or parable having more than one conclusion or interpretation or "moral," then it is unlikely that anything about the literary shape of this parable would have given the authorial audience any reason to question its rhetorical unity. Far from a clear sign of redactional disruption and separate social settings, according to the *Progymnasmata* a conclusion with multiple interpretations or applications was a conventional and acceptable way to end a fictitious story imaging truth.

Luke 16:8–9 corresponds remarkably to the three episodes and three main characters of the story. This fits what Theon says elsewhere about attending to the perspective of the characters/speakers (*Prog.* 75–76). Verse 8a addresses the parable from the perspective of the *master*, who praises the manager (assuming here that the "master" refers to the householder in the parable and not to Jesus himself; so Scott 1989, 257; contra Jeremias 1972, 45–47): all of God's people will be called to give a reckoning of the nature of their service to him. Verse 8b is from the perspective of the *manager* and comments on his shrewdness: **Because the people of this age are more shrewd with their contemporaries than are the children of light** (16:8b). Preparation for that reckoning should involve a prudent use of all our resources, especially in the area of finances. Verse 9 is from the point of view of the *debtors* and describes the grace that the debtors experience: **And I tell you, make friends for yourselves using worldly wealth in order that when it is used up you will be welcomed into eternal dwellings** (16:9). At Qumran "wealth" or "mammon" could refer to the money of those outside the community (1QS 5.14–20; 9.8–9; see Fitzmyer 1981–85, 2:1109–10). By paying their bills (at least partially), the debtors in the parable made friends with the manager (and by proxy, also the master). Such prudence, demonstrating a life of true discipleship, will be rewarded with eternal life and joy.

Finally, the conclusion (16:10–13) represents a form of the lesser-to-greater argument: **One who is faithful in little is also faithful in much** (16:10a). Verses 11 and 12 replace "little" with **earthly riches** and **another's** (that which is loaned from God) and replace "much" with **true** (i.e., heavenly) **riches** and **one's own** (that which will last into eternity). The move from lesser to greater is from material possession to the "true wealth" of spiritual truth. Jesus ends the application with the reminder that one is not able to serve two masters without hating one and loving the other. Once again, the disciple is called to choose God above all else.

On the Lovers of Money and the Law and the Prophets (16:14–18)

16:14–18. Jesus continues the theme regarding the abuse of wealth by turning his attention to the Pharisees who are listening to him:

> Now, the Pharisees, who were lovers of money, were listening to all these things and were ridiculing him. So he said to them, "You are men who justify yourselves before people, but God knows your hearts. [I say this] because what is exalted among people is an abomination in the Lord's opinion. The Law and the Prophets [testified] until John. Since then, the kingdom of God has been preached, and everyone is using violence against it. It is easier for heaven and earth to pass away than for one stroke of the law to fail. Everyone who divorces his wife and marries another woman commits adultery, and the one who marries a woman who has been divorced from her husband commits adultery." (16:14–18)

Luke 16:14–18 occupies the center of the chapter; these verses are tied into what precedes them (the parable of the unrighteous manager and its interpretations) by the reference to the Pharisees, whom Luke calls lovers of money and who scoff at Jesus's claim that one could not serve both God and mammon. Although many have understood the logion on divorce "to move to an entirely different topic" (so Fitzmyer 1981–85, 2:1119), the saying on divorce, in its current Lukan form, fits well within the theme of wealth (so Nolland 1989–93, 2:821–22). Whereas the related saying in Mark 10:2–9 addresses divorce only, here the subject is divorce and remarriage. Further, Nolland notes that some Greek fathers interpreted the first "and" in a final sense ("dismisses in order to marry"). In the first half of 16:18 Jesus is condemning anyone who, for financial reasons (e.g., the prospective wife has a larger dowry), dismisses his wife. Though the wife presumably could not initiate divorce, she could certainly provoke it, and she might well do so in order to better herself with a more wealthy paramour waiting in the wings for her to extricate herself from marriage. In either case, the pain of divorce is compounded by the potential abuse of the love of money.

The Inequity of Wealth and Poverty in This Life (16:19–31)

16:19–26. The parable divides into two parts, both of which feature *topoi* that would have been widely recognized in the ancient world. The first part, 16:19–26, deals with the reversal of fortunes.

> Now, a certain man was rich, and he dressed himself in purple cloth and fine linen and partied lavishly each day. And a poor man named Lazarus had been placed

at his gate, full of sores and longing to satisfy his hunger with what fell from the rich man's table. Instead, the dogs were even coming and licking his sores!

Now it happened that the poor man died and he was carried away by angels to Abraham's side. Then the rich man also died and was buried. In Hades, when he looked up, being in torment, he saw Abraham from a distance and Lazarus at his side. So he called out and said, "Father Abraham! Take pity on me and send Lazarus so that he can wet the tip of his finger with water and cool my tongue, since I am in anguish in these flames." Abraham replied, "Child, remember that you received your good things during your life, and Lazarus likewise (received) bad things, but now he is being comforted and you are in anguish. Besides all these things, a great chasm has been put in place between us and you so that those wanting to go over to you from here are not able to, nor could they cross over from there to us."

H. Gressmann was the first scholar to note parallels with an Egyptian folk story of Setme and Si-Osiris and its later Jewish derivatives (1918). In the story, a miraculously reincarnated Si-Osiris takes his father on a tour of Amente, the realm of the dead, in which they see the reversal of fortunes of a rich man and a poor beggar, whose two funerals the father and son have witnessed before their sojourn to Amente. In the realm of the dead, the rich man is in torment and pain, while the poor beggar now sits, robed in the rich man's fine garments, near the throne of the ruler of the dead.

Richard Bauckham argues that the general theme of the reversal of fortunes was not limited to the Egyptian tale and its derivatives but was a pervasive theme in the Greco-Roman world (1991). What is the reason for this reversal of fortunes? Unlike many of the parallel stories, the Lukan parable does not claim that the reversal is due to the poor man's piety. Rather, Luke points to the injustice of the social system that allows for such economic inequity to exist. That does not mean the rich man has no personal culpability; he does, after all, know the name of the poor man—a fact revealed in the scene of their afterlife. Jesus's words both appeal to popular notions of an eschatological reversal of fortunes and provide social commentary on the inequities and injustices of the social and economic systems of his day. Yet the resources to resolve such inequities are already in the possession of Jesus's (and Luke's) hearers, a point made in the second half of the parable.

16:27–31. The second part of the parable, 16:27–31, deals with the general topic of the return of a recently dead person with a message for the living.

Then he said, "I ask you then, Father, that you send him to my father's house—for I have five brothers—so that he might alert them so that they too will not come to this place of torment." But Abraham said, "They have Moses and the Prophets. Let them pay attention to them!" Then he replied, "No, Father Abraham! But if someone from the dead goes to them, then they will repent." But he said to him, "If they do not pay attention to Moses and the Prophets, they will not be convinced even if someone rises from the dead!"

The similarity between the second half of the parable and the Egyptian folklore, so often appealed to as a parallel for the parable's first half, has largely been ignored. In both stories, a venue is imagined in which this reversal of fortunes can be reported to the realm of the living in the hopes of effecting change. The difference, and it is an important one, is that in the Egyptian (and Jewish) stories, the message is received by those among the living, while Abraham refuses the rich man's request that his brothers be informed of his eternal fate. A most interesting parallel occurs in the *Book of Jannes and Jambres*, a second- or third-century AD text of Jewish or Christian origins (cited by Bauckham 1991, 241).

Jannes and Jambres were the names given in Jewish tradition to the Egyptian magicians who opposed Moses (cf. CD 5.19). As punishment for opposing Moses, Jannes dies and is buried by his brother, Jambres, only to be recalled by Jambres through necromancy and the use of magic books. The soul of Jannes appears and urges Jambres to avoid his fate in Hades: "make sure you do good in your life to your children and friends; for in the netherworld no good exists, only gloom and darkness" (*OTP* 2:440–41).

The parallels with the parable in Luke are striking (a message from a dead brother tormented in Hades to his living relative[s], revealing his fate and urging his brother[s] to repent and avoid his fate), as are the differences (the rich man asks Abraham to send Lazarus, there is no use of necromancy, and most significant, the request for such communication is denied). One need not assume direct knowledge of this particular story on the part of Jesus or Luke (or their audiences) in order to make the assumption that the ancient auditor of the parable of the rich man and Lazarus—given the widespread number of stories in which the recently dead (or their representatives), in some fashion or another, communicate their fate to those still living—might reasonably expect the rich man's brothers to benefit from the knowledge of the fate of their recently deceased brother. The refusal of this request would surely have stopped the audience in their tracks.

Abraham's refusal to grant the rich man's request via some apocalyptic revelation, in effect, thwarts all the audience's expectations. But why did Abraham refuse the request? Because the rich man has had the remedy in the form of Moses and the Prophets all along. "If they refuse to see how the situation contradicts God's justice on the evidence of the scriptures, no purported revelation of the fate of the dead will convince them" (Bauckham 1991, 246).

Forgiveness, Faith, and Duty (17:1–10)

17:1–10. This section combines material found in all three Synoptics (Luke 17:1–3a//Mark 9:42//Matt. 18:6–7 and Luke 17:5–6//Matt. 17:19–21; cf. Mark 9:28–29), material found in double tradition (Luke 17:3b–4//Matt. 18:15), and material that is uniquely Lukan (Luke 17:7–10). Jesus addresses the disciples' responsibility not to be a stumbling block, the need to rebuke and forgive, and the requirements of faithful living. **Then he said to his disciples, "It is impossible for stumbling blocks not to come, but woe to the one through whom they come! It would be better for that one if a millstone were hung around the neck and she or he were hurled into the sea than that she or he should cause one of these little ones to stumble! Guard yourselves!"** (17:1–3a). Jesus acknowledges that temptations (*skandala*; lit., "stumbling blocks"; cf. LXX Ps. 68:22; Lev. 19:14) are inevitable but issues a warning to those responsible, especially for causing "little ones" to stumble. "Little ones" is a favorite term in Matthew to describe new or vulnerable believers (Matt. 10:42; 18:6, 10, 14; cf. Mark 9:42), but it occurs only here in Luke (Johnson 1991, 258). In its Lukan context the "little ones" refer primarily to the poor, who are economically and socially vulnerable, like Lazarus (16:19–31; see Culpepper 1995, 321), although weaker disciples and even children may be in view also (Just 1996–97, 2:643). The warning regarding the millstone around the neck was proverbial (Jer. 51:63; Josephus, *Ag. Ap.* 1.307; Marshall 1978, 641; see the sidebar).

Millstones

Figure 20. Millstones from Capernaum

Millstones in ancient Judea were typically made of basalt and consisted of two stones. The top stone was shaped like a cone and rotated over a lower, inverted cone. The top stone had a hole into which the grain was inserted. A "ludicrous and comic image" is produced if the audience imagines that the offender's head is inserted through the hole (Culpepper 1995, 321).

Jesus continues: **If your brother or sister sins, rebuke them; and if he or she repents, forgive them. Even if they should sin against you seven times in a day and return to you seven times, saying, "I'm sorry," you must forgive them** (17:3b–4). Jesus calls his disciples to be "appropriately confrontational and unstintingly forgiving" (Vinson 2008, 538). The reference to forgiving seven times a day lacks the hyperbole of Matthew ("seventy times seven"; 18:22 RSV) but still suggests that the disciples are to respond with boundless forgiveness, thus extending Jesus's Isaianic ministry (Carroll 2012, 341). The call to forgiveness was "within the framework of Jewish piety" (Johnson 1991, 258–59). "If anyone sins against you, speak to him in peace. . . . If anyone confesses and repents, forgive him" (*T. Gad* 6.3–4, cited by Bock 1994–96, 2:1387; cf. *'Abot R. Nat.* 41). Such endless mercy was lavishly illustrated by the parable of the loving father (Luke 15:11–32).

The apostles are singled out for the first time since Luke 9:10: **So the apostles said to the Lord, "Increase our faith!"** (17:5). Given the demands laid down regarding the wideness of mercy required by believers, it is no surprise that the apostles request that Jesus add to their faith. What is surprising is Jesus's response: **The Lord replied, "If you had faith like a mustard seed, you would say to this mulberry tree, 'Be uprooted and planted in the sea,' and it would obey you"** (17:6). Earlier, Jesus was more than willing to help the apostles when they requested help in understanding the parables (8:9), but now he abruptly questions the assumption that they simply need to "top off" the faith they already have. Instead, Jesus argues, if they had the faith of a mustard seed (which they do not), then they could transplant a tree (which they cannot). Whether the tree is a mulberry or a sycamore (the Greek is *sykaminos*; cf. 1 Kings 10:27; 1 Chron. 27:28), the point is that it is a relatively large tree, but only a small amount of faith is required to move it (cf. 1 Cor. 13:2). Furthermore, planting a tree in the sea is as paradoxical as a camel going through the eye of a needle; both "graphically and hyperbolically" illustrate that even a little faith can do amazing feats (Bock 1994–96, 2:1391).

Jesus then uses a master/slave analogy (cf. Luke 12:35–40, 42–48; 13:25–27; 14:16–24; 16:1–13; cited by Johnson 1991, 259) to illustrate his last point about the disciple's duties. He is not condoning (nor condemning) slavery but "simply assuming the social system of his world" (Carroll 2012, 342):

> Who among you is a person who has a slave who has been plowing or tending sheep, and who will say to him as he comes in from the field, "Come at once and take a seat at the table!" Instead, won't you say to him, "Prepare my meal, and after you get dressed wait on me until I have had my meal; and after that you'll have your meal"? You don't thank the slave because of what he did, do you? (17:7–9)

The scenario is that of a master who owns one slave, who is responsible for both agricultural (plowing, shepherding) and domestic (preparing meals) duties (Talbert 1982, 163). Jesus begins by placing his hearers in the position of the master who has no obligation to thank the slave for what he is supposed to do. "If a human master can make such demands on his servants how much more can God expect of Christian servants in his Kingdom?" (Fitzmyer 1981–85, 2:1146). Jesus then places the audience in the role of the servant: **Likewise, you also, when you have done everything you were ordered to do, should say, "We are insignificant slaves; we have simply done what we were obligated to do"** (17:10). The story disabuses the disciples of any claims to entitlement based on service. The slightest impulse toward faith makes these seemingly impossible commandments achievable, but "it is impossible to go beyond what is expected" (Talbert 1982, 163). Luke's authorial audience may also hear in the activities of the servant the duties of the leaders of the

Christian communities: plowing (1 Cor. 9:10), tending the flock (1 Cor. 9:7), and serving the community meal (1 Cor. 11). These are the obligations of the servants/leaders, for which they are owed no special merit (Marshall 1978, 645).

Theological Issues

Although scholars disagree regarding the specific details, there is common consensus that the ancient world was infamous for its inequity in wealth distribution (Longenecker 2010). Thus, the situation of extreme wealth living beside extreme poverty presumed in Jesus's parable of the rich man and Lazarus reflects the larger socioeconomic reality of Luke's world. But those inequities are not confined to antiquity. In contemporary America, the chasm between the wealthy and those in poverty is greater than it has ever been since the period just before the Great Depression. Yet most Americans are unaware of how deep the divide really is. Harvard business professor Michael Norton and Duke psychology professor Dan Ariely have concluded that nine out of ten Americans badly underestimate how inequitable the distribution of wealth really is in contemporary America (2011). Using a working definition of wealth as the "total value of everything someone owns minus any debt that he or she owes" (Norton and Ariely 2011, 9), most respondents underestimated the wealth possessed by the richest 20 percent. Nine out of ten respondents forecast that the top quintile controlled about 59 percent of the wealth. This is a far cry from a socialist society in which all the wealth is evenly distributed across the entire population, but it is even further from the reality in which we live. In reality, the wealthiest 1 percent of Americans control 40 percent of the wealth and the middle 80 percent has only 7 percent of the wealth. The lowest quintile barely registers on the scale. Both the rich man and Lazarus are alive and well (or not so well) in the contemporary American economic landscape.

What was the ideal "just" society for most of the survey participants? Regardless of gender, political party, and income level, the participants preferred a more equitable distribution of wealth than currently exists. The participants were asked to choose the kind of "just" society (in a Rawlsian sense) in which they would like to live if they knew they "would be randomly assigned to a place in the distribution," and "could end up anywhere in this distribution, from the very richest to the very poorest" (Norton and Ariely 2011, 10). In that scenario, 90 percent of the respondents would choose to live in a society in which the wealthiest quintile controlled just 32 percent of the wealth.

The results of the survey were made available in a YouTube video, uploaded in March 2013 under the title "Wealth Inequality in America" by a poster known as "politizane" (http://www.youtube.com/watch?v=QPKKQnijnsM). The video immediately went viral and was seen by nearly seven million viewers. What will happen now that the misconception of wealth distribution in

America has been exposed? The first step for the rich man was to open his eyes to Lazarus, who was lying at his door day after day after day. Certainly, to achieve a more equitable distribution of wealth that most people, regardless of their social location, desire will require going beyond individual acts of charity relief. Ron Sider, Philip N. Olson, and Heidi Rolland Unruh have argued that, for Christians, expressions of charity need to be seen alongside other efforts aimed at social change. They arranged their comments around the old proverb, "Give a hungry person a fish and you feed him or her for a day. Teach a hungry person to fish and you feed him or her for a lifetime":

1. *Relief* (giving a hungry person a fish) involves directly supplying food, clothing, or housing to someone in urgent need.
2. *Individual development* (teaching a person to fish) includes transformational ministries that empower a person to improve physical, emotional, intellectual, relational, or social status.
3. *Community development* (giving a person fishing equipment) renews the building blocks of a healthy community, such as housing, jobs, health care, and education.
4. *Structural change* (helping everyone get fair access to the fish pond) means transforming unfair political, economic, environmental, or cultural institutions and systems (Sider, Olson, and Unruh 2002, 86).

Poverty relief must be sought in tandem with structural changes in unjust systems. The problems are complex, and the way forward is not altogether clear, but Jesus's parable of the rich man and Lazarus asks: if we ignore the evidence we already have, would it make any difference if One raised from the dead pointed out the injustices of our culture?

Luke 17:11–18:30

Jesus's Teaching about the Kingdom

Introductory Matters

The next major unit, Luke 17:11–18:30, parallels the following unit, 18:31–19:44, in its structure (modifying Talbert 1982, 164).

A. Both units begin with a description of Jesus's movement to Jerusalem (17:11; 18:31–34), followed by healing/conversion stories (17:12–19 [one continuous story]; 18:35–19:10 [two stories]).
B. Jesus then gives eschatological teachings about the kingdom of God (17:20–18:8; 19:11–27).
C. Jesus's teaching regarding the appropriate human responses to God follow next (18:9–30; 19:28–44).

Tracing the Narrative Flow

The Healing of Ten Lepers and the Conversion of One (17:11–19)

17:11–19. The story includes a geographical note (17:11), a healing story (17:12–14), and a conversion story (17:15–19). **And it happened as he was going to Jerusalem that he traveled between Samaria and Galilee** (17:11). The reference to Jerusalem points the audience "toward the culmination of his [Jesus's] ministry in Jerusalem rather than to his current route" (Culy, Parsons, and Stigall 2010, 547). The border "between Samaria and Galilee" is "liminal space," a kind of "no man's land" (Carroll 2012, 343). **And as he**

was entering a village, ten lepers met him, who stood a distance away (17:12). Given the location, it would be impossible to know immediately whether the village he enters is Jewish or Samaritan (Vinson 2008, 545). Leprosy was a skin disease (not to be confused with modern Hansen's disease; Vinson 2008, 546), the symptoms of which are described in detail in Lev. 13. Their shared disease causes them to travel in isolation from others (Lev. 13:45; Num. 5:2) and in a group (cf. 2 Kings 7:3), even though they are of mixed nationalities (cf. 17:16–18). Luke reports: **They shouted, saying, "Jesus! Master! Take pity on us!"** (17:13). In contrast to their subsequent response to the healing, the lepers raise their voices in unison (lit., "lifted the voice"; see Culpepper 1995, 326). Of all the characters in Luke, only the lepers here, the blind beggar (18:38), and the penitent thief (23:42) refer to Jesus as "Jesus," and the lepers are the only nondisciples to refer to him as "Master" (*epistata*; cf. 5:5; 8:24, 45; 9:33, 49; Johnson 1991, 260). Mercy, of course, is the trademark virtue of discipleship, and Jesus responds to their petition: **When he saw them, he said to them, "Go and show yourselves to the priests!" And it happened that as they were going away, they were healed** (lit. "were made clean"; 17:14). The command to present themselves to the priests recalls the previous healing of a leper in

---

Luke 17:11–18:30 in the Narrative Flow

Jesus's origins and training (1:1–4:13)

Jesus's mighty words and deeds in Galilee (4:14–9:50)

Jesus's mighty words and deeds along the way (part 1) (9:51–14:35)

Jesus's mighty words and deeds along the way (part 2) (15:1–19:44)

   The character of God and the "lost" parables (15:1–32)

   The use and abuse of wealth (16:1–17:10)

▶**Jesus's teaching about the kingdom (17:11–18:30)**

    The healing of ten lepers and the conversion of one (17:11–19)

    The kingdom of God: now and not yet (17:20–18:8)

       The present reality of the kingdom (17:20–21)

       The coming of the Son of Man (17:22–25)

       Analogies from Scripture regarding the eschaton (17:26–30)

       Warnings regarding the end (17:31–37)

       The parable of the widow and the unjust judge (18:1–8)

    Responding to God (18:9–30)

       The Pharisee and the tax collector (18:9–14)

       Receiving the kingdom of God as a child (18:15–17)

       The rich ruler (18:18–30)

Luke (5:12–16, esp. v. 14), and the story more generally echoes the healing of Naaman the Syrian, who was cleansed from leprosy by Elisha (2 Kings 5) and whose story Jesus has already mentioned in his Nazareth sermon (Luke 4:27). As they were presumably going to the priests as Jesus instructed, they were healed. Nothing more is heard from nine of them.

But Luke reports about the other: **One of them, when he saw that he had been cured, came back glorifying God with a loud voice. He fell on his face at the feet of Jesus, thanking him. And he was a Samaritan** (17:15–16). "Seeing" plays a key role here. Jesus "sees" the lepers and perceives an opportunity to be merciful (17:14); now the leper "sees" that he has been cured and recognizes that mercy had been granted (Culpepper 1995, 326). The leper in Luke 5:12 fell on his face in petition; the leper here falls on his face in gratitude. Glorifying God is the "standard response" to the "working of a wonder" in Luke (Johnson 1991, 260). What surprises the audience (and Jesus) is the statement at the end that he is a Samaritan. Jesus's surprise is expressed in a series of rhetorical questions (see *Rhet. Her.* 4.15.22): **Then Jesus responded and said, "Weren't ten men healed? So, where are the other nine? Have none of them come back to give glory to God except this foreigner?"** (17:17–18). The animosity between Jews and Samaritans in antiquity is well-known and well documented (see Josephus, *Ant.* 9.29; *m. Qidd.* 4.3; John 4:8–9; Parsons 2008a, 113–18). Their ethnic status vis-à-vis Judaism was ambiguous. Here Jesus refers to the leper as a "foreigner" (*allogenēs*; cf. Lev. 22:10–13, 25), again recalling the story of Naaman. Since only the Samaritan, the "foreigner," the "Other," has returned to "give glory to God," Jesus says to him, **Get up and go on your way. Your faith has delivered you** (17:19). The word translated "delivered" is *sōzō*, which, as we have seen, can mean "heal" or "save"; here the primary emphasis is on the Samaritan leper's spiritual salvation or "deliverance," which has set him apart from the other nine.

The Kingdom of God: Now and Not Yet (17:20–18:8)

The next unit is composed of five sections: the present reality of the kingdom (17:20–21); the coming of the Son of Man (17:22–25); analogies from Scripture regarding the eschaton (17:26–30); warnings regarding the end (17:31–37); and the parable of the widow and the unjust judge (18:1–8).

17:20–21. *The present reality of the kingdom.* **Now, when he was asked by the Pharisees when the kingdom of God was coming . . .** (17:20a). The setting of this scene is not specified; the topic is the coming of the kingdom of God. There is nothing to suggest the Pharisees are testing Jesus or speaking contemptuously to him; after all, they do believe in resurrection and the age to come (Fitzmyer 1981–85, 2:1160). **Jesus responded to them and said, "The kingdom of God does not come in an observable manner. Nor will people say, 'Here it is!' or 'There it is!'"** (17:20b–21a). The kingdom has been the topic of conversation previously. The kingdom of God has come near (10:9, 11; cf.

9:27); it has reached Jesus's audience (11:20). Here Jesus adds the point that the kingdom does not come "in an observable manner"; people will not be able to point and say, "Here it is." Jesus rejects any kind of sign-seeking mentality; there are no telltale signs of God's realm that permit ready prognostication (Carroll 2012, 346; Fitzmyer 1981–85, 2:1161). Although the noun *paratērēsis* (observable manner) occurs only here in the NT (cf. Diodorus Siculus, *Bibl. hist.* 1.9.6; 1.28.1; 5.31.3), Luke uses its cognate, the verb *paratēreō*, to describe the Pharisees watching Jesus closely in order to find fault in his deeds or words (6:7; 14:1; 20:20). They watch, but they cannot see with discernment (Carroll 2012, 346). If they were able to see, they would know the truth of Jesus's next words: **For the kingdom of God is in your midst!** (17:21b). The words "among you" (*entos hymōn*) are unusual and have been interpreted in several ways (see Fitzmyer 1981–85, 2:1161, for the possibilities). The translation offered here, "in your midst," makes the most sense of the immediate Lukan context (including the use of the plural "you"). The kingdom of God is present in Jesus's words and deeds, but the Pharisees, despite their scrutinizing Jesus's every movement, are unable to see it (Johnson 1991, 263).

17:22–25. *The coming of the Son of Man.* Jesus then turns the topic to the coming of the Son of Man. **Then he said to the disciples, "The days are coming when you will long to see one of the days of the Son of Man, but you will not see it"** (17:22). The desire for deliverance is heightened by reference to "*one* of the days" (Culpepper 1995, 381); it also parallels the days of Noah (17:26) and Lot (17:28). Once again, Jesus reminds them that the desire to see does not guarantee its fulfillment: **People will say to you, "It is there!" [or] "It is here!" Do not go out or pursue these things** (17:23). Such declarations have nothing to do with deliverance (Fitzmyer 1981–85, 2:1169). Rather, the appearance of the Son of Man will be as sudden as a flash of lightning: **For just as lightning that flashes shines from one end of the sky to the other, so shall the Son of Man be [on his day]** (17:24). Jesus then grounds his predictions about the timing of the Son of Man's coming in his rejection and suffering: **First, however, it is necessary for him to suffer many things and to be rejected by this generation** (17:25). Jesus holds in tension the present reality of the impending passion and the fulfillment of the kingdom's coming in the apocalyptic appearance of the Son of Man (Culpepper 1995, 329).

17:26–30. *Analogies from Scripture regarding the eschaton.* Jesus turns to two analogies from Scripture to clarify his point; Noah and Lot are cited together elsewhere (Wis. 10:4–8; *T. Naph.* 3.4–5; Philo, *Mos.* 2.52–56): **And just as it was in the days of Noah, so also it will be in the days of the Son of Man—they were eating, drinking, marrying, and being given in marriage until the very day Noah entered the ark and the flood came and destroyed everyone** (17:26–27). In Second Temple Jewish texts, Noah is a model of righteousness. Noah says of himself: "During all my days I practiced truth" (1QapGen^{ar} 6.2; cited by Fitzmyer 1981–85, 2:1170; cf. 2 Pet. 2:5). The activities

> **Up on the Roof**
>
> In Luke 17:31, Jesus underscores the urgent response required when the Son of Man is revealed by picturing a person on the rooftop of the house. That person will not have time to enter the house and retrieve his or her possessions. The image may further imply running across the flat rooftops of connected houses in a city in "parkour-like" fashion to make a hasty escape. Josephus records a scene reminiscent of this one in his description of a battle between Antiochians and Jews. Jewish soldiers had positioned themselves on the roofs of palace buildings and were hurling missiles at the Antiochians below. In order to flush out the Antiochians the Jewish soldiers set the houses on fire. Josephus recounts:
>
>> "As the houses were close together and mostly built of wood, the flames spread over the whole city and entirely consumed it. Thereupon the Antiochians, being unable to give help or to control the fire, turned to flight. But the Jews, leaping from roof to roof [apo dōmatos epi dōma diapēdōntōn], pursued them in this manner, and a very strange manner of pursuit it was." (Ant. 11.140, trans. R. Marcus 1937)
>
> So too might an audience living in an ancient suburb have imagined those trying to escape the impending judgment described by the Lukan Jesus.

of Noah's contemporaries—eating, drinking, marrying, and being given in marriage—are not unusual events, and certainly not intrinsically evil. In Luke, however, they are activities that can produce anxiety (12:29) or distract believers from the requisite vigilance (12:19, 45; 14:20; 20:35). Thus Jesus uses an implicit *synkrisis* to criticize those living in the days of the Son of Man and to warn them that such nonchalance may lead also to their destruction (Fitzmyer 1981–85, 2:1171).

The example of Lot is used to make a similar point (17:28–30). Here Jesus next alludes to the story of Lot in Sodom (Gen. 19:1–26). To the activities of "eating and drinking" are added commercial activities: **buying, selling, planting, and building** (17:28), which are also signs of inattentiveness (12:18–19; 14:18–19; 19:45; cf. Ezek. 16:46–52; Fitzmyer 1981–85, 2:1171). **Fire and sulfur** (Luke 17:29) allude to Gen. 19:24 but are also apocalyptic signs of judgment (Deut. 29:23; Job 18:15; Ps. 11:6; Isa. 30:33; 3 Macc. 2:5) that will accompany the revelation of the Son of Man. As then, so now, allowing the daily activities of family and commerce to become distractions will prove disastrous.

17:31–37. *Warnings regarding the end.* The eschatological warnings continue in the next section. This section further divides into two units: two examples of what to expect "on that day" (17:31–33) and two examples that will occur "on that night" (17:34–37). **On that day, let the one who is on the roof, and the belongings are in the house, not go down to take them; and the one in the**

field, likewise, let that one not turn back (17:31). Both examples (one placing the hearer on the rooftop, the other in a field) insist on decisive action. The first example connects the preservation of life with the abandonment of possessions, a theme already addressed in the Third Gospel (12:13–21, 31–34; 16:19–31). The image suggests that access to the roof is by means of an outside staircase; the disciple is not to waste time entering the house to collect possessions (Fitzmyer 1981–85, 2:1171). The second example urges the believer to flee without looking back. The reference to "turning back" alludes to Gen. 19:26 LXX ("looked upon the things left behind" [*eis ta opisō*]) and explains Jesus's next admonition: **Remember Lot's wife!** (17:32). While fleeing the destruction of Sodom, Lot's wife disobeyed the command not to look back or tarry (Gen. 19:17) and was immediately turned into a pillar of salt (Gen. 19:26; Josephus claims to have seen the pillar of salt [*Ant.* 1.204]; attempts were often made to identify the pillar; see *1 Clem.* 11; Irenaeus, *Haer.* 4.31.3; Cyril of Jerusalem, *Catech.* 19.8; cited by Plummer 1903, 409). Jesus concludes this section with a traditional proverb: **Whoever tries to preserve their life will lose it; and whoever loses their life will preserve it** (17:33; cf. Matt. 10:39; Luke 9:2; John 12:25).

Jesus continues his warnings of what will happen, though the temporal reference changes from "on that day" to "on that night." Efforts to identify "that night" with any specific moment have been unconvincing (Plummer 1903, 409): **I tell you, on that night two people will be in one bed; one will be taken, and the other left behind. Two women will be grinding together; one will be taken, the other left behind** (17:34–35). The reference to "two . . . in one bed" could be a reference to two reclining on a couch to dine, though the nocturnal reference suggests that the translation of *klinē* as "bed" is more likely (cf. 5:18; 8:16). The reference also could be to a husband and wife asleep in bed, although two men is "probably the meaning" (Plummer 1903, 409). In any case, "the image has no sexual overtones and reflects less affluent times when people did not enjoy the luxury of private bedrooms" (D. Garland 2011, 701; cf. Luke 11:7). The point with this example as with the second (two women grinding meal together) is that despite the proximity of the two persons, one is taken and one is left (17:36, "Two men will be in the field; one will be taken and the other left," which is missing in most manuscripts [𝔓75 A B E G], makes the same point). While it is not certain whether one is taken from or to destruction, the context (Noah and Lot were delivered and taken from destruction) suggests that the ones taken are taken from the bed and the field and are thus delivered "from destruction" (Fitzmyer 1981–85, 2:1172).

Jesus's words prompt the disciples to pose a question: **They responded and said to him, "Where, Lord?"** (17:37a). The meaning of Jesus's response to the disciples hinges on the understanding of the question (contra many commentaries, which seem to ignore the immediate context; e.g., O'Day 2004, 293–96). The disciples may be asking, "Where will the Son of Man appear?"

(cf. 17:24; for an interpretation along these lines, see Culpepper 1995, 333). The more immediate context of those taken (in deliverance) and those left (in judgment) suggests that the disciples are inquiring as to the final destination of those taken from destruction.

To the disciples' question Jesus responds with an unelaborated, responsive *chreia* (see Theon, *Prog.* 98; see also Luke 12:15a): **Where the body is, there also will the eagles gather** (17:37b; cf. Matt. 24:28). Once again, this saying is open to multiple interpretations, the most common among modern interpreters being that of an aphorism drawn from nature (see Bock 1994–96, 2:1439). While "body" (*sōma*) can refer generally in Luke's writings to a physical body (12:4, 22, 23) or even a corpse (Acts 9:40), it is also used to refer to Jesus's crucified body in Luke (24:3, 23), not just to any "corpse" (for which there is a Greek word, *ptōma*, used in the parallel passage to Luke 17:37 in Matt. 24:28). Coupled with its metaphorical sense in the Lord's Supper scene (22:19) and the use of the definite article here ("*the* body"), in its Lukan context the reference is to the body of the Lord—and not just the crucified body, but the crucified and resurrected body of the Lord (Bridge 2003, 51–52). But who or what are the eagles? While some have seen an allusion here to the eagle as the symbol of Rome (Carter 2003), that interpretation seems to fit the Matthean context better than the Lukan one (O'Day 2004, 297n30). Here the Lukan Jesus seems to be drawing on the biblical tradition that one function of the eagle is to deliver the believers to the Lord (Exod. 19:4; cf. Deut. 32:10–12; *1 En.* 96.1–2; 4Q504 [frg. 6] 6–8; cited by D. Garland 2011, 702). Eventually, in patristic interpretation, the eagles become a symbol of the righteous themselves ("He says not vultures or crows, but 'eagles,' showing the lordliness and royalty of all who have believed in the Lord's passion"; Thomas Aquinas, *Catena aurea* on Matt. 24:28, cited by O'Day 2004, 302). "Where are the righteous going?" the disciples ask. "They are being gathered to the glorified body of the Lord!" the Lukan Jesus replies.

18:1–8. *The parable of the widow and the unjust judge.* Jesus next tells a parable that has become known as the parable of the widow and the unjust judge: **Then he told them a parable in order to highlight the need for them to always pray and not lose heart** (18:1). Whatever the original context of the parable (Reid 1996, 190, suggests Jesus told the story originally to portray God as "relentlessly pursuing justice," much as Luke 15 depicts God as a housewife seeking a lost coin), Luke has framed it in such a way as to illustrate the need for prayer (and thus connects it with the parable of the friend at midnight; 11:5–8). There the point was to pray shamelessly; here the exhortation is to pray always (cf. Phil. 4:6–7). Luke frames the story as an example of how to pray and not lose heart; however, that does not eliminate the relentless pursuit of justice as an important element of the story in its final form.

The first character introduced is the judge: **There was a judge in a particular city who did not fear God or care about people** (18:2). The negative characterization is a stock description in antiquity for corrupt leadership. Josephus describes King Jehoiakim as "neither reverent toward God nor fair toward human beings" (*Ant.* 10.283, trans. Marcus 1937). Dionysius of Halicarnassus portrays certain Roman conspirators as "neither fearing the wrath of the gods nor regarding the indignation of men" (*Ant. rom.* 10.10.7, trans. Cary 1947; see also Livy, *Hist.* 13.12.3.4–5; Cotter 2005, 331). In contrast to the disdain shown by corrupt leaders toward things human and divine are the words of Jehoshaphat to his newly appointed judges: "Consider what you are doing, for you judge not on behalf of human beings but on the LORD's behalf; he is with you in giving judgment. Now, let the fear of the LORD be upon you; take care what you do, for there is no perversion of justice with the LORD our God, or partiality" (2 Chron. 19:6–7).

Next, Jesus introduces the second character of his story: **There was also a widow in that city, and she kept coming to him, saying, "Give me justice from my enemy!"** (18:3). Widows, because of their vulnerable position in society, were the focus of specific mandates for compassionate justice (Deut. 24:17; Isa. 1:17; see Carroll 2012, 355). That a widow, then, would be required to argue her own case is "startling," since such courtroom adjudication was traditionally the domain of men (Reid 1996, 190). The legal issue is unspecified, and the adversary is unnamed (Carroll 2012, 355). Nonetheless, some have suggested that the complaint may have been against the widow's nearest male relative, who should have been serving as her protector (Reid 1996, 190), or, similarly, perhaps the woman was recently widowed and the issue related to the financial settlement of her husband's estate (D. Garland 2011, 709). If inheritance laws preserved in later rabbinic materials were in force at this time, then the woman could not have inherited her husband's estate directly (*m. B. Bat.* 8.1). Perhaps the executor of the estate refused even to allow her to be maintained by the estate, again a right stipulated in later rabbinic tradition (*m. Ketub.* 11.1; 12.3; see D. Garland 2011, 709). Whatever the reason, the widow has been denied justice (cf. Exod. 22:22–24; Deut. 10:18; Mal. 3:5; Ruth 1:20–21), and, in apparent desperation, she "seeks not the punishment of her opponent, but the settling of her rights" (Fitzmyer 1981–85, 2:1179). With persistence as "her only weapon" (Fitzmyer 1981–85, 2:1179), she joins Ruth, Tamar, and other widows who take proactive and assertive action in their own behalf (Reid 1996, 193).

Initially, the judge is callous to her appeals: **For a time he was not willing to do so, but after a while he said to himself, "Although I don't fear God or care about people, yet because this widow is causing trouble for me, I will give her justice"** (18:4–5a). The judge's refusal to aid the widow reflects the deluded reasoning of the ungodly recorded in Wis. 2:10–11 ("Let us oppress the righteous poor man; let us not spare the widow or regard the gray hairs of the aged. But let our might be our law of right") and further contributes to his negative characterization (D. Garland 2011, 709). It is not out of any sense of justice, but simply in an effort to escape the trouble she is causing him, that he decides to "give her justice." The last part of the judge's soliloquy is interesting. He rationalizes his reluctant administration of justice: **so that she will not in the end shame me by her coming** (18:5b). The word translated "shame" (*hypōpiazō*) has been translated "wear out" (NRSV) or "weary" (KJV). The word carries the literal connotation of "pummel" or "strike under [the eye]" (cf. 1 Cor. 9:27; Fitzmyer 1981–85, 2:1179), which in some ancient texts has taken on the metaphorical sense of "blacken the face" (like the modern metaphor, to suffer a "black eye") or "put to shame" (Plutarch, *Fac.* 921–22; see Derrett 1972). Some interpreters, however, have concluded that the judge, who does not care about humans (18:4), would not care about possibly tarnishing his reputation and instead fears physical violence on the part of the woman (Vinson 2008, 564; Reid 1996, 190). Still others understand as "sexist sarcasm" the words of the judge, whose lack of a moral compass renders him capable of most anything (Schottroff 1995, 104). Concern for shame, whether sincere or sarcastic, seems the more likely reading.

The Lukan Jesus now relates the parable to the issue of theodicy: **Then the Lord said, "Hear what the unjust judge says! So won't God certainly give justice to his chosen ones who cry out to him day and night? Indeed, he is patiently waiting for them"** (18:6–7). Jesus invites a surprising comparison between the "unjust judge" and God (Jeremias 1972, 156). The real point of comparison, of course, is one of contrast. The reference to those "who cry out day and night" recalls the persistence of Anna, who worshiped, fasted, and prayed day and night for the redemption of Israel (2:36–38), and echoes the psalmist who despaired at the inaction of God in the face of suffering:

> O Lord, the God of my salvation,
>   I have cried out by day and in the night before You.
> Let my prayer come before You;
>   Incline Your ear to my cry!
> For my soul has had enough troubles,
>   And my life has drawn near to Sheol. . . .
> But I, O Lord, have cried out to You for help,
>   And in the morning my prayer comes before You.
> O Lord, why do You reject my soul?
>   Why do You hide Your face from me?
>   (Ps. 88:1–3, 13–14 NASB; cf. *3 Bar.* 1.2;
>   2 Esd. [*4 Ezra*] 4:23–25)

The judge gives justice out of exasperation; God gives justice to "his chosen" out of his patience. Long-suffering is a frequently mentioned attribute of God in the LXX (Exod. 34:6; Num. 14:18; Neh. 9:17; Pss. 7:12; 85:15; 144:8; Wis. 15:1). But what is God waiting for? God's tardiness is grounded in his patience toward the wicked, but the inaction "feels like callousness to the suffering" (Vinson 2008, 565). Jesus reassures them: **I tell you, he will give them justice suddenly!** (18:8a). The phrase *en tachei* can mean "suddenly," in the sense that when divine justice does come it will come swiftly (Johnson 1991, 271), or it could mean "soon," in the sense that vindication is temporally near (Nolland 1989–93, 2:870). Jesus then turns the tables with this question: **Nevertheless, when the Son of Man comes, will he find faith on the earth?** (18:8b). Jesus shifts the discussion from the faithfulness of God, in which he has utter confidence, to the question of human faithfulness. What will the Son of Man find when he comes?

Responding to God (18:9–30)

The next unit contains three pericopae: the parable of the Pharisee and the tax collector (18:9–14); Jesus's teaching about receiving the kingdom of God as a child (18:15–17); and the story of the rich ruler (18:18–30). Each story describes appropriate and inappropriate responses to Jesus's message.

18:9–14. *The Pharisee and the tax collector.* Jesus tells a second parable: **Then he also spoke this parable to some who had confidence in themselves that they were righteous and looked with contempt on the rest** (18:9). The description of those to whom Jesus directs this parable is remarkably similar to that of the unjust judge in the previous parable. The judge did not fear God and did not have regard for others (18:2). The unnamed audience trust in themselves (rather than God) and despise others. The judge, however, was well aware of his dispositions (18:4); those who are the target of Jesus's teaching are presumably clueless, thinking they are righteous (Vinson 2008, 567). Presumably these self-righteous include Pharisees in Jesus's audience (cf. 15:2; 16:13–14). Pharisaic self-confidence was criticized by other Jewish writers (Josephus, *J.W.* 1.110; see Jeffrey 2012, 216), but it would be misleading to assume that either only or all Pharisees fit this description; already in Israel's Scriptures, one finds general criticism of any who trust in their own righteousness (Ezek. 33:13; see Fitzmyer 1981–85, 2:1185–86).

Like the previous parable, this one contains two characters: **Two men went up to the temple to pray; one was a Pharisee, and the other a tax collector** (18:10). The reference to going to the temple to pray is presumably a reference to the Tamid, the daily worship service (Num. 28:2–8; Jdt. 9:1; *m. Tamid* 5.1; cf. Luke 1:10, 21). The authorial audience, familiar with Luke's Gospel to this point, is already predisposed to view the Pharisee negatively (e.g., Luke 7; 11; 14) and the tax collector positively, at least as open to Jesus's teachings (cf. 5:27).

The portrayal of each confirms these initial impressions: **The Pharisee stood and prayed these things to himself** (18:11a). The phrase *statheis pros heauton tauta proseucheto* (translated here: "stood and prayed these things to himself") could be translated this way: the Pharisee, "standing by himself, prayed these things" (in parallel with the tax collector, who stood at a distance). More likely, the phrase refers to the Pharisee praying to himself, but even here there is disagreement regarding the sense: it has been variously understood to refer to the Pharisee (1) praying quietly "to himself"; (2) praying in reference to himself with an eye toward the tax collector (and others); or (3) talking to himself rather than praying to God (Johnson 1991, 272). The use of the first person throughout the prayer, as well as the generally negative connotations of the prayer, supports one of the latter two options. The prayer begins in a promising—and traditional (see Pss. 18:1–3; 118:1)—way, with thanksgiving: **O God, I thank you** (18:11b); then it quickly veers off into an insidious comparison: I thank you **that I am not like other people—swindlers, unjust, adulterers—or even like this tax collector** (18:11c). There is nothing wrong with thanking God for one's progress in spiritual matters, but it need not require comparing one's success with others' failures (Vinson 2008, 569). The Pharisee's prayer is a kind of parody of other Jewish prayers, which thank God, not for their own accomplishments in comparison to others (as here), but for placing them in a particular situation (and not in others; cf. 1QpHab 15.34–35; *t. Ber.* 6.18; *b. Ber.* 28b; Doran 2007, 266–67). Here, though, the Pharisee thanks God that he is not like others, assuming an air of moral superiority. The first three contrasts—swindlers, unjust, adulterers—seem generally to refer to those who violate the Decalogue (Fitzmyer 1981–85, 2:1187), but the last is with the tax collector in view; it is a "portrait of prayer with peripheral vision" (Johnson 1991, 272).

The Pharisee proceeds to extol his own virtues (an exercise not unknown even among Christian Pharisees; cf. Phil. 3:4–6): **I fast twice a week; I give a tithe from everything I acquire** (18:12). Again, the Pharisee's acts of piety, in and of themselves, are laudable. The Torah mandated fasting once a year, and Jews were widely known in antiquity for their asceticism. In his description of Augustus's modest lifestyle, Suetonius remarks that "not even a Jew ... fasts so scrupulously" (*Aug.* 76, trans. Rolfe 1914). The Pharisee of Jesus's parable would be noteworthy even among those so noted for their encratic lifestyle; he fasts twice a week (cf. *Did.* 8.1). Furthermore, whereas the Torah required tithes be paid on what one produced (Deut. 14:22–29), this Pharisee tithes not only on what he produces but on all that he purchases as well (Carroll 2012, 360). Like the Pharisees Jesus has described in 11:42, however, something is missing in this Pharisee's religious life. The Pharisee of the parable "exemplifies ... the need for mercy of the self-approved righteous, even if they do not recognize their need" (Carroll 2012, 360).

The tax collector stands in contrast in nearly every way: **The tax collector, on the other hand, who stood at a distance, was not even willing to look up to heaven. Instead, he was beating his chest and saying, "O God, may you be favorably disposed toward me, the sinner"** (18:13). Whereas the majority of the text (29 of 36 words) describing the Pharisee is devoted to the content of his prayer, the tax collector's prayer in Greek consists of only six words. Nineteen of the twenty-nine words used to portray the tax collector are devoted to a description of his posture in prayer (Carroll 2012, 359). He stands at a distance; the audience is perhaps to imagine him standing on the periphery of the Court of Israel. He will not raise his eyes toward heaven, a typical posture of prayer (Ps. 123:1; *1 En.* 13.5; cf. Mark 6:41; 7:34; D. Garland 2011, 718; Fitzmyer 1981–85, 2:1188). He beats his chest in repentance (Luke 23:48; cf. *Jos. Asen.* 10.17), and he cries out. Such an act of repentance was not without its cost: he would be expected to make restitution to those whom he cheated (cf. 19:8); he would risk suffering the hostile wrath of the Romans, whose services he would have abandoned; and he would lose his (presumably profitable) livelihood (Talbert 1982, 170). The verb *hilaskomai* is translated here as "be favorably disposed" (i.e., "propitiated") in order to capture the sacrificial context of the temple in which it is uttered (Hamm 2003, 224; cf. the similar prayer of supplication by Rabbi Bibi ben Adaye in *Lev. Rab.* 3.3, cited by Doran 2007, 268: "Forgive me all my transgressions and grant me atonement for all my sins"). By acknowledging his sinfulness, he has aligned himself with other characters in Luke (Peter, 5:8; the prodigal son, 15:18; the thief on the cross, 23:40–41). But the tax collector of the parable raises the stakes by describing himself as "*the* sinner" (*hamartōlō*, with the definite article, *tō*), suggesting he views himself as the worst sinner of all (Wallace 1996, 222–23; similar *in sensu* to 1 Tim. 1:15).

Jesus finally makes the point of the parable explicit: **I tell you, this man, rather than that one, went down to his home justified** (18:14a). Only God can "justify," that is, put one in right relationship with him. By adopting a posture of vulnerable humility and confessing his sin, the tax collector, and not the Pharisee, receives the only kind of justification that matters (for a different reading that understands the tax collector to be more justified than the Pharisee, see Doran 2007). Self-justification leads only to self-delusion; still, it is tempting for Jesus's audience (then and now) to become the Pharisee of the parable and thank God that they (we) are not like the Pharisee (see González 2010, 213). Jesus ends his teaching by repeating one of the themes of the travel narrative (see the introduction to Part 3: Luke 9:51–14:35): **For, all who exalt themselves will be humbled; and those who humble themselves will be exalted** (18:14b; cf. 14:11; Ezek. 21:26).

18:15–17. *Receiving the kingdom of God as a child.* Jesus gives another example about the proper response to God's reign, although judging from the history of interpretation, the point seems a bit ambiguous: **Now, people were also bringing babies to him so that he could touch them; but when the disciples saw this, they started scolding them** (18:15). People, presumably parents, bring their babies (*brephē*; cf. 1:41, 44; 2:12, 16) to be touched by Jesus, evidently for healing or blessing or both. Luke does not explain why the disciples scold the parents. Perhaps they see the rich ruler in line to speak to Jesus (cf. 18:18–23), and wish to disperse these "little ones" so that Jesus may encounter one holding a much higher social status. In any case, the disciples evidently have not understood Jesus's earlier teaching about receiving children (cf. 9:46–48), so now their actions "betray their failure to grasp what Jesus's enactment of the reign of God is doing to conventions of status and honor" (Carroll 2012, 361). The Lukan Jesus does not rebuke the disciples, as he does in the parallel passage in Mark 10:14, but rather he keeps the focus here on the children: **So, Jesus called for them, saying, "Allow the children to come to me, and do not prevent them, for the kingdom of God belongs to such as these"** (18:16). Jesus says that the kingdom of God belongs not to these children, but "to such as these" (Fitzmyer 1981–85, 2:1194).

He then offers these words: **I assure you, whoever does not receive the kingdom of God like a child will certainly not enter it** (18:17). This pronouncement has been variously understood (see Clark 2002, 236–38; Carroll 2012, 362):

1. Receive the kingdom as a child would receive the kingdom (Culpepper 1995, 344). This interpretation suggests that the believer must adopt childlike qualities of simplicity and humility, but it presumes a kind of conscious capacity that infants do not possess (Fitzmyer 1981–85, 2:1193). Further, this interpretation appears based on a modern view of children not shared in late antiquity (D. Garland 2011, 729).
2. Receive the kingdom as one should receive a child. In this view, the emphasis is not on the spiritual condition of the one entering the kingdom but rather on the character of the kingdom. Hospitality and reception of the vulnerable and the marginalized, represented here by children, are marks of the kingdom (Johnson 1991, 280). In the background may lie a critique of the practice, evidently widespread in the Roman Empire, of abandoning unwanted infants, exposing them to death. Later, Christians will be distinguished as those who "do not expose infants once they are born" (*Diogn.* 56, cited by Vinson 2008, 575).
3. Receive the kingdom as though one were a child. Here the emphasis is not on some innate quality of humility possessed by children but on the utter helplessness and dependence of an infant. One must, like the tax collector in the previous parable, render oneself totally vulnerable in order to be justified by and before God (D. Garland 2011, 729).

The grammar of the sentence supports each of the last two readings (the neuter *paidion* can be either the object or subject of an implied *dechomai*); thus the Lukan Jesus may have both readings in view, a violation of rhetorical convention (see Theon's caution against such ambiguities; *Prog.* 81–82) in service of theological insight. The one who becomes totally dependent on God's grace in order to enter the kingdom of God finds that kingdom populated by those marginalized and rendered vulnerable in this life.

The rich ruler (18:18–30). The next unit has two parts: (1) a dialogue with a rich ruler (18:18–23) and (2) a dialogue with the disciples (18:24–30).

18:18–23. The section begins with a question Jesus has heard before (cf. 10:25): **Then a certain leader questioned him, saying, "Good Teacher! What must I do to inherit eternal life?"** (18:18). The question was originally posed by a lawyer; Jesus answered with the parable of the good Samaritan. This time, the interrogator is a "leader" (*archōn*), a term variously associated with religious (8:41; 14:1; 23:13, 35; 24:20), political (12:58), and even demonic (11:15) rulers. The question regarding eternal life was not uncommon in Second Temple Judaism ("those who fear the Lord shall rise up to eternal life," *Pss. Sol.* 3.12, *OTP* 2:655; cf. *1 En.* 37.4; 40.9; 58.3; Dan. 12:2). At first Jesus ignores the question and focuses on the title with which the leader has addressed him: **Jesus said to him, "Why do you call me good? No one is good except one, namely, God"** (18:19). Jesus here uses the rhetorical figure of *correctio*, which retracts what was said and replaces it with a more appropriate statement (*Rhet. Her.* 4.26.36). The Lukan Jesus uses the figure to shift the attention away from himself to God (see Fitzmyer 1981–85, 2:1199, for other interpretive options) and to cause the ruler (and the audience) to "ponder the relationship between Jesus, God, and the good" (Reich 2011, 94). Debates regarding "the good" were, of course, common in ancient philosophy (see Cooper 2004). Jesus's response echoes a common refrain in the Psalter (cf. Pss. 34:8; 100:5; 106:1; 107:1; 118:1–4, 29; 136:1) and asserts that true goodness resides with God alone (see Carroll 2012, 363) and that "entrance into the reign of God only comes via the miracle of God's grace" and not through moral goodness per se (D. Garland 2011, 730).

Jesus then turns explicitly to the question at hand: **You know the commands: Do not commit adultery; do not murder; do not steal; do not give false testimony; honor your father and mother** (18:20). Jesus quotes a portion of the Decalogue (Exod. 20:12–16; Deut. 5:16–20) that deals with "human interactions" (Carroll 2012, 364). The list in Luke reverses the Markan order of the first two commandments and omits the fifth ("do not defraud"; Mark 10:19; cf. Rom. 13:9); the Lukan order agrees with Philo (*Decal.* 51; see Fitzmyer 1981–85, 2:1199). The ruler responds: **Then he said, "I have carefully kept all these from my youth"** (18:21). Unlike the lawyer in Luke 10, who posed his question in order to "test" Jesus, there is nothing here to indicate that the ruler is anything other than a "genuinely pious Jew" (Jeffrey 2012, 221). Still, his faith has a flaw: **When Jesus heard this, he said to him, "You still lack one thing. Sell everything you have, and distribute the proceeds to the poor, and you will have treasure in heaven. Then come, follow me"** (18:22). Despite his piety, the ruler is, from the Lukan point of view, an idolater whose possessions have prevented him from keeping the first commandment to have no other gods before Yahweh God (Exod. 20:3). The ruler's possessions hinder him from experiencing the eternal life he desires. Jesus's words reveal that he has tried to worship God *and* mammon (cf. 16:13; Talbert 1982, 172). "To receive the treasure he wants, the ruler must give up the treasure he has"

(D. Garland 2011, 730). **When the man heard these things, he became very sad; for he was extremely wealthy (18:23).** Though he is saddened by Jesus's remarks about selling his possessions, the audience is not informed that the ruler in Luke's account departs (contra Mark 10:22; Matt. 19:22). When Jesus follows up with his aphorism about the difficulty (but not the impossibility) of rich people getting into heaven and camels passing through a needle's eye, the narrator reports that Jesus is looking at the rich ruler (18:24). This story joins with the unfinished stories of the prodigal son and the good Samaritan to insist that the possibility is left open that the character (not to mention the authorial audience) may still respond favorably to Jesus's invitation to join the banquet, to perform acts of charity, and to redistribute possessions to care for the poor.

18:24–30. In the second subunit, Jesus engages in conversation with his followers over his observation prompted by the ruler's response: **When Jesus saw him [becoming very sad], he said, "How difficult it is for those who have wealth to enter the kingdom of God! Indeed, it is easier for a camel to go through the eye of a needle than for a rich person to enter the kingdom of God" (18:24–25).** Once again (cf. 6:41–42), Jesus engages in hyperbole to make his point (see *Rhet. Her.* 4.33.44). Earlier efforts to soften the rhetorical force of the image of a camel passing through a needle's eye have mostly been dismissed (Nolland 1989–93, 2:890). There is no literary or archaeological evidence of a small entrance in the city walls of Jerusalem called the "Needle's Eye" that required a traveler to lead a camel through on its knees. Further, changing the word from camel (*kamēlos*) to rope (*kamilos*) does not remove the hyperbole; it simply lessens its rhetorical effect. Instead, Jesus's point is that, humanly speaking, it is as difficult for a rich person to enter the kingdom as it is for the largest known Palestinian animal to pass through the smallest known opening (see Fitzmyer 1981–85, 2:1205).

The hyperbole gives rise to a question and answer dialogue (see Theon, *Prog.* 89; see also *Rhet. Her.* 4.52.65): **Then those who heard said, "So, who can be saved?" He replied, "The things that are impossible with people are possible with God" (18:26–27).** Jesus's response takes the form of an antithesis ("impossible"/"possible"; see *Rhet. Her.* 4.15.21; Quintilian, *Inst.* 9.3.81–86) and pivots on the incredulity of the hyperbole. What is impossible from a human point of view (e.g., a camel passing through a needle's eye or a rich person entering the kingdom of God) is possible with God. In other words, God can do what people cannot (Carroll 2012, 365). Possessions are neither inherently good (as the theology of the Deuteronomistic history insists) nor inherently evil (as presumed in certain prophetic circles). Jesus's words, rather, echo that scriptural stream that presumes a neutral attitude toward possessions per se (cf. Prov. 30:7–9). It is the idolatrous attachment to material possessions that hinders one from proper attachment to the way of Jesus (Talbert 1982, 173).

A second dialogue follows: **Then Peter said, "We have left what we had and followed you!"** (18:28). Peter's words recall the episode in which Peter, James, and John respond to Jesus's invitation to follow and "leave everything" (*aphentes panta*; 5:11); here, Peter says "we have left what we had" (*aphentes ta idia*; lit., "our own things"). Jesus reassures him: **I assure you that there is no one who has left home or wife or siblings or parents or children for the sake of the kingdom of God who will not receive [back] many times over in this life and in the coming age eternal life!** (18:29–30). Unswerving commitment to God's rule will have its rewards, present and future.

Theological Issues

As noted in the introduction to Luke 9:51–14:35, many of these parables in the travel narrative have a theocentric emphasis, focusing squarely on the character of God and the nature of God's reign. It is appropriate to rehearse and summarize the points made by the parables. The three "lost" parables of chapter 15 contribute to defining the qualities of God. Two of the images are traditional: God is like a good shepherd (15:3–7; cf. Ps. 23) who seeks out the sheep that is lost. God is like a loving father who welcomes his wandering children back home (15:11–32). But God is also like the housewife who is relentless in her search for a lost coin (15:8–10). The primary quality on display here is God's commitment to seek out the lost.

Defending the character of God is an aspect of three other parables. Issues typically associated with theodicy are raised. In the parable of the friend at midnight (11:5–13), God is indirectly compared to the "sleeping" friend. In Israel's Scriptures and later Jewish tradition, the image of sleep was used to depict the inactivity of God in the face of human suffering (Pss. 44:23; 78:65; *b. Soṭah* 48a). In the parable, Jesus concludes that if a sleeping friend will reluctantly answer the shameless petition of one in need, how much more does God, who knows how to give good gifts to his children, wish to answer these requests for relief from suffering (11:9–13). In the parable of the barren fig tree (13:1–7), Jesus turns on its head the question of human and natural evil raised by the religious authorities. The absence of God's judgment is a sign, not of God's approval, but of God's mercy. And with that divine mercy comes the human obligation to act responsibly with the time and resources so graciously given. In the parable of the persistent widow and the unjust judge (18:1–8), the judge grants justice reluctantly and out of exasperation; God grants justice out of his very character. If he delays while those are crying out day and night, again it is only to allow a time for repentance and restoration.

This kind of loving, merciful, and just God expects his people to exhibit similar traits and to belong to a certain kind of kingdom. Jesus's answer to the question "Who is my neighbor?" takes the form of the parable of the good Samaritan (10:25–37). In God's kingdom, the definition of "neighbor" explodes the traditional ethnic and racial boundaries. A neighbor is anyone willing to extend help. Such help may come from the most unlikely and unwelcomed source. If you are a first-century Jew, the neighbor is a Samaritan (and vice versa). If you are a twenty-first-century Jew, the neighbor may be a Palestinian (and vice versa). If you are the Grand Dragon of the KKK (Ku Klux Klan), the neighbor could be the leader of the NAACP (National Association for the Advancement of Colored People) (and vice versa). In God's neighborhood, the neighbor may be the one you would like help from the very least. Similarly, in the parable of the big dinner (Luke 14:15–24), those invited to the eschatological banquet will include those who are usually excluded, those living in the marginalized areas outside the city walls, in the highways and byways. This image is powerfully rendered in the scene at the end of the film *Places of the Heart*, in which communion is passed from person to person, black and white, victim and victimizer, living and dead. "Peace of God" are the last words spoken by Wylie, a young African American, to the sheriff, whom Wylie accidentally killed, a reconciliation realized in the eschatological banquet that is unimaginable in this life. Finally, God's kingdom will be populated by those who humbly seek God's forgiveness, like the tax collector in Luke 18, who trusts in God and not self for justification. Through the parables of the travel narrative, the Lukan Jesus paints a picture of the character and qualities of God and the character and qualities of those who follow this God.

Luke 18:31–19:44

Drawing Near to Jerusalem

Introductory Matters

This next section, 18:31–19:44, parallels the previous section (see "Introductory Matters" for Luke 17:11–18:30). It consists of a travel notice (with passion prediction; 18:31–34), a healing and conversion story (18:35–19:10), the parable of the evil tyrant and Jesus's eschatological teaching (19:11–27), and the "triumphal entry" and (in)appropriate responses to Jesus (19:28–44). With this section, Jesus's long journey to Jerusalem comes to an end, though in a real sense, his journey back to the Father is just beginning.

Tracing the Narrative Flow

The Way of Jesus (18:31–34)

18:31–34. Once again (cf. 17:11; "Introductory Matters" above), the audience is reminded that Jesus's destination is Jerusalem: **Then Jesus took the Twelve aside and said to them, "We are going to Jerusalem, and everything that has been written through the prophets regarding the Son of Man will be fulfilled!"** (18:31). The reference to the fulfillment of the prophets' writings is an addition to the parallel passage in Mark (10:32–34) and anticipates later references to events of the passion fulfilling Scripture (see 22:37; 24:44, 46). What OT passages does the Lukan Jesus have in mind? Isaiah 53 is explicitly quoted in Luke 22:37, and in his second volume (Acts 4:25–26) Luke has disciples quote Ps. 2 as a scriptural reference for Roman participation in Jesus's

> **Luke 18:31–19:44 in the Narrative Flow**
>
> **Jesus's origins and training (1:1–4:13)**
> **Jesus's mighty words and deeds in Galilee (4:14–9:50)**
> **Jesus's mighty words and deeds along the way (part 1) (9:51–14:35)**
> **Jesus's mighty words and deeds along the way (part 2) (15:1–19:44)**
>   The character of God and the "lost" parables (15:1–32)
>   The use and abuse of wealth (16:1–17:10)
>   Jesus's teaching about the kingdom (17:11–18:30)
> ▶ Drawing near to Jerusalem (18:31–19:44)
>   The way of Jesus (18:31–34)
>   Stories of healing and conversion (18:35–19:10)
>   The healing of the blind man (18:35–43)
>   The conversion of Zacchaeus (19:1–10)
>   The parable of the evil tyrant (19:11–27)
>   The "triumphal" entry (19:28–44)

death. The passion prediction that immediately follows seems to draw on Isa. 50:6 LXX (and perhaps also Zeph. 3:11–12; see Bock 1994–96, 2:1497) in its language (see below). More likely, the Lukan Jesus has in mind the entire prophetic pattern of the Jewish Scriptures, which point forward to the Messiah's coming (see Juel 1988). Jesus then gives the fourth prediction of his impending passion (cf. 9:22, 44, 17:25; see also 12:50; 13:32–33): **Indeed, he will be handed over to the gentiles and will be ridiculed, mistreated, and spit on. After they have whipped him, they will kill him; and on the third day he will rise again** (18:32–33). Luke omits Mark's reference to the Jewish leaders' participation in Jesus's death, choosing instead to focus on the gentiles' (i.e., the Romans') role in the passion. This prediction is the most detailed of all, covering his trial, execution, and resurrection. Jesus specifies that the Son of Man will be ridiculed, mistreated, spit on, scourged, and killed. Of those activities, Jesus is explicitly ridiculed (by Herod [23:11] and soldiers [23:36]), mistreated (22:63), and, of course, killed (23:46). Pilate threatens to have him scourged (23:22), but this event is not recorded in Luke, nor is the detail that he was spit on (cf. Mark 14:65). Luke's language reflects Mark 10:32–33 (which itself seems to reflect Isa. 50:6), and Luke evidently made no attempt to conform the prediction to the details of the passion, or vice versa (Bock 1994–96, 2:1497). Despite the prediction's specificity, the apostles are unable to comprehend Jesus's words: **But they understood none of these things. This matter had been hidden from them, and they were not grasping what** was being said (18:34). Like Jesus's parents (Luke 2:50), the disciples do not understand Jesus's explanation regarding his vocation still to be about the Father's business. The language alternates between describing their inability to understand as the result of human failure ("they did not understand") and divine purpose ("this matter was hidden from them"), much like the story of the exodus alternates between Pharaoh hardening his own heart and God hardening it (cf., e.g., Exod. 7:3; 8:15). The significance of Jesus's death could not be comprehended by human reason but could be made intelligible only through divine reason (Craddock 1990, 216).

Stories of Healing and Conversion (18:35–19:10)

The two Jericho stories of the blind man (18:35–43) and Zacchaeus (19:1–10) parallel the healing and conversion of the Samaritan leper (17:11–19).

18:35–43. *The healing of the blind man.* The story of the blind man in Luke is the fourth miracle recorded in the travel narrative (13:10–17; 14:1–6; 17:11–19) and closely parallels the story in Mark 10:46–52 (on the various ramifications of blindness in antiquity, see Hartsock 2008). There are variations between the accounts, which may be explained as the result of the rhetorical technique of "paraphrase" (*paraphrasis*), in which a writer would "change the form of expression while keeping the thoughts" (Theon, *Prog.* 107P, trans. Kennedy 2003, 70; see also Aphthonius, *Prog.* 23; Quintilian, *Inst.* 1.9.2; Suetonius, *Gramm.* 4; see also comments on Luke 1:77). According to Theon, "all ancient writers seem to have used paraphrase in the best possible way, rephrasing not only their writings but those of each other" (*Prog.* 62, trans. Kennedy 2003, 6). The changes (by addition, subtraction, and substitution; see Theon, *Prog.* 107P–108P) and their significance will be noted below.

Luke begins with this notice: **Now it happened as he was approaching Jericho that a blind man was sitting beside the road begging** (18:35). The first change to note is that Luke has omitted the intervening narrative in Mark (10:35–45) that occurs between the travel notice and passion prediction (Mark 10:32–34//Luke 18:31–34) and the current story of the healing of the blind man. This variation juxtaposes the disciples' inability to perceive Jesus's teaching with the story of the blind man's (in)sight (Craddock 1990, 217). Second, the story in Luke takes place as Jesus enters Jericho rather than as he exits from it, tying the healing story closely to the narrative about Zacchaeus that follows, which also takes place in Jericho (the only other locale specified to this point in the travel narrative except for Jerusalem). Finally, the name, Bartimaeus, drops out in Luke, leaving only the image of a beggar. Begging was a cause for shame: the dishonest steward exclaims, "I'm ashamed to beg" (16:3); Epictetus remarks: "A Cynic who excites pity is regarded as a beggar . . . everybody takes offense at him" (*Diatr.* 3.22.89, cited by Johnson 1991, 283). The blind man's anonymity in Luke allows him to serve as a type of those who recognize their neediness "not simply for alms but also for the sight of salvation" (Brookins 2011, 84).

Luke continues: **When he heard a crowd going by, he asked what was happening. They informed him that Jesus the Nazarene was going by. So, he cried out, saying, "Jesus! Son of David! Take pity on me!"** (18:36–38). When the blind man is told that Jesus the Nazarene is passing by, he makes some quick deductions. Presumably he has heard about Jesus's healing ministry (4:18; 7:21), and while there was no clear understanding in early Judaism that the Messiah would perform miracles (but see 4Q521; Novakovic 2003, 169–84), that identification is unambiguous in Luke. The demons whom Jesus exorcises know, as a result of his healing ministry, that he is the Christ (4:41). Likewise, when the disciples of John the Baptist come to Jesus, seeking "the Coming One" (7:20), Jesus's response is to cure many diseases and plagues, including blindness, thus making a link "between his miracles and his messianic identity" (Novakovic 2003, 178). The blind man also makes the connection between Jesus's messianic identity and his ability to heal, and thus confesses Jesus to be the "Son of David" and begs for mercy, presumably in the form of healing. Although blind, he has insight into Jesus's identity (though the precise meaning of the title "Son of David" will be taken up again at 20:41–44), and he stands in contrast with the disciples, who "understood none of these things" (18:34).

His words irritate some in the crowd: **Those who were in the front [of the crowd] were scolding him so that he would be quiet** (18:39a). The story parallels the story of the little children (18:15–17). Like the disciples who tried to prevent the helpless infants from being brought to Jesus, so now there are those who seek to prevent the vulnerable blind man from being brought to Jesus (Johnson 1991, 287). Once again Luke paraphrases the Markan account by substituting "those who were in the front" for the "many" (Mark 10:48). Are "those who are in the front" seeking to be "first in importance," thus usurping Jesus's role as leader (Brookins 2011, 82)? Jesus has warned against persons like that (13:30) and will do so again (22:24–27). The harsh picture of "those who were in the front" finds no relief as Luke further paraphrases Mark by deleting the words of comfort offered to the blind man by the crowd ("Take heart; rise; he is calling you"; Mark 10:49). The blind man is undeterred: **but he kept on shouting all the more, "Son of David! Take pity on me!"** (18:39b). And just as Jesus received the little children (18:16), he receives the blind man: **Then Jesus stopped and ordered him to be brought to him. When he came near, he asked him, "What do you want me to do for you?"** (18:40–41a). Jesus's authority is enhanced when Luke substitutes "ordered" (*ekeleusen*) for the more mundane "said" (Mark 10:49). Further, Luke replaces the honorific title "rabbi" (*rabbouni*; Mark 10:51) with the more theologically freighted "Lord" (*kyrios*; Brookins 2011, 80; Bock 1994–96, 2:1510). The blind man's desire is simple: **He replied, "Lord, that I might see again"** (18:41b).

Jesus responds immediately: **Then Jesus said to him, "See again! Your faith has delivered you"** (18:42). Luke has replaced the ambiguous "Go your way" in Mark (10:52 RSV) with the command "See again!" The effect is twofold. First, it removes any ambiguity as to whether the man is obeying or disobeying Jesus's command (see Smith 2005, 132–33). Second, it underscores Jesus's authority. Jesus does not lay hands on the man; he does not mix spit with clay. He simply speaks, and the healing is accomplished by fiat. The man has perceived Jesus's identity as "Son of David," and he persists in following his convictions; Jesus commends him for both (Bock 1994–96, 2:1510). His faith has delivered him, both physically and spiritually. The healing itself is no less spontaneous: **Immediately, he could see again** (18:43a). Luke also observes: **he began following Jesus, glorifying God** (18:43b); this indicates that the healing story is also a discipleship story—the beggar becomes a disciple. Luke's last paraphrase is an addition missing from Mark (and Matthew): **When all the people saw this they gave praise to God** (18:43c). This addition introduces a subtle contrast with 18:36–39. Those in front (18:39) of the crowd (*ochlos*; 18:36) were rebuking the blind man; now it is the people (*laos*) who praise God for what they see (Brookins 2011, 82). Luke, borrowing the term from the Septuagint, uses "people" when referring to God's elect. So the story ends with the note that those from among the crowd who are acting as the people of God (in contrast to those who would "go in front" [18:39]) praise God on the basis of what they have witnessed (on the distinction between "crowd" and "people" elsewhere in Luke, see comments in "Theological Issues" at the end of the chapter on 22:1–23:49).

19:1–10. *The conversion of Zacchaeus.* Jesus's journey through Jericho continues: **After entering Jericho, Jesus was passing through the city** (19:1). Here he encounters a chief tax collector named Zacchaeus: **And a man by the name of Zacchaeus was there. He was a chief tax collector—and he was rich!** (19:2). Zacchaeus's occupation and socioeconomic status paint a negative picture of him for the authorial audience. Zacchaeus holds the position of tax collector—indeed, *chief* tax collector—in Jericho, a much despised occupation in Judea (see *m. Ṭehar.* 7.6: "If tax-gatherers entered a house [all that is within it] becomes unclean" (trans. Danby 1933, bracketed material original) and throughout the Roman Empire (see Plutarch, *Curios.* 518E; Josephus, *J.W.* 7.218; see also Dio Cassius, *Hist. Rom.* 65.7.2). The internal evidence of Luke's Gospel confirms this negative characterization of the position of tax collector found in other first-century witnesses. Repeatedly in Luke, tax collectors are coupled with the generic category of "sinners" "as a religious metaphor for those who display the proper spirit of contrition and repentance" (Neale 1991, 177; cf. Luke 5:30; 7:34; 15:1; 18:11). The epithet "rich" would also have been heard negatively, a point confirmed by the other occurrences in Luke of the term "rich," which have a uniformly negative connotation (6:24; 12:16–21; 14:12; 16:1–13; 18:25; 21:1–4). Zacchaeus's wealth, then, would have been interpreted negatively as something that he most likely gained at the expense of others and that served as an impediment to his salvation.

In the context of late antiquity, the third descriptor of Zacchaeus would also have been perceived as a negative quality: **Now, he was trying to see who Jesus was but was unable to because of the crowd, since he was short in stature** (19:3). Why mention that Zacchaeus is "short in stature"? In ancient physiognomy (see comments on Luke 11:33–36; 13:10–11), smallness in physical stature was generally seen as reflective of "smallness in spirit" (*mikropsychia*). Pseudo-Aristotle claims: "These are the marks of a small-minded person. He is small-limbed, small and round, dry, with small eyes and a small face, like a Corinthian or Leucadian" (*Physiog.* 808a.30, trans. Hett 1936). Conversely, "greatness of soul" was associated with great physical stature (see Aristotle, *Eth. nic.* 4.3.1123b.7; 4.8.1128a.8–13). But what does "smallness in spirit" suggest? The term has several semantic possibilities, with each meaning containing suggestive material for reflection in relation to Zacchaeus. According to Aristotle, "he that rates himself too high is vain, he that rates himself too low, small-spirited" (*Eth. eud.* 1233a.16–20, trans. Rackham 1935). Others saw small-mindedness as a form of greed. For Chrysostom, "small-mindedness" was related to "pettiness" (*Hom. Gal.* 1.3; *Hom. Matt.* 10.1) or "greediness" (*Hom. Rom.* 18.7). Both low self-expectations and greediness can be seen in our story. In the profession of tax collector, Zacchaeus's low expectations could live happily with his greediness. In first-century Judea, tax collectors were puppets of the Roman government. They were viewed as traitors by their fellow country folk, since they made their living by overcharging on the taxes and keeping the overage for themselves. And Zacchaeus has done quite well. "Zacchaeus" may be a diminutive form of the name Zechariah, which means "pure" or "innocent," thus increasing the irony of the story (Marshall 1978, 696). Zacchaeus has been conditioned to have low expectations of himself, and Zacchaeus, the short man, "sells himself short," in terms of living up to his name. Zacchaeus grew up and took the only job open to someone like himself, an occupation that is anything but "pure" and "innocent."

> **Cyril of Alexandria on Zacchaeus**
>
> Even if these connotations are lost on the modern reader, it seems that the ancient audience, living in a world in which the physiognomic consciousness prevailed, would naturally interpret Zacchaeus's small stature as reflective of a small-spiritedness that accounts for both his occupation (he has "rated himself too low"; see Aristotle, *Eth. eud.* 1233a.16–20; see also comments on 19:3) and his greed. Consider the brief comment of Cyril of Alexandria in this light: "He [Zacchaeus] was short of stature, not merely in a bodily point of view but also spiritually" (*Comm. Luke,* homily 127, trans. Smith 1983).

Further, the Roman elite were obsessed with what they considered the "monstrous" (R. Garland 1995, 48–49), which included a fascination with the movements of the physically diminutive. Lucian gives a vivid account of a clown named Satyrion, an "ugly fellow" who "danced, doubling himself up and twisting himself about to cut a more ridiculous figure" (*Symp.* 18, trans. Harmon 1913). In this context, the image of Zacchaeus running ahead of the crowd suggests a cruel mockery: **So he ran on up ahead and climbed a sycamore tree in order to see him, because he was about to go by there** (19:4). The widespread rhetorical appeal to physical characteristics (including shortness) in invectives, along with the physiognomic condemnation of diminutive stature, suggests that the figure of Zacchaeus would have been viewed as a laughable, perhaps despicable, character (Plutarch, *Lib. ed.* 2; Cicero, *De or.* 2.60.245; see Parsons 2011, 98–101). For Luke's audience, then, the reference to Zacchaeus's shortness would have suggested, at the least, another cruel joke deriding the deformed.

Jesus arrives: **When he came to that place, Jesus looked up and said to him, "Zacchaeus, hurry and come down! For I must stay at your house today!"** (19:5). There is a certain necessity about the encounter between Jesus and Zacchaeus. **So, he quickly came down and gladly welcomed him** (19:6). Zacchaeus responds immediately by offering Jesus hospitality in his home. But not everyone is pleased by this development. **When everyone saw this, they began grumbling, saying, "He has gone in to stay with a sinful man!"** (19:7). The comment by the townspeople of Jericho may take on additional meaning in light of the ancients' understanding of congenital deformity as divine judgment. Zacchaeus is a sinner not only because he has cheated people in his role as chief tax collector, as most commentators observe, but also because his physical smallness is regarded as the result of sin. Congenital birth defects, and even infant mortality, were associated with sinfulness in the writings of Jews (2 Sam. 12:15b–23; *Ruth Rab.* 6.4), Christians (John 9:2), and Greeks (Hesiod, *Op.* 1.235; Herodotus, *Hist.* 1.105; 4.67; see also SEG 18.561.7). Thus, Luke's authorial audience would naturally have heard a double entendre in the crowd's pronouncement of Zacchaeus's sinfulness: he was born a sinner (as divine punishment), and he lived as a sinner (by cheating his fellow country folk out of their money). Unlike blindness or lameness, leprosy or dropsy, shortness was an irreversible punishment (cf. Luke 12:25). Both John the Baptist and Jesus grew in stature and wisdom (1:80; 2:52), but Zacchaeus did *not* grow in stature, and he did *not* become strong in spirit, and he certainly did *not* increase in human favor.

Zacchaeus responds: **Now, Zacchaeus stood up and said to the Lord, "Half of my belongings, Lord, I am giving to the poor! And if I have extorted anything from anyone, I am paying it back fourfold"** (19:8). How are we to understand Zacchaeus's words? Is he defending himself against the accusations of the crowd—that is, does he customarily give half of his possessions to the poor (taking the present tense verbs as iterative?; see Mitchell 1990)?

Or is Zacchaeus resolving to change his behavior based on his encounter with Jesus? In other words, is this a conversion story? The latter, traditional view takes the verb as "futuristic," as does the NRSV ("I will give to the poor"), and sees Zacchaeus's statement as a resolve for the future and as indicative of his moral transformation. The rhetorical effect of Zacchaeus's negative characterization confirms the traditional view: Luke's audience would have heard the story of Zacchaeus as a conversion narrative (so Hamm 1988; 1991, 249–52; contra Mitchell 1990). The blind beggar responds to salvation with joy (18:43); Zacchaeus responds with restitution of past wrongs. Both responses are appropriate (Talbert 1982, 175–76).

The last word belongs to Jesus: **Then Jesus said to him, "Today, salvation has come to this house, because he also is a son of Abraham!"** (19:9). This is a healing story no less marvelous than any of the other healings recorded in the Gospels. To be sure, when Zacchaeus walked out of his house that day, even with his head held high he was not one cubit taller than he was when he entered it (cf. Luke 12:25). But the spiritual healing was real nonetheless. Hopefully, Zacchaeus was not the only one healed in Jericho that day. Jesus announces: "Today, salvation has come to this house." Jesus's name, Yeshua, means "salvation," and in one sense "salvation" *has* come to this house in the very person of Jesus. And that salvation has come for the whole house, everyone gathered in it (and around it), not just Zacchaeus.

When Jesus spoke these words, **the Son of Man came to seek and to save the lost** (19:10), the authorial audience might reasonably imagine that the walls of prejudice and bias of some of those living in Jericho came tumbling down, and they recognized Zacchaeus for what he was: "a son of Abraham." And their transformation was no less real than that of Zacchaeus. Luke has spared no insulting image to paint Zacchaeus as a pathetic, even despicable, character. The image of a traitorous, small-minded, greedy, physically deformed tax collector sprinting in an ungainly manner ahead of the crowd and climbing a sycamore tree is derisive and mocking. But as much as Luke exploits these conventional tropes, his intention is to reverse them in the conclusion to his story. With Jesus's pronouncement of salvation, the stranglehold of physiognomic determinacy is broken, and the ridicule is turned against itself. Just because Zacchaeus is small in stature does not mean he must be small in spirit. Just because he is pathologically short does not mean he is to be excluded from the family of God.

The Parable of the Evil Tyrant (19:11–27)

19:11–27. The story of Zacchaeus is followed by a parable. A similar parable is recorded in Matt. 25:14–30. Several features of the Lukan version suggest that the story reflects a common topic among ancient rhetoricians, the *topos* of the evil tyrant. According to Theon, a *topos* "is speech amplifying something that is acknowledged to be either a fault or a brave deed; it is of two kinds;

one is an attack on those who have done evil deeds, for example, a tyrant [!], traitor, murderer, profligate; the other in favor of those who have done something good; for example, a tyrannicide, a hero, a lawgiver" (Theon, *Prog.* 106.1, trans. Kennedy 2003, 42–43). Aphthonius even gives as his examples of commonplace a speech against evil tyrants (*Prog.* 18R–21R). First (contra Matthew), Luke prefaces the parable by noting that Jesus tells the parable to clarify the character of the kingdom: **Now, while they were listening to these things, Jesus went on and told a parable, because he was approaching Jerusalem and they thought that the kingdom of God was going to appear right away** (19:11). Other aspects of the parable itself support this view. **So he said, "A nobleman went to a distant country to receive a kingdom for himself and then return"** (19:12). The Lukan Jesus reports that a nobleman was preparing to travel to a distant place to "receive a kingdom" (contra Matt. 25:14, which states simply that a man was going on an unspecified journey). Before departing, he gave various assignments (or tests?) to his servants by distributing minas (= 100 drachmas): **He first called ten of his slaves, gave them ten minas, and said to them, "Do business with this money while I'm gone"** (19:13). The first sign of trouble now appears: **Now, his subjects hated him, and they sent a delegation after him to say, "We don't want this man to rule over us!"** (19:14). Their efforts to undermine his appointment apparently fail, and the new king calls for an accounting from his slaves: **And it happened that as he returned, after receiving his kingdom, he called for these slaves to whom he had given the money to be summoned for him so that he might know what they had earned** (19:15). The first results are acceptable to the king, and the slaves are duly rewarded: **The first one came in, saying, "Master! Your mina has earned ten minas!" The master said to him, "Well done, good slave! Because you have been faithful in the smallest of things, you are given authority over ten cities!" Then the second one came, saying, "Your mina, Master, has made five minas!" So he said to this one also, "You will be over five cities!"** (19:16–19). In both cases, the reward is commensurate with the investment. The reason (or one of them) that the subjects have sought to undermine the nobleman's appointment as their king, however, now becomes apparent: **Then another one came, saying, "Master, here's your mina, which I was keeping stored away in a cloth! For, I was afraid of you, because you are a hardnosed man. You take away what you did not put aside, and you reap what you did not sow"** (19:20–21). This slave is so afraid of the king that, rather than risk losing any part of the investment, he has simply hidden it and returned the money to the king. His fears are not the result of paranoia. **He said to him, "I will judge you based on what you yourself have said, you wicked slave! You knew that I was a hardnosed man, did you, who takes away what I did not put aside and reaps what I did not sow? So then, why did you not deposit my money in the bank? Then when I came back I could have at least gotten it back with interest!" And to those standing by he said, "Take the mina away from him, and** give it to the one who has ten minas!" (19:22–24). The king does not deny the slave's characterization of him as "hardnosed"—and his actions confirm it.

His judgment seems unfair to the subjects observing the encounter: **They said to him, "Master, he has ten minas already!"** (19:25). The king is unrelenting: **I tell you, to everyone who has, more will be given, but from those who do not have much, even what they do have will be taken away!** (19:26). The judgment sounds harsh but up to this point is consistent with Jesus's theme of impending eschatological judgment elsewhere in the Third Gospel (most recently 17:1, 26–30; 18:16–17). To this point in the story, Matthew's version is harsher. In Luke the slave simply has his mina taken away; in Matthew, he is thrown into the "outer darkness" (25:30). The Lukan version, however, now takes an ominous turn. **However, these enemies of mine who did not want me to rule over them, bring them here and slaughter them before me!** (Luke 19:27). To this point, the authorial audience has no idea that the new king knows about the efforts of his would-be subjects to thwart his appointment. But he does know, and his response is as brutal as it is sudden. As a commonplace against tyrants, the actions in Jesus's parable of the evil tyrant, who orders the execution of those who object to his unjust treatment of the third servant, are *not* to be seen as reflecting the impending eschatological judgments of a righteous God (Culpepper 1995; Vinson 2008). The audiences of both Jesus and Luke, experienced as they were in the unjust actions of evil tyrants, easily recognized in Jesus's parable the truth of how easily power is abused by those who wield it.

The "Triumphal" Entry (19:28–44)

19:28–44. Thus, the parable in Luke 19 sets the stage for an invective/encomium *synkrisis* with the next story. Over against the typical behavior of evil tyrants stands Jesus as a benevolent ruler. The story begins with Jesus in the lead: **When he had said these things, he went in front of them going up to Jerusalem** (19:28). He then prepares for his entry into the city: **And it happened when he came near to Bethphage and Bethany at the hill called the Mount of Olives that he sent two of his disciples, saying, "Go into the village across from here, where you will find a colt tied up when you enter, on which no person has ever sat. Untie it, and bring it here. And if anyone should ask you, 'Why are you untying it?' say this: 'The Lord needs it'"** (19:29–31). The events unfold for the two unnamed disciples just as Jesus has foretold: **So, those who had been sent went away and found it just as he had told them. Then, while they were untying the colt, its masters said to them, "Why are you untying the colt?" They replied, "The Lord needs it." So, they brought it to Jesus, and after throwing their garments on the colt they helped Jesus mount it** (19:32–35). Jesus is now prepared for his triumphal entry into the city.

Three intertextual elements of Luke's version of Jesus's entry into Jerusalem indicate the evangelist's intent to depict the multitude's conviction that they are celebrating the arrival of a king into the Holy City. An examination of the scriptural references to which these events allude will demonstrate how the pilgrims accompanying Jesus mistake his entry into Jerusalem for the triumphal procession of a conquering hero into the city of destiny, Jerusalem. Those around Jesus do not yet understand the contrast between the parable and Jesus's kingdom. The first point to notice is the spreading of the garments (missing are the "leafy branches"; cf. Mark 11:8b): **Now, as he was going along, they were spreading their garments under him on the road** (19:36). The spreading of garments before a royal figure reflects the nationalistic zeal on the part of the crowds. For example, when it was revealed that Jehu had been anointed to be king over Israel, the people responded by taking their garments and placing them before the new king-designate while shouting, "Jehu is king" (2 Kings 9:13).

The second scriptural allusion is to Ps. 118, of which the crowd sings a part: **Then, when he had already come near to the descent from the Mount of Olives, the whole throng of disciples joyfully began to praise God with a loud voice concerning all the incredible miracles they had seen, saying, "Blessed is the Coming One, the king who comes in the name of the Lord! Peace in heaven, and glory in the highest places!"** (19:37–38). According to *m. Sukkah* 4.5, Ps. 118 belonged to the Feast of Tabernacles, although it played a prominent role in the liturgy of the feasts of Passover and Dedication. It concludes the Hallel Psalms (113–18) and has the distinction of being the most quoted psalm in the NT. The part of the psalm quoted by the crowds at Jesus's entry (Ps. 118:26) was originally a reference either to the king as he approaches the temple to worship God or, more likely, to any pilgrim who comes to the temple (see 2 Sam. 6:18). In the Gospels, however, the phrase "he who is to come" is understood as a title for Jesus (Luke 7:19; 13:35; cf. Matt. 11:3; 23:39); thus, the psalm was invested with messianic meaning by the Gospel writers.

That the disciples in Luke conceived Jesus's entry into the city as a "royal entry" is evident in the addition of the title "king" to the quotation from the psalm (cf. Matt. 21:9; Mark 11:9). The Lukan "throng of disciples" are not proclaiming that the "kingdom of David" is coming (so Mark); rather, they are voicing, in chorus-like fashion, the conviction that the king himself has come to visit the Holy City. For those characters viewing the scene in Luke, the festive atmosphere surrounding the arrival of Jesus is not unlike that of the triumphal procession of the Roman general fresh from victory (see Josephus, *J.W.* 132–57) or the royal arrival of a newly appointed king (see 2 Sam. 6:1–5). To be sure, the celebration is neither as extravagant nor as elaborate as a *triumphus*; nevertheless, the pilgrims traveling with Jesus, along with others who have come out of the city to greet him, believe his entry into Jerusalem marks the arrival of their conquering king. That this fundamental misunderstanding of the significance of Jesus's entry includes "the whole throng of disciples," rather than simply the crowd milling about, makes the misapprehension that much more tragic.

Figure 21. Dominus Flevit Church, Which Commemorates Jesus Weeping over Jerusalem

The young colt on which Jesus rides evokes the messianic prophecy in Zech. 9:9: "See, your king is coming to you, his cause won, his victory gained, humble and mounted on a donkey, on a colt, the foal of a donkey" (REB). Luke records that the colt is one on which no one has yet ridden (19:30). From the point of view of the crowds gathered there, this action is indicative of Jesus's royal and messianic status, since a true king would not choose an animal previously ridden, both to avoid possible contamination and to preserve his royal dignity. According to *m. Sanh.* 2.5, no commoner was permitted to ride an animal once a king had ridden it.

No matter how much evidence the crowds marshal in defense of their view of Jesus as a political leader entering occupied Jerusalem to conquer its oppressors, from the point of view of the Lukan narrator, this hope is misplaced. Indeed, Jesus is a king, but not the kind of king the crowds so desperately desire. As he begins the last week of his earthly ministry, Jesus enters the city of Jerusalem with all the apparent trappings of a royal entry. Garments are strewn in his path, psalms are sung to his glory, and a colt is provided for his transport. But Jesus is willing to accept this royal procession only if the crowds are willing to accept his definition of "king," a term he will define by his example during this last week, in a manner that stands in direct contrast to the cruel actions of the evil tyrant in the previous parable.

Not everyone is convinced of Jesus's messianic status, however. **Then some of the Pharisees from the crowd said to him, "Teacher, reprimand your disciples!"** (19:39). The Pharisees who try to silence the messianic cries of Jesus's followers recall the efforts of the disciples to rebuke those bringing infants to Jesus (18:15) and the leaders of the crowd who sought to silence the blind man (18:39; D. Garland 2011, 742). Jesus is defiant in his retort: **He responded and** said, "I tell you, if these become silent, the stones will cry out!" (19:40). The people, including his disciples, want a nationalistic, messianic, militaristic king who will save them from their oppressors and restore political freedom at whatever cost. Jesus, on the contrary, sees his reign not as nationalistic but as universal. His mission includes not only proclaiming release to the captives but also recovery of sight to the blind and good news to the poor (cf. Luke 4:18–19). His crown is a crown of thorns; his throne, a splintery cross. His exaltation does not come in riding a horse-drawn chariot amid the cheers of family and friends; rather, he finds his glory in being raised up on a cross amid the jeers of the masses. Through his death and resurrection this one who refuses to be an earthly king makes his royal entry by way of a cross and empty tomb. Like John the Baptist before him (3:8), Jesus declares that if humans fail to bear witness to this kind of king, the very stones themselves will cry out.

> **Inflection and Jesus's Lament**
>
> Luke here again employs inflection (*polyptoton*, or *klisis*), in which the subject of Jesus's words is inflected in all cases (cf. Theon, *Prog.* 74.24–35; 85.29–31; Quintilian, *Inst.* 9.1.34). In a short space, the second-person personal pronoun "you" (*sy*) occurs in the nominative (19:42), genitive (19:42, 43, 44 [2x]), dative (19:43, 44 [2x]), and accusative cases (19:43 [3x], 44) for a total of twelve times. The use of inflection increases the pathos of the calamities that Jesus predicts will befall those listening to him.

Jesus finally approaches the city, and Luke describes a poignant scene (see fig. 21): **Now, when he drew near, he saw the city and wept over it, saying, "If you, yes you, had known on this day the things that lead to peace—but as it is they have been hidden from your eyes!"** (19:41–42). His lament (cf. Luke 13:34) is immediately followed by a warning: **For the days will come upon you when your enemies will put up a barricade against you, surround you, and hem you in from every side. They will completely destroy you and your children within you, and they will not leave one stone on another stone within you, because you did not recognize the time of your visitation** (19:43–44). The description is so detailed that many commentators have concluded that this is a prophecy recorded after the fact (*vaticinium ex eventu*). The travel narrative has come to a close, but Jesus's journey, in its deepest sense, only now begins.

Theological Issues

The story of Zacchaeus (19:1–10) is one of several in Luke/Acts in which the relationship between one's outer physical appearance and inner moral character is examined (see Luke 13; Acts 3–4; 8). This relationship was the subject of ancient physiognomy (see Parsons 2011). Despite our unfamiliarity with the term "physiognomy," our contemporary culture is certainly not immune to the practice of it. One can purchase a Digital Physiognomy software package online that "determines a person's psychological characteristics and presents a detailed character analysis of that person in a graphic format" (http://www.uniphiz.com/physiognomy.htm).

The post-9/11 politics and ethics of racial profiling continue to be hotly debated (Meeks 2000) and have reached a new level of intensity since the fatal shooting of Trayvon Martin in 2012 and the subsequent trial of George Zimmerman in Florida. On high school and university campuses across the United States, young women struggle with eating disorders based on issues of body image and self-esteem. All these practices have their roots in the ancient practice of physiognomy, which assumes a direct correlation between the outer physical body and inner moral character. However, we also live in a contemporary context that knows the "emancipation proclamation" embodied in the Americans with Disabilities Act of 1990, which seeks to create a legal, moral, religious, and cultural context in which disabled persons may live fully and with dignity.

How Luke addressed these issues is relevant for the contemporary church. Luke uses physiognomic conventions in order to subvert them. For the Lukan Jesus, one's moral character is *not* determined by the color, shape, size, or limitations of one's body. Luke has radically redrawn the map of who is in and who is out. He has done so under scriptural warrant, based on his understanding of the implications of the Abrahamic covenant for those so often excluded, whether because of physical condition or ethnic and racial identity. For Luke, God's covenant people can be a "blessing to the nations" only by including those gentiles in the community itself. Luke's vision of this Abrahamic community is based also on his understanding of the teachings of Jesus, which include holding up an otherwise despised Samaritan as an example to follow (Luke 10) and declaring a "bent woman" and a "short man" as daughter and son of Abraham. For Luke, finally, the covenant messianic community, the "whole" body of Christ, includes even, perhaps especially, those who do not themselves have, in the eyes of the larger culture, a "whole" body. The kingdom of God belongs to these, and they to God's covenant community.

PART 5

Luke 19:45–24:53

Jesus in Jerusalem: Teachings, Death, and Resurrection

The fifth and final unit of Luke's Gospel (19:45–24:53) consists of three sections: Jesus in and around the temple (19:45–21:38); the meaning and manner of Jesus's death (22:1–23:49); and Jesus's burial, empty tomb, and postresurrection appearances (23:50–24:53). The first section, 19:45–21:38, continues the focus on Jesus's public words and deeds and deals specifically with Jesus's activities in and around the temple. The last two sections deal with the death and postmortem events related to the protagonist of the biography.

Luke 19:45–24:53 in Context

Jesus's origins and training (1:1–4:13)

Jesus's mighty words and deeds in Galilee (4:14–9:50)

Jesus's mighty words and deeds along the way (part 1) (9:51–14:35)

Jesus's mighty words and deeds along the way (part 2) (15:1–19:44)

▶ **Jesus in Jerusalem: teachings, death, and resurrection (19:45–24:53)**

    Jesus in and around the temple (19:45–21:38)

    The meaning and manner of Jesus's death (22:1–23:49)

    Jesus's burial, empty tomb, and postresurrection appearances (23:50–24:53)

Luke 19:45–21:38

Jesus in and around the Temple

Introductory Matters

This section is held together with notices that the people were listening to Jesus's teachings in the temple (19:45–48; 21:37–38). In between are the following scenes: the debate over Jesus's authority (20:1–8); the parable of the vineyard (20:9–19); the debate over paying tribute to Caesar (20:20–26); the debate with the Sadducees (20:27–44); Jesus's observations about widows (20:45–21:4); Jesus's predictions regarding the temple and Jerusalem (21:5–28); and Jesus's parable and pronouncement (21:29–38).

Tracing the Narrative Flow

Jesus in the Temple (19:45–48)

19:45–48. Jesus returns to the temple for the first time in Luke since he was a boy of twelve, still engaging the religious leaders and still seeking to be about his Father's business (Luke 2:46–49; cf. Mal. 3:1–2). Compared to Mark 11:15–17, Luke's version of the cleansing of the temple is brief (65 Greek words in Mark compared to 25 in Luke). The reference to Jesus entering the city (Mark 11:15) is omitted, as are the violent details of the cleansing (Mark 11:15c–d). The prohibition by Jesus, disallowing anyone to carry vessels through the temple (Mark 11:16), as well as the end of the citation from Isa. 56:7 ("for all peoples"; cf. Mark 11:17a), are deleted. The latter omission may reflect Luke's view that the temple, now destroyed by the time of Luke's writing, can play

> **Luke 19:45–21:38 in the Narrative Flow**
>
> **Jesus's origins and training (1:1–4:13)**
>
> **Jesus's mighty words and deeds in Galilee (4:14–9:50)**
>
> **Jesus's mighty words and deeds along the way (part 1) (9:51–14:35)**
>
> **Jesus's mighty words and deeds along the way (part 2) (15:1–19:44)**
>
> **Jesus in Jerusalem: teachings, death, and resurrection (19:45–24:53)**
>
> ▶ Jesus in and around the temple (19:45–21:38)
>
>   Jesus in the temple (19:45–48)
>
>   The debate over Jesus's authority (20:1–8)
>
>   The parable of the vineyard and its implications (20:9–19)
>
>   The tribute to Caesar (20:20–26)
>
>   The debate with the Sadducees (20:27–44)
>
>   Jesus's observations about widows (20:45–21:4)
>
>   The temple's beauty and demise and the eschatological discourse (21:5–28)
>
>   Parable and pronouncement (Luke 21:29–38)

no part in the gentile mission. Finally, the story of Jesus cursing the fig tree, which frames the temple incident in Mark (11:12–14, 20–25), is likewise deleted (Fitzmyer 1981–85, 2:1261). What remain are Jesus's prophetic act and words: **Then he entered the temple and began to throw out those who were selling things there, saying to them, "It is written, 'My house will be a house of prayer,' but you have made it a den of thieves!"** (19:45–46). Mark's version (with its violent actions, addition of "all the nations," and framing narrative of the cursing of the fig tree) is harsher and suggests that Jesus's actions symbolize a cursing of the temple, which failed in its mission to be a place of multinational and ethnically inclusive prayer, and has rather been co-opted as a nationalist stronghold (interpreting *lēstēs* as a political insurrectionist; so Barrett 1975, 16). Luke's version, however, still maintains some teeth in its critique by depicting Jesus as expelling (*ekballō*) the money changers. This is the Greek word used for exorcisms in Luke (9:40, 49; 11:14, 15, 18, 19, 20; 13:32), making the money changers comparable to "unclean spirits who profane the holy place" (Johnson 1991, 299). The Lukan Jesus combines Isa. 56:7 ("my house shall be a house of prayer") with Jer. 7:11 ("but you have made it a den of thieves") to level his prophetic critique against the institution. Such intra-Jewish criticism of the financial dealings of the temple was not unknown: those at Qumran viewed such practices as a defilement of the temple (CD 6.15–16; 1QpHab 9.1–7); later rabbinic Judaism, however, was uncompromising in its support of money changers providing the necessary coinage for the annual temple tax (*m. Šeqal.* 1.3; see Johnson 1991, 299–300).

Luke inserts the notice that Jesus **was teaching day by day in the temple** (19:47a), which subtly shifts the focus of the religious leaders' rage from this one particular prophetic act of cleansing the temple to Jesus's daily activity of teaching in the temple: **And the chief priests and scribes, along with the** other prominent ones of the people, were trying to kill him (19:47b). They are unable to act: **they could not figure out what to do, for all the people were captivated listening to him** (19:48). This last notice draws a sharp distinction between the "people" who accept Jesus and his message (7:29) and the leaders who have rejected him (7:30; see Johnson 1991, 300), a division that will deepen in the next episode and continue through the course of the passion narrative.

The Debate over Jesus's Authority (20:1–8)

20:1–8. The controversy between Jesus and the religious authorities continues in the next scene: **And it happened on one of the days as he was teaching the people in the temple and preaching the gospel that the chief priests and scribes came up with the elders and said to him, "Tell us by what sort of authority you are doing these things, or who the person is who gave you this authority!"** (20:1–2). The generalized reference to Jesus's teaching in 20:1 raises questions as to what the religious leaders are referring to when they ask "by what sort of authority are you doing *these things*?" On the one hand, the close proximity to 19:47–20:1a would suggest that they have primarily his teaching and preaching in mind. The use of the word "do" instead of "say," on the other hand, cautions against excluding the cleansing of the temple (although it is less the focus here than in Mark 11:27–28). It is better, perhaps, to include both Jesus's deeds and his teaching as the objects of the leaders' criticism (Fitzmyer 1981–85, 2:1273). The issue of Jesus's authority has already been addressed in the dispute over his healing of the paralytic in 5:17–26.

> **Repartee between Ptolemy and the Pedant**
>
> "So also Ptolemy, when he was jeering at a pedant for his ignorance, asked him who was Peleus' father; and the pedant replied, 'I shall tell you if you will first tell me who was the father of Lagus.' This was a jest at the dubious birth of the king, and everyone was indignant at its improper and inopportune character; but Ptolemy said, 'If it is not the part of a king to take a jest, neither is it to make one.'" (Plutarch, *Cohib. ira* 458A–B, trans. Helmbold 1939)
>
> In this dialogue reported by Plutarch, Ptolemy I questions a pedant (*grammatikon*) regarding the identity of Peleus's father, about which there was no consensus in antiquity. The pedant retorts by asking Ptolemy to identify the father of Lagus, the rumored father of Ptolemy. Lagus's obscure birth was the source of some embarrassment for Ptolemy and his supporters (see Danker 1988, 317).

Jesus responded and said to them, "I too will ask you something, and you answer me: Was John's baptism from heaven or from people?" (20:3–4).

Answering a question with a question was certainly a strategy associated with later rabbinic disputes (*Lev. Rab.* 34.3; *b. Šabb.* 101a; 119a), but it was not unknown in larger Greco-Roman circles (Epictetus, *Diatr.* 2.23; cited by Johnson 1991, 308).

Indeed, public debates such as the one between Jesus and the religious authorities and Ptolemy and the pedant were so commonplace in antiquity that they could become the object of ridicule. Erasmus observes that Jesus "blunted their malice as if driving out one nail with another (*Clavum clavo pellere*)" (*Paraphrases on Luke* [on 20:1–6], trans. Phillips 2003, 158). Jesus's response is more than a clever repartee, however. The issue of the origins of John's baptism implies also a question regarding the source of John's mission and message, with which Jesus has previously identified (3:21–22). Is the source of John's authority divine or human?

The religious authorities recognize that Jesus has posed to them a "horned question" (*cornuta interrogatio*; Erasmus, *Paraphrases on Luke*, trans. Phillips 2003, 157): **So, they discussed it with each other, saying, "If we say, 'From heaven,' he will say, 'Why didn't you believe him?' But if we say, 'From people,' all the people will stone us. For, they are convinced that John was a prophet"** (20:5–6). The religious authorities' response presumes that they did not, in fact, believe in John's mission and message; further, it reflects the rhetorical figure of *hypophora*, which "occurs when we enquire of our adversaries, or ask ourselves, what the adversaries can say in their favour, or what can be said against us; then we subjoin what ought or ought not to be said—that which will be favorable to us, or by the same token, be prejudicial to the opposition" (*Rhet. Her.* 4.23.33–24.34, trans. Caplan 1954). The religious authorities choose to take the fifth amendment: **So they answered that they did not know from where it came** (20:7). In reality it is the truth, not stoning, that they fear. Jesus likewise refuses to continue in the debate: **Then Jesus said to them, "Neither will I tell you by what authority I do these things"** (20:8). "Both in the counter-question and in the refusal Jesus, in effect, challenges the authorities to recognize his authority. Implied: he knows clearly what authority he has, who has commissioned him, and, in fact, who he really is" (Fitzmyer 1981–85, 2:1276).

The Parable of the Vineyard and Its Implications (20:9–19)

20:9–19. This debate with the religious leaders over Jesus's authority is in the background of the parable of the vineyard, which he tells to the "people" (20:9–16; cf. Mark 12:1–12; Matt. 21:33–46; *Gos. Thom.* 65). The parable, in its Lukan form, is an allegory of salvation history "as Luke sees it" and "implies that the bureaucracy recognized him but rejected him because they were unwilling to relinquish control over the vineyard to its rightful owner" (Talbert 1982, 189). The owner, even though the tenants have injured his three servants, is hopeful that they will respect his son (so also *Gos. Thom.* 65; but

Figure 22. Palestinian Vineyard

cf. Mark 12:6, where the assertion is unqualified). The rejection of the "beloved son" in the parable does not result in the destruction of the vineyard but results in the removal of the corrupt tenants/leaders who have refused to recognize the authority the vineyard's owner invested in his servants and his son. In the larger story recorded in Luke's two volumes, control of the vineyard will be given to others, namely, the apostles (the description of the vineyard in Luke lacks the allusion to Isa. 5 found in Mark 12:2//Matt. 21:33).

The response of the people is visceral; what Jesus has described is unimaginable: **When they heard this, they said, "May it never be!"** (20:16b). But Jesus offers no words of comfort: **Then he looked at them and said, "What, then, does this mean where it says, 'The stone that the builders rejected, this one has become the cornerstone'? Everyone who falls on that stone will be broken in pieces; and on whomever it falls, it will crush them"** (20:17–18). He changes the metaphor from agriculture to construction (citing Ps. 118:22–23; cf. 1 Pet. 2:7), but the message remains the same: woe to those who reject the beloved Son/cornerstone. One hears in the consequence of falling on the cornerstone (or vice versa) an echo of *Esther Rab.* 3.6: "Should the stone fall on the crock, woe to the crock. Should the crock fall on the stone, woe to the crock. In either case, woe to the crock" (cited by Talbert 1982, 189).

Having elicited a response from the people to his parable (20:16), Jesus provokes a response from the religious leaders with his last words: **So the scribes and chief priests were trying to lay their hands on him at that time—yet they were afraid of the people—for they knew that he had spoken the parable against them** (20:19). Even though they know that the parable is directed against them and their leadership, the religious authorities are again reluctant to act against Jesus, fearing the people (cf. 19:47–48).

The Tribute to Caesar (20:20–26)

20:20–26. The religious authorities descend to new depths when they send "spies" to trick Jesus into saying something that might be judged to be politically subversive: **Now, they watched him closely and sent spies who pretended to be upstanding men in order that they might catch him saying something wrong and thus hand him over to the power and authority of the governor** (20:20). This description signals for the audience the insincerity of their question: **They asked him, "Teacher, we know that you speak and teach rightly, and do not show partiality, but instead truly teach the way of God. Is it lawful for us to pay tribute tax to Caesar or not?"** (20:21–22). Jesus's antagonists ask a "horned question" of their own (cf. 20:5–6) in an attempt to ensnare Jesus. The tribute tax to Caesar was very controversial (see Josephus, *J.W.* 2.117–18). If Jesus said that it was not necessary to pay the tribute tax (on the historical context of the Roman tribute tax, see Udoh 2005), then the pro-Roman contingent of his audience would see this response as supporting civil disobedience and perhaps even revolution. If he said yes, then his response could be taken as approval of his compatriots continuing to live obediently under foreign domination; it might even be viewed by some as a violation of the first commandment, to have no other gods before Yahweh God (Ball 2003, 14; cf. Owen-Ball 1993). Jesus, however, is not duped: **Since he detected their craftiness, he said to them, "Show me a denarius. Whose image and inscription does it have?" They replied, "Caesar's"** (20:23–24). The coin he requests is presumably a denarius bearing the image of Tiberius, the current emperor, and the inscription TI CAESAR DIVI AVG F AVGVSTVS ("Tiberius Caesar, Augustus, son of the Divine Augustus").

His next words are not only a brilliant evasion of the snare laid for him but also a profound, if enigmatic, statement regarding the believer's civil and religious allegiances (on various interpretations of the passage, see Derrett 1970, 318): **Then he said to them, "So then, give back to Caesar what belongs to Caesar, and to God what belongs to God"** (20:25). If the coin belongs to Caesar because it bears the image (*eikona*) and inscription (*epigraphēn*) of Caesar, then Jesus's assertion regarding Caesar raises the question: what "belongs to God"? Jesus's (and Luke's) audience knows from Scripture that humans bear the *image* of God (Gen. 1:26). Furthermore, at least some of those in Jesus's audience carried with them the *inscription* of God by virtue of the *tefillin* (small leather boxes containing parchment bits of Torah), which they were obligated to wear (Deut. 6:5–8). Thus, they may owe taxes to Caesar, but they owe their very selves to God, and that allegiance takes precedence over any other relationship or allegiance. Certainly Jesus's words cannot be used to discourage all forms of civil disobedience, as has sometimes been the case in the history of the passage's interpretation (see Barth 1989, 273–74), nor does it provide scriptural warrant for a two-realms view. "The passage does not specify the precise nature of a Christian's duty regarding civil taxes or regarding civil obligations in general. The passage does suggest, however, that Christians shouldn't respond to civil issues without considering, first and foremost, their religious duty in the matter" (Ball 2003, 17). This reading of Jesus's saying goes back at least to Tertullian, who argues the believer is to render "the image of Caesar, which is on the coin, to Caesar, and the image of God, which is on man, to God; so as to render to Caesar indeed money, to God yourself" (*Idol*. 15, ANF 3:70). Finally, that "the earth is the Lord's and all that is in it" (Ps. 24:1) demands that disciples recognize that their ultimate citizenship and allegiance belongs finally to the Lord God. The force and logic of Jesus's rhetoric have rendered them impotent to respond (see comments on Luke 10:26; 20:5–6, on the rhetorical figure of *hypophora*): **So, they were not able to catch him saying something wrong in front of the people, and, amazed at his answer, they fell silent** (20:26). But not all in their group have given up on the effort to trick him.

The Debate with the Sadducees (20:27–44)

20:27–40. Sadducees are Jesus's next verbal sparring partners:

> Then some of the Sadducees, who say there is no resurrection, came to him and asked him, saying, "Teacher, Moses wrote for us that if someone's brother who is married dies, and he was childless, his brother should marry his wife and produce offspring for his [deceased] brother. So then, there were seven brothers. The first one married and died childless. The second and then the third married her; likewise the rest of the seven did not leave any children and died." (20:27–31)

This is the first and only appearance of the Sadducees in the Third Gospel (but cf. Acts 4:1; 5:17; 23:6, 7, 8). The narrator informs the audience that they do not believe in the resurrection of the dead (cf. Josephus, *Ant*. 18.16–17; *J.W.* 2.164–65; Acts 23:8), revealing the insincerity of their question. Their inquiry may have been a stock question to expose the fallacy of their opponent's view, similar perhaps to the Sadducees' tongue-in-cheek question posed to Pharisees and preserved in later rabbinic material: "Do the resurrected have to go through ritual cleansing because they had contact with a corpse?" (*b. Nid*. 70b, cited by D. Garland 2011, 807). The story has echoes of the widow in Tobit whose seven previous husbands have died in the bridal chamber before she marries Tobias (Tob. 7:11). The riddle posed by the Sadducees is a parody of levirate marriage (Deut. 25:5), the purpose of which was to provide for widows and insure that the property and inheritance remained in the deceased's family (see Josephus, *Ant*. 4.254–55).

The Sadducees ignore these aspects of the regulation and rather press their question in a *reductio ad absurdum* argument (Jeffrey 2012, 239). **Last of all, the woman also died. So then, at the resurrection whose wife will the woman be? For all seven had her as a wife!** (20:32–33). The Sadducees' question to

Jesus rests on two assumptions (D. Garland 2011, 808): (1) The question presumes that the age to come will be like the present age, that is, there will be marriages in the next age. (2) The question assumes that the parties involved will all be resurrected (which, of course, the Sadducees do not actually believe).

Jesus challenges both assumptions (though the opening admonition in Mark 12:24 is omitted): **Jesus said to them, "The people of this age marry and are given in marriage, but those who are found worthy to experience that age and the resurrection from the dead neither marry nor are given in marriage. For they are no longer able to die, because they are like the angels and are God's children, since they are children of the resurrection"** (20:34–36). Marriage in "this age," according to the Torah, is necessary for producing offspring and establishing posterity (Jeffrey 2012, 239), but since there is no death in the age to come, there is no need for marriage (cf. *2 Bar.* 5.1–10; *1 En.* 104.4; 1 Cor. 7; cited by Talbert 1982, 195). The concern in the age of resurrection is "not the parenthood of a brother, but the Parenthood of God" (Danker 1988, 322). Those worthy of the age to come will be "like angels" (*isangeloi*; a hapax in the NT), who *should not* marry or have sex, even if they can (Gen. 6:1–4; *1 En.* 15.1–7; see Vinson 2008, 627). But is everyone worthy of the resurrection? Here as elsewhere (Luke 13:23–24; 18:24–27), the Lukan Jesus suggests that not all will be "worthy to experience that age and the resurrection from the dead" (20:35).

Jesus then goes on to offer more evidence for the belief in resurrection: **But that the dead are raised even Moses made known at the bush when he called the Lord the God of Abraham, and the God of Isaac, and the God of Jacob. He is not the God of the dead but the God of the living. For all of us are alive in his sight** (20:37–38). Since Moses does not refer to God in this way, the "bush" most likely is an allusion to the scriptural "passage about the bush" (Culy, Parsons, and Stigall 2010, 637). In an episode reported in the Babylonian Talmud, Gamaliel, a first-century "rabbi," appealed to Deut. 11:21 (among other texts), which speaks in the present tense of promises made to the patriarchs, as scriptural evidence for the doctrine of resurrection. Although also referring to Scripture, the logic of Jesus's argument turns on the character of God rather than biblical interpretation. God is the God "of the living"; therefore, the ancestors Abraham, Isaac, and Jacob must be alive (cf. 4 Macc. 7:19; 16:25). What is not clear is whether the Lukan Jesus is assuming some kind of Platonic view of the immortality of the soul or an ongoing interim, soulful (but not corporeal) postdeath existence before the final judgment (Carroll 2012, 407). In other words, does the operative question belong to Plato ("If a person dies, is that one still alive?") or Job ("If someone dies, will they live again?"; 14:14 NIV). The evidence would seem to point toward the latter (cf. Luke 16:19–31; 23:39–43): "Luke's Jesus definitely believes that the dead are raised, and may also believe that they live on after death in a temporary place of blessings or punishment, while they await the final disposition at the last day" (Vinson 2008, 630). Jesus's answer seems to satisfy his interlocutors: **Then some of the scribes responded and said, "Teacher, you have spoken well." Indeed, they did not dare to ask him anything anymore** (20:39–40). Jesus, however, is not quite finished with the conversation.

20:41–44. They initially raised the question of the correct way to interpret Scripture; Jesus presents his own scriptural conundrum. Jesus turns the traditional assumption that the Messiah will come from the Davidic line (2 Sam. 7:12–14; *Pss. Sol.* 17.21; Rom. 1:3) into a question: **Then he said to them, "How is it that they say that the Christ is the son of David?"** (20:41). Within the narrative of Luke, the association of Jesus with the house of David has already been established (1:69; 2:4; 3:23–31), and the implied identification of the Lukan Jesus with the messianic role of David's son is shared with the audience. Jesus then quotes Ps. 110:1: **For David himself says in the book of Psalms, "The Lord said to my lord, 'Sit at my right hand until I put your enemies under your feet'"** (20:42–43). While there is little evidence that Ps. 110, traditionally understood to be a "royal" psalm (in celebration of the coronation of the king), was read messianically in pre-Christian Second Temple Judaism, it was common in Christian exegesis to read the psalm as referring to the Lord God speaking to the Lord Jesus (so *Barn.* 12.11 says explicitly, "The Lord said to Christ, my Lord" [*ANF* 1:145]). Jesus then poses his riddle: **David calls him Lord. So how is he his son?** (20:44). No answer is given to this rhetorical question, but the answer is clear: Jesus, David's son, will become David's Lord by his resurrection and exaltation. This argument will be made clearly in Luke's second volume (Acts 2:34–35; 13:22–23, 33–37) and is an argument that the Sadducees, given their views on resurrection in general, simply cannot accept.

Jesus's Observations about Widows (20:45–21:4)

20:45–21:4. Having exposed the fallacy in the religious leaders' logic concerning the resurrection (20:27–40) and their faulty exposition of Scripture (20:41–44), Jesus now turns to a critique of their religiosity (Talbert 1982, 195): **Now, as all of the people were listening, he said to his disciples, "Beware of the scribes who like to walk around in long robes and love being greeted in the marketplace and receiving the most important seats in the synagogues and seats of honor at banquets, who devour the homes of widows and pray on and on for show. These men will receive a more severe judgment than others!"** (20:45–47). The way of life of the religious leaders, or at least some of them, had devolved to the point where they were outwardly pious but inwardly corrupt, preying on the vulnerable in society while praying merely for show. This is a charge Jesus has leveled before (11:37–41). The warning now, however, is directed toward the disciples (within the people's hearing; 20:45) not to become like those who practice such insincere "piety." Abandoning the pursuit of justice for the show of pious practice will result in "severe judgment."

The scene continues; having just criticized the scribes for their pretense at wealth (wearing long robes, seeking status), Jesus now notices those who are truly wealthy (Vinson 2008, 640): **Now, when he looked up he saw the rich tossing their gifts into the treasury** (21:1). According to later tradition (*m. Šeqal.* 6.5), there were thirteen receptacles to receive the various temple offerings, and for the purposes of the story, it was irrelevant whether the offerings were for administering temple worship, for maintaining the temple buildings, or for alms (D. Garland 2011, 817). What mattered was the show of conspicuous wealth. Some of the receptacles were brass, which no doubt made a loud sound when large sums of coins were tossed in. Was Jesus's attention drawn to the noise made by the large gifts ringing in the receptacles (D. Garland 2011, 818)? Jesus then notices another figure also making an offering: **And he saw a poor widow tossing two leptons there** (21:2). Luke has a special concern for widows. Already Jesus has shown compassion to a widow (7:11–17) and used a widow as an exemplary model of persistence (18:1–8). In the immediate context, there was told a story about a woman widowed seven times (20:27–33), along with the image of the exploitation of widows' houses (20:47; cf. Carroll 2012, 410). This widow has made an offering of two lepta, the value of which was next to nothing, only 1/64th as much as a day laborer would earn in a single day.

Jesus comments on the contrast between the two gifts: **I tell you for certain, this poor widow put in more than everyone! For all of these out of their abundance tossed money into the receptacle for gifts, but this widow, out of her meager possessions, put in all the livelihood that she had!** (21:3–4). Through antithesis (see *Rhet. Her.* 4.15.21), Jesus contrasts the actions of the wealthy and the widow, but commentators are divided as to whether Jesus's comments are to be viewed as lament or praise (see Fitzmyer 1981–85, 2:1320–21, for various options). Was the widow exhibit A of the exploitation produced by an oppressive temple economic system, or was she being praised for her act of piety? Given the positive role of widows in the Lukan narratives, it seems most likely that Jesus intends to praise the woman's act of piety. She has given her whole livelihood. This is what it looks like to render to God what is God's. According to Jesus, the true value of a gift is how much is kept back by the giver, how much the gift costs the giver to give. In that regard, the woman's gift is far superior to all the others. So on one level Jesus commends the piety of the widow. But the act is not done in a vacuum. The act leaves her destitute, with the "status of a beggar" (Danker 1988, 327). If the religious establishment to which she has just given her whole life ignores her need, then her house will indeed be devoured. To avoid this kind of systemic abuse, the religious authorities must step up and care for those whose sacrificial giving out of devotion and piety has left them vulnerable (see Vinson 2008, 641). Jesus holds out little hope that the current temple system is capable of such care. Jesus has already called it a den of thieves (19:46), and he is about to predict its devastation (21:6). But that should not mislead the authorial audience into a false and arrogant attitude of being better than those in charge of the temple complex. All too soon, the followers of Jesus will face the same problem; they have neglected the needs of widows (Acts 6:1–6). What will they do then?

The Temple's Beauty and Demise and the Eschatological Discourse (21:5–28)

Jesus's eschatological discourse is structured in two dialogues (21:5–6; 21:7–28; cf. Carroll 2012, 412). First, someone in the audience comments on the beauty of the temple (21:5) and Jesus responds briefly by predicting its destruction (21:6). Next, another anonymous person in the audience asks when Jesus's prediction will take place (21:7), to which Jesus gives a longer response, first describing events that will precede the temple's demise (21:8–11). Then, in a parenthetical flashback, Jesus describes a period of testing and persecution that the disciples will face before the destruction of temple and city (21:12–19). In 21:20–24, Jesus describes the destruction of Jerusalem, finally directly addressing the question posed in 21:7, and 21:25–28 elaborates on the apocalyptic imagery of 21:10–11, providing a basis of hope for Jesus's followers that their redemption is to be found in the midst of the persecution and judgment.

21:5–6. While Jesus is warning of the consequences of ignoring acts of piety, like that of the widow, which leave the vulnerable even more destitute, "some" are remarking on the beauty of the temple and its votive offerings (2 Macc. 9:16; 3 Macc. 3:17): **While some were saying about the temple that it was decorated with beautiful stones and offerings, he said, "These things that you**

Perceptions of Giving in Antiquity

The widow's generosity in Luke 21:1–4 would have been celebrated in Jewish and Greco-Roman circles:

> "[God] requires no sacrifice, or should they offer any, however modest, more gladly does He welcome this homage from poverty than that of the wealthiest." (Josephus, *Ant.* 6.149, trans. Thackeray and Marcus 1930)

> "More than once I see poor people who are wiser than the rich and who give offerings to the gods with their weak hands; yet they are more pious than those who sacrifice oxen." (Euripides, *Danae* frg. 327, cited by Bovon 2002–13, 3:93)

> "Generosity is not measured in the amount given; it depends on the attitude of the donor. People who are truly generous give in proportion to what they actually have. It is possible, therefore, that a person who gives a little out of small resources is more generous than another." (Aristotle, *Eth. nic.* 4.2.29, cited by Danker 1988, 328; see also *Lev. Rab.* 107a)

see—**the days will come when not one stone will be left upon another, not one that will not be torn down**" (21:5–6). It would appear that, despite Jesus's words, some of those in the temple are more concerned with the beauty of the temple surroundings than with caring for the marginalized within its walls. They marvel at the beauty of the outside of the cup, while ignoring the wicked exploitation that lies within (cf. 11:39–41). Jesus responds by predicting the demise of the temple (cf. the same image in 19:44 in reference to Jerusalem).

21:7–11. The setting of the next section continues to be the temple (rather than the Mount of Olives; cf. Mark 13:3//Matt. 24:3), and the section begins with another question, one that follows naturally on Jesus's previous comment: **So they asked him, "Teacher, when, then, will these things happen? And what will the sign be when these things are about to take place?"** (21:7). Once again, the questioners are not explicitly identified, but the address of Jesus as "teacher" suggests that it is not the disciples who are speaking. This is the eleventh and final time that Jesus is addressed as "teacher" in Luke's Gospel; never is the speaker one of Jesus's followers (Culpepper 1995, 399). Jesus will return to the question (21:20–24) but chooses to respond first by warning them not to assume too readily that the end is imminent: **Watch out that you are not deceived! For many will come in my name, saying, "I am [the messiah]," and "The time is near." Do not follow them! And when you hear of wars and rebellions, do not be alarmed. For it is necessary for these things to happen first; but the end will not immediately follow** (21:8–9). Jesus earlier issued a similar warning not to follow false prophets who are quick to point to signs of the end (17:23). Josephus provides a sampling of prophetic proclamations during the siege of Jerusalem (*J.W.* 6.285–87, 300–309; cited by Johnson 1991, 321). Jesus argues that "wars and rebellions" must "happen first," and even then "the end will not immediately follow": **Then he proceeded to say to them: "Nation will rise against nation, and kingdom against kingdom. And there will be both powerful earthquakes and famines and plagues all over the place. There will be both fearful events and great signs from heaven"** (21:10–11). Whether the "end" refers to the end of the temple or the end of time is a false dichotomy, especially in light of the use of traditional apocalyptic imagery of natural disasters, like earthquakes, plagues, and famines (cf. Isa. 14:30; 51:19; Ezek. 36:29–30; Zech. 14:5; Amos 8:11–12; 2 Esd. [*4 Ezra*] 16:18–22; *T. Jud.*

> **Josephus on the Temple**
>
> "The exterior of the building wanted nothing that could astound either mind or eye. For, being covered on all sides with massive plates of gold, the sun was no sooner up than it radiated so fiery a flash that persons straining to look at it were compelled to avert their eyes as from solar rays." (Josephus, *J.W.* 5.222, trans. Thackeray 1928)

23.3; on the lyrical use of the near homonyms *limoi* and *loimoi*, see Culy, Parsons, and Stigall 2010, 646). Rather, the Lukan Jesus paints "the coming historical conflict (including the siege of Jerusalem) onto a wider, indeed cosmic, canvas, the first broad strokes of an eschatological vision given fuller description in vv. 25–28" (Carroll 2012, 416).

21:12–19. The next section (21:12–19) begins with "before all these things," a "key editorial insertion" that enables "Luke to place Jesus' predictions of his followers' sufferings before the fall of the city" (Johnson 1991, 321):

> Before all these things, they will lay their hands on you and persecute you, so that you are handed over to synagogues and prisons—yes, you will be brought before kings and governors on account of my name. This will result for you in opportunities for testimony. So then, determine in your hearts not to prepare in advance to defend yourself. For I will give you words and wisdom that none of those who are against you will be able to withstand or oppose. You will be betrayed even by parents and siblings, relatives and friends. And they will put some of you to death. And you will be hated by all people because of my name. (21:12–17)

Later, when Luke composes his second volume, he will use these predictions of Jesus as a template to describe the specific experiences of Jesus's first followers (Culpepper 1995, 400–401; see table 7). Further, that the disciples serve as witnesses will prove to be a major theme throughout Acts.

Table 7. Shaping the Story of Jesus's First Followers

Prediction in Luke 21:12–17	Fulfillment in Acts
Arrested ("lay their hands on you")	4:3; 5:18; 12:1; 21:27
Persecuted	7:52; 8:3; 9:4–5; 12:4; 22:4, 7–8; 26:11, 14–15
Conflict in synagogues	6:9; 9:2; 13:44–51; 17:1–5; 19:8–10
Imprisoned	5:18; 12:3–5; 16:19–24; 21:27–36; 28:16
Brought before kings and governors	12:1; 13:6–12; 18:12–17; 23:24–33; 24:1, 10; 25:13–26; 26:2, 27, 30
Given words to speak (see also Luke 12:11–12)	18:9–10; 23:11
None can withstand or oppose	6:10; 13:8–12
Executed	7:59–60; 12:2

Jesus balances his prediction of impending perils with a promise of divine protection: **But not even a hair of your head will be destroyed. By your endurance you must gain your lives** (21:18–19). The promise that not even a hair on the head will be harmed is a metaphor drawn from Scripture (2 Sam. 14:11; 1 Kings 1:52) and used earlier by Jesus (Luke 12:7). Patience is commonly connected to persecution in early Christian tradition (e.g., Rom. 5:3–4; 8:25; 2 Cor. 1:6; Col. 1:11; 1 Thess. 1:3; 2 Thess. 1:4; see Johnson 1991, 323), and it was also extolled in the larger Greco-Roman world (Archilochus, *Carm.* 67a; Seneca, *De tranquillitate animi*; Horace, *Carm.* 2.3.2; 2.10.21–22; cited by Danker 1988, 332).

21:20–28. The final section of this unit (21:20–28) of Jesus's discourse begins with a notice of the destruction of Jerusalem (21:20) and ends with the restoration of the audience (21:28). The first subunit (21:20–24) provides a delayed answer to the question raised in 21:7: "When, then, will these things happen?" **Now, when you see Jerusalem surrounded by armies, then know that its desolation is near!** (21:20). When Rome has encircled the walls of the city, then the destruction of Jerusalem is inescapable. Josephus describes the Roman siege of Jerusalem in gruesome detail (*J.W.* 4.326–33; 5.420–38, 512–18). At that time, Jesus asserts, it will be necessary to abandon the city: **At that time, those in Judea must flee to the mountains; those inside Jerusalem must get out; and those out in the fields must not go back into the city, because these are days of vengeance: everything that has been written will be fulfilled** (21:21–22). This abandonment is not a "cowardly retreat but a deliberate break with Jerusalem and the false theology of security that views it as sacrosanct and inviolable" (D. Garland 2011, 833). The time for retribution (cf. Jer. 46:10; Hosea 9:7) against the city that has killed the prophets (13:34) and rejected the things that make for peace (19:42–44) has come (Carroll 2012, 418). And there is more, Jesus says, and it is worse: **Woe to those who are pregnant or nursing in those days!** (21:23a). The effects of war on expectant and nursing mothers are especially horrible (Amos 1:13; Lam. 2:11–12, 20; Josephus, *J.W.* 6.201–22; see Johnson 1991, 323). **For there will be great distress on the earth and wrath for this people** (21:23b). Is the "wrath for this people" the wrath of Rome or of God? Most likely it is God's wrath through the agency of Rome. "Engagement with prophetic texts that picture Jerusalem's (and the first temple's) demise as the working out of divine judgment on a recalcitrant city" suggests that "divine wrath is in evidence" (Carroll 2012, 418). Jesus concludes this section on an ominous note: **They will fall by the edge of the sword and be taken captive into all the nations; and Jerusalem will [continue to be] trampled down by the gentiles until the times of the gentiles are complete** (21:24). Jesus's words are replete with intertextual echoes: falling by the "edge of the sword" (2 Sam. 15:14 NRSV; cf. Jer. 16:4); "taken captive" into all the nations (1 Macc. 5:13; 8:10; cf. fig. 23); and "trampled down" by the gentiles (Zech. 12:3; Dan. 8:13). While the phrase "until the times of the gentiles are

Figure 23. Arch of Titus, Erected in Honor of Titus's Siege of Jerusalem

complete" could refer to the gentile mission (cf. Luke 24:47; Rom. 11:25–27; Tob. 14:6; so D. Garland 2011, 834), in this context in which Rome is functioning as an agent of God's wrath, it more likely refers to the period of foreign domination, which will also come to an end (cf. Dan. 2:21; 9:24–27). The judgment on Rome will correspond to the judgment on Jerusalem (Nolland 1989–93, 3:1006). "The time of the pagans will give way to the coming of the Son of Man" (Schneider 1977, 2:424).

Jesus seamlessly transitions to cosmic eschatological images that are no longer confined to Jerusalem and its environs (Carroll 2012, 420): **There will be signs in the sun and moon and stars, and on earth the nations will be distressed as they have great anxiety from the noise of the sea and its waves, so that people will be fainting from fear and from the thought of what is coming upon the world. For the powers of the heavens will be shaken** (21:25–26). Josephus describes in some detail the heavenly portents that accompany the fall of Jerusalem (*J.W.* 6.288–300). Here the cosmic "signs" are vague portents in the "sun and moon and stars," which nonetheless convey the "climatic judgment upon the nations" (Nolland 1989–93, 3:1006). The deafening noise of the roaring sea (cf. Isa. 17:12) produces anxiety and even fainting among the gentiles over the prospects of the impending judgment (2 Esd. [*4 Ezra*] 6:17). The portents even impact the heavenly powers (cf. Isa. 34:4; Joel 2:10; Hag. 2:6, 21; see also Carroll 2012, 420).

What is judgment for some, however, is redemption for others: **And then they will see the Son of Man coming in a cloud with great power and glory. Now, when these things begin to happen, stand up straight, and lift your heads, because your redemption is approaching** (21:27–28). Jesus's eschatological discourse proper ends with the glorious and victorious coming of the Son of Man (cf. Dan. 7:13–14), who brings liberation and redemption. Luke here omits the reference in Mark to the gathering of the elect by angels (Mark 13:27); rather, the Lukan Jesus commands that his followers "stand up straight" (*anakypsate*). This is the same word used to describe the "bent woman" who could not "stand up straight" because she was bound by Satan (Luke 13:11; see Johnson 1991, 328). Thus the Son of Man gives freedom from the bonds of evil and enables his followers to stand tall and lift their heads. It is a glorious and beautiful vision of the end, fully in God's control.

Parable and Pronouncement (21:29–38)

21:29–33. Jesus continues his teaching with a parable (21:29–33) and an exhortation (21:34–36): **Then he told a parable to them: "Look at the fig tree and all the other trees. When they have already sprouted leaves, you see for yourselves and know that the summer is now near. Thus, you also, when you see these things happening, know that the kingdom of God is near"** (21:29–31). Jesus tells a parable to further clarify his eschatological teaching. Just as his hearers know summer is near when the trees begin to bud (notice Luke includes "all the other trees" and not just the fig tree, as does Mark 13:28), so when they see "these things happening" (esp. the aforementioned portents) they will know that the kingdom of God, that is, the eschaton, is near (9:26–27; 11:2; 14:15; 17:20–21; 19:11; 22:30; see D. Garland 2011, 836). Jesus then goes on to reassure his audience of the reliability and durability of his words: **I assure you that this generation will certainly not pass away until all these things take place! Heaven and earth will pass away, but my words will never pass away!** (21:32–33). For the authorial audience, "prophetic prediction in Jesus' time, then, becomes historical fulfillment in Luke's lifetime" (Carroll 2012, 419). Thus, "the fact that these events had occurred, and in a way consistent with the words of Jesus, must have had a powerful impact" (Johnson 1991, 326). But Jesus also asserts that "this generation" will not pass away until these things take place. What does he mean by "this generation"? Within the Lukan context, "this generation" most likely refers to the generation that will witness the signs of the end time outlined in the eschatological discourse (for other options, see Fitzmyer 1981–85, 2:1353). Neither that generation nor Jesus's words will pass away before these things are fulfilled.

21:34–36. With that in mind, Jesus offers the following admonition: **So, guard yourselves so that your hearts will not be weighed down with carousing and drunkenness and the cares of everyday life, and so that that day will not come upon you suddenly, like a trap. For it will come upon everyone who lives on the face of the entire earth** (21:34–35). Jesus warns his listeners to refrain from distracting, degrading, mundane pursuits, described in the conventional moral language of "carousing and drunkenness and the cares of everyday life" (Luke 12:19, 22–31; 1 Thess. 5:7; Rom. 13:13). Otherwise that day will come "suddenly" (Luke 17:24), like a "trap" (Isa. 24:17–18; cf. Ps. 34:7–8; Prov. 12:13), on "everyone" (cf. 21:25–26). In contrast to the drunken stupor of the careless and immoral life, Jesus's appeal is for his followers to be awake and alert (cf. 1 Thess. 5:6; 1 Pet. 4:7): **So, be alert at all times, and plead that you might be able to escape all these things that are about to happen and to stand before the Son of Man** (21:36). From the Lukan Jesus's point of view, knowledge of and confidence in the future find their significance as a motivation for followers, challenged and chastised by crisis, to remain morally vigilant and faithful and to "stand before the Son of Man."

21:37–38. The section ends with a summary statement of Jesus's temple teaching being positively received by the "people," which forms an *inclusio* with the beginning of the unit (19:45–48): **Now, he was teaching in the temple during the day, but at night he was going out and spending the night on the hill called the Mount of Olives. And all the people were coming to him early in the morning to listen to him at the temple** (21:37–38). Jesus went out to the Mount of Olives only at night; thus the summary reminds the authorial audience that the entirety of the eschatological discourse, including its criticism of the temple, has occurred within the temple precincts (contra Mark 13:3). Certainly, the image of a solitary figure standing within the very walls of the institution he is criticizing would be well-known to anyone familiar with Israel's Scriptures (cf. esp. Jer. 7), but it would not have been unknown to those familiar only with pagan literature (Cicero, *Div.* 1.1–2; Philostratus, *Vit. Apoll.* 1.2; cited by Johnson 1991, 325).

Theological Issues

In *The Return of the King*, J. R. R. Tolkien's final volume in The Lord of the Rings trilogy, Samwise Gamgee, Shire gardener and faithful companion and servant of Frodo Baggins, is awakened from a deep sleep by Gandalf the White Wizard after the ring has been destroyed at Mount Doom. Sam is surprised to find both that he is alive and that Gandalf is with him. He says, "Gandalf! I thought you were dead! But then I thought I was dead myself. Is everything sad going to come untrue? What's happened to the world?" (Tolkien 1957, 230). Sam's questions resonate with the great reversal that has shaped Luke's understanding of apocalyptic theology and that is so deeply embedded in Christian eschatology. For those who follow Jesus, the sadness of the world, broken by evil and torn by sin, will "become untrue" when the Son of Man returns in glory and power. As Gandalf puts it in his response to Sam: "A great Shadow has departed" (Tolkien 1957, 230).

Luke's vision is no less powerful and evocative: those who have been bent under the bonds of evil and trampled down under the curse of sin are bid to "stand up straight" and to "lift their heads" to their coming redemption (Luke

21:28). "This hope of eternal beatitude preserves Christians from discouragement, sustains them when they have been abandoned, protects them from the selfishness of despair, and prompts them to acts of charity" (Wood 2003, 144).

With such a hopeful vision of the end before us, why is it that so many contemporary Christians find so little inspiration in Christian eschatology? Justo González puts the problem this way: "We prefer a 'gospel' without eschatology—a 'good news' without hope—because for many of us such 'good news' is not so good. We prefer a gospel without eschatology, because the good news of the great reversal that Luke has been proclaiming all along does not seem so good to us" (2010, 239). González then offers the following remedy for those of us who find ourselves on the wrong side of the great reversal, looking more at judgment than at redemption:

> What then about those of us who are not poor or disinherited, whose religion makes us socially respectable, whose mainline churches are the moral and social mainstay of our communities? If all that Luke says about the great reversal is true, there is only one way open to us: solidarity. The doctor of the law cannot suddenly become a Samaritan. He is who he is. The only alternative left to him is to act like the good Samaritan. The Pharisee cannot leave behind his faith, his piety, and his obedience to the law. The only alternative left to him is to join "sinners" in their pain and their trust to God. . . . Within this context, eschatology is a glimpse into that future so glorious that we cannot fully envision it or understand it, but for which we still hope and for which we live. (2010, 240, 242)

Our Christian hope is that the time will come in the future when the sad things become untrue and when we will finally be able to stand up straight and lift our heads to the redemption that awaits us. That conviction shapes and informs the way we live in the present. "God's future is God's call to the present, and the present is the time of decision in light of God's future" (Bornkamm 1960, 93).

Luke 22:1–23:49

The Meaning and Manner of Jesus's Death

Introductory Matters

The next major section also addresses a common topic in encomiastic biography, namely, the manner and meaning of the protagonist's death (see Theon, *Prog.* 78). This unit (22:1–23:49) consists of five scenes: the preparations for the Passover (22:1–13); the Last Supper (22:14–38); the prayer and arrest in Gethsemane (22:39–53); the trials of Jesus (22:54–23:25); and the death of Jesus (23:26–49).

Tracing the Narrative Flow

The Preparations for the Passover (22:1–13)

22:1–6. The Lukan passion narrative begins on an ominous note: **Now, the Feast of Unleavened Bread, which is called Passover, was approaching. And the chief priests and scribes were looking for how they might get rid of him** (22:1–2a). The motive of the religious leaders for "getting rid" of Jesus, as well as their delay in doing so, is explained in the next line: **For they were afraid of the people** (22:2b). The conflict moves to another level when Luke notes that **Satan then entered into Judas, called Iscariot, who was one of the Twelve; and he went off and spoke with the chief priests and temple officers about how he might hand him over to them** (22:3–4). Although Conzelmann's notion of Jesus's "Satan-free ministry" (1961, 80–81, 156–57) has long since been discarded (see Garrett 1989, 41–43), the reemergence of Satan into the

> **Luke 22:1–23:49 in the Narrative Flow**
>
> Jesus's origins and training (1:1–4:13)
>
> Jesus's mighty words and deeds in Galilee (4:14–9:50)
>
> Jesus's mighty words and deeds along the way (part 1) (9:51–14:35)
>
> Jesus's mighty words and deeds along the way (part 2) (15:1–19:44)
>
> Jesus in Jerusalem: teachings, death, and resurrection (19:45–24:53)
>
>   Jesus in and around the temple (19:45–21:38)
>
> ▶ The meaning and manner of Jesus's death (22:1–23:49)
>
>   The preparations for the Passover (22:1–13)
>
>   The Last Supper (22:14–38)
>
>   The prayer and arrest in Gethsemane (22:39–53)
>
>   The trials of Jesus (22:54–23:25)
>
>   The death of Jesus (23:26–49)

story line (missing in both Matthew and Mark) does suggest that "at the passion Satan takes the offensive again" (Garrett 1989, 46). The collaboration of the religious authorities with Satan sets the stage for a cosmic battle in which God and his agent, Jesus, are pitted against the dark powers (cf. 22:53). A deal is struck: **They were delighted and agreed to give him money (22:5)**. Since the main verb in the next clause, **and he accepted the offer (22:6a)**, refers to Judas's agreement, the sense of *syntithēmi* ("agreed"; 22:5) here is that of agreement among the Jewish leaders rather than between them and Judas (Culy, Parsons, and Stigall 2010, 663–64). Judas, as Satan's agent, looks for the opportune time to betray Jesus (cf. 4:13!): **he began looking for a good time to hand him over to them, when a crowd was not present (22:6b)**.

22:7–13. The next unit describes the preparations for Jesus's last meal with his followers (22:7–13), and the one following portrays the meal itself, which involves Jesus's last extended speech to his disciples (22:14–38; cf. Talbert 1982, 206). Luke begins by setting the scene: **Now, the Day of Unleavened Bread arrived, on which it was necessary to sacrifice the Passover lamb (22:7)**. The "Day of Unleavened Bread" refers to the general time period for the seven-day feast, during which the slaughter of the Passover lamb occurs, and it may be Luke's subtle correction of Mark, who seems to suggest (incorrectly) that the Passover lambs were slaughtered on the first day of the feast (cf. Mark 14:12; D. Garland 2011, 852). While the slaughter of the lambs is not technically a "sacrifice" (Bovon 2002–13, 3:142; though cf. Exod. 12:6, 21 LXX), the use of that term (*thyesthai*), along with the notice that "it was necessary," echoes the divine necessity of Jesus's sacrificial death (cf. 9:22; 13:33; 17:25; 22:37; 24:7, 26, 44). Luke is less interested in the details associated with the slaughter of the Passover lambs (cf. *m. Pesaḥ.* 5) and much more interested in the general setting, for by linking Jesus's exodus (9:30–31) with the Passover, Luke is commemorating "the exodus liberation of the people from Egypt" in the story of Jesus's passion (Carroll 2012, 426). Further, in Luke's version, Jesus is in charge of the details of his last week:

So, he sent Peter and John, saying, "Go and prepare the Passover meal for us, so that we can eat it" (22:8; contrast Mark 14:12, in which it is the disciples' question regarding the place for the meal that prompts Jesus's response). It is appropriate that Peter and John are sent to prepare the Passover meal, since they (along with James) were with Jesus at the transfiguration, in which his passion was described as an "exodus" (9:31; see above). By accepting this task, Peter and John become servants who ready the table for others (cf. 22:24–27; Green 1997, 313), a task they will later reject (Acts 6:1–6). The disciples' question is logical: **They said to him, "Where do you want us to prepare it?"** (22:9).

Jesus responds with these instructions: **Then he said to them, "After you enter the city, a man carrying a jar of water will meet you! Follow him into the house that he enters, and say to the owner of the house, 'The teacher says to you, "Where is the guest room where I may eat the Passover meal with my disciples?"' He will show you a large upstairs room that is furnished [with what we need]. Prepare the meal there"** (22:10–12). Some commentators suggest that the sight of a man carrying a water jar would have been unusual, since this was typically "women's work" (cf. John 4) and thus Peter and John could easily pick out the person (Culpepper 1995, 416). But male slaves could also perform domestic duties (cf. Luke 17:7–8), and, in fact, their use was a kind of "conspicuous consumption," since they were generally more expensive (Saller 2003, 196). In any case, the point is moot, since Jesus says that the man will meet the disciples and not vice versa (Nolland 1989–93, 3:1033). While it is possible that Jesus's words suggest that he has prearranged with a householder (who knows Jesus as "the teacher" from his public speaking?) to prepare a room for Jesus to dine with his friends, it is more likely a matter of "prescient discernment" (Carroll 2012, 428), designed to depict Jesus as "master of his destiny" (Bovon 2002–13, 3:145), or, better, as "the prophet who anticipates his own death and . . . exercises direction" (Johnson 1991, 335–36). The householder "has no choice but to yield to the demands of the other master" (Bovon 2002–13, 3:144). The large upper room is a "guest room" (*katalyma*; 22:11; cf. comments on Luke 2:7b), no doubt in great demand in light of the crowds swelling the population of Jerusalem during Passover (Josephus's estimation of 2.5 million pilgrims is an exaggeration [see *J.W.* 6.420–26], but it is likely that the number of residents tripled during the festival; see Carroll 2012, 426). Peter and John obey: **they went and found things just as he had told them, and they prepared the Passover meal** (22:13). The words of the Prophet are fulfilled.

The Last Supper (22:14–38)

22:14–23. The next unit (22:14–23) describes what has come to be known in Christian tradition as the Lord's Supper, or Eucharist. The passage begins: **And when the hour came, he sat down to eat, and the apostles sat down with him** (22:14). Luke's note contains three differences from Mark's version (Johnson 1991, 337). First, while Mark records that Jesus gathered with his disciples "when it was evening" (Mark 14:17 NRSV), Luke reports that the "hour came." The reference to the "hour" is more than a simple chronological reference but rather suggests, in Johannine-like fashion (cf. John 13:1), "a solemn chiming of the hour heralding the doom-laden events to come" (D. Garland 2011, 853; cf. Luke 22:53). Second, Luke refers to Jesus's followers as "the apostles" rather than the "Twelve" (Mark 14:17), perhaps echoing the role of Peter and John, whom Jesus sent (*apostellō*; 22:8) to prepare the meal. Finally, whereas Mark notes that "they [the Twelve and Jesus] were at table" (Mark 14:18 NET), Luke reports that "Jesus sat down to eat, and the apostles sat down with him," keeping the focus on Jesus and his role as teacher and host (Johnson 1991, 337; Culy, Parsons, and Stigall 2010, 668).

Jesus speaks to his friends: **I have greatly desired to eat this Passover meal with you before I suffer. For I tell you, I will certainly not eat it again until it finds its fulfillment in the kingdom of God** (22:15–16). Two items in Jesus's speech are rather ambiguous. Did Jesus actually participate in the meal with the disciples? Some take the Semitic idiom "I have greatly desired" (*epithymia epethymēsa*; an example of rhetorical "doubling"; see Quintilian, *Inst.* 9.3.28–29) as an expression of an unfulfilled wish (see D. Garland 2011, 854; some scribes [C K N P W] evidently inserted "no longer" [*ouketi*] to avoid this interpretation). More likely, Jesus does share in the meal but is nonetheless looking forward to the eschatological banquet (cf. the reference to "from this time" in 22:18; Culpepper 1995, 418). What is the referent of the second part of Jesus's statement, "I will not eat *it*, until *it* finds fulfillment"? While some (Parker 1997, 155) seem to think Jesus is referring to this newly inaugurated "Last Supper," most commentators take the pronoun (*auto*) to refer to the Passover meal, thus giving the Passover meal an eschatological overtone. And Luke is more interested in this eschatological dimension of Passover than in detailing the various constituent Passover components of Jesus's last meal (for that, see Culpepper 1995, 419; Jeremias 1966, 216). "The meal then that had been a celebration of God's deliverance of Israel will henceforth point toward the fulfillment of God's redemptive work in the kingdom" (Culpepper 1995, 419). The notion of an eschatological banquet was firmly rooted in Israel's Scriptures (Isa. 25:6–8; 55:1–2; 65:13–14) and Second Temple Jewish texts (*1 En.* 62.14; *2 Bar.* 29.4; 1QSa 2.12–21) and is certainly familiar to Luke (13:29; 14:15–24), although connecting the Passover meal to the eschatological banquet appears distinctive to Luke (Fitzmyer 1981–85, 2:1397).

This forward-looking aspect of Passover continues in Jesus's next words (in an example of *synonymy*, or repetition of the same thought in different words; see *Rhet. Her.* 4.18.38; Quintilian, *Inst.* 9.3.45–46): **And when he had received the cup, he gave thanks and said, "Take this, and share it among yourselves. For I tell you, I will certainly not drink from the fruit of the vine from this time until the kingdom of God comes"** (22:17–18). The reference to the "fruit of the vine" continues the Passover imagery, since apparently it

Early Traditions regarding the Sequence of the Bread and the Cup

Five texts recount Jesus's last meal, which cluster around three traditions (Parker 1997, 153): (1) Mark 14:18–25//Matt. 26:21–29, in which the prediction of betrayal precedes the meal and in which the cup is described as blood poured out for many; (2) the longer text of Luke 22:15–23, which has cup/bread/cup (on multiple cups in later practices, see Justin Martyr, *1 Apol.* 65–67)/1 Cor. 11, both of which describe the meal as a "memorial"); and (3) the shorter text of Luke (minus vv. 19b–20), which, uniquely among the canonical texts, has the cup precede the bread and makes no explicit reference to Jesus's death (but see above). The cup/bread sequence is not unprecedented in early Christian literature, however. The *Didache*, a late first- or early second-century document, reports:

"Now concerning the Eucharist, give thanks as follows. First, concerning the cup:

"We give you thanks, our Father,
for the holy vine of David your servant,
which you have made known to us
through Jesus, your servant;
to you be the glory forever.

"And concerning the broken bread:

"We give you thanks, our Father,
for the life and knowledge
that you have made known to us
through Jesus, your servant;
to you be the glory forever."

(*Did.* 9.1–3, trans. Holmes 2007, 357, 359)

If the *Didache* is reflecting early liturgical practice (cf. Fitzmyer 1981–85, 2:1397, who remains skeptical), then we may have evidence for the shorter text of Luke circulating very early, if not originally. In any case, many interpreters who opt for the shorter reading do so in part in order to remove the explicit reference to Jesus's death having any kind of atoning significance, since that view is otherwise missing in Luke's narratives (Carroll 2012, 432–33; Parker 1997, 153–55). As we see above, however, what remains in Luke 22:15–23, even stripped of any kind of liturgical elaboration, is not devoid of references to Jesus's suffering, the necessity of which can best be explained as integral to God's redemptive plan for a fallen world, and this interpretation fits within Luke's larger argument regarding the redemptive, even vicarious, nature of Jesus's suffering (see Parsons 2008a).

recalls one of the paschal blessings ("Blessed art thou, O Lord our God, king of the universe, creator of the fruit of the vine," cited by Johnson 1991; see *m. Ber.* 6.1), but again the emphasis is on the eschatological context: Jesus says he will not drink the cup until he does so in the kingdom of God. The shared cup symbolizes intimate communion and a shared destiny between Jesus and his followers (cf. Ps. 16:4–5); it binds them to Jesus's death (cf. 22:42; D. Garland 2011, 854; Danker 1988, 345).

Next, Jesus turns to the bread: **And when he had taken the bread, he gave thanks and broke it. Then he gave it to them, saying, "This is my body"** (22:19a; on the text-critical issues surrounding 22:19b–20, omitted here, see Martin 2005, 291). Once again, Jesus partakes in gestures (taking, giving thanks over, breaking, and distributing the bread) reminiscent of a *"chreia* of action" (see comments and the sidebar *"Chreiae* of Action" at Luke 9:16). Jesus elaborates the action with a simple but profound declaration: "This is my body." The broken bread is a powerful foreshadowing of Jesus's suffering and death, now only a matter of hours away (22:63–65; 23:33). Jesus turns the spotlight on his followers: **"Nevertheless, the hand of the one who betrays me is with me at the table! For the Son of Man will go in accord with what has been determined, but woe to that man through whom he is betrayed!" Then they began to discuss with each other who among them, in light of what he had said, could possibly be the one who was about to do this** (22:21–23). That the fate of the Son of Man is according to God's divine plan does not excuse human participation in the impending events. Certainly within the overall narrative of Luke, the audience will recognize that the hand that betrays is primarily that of Judas (22:3–6, 47–48), but given the disciples' responses to his accusation (cf. esp. 22:24–27), it is not inappropriate to conclude that the betraying hand has twelve names (Clivaz 2002, 416).

22:24–34. The conversation next takes a jarring turn and should be viewed as an intensification of the disciples' query recorded in 22:23. In denying that they are the betrayer, the disciples quickly move to the other end of the spectrum by arguing over who appears to be the greatest: **Now there was, in fact, an argument among them regarding which of them was considered to be the greater** (22:24). The phrasing and placement of this controversy are Lukan, but the substance of the argument is found also in Mark 10:43–44//Matt. 18:1 (cf. Luke 9:46; Johnson 1991, 344). The Greco-Roman symposia tradition of teaching, controversy, and resolution forms a broad framework within which to understand this present text. "The shocking contrast . . . highlights with dark humor, the disciples' failure . . . to grasp what is happening, what Jesus' destiny is, and what his messianic vocation means for their common life" (Carroll 2012, 438). Jesus responds: **The kings of the gentiles rule over them, and those who exercise authority over them are called benefactors** (22:25). Benefaction was widespread in antiquity and operated on all levels of society (Danker 1988, 347–48). Certainly there were ample examples of tyrants who exploited their power: "the largess of an emperor always comes at someone's expense" (Vinson 2008, 681, see also 707n22 where he cites *Res gest. divi Aug.* 16). But Jesus's critique here seems to go deeper, questioning the system of reciprocity and the hierarchical client/patron pattern that undergirded benefaction. "Luke wishes to pinpoint something negative about ordinary patterns of ruling (not just oppressive rule) and usual concerns for public honor (not just improper acquisition of titles)" (Nelson 1994, 154).

The status quo of performing some beneficent act in expectation of something in return is questioned at its roots: **But you are not to be that way. Let the greatest among you be like the youngest, and the leader among you like the one who serves** (22:26). The use of the rhetorical figure of *similitudo* to draw a comparison/contrast is not unusual (see *Rhet. Her.* 4.45.59–48.61), but the specific contrast between the "greatest" and the "youngest" (*neōteros*) is unexpected; one expects the more common contrast of greatest/least. Here, Jesus recalls the previous argument among the disciples as to who is the greatest (9:46), when Jesus responded by putting a child in the midst of them (9:47) and asserting that the one who is least among all of you, this one is truly great (9:48), thus equating the "young" with the "least." He may also be alluding to the theme of the favored younger ones that runs throughout the biblical narrative (Gen. 27:15, 36; 37:3; 42:13; 48:14, 19; 1 Sam. 17:14; Luke 15:11–32; cited by Johnson 1991, 344). Jesus calls for "a profound reformation of the idea of greatness and leadership, he does not call for its elimination" (Nelson 1994, 156). He then extends his argument with two rhetorical questions and a statement: **For who is greater, the one who sits at the table or the one who serves? Is it not the one who sits at the table? But I am among you as one who serves** (22:27). Jesus now has provided several contrasting pairs (Nelson 1994, 133):

the greatest	the youngest (22:26b)
the leader	the servant (22:26c)
the diner	the table servant (22:27a)
the diner	Jesus the table servant (22:27b–c)

With these comparisons Jesus offers a reappraisal of power and authority. The "disciples are interested in titles; Jesus offers them towels" (D. Garland 2011, 868). The ultimate example of leadership is Jesus himself, who serves them both in the immediate context of the Last Supper and throughout his entire public ministry, a service that will culminate in his suffering and death (Nelson 1994, 166–69).

Jesus turns his attention back to the disciples: **You are the ones who have stuck with me in my trials** (22:28). From the time of their calling in Luke 5, the disciples have been with Jesus as he has faced a variety of adversaries: "rejection by his beloved Jerusalem, hostility and opposition from Jewish sects and leaders, dullness and disbelief of his generation, and clashes with demonic powers" (Nelson 1994, 196). Furthermore, the disciples will be depicted in a more favorable light in the ensuing passion narrative than they are in Matthew and Mark; they do not, for example, forsake Jesus and flee at his arrest.

As a result of their faithfulness, Jesus rewards them (Johnson 1991, 345): **So I confer a kingdom on you, just as my Father conferred it on me, so that you might eat and drink at my table in my kingdom, and you will sit on thrones judging the twelve tribes of Israel** (22:29–30). He gives them a kingdom (cf. 12:32–33), which his Father has given him, but it is a sharing of authority, not a transfer of it. And if the king is different by being one who serves, so too is this kingdom different. The image of dining in the eschatological kingdom (see above) is one of inclusion, not privilege (Senior 1989, 74). This banquet at Jesus's table in Jesus's kingdom will include those from east and west (13:29), the disenfranchised (14:21–23)—indeed, any sinner who repents (cf. 7:34). The omission of a reference to the twelve thrones (cf. Matt. 19:28) implicitly acknowledges the impending defection of Judas (Carroll 2012, 440); nonetheless, the remaining apostles will "judge," here with the connotation of "rule" (Fitzmyer 1981–85, 2:1419), which "is defined paradoxically as 'serving'" (Culpepper 1995, 426). This passage is a "pivot point" in discipleship, where by virtue of "leading *and* following, ruling *and* serving . . . the Lukan apostles here stand both in *and* under authority" (Nelson 1994, 240, my emphasis).

Jesus next turns his attention to Simon Peter: **Simon, Simon, Satan has demanded to sift you all like wheat!** (22:31). Peter has not been referred to as Simon since the narrative describing his call as a disciple (cf. 5:1–10; 6:14); this fact coupled with the repetition of his name, "Simon, Simon," has led some to suggest that Jesus "gently chides" Peter in his opening address (Fitzmyer 1981–85, 2:894, 1424). The repetition of the name, however, is better understood as an example of *conduplicatio*, a rhetorical device used to indicate compassion or pity (see *Rhet. Her.* 4.28.38; see also comments on Luke 10:41–42; contra BDF §493.1). Thus, the double address is better interpreted as deepening the pathos (Carroll 2012, 441) or signaling "the seriousness of the situation" (Bock 1994–96, 2:1742; cf. Luke 8:24; 10:41; 13:34; Acts 9:4 and parallels). Although Simon is singled out in the address, it is as the leader of the disciples. Satan, Jesus says, has asked to "sift you all." The pronoun is plural and refers more broadly to the band of disciples (Kwong 2005, 176). Satan, who has already "entered into Judas" (22:3), desires to have all the disciples, but his power is limited: he must ask permission to "sift" God's followers (cf. Job 1:8–12; 2:2–5). The specific meaning of the metaphor of sifting is not wholly clear (see Luke 3:17 for a similar image of separating wheat and chaff and Marshall 1978, 820–21, for various interpretive options). However, it is clear that Satan's intended goal is not simply the testing of the disciples' faith but its destruction. This is made clear in Jesus's next comment: Jesus's prayer is that faith will not "fail."

Jesus shifts to the second-person singular, so that the focus is on Peter again, but as the representative and leader of the disciples: **But I have pled for you, [Simon], that your faith may not fail. And you, when you have turned back, strengthen your brothers** (22:32). Although Satan's desire will ultimately be thwarted (cf. the similar theme in *T. Benj.* 3.3), this "does not mean that he [Peter] will not temporarily fail in his commitment" (Crump 1992, 156), as evidenced by Jesus's reference to Peter's "turning back" (*epistrepsas*). Peter will fulfill Jesus's imperative to "strengthen" the believers in the pages of Acts (cf. Acts 1:16–25; 2:14–39; 4:8–13). Peter responds: **But he said to him, "Lord, I am ready to go with you even to prison and to death!"** (22:33). The protest here is missing the negative context of Mark 14:26–27//Matt. 26:31 (and is thus closer to John 13:37; see Johnson 1991, 346), where in a gesture of "competitive braggadocio" (D. Garland 2011, 868), Peter exclaims, "Even if all fall away, I will not!" Peter will, in fact, go to prison (Acts 4:3; 12:3) and eventually, according to church tradition, suffer a martyr's death for his faith. But not now; now Peter's impetuous claim of readiness for prison and death sounds hollow in light of his impending acts of denial, which Jesus foretells: **I tell you, Peter, a rooster will not crow today until you have denied three times that you know me!** (22:34). The prediction of denial is slightly softened in that Jesus has already offered him intercession and (implied) forgiveness (22:32) and by Luke's nuance that Peter will not deny Jesus himself (cf. Mark 14:30) but will deny knowing him, or that he was one of his followers (22:58), or that he knows what his accusers mean (22:60; D. Garland 2011, 868). Still, there may be some irony in that Jesus addresses Simon as Peter—"rock"—the name he gave him at his call (6:14). Nevertheless, although the "rock" will temporarily crumble, he will, so Jesus predicts and prays, turn back and strengthen the believers. But the audience does well to remember that Peter's "rocklike strengthening will come ... not from his character but from Jesus' prayer" (Fitzmyer 1981–85, 2:1426).

22:35–38. The final exchange between Jesus and the disciples before they go out to the Mount of Olives is unique to Luke and "most enigmatic" (Culpepper 1995, 429). Why does Jesus contrast the current circumstance with the disciples' previous missions? Are his words regarding the sword intended literally (as the disciples take them) or metaphorically? Who are the "lawless" ones among whom Jesus will be numbered (and thus fulfill prophecy)? And what is the meaning of Jesus's final statement, "It is enough"? With these questions in mind, we turn to the text.

Jesus engages the disciples in a question and answer: **"When I sent you without a wallet, a travel bag, or extra sandals, you didn't lack anything, did you?" They replied, "Nothing"** (22:35). Jesus reminds them of their previous missions, in which they were instructed to take nothing with them (10:4; cf. 9:3). Even though they were lacking in everything by way of provision, they affirm that, in fact, they lacked nothing (cf. Josephus's description of the

Essenes in *J.W.* 2.124; cited by D. Garland 2011, 870). The providential protection Jesus promised them had worked, and they received hospitality in the form of food, drink, and shelter, presumably from at least some of those to whom they ministered (10:6–8; cf. 9:4).

Now things have changed. **He said to them, "But now, the one who has a wallet, let him take it along. Likewise also a travel bag. And the one who does not have one, let him sell his cloak and buy a sword"** (22:36). The adversative *alla nyn* ("but now") indicates a drastic change in the times. Before, the disciples went out like "lambs surrounded by wolves" (10:3), but now it is much worse. Before, they were to sell and give alms; now those who have a wallet and a travel bag are to take them, and those who have no sword are to sell clothing and buy one. Some think the sword in antiquity was "standard equipment for a traveler" and was necessary for self-defense in perilous times (Culpepper 1995, 430). Others see the command to buy a sword as a "metaphorical indication of a new situation of hostility" (Moo 1983, 134). In favor of the metaphorical interpretation is the fact that Luke has already used "sword" in this kind of symbolic way to indicate division or hostility. Simeon tells Mary that "a sword will go through your very own soul" (2:35; see also 12:49–53, which understands the "sword" of Matt. 10:34 to refer to "divisions"; see D. Garland 2011, 871). Thus, the "purse, bag, and sword are quasi-symbolic ways of concretizing the necessary readiness for such contingencies" (Brown 1994, 1:270).

Jesus continues, interpreting the current circumstances in light of Scripture, specifically Isaiah (cf. Luke 4:14–30): **For I tell you, it is necessary for this passage that was written to be fulfilled in me: "He was counted with the lawless." For indeed the things written about me are coming to completion** (22:37). Until now, Jesus has spoken of his passion using the circumlocution the "Son of Man," and those predictions have increasingly become more detailed and specific (9:22, 44; 18:31). Now, for the first time, Jesus explicitly claims that Isa. 53:12 is being fulfilled, coming to completion "in me"—he is the Isaianic Servant. But who are the "lawless"? It could refer to those who arrest Jesus (22:52), or to the evildoers with whom he is crucified (23:32–33), or even to his executioners, the "lawless" ones who put him to death (Acts 2:23; cf. Brown 1994, 1:270). Perhaps the "lawless" ones are the disciples, who, we are about to learn, are brandishing swords like lawless brigands. Perhaps there is no need to choose, for the things written about Jesus are coming to completion through and despite the actions of all these "outlaws"—the arresting party, the two criminals, and the Romans who carry out the execution.

But before we can ponder this question too long, the disciples, who presumably have been so fixated on Jesus's words about swords that they have missed entirely the references to Jesus's sacrifice, blurt out: **Lord, here are two swords!** (22:38a). This passage, in part, explains where the sword used to cut off the ear of the high priest's servant comes from (22:49–50), but more important, it shows how deeply the disciples have misunderstood Jesus's reference to the sword. He means the reference to be taken metaphorically (or, less likely, as a reference to the traveler's equipment necessary for self-defense). The disciples, however, think Jesus has authorized them to carry concealed weapons. Does Jesus already know that they have these weapons in their possession, and has he approached the topic in order to flush them out (much as he did with regard to his prediction about his betrayal)?

In any case, Jesus's response is cryptic, almost to the point of being indecipherable. He says, literally, **It is** *hikanon* ("enough" or "appropriate"; 22:38b). The words can be taken dismissively, "Enough of that!" (Culpepper 1995, 430; Brown 1994, 1:270). The words could be ironic, "That's more than enough" (Fitzmyer 1981–85, 2:1434), an interpretation that goes back at least to Cyril of Alexandria (Jesus "ridicules their speech . . . two swords are enough to bear the brunt of the war about to come upon them"; *Comm. Luke*, homily 145, trans. Smith 1983, 580). Or it could be an expression of exasperated sarcasm, "It's appropriate" (i.e., it's fitting that you [mis]understand this way, because that's the way you typically [mis]understand; Brown 1994, 1:271). Given the ways in which the disciples' behavior has been characterized in this passage, this last interpretation is compelling. The disciples, despite being praised for sticking with Jesus in trials (22:28), have questioned (accused?) one another regarding the identity of the betrayer (22:23), argued over which of them is the greatest (22:24), and had their leader deny that he will be the denier (22:33). It is little wonder that they misconstrue Jesus's words in this way.

> **A Brief History of Misunderstanding: Jesus's Teaching regarding the Two Swords**
>
> The disciples are not the only ones who have misunderstood Jesus's reference to the swords. Raymond Brown has noted: "The text has been (mis-)used as a general declaration of the right of Christians to bear arms; as support for the right of the medieval papacy to exercise both material and spiritual power (two swords); and as a proof that Jesus encouraged armed revolution!" (1994, 1:270n7). Or as David Garland has observed, more generally: "When Jesus uses metaphors, he is taken literally, when he gives direct commands, he is taken metaphorically" (2011, 872).

The Prayer and Arrest in Gethsemane (22:39–53)

22:39–46. Luke 22:39–46 is critical for understanding the Lukan passion narrative. As Joel Green notes: "Jesus' struggle on the Mount of Olives is presented by Luke as the watershed in the passion narrative" (Green 1997, 777). Whether in these verses Luke has redacted Mark (e.g., Linnemann 1970, 34–70), is working with non-Markan sources (e.g., V. Taylor 1972, 69–72), or has combined Mark with various oral traditions (e.g., Soards 1987a), the focus of the scene is on the efficacy of prayer. Luke begins the passage with a transitional sentence: **Leaving there, he went to the Mount of Olives in accord with his custom, and the disciples followed him** (22:39). Jesus leaves the site of the Last Supper and goes to the Mount of Olives "in accord with his custom." What is that custom? Several times earlier in the Gospel, Jesus is depicted as going to a mountain for the purpose of prayer (6:12; 9:28). This particular mountain, the Mount of Olives, was part of a mountain range running parallel to Jerusalem across the Kidron Valley (Brown 1994, 1:125). There are a number of references to this site in the OT, most notably Zech. 14, when "the feet of the Lord stand on the Mount in the scene of judgment" (Brown 1994, 1:125). That scene will shape the background for Luke's account of Jesus's ascension from the Mount of Olives later, in Acts 1:9, 12. More relevant to Luke 22:39 is the reference to the Mount of Olives in 2 Sam. 15, in which David, betrayed by his trusted adviser Ahithophel, crosses the Kidron (2 Sam. 15:23 LXX), goes up the Ascent of Olives, and there weeps and prays to God (Glasson 1973–74; Trudinger 1974–75; Brown 1994, 1:125). The connection to prayer is further strengthened: **Now, when he arrived at the place . . .** (22:40a). "The place" suggests a specific location, not just the locale of his impending arrest, but probably also "the place where Jesus was wont to pray during the last nights of his life" (Stanley 1980, 214). The reference also echoes Luke 11:1 ("while he was praying in a certain place").

Jesus instructs the disciples to pray for something specific: **Pray that you are not overcome by temptation** (22:40b; cf. 22:46). The use of the term *peirasmos* ("temptation," or perhaps better, "trial") suggests a cosmic setting for an eschatological struggle against diabolic forces. In the Lukan temptation narrative (4:1–13), the term occurs in both its verbal and nominal forms. Jesus is led by the Spirit to be "tempted"/"tried" by the devil (4:2), and at the end of the

Figure 24. Grotto of Gethsemane, Traditional Site of Jesus's Prayer at Gethsemane

account, in a passage peculiar to Luke, the narrator records that "the devil had carried out every temptation [*peirasmon*]" (Luke 4:13). Clearly the temptation in Luke is a trial or ordeal against demonic forces. Likewise in the explanation of the parable of the sower in Luke (which has already mentioned the activity of the devil in 8:12), we find that there are those whose faith has no roots and who in the "time of temptation/trial fall away" (8:13). So also in the Lukan version of the Lord's Prayer, Jesus teaches the disciples to pray, "And do not bring us into trial [*peirasmon*]" (11:4), which should probably be understood as an eschatological struggle for the kingdom (Brown 1961).

Furthermore, we see Satan has already been mentioned twice in the immediate context: Satan has "entered into Judas" (22:3) and has demanded to have Simon Peter in order that he might sift him like wheat (22:31). Jesus has also mentioned the trials that he and his followers face and has suggested that victory over these trials will result in Jesus and his disciples eating and drinking at the eschatological banquet when Jesus receives his kingdom and the disciples "sit on thrones judging the twelve tribes of Israel" (22:30). Brown's conclusion seems correct: "The scene on the Mount of Olives, then, is a crucial moment

---

"If You Decide to Take This Cup away from Me . . ."

David Stanley has made the intriguing suggestion that the original text of Luke 22:42 may be preserved in a variant reading. Some manuscripts replace the imperative *parenenke* ("[you] take") with a complementary infinitive, either aorist *parenenkai* ("to take"; cf. [ℵ] K L f¹³) or present tense *parenenkein* (A W Ψ 𝔐). Stanley (1980, 216; cf. BDF §482) suggests that the resulting text causes Jesus's prayer to break off unfinished ("Father, if you decide to take this cup away from me . . . However, not my desire, but may yours continue to be done!"). This rhetorical technique is known as *aposiopesis* (Latin: *praecisio* or *reticentia*) and "occurs when something is said, then the rest of what the speaker had begun to say is left unfinished" (*Rhet. Her.* 4.30.41, trans. Caplan 1954). Quintilian suggests that this rhetorical figure reflects the speaker's "passion" or "anger" or "anxiety" or "scruple" (*Inst.* 9.2.54, trans. Butler 1922). What Jesus omits, according to Stanley (1980, 217), is something like this: "If you decide to take away this cup . . . [I should prefer that!]." The result of this reading is that "Luke's hint (through aposiopesis) of the intense quality of Jesus' experience makes plausible . . . that in his prayer Jesus is represented as praying also for the gift of endurance and persevering prayer for the disciples" (Stanley 1980, 217; contra Brown 1994, 1:171n10, who concludes that the "choice makes no difference in meaning"). If the reading is not original it still perhaps reflects a scribe who is sensitive to, and seeks to communicate, Jesus's struggle in the garden.

in the great *peirasmos*. . . . If we think of *peirasmos* as the final trial, both Jesus and the disciples are confronted with entering it" (Brown 1994, 1:161).

Next, **Jesus withdrew from them about a stone's throw, knelt down, and began praying** (22:41). We are then given the content of the prayer: **Father, if you are willing, take this cup from me. Nevertheless, may it be not my will but rather yours that is done** (22:42). Jesus's prayer should be understood as a prayer not to enter into the final trial. Yet even in his request that the cup of death and suffering be removed, one finds expressed Jesus's obedient affirmation that his future lies in God's hands (Green 1997, 780). Jesus addresses God as "Father" (*pater*; cf. Mark's "Abba"), recalling the opening address of the Lukan version of the dominical prayer (11:2). Luke's audience will also notice that Jesus uses the term *boulomai* ("will" or "decide"), a favorite Lukan word (16 of 37 occurrences are in Luke and Acts). This term reflects Luke's emphasis on Jesus's ultimate obedience to the preordained "plan of God" (*boulē tou theou*; cf. Luke 7:29–30 and the fuller development of the theme in Acts, e.g., 2:23; 4:28; 5:38–39; 13:36; 20:27; see Squires 1993, 1–2). A similar theological point is made by the writer of Hebrews: "Although he was a Son, he learned obedience through what he suffered" (Heb. 5:8).

Luke 22:43–44 is textually doubtful and thus is bracketed (or omitted) in most Greek texts and English translations: [[**Then an angel from heaven appeared to him to strengthen him. And being in agony he was praying all the more earnestly. Indeed, his sweat was like drops of blood falling on the ground.**]] The evidence against this inclusion is impressive ($\mathfrak{P}^{75}$ ℵ¹ A B N R T W 579 pc) and scholarly opinion is divided (see Bock 1994–96, 2:1763–64). Claire Clivaz has recently mounted an argument in favor of the authenticity of the verses (2010; see below). The verses make explicit that God's answer is not to grant the request but rather to send an angel to strengthen him (22:43). Although ministering angels are present in the temptation narratives of both Mark (1:13) and Matthew (4:11), Luke omits this detail from his version (4:13). Just as Jesus has cited Deuteronomy in response to Satan's trials, so now, in the detail of the ministering angel, the narrator echoes another passage in Deuteronomy: "Let all the angels of the Lord strengthen themselves in him" (Deut. 32:43 LXX). The angel stands as a reminder that Jesus must indeed enter this final trial, but not without divine help.

Jesus responds to this divine act of strength in the time of his final trial by "praying all the more earnestly" (22:44). Jesus's "agony" (*agōnia*; 22:44) in this context reflects more the strenuousness of his prayer than any sense of being distraught (as does Mark's reference to Jesus being "sorrowful unto death"), though it does not suggest Jesus is totally devoid of any emotion (contra Neyrey 1980). This exertion in prayer is part of Jesus's training (almost as an athlete) and preparation (Gamba 1968, 159–66). Clivaz concludes that originally the depiction of Jesus as a "great wrestler" was read against the background of the story of Jacob wrestling with the angel/God (Gen. 32; cf. Origen, *Mart.*

29.32–37; *Cels.* 1.69; cited by Clivaz 2010, 546–47). The reference to Jesus's sweat being "like drops of blood" graphically fills out this picture of Jesus's exertion. Once again Luke employs the strategy of ekphrastic language (see Luke 9; 24; Acts 2), here specifically using metaphors to paint pictures with words (cf. "tongues as if of fire," Acts 2:3; or "about a stone's throw," just three verses earlier in Luke 22:41; see also Luke 3:22; 10:18; 11:44; 22:31). The intense struggle associated with bloody sweat was recognized by several ancient writers, such as Photius, Theophylact, Euthymius, and Zigabenus (see Brown 1994, 1:185n8). Further, bloody sweat could be viewed as a sign of divine healing following such intense struggle (cf. Aelius Aristides, *Hier. log.* 4.17; cf. Clivaz 2010, 424–30). According to Clivaz, the image of Jesus struggling, "Jacob-like," with/against the angel and with/against the Father in our behalf, was co-opted by Alexandrian gnostics into a gnostic framework in which Jesus the archangel fights the "Demiurge at the Place, and helping the psychic Christ to go through the Place" (Clivaz 2010, 638). Unable to hear these verses as anything other than an expression of their opponents' views, proto-orthodox Christians in Alexandria excised the verses, resulting in a manuscript tradition represented by $\mathfrak{P}^{75}$ (Clivaz 2010, 603–7).

In comparison with the Markan and Matthean passages, Luke presents a more positive portrayal of the disciples and their actions in the garden: **When he got up from praying, he went to the disciples and found them sleeping because they were worn out from grief** (22:45). Mark and Matthew record that Jesus finds the disciples asleep three times, underscoring their failure, in contrast to Jesus, to prepare for the events that are to follow (Mark 14:32–42; Matt. 26:36–46). Luke, on the contrary, notes only once that the disciples are sleeping and, furthermore, gives a reason for their slumber: they are asleep "from grief" (Luke 22:45; contra Mark and Matthew, who give no reason for their sleep). **And he said to them, "Why are you asleep? Get up and pray, so that you do not enter temptation"** (22:46). The focus in Luke, then, is not on the disciples' failure in the garden but rather on Jesus's exhortation for them to follow his example and pray. Luke's presentation of the disciples in the garden can be taken as "another example of the benevolent outlook on apostleship" (Brown 1994, 1:68). Thus, Joel Green's comments are on target when he claims that we find in this scene "the critical point at which faithfulness to the divine will is embraced definitively in the strenuousness of prayer" (Green 1997, 777). This conclusion is true whether one views the garden scene as portraying Jesus as a Suffering Servant (so Green 1997, 41–42), or as a martyr (Brown 1994, 1:187–90; Talbert 1982, 212–14), or as a Socratic philosopher (Sterling 2001).

22:47–53. The betrayal and arrest scene (22:47–53) is found in all four canonical Gospels, with some interesting variations (Matt. 26:47–56//Mark 14:43–52//Luke 22:47–53//John 18:1–11). All three Synoptics agree that while Jesus is still speaking with the disciples about their lack of preparation for the impending events, Judas arrives with a group: **While he was still speaking, a crowd**

arrived! **The one called Judas, one of the Twelve, was in front of them, and he came up to Jesus to kiss him** (Luke 22:47; cf. Matt. 26:47//Mark 14:43). In each of the accounts, Judas approaches to kiss Jesus, the prearranged sign to indicate which of the men is to be arrested. In both Matthew and Mark, Judas prefaces his kiss with a simple salutation: "Greetings, Rabbi!" (Matt. 26:49 NRSV); "Rabbi!" (Mark 14:45). Judas delivers the ill-fated kiss in Matthew and Mark, but in Luke Jesus addresses him before Judas actually kisses Jesus: **Jesus said to him, "Judas, are you betraying the Son of Man *with a kiss*?"** (Luke 22:48). This slight change in Luke allows Jesus to take the initiative in the encounter with the high priests.

In all *four* Gospel accounts, one of Jesus's followers suddenly draws a sword and cuts off the ear of the high priest's servant (in John, we are told the names of those involved: Peter is the assailant, Malchus the victim; John 18:10). In Luke, the action is preceded by a question: **When those around him saw what was going to happen, they said, "Lord, should we actually strike with our swords?"** (22:49; cf. 22:38, above). Before Jesus can answer, someone acts: **a certain one of them struck the slave of the high priest and cut off his right ear** (22:50). Luke adds the interesting detail that it was the right ear of the slave. Older interpreters (e.g., Hobart 1882) have taken this as evidence of the author's medical interest and additional proof that the author was none other than Luke the Beloved Physician. A more convincing reading, however, is that the right ear is mentioned to imply that the slave has been struck from behind. After all, assuming that the assailant was right-handed (a rather widespread assumption in antiquity, given the negative connotations that accompanied left-handedness), it would have been nearly impossible to cut off the slave's ear while facing him without also slicing his nose. This interpretation receives support from the logion in Matthew's Sermon on the Mount, where Jesus says, "But if anyone strikes you on the right cheek, turn the other also" (Matt. 5:39). Being struck on the right cheek (again presuming a right-handed assailant) implies being struck with the back of the hand, a gesture that in Judaism added insult to injury (four times over; see *m. B. Qam.* 8.6). So also Luke, in our text, with the detail of the right ear, implies that the slave was hit from behind in what was an act not only of violence but of cowardice as well. Jesus's immediate response varies in all four accounts. According to Luke, **Jesus responded and said, "Stop this!" And he touched his ear and healed him** (22:51). This stands as the only miracle Jesus performs in the passion narrative.

Perhaps in an effort to soften the negative picture of the disciples, Luke omits the stark note added by both Matthew and Mark: "Then all of them/the disciples deserted him and fled" (Matt. 26:56b//Mark 14:50 NRSV). Instead, Jesus turns his attention to the group who have come out to arrest him: **Then Jesus said to the chief priests, officers from the temple, and elders who had come to him, "Have you come with swords and clubs like you would come** after a criminal? Day after day while I was with you in the temple you did not lay hands on me; but this is your hour, and the authority of darkness is at work" (22:52–53). Jesus's words make clear that the conflict is one of cosmic dimensions. It is not simply a squabble between temple authorities and a religious "rebel"; it is a struggle between, on the one hand, God and his agent, Jesus, and on the other hand, anti-God forces who labor under "the authority of darkness."

The Trials of Jesus (22:54–23:25)

22:54–65. With little more fanfare, **they arrested him, led him away, and brought him into the house of the high priest** (22:54a). The identity of the "they" is unclear; presumably it refers to the religious authorities who have accompanied Judas and who are later described as those who "were holding Jesus" (22:63; see Fitzmyer 1981–85, 2:1464). Luke does not identify the high priest here (though cf. Luke 3:2; in Matt. 26:57 and John 18:13 he is identified as Caiaphas). The important note for the subsequent narrative is that **Peter was following at a distance. Now, they had lit a fire in the middle of the courtyard and sat down together, and Peter was sitting among them** (22:54b–55). This note sets the stage for Peter's denial. Unlike Mark 14:53–65 (and Matt. 26:57–68), which presents Peter's denial in an intercalation with the interrogation of Jesus, Luke, perhaps for reasons of literary economy, presents the episode in one continuous scene, simplifying Mark's sequence (Brown 1994, 1:423). Peter's first accuser is a servant girl (cf. Peter's other frustrating encounter with another maidservant in Acts 12:12–17): **When a servant girl saw him sitting toward the light of the fire and looked closely at him, she said, "This man was also with him!"** (22:56). Presumably she recognizes him in the firelight as he sits facing the fire (see Culy, Parsons, and Stigall 2010, 695); she addresses Peter in third person ("this man"), thus making her accusation a public one.

Peter responds with his first denial: **But he denied it, saying, "Woman, I don't know him!"** (22:57). Each of Peter's responses begins with the rhetorical figure of *exclamatio*, in which the speaker expresses indignation or grief by means of an address to an individual (see *Rhet. Her.* 4.15.22; here, the vocative "Woman!"; cf. "Man!" in 22:58, 60; see also 5:20; 13:12). The language ("I don't know him") is shaped to reflect Jesus's prediction in 22:34 (you will deny that "you know me").

The second accusation is made to, and not about, Peter. **Then, after a short time, another person who saw him said, "You are one of them too!"** (22:58a). Peter's second denial, **Man, I am not!** (22:58b), contrasts with Jesus's words in 22:70: "I am!" (Brown 1994, 1:603). Luke continues: **After about an hour had passed, another person started insisting it was so, saying, "This man was surely also with him! For he too is a Galilean"** (22:59). There is a certain irony in the wording of this third accusation that Peter was "with" (*meta*) Jesus and Peter's earlier pledge of loyalty to Jesus that he was ready to go "with" (*meta*) him to prison and to death (22:33). It is unclear if the third accuser recognizes that Peter is a Galilean because of his speech (so Matt. 26:73) or his appearance. Pilate, of course, will attempt to use this Galilean provenance as an opportunity to transport the problem of Jesus to Herod (23:6). Once again Peter refuses to acknowledge any participation in the Jesus movement: **Man, I don't know what you are talking about!** (22:60a). As the sound of his denial is ringing throughout the courtyard, Jesus's prediction is fulfilled: **immediately, while he was still speaking, a rooster crowed** (22:60b). Some modern scholars have (rather humorously) attempted to determine the exact time of the denial by keeping watch through the night in Jerusalem and making careful notation of cocks' crowing! Surely Cicero's judgment is more reasonable here: "Is there any time, night or day, that cocks do not crow?" (*Div.* 2.26.56, cited by Brown 1994, 1:607). At any rate, it is the fulfillment of Jesus's prophecy, not its timing, that is of paramount importance to Luke.

The scene ends with Peter's recognition of the prophecy's fulfillment: **and the Lord turned around and looked straight at Peter, and Peter remembered the statement of the Lord, when he said to him, "Before a rooster crows today you will deny me three times." And he went outside and wept bitterly** (22:61–62). Only Luke records that Peter's remembrance of Jesus's words is prompted by Jesus himself turning and looking at Peter (and not the cock's crow); Peter has denied Jesus in the presence of Jesus. But the authorial audience would understand that Jesus's look of empathy stands in contrast to the maidservant's accusing glare at the beginning of the story (D. Garland 2011, 892). And although Peter's tears are a sign of bitter remorse, they are not without hope. Perhaps in seeing Jesus "turn" (*strephō*), Peter remembers the other prophecy, that he too will "turn again" (*epistrephō*, 22:32; see Brown 1994, 1:608).

The scene turns quickly to Jesus: **Meanwhile, the men who were holding Jesus in custody were ridiculing him and beating him** (22:63). The "timing and locale of the mockery scene differs from that of the other Gospels" (Brown 1994, 1:581). Here the abuse occurs in the night before the trial by the Sanhedrin; in the others it occurs during or at the end of the interrogation. Here the mockery presumably occurs in the same courtyard in which Peter has just denied Jesus; in the others it occurs in the place of the interrogation (Brown 1994, 1:581). The mockery takes the form of a cruel game: **After they had blindfolded him, they began asking him, saying, "Prophesy! Who is the one who hit you?"** (22:64). The scene resembles an ancient form of blindman's bluff (perhaps a combination of *chalkē myia* and *kollabismos*) described by Pollux in which persons are blindfolded and asked to guess who is striking them with husks of papyrus (*Onom.* 9.123, 129; cited by Miller 1971, 309–11). Rather than demanding Jesus to "guess" who struck him, however, Jesus's mockers demand that he "Prophesy!" It is Jesus's "prophetic ministry that is challenged by derision" and "not his talents as a soothsayer" (Bovon 2002–13, 3:234). The irony, of course, is that this ridicule is happening at the very time when the authorial audience realizes that Jesus's prophecies are coming to fulfillment: he has been betrayed (22:21; cf. 22:47–53), denied (22:34; cf. 22:54–62), reckoned with transgressors (22:37; cf. 22:52), beaten and mocked (18:32; cf. 22:63)—and there is more to come. Through the placement of the mockery of Jesus's prophetic ministry in the context of its obvious fulfillment, the mockery, for the authorial audience, is itself mocked. The "mockery is reversed and the derided victim demands to be taken seriously" (J. Marcus 2006, 86). The scene ends with Jesus's mockers **saying many other things against him, slandering him** (22:65). The reference to "slandering" is literally "blaspheming" and "centers on his reputation as a prophet" (Carroll 2012, 451).

22:66–71. The scene and locale abruptly change in this next unit: **When it was day, the ruling body of elders of the people gathered, both the chief priests and the scribes, and they brought him in to their council** (22:66). In Luke the interrogation of Jesus by the Jewish authorities does not have the trappings of a nocturnal and impromptu (and perhaps illegal?) trial. Rather, it occurs during the "day" before the "ruling body" of the people. But neither does Luke paint the picture of a formal trial; there are no formal witnesses and no appointed

"Who Is the One Who Hit You?" A Major "Minor Agreement"?

François Bovon has labeled Luke 22:64//Matt. 26:68 a "major *minor agreement*" (2002–13, 3:227). For advocates of the two-source theory, this verse represents something of a conundrum. Matthew and Luke agree with each other against Mark in including these five Greek words (*tis estin ho paisas se*). Typically such agreements would be assigned to Q, but since Q purportedly had no passion narrative, most two-source theorists have concluded that the textual tradition of Luke has been contaminated with the secondary addition of the statement, which was original to Matthew (so Grundmann 1966, 417; Ernst 1993, 615; Bovon 2002–13, 3:227; contra Bock 1994–96, 2:1804–5; Fitzmyer 1981–85, 2:1465). Raymond Brown, recognizing the weaknesses of the text-critical solution, has suggested that the ancient game of blindman's bluff (see the comments for 22:64) was known in antiquity by the question "Who hit you?" and thus both Matthew and Luke independently refer to the game by its well-known question (analogous to the American playground game "Who's It?"; Brown 1994, 1:579). Unfortunately, there is no evidence from antiquity that this game was known by this question. Another alternative, of course, would be to conclude (as advocates of the Farrer Hypothesis do) that Luke knows the saying from his acquaintance with Matthew (Goodacre 2002).

judge. The setting is more like a "short informal hearing" (D. Garland 2011, 899). "They" (perhaps those who had been holding Jesus?; cf. 22:63) brought him in to the council (lit., "Sanhedrin"). As with the modern-day term "Supreme Court," it is not clear whether the reference is to the place where the Sanhedrin met or to the tripartite body of elders, chief priests, and scribes. The extent of the legal powers of such a group in the first century is obscured by a lack of evidence (Bovon 2002–13, 3:242). It seems clear enough, however, that many of the "everyday chores" of the provincial Roman administration were carried out by the "local council" (D. Garland 2011, 900).

They waste no time beginning their questioning: **If you are the Christ, tell us!** (22:67a). Jesus's response is initially evasive: **Then he said to them, "If I should tell you, you would certainly not believe me. And if I should ask you, you would certainly not answer"** (22:67b–68). Jesus's refusal to answer recalls his earlier encounter with religious authorities in 20:1–8 (see also John 10:24–25 and the parallel construction in Jer. 38:15). "Today's question was not much different from yesterday's question" (Bovon 2002–13, 3:243). The question is a trap, and Jesus refuses to answer their question since any answer, given their obstinance, would be "pointless" (Bock 1994–96, 2:1795).

Jesus's reluctance to respond makes his next statement rather surprising: **From now on the Son of Man will be seated at the right hand of the power of God** (22:69). While Jesus's response to the question about the "Christ" was ambiguous, his claim regarding the Son of Man is certainly not (cf. the figure of "frank speech," *licentia*; *Rhet. Her.* 4.36.48). The saying in both Luke and Mark (and Matthew) combines Dan. 7:13 with Ps. 110:1, but Luke's version of the saying is different from Mark's in a couple of significant ways (see Just 1996–97, 2:886).

Luke 22:69	Mark 14:62b
From now on	*You will see*
the Son of Man	the Son of Man
will be seated at the right hand	seated at the right hand
of the power of God	of Power
	and coming with the clouds of heaven.

The shift is away from what Jesus's interlocutors "will see" in a future event ("coming with the clouds of heaven"), since the Lukan Jesus despairs of what his opponents are able to see. Rather, the focus is on Jesus's "installation in a position of power 'from now on', whether Jesus' examiners recognize it or not" (Carroll 2012, 452). Furthermore, "Jesus, who has just refused to give a direct answer to a malicious question, announces to all who are willing to hear it in faith that the Son of Man, who shares the human condition (7:34), enjoys divine authority (5:24), and has agreed to follow the path that leads to death (18:31–33), will soon be exalted" (Bovon 2002–13, 3:244).

Jesus's words prompt his interrogators to pose a second question: **Then all of them said, "Are you, then, the Son of God?"** (22:70a). In Mark 14:61// Matt. 26:63, the high priest combines the titles Christ/Son of God (Matthew: "Blessed One") into one question, so it is tempting here to see Luke dividing the titles into political ("Christ") and religious ("Son of God") categories (so D. Garland 2011, 901). But there is no basis for that distinction in the Third Gospel (and indeed, in the larger Greco-Roman culture, the association of the title "son of God" with the emperor was not unknown; e.g., Virgil, *Aen.* 6; and comments on Luke 2:1–7). Rather, in Luke, the titles "Christ" and "Son of God" are near semantic equivalents (cf. 4:41), or more precisely, they are carefully coordinated: The people muse about the identity of Jesus as the Messiah in 3:15, but the divine voice pronounces him "beloved Son" in 3:22. Similarly, Peter confesses Jesus to be the Christ in 9:20, while the divine voice proclaims him the "chosen Son" in 9:35. Thus "one seems to need divinely revealed knowledge to interpret 'the Messiah' correctly as a title that fully identifies Jesus as the Son of God" (Brown 1994, 1:472), knowledge the religious authorities are notably lacking here. Thus when Jesus says to them, **You are saying that I am** (22:70b), Luke intends to convey that his accusers "are actually saying it [i.e., that Jesus is the Son of God], even if they don't believe it" (Fitzmyer 1981–85, 2:1463).

The opponents exclaim: **Why do we still need witnesses? For we ourselves have heard it from his own mouth** (22:71). The interrogators interpret Jesus's rather ambiguous response as an admission of guilt. They need no other witnesses; Jesus himself has provided all the testimony they need. The lack of (false) witnesses (cf. Mark 14:55–59) allows the focus in Luke to be on Jesus's identity and mission (Neagoe 2002, 64). Jesus, who begins the scene as the accused on trial, ends by being both witness ("You are saying that I am") and judge ("seated at the right hand of the power of God"; see Bock 1994–96, 2:1797).

23:1–5. The scene shifts to the interrogation before Pilate (23:1–5): **the whole group of them got up and brought him to Pilate** (23:1). The "whole group" apparently refers to the assembly who have arrested, mocked, and interrogated Jesus (22:52, 63, 66; see Just 1996–97, 2:892). Pilate has appeared earlier in the narrative, at 3:1, where he is described as "governor of Judea" (on his prefecture, see Brown 1994, 1:693–705), and at 13:1, which records Pilate's massacre of some praying Galileans. The scene is a trial *extra ordinem* ("outside the system"), and the general principle at play is that of maintaining order in the province rather than the observance of any particular law (Brown 1994, 1:718). After all, Jesus is not a Roman citizen, and therefore Pilate has broad discretionary powers in dealing with, and disposing of, this problem. The gathered group immediately begins to accuse him: **We found this man misleading**

our people, forbidding them to pay tribute to Caesar, and claiming himself to be the Messiah, a king! (23:2). Rather than construing the accusation as consisting of three separate charges, it is better to view it as a single, primary charge that Jesus is misleading the people (cf. *b. Sanh.* 43a), for which they provide two examples (Brown 1994, 1:738). The general charge of "misleading" has biblical echoes: Pharaoh charges Moses and Aaron with misleading the people (Exod. 5:4 LXX); Ahab accuses Elijah of misleading Israel (1 Kings 18:17). Later, Paul will be charged with a similar crime (see Acts 23:2–8). The deception here allegedly consists of Jesus's forbidding the paying of taxes to Caesar, a clear distortion of Jesus's teaching in 20:25 and of how he associated with tax collectors (5:27–30; 15:1–2; 19:1–10; Johnson 1991, 364). Likewise, the charge that Jesus has unambiguously referred to himself as "Messiah" is misleading (Brown 1994, 1:740), especially as it has been translated into the more politically charged title "king."

Unsurprisingly, it is only this second example, of Jesus purportedly misleading the people by claiming to be a king, that catches Pilate's attention: **So Pilate asked him, saying, "Are you the king of the Jews?"** (23:3a). This question is the same in all four Gospels (Mark 15:2//Matt. 27:11//John 18:33), but Jesus's answer varies. Here, he gives another typically ambiguous reply: **He responded and said to him, "You are saying so"** (23:3b; some manuscripts [e.g., Codex W] and translations render this as a question: "Are you saying so?"; see Culy, Parsons, and Stigall 2010, 704). Despite the similarity in the ambiguity, Pilate seems to interpret the "you are saying" in exactly the opposite way that the Sanhedrin did (22:70–71; see Carroll 2012, 456). In any case, Jesus's response gives Pilate the opportunity to acknowledge what is transparent to any whose minds are not already set against Jesus: **Then Pilate said to the chief priests and the crowds, "I find no cause for legal action relating to this man"** (23:4). The crowds (*ochloi*) reappear for the first time since they participated in Jesus's arrest (see "Theological Issues" at the end of this chapter). Whatever the force intended by Jesus's elliptical response, Pilate for the first of three times declares he finds no punishable offense in Jesus—"whatever Jesus or his followers may claim about him, he is not, as his accusers assert, a claimant to political power of a sort to trouble the Roman purview" (Jeffrey 2012, 269). The opponents respond by repeating their accusation: **But they persisted, saying, "He is stirring up the people by teaching throughout all of Judea, starting from Galilee all the way to here!"** (23:5). The authorial audience, of course, knows that Jesus has neither misled nor stirred up "all of Judea" (hyperbole; see *Rhet. Her.* 4.33.44) with his teaching; rather, he has led them in a way that has annoyed those accusing him (cf. 19:47–48; 20:6, 19, 26; 21:38; 22:2; see also Brown 1994, 1:739). It is true, however, that "Jesus will be crucified because of his catechesis" (Just 1996–97, 2:897). Perhaps because Jesus did not preach there (9:52–53), Samaria is omitted from the trajectory of Jesus's "troublemaking."

23:6–12. The reference to Jesus's Galilean ministry allows Luke to anticipate the introduction of Herod, the tetrarch of Galilee (23:6–12): **Now when Pilate heard this, he asked if the man was a Galilean; and when he found out that he was from Herod's jurisdiction, he sent him to Herod, who himself was also in Jerusalem at that time** (23:6–7). This "Herod" is Herod Antipas, the son of Herod the Great (cf. 3:19–20; 9:2–9; 13:31–37). He is in the city presumably for the Passover Festival. But why does Pilate send Jesus to Herod (see Fitzmyer 1981–85, 2:1480)? Does he sense an opportunity to rid himself of the problem by transferring Jesus to Herod in whose province he resides? Is Pilate wishing to honor Herod, or at least is he seeking a diplomatic way to neutralize an old enemy (cf. 23:12b)? Or is he seeking an independent evaluation from someone who has a legal relationship to Jesus (Brown 1994, 1:766; cf. Festus, who consults the visiting Herod Agrippa over the issue of Paul in Acts 25; Bovon 2002–13, 3:262)? It is finally impossible to decide among the options. However, a prefect evidently had jurisdiction over the people of his province only while in the province; in Jerusalem, Herod was "a private person without jurisdiction over Jesus" (Brown 1994, 1:765). Thus, Pilate was presumably making an impromptu decision to delegate the investigation without ceding final jurisdiction. That does not eliminate the strong possibility that he was also operating out of self-interest, hoping to insinuate Herod into the issue. In any case, there are echoes here of Ps. 2:2, in which "the kings of the earth" and the "rulers" take counsel against the "Lord and his anointed" (NRSV; an allusion made explicit by Luke later in Acts 4:25–26).

Whatever Pilate's motive, Herod is pleased to be involved: **When Herod saw Jesus, he was very glad, for he had been wanting to see him for some time, because he had heard about him and was hoping to see some sign performed by him** (23:8). Herod's interest in Jesus is neither new (cf. 9:7–9) nor innocuous. From the episode of the beheading of John the Baptist (3:19–20), the authorial audience already knows that Herod is capable of "evil things" (3:19 NRSV). And although the Pharisees are not the most reliable group in Luke, there is no reason to doubt their warning to Jesus that Herod was seeking to kill him (13:31). Herod's malicious intent is already hinted at by reference to his "power" (23:7; translated here "jurisdiction"), the same word (*exousia*) used to describe the dark hour that has descended (22:53). Herod's desire to see Jesus perform a sign aligns him with the "evil generation," who seek, like Satan, to test him (11:16; cf. 4:9–12; D. Garland 2011, 906; Brown 1994, 1:770).

Herod questioned him at length, but he did not answer him at all (23:9). Were it not for Herod's malicious intent, the emotions that Jesus produces in Herod (rejoicing, wishing, hoping, questioning) might seem merely childish (Brown 1994, 1:769). Certainly, Herod's hyperactivity stands in contrast to Jesus's silence, a silence that recalls not only the silence of Isaiah's Suffering Servant (Isa. 53:7; cf. 1 Pet. 2:22–25; Johnson 1991, 366) but also the resolved silence of the threatened philosopher Diogenes Laertius (*Vit. phil.* 3.19; 9.15; Danker

1988, 365). And, after all, Jesus has already answered this "fox" (13:32–33); there is no need for further words (Brown 1994, 1:710).

At this point the religious leaders, who have been watching from the sidelines, resume their accusations: **Now the chief priests and scribes had been standing there vehemently accusing him** (23:10). Luke does not specify the charges, but they must have been similar to those lodged before Pilate (23:2, 5). Herod then joins in the ridicule of Jesus: **Then, after Herod had [also] treated him with contempt, along with his soldiers, and made fun of him, he put elegant clothes on him and sent him back to Pilate** (23:11). Commentators are divided as to whether Jesus's robing was part of the mockery or indicated something else. Influenced by Mark 15:17–20 (in which the soldiers clothe Jesus in a purple robe and crown of thorns, later removing the robe), some see the "elegant" (*lampran*; lit., "shining" or "white"; cf. the adverbial form in 16:19; see also James 2:2–3) clothes as a way of ridiculing Jesus's purported kingship (Bock 1994–96, 2:1821). More likely, Herod, frustrated that Jesus refuses to perform any signs, creates a "sign" himself; the robe is a sign of Jesus's innocence (Fitzmyer 1981–85, 2:1480; Just 1996–97, 2:903; Brown 1994, 1:776). At least that is evidently the way in which Pilate will interpret it (23:15). Given the "carnivalesque" context of Herod's interrogation (Carroll 2012, 458), however, it is fair to conclude that Herod also intends to humiliate Jesus with the act.

The conclusion to the scene is a bit puzzling: **And so Herod and Pilate became friends with one another on that day. For previously they had been in a state of enmity with each other** (23:12). That there was enmity between Pilate and Herod is hinted at earlier in the narrative. Pilate killed Galileans at prayer, presumably without Herod's consent (13:1). Philo also records demonstrations led by Herodian princes against Pilate (Philo, *Legat.* 299–305). Further, Pilate would have had good reason to befriend Herod, if Josephus's report of good relations between the Herodians and the Julio-Claudian imperial family were true (*J.W.* 1.398–400). But why does Luke bother to mention it? That he intends to symbolize the effects of Jesus on Jewish (Herod) and gentile (Pilate) relations, despite the popularity of this interpretation in patristic exegesis, is unlikely. More probable is that Luke is parodying the *topos* of friendship, the lowest form of which, according to Aristotle, was utilitarian (*Eth. nic.* 8.4.2–6), which was based on self-interest and dissolved as soon as its profit ceased.

23:13–25. Pilate now takes the initiative: **Then Pilate summoned the chief priests, the other officials, and the people and said to them, "You brought this man to me as one who was leading the people astray"** (23:13–14a). The "people" are the surprising part of the group summoned by Pilate. The word is consistently used in the Third Gospel to refer to the people of Israel, the people of God (cf. the exception in Acts 15:14, which confirms the rule), and until this point in the narrative, references to the "people" have been favorable (19:47–48; 20:6, 19, 45; 21:38; 22:2; see Brown 1994, 1:790). "There is no MS support for a suggested emendation to 'leaders of the people' [cf. Rau 1965], but the mere attempt indicates how striking and bothersome this exception is" (Johnson 1991, 370). Perhaps Pilate wishes them to hear the previous charge by the religious leaders that Jesus is "leading the people astray" (even going so far as to change the charge in 23:2 from "perverting the nation" to "leading the *people* astray"; Bovon 2002–13, 3:250; Culpepper 1995, 447). The question as to whether the people will defend Jesus or confirm the allegations is quickly answered when they all join together in Jesus's condemnation (23:18). Although in the narrative of the Third Gospel Luke labors to place most of the responsibility for Jesus's death on the religious and political leaders, he cannot ignore altogether the role of the people in the events that transpire (cf. esp. Acts 2:23; 3:13–14; a role explained by their "ignorance" [3:17]; see Johnson 1991, 370).

Next Pilate gives his judgment regarding Jesus: **I have examined him before you and found no cause for legal action relating to this man with respect to the things you are accusing him of doing!** (23:14b). The use of legal language—"examine" (*anakrinō*); "cause [for legal action]" (*aition*)—lends a certain solemnity to the verdict and suggests a public judicial examination. The fronting of *outhen* in the Greek word order (lit., "*nothing* did I find in this man") further emphasizes Pilate's legal findings (Culy, Parsons, and Stigall 2010, 711). Now Pilate is able to add a second witness (cf. Deut. 19:15) who corroborates the judgment of innocence: **Then again, neither did Herod, for he sent him back to us!** (23:15a). The placement of the phrase "neither did Herod" again is emphatic, perhaps because Herod is a supposed expert in Jewish matters (Bovon 2002–13, 3:280), or perhaps Pilate knows that Herod's verdict of innocence will shock some in the audience who know that Herod earlier sought to kill Jesus (13:31). This sets the stage for Pilate's final summation: **Obviously, nothing worthy of death has been done by him!** (23:15b). The Greek *kai idou* (lit., "and behold") is rendered here "obviously" (see Fitzmyer 1981–85, 2:1485; Culy, Parsons, and Stigall 2010, 712) and reflects Pilate's (futile) attempt to close the book on the case. "Death" is mentioned for the first time in the Lukan passion narrative and foreshadows what is to follow.

Pilate concludes his verdict with his proposed penalty: **So then, I will have him punished and then release him** (23:16; on the omission of 23:17, see the sidebar). The verdict is concise (employing the figure of *brevitas*, which expresses an idea in the minimum number of essential words; see *Rhet. Her.* 4.54.68). The word "punished" (*paideusas*) typically means "instruct" or "educate." Since such education in antiquity could be accompanied by the rod, the word could take on the primary connotation of "whipping," with "education" as a secondary by-product (cf. the chastising with whips in LXX 1 Kings 12:11, 14; 2 Chron. 10:14). This "whipping" (*fustigatio*) was intended as the final punishment and served as a preventative warning against future offenses (Bovon 2002–13, 3:281; cf. 2 Cor. 6:9). It was a less severe punishment than the flogging (*flagellatio*), which was part of the process of Roman crucifixion (cf. Mark 15:15; Brown 1994, 1:851). That is not to say, however, that such "education by whipping" was not brutal; Josephus, for example, speaks of Jesus bar Ananias as being "whipped until his bones were laid bare" (*J.W.* 6.303–4, cited by D. Garland 2011, 908).

It is thus an "appalling euphemism" (Culpepper 1995, 448), but there is no evidence that Pilate is able to carry out this punishment, because the crowd immediately reacts: **But they shouted all together, saying, "Take this man away! Release Barabbas to us!"** (Luke 23:18). The crowd presumably includes the religious authorities, along with the people mentioned in 23:13 (see also 23:35, 48). When the people raise their voices in unison with the religious authorities, "it becomes clear that the chief priests . . . are the ones who have 'perverted the people'" and not Jesus (Culpepper 1995, 447). Their plea that Pilate take "this man [a derisive term] away" suggests that he be "taken away" from life, and it echoes Isa. 53:8 ("by a perversion of justice he was taken away"; cf. Acts 8:33) and picks up on Pilate's passing reference to "death" (23:15). Barabbas is named in all four Gospels. The name is a patronym meaning "son of Abba," like Bartimaeus ("son of Timaeus"; Mark 10:46) or Barjonah ("son of Jonah"; Matt. 16:17). Evidence that Abba was a personal name exists in literary texts and inscriptions (see Brown 1994, 1:799–800; Fitzmyer 1981–85, 2:1490), but early Christians soon noted the irony that Pilate offers the crowd a choice between Jesus, the authentic "son of the Father," and Barabbas, a rioting, murderous, and therefore counterfeit "son of a father." This contrast was even more biting if Barabbas's first name was also Jesus, as several manuscripts attest at Matt. 27:17 (a reading that, according to Brown 1994, 1:798–99, is now preferred by most scholars). Luke adds a parenthetical note about Barabbas, concerning not his name but the reason for his imprisonment: **(He was the one who on account of a revolt that occurred in the city and murder had been thrown in prison)** (23:19). This information identifies

> ### Luke 23:17 and the *Privilegium Paschale*
>
> Some of the oldest and best manuscripts ($\mathfrak{P}^{75}$ ℵ A B), along with most modern translations and critical editions of the Greek NT, omit 23:17 ("For it was necessary that he release one to them at the feast"). The missing verse likely borrows from the other Gospels (Mark 15:6//Matt. 27:15//John 18:39). This "Passover privilege" (*privilegium paschale*) is unknown outside the Gospels (Fitzmyer 1981–85, 2:1485). Its secondary addition was presumably motivated by an attempt to explain the introduction of Barabbas in the next verse and to conform the Third Gospel with the other three. Luke, however, seems less interested in the origins of the custom to release a prisoner at Passover than in the "odious comparison between Jesus and Barabbas" (Bovon 2002–13, 3:277n10; cf. Luke 23:19, 25).

Barabbas as one who participated in a local riot that included deathly violence. The contrast with Jesus could not be more sharply drawn, and it is a contrast to which Luke will return at the end of the passage (23:25).

Pilate makes another attempt to keep his public announcement from devolving into a mob scene: **Once again Pilate called out to them, wanting to release Jesus** (23:20). But again, his efforts are futile and further evidence of his weakness (D. Garland 2011, 809): **But they kept shouting back, saying, "Crucify! Crucify him!"** (23:21). The rhetoric has moved quickly in crescendo-like fashion, from a judgment that Jesus is to be released to a cry that he be taken away (from life) to the full-throated demand that he be crucified (Bovon 2002–13, 3:283). The repetition of the verb "crucify" is unique to Luke (cf. Mark 15:14//Matt. 27:22) and reflects the rhetorical figure *conduplicatio*: "The reiteration of the same word makes a deep impression upon the hearer and inflicts a major wound upon the opposition—as if a weapon should repeatedly pierce the same part of the body" (*Rhet. Her.* 4.28.38, trans. Caplan 1954).

Pilate resists again but is beginning to show the effects of this verbal assault: **So, he said to them a third time, "What has this man done wrong? I have found no grounds for the death sentence relating to him! Therefore, I will have him punished and then release him"** (23:22). Luke reminds the reader that this is the third time Pilate has pronounced Jesus innocent, but he adds nothing new in defense of his decision; in fact, "Pilate's last words in the Gospel are his hollow declaration that he will release Jesus" (Culpepper 1995, 449). **But they kept up the pressure, with loud voices asking for him to be crucified; and their voices prevailed** (23:23). The crowds continue their rhetorical barrage until Pilate is forced to succumb: **So Pilate decided that their request should be granted** (23:24). The effect of Pilate's capitulation to the crowd is certainly not to excuse his actions. Pilate is depicted as "pitifully weak" and "all the more culpable for executing one he knows to be innocent"; he is a "pawn in the hands of those he is supposed to rule" (D. Garland 2011, 909). The story ends on this note of lament: **He released the one who had been thrown in prison for the revolt and murder, whom they had been asking for, and he handed Jesus over to their will** (23:25). The repetition of the information regarding Barabbas is striking. It effectively draws a sharp contrast between the criminal released and the innocent person now condemned to death (Culy, Parsons, and Stigall 2010, 716). In effect, Pilate has surrendered to the mob, "Let their will [*thelēmati*] be done"—the exact opposite of Jesus's prayer on the Mount of Olives (22:42; see Bovon 2002–13, 3:284). Little do they know that, in the end, it is not their will but God's "will" that triumphs (D. Garland 2011, 909; cf. Acts 2:23).

The Death of Jesus (23:26–49)

Luke 23:26–49 divides into three units: Jesus's address to the so-called daughters of Jerusalem on the way to Calvary (23:26–32), the account of Jesus's crucifixion and the exchange with the criminals with whom he is executed

(23:33–43), and the narrative depicting the death of Jesus and the events immediately surrounding his death (23:44–49).

23:26-32. While the frame around Luke 23:26–32 is borrowed from Mark 15:20b ("And when they had led him away" . . . "brought to be executed with him"; Brown 1994, 2:918), much of the content in between is unique to Luke among the canonical Gospels.

Whatever the origins of the pericope, what is its purpose in Luke? The story begins by making reference to Simon: **And when they had led him away, they seized Simon, a Cyrenian who was coming in from working in the field, and put the cross on him to carry behind Jesus** (23:26). This story of Simon bearing Jesus's cross occurs also in Mark 15:15 and Matt. 27:26. In Mark, Simon is remembered as "the father of Alexander and Rufus," presumably because this family was known to Mark's readers. Luke also depicts Simon as a disciple of Jesus, albeit in a more subtle fashion. Simon carries the cross "behind" (*opisthen*) Jesus, placing him in the position of a disciple (see Luke

---

Luke and the *Gospel of Thomas*

There are some interesting parallels between lines from this unit and other early Christian literature, most notably the *Gospel of Thomas* (Schürmann 1963, 241, 250–51; Schrage 1964, 164–68). The following line-by-line diagram allows for a comparison between Luke 11:27–28/23:29 and *Gos. Thom.* 79 (adapted from Soards 1987b, 233–34):

	Luke	*Gospel of Thomas*	
11:27a	As he said these things		
11:27b	A woman from the crowd, lifting up her voice, said to him,	A woman from the crowd said to him,	79a
11:27c	"Blessed is the womb that bore you	"Blessed is the womb that bore you	79b
11:27d	and the breasts that you sucked."	and the breasts that nourished you."	79c
11:28a	But he said,	He said to [her],	79d
11:28b	"Rather, blessed are those who hear the word of God and observe it.	"Blessed are those who have heard the word of the Father and have kept it in truth.	79e
23:29a	For look! Days are coming in which they will say,	For there will be days when you will say,	79f
23:29b	'Blessed are the barren and the wombs that did not bear	'Blessed is the womb which has not conceived	79g
23:29c	and the breasts that did not feed.'"	and the breasts that have not suckled.'"	79h

Many scholars see here a common tradition, which Luke has adapted for his purposes in this story (Soards 1987b, 236–37).

9:23: "If anyone would come after me, let him deny himself and take up his cross daily and follow me" [ESV]). This also fits the Lukan concept of Jesus as a "leader" (*archēgos*; see Acts 3:15; 5:31; Talbert 1982, 219). In this regard, Simon fits well with the penitent thief and the Roman centurion who identify positively with Jesus.

Simon in Luke also is "a positive figure who helps the transition to the description of others not opposed to Jesus whom Luke will now introduce" (Brown 1994, 2:918), the crowd of the people and daughters of Jerusalem: **Now, a large crowd of people was following him, including women who were beating their breasts and wailing for him** (23:27). Because they lament and weep for Jesus, it would be a mistake to suggest, as some have done, that the women "symbolize the element of Israel which continually rejected God's messengers" (Neyrey 1985, 110). However, the women need not be viewed as "disciples" of Jesus (this role seems specifically reserved for the women from Galilee; Luke 23:49, 55) in order to be viewed positively as sympathizers with Jesus. Rather, "the lament of the women is a counterpoint to the terrible rejection of Jesus by the leaders and people narrated in the previous scene. Through their grief, these Jewish people extend compassion to him" (Senior 1989, 120).

Despite their compassion, Jesus's words to the women in 23:28–30 should be viewed as words of judgment, not consolation: **Jesus turned toward them and said, "Daughters of Jerusalem! Do not cry for me. Instead, cry for yourselves and for your children, because days are coming in which people will say, 'Blessed are the barren, and the wombs that have not given birth, and the breasts that have not nursed!' At that time, people will start saying to the mountains, 'Fall on us!' and to the hills, 'Cover us!'"** (23:28–30). Therefore, Jesus's words reflect a deep tradition within Jewish thought. Luke 23:30 is an allusion to Hosea's words of judgment on unfaithful Israel: "and they shall say to the mountains, 'Cover us!' and to the hills, 'Fall upon us!'" (Hosea 10:8 RSV). The view that it is better not to have children than to subject them to the calamities associated with the "last days" is likewise deeply rooted in Jewish (and later Christian) apocalyptic thought. Second Baruch states:

> And you, wives, do not pray to bear children,
> For the barren will rejoice more.
> And those who have no children will be glad,
> And those who have children will be sad.
> For why do they bear in pains only to bury in grief?
> Or why should men have children again?
> (10.13b–16, *OTP* 1:624; cf. *Apoc. El.* 2.38;
> see also Pitre 2001).

Furthermore, this lament over the "daughters of *Jerusalem*" echoes other words of Jesus in Luke (21:23–24; cf. 13:34–35; 19:41–44).

The next verse, **since if they are doing these things to green wood, what will happen to the dry wood?** (23:31) has given rise to multiple interpretations (see the sidebar). There are echoes here of Hosea 9:16: "Ephraim is stricken, their root is dried up, they shall bear no fruit. Even though they give birth, I will kill the cherished offspring of their womb." Thus, Jesus's proverb about green and dry wood "makes perfect sense if it is read in light of Hosea's claim that 'their [Ephraim's] root' is dried up in 9.16 [LXX]. Hosea is using the imagery of dryness and infertility to depict the coming period of barrenness and judgment. Similarly, Jesus is simply contrasting the present age of fertility/peace ('green wood') with a coming period of barrenness/judgment ('dry wood')" (Pitre 2001, 71). And while mercy stands at the center of Luke's overall portrait of Jesus, that portrayal is not inconsistent with God's judgment, which is an important aspect of Jesus's prophetic warning against Jerusalem because of its unfaithfulness. "Looking only at Jesus' words to the women, one could conclude that there is no invitation to repentance here. The 'weeping' Jesus speaks of are not tears of repentance like Peter's (22:62) but tears of lament and grief over tragedy. But when this incident is put in the wider context of the Passion narrative and Luke's Gospel, the implication of repentance cannot be excluded" (Senior 1989, 125). Luke frames the story by utilizing the second part of Mark 15:20b: **Now, two other criminals were also being brought to be executed with him** (23:32). The stage is set for Jesus's crucifixion and death.

> **Interpreting Luke 23:31**
>
> Joseph Fitzmyer has offered four possibilities for interpreting the proverb: (1) "If the Romans so treat me, whom they admit to be innocent, how will they treat those who revolt against them?"; (2) "If Jews so treat me who have come to save them, how will they be treated for destroying me?"; (3) "If human beings so behave before their cup of wickedness is full, what will they do when it overflows?"; (4) "If God has not spared Jesus, how much more will Judaism, if impenitent, learn the seriousness of divine judgment?" (1981–85, 2:1498–99).

23:33–43. Luke 23:33–43 further subdivides into two units. The first, 23:33–39, records the continued mocking of Jesus and parallels Matt. 27:33–44 and Mark 15:22–32; the second, 23:40–43, is about the so-called penitent thief and is uniquely Lukan.

By echoing various OT passages, especially in the Psalms, the narrator highlights the rejection of Jesus in the first section. From the narrator's perspective:

When they came to the place called The Skull, there they crucified him and the two criminals, one on his right and one on his left (23:33) fulfills Isa. 53:12 ("and was numbered with the transgressors"; see also Luke 22:37).

- Then, as they separated his garments they cast lots for them (Luke 23:34b; on the omission of 23:34a, see the sidebar) fulfills Ps. 22:18 ("They divide my clothes among themselves, and for my clothing they cast lots").
- And the people stood there watching. The [Jewish] officials were, in fact, sneering at him and saying, "He saved others! Let him save himself, if this man really is God's Messiah, the Chosen One!" (Luke 23:35) fulfills Ps. 22:7 ("All who see me mock at me"; see also Wis. 2:18).
- Even the soldiers ridiculed him by coming up to him, offering sour wine to him, and saying, "If you are the king of the Jews, save yourself!" (Luke 23:36–37) fulfills Ps. 69:21 ("They gave me poison for food, and for my thirst they gave me vinegar").

The audience cannot miss the irony of these characters uttering a truth that they themselves do not believe or understand (otherwise, they would know that the proof of Jesus's kingship is to be found in his saving others, not himself). The very sign above Jesus's head likewise bears witness to his kingship: **There was, in fact, an inscription above him: "This is the king of the Jews"** (23:38).

The narrator presents the groups who are mocking Jesus in descending order of social status: first the religious leaders scoff at Jesus (23:35), next the soldiers mock him (23:36–37), and finally, as the humiliation reaches its nadir, Jesus's fellow condemned man ridicules him: **One of the criminals who had been hung there was berating him and saying, "You're the Messiah, are you? Save yourself and us too!"** (23:39).

There is some relief in this otherwise stark story of ridicule and mockery, which after all is provided a setting in Luke referred to simply as "The Skull" (23:33; cf. Matt. 27:33//Mark 15:22, where the name Golgotha is given). The people, in contrast to the religious authorities, are depicted as watching, but not participating in, these degrading events (23:35). This brief reference stands within a carefully

> **The Question of Luke 23:34a**
>
> If Luke 23:34a is original to the text, then there is a second positive note in the midst of the portrayal of the extreme humiliation of Jesus (a humiliation that extends all the way back to the beginning of chapter 23). Jesus prays: [[**Father, forgive them, for they do not know what they are doing**]] (23:34a). The theme of forgiveness is consistent with Jesus's comments elsewhere in the Third Gospel (4:18; 5:23–24; 6:27–28; 7:47; 11:4; 17:3). However, a number of the oldest and best manuscripts do not contain this verse ($\mathfrak{P}^{75}$ ℵ¹ B D W *al*), prompting the question as to why a scribe would omit such a profoundly evocative utterance by Jesus. I have argued elsewhere that the saying was a genuine, free-floating agraphon that eventually found its place in canonical Luke (because it fits so well with this aforementioned theme of forgiveness) as the seventh saying of Jesus from the cross (see Parsons and Whitlark 2006 for this and other arguments).

developed portrayal of the role of the people in Jesus's death in Luke. At first, they are implicated along with the chief priests and leaders in conspiring for Jesus's death (23:13), they join in the cries for the release of Barabbas (23:18), and finally, in response to Pilate's offer to release Jesus, shout, "Crucify! Crucify him!" (23:21). But unlike the religious leaders, who maintain a consistent opposition to Jesus throughout the Lukan passion, the people show signs of a change of heart and mind, at least to the point of refusing to participate in the events surrounding Jesus's death. Even though they have clamored for his death, the narrator reports that "a great number of the people followed him" (23:27) on the route to the place called The Skull. Whatever their reason for following along Jesus's path, the people, in contrast to their leaders, have placed themselves in a position to remain open to the plan of God.

That they fall short of complete repentance is because Luke knows that as the "people" of God, they have not yet joined the newly constituted community; this story Luke will tell later, in the pages of Acts.

The second part of this unit, 23:40–43, is unique to Luke's Gospel. The other criminal speaks: **But the other one responded and said to him in rebuke, "Don't you fear God, since you are under the same sentence?"** (23:40). By "rebuking" the malefactor, the penitent thief fulfills the words of Jesus originally addressed to his disciples: "if your brother sins, rebuke him" (17:3). The criminal then pronounces Jesus, in contrast to his fellow victims, innocent of all charges: **We, in fact, have been rightly condemned, for we are receiving the consequences that are appropriate for what we did; but this man has done nothing wrong** (23:41; on the theme of Jesus's innocence, see comments in "Theological Issues" at the end of this chapter).

The "penitent thief" gets his name from his next utterance: **Jesus, remember me when you come into your kingdom** (23:42). This request for remembrance echoes past petitions: Hannah (1 Sam. 1:11), Nehemiah (Neh. 5:19), Job (Job 14:13), the psalmist (Ps. 25:7), and Jeremiah (Jer. 15:15) all cried out to God: "Remember me!" Some have viewed the plea of the criminal as a request for

---

Paradise

Second Temple Jewish texts bear witness to the use of "paradise" in three "interrelated and partially overlapping notions": (1) as a reference to the biblical garden of Eden; (2) as the temporary abode of the righteous dead; and (3) as the eschatological venue of the world to come (Bockmuehl 2010, 195). While Luke holds to a belief in a general resurrection before the last judgment (Acts 4:2; 17:32) as well as a resurrection of the righteous (Luke 14:14), here he reveals his belief in a temporary but joyful abode for the righteous before the final resurrection (1 En. 22; T. Ab. 20.18–19). Here, the Lukan Jesus refers to it as "paradise"; earlier he describes it as the "bosom of Abraham" (Bovon 2002–13, 3:313).

a kind of "royal clemency," but Jesus in his response goes beyond that request for pardon: **I assure you, today you will be with me in paradise!** (23:43). As in some pagan (Plato, *Apol.* 39) and Jewish (*b. 'Abod. Zar.* 18a) sources, Jesus's martyrdom produces a convert. Salvation here is depicted in terms of immediacy and solidarity. The use of the word "today" echoes especially the words spoken by Jesus to Zacchaeus: "Today, salvation has come to this house, because he also is a son of Abraham" (19:9; see also 2:11 and 4:21). The import is one of immediacy, not of chronological specificity. Salvation is also expressed here as a kind of "withness," a solidarity with Jesus. Jesus offers words of comfort that far exceed the criminal's request; he will be with him in paradise (cf. 2 Cor. 12:2, 4; Rev. 2:7).

23:44–49. The powerful story in Luke 23:44–49 has fittingly been called the Gospel in miniature. It carries many of the messages so dear to Luke: the kingship of Jesus, his innocence, and the importance of forgiveness, repentance, and prayer. Jesus does not seek this martyr's death (cf. 23:1–25), but when it comes neither does he refuse it (cf. Justin Martyr, *2 Apol.* 12). This text legitimates the mission of Jesus, the faithful and righteous martyr, whose life and death have saving efficacy.

Luke begins the death scene with this word: **Now, it was already the sixth hour, and darkness covered the whole land until the ninth hour, because the sun gave out** (23:44–45a). Pseudo-Hermogenes advises that in an encomium the writer should note "if there was anything unusual" about the protagonist's death (*Prog.* 16). Other writers have observed such natural phenomenon accompanying the demise of great men (e.g., Plutarch, *Rom.* 27.6: "the light of the sun was eclipsed," cited by Brown 1994, 2:1043; Pliny the Elder, *Nat.* 2.30; Ovid, *Metam.* 15.787; Virgil, *Georg.* 1.467; Josephus, *Ant.* 14.309). The signs that Herod has futilely demanded (23:8) "now abound at Jesus' death" (D. Garland 2011, 927). Efforts to link Luke's account to known solar eclipses (prompted by Luke's use of the Greek word *eklipontos*) have proven futile (see Brown 1994, 2:1038–40); rather, Luke understood the event as an eschatological sign occurring in the natural world—indeed, the whole natural world, the "whole land." The universal effects of Jesus's death on the natural world parallel the universal effects of Jesus's birth on the political world (cf. Luke 2:1). In one sense, the darkness is evidence that the "power of darkness" has come (22:53); in another sense, the darkness is a sign of the "divine displeasure" at the unfolding events (Marshall 1978, 873; cf. Joel 2:10, 31; Amos 5:18; 8:9; Zeph. 1:15). The darkness is accompanied by another sign: **And the curtain of the temple was torn down the middle** (23:45b). Is the tearing of the temple veil a positive sign (all now have access to God) or a negative one (foreshadowing the temple's destruction) (see Johnson 1991, 379)? Coupled with the darkness, the primary significance is probably negative: it is evidence of God's judgment that the temple will no longer hold its central role as representing the locus of divine presence. One consequence of that judgment, however, at least for gentiles, is that access to God is now open to all (cf. Eph. 2:14–21; on which temple curtain Luke imagines is torn, see Fitzmyer 1981–85, 2:1518).

Jesus's death is recounted straightforwardly: **Then Jesus cried out with a loud voice and said, "Father, into your hands I commit my spirit." And when he had said this, he breathed his last** (23:46). Whereas Jesus quotes Ps. 22:1 (21:2 LXX) in Mark, he quotes Ps. 31:5 (30:6 LXX) in Luke. Both psalms speak of God's deliverance of the psalmist from enemies, but the Markan Jesus quotes the "most desperate verse," while the Lukan Jesus cites the "most trusting verse" of the respective psalms (Brown 1994, 2:1067). It is this note of assurance, in which Jesus proclaims that he is placing his "spirit," that is, his whole self, into God's hands, that serves as the "denouement of the Passion Narrative"—not the account of the religious authorities seeking to lay "hands" on Jesus (20:19; cf. 22:53) or even Jesus's prediction that the Son of Man would be given over into the "hands" of sinful ones (9:44; see Brown 1994, 2:1068). Jesus begins with the word "Father," which recalls his first words in the Gospel (Luke 2:49, to be about his Father's business) and which was characteristic of his previous prayers (10:21; 22:42; cf. 11:2; Bovon 2002–13, 3:327). Furthermore, in Mark, Jesus's address to God moves in the direction of increasing alienation, from "Father" (14:36) to "My God" (15:34), but in Luke, Jesus remains "utterly consistent" (Luke 22:42; 23:34 [v.l.]; 24:49; cf. Justin Martyr, *Dial.* 105; Brown 1994, 2:1068).

There are three immediate responses to Jesus's death: **Now, when the centurion saw what had happened, he began glorifying God, saying, "Surely this man was upright!" And all the crowds that had come together for this spectacle, when they saw the things that had happened, returned home, beating their chests. All those who knew him had been standing at a distance, and the women who had followed him from Galilee [were also standing there] watching these things** (23:47–49). Strictly speaking, the events following the death of the protagonist in an encomiastic biography would constitute a separate topic (e.g., "what followed death"; see Theon, *Prog.* 78; Ps.-Hermogenes, *Prog.* 16). But those events are often associated with events (much) later, such as "posthumous votes of thanks, or statues erected at the public expense" (Quintilian, *Inst.* 3.7.17, trans. Butler 1920) or funeral games in the protagonist's honor or an oracle concerning the person's bones (Ps.-Hermogenes, *Prog.* 16–17; see Shuler 1982, 54). Thus, the burial, empty tomb stories, and postresurrection appearances will be treated in the next section as part of those posthumous events. Here in Luke these immediate responses are tied directly to Jesus's death and parallel responses prior to the death.

Theological Issues

The responses to Jesus on the cross form a kind of triptych, which can be diagrammed as follows. There are three parties who are favorable to Jesus after his death, which parallel the three favorable responses toward Jesus before his death (Brown 1994, 2:1160).

Table 8. A Triptych of Favorable Acts and Attitudes toward Jesus

Before Jesus's death	After Jesus's death
A. Simon who carries Jesus's cross (23:26)	A. the centurion who praises Jesus as an upright man (23:47)
B. the large group of people who follow Jesus, including women who mourn for Jesus on the way to Calvary (23:27)	B. the crowds who return home beating their breasts (23:48)
C. two criminals, one of whom is later sympathetic toward Jesus (23:32, 39–43)	C. Jesus's acquaintances and the women from Galilee who stand at a distance and observe (23:49)

We consider each of the responses following Jesus's death in turn.

A. *The centurion*. The authorial audience will notice at least two differences between Mark's presentation of the centurion and his confession and Luke's version. (1) The centurion in Luke "began glorifying God" (23:47); this was the typical reaction to Jesus's demonstrations of power (4:15; 5:25–26; 7:16; 13:13; 17:15; 18:43) and forms an *inclusio* with the shepherds who glorified God at Jesus's birth (2:20; see Culpepper 1995, 462; Brown 1994, 2:1161). (2) The centurion pronounces Jesus "upright" or "righteous" (*dikaios*), rather than the "Son of God" as in Mark. In Greco-Roman thought, the "upright" one fulfilled all obligations and duties (see Polybius, *Hist*. 2.10.5; 3.116.9; Plato, *Resp*. 361e–362a; cited by Danker 1988, 382). In Israel's Scriptures, the title "Righteous One" has messianic connotations (Jer. 23:5; Zech. 9:9; *Pss. Sol*. 17.32; cf. Ps. 31:18 LXX), and it is taken up in early Christianity and applied to Jesus (Acts 3:15; 7:52; 22:14; James 5:6; 1 Pet. 3:18; 1 John 2:1).

Innocence is also within the semantic range of *dikaios* (Brown 1994, 2:1163). This theme of Jesus's innocence is a major one in Luke's passion narrative. Three times, Pilate pronounces the innocence of Jesus (23:4, 14, 22). Also, the narrator makes it a point to note that the last attempt Pilate makes to release Jesus is the "third time" he has pronounced Jesus innocent of any wrongdoing (23:22a). Likewise Herod, to whom Pilate has sent Jesus (since as a Galilean Jesus is under Herod's jurisdiction), pronounces Jesus innocent and returns him to Pilate (23:15; cf. 23:6–12). Finally too, the centurion in Luke recognizes Jesus's innocence (23:47). Luke emphasizes that the death of Jesus is the death of a martyr, the unjust murder of an innocent and "righteous" man by the religious and political establishment.

B. *The crowds*. Likewise "all the crowds," when they saw the "things that had happened" (including now the centurion's confession) returned home "beating their breasts" (23:48). The gesture is one of repentance (cf. 18:13), but for what does the crowd repent? It seems that Luke has distinguished between the "people" (*laos*), who function as the people of God, and the indeterminate "crowds" (*ochloi*), who include the "people" (*laos*) but who do not act as the people proper. At the beginning of the Lukan passion narrative, the people and the crowds seem indistinguishable (cf. 22:2, 6). But as the narrative progresses, their roles are disaggregated. It is the "crowd" that Judas leads to arrest Jesus (22:47), and it is the "crowd" Pilate addresses in 23:4. So it is for their part in the arrest and condemnation of Jesus that the "crowd" repents and beats their breasts. But this is not the crowd as the chosen people, for Luke knows that the "people" have not yet repented *as* the chosen people (cf. Acts 28). Although initially the "people" were feared to be on Jesus's side (22:2), eventually they reach their nadir when they join in with the religious authorities in calling out for Jesus's death (23:13, 14). They are found again as part of the group who are "following" Jesus, and they finally refuse to participate in the authorities' mocking and crucifixion of Jesus (23:35). Thus they are partially exonerated from full participation in Jesus's condemnation and death, but they cannot, in Luke's view, come to full repentance in their role as the people, even though they can participate as individuals in the "crowd," which does, in fact, express remorse.

C. *The women (and acquaintances)*. Finally, Jesus's acquaintances are standing there (23:49). The identity of these acquaintances (*gnōstoi*; lit., "those known to him") is not clear. Presumably it included acquaintances who were not relatives (cf. the distinction between relatives and acquaintances at Luke 2:43–44). Is there perhaps some mild criticism implied in the description of them standing "at a distance," perhaps echoing the isolation of the persecuted one from his acquaintances in Ps. 88:8 (cf. Ps. 38:11)? The best that can be said is that they still stand and watch and at least do not flee. Whatever criticism may be intended, it is muted and does not apply to the "women who had followed him from Galilee" (cf. 8:1–3), who are poised to participate fully in the surprising events that are to follow. For Luke's audience, these three responses are paradigmatic for understanding Jesus's death within the Lukan narrative.

Luke 23:50–24:53

Jesus's Burial, Empty Tomb, and Postresurrection Appearances

Introductory Matters

Much of the previous work on the resurrection narratives in the canonical Gospels focuses on issues of the existence (or not) of pre-Gospel oral traditions and questions of historicity (see Fuller 1971; C. F. Evans 1970; Wright 2003; see also Allison 2005, 198–350, for a survey of the various options). From the time of D. F. Strauss in the nineteenth century (and before; cf. Reimarus in the eighteenth century), skeptics have doubted the claims of the Gospels that the tomb was empty and that Jesus made postmortem appearances to his followers (e.g., Strauss 1835–36; Lüdemann 1994). Others have claimed that the root of the issue is found in the story of Jesus's burial, concluding that "the historicity of the empty tomb story is dependent to a large extent on the historicity of the burial story" (Barclay 1996, 23; cited by Allison 2005, 352). Thus, the burial, empty tomb, and appearance narratives were late and legendary developments (Crossan 1974) or the result of redactional activity on the part of the evangelists to depict Jesus as "hero-like" (Collins 1997) or to confirm the conviction that God had vindicated his eschatological prophet.

These conclusions have been challenged from various quarters. Form-critical studies have concluded that the empty tomb narratives are based on an ancient tradition that attests to women finding that the body of Jesus was missing from its tomb on the first Easter (Bode 1970) and, likewise, that Jesus's appearances to his followers recorded in Matthew, Luke, and John share a common *Gattung*, or literary form, that is rooted in ancient tradition (Alsup 1975). N. T. Wright has mounted the most recent and vigorous defense that the "best historical explanation" for the rise of early Christianity "is that Jesus was indeed bodily raised from the dead" (2003, 8; cf. Allison's more nuanced claims, 2005, 344–50). Some historians would modify Wright's conclusion (perhaps earning his disapproval) to make the more modest claim that the earliest Christians *believed*—totally and fully—that Jesus was bodily raised and appeared to his followers. From that conclusion, it remains a step of faith, but not—given the patient historical work cited above—an unreasonable one, for the modern believer to conclude that those first followers were, indeed, right. That is the position of this commentary. But belief in the historicity of the events narrated in the Gospels concerning the burial, empty tomb, and appearance stories does not necessarily guarantee that we will adequately grasp the rhetorical shape or theological import of those narratives in their portrayal of Jesus.

What is sometimes lost in this debate is an analysis of the rhetoric of the resurrection narratives themselves. What were the evangelists seeking to argue in their presentation of empty-tomb and postmortem-appearance stories? Specifically, what were Luke's points regarding Jesus's resurrection? We are reminded that one of the progymnastic topics for encomiastic biography was the events associated with the protagonist following death. Pseudo-Hermogenes recommends: "You will examine also the events after death: if they held games in his honor, as for Patroclus (*Il.* 23); if there was an oracle about his bones, as with Orestes; if he had famous children, as did Neoptolemus" (*Prog.* 16–17, trans. Kennedy 2003, 82). These postmortem events, like the corresponding details of the prepublic career, are intended to disclose some aspect(s) of the protagonist's essential character (the following examples are drawn from Martin 2008, 25–36). And in practice, ancient biographers were attentive to details of important events occurring after death. In his *Parallel Lives*, Plutarch often recounts the honorable burial afforded his subjects by their devotees (e.g., *Alc.* 39.4a; *Cor.* 3.5–6). Further, Plutarch describes how Coriolanus's death was mourned by women for ten months (*Cor.* 39.5–6). In the case of Apollonius, Philostratus includes reference to his honorable burial and postmortem appearances (*Vit. Apoll.* 8.31). The Jewish biographer Philo likewise attends to postmortem events in his life of Moses. Philo recounts how Moses was

> told how he was buried with none present, surely by no mortal hands but by immortal powers, how also he was not laid to rest in the tomb of his forefathers but was given a monument of special dignity which no man has ever seen, how all the nation wept and mourned for him a whole month and made open display, private and public, of their sorrow, in memory of his vast benevolence and watchful care for each one of them and for all. (*Mos.* 2.291b, cited by Martin 2008, 32n41)

Of course, the events after the death of Jesus are a necessary part of the story in understanding Jesus's "essential character" as the crucified and bodily risen Lord, whom God has vindicated as Israel's Messiah.

Tracing the Narrative Flow

Luke narrates four events after Jesus's death: his burial (23:50–56); the empty tomb (24:1–11); and two postresurrection appearances to his followers, first to Cleopas and his companion (24:13–35) and finally to the Eleven (24:36–53).

The Burial of Jesus (23:50–56)

23:50–56. The first event recorded after Jesus's death is his burial. Luke's version omits several details from Mark's account (Fitzmyer 1981–85, 2:1523–24): Joseph of Arimathea's courage (Mark 15:43), Pilate's concern regarding the confirmation of Jesus's death (15:44–45), Joseph's purchase of a burial cloth (15:46a), the closing of the tomb (15:46d), and the naming of the women (at this point in the narrative, but see the partial list in Luke 24:10). Luke does, however, include several additional details regarding the characterization of Joseph of Arimathea: **There was a man by the name of Joseph, who was a council member, a good and just man (this man had not consented to their plan or actions) from Arimathea, a city of the Jews, who was anticipating the kingdom of God** (23:50–51). To Mark's note that Joseph was a member of the council (Mark 15:43a), Luke adds that he "had not consented to their plan or actions." To Mark's observation that Joseph "was also himself waiting expectantly for the kingdom of God" (Mark 15:43b), Luke adds that he was "a good and just man." Mark refers to Arimathea, Joseph's city of origin (Mark 15:43a); Luke notes that it is a "city of the Jews." Each addition connects to features from Luke's larger

---

Luke 23:50–24:53 in the Narrative Flow

Jesus's origins and training (1:1–4:13)

Jesus's mighty words and deeds in Galilee (4:14–9:50)

Jesus's mighty words and deeds along the way (part 1) (9:51–14:35)

Jesus's mighty words and deeds along the way (part 2) (15:1–19:44)

Jesus in Jerusalem: teachings, death, and resurrection (19:45–24:53)

   Jesus in and around the temple (19:45–21:38)

   The meaning and manner of Jesus's death (22:1–23:49)

▶ Jesus's burial, empty tomb, and postresurrection appearances (23:50–24:53)

   The burial of Jesus (23:50–56)

   The empty tomb (Luke 24:1–11)

   Postresurrection appearance: On the road to Emmaus (24:13–35)

   Postresurrection appearance: to the disciples (Luke 24:36–53)

narrative. That Joseph has not participated in the council's plot (22:4–5) or actions (22:66–71; 23:18) recalls Simeon's prophecy that Jesus would lead to "the fall and rise of many in Israel" (2:34) and aligns Joseph with those who would "rise." Further, Joseph's characterization as a "good and just man" who "was anticipating the kingdom of God" recalls the characterization of this same Simeon, who "was righteous and devout, waiting for the consolation of Israel" (2:25; see also Elizabeth [1:6] and Jesus [23:47], who are also described as *dikaios*; Danker 1988, 383). Luke is also more interested in Joseph's moral character than his social standing (contra Matt. 27:57). Finally, Luke's addition that Arimathea (on its possible location, see Fitzmyer 1981–85, 2:1526) is "a city of the Jews" is complementary to the women who were from Galilee (23:49, 55) and is a subtle reminder that the one who comes to bury Jesus is an "outsider" and not one of his disciples (see Brown 1994, 2:1228; in contrast to Matt. 27:57 and John 19:38, both of which call Joseph a "disciple"). Joseph's role as a disciple is further embellished in later apocryphal Gospels (see *Gos. Pet.* 2; *Acts Pil.* 12–17; *Narrative of Joseph of Arimathea* 5; Brown 1994, 2:1232–34).

Joseph went to Pilate and requested the body of Jesus. Then he took down [the body from the cross], wrapped it in linen, and placed him in a rock-hewn tomb where no one had ever been laid (23:52–53). Providing proper burial for a corpse was not only viewed as a pious duty among Jews (Tob. 1:17; 2:7; Josephus, *Ag. Ap.* 2.211; see C. A. Evans 2005, 233–48), but it was also a widely recognized responsibility in antiquity (e.g., Sophocles's *Antigone*). Even though Romans typically refused burial to criminals executed by the state (Tacitus, *Ann.* 6.29; cf. Petronius, *Sat.* 111–12; Philo, *Flacc.* 83–84; see also Brown 1994, 2:1207–9), Joseph comes both out of "respect and pity" (Brown 1994, 2:1255) and as a law-observant Jew seeking to give Jesus a proper burial (cf. Deut. 21:22–23), and he is able to secure permission to bury Jesus, perhaps because Pilate has never been convinced of any wrongdoing on Jesus's part (see above and Brown 1994, 2:1209–11 on whether Jews would have considered Jesus worthy of an "honorable burial"). The note that Joseph places Jesus's body in a "tomb where no one had ever been laid" recalls the so-called triumphal entry, in which Jesus rode into the city on a colt "on which no person has ever sat" (19:30). Here also is an implicit comparison, or *synkrisis*, typical of encomiastic narrative ("The best source of argument in encomia is derived from comparisons, which you will utilize as the occasion may suggest"; Ps.-Hermogenes, *Prog.* 17, trans. Kennedy 2003, 82). Those Jews who could afford tombs in the late Second Temple period practiced secondary burials; that is, corpses were placed in a large tomb (often for extended families; see fig. 25) and when the flesh had decayed, the bones were placed in an ossuary, or bone-box. This allowed for tombs to be reused (see Magness 2005). The tomb to which Joseph has access, however, has never been used and thus, in implicit comparison to others, proves "a grave worthy of Jesus" (Fitzmyer 1981–85, 2:1525).

Figure 25. Traditional Site of Jesus's Burial

Luke then gives the temporal framework: **It was the day of preparation, and the Sabbath was approaching** (23:54). The day of preparation here refers to the day before the Sabbath (Thursday evening to Friday evening), and "Joseph had little time to do all that was necessary to bury Jesus" (D. Garland 2011, 940). Furthermore, according to Israel's Scriptures, corpses were not supposed to be left hanging overnight, under threat of defiling the whole land (Deut. 21:23). It is within this context of a heightened sense of urgency that Luke reports: **The women who had come with him from Galilee followed along behind and observed the tomb and how his body was placed in it** (23:55). These women (some of whom are named later, in 24:10) have provided for Jesus during his public ministry (8:2–3); now they seek to provide for him in death. Mark emphasizes "where" the body was laid (15:47); here the women observe "how" (*hōs*) the body was placed—that is, the manner with which it was placed (see Culy, Parsons, and Stigall 2010, 732–33). Presumably in his hurry to get Jesus's corpse in the tomb before sundown, Joseph has neglected to wash (cf. *Gos. Pet.* 6.21–24) and especially to anoint the body (23:53; see Fitzmyer 1981–85, 2:1530). So the women **returned [home] and prepared aromatic oils and scented ointments** (23:56a). There is no mention that the women have to purchase spices (contra Mark 16:1), but it is not clear how the women have time to make these preparations before the Sabbath begins (in Mark, these activities occur *after* the Sabbath); perhaps the exception that allowed for the preparation of a corpse even on the Sabbath, which is expressed in the Mishnah, was current also in the first century: "They may make ready [on the Sabbath] all that is needful for the dead, and anoint it and wash it" (*m. Šabb.* 23.5, cited by Fitzmyer 1981–85, 2:1530; see also D. Garland 2011, 940; but cf. Brown 1994, 2:1258). This unit ends with: **But they rested during** the Sabbath in accord with the command (23:56b). As the characterization of Joseph as "good and just" reaches back to the infancy narrative (see above), so the characterization of the women as Torah-obedient Jews points forward to the final depiction of the disciples who are "continually in the temple praising God" (24:53).

The Empty Tomb (24:1–11)

24:1-11. These women who were last at the cross in Luke's Gospel (23:49, 55) are first at the tomb on Sunday morning: **On the first day of the week, very early in the morning, they came to the tomb** (24:1a). By implication, Luke agrees with Mark (16:1) that the purpose in their coming is to anoint Jesus's body with **the same aromatic oils that they had prepared** (24:1b; cf. 23:56). One might have expected the Eleven to give attention to the corpse. But after all, the apostles are long gone, and only the women remain. But they soon discover there is no body to anoint! What remains for these women is far more important; they are the ones who will discover that Jesus's tomb is empty: **They found the stone rolled away from the tomb, but when they entered it, they did not find the body of Jesus** (24:2–3; on the addition of "Lord" in the manuscript tradition, along with other variants in this chapter, see the introduction).

As they ponder this event, they realize they are not alone: **And it happened that while they were perplexed about this, two men in bright shining clothing suddenly stood by them!** (24:4; on the function of the "two men," see the sidebar "'Behold, Two Men'" at Luke 9:30). The women's perplexity quickly shifts to fear: **And as they were very frightened and were falling down to the ground [in fear], the men said, "Why are you looking for the living among the dead?"** (24:5a; on the omission of 24:5b, see the introduction). The men (later identified as a "vision of angels"; 24:23) know why the women are there, but they are looking in the wrong place. The two men in Luke prompt the women to remember Jesus's words: **Remember how he told you while he was still in Galilee, saying that the Son of Man must be handed over into the hands of sinful men, be crucified, and on the third day rise again** (24:6–7). Whereas during his ministry Jesus's followers were caught up by the first half of this prediction, the so-called passion part of the prediction, the emphasis now clearly falls on the latter part: "on the third day" he will "rise again."

Thus prompted, **they remembered what he had said, and when they returned from the tomb they reported all these things to the Eleven and all the rest** (24:8–9). Luke finally specifies the identity of (most of) the women: **Now, Mary Magdalene, Joanna, Mary the mother of James, and the rest of the women with them were the ones involved** (24:10a). Mary Magdalene and Joanna are also mentioned in Luke 8:2–3; Susanna, who is mentioned there, is absent, at least by name, here (cf. 23:55). The number of unnamed women who accompanied these three may be large; Luke 8:3 refers to the "many" (*pollai*) women who supported Jesus during his Galilean ministry. Despite their number (John has only Mary Magdalene; Matthew has the Magdalene and the "other" Mary; Mark has Mary Magdalene, Mary the mother of James, and Salome), their story is not well received: **They were telling these things to the apostles, but these words seemed like complete nonsense to them; and they would not believe them** (24:10b–11; on the omission of 24:12, see the introduction).

Postresurrection Appearance: On the Road to Emmaus (24:13–35)

The story of the road to Emmaus is one of the most powerful stories in the Bible and certainly one of Luke's greatest achievements as a storyteller. The story divides into two parts, the walk to Emmaus (24:13–27) and the meal at Emmaus (24:28–35). The entire story is framed with a chiastic structure that initiates the movement of the story away from Jerusalem and brings it to a full stop with the Emmaus disciples' return to Jerusalem:

A Disciples go away from Jerusalem (24:13)
  B Disciples talk with each other (24:14)
    C Jesus comes near (24:15)
      D Disciples' eyes are kept from recognizing Jesus (24:16)
      D′ Disciples' eyes are opened and they recognize Jesus (24:31a)
    C′ Jesus vanishes (24:31b)
  B′ Disciples talk with each other (24:32)
A′ Disciples return to Jerusalem (24:33)

24:13–27. The story begins with two, as of yet, unnamed followers of Jesus traveling to an obscure village outside Jerusalem: **Now, two of them on that same day were going to a village about seven miles away from Jerusalem named Emmaus** (24:13). That these two are followers of Jesus is suggested in the language "two of them," that is, two of the followers of Jesus. Scholars have never been able to locate this village with any certainty (see the catalog of possibilities in Riesner 2007), and in terms of the plot of the story, it is enough for the hearer to know that it is "about seven miles away from Jerusalem," that is, long enough for them to engage in deep conversation over the events of the day: **and they were talking with each other about all these things that had happened** (24:14). But then their conversation takes an unexpected turn: **And it happened that while they were talking and debating Jesus himself came up and began accompanying them** (24:15). The travelers are unaware of this Christophany: **their eyes were obstructed—that is, they did not recognize him** (24:16). The theme of a deity appearing to unsuspecting mortals would have been well-known to the ancient audience (see, e.g., Ovid, *Metam.* 8.611–725). The use of the passive voice also suggests that the disciples' blindness was the result of a divine act.

Jesus wastes no time in cutting to the chase: **Then he said to them, "What are these matters that you are discussing with each other as you walk?"** (24:17a). Before giving their response, the narrator builds the drama: **And they stopped walking, being gloomy** (24:17b). The response is ironic, even comical: **The one named Cleopas responded and said to him, "Are you the only one staying in Jerusalem and yet not knowing what has happened there in these past few days?"** (24:18). Of course, the audience knows that Jesus is the *only one* who *does* know the full details of what has transpired in Jerusalem over the past few days. Jesus seems to egg them on: **What sort of things?** (24:19a). They take the bait and continue: **The things pertaining to Jesus the Nazarene, who was a man—actually, a prophet!—powerful in word and deed before God and all the people, and how our chief priests and officials handed him over for the death sentence, and they crucified him** (24:19b–20). This summary of events would have been heard favorably by the authorial audience, who expected integrity between what a leader did ("powerful in deed") and what he said ("and word") before God and the people. The two explicitly claim that the responsibility for Jesus's death lay squarely with their chief priests and leaders rather than the "people" who witnessed Jesus's deeds and words. The reference to Jesus being "*handed over* for the death sentence" also effectively insinuates the role that the Romans played in conspiring for Jesus's death. The objective summary of events quickly gives way to their reaction to it: **We had been hoping that he was the one who was going to liberate Israel** (24:21a). Their despair is poignant, almost palpable. The hope for Israel's deliverance (from spiritual oppression? from the Romans? from exile?) they once placed in Jesus lies shattered by the events they have attempted to describe dispassionately.

The remainder of their speech, however, discloses to the audience that their temporary inability to see Jesus is more than physical. They glibly report: **But instead, along with all these things, it is now the third day since these things happened!** (24:21b). Apparently they are unaware of the significance of the chronology, even though the audience could hardly miss the import of "the third day" (cf. 24:7). Furthermore, they are unwilling and unable to accept the testimony of others: **More than that, some women from our group astounded us. After being at the tomb early in the morning and not finding his body, they came saying, in fact, that they had seen a vision of angels, who said that he is alive! Some of the men with us went off to the tomb and found it that way, just as, in fact, the women had said! But they did not see him** (24:22–24). Even though some of their other (presumably male) companions confirmed that the tomb was empty, the Emmaus disciples, lacking empirical evidence ("they did not see him"), simply cannot see the conclusion to which their story irresistibly draws the audience—Jesus has been raised from the dead, just as he promised, just as the angels claimed, and just as the empty tomb indirectly attested. And, of course, they make this "nonconfession" of faith to the very one whose presence in this story confirms his resurrection for the audience.

Jesus finally blurts out what the audience is feeling: **How foolish you people are and how slow in heart to believe all that the prophets have said!** (24:25). It is significant that the risen Jesus does not remind these pilgrims of what he himself predicted regarding his death and resurrection (Luke 9:22, 44; 18:32), nor does he point to some heavenly revelation; rather, the resurrected Christ turns their attention back to "the patient exposition of Israel's scriptures" (R. Hays 2002, 415) and proceeds to instruct the disciples in what "the prophets have said," specifically regarding the divine necessity: **Wasn't it necessary for the Christ to suffer these very things and then enter into his glory?** (24:26; on the "necessity" of Christ's suffering, see Bass 2009). Here is a clear example of early Christian messianic exegesis, delivered by the Messiah himself. **And beginning with Moses and all the prophets, he explained to them the things written about himself in all the Scriptures** (24:27; see Doble 2006). The "whole story of Israel builds to its narrative climax in Jesus" (R. Hays 2002, 416). This pattern of scriptural exposition followed by a meal with the disciples is reversed in the scene that follows (24:36–49). Jesus eats a meal with the disciples and then expounds the Scriptures to them regarding the suffering and resurrection of the Messiah (24:44–46; see below).

24:28–35. The second section of this unit, the meal at Emmaus, begins with another strange twist. **They came near to the village where they were going, and he pretended like he was going farther** (24:28). Is he toying with them, trying to wrest a dinner invitation from them (which he does)? Does the text echo the OT scene where God disclosed his glory by passing by Moses (cf. Exod. 33:21–23; also Mark 6:48)? Whatever the motive, the travelers do urge Jesus strongly: **Stay with us, since it is almost evening and the day is already ending** (24:29a). He complies: **he went in to stay with them** (24:29b). Again an ironic situation quickly develops: the guest becomes the host. **And it happened that as he was seated with them he took bread and blessed it. Then, after breaking it, he began giving it to them** (24:30). These four gestures—taking, blessing, breaking, and giving the bread—recall earlier meal scenes: the feeding of the five thousand (9:16) and the Last Supper (22:19, though there he "gave thanks" rather than "blessed"), and function here as a "*chreia* of action" (see comments on Luke 9:10–17). The Emmaus disciples notice the similarities as well: **After that, their eyes were opened, and they recognized him** (24:31a). It is the combination of communal meal and scriptural exposition that leads finally and fully to their recognition of the identity of their guest/host (see R. Hays 2002 and, from a Catholic perspective, Martini 1999). Their inability to recognize Jesus was presumably due more to their "blindness" than to some kind of polymorphic state of Jesus's resurrected body (see Foster 2007; for the view that Justin Martyr's *Dialogue with Trypho* depicts Jesus in the polymorphic form of an "old man" and is based on the road to Emmaus scene, see Hofer 2003).

> ### Simon Peter as Cleopas's "Companion"?
>
> In the Lukan text as we have it, Cleopas's companion is unnamed, and there are good literary and theological reasons for concluding that this was Luke's intent (see "Theological Issues," below). That, however, has not stopped biblical scholars across the centuries from attempting to identify him as Luke, Cleopas's wife, and so on (see Metzger 1980, 40–41; Hornik and Parsons 2007, 130–33). One of the oldest traditions is the identification of the unnamed disciple with Simon Peter. Codex D (Bezae), a fifth-century, bilingual manuscript, reads *legontes* (nominative plural) rather than *legontas* (accusative plural) in Luke 24:34 where the Emmaus pilgrims meet the eleven apostles. (The Latin, *dicentes*, since it is both nominative and accusative in form, is ambiguous on this point.) The use of the nominative plural (*legontes*) would assign the statement "The Lord has risen indeed, and has appeared to Simon!" to the Emmaus disciples and would imply that Simon Peter was the other (to this point unnamed) disciple. The omission in Codex D of Luke 24:12, where Peter visits the empty tomb, goes hand-in-hand with this variant in 24:34, since Simon Peter could not have discovered the tomb empty and also be, as Codex D presumes, one of the disillusioned Emmaus disciples. Origen, presumably following a tradition represented by Codex D, seven times identifies Cleopas's companion as Simon (Peter) (Origen, *Comm. Jo.* 1.5.30; 1.8.50; *Cels.* 2.62, 68; *Hom. Jer.* 20 [2x]; *Fr. Luc.* 36). This view has not been without support in (older) critical scholarship (see Annand 1958; Sawyer 1949–50; Crehan 1953; Huffman 1945, 221–26).

No sooner have they recognized Jesus than he has **disappeared from their sight** (24:31b). They reflect on what has just happened: **Weren't our hearts burning [in us] as he was speaking to us on the road, as he opened the Scriptures for us?** (24:32). Immediately, **they got up at that hour and returned to Jerusalem** (24:33a). They find the disciples, who have news of their own: **They found the Eleven gathered together and those with them, who were saying that the Lord had truly been raised and appeared to Simon** (24:33b–34). The scene ends: Cleopas and his companion **proceeded to explain the things that had happened on the road and how he was made known to them in the breaking of bread** (24:35).

What was the meaning of this story, often considered the most beautiful story in Luke's Gospel, for the authorial audience? Primarily, the story was to give witness to the fact that following his brutal death, a death that left his followers disillusioned and disheartened, the risen Jesus appeared to his disciples to explain, on the basis of Scripture, how the events of the preceding few days fit into the plan of Israel's God (for the contemporary relevance, see "Theological Issues" at the end of this chapter).

Postresurrection Appearance: To the Disciples (24:36–53)

24:36–53. In the last major section of Luke's Gospel, Jesus makes his final appearance to the disciples. The scene begins where the Emmaus story left off. The disciples have been talking about the appearances of Jesus to Simon and to the Emmaus pilgrims. Suddenly, Jesus stands among them: **Now, while they were saying these things, he suddenly stood among them** (24:36a; on the omission of 24:36b, see the introduction). Their response is typical of postresurrection appearances (cf. Matt. 28:17): **But being startled and terrified, they began to think they were seeing a ghost** (24:37). Given the accounts of postmortem appearances by apparitions (see Prince 2007), such a response is not surprising. Jesus responds with a gentle reproof and an invitation for them to touch and see that he is no apparition: **Then he said to them, "Why are you troubled? And why do doubts arise in your hearts? Look at my hands and my feet; see that it is me. Touch me and see [that it is true], because a ghost does not have flesh and bones, as you can see I have"** (24:38–39; on the omission of 24:40, see the introduction).

Luke continues: **And while they were still unable to believe what was happening because of their joy, and were amazed, he said to them, "Do you have anything to eat here?"** (24:41). Many commentators see in this question a continuation of the Lukan emphasis on the corporeality of the resurrection, previously seen in the invitation to the disciples to touch Jesus's body in order to disprove that he is only a phantom (e.g., Johnson 1991, 402; D. Garland 2011, 906). In this view, Jesus offers to consume food before the disciples to demonstrate the bodily nature of his resurrection. Luke may indeed be clarifying the distinction between postmortem appearances of apparitions (see above) and the corporeal nature of Jesus's resurrection appearance (cf. the similar theme in John 20:24–29).

The Gospel storyteller's concerns, however, go beyond establishing Jesus's bodily resurrection. The disciples respond to Jesus's request: **they gave him a piece of broiled fish** (24:42). Most translations read something like, "which he took and ate before their eyes" (24:43; cf. NRSV). Such a rendering suggests that only Jesus ate the fish, while the disciples were passive onlookers. The only other time the Greek construction translated "ate before their eyes" is found in Luke's Gospel is at 13:26. There the phrase is translated, "We ate and drank in your presence [*enōpion sou*]" and clearly refers to a shared meal. The same understanding should apply here as well, and the verse is better translated as follows: **which he took and ate *with them*** (24:43). So the image here is not of Jesus seeking simply once more to demonstrate his bodiliness. Rather, here we find the resurrected Lord seizing one last opportunity to dine with his disciples.

This reading is consistent with the theme of food and meals that runs throughout Luke's Gospel. Only Luke reports that at Jesus's birth he was placed in a manger, a feeding trough (see Luke 2:7, 12, 16), and provides a vivid image drawn from the very beginning of Jesus's earthly existence. For Luke, Jesus, born in a feeding trough, is food for the world (see comments on Luke 2:7b). Luke develops this theme in ways distinct from John. John favors the rhetorical device of "telling," that is, having his protagonist Jesus make explicit theological claims about being sustenance for the world: "I am the bread of life" (John 6:35); "I am the living bread that has come down from heaven; if anyone eats this bread, he will live forever. The bread which I shall give is my own flesh" (John 6:51 REB); "Whoever eats my flesh and drinks my blood has eternal life. . . . My flesh is real food; my blood is real drink. Whoever eats my flesh and drinks my blood dwells in me and I in him" (John 6:54–56 REB); "Those who drink of the water that I will give them will never be thirsty" (John 4:14).

Luke, however, employs the rhetorical device of "showing," that is, having Jesus engage in actions that demonstrate that he is sustenance for the world. This is not to say that John never employs the strategy of showing (cf. the wedding feast at Cana, John 2; the feeding of the 5,000, John 6) or that Luke never uses the technique of telling ("Blessed are those who are hungry now, for you will be satisfied"; Luke 6:21; "This is my body"; Luke 22:19; see also the parable of the banquet in Luke 14 and the parable of the rich man and Lazarus in Luke 16), but John clearly favors telling, while Luke prefers showing. Most of the showing in Luke occurs in the context of table fellowship. Jesus dines with Levi, a tax collector, and other sinners (Luke 5), and with Pharisees (Luke 7; 11; 14). He feeds the multitudes (Luke 9) and individuals (Luke 8:55). He eats with Mary and Martha (Luke 10) and presumably with Zacchaeus (Luke 19). He dines with disciples in Jerusalem (Luke 22) and Emmaus (Luke 24).

Such indiscriminate dining leads to sharp criticism of both Jesus and his disciples. The Pharisees complain to the disciples: "On what basis do you eat and drink with tax collectors and sinners?" (5:30). Later, they direct their objections at Jesus: "This man welcomes sinners and eats with them!" (15:2). Jesus himself states the opposition viewpoint very clearly: "and you say, 'The man is a glutton and a drunk, a friend of tax collectors and sinners!'" (7:34). To share a meal with someone, whether in antiquity or today, implies acceptance of that person. In Luke, the way Jesus eats—with sinners and tax collectors, with religious authorities and disciples—leads directly to his death. Such inclusivism was not to be tolerated.

Jesus does not want his disciples to forget how (or with whom) to eat. So in Luke, Jesus has two "Last Suppers." At the first (Luke 22), Jesus, reclining at table, engages his disciples in a discussion reminiscent of the Platonic symposium. The topic is true greatness (22:26). The point is clear: "eating and drinking" at Jesus's messianic table in his kingdom (22:30) demands radical inclusion at the ordinary table, an inclusiveness that transcends racial, social, and gender barriers. And so the last "Last Supper" (Luke 24), where Jesus eats broiled fish with his disciples, not only is a reminder of the corporeal nature of Jesus's own resurrected body, but, standing as it does in a sequence of suppers, no doubt also serves to remind the disciples of the radical inclusivity of the "body," the church, which remains behind to continue the work of the resurrected Christ. And so he took fish and ate it with them.

Jesus then gives his disciples a model of scriptural interpretation. **Then he said to them, "These were my words that I spoke to you while I was still with you, that it is necessary for everything that was written about me in the Law of Moses and the Prophets and the Psalms to be fulfilled"** (24:44). He makes it clear that what the Law, Prophets, and Psalms say about him deals specifically with his suffering: **Then he opened their minds to understand the Scriptures and said to them, "Thus it was written, that the Christ would suffer, and rise from the dead on the third day"** (24:45–46). Commentators since Hans Conzelmann have often overemphasized the lack of any notion of vicarious suffering in Luke. But here (see also Acts 8), the suffering of the Messiah leads inevitably to **repentance for the forgiveness of sins, which would be preached in his name in all nations, beginning at Jerusalem** (24:47). Jesus's interpretation of Scripture leads from exposition to application: **You [the disciples] are witnesses of these things** (24:48). Jesus then gives the disciples a promise: **I am sending you what my Father promised** (24:49a). He then gives them a command, but unlike in Matthew, in which the disciples are commissioned to "go and make disciples," in Luke, the disciples are to *stay* **in the city** (24:49b). The delay, however, is only temporary. They are simply to wait until they **are clothed with power from on high** (24:49c), a wait that ends with the events at Pentecost (Acts 2).

The last scene in Luke (24:50–53) brings closure to the story. **Jesus brought them out as far as Bethany** (24:50a), where he completes his "exodus" (cf. 9:30). He gives them one final "priestly" blessing: **and, raising his hands, he blessed them** (24:50b, doing what Zechariah was unable to do [Luke 1:22]; see Mekkattukunnel 2001). Luke continues: **while he was blessing them, he departed from them** (24:51a; on the textual variant in 24:51b, "and he was brought up into heaven," see the introduction). The disciples return to the temple in Jerusalem, where the story began (Luke 1:5–23): **And they returned to Jerusalem with great joy; and they were continually in the temple praising God** (24:52–53; on the possibility that the idiom translated "continually" [*dia pantos*] is better rendered "regularly" in a cultic setting, see Hamm 2004). This literary circularity provides a sense of completion (Parsons 1987).

Luke has artistically employed another strategy to indicate that the story is now complete. He introduces some "space" between the audience and the scene. The audience is allowed close enough to see what Jesus is doing (lifting his hands, blessing the disciples), but not close enough to hear—there is no dialogue in this closing scene (contrast Matt. 28:16–20). The effect is to usher the audience out of the symbolic world of the narrative and back into the real world. The task of proclaiming "repentance for the forgiveness of sins ... in all nations" (Luke 24:47), a theme reiterated in the book of Acts, remains for those who, having heard, now wish to be "servants of the gospel" (Luke 1:2).

Theological Issues

"Emmaus never happened; Emmaus always happens" (Crossan 1994, 197). "Emmaus *did* happen. . . . Emmaus *will never happen again*" (Wright 2003, 658). These two views could hardly stand farther apart. For Crossan, Emmaus—indeed, the entire resurrection narrative—functions like a parable to challenge and comfort contemporary believers in their spiritual and existential existence. For Wright, Emmaus—indeed, the entire resurrection narrative—rests on historical bedrock with its primary purpose to bear faithful witness to the unique events of that first Easter. Wright seems to have the upper hand in describing Luke's purposes, but that does not mean, as Wright himself admits, that there are not "multiple resonances in Christian experience which the stories set up" (Wright 2003, 657). Now that we have examined Luke's primary purpose in the previous section, it is appropriate to try to hear some of the "resonances which echo out . . . from the original event itself" (Wright 2003, 657).

Christian hope is the foundation of the Christian faith. The story of Emmaus begins as a story of fundamental and irreducible loss. The Emmaus travelers were mourners, disillusioned over the disappointment of what might have been. Jesus (and God) had failed to meet their expectations. The person they fervently believed would become the new king of Israel not only wasn't ruling Israel but also was in his grave. The candle of their messianic hopes had been snuffed out. His closest followers were in hiding. Their homeland was still ruled by Romans. The kingdom of God that Jesus had said was already present now seemed infinitely distant.

Luke has captured the hopelessness of their situation: "We *had hoped* he was the one to redeem Israel," suggesting that they had at that point ceased to hope. Their loss of hope was corporate and pervasive. Augustine understands it this way as well: "'We,' they said, 'had hoped that he was the one to redeem Israel.' O my dear disciples, you had hoped! So now you no longer hope? Look, Christ is alive! Is hope dead in you?" (Augustine, *Serm.* 235.2, trans. Hill 1993b). In one sense, Emmaus is a "one off" story never to be repeated; it is a devastating, historical event with wide-ranging consequences, not unlike the Babylonian destruction of the temple (cf. Ps. 137)—Wright is right. Emmaus speaks powerfully to a cynical culture that has relegated eschatological hope to a quaint idea of a bygone day. Emmaus proclaims boldly, "In the end (as in the beginning), God!"

But in another secondary and derivative way, the loss expressed on the road to Emmaus can inform our articulations of more personal but no less intense experiences of loss. We all do travel the road to Emmaus, and in that sense, Crossan is right too. Certain kinds of losses are, simply put, catastrophic—loss of limb, loss of marriage, loss of job or home, loss of health, and certainly, as the Emmaus disciples knew, loss of a loved one. These catastrophes take no particular aim at the wicked and no particular detour around the righteous, and they are stubbornly resistant to any facile answers to the question "Why?" Nor is there any one-size-fits-all self-help plan for dealing with such loss. But we do have resources to draw on from our faith tradition in times of loss. And the witness of Scripture is one of those resources. Emmaus provides several clues about the relationship of hope and loss in life after Easter. We begin with the recognition that the Emmaus path to spiritual illumination and growth is a downward one. This truth is hard to hear in a culture that values and honors those whose blind ambitions lead them upward and onward. Loss and failure are to be avoided at all costs, and this escapism and denial can lead down a self-destructive path. The path to wholeness, however, is downward as we turn to embrace the loss and pray for transforming grace. The old Shaker hymn is surely right: "'Tis a gift to be simple, 'tis a gift to be free, 'tis a gift to *come down* where we *ought* to be."

At the end of the story, Christ makes himself known to Cleopas and his companion around the table in the breaking of bread. Immediately they return to Jerusalem to share their experience of hearts strangely warmed; the inward journey must always lead outward. We sink down in the fragile hope that we are sinking not into the abyss but into the deep, deep love of God, who surrounds us, who is above and beneath us, before and behind us—in whom hope floats with an unexpected and undeserved buoyancy.

Luke's audience lived at a time when the apostles, the living links to Jesus, were dying or were already dead, and presumably no one in his audience knew the earthly Jesus; neither did the author himself. Parousia hope was fading. Yet the Emmaus story reminds them that one need not be an apostle to experience an epiphany of Christ. One could be so little known that one's name is forgotten. Indeed, leaving the one disciple unnamed is an invitation to the reader to participate in its story—to inscribe himself or herself into the narrative. One need not sit at the feet of the earthly Jesus in order to know him. Christ continues to make himself known in the Eucharist, in the "breaking of the bread" (see Acts 2:42, 46; 20:7, 11). One need not be in the religious center of Jerusalem (or anywhere else) for a religious revelation. One might experience the presence of the resurrected Christ in one's own home. So Luke encourages his audience, then and now, to take heart in that the resurrected Lord revealed himself through the faithful exposition of Scripture, in an obscure place, in a humble home, in a shared meal to little-known followers who had experienced devastating loss. He continues to come to us in Word and at Table. So goes the good news!

Bibliography

Aker, Ben. 1988. *New Directions in Lucan Theology: Reflections on Luke 3:21–22 and Some Implications*. Peabody, MA: Hendrickson.

Alexander, Loveday. 1993. *The Preface to Luke's Gospel: Literary Convention and Social Context in Luke 1.1–4 and Acts 1.1*. Society for New Testament Studies Monograph Series 78. Cambridge: Cambridge University Press.

Allison, Dale C., Jr. 1987. "The Eye Is the Lamp of the Body (Matthew 6:22–23 = Luke 11:34–36)." *New Testament Studies* 33:61–83.

———. 1999. "Behind the Temptations of Jesus: Q4:1–13 and Mark 1:12–13." In *Authenticating the Activities of Jesus*, edited by Bruce Chilton and Craig A. Evans, 195–213. Leiden: Brill.

———. 2000. *The Intertextual Jesus: Scripture in Q*. Harrisburg, PA: Trinity.

———. 2002. "Rejecting Violent Judgment: Luke 9:52–56 and Its Relatives." *Journal of Biblical Literature* 121:459–78.

———. 2005. *Resurrecting Jesus: The Earliest Christian Tradition and Its Interpreters*. London: T&T Clark.

———. 2008. "Healing in the Wings of His Garment: The Synoptics and Malachi 4:2." In *The Word Leaps the Gap: Essays on Scripture and Theology in Honor of Richard B. Hays*, edited by J. Ross Wagner, C. Kavin Rowe, and A. Katherine Grieb, 132–46. Grand Rapids: Eerdmans.

Alsup, John. 1975. *Post-Resurrection Appearance Stories in the Gospel Tradition*. London: SPCK.

André, Jacques, ed. 1981. *Traité de physiognomonie: Anonyme latin*. Paris: Les Belles Lettres.

Annand, Rupert. 1958. "'He Was Seen of Cephas': A Suggestion about the First Resurrection Appearance to Peter." *Scottish Journal of Theology* 11:180–87.

Arterbury, Andrew E. 2005. *Entertaining Angels: Early Christian Hospitality in Its Mediterranean Setting*. Sheffield: Sheffield Phoenix.

Babbitt, Frank Cole, trans. 1927. *The Education of Children. How the Young Man Should Study Poetry. On Listening to Lectures. How to Tell a Flatterer from a*

Friend. How a Man May Become Aware of His Progress in Virtue. Vol. 1 of *Plutarch: Moralia*. Loeb Classical Library 197. London: Heinemann.

Bailey, Kenneth E. 1976. *Poet and Peasant: A Literary-Cultural Approach to the Parables in Luke*. Grand Rapids: Eerdmans.

———. 1979. "The Manger and the Inn: The Cultural Background of Luke 2:7." *Theological Review* 2:33–44.

———. 1980. *Through Peasant Eyes: More Lucan Parables, Their Culture and Style*. Grand Rapids: Eerdmans.

———. 2008. *Jesus through Middle Eastern Eyes: Cultural Studies in the Gospels*. Downers Grove, IL: InterVarsity.

Balch, David L. 1995. "Paul in Acts: '. . . You Teach All the Jews . . . to Forsake Moses, Telling Them Not to . . . Observe the Customs' (Acts 21,21)." In *Panchaia: Festschrift für Klaus Thraede*, edited by Manfred Wacht, 11–23. Münster: Aschendorff.

Balch, David L., and Carolyn Osiek. 1997. *Families in the New Testament World: Households and House Churches*. Louisville: Westminster John Knox.

Ball, David T. 2003. "What Jesus Really Meant by 'Render unto Caesar' (It's Not about Taxes)." *Bible Review* 19(2):14–17, 52.

Barclay, John M. G. 1996. "The Resurrection in Contemporary New Testament Scholarship." In *Resurrection Reconsidered*, edited by Gavin D'Costa, 13–30. Oxford: Oneworld.

Barr, Beth A., Bill J. Leonard, Mikeal C. Parsons, and C. Douglas Weaver. 2009. *The Acts of the Apostles: Four Centuries of Baptist Interpretation*. Waco: Baylor University Press.

Barrett, C. K. 1975. "The House of Prayer and the Den of Thieves." In *Jesus und Paulus: Festschrift für Werner Georg Kümmel zum 70sten Geburtstag*, edited by E. Earle Ellis and Erich Grässer, 13–20. Göttingen: Vandenhoeck & Ruprecht.

———. 1994–98. *A Critical and Exegetical Commentary on the Acts of the Apostles*. 2 vols. International Critical Commentary. Edinburgh: T&T Clark.

Barth, Karl. 1989. "The Christian Community and the Civil Community." In *Karl Barth: Theologian of Freedom*, edited by Clifford Green, 265–95. Making of Modern Theology. San Francisco: Harper & Row.

Bass, Kenneth. 2009. "The Narrative and Rhetorical Use of Divine Necessity in Luke-Acts." *Journal of Biblical and Pneumatological Research* 1:48–68.

Basser, H. W. 1998. "The Jewish Roots of the Transfiguration." *Bible Review* 14:30–35.

Bauckham, Richard. 1991. "The Rich Man and Lazarus: The Parable and the Parallels." *New Testament Studies* 37:225–46.

———. 1998a. "For Whom Were Gospels Written?" In *The Gospels for All Christians: Rethinking the Gospel Audiences*, edited by Richard Bauckham, 9–48. Grand Rapids: Eerdmans.

———. 1998b. "The Scrupulous Priest and the Good Samaritan: Jesus' Parabolic Interpretation of the Law of Moses." *New Testament Studies* 44:475–89.

Bauer, Johannes Baptist. 1963. "'Wer sein Leben retten will . . .': Mk 8,35 Parr." In *Neutestamentliche Aufsätze: Festschrift für Prof. Josef Schmid zum 70. Geburtstag*, edited by Josef Blinzler, Otto Kuss, and Franz Mussner, 7–10. Regensburg: Pustet.

Beasley-Murray, George. 1973. *Baptism in the New Testament*. Grand Rapids: Eerdmans.

Beavis, Mary Ann. 1990. "Parable and Fable." *Catholic Biblical Quarterly* 52:473–98.

———. 1992. "Ancient Slavery as an Interpretative Context for the New Testament Servant Parables, with Special Reference to the Unjust Steward (Luke 16:1–8)." *Journal of Biblical Literature* 111:37–54.

Betz, Hans Dieter. 1995. *The Sermon on the Mount: A Commentary on the Sermon on the Mount*. Hermeneia. Minneapolis: Fortress.

Beutler, Christian. 1991. *Der älteste Kruzifixus: Der entschlafene Christus*. Frankfurt am Main: Fischer Taschenbuch.

Bird, Michael. 2007. "The Unity of Luke-Acts in Recent Discussion." *Journal for the Study of the New Testament* 29:425–48.

Blomberg, Craig L. 1990. *Interpreting the Parables*. Downers Grove, IL: InterVarsity.

Bock, Darrell L. 1994–96. *Luke*. 2 vols. Baker Exegetical Commentary on the New Testament. Grand Rapids: Baker Academic.

Bockmuehl, Markus. 1998. "'Let the Dead Bury Their Dead' (Matt. 8:22/Luke 9:60): Jesus and the Halakah." *Journal of Theological Studies* 49:553–81.

———. 2005. "The Making of Gospel Commentaries." In *The Written Gospel*, edited by Markus Bockmuehl and Donald A. Hagner, 274–95. New York: Cambridge University Press.

———. 2006. *Seeing the Word: Refocusing New Testament Study*. Studies in Theological Interpretation. Grand Rapids: Baker Academic.

———. 2010. "Locating Paradise." In *Paradise in Antiquity: Jewish and Christian Views*, edited by Markus Bockmuehl and Guy G. Stroumsa, 192–209. New York: Cambridge University Press.

Bode, Edward Lynn. 1970. *The First Easter Morning: The Gospel Accounts of the Women's Visit to the Tomb of Jesus*. Analecta biblica 45. Rome: Biblical Institute.

Bonhoeffer, Dietrich. 1948. *The Cost of Discipleship*. Translated by R. H. Fuller. New York: Macmillan.

Boring, M. Eugene, Klaus Berger, and Carsten Colpe, eds. 1995. *Hellenistic Commentary to the New Testament*. Nashville: Abingdon.

Bornkamm, Günther. 1960. *Jesus of Nazareth*. Translated by Irene McLuskey and Fraser McLuskey with James M. Robinson. New York: Harper.

Bosold, Iris. 1978. *Pazifismus und prophetische Provokation: Das Grussverbot Lk 10,4b und sein historischer Kontext*. Stuttgarter Bibel-Studien 90. Stuttgart: Katholisches Bibelwerk.

Bovon, François. 1993. "The Role of the Scriptures in the Composition of the Gospel Accounts: The Temptations of Jesus (Lk 4:1–13 par) and the Multiplication of the Loaves (Lk 9:10–17 par)." In *Luke and Acts*, edited by Gerald O'Collins and Filberto Marconi, translated by Matthew J. O'Connell, 26–31, 215–16. New York: Paulist Press.

———. 2001. "Names and Numbers in Early Christianity." *New Testament Studies* 47:267–88.

———. 2002–13. *Luke*. Translated by Christine M. Thomas, Donald S. Deer, and James Crouch. 3 vols. Hermeneia. Minneapolis: Fortress.

Braun, Willi. 1995. *Feasting and Social Rhetoric in Luke 14*. Cambridge: Cambridge University Press.

Brawley, Robert L. 1992. "Canon and Community: Intertextuality, Canon, Interpretation, Christology, Theology, and Persuasive Rhetoric in Luke 4:1–13." In *SBL Seminar Papers, 1992*, 419–34. Society of Biblical Literature Seminar Papers 31. Atlanta: Scholars Press.

———. 1995. *Text to Text Pours Forth Speech: Voices of Scripture in Luke-Acts*. Indiana Studies in Biblical Literature. Bloomington: Indiana University Press.

———. 1999. "Abrahamic Covenant Traditions and the Characterization of God in Luke-Acts." In *The Unity of Luke-Acts*, edited by Jozef Verheyden, 109–32. Louvain: Peeters.

Bridge, Steven L. 2003. *"Where the Eagles Are Gathered": The Deliverance of the Elect in Lukan Eschatology*. Journal for the Study of the New Testament Supplement Series 240. London: Sheffield Academic.

Brookins, Timothy A. 2011. "Luke's Use of Mark as παράφρασις: Its Effects on Characterization in the 'Healing of Bartimaeus' Pericope (Mark 10.46–52/Luke 18.35–43)." *Journal for the Study of the New Testament* 34:70–89.

Brown, Raymond E. 1961. "The Pater Noster as an Eschatological Prayer." *Theological Studies* 22:175–208.

———. 1966–70. *The Gospel according to John*. 2 vols. Anchor Bible 29–29A. Garden City, NY: Doubleday.

———. 1977. *The Birth of the Messiah: A Commentary on the Infancy Narratives in Matthew and Luke*. New York: Doubleday.

———. 1994. *The Death of the Messiah: From Gethsemane to the Grave; A Commentary on the Passion Narratives in the Four Gospels*. 2 vols. New York: Doubleday.

Brueggemann, Walter. 1982. *Genesis*. Interpretation. Louisville: John Knox.

Bultmann, Rudolf. 1928. *The New Testament and Mythology and Other Basic Writings*. Translated by Schubert M. Ogden. Philadelphia: Fortress.

———. 1968. *The History of the Synoptic Tradition*. Translated by John Marsh. New York: Harper & Row.

Burridge, Richard. 1992. *What Are the Gospels? A Comparison with Graeco-Roman Biography*. Cambridge: Cambridge University Press.

———. 2004. *Jesus Now and Then*. Grand Rapids: Eerdmans.

Butler, H. E., trans. 1920. *The Institutio Oratoria of Quintilian*. Vol. 1. Loeb Classical Library 124. London: Heinemann.

———, trans. 1921. *The Institutio Oratoria of Quintilian*. Vol. 2. Loeb Classical Library 125. London: Heinemann.

———, trans. 1922. *The Institutio Oratoria of Quintilian*. Vol. 3. Loeb Classical Library 126. London: Heinemann.

Cadbury, Henry J. 1920. *The Style and Literary Method of Luke*. Cambridge, MA: Harvard University Press.

———. 1921. "The Purpose Expressed in Luke's Preface." *The Expositor* (June): 431–41.

———. 1922a. "The Tradition." In *The Beginnings of Christianity*, edited by F. J. Foakes Jackson and Kirsopp Lake, 2:209–64. London: Macmillan.

———. 1922b. "Commentary on the Preface of Luke." In *The Beginnings of Christianity*, edited by F. J. Foakes Jackson and Kirsopp Lake, 2:489–510. London: Macmillan.

———. 1922c. "The Knowledge Claimed in Luke's Preface." *The Expositor* (December): 401–20.

———. 1933. "Lexical Notes on Luke-Acts 5: Luke and the Horse-Doctors." *Journal of Biblical Literature* 52:55–65.

Callan, Terrance. 1985. "The Preface of Luke-Acts and Historiography." *New Testament Studies* 31:576–81.

Calvin, John. 1972. *A Harmony of the Gospels: Matthew, Mark and Luke*. Translated by A. W. Morrison. Vol. 1 of *Calvin's New Testament Commentaries*. Edited by D. W. Torrance and T. F. Torrance. Grand Rapids: Eerdmans.

Campbell, Constantine R. 2007. *Verbal Aspect, the Indicative Mood, and Narrative: Soundings in the Greek of the New Testament*. Studies in Biblical Greek 13. New York: Peter Lang.

Caplan, Harry, trans. 1954. *Cicero: Rhetorica ad Herennium*. Loeb Classical Library 403. Cambridge, MA: Harvard University Press.

Caragounis, Chrys C. 2006. *The Development of Greek and the New Testament: Morphology, Syntax, Phonology, and Textual Transmission*. Grand Rapids: Baker Academic.

Carlson, Stephen C. 2004. "Putting Luke 2:2 in Context." *Hypotyposeis: Sketches in Christian Origins*, December 31. http://www.hypotyposeis.org/weblog/2004/12/putting-luke-22-in-context.html.

Carroll, John T. 2008. "'What Then Will This Child Become?': Perspectives on Children in the Gospel of Luke." In *The Child in the Bible*, edited by Marcia Bunge, Terence E. Fretheim, and Beverly Roberts Gaventa, 177–94. Grand Rapids: Eerdmans.

———. 2012. *Luke: A Commentary*. New Testament Library. Louisville: Westminster John Knox.

Carter, Warren. 1996. *Matthew: Storyteller, Interpreter, Evangelist*. Peabody, MA: Hendrickson.

———. 2003. "Are There Imperial Texts in the Class? Intertextual Eagles and Matthean Eschatology as 'Lights Out' Time for Imperial Rome (Matthew 24:27–31)." *Journal of Biblical Literature* 122:467–87.

Cary, Earnest, trans. 1947. *Dionysius of Halicarnassus: Roman Antiquities*, Books 9.25–10. Loeb Classical Library 378. Cambridge, MA: Harvard University Press.

Clark, Ronald R., Jr. 2002. "Kingdom, Kids, and Kindness: A New Context for Luke 18:15–17." *Stone-Campbell Journal* 5:235–48.

Clivaz, Claire. 2002. "Douze noms pour une main: Nouveaux regards sur Judas à partier de Lc 22.21–2." *New Testament Studies* 48:400–416.

———. 2010. *L'ange et la sueur de sang (Lc 22,43–44): Ou comment on pourrait bien encore écrire l'histoire*. Louvain: Peeters.

Cohen, A., trans. 1936. "*Soṭah*: Translated into English with Notes, Glossary and Indices." In *The Babylonian Talmud, Nashim VI: Nazir. Soṭah*. London: Soncino.

Cohen, Shaye J. D. 1991. "Menstruants and the Sacred in Judaism and Christianity." In *Women's History and Ancient History*, edited by Sarah B. Pomeroy, 273–99. Chapel Hill: University of North Carolina Press.

Coleridge, Mark. 1993. *The Birth of the Lukan Narrative: Narrative as Christology in Luke 1–2*. Sheffield: JSOT Press.

Collins, Adela Yarbro. 1997. "Apotheosis and Resurrection." In *The New Testament and Hellenistic Judaism*, edited by Peder Borgen and Soren Giversen, 88–100. Peabody, MA: Hendrickson.

Colson, F. H., trans. 1935. *On Abraham. On Joseph. On Moses.* Vol. 6 of *Philo.* Loeb Classical Library 289. Cambridge, MA: Harvard University Press.

———, trans. 1962. *The Embassy to Gaius. General Indexes.* Vol. 10 of *Philo.* Loeb Classical Library 379. Cambridge, MA: Harvard University Press.

Conyers, A. J. 2001. "Rescuing Tolerance." *First Things* 115:43–46.

Conzelmann, Hans. 1961. *The Theology of St. Luke.* New York: Harper.

Cooper, John M. 2004. *Knowledge, Nature, and the Good: Essays on Ancient Philosophy.* Princeton: Princeton University Press.

Corley, Kathleen E. 1989. "Were the Women around Jesus Really Prostitutes?" In *SBL Seminar Papers, 1989*, 487–521. Society of Biblical Literature Seminar Papers 28. Atlanta: Scholars Press.

———. 1993. *Private Women, Public Meals: Social Conflict in the Synoptic Tradition.* Peabody, MA: Hendrickson.

Cosgrove, Charles H. 2005. "A Woman's Unbound Hair in the Greco-Roman World, with Special Reference to the Story of the 'Sinful Woman' in Luke 7:36–50." *Journal of Biblical Literature* 124:675–92.

Cotter, Wendy J. 1999. *Miracles in Greco-Roman Antiquity: A Sourcebook for the Study of New Testament Miracle Stories.* London: Routledge.

———. 2005. "The Parable of the Feisty Widow and the Threatened Judge (Luke 18.1–8)." *New Testament Studies* 51:328–43.

Couroyer, Bernard. 1970. "De la mesure dont vous mesurez il vous sera mesuré." *Revue biblique* 77:366–70.

Craddock, Fred B. 1990. *Luke.* Interpretation. Louisville: Westminster John Knox.

Crehan, Joseph H. 1953. "St Peter's Journey to Emmaus." *Catholic Biblical Quarterly* 15:418–26.

Cribiore, Raffaella. 2001. *Gymnastics of the Mind: Greek Education in Hellenistic and Roman Egypt.* Princeton, NJ: Princeton University Press.

Crossan, John Dominic. 1974. "Servant Parables of Jesus." *Semeia* 1:17–62.

———. 1994. *Jesus: A Revolutionary Biography.* San Francisco: HarperSanFrancisco.

Crump, David. 1992. *Jesus the Intercessor: Prayer and Christology in Luke-Acts.* Tübingen: Mohr Siebeck.

Culpepper, R. Alan. 1983. *Anatomy of the Fourth Gospel: A Study in Literary Design.* Philadelphia: Fortress.

———. 1994. "Seeing the Kingdom of God: The Metaphor of Sight in the Gospel of Luke." *Currents in Theology and Mission* 21:434–43.

———. 1995. "Luke." In *The New Interpreter's Bible*, edited by Leander E. Keck, 9:1–490. 12 vols. Nashville: Abingdon.

Culy, Martin M. 1989. "A Typology of Relative Clauses in Koine Greek." In *Work Papers of the Summer Institute of Linguistics, University of North Dakota Session* 33, edited by R. A. Dooley and J. A. Bickford, 67–92. Dallas: Summer Institute of Linguistics.

———. 2010. *Echoes of Friendship in the Gospel of John*. Sheffield: Sheffield Phoenix.

Culy, Martin M., Mikeal C. Parsons, and Joshua J. Stigall. 2010. *Luke: A Handbook on the Greek Text*. Waco: Baylor University Press.

Dahl, Nils Alstrup. 1952. "Parables of Growth." *Studia theologica* 5:132–66.

———. 1966. "The Story of Abraham in Luke-Acts." In *Studies in Luke-Acts*, edited by Leander E. Keck and J. Louis Martyn, 139–58. Nashville: Abingdon.

Danby, Herbert. 1933. *The Mishnah: Translated from the Hebrew with Introduction and Brief Explanatory Notes*. Oxford: Oxford University Press.

Danker, Frederick W. 1960–61. "The *Huios* Phrases in the New Testament." *New Testament Studies* 7:94.

———. 1982. *Benefactor: Epigraphic Study of a Graeco-Roman and New Testament Semantic Field*. St. Louis: Clayton.

———. 1988. *Jesus and the New Age: A Commentary on St. Luke's Gospel*. Philadelphia: Fortress.

Darr, John A. 1998. *Herod the Fox: Audience Criticism and Lukan Characterization*. Sheffield: Sheffield Academic Press.

Dean-Jones, Lesley Ann. 1994. *Women's Bodies in Classical Greek Science*. Oxford: Oxford University Press.

De Boer, Esther A. 2002. "The Lukan Mary Magdalene and the Other Women Following Jesus." In *A Feminist Companion to Luke*, edited by Amy-Jill Levine and Marianne Blickenstaff, 140–60. Sheffield: Sheffield Academic Press.

De Lacy, Phillip H., and Benedict Einarson, trans. 1959. *On Love of Wealth. On Compliancy. On Envy and Hate. On Praising Oneself Inoffensively. On the Delays of the Divine Vengeance. On Fate. On the Sign of Socrates. On Exile, Consolation to His Wife*. Vol. 7 of *Plutarch: Moralia*. Loeb Classical Library 405. Cambridge, MA: Harvard University Press.

Derrett, J. Duncan M. 1970. *Law in the New Testament*. London: Darton, Longman, & Todd.

———. 1972. "Law in the New Testament: The Parable of the Unjust Judge." *New Testament Studies* 18:178–91.

Dibelius, Martin. 1971. *From Tradition to Gospel*. Translated by Bertram Lee Woolf. Library of Theological Translations. Cambridge: Clarke.

Dillon, Richard J. 1991. "Ravens, Lilies, and the Kingdom of God (Matthew 6:25–33/ Luke 12:22–31)." *Catholic Biblical Quarterly* 53:605–27.

Doble, Peter. 2006. "Luke 24.26, 44—Songs of God's Servant: David and His Psalms in Luke-Acts." *Journal for the Study of the New Testament* 28:267–83.

Dobson, Brian. 1974. "The Significance of the Centurion and the 'Primipilaris' in the Roman Army and Administration." *Aufstieg und Niedergang der römischen Welt: Geschichte und Kultur Roms im Spiegel der neueren Forschung* 1:392–434. Part 2, *Principat*, 1. Edited by Hildegard Temporini. Berlin: de Gruyter.

Dodd, C. H. 1961. *The Parables of the Kingdom*. New York: Scribners.

Dodson, Derek S. 2009. *Reading Dreams: An Audience-Critical Approach to the Dreams in the Gospel of Matthew*. London: T&T Clark.

Donahue, John R. 1971. "Tax Collectors and Sinners: An Attempt at Identification." *Catholic Biblical Quarterly* 33:39–61.

Donald, Trevor. 1963. "The Semantic Field of 'Folly' in Proverbs, Job, Psalms, and Ecclesiastes." *Vetus Testamentum* 13:285–92.

Donaldson, Terence L. 1985. *Jesus on the Mountain: A Study in Matthean Theology*. Sheffield: JSOT Press.

Doran, Robert. 2007. "The Pharisee and the Tax Collector." *Catholic Biblical Quarterly* 69:259–70.

Du Plessis, I. I. 1974. "Once More: The Purpose of Luke's Prologue (Lk 1:1–4)." *Novum Testamentum* 16:259–71.

Ehrman, Bart D. 1993. *The Orthodox Corruption of Scripture: The Effect of Early Christological Controversies on the Text of the New Testament*. New York: Oxford University Press.

———, trans. 2003. *Epistle of Barnabas. Papias and Quadratus. Epistle to Diognetus. The Shepherd of Hermas*. Vol. 2 of *The Apostolic Fathers*. Loeb Classical Library 25. Cambridge, MA: Harvard University Press.

Ellis, E. Earle. 1974. *The Gospel of Luke*. New Century Bible Commentary. Grand Rapids: Eerdmans.

Emmrich, Martin. 2000. "The Lucan Account of the Beelzebul Controversy." *Westminster Theological Journal* 62:267–79.

Erickson, Richard J. 1993. "The Jailing of John and the Baptism of Jesus: Luke 3:19–21." *Journal of the Evangelical Theological Society* 36:455–66.

Eriksson, Anders. 2005. "The Old Is Good: Parables of Patched Garment and Wineskins as Elaboration of a Chreia in Luke 5:33–39 about Feasting with Jesus." In *Rhetoric, Ethic, and Moral Persuasion in Biblical Discourse*, edited by Anders Eriksson and Thomas Olbricht, 52–72. New York: T&T Clark International.

Ernst, Josef. 1993. *Das Evangelium nach Lukas*. 2nd ed. Regensburg: Pustet.

Esler, Philip Francis. 1987. *Community and Gospel in Luke-Acts: The Social and Political Motivations of Lucan Theology*. Cambridge: Cambridge University Press.

Evans, C. F. 1970. *Resurrection and the New Testament*. London: SCM.

Evans, Craig A. 1987. "'He Set His Face': Luke 9:51 Once Again." *Biblica* 68:80–84.

———. 1990. *Luke*. Understanding the Bible Commentary Series. Grand Rapids: Baker Books.

———. 2005. "Jewish Burial Traditions and the Resurrection of Jesus." *Journal for the Study of the Historical Jesus* 3:233–48.

Ewald, Marie Liguori, trans. 1964. *The Homilies of St. Jerome, Vol. 1 (1–59 on the Psalms)*. Fathers of the Church. Washington, DC: Catholic University of America Press.

Fee, Gordon D. 1981. "'One Thing Is Needful': Luke 10:42." In *New Testament Textual Criticism: Its Significance for Exegesis; Essays in Honour of Bruce M. Metzger*, edited by Eldon Jay Epp and Gordon D. Fee, 61–75. Oxford: Clarendon.

Fiore, Benjamin. 1997. "The Theory and Practice of Friendship in Cicero." In *Greco-Roman Perspectives on Friendship*, edited by John T. Fitzgerald, 59–76. Atlanta: Scholars Press.

Fitzmyer, Joseph A. 1981–85. *The Gospel according to Luke*. Anchor Bible 28–28A. Garden City, NY: Doubleday.

Flannery-Dailey, Frances. 2004. *Dreamers, Scribes, and Priests: Jewish Dreams in the Hellenistic and Roman Eras*. Leiden: Brill.

Forbes, Greg. 2000. *The God of Old: The Role of the Lukan Parables in the Purpose of Luke's Gospel*. Journal for the Study of the New Testament Supplement Series 198. Sheffield: Sheffield Acadamic Press.

Foster, Paul. 2007. "Polymorphic Christology: Its Origins and Developments in Early Christianity." *Journal of Theological Studies* 58:66–99.

Fowler, Robert M. 1991. *Let the Reader Understand: Reader-Response Criticism and the Gospel of Mark*. Minneapolis: Fortress.

Frye, Northrop. 1982. *The Great Code: The Bible and Literature*. London: Routledge & Kegan Paul.

Fuller, Reginald H. 1971. *The Formation of the Resurrection Narratives*. London: SPCK.

———. 1974. *Preaching the New Lectionary: The Word of God for the Church Today*. Collegeville, MN: Liturgical Press.

Funk, Robert W. 1974. "The Good Samaritan as Metaphor." *Semeia* 2:74–81.

Gamba, G. G. 1968. "Agonia di Gesù." *Revista Biblica* 16:159–66.

Gamble, Harry Y. 1985. *The New Testament Canon: Its Making and Meaning*. Philadelphia: Fortress.

———. 1995. *Books and Readers in the Early Church: A History of Early Christian Texts*. New Haven: Yale University Press.

García Martínez, Florentino. 1996. *The Dead Sea Scrolls Translated: The Qumran Texts in English*. 2nd ed. Leiden: Brill.

Garland, David E. 2011. *Luke*. Zondervan Exegetical Commentary on the New Testament. Grand Rapids: Zondervan.

Garland, Robert. 1995. *The Eye of the Beholder: Deformity and Disability in the Graeco-Roman World*. Ithaca, NY: Cornell University Press.

Garnsey, Peter, and Richard Saller. 1987. *The Roman Empire: Economy, Society, and Culture*. Berkeley: University of California Press.

Garrett, Susan R. 1989. *The Demise of the Devil: Magic and the Demonic in Luke's Writings*. Minneapolis: Fortress.

———. 1991. "'Lest the Light in You Be Darkness': Luke 11:33–36 and the Question of Commitment." *Journal of Biblical Literature* 110:93–105.

Gathercole, Simon. 2003. "Jesus' Eschatological Vision of the Fall of Satan: Luke 10,18 Reconsidered." *Zeitschrift für die neutestamentliche Wissenschaft und die Kunde der älteren Kirche* 94:143–63.

———. 2005. "The Heavenly ἀνατολή (Luke 1:78–9)." *Journal of Theological Studies*, n.s., 56:471–88.

Geldenhuys, Norval. 1951. *Commentary on the Gospel of Luke*. New International Commentary on the New Testament. Grand Rapids: Eerdmans.

Glasson, Thomas Francis. 1973–74. "Davidic Links with the Betrayal of Jesus." *Expository Times* 85:118–19.

Gleason, Maud W. 1995. *Making Men: Sophists and Self-Presentation in Ancient Rome*. Princeton, NJ: Princeton University Press.

González, Justo L. 2010. *Luke*. Belief: A Theological Commentary on the Bible. Louisville: Westminster John Knox.

Goodacre, Mark. 2002. *The Case against Q: Studies in Markan Priority and the Synoptic Problem*. Harrisburg, PA: Trinity.

Goodman, Martin. 1983. *State and Society in Roman Galilee*. Totowa, NJ: Rowman & Allenheld.

Gowler, David B. 2003. "Text, Culture, and Ideology in Luke 7:1–10: A Dialogic Reading." In *Fabrics in Discourse: Essays in Honor of Vernon K. Robbins*, edited by David B. Gowler, L. Gregory Bloomquist, and Duane F. Watson, 89–125. Harrisburg, PA: Trinity.

Gray-Fow, Michael. 1986. "Pederasty, the Scantinian Law, and the Roman Army." *The Journal of Psychohistory* 13:449–60.

Green, Joel B. 1989. "Jesus and a Daughter of Abraham (Luke 13:10–17): Test Case for a Lucan Perspective on Jesus' Miracles." *Catholic Biblical Quarterly* 51:643–54.

———. 1994. "The Problem of a Beginning: Israel's Scriptures in Luke 1–2." *Bulletin for Biblical Research* 4:61–85.

———. 1997. *The Gospel of Luke*. New International Commentary on the New Testament. Grand Rapids: Eerdmans.

———. 1999. "From 'John's Baptism' to 'Baptism in the Name of the Lord Jesus': The Significance of Baptism in Luke-Acts." In *Baptism, the New Testament, and the Church: Historical and Contemporary Studies in Honour of R. E. O. White*, edited by Stanley E. Porter and Anthony R. Cross, 157–72. Sheffield: Sheffield Academic Press.

Gregory, Andrew. 2003. *The Reception of Luke and Acts in the Period before Irenaeus: Looking for Luke in the Second Century*. Wissenschaftliche Untersuchungen zum Neuen Testament 2/169. Tübingen: Mohr Siebeck.

Gressmann, Hugo. 1918. *Vom reichen Mann und armen Lazarus: Eine literargeschichtliche Studie*. Abhandlungen der königlichen preussischen Akademie der Wissenschaften: Philosophische-historische Klasse 7. Berlin: Königliche Akademie der Wissenschaften.

Grundmann, Walter. 1966. *Das Evangelium nach Lukas*. 4th ed. Theologischer Handkommentar zum Neuen Testament 3. Berlin: Evangelische Verlagsanstalt.

Gutwenger, Engelbert. 1946. "The Anti-Marcionite Prologues." *Theological Studies* 7:393–409.

Hamm, Dennis. 1988. "Luke 19:8 Once Again: Does Zacchaeus Defend or Resolve?" *Journal of Biblical Literature* 107:431–37.

———. 1991. "Zacchaeus Revisited Once More: A Story of Vindication or Conversion?" *Biblica* 72:248–52.

———. 2003. "The Tamid Service in Luke-Acts: The Cultic Background behind Luke's Theology of Worship (Luke 1:5–25; 18:9–14; 24:50–53; Acts 3:1; 10:3, 30)." *Catholic Biblical Quarterly* 65:215–31.

———. 2004. "Praying 'Regularly' (Not 'Constantly'): A Note on the Cultic Background of *Dia Pantos* at Luke 24:53, Acts 10:2 and Hebrews 9:6, 13:15." *Expository Times* 116:50–52.

Hanks, Tom. 2000. *The Subversive Gospel: A New Testament Commentary of Liberation*. Cleveland: Pilgrim Press.

Hanson, Ann Ellis. 1990. "The Medical Writers' Woman." In *Before Sexuality: The Construction of Erotic Experience in the Ancient Greek World*, edited by David M. Halperin, John J. Winkler, and Froma I. Zeitlin, 309–38. Princeton, NJ: Princeton University Press.

Hanson, John. 1980. "Dreams and Visions in the Graeco-Roman World and Early Christianity." *Aufstieg und Niedergang der römischen Welt: Geschichte und Kultur Roms im Spiegel der neueren Forschung* 23.2:1395–1427. Part 2, *Principat*, 23.2. Edited by Wolfgang Haase. Berlin: de Gruyter.

Harmon, A. M., trans. 1913. *Phalaris. Hippias or The Bath. Dionysus. Heracles. Amber or The Swans. The Fly. Nigrinus. Demonax. The Hall. My Native Land. Octogenarians. A True Story. Slander. The Consonants at Law. The Carousal (Symposium) or The Lapiths*. Vol. 1 of *Lucian*. Loeb Classical Library 13. London: Heinemann.

Hartman, Lars. 1997. *Into the Name of the Lord Jesus: Baptism in the Early Church*. Edinburgh: T&T Clark.

Hartsock, Chad. 2008. *Sight and Blindness in Luke-Acts: The Use of Physical Features in Characterization*. Leiden: Brill.

Hawkins, John C. 1911. "Three Limitations to St. Luke's Use of St. Mark's Gospel." In *Studies in the Synoptic Problem by Members of the University of Oxford*, edited by William Sanday, 29–60. Oxford: Clarendon.

Hays, Christopher M. 2010. *Luke's Wealth Ethics: A Study in Their Coherence and Character*. Wissenschaftliche Untersuchungen zum Neuen Testament 2/275. Tübingen: Mohr Siebeck.

Hays, Richard B. 2002. "Can the Gospels Teach Us How to Read the Old Testament?" *Pro Ecclesia* 11:402–18.

Heil, John Paul. 1999. *The Meal Scenes in Luke-Acts: An Audience-Oriented Approach*. Atlanta: Society of Biblical Literature.

Helmbold, W. C., trans. 1939. *Can Virtue Be Taught? On Moral Virtue. On the Control of Anger. On Tranquility of Mind. On Brotherly Love. On Affection for Offspring. Whether Vice Be Sufficient to Cause Unhappiness. Whether the Affections of the Soul are Worse Than Those of the Body. Concerning Talkativeness. On Being a Busybody*. Vol. 6 of *Plutarch: Moralia*. Loeb Classical Library 337. Cambridge, MA: Harvard University Press.

Hemer, Colin J. 1989. *The Book of Acts in the Setting of Hellenistic History*. Wissenschaftliche Untersuchungen zum Neuen Testament 2/49. Tübingen: Mohr Siebeck.

Hengel, Martin. 2000. *The Four Gospels and the One Gospel of Jesus Christ*. London: SCM.

Hester, David C. 1977. "Luke 4:1–13." *Interpretation* 31:53–59.

Hett, W. S., trans. 1936. *Aristotle: Minor Works: On Colours. On Things Heard. Physiognomics. On Plants. On Marvellous Things Heard. Mechanical Problems. On Indivisible Lines. The Situations and Names of Winds. On Melissus, Xenophanes, and Gorgias*. Loeb Classical Library 307. Cambridge, MA: Harvard University Press.

Hicks, R. D., trans. 1925a. *Diogenes Laertius: Lives of Eminent Philosophers, Books 1–5*. Loeb Classical Library 184. London: Heinemann.

———, trans. 1925b. *Diogenes Laertius: Lives of Eminent Philosophers, Books 6–10*. Loeb Classical Library 185. London: Heinemann.

Hill, Edmund, trans. 1993a. *Sermons, (184–229z) on the Liturgical Seasons*. Vol. 3.6 of *The Works of St. Augustine: A Translation for the 21st Century*. New Rochelle, NY: New City.

———, trans. 1993b. *Sermons, (230–272b) on the Liturgical Seasons*. Vol. 3.7 of *The Works of St. Augustine: A Translation for the 21st Century*. New Rochelle, NY: New City.

———, trans. 1994. *Sermons, (273–305A) on the Saints*. Vol. 3.8 of *The Works of St. Augustine: A Translation for the 21st Century*. Hyde Park, NY: New City.

Hobart, William Kirk. 1882. *The Medical Language of St. Luke*. Dublin: Hodges, Figgis.

Hock, Ronald F. 1995. *The Infancy Gospels of James and Thomas*. Santa Rosa, CA: Polebridge.

———. 1998. "Why New Testament Scholars Should Read Ancient Novels." In *Ancient Fiction and Early Christian Narrative*, edited by Ronald F. Hock, J. Bradley Chance, and Judith Perkins, 121–38. Society of Biblical Literature Symposium Series 6. Atlanta: Scholars Press.

———. 2003. "The Parable of the Foolish Rich Man (Luke 12:16–20) and Graeco-Roman Conventions of Thought and Behavior." In *Early Christianity and Classical Culture: Comparative Studies in Honor of Abraham J. Malherbe*, edited by John T. Fitzgerald, Thomas H. Olbricht, and L. Michael White, 181–96. Supplements to Novum Testamentum 110. Leiden: Brill.

Hock, Ronald F., and Edward N. O'Neil. 1986. *The Progymnasmata*. Vol. 1 of *The Chreia in Ancient Rhetoric*. Society of Biblical Literature Texts and Translations 27. Atlanta: Scholars Press.

Hoehner, Harold W. 1972. *Herod Antipas*. New York: Cambridge University Press.

Hofer, Andrew. 2003. "The Old Man as Christ in Justin's *Dialogue with Trypho*." *Vigiliae Christianae* 57:1–21.

Holmes, Michael W., ed. and trans. 2007. *The Apostolic Fathers: Greek Texts and English Translations*. 3rd ed. Grand Rapids: Baker Academic.

Hooker, Morna D. 1997. *The Signs of a Prophet: The Prophetic Actions of Jesus*. Harrisburg, PA: Trinity.

Hornik, Heidi J., and Mikeal C. Parsons. 2003. *Illuminating Luke: The Infancy Narrative in Italian Renaissance Painting*. Harrisburg, PA: Trinity.

———. 2007. *The Passion and Resurrection Narratives in Italian Renaissance and Baroque Painting*. Vol. 3 of *Illuminating Luke*. Harrisburg, PA: Trinity.

Hornsby, Teresa J. 1998. "Why Is She Crying? A Feminist Interpretation of Luke 7:36–50." In *Escaping Eden: New Feminist Perspectives on the Bible*, edited by Harold C. Washington, Susan Lochrie Graham, and Pamela Thimmes, 91–103. Sheffield: Sheffield Academic Press.

Hubbard, Benjamin J. 1978. "The Role of Commissioning Accounts in Acts." In *Perspectives on Luke-Acts*, edited by Charles H. Talbert, 187–98. Danville, VA: Association of Baptist Professors of Religion.

Hubbell, H. M., trans. 1949. *Cicero: On Invention. The Best Kind of Orator. Topics.* Loeb Classical Library 386. Cambridge, MA: Harvard University Press.

Huffman, Norman A. 1945. "Emmaus among the Resurrection Narratives." *Journal of Biblical Literature* 64:205–26.

Humphrey, Edith M. 2007. *And I Turned to See the Voice: The Rhetoric of Vision in the New Testament*. Grand Rapids: Baker Academic.

Humphrey, Hugh M. 1991. "Temptation and Authority: Sapiential Narratives in Q." *Biblical Theology Bulletin* 21:43–50.

Isaac, Benjamin. 1990. *The Limits of Empire: The Roman Army in the East*. Oxford: Clarendon.

Jeffrey, David Lyle. 2012. *The Gospel of Luke*. Brazos Theological Commentary on the Bible. Grand Rapids: Brazos.

Jeremias, Joachim. 1963. *The Sermon on the Mount*. Philadelphia: Fortress.

———. 1966. *The Eucharistic Words of Jesus*. New York: Scribner.

———. 1969. *Jerusalem in the Time of Jesus: An Investigation into Economic and Social Conditions during the New Testament Period*. Philadelphia: Fortress.

———. 1972. *The Parables of Jesus*. New York: Scribner.

Jervell, Jacob. 1972. *Luke and the People of God: A New Look at Luke-Acts*. Minneapolis: Augsburg.

———. 1984. "The Daughters of Abraham: Women in Acts." In *The Unknown Paul: Essays on Luke-Acts and Early Christian History*, 146–57, 186–90. Minneapolis: Augsburg.

Johnson, Luke Timothy. 1977. *The Literary Function of Possessions in Luke-Acts*. Society of Biblical Literature Dissertation Series 39. Missoula, MT: Scholars Press.

———. 1979. "On Finding the Lukan Community: A Cautious Cautionary Essay." In *SBL Seminar Papers, 1979*, 1:77–100. 2 vols. Society of Biblical Literature Seminar Papers 16. Chico, CA: Scholars Press.

———. 1991. *The Gospel of Luke*. Sacra Pagina 3. Collegeville, MN: Liturgical Press.

———. 2005. "Literary Criticism of Luke-Acts: Is Reception History Pertinent?" *Journal for the Study of the New Testament* 28:159–62.

Juel, Donald. 1988. *Messianic Exegesis: Christological Interpretation of the Old Testament in Early Christianity*. Philadelphia: Fortress.

Just, Arthur A. 1993. *The Ongoing Feast: Table Fellowship and Eschatology at Emmaus*. Collegeville, MN: Liturgical Press.

———. 1996–97. *Luke*. 2 vols. Concordia Commentary. St. Louis: Concordia.

———, ed. 2003. *Luke*. Ancient Christian Commentary on Scripture. Downers Grove, IL: InterVarsity.

Kähler, Christoph. 1994. "Satanischer Schriftgebrauch: Zur Hermeneutik von Mt 4,1–11/Lk 4,1–13." *Theologische Literaturzeitung* 119:857–67.

Karris, Robert J. 1985. *Luke: Artist and Theologian; Luke's Passion Narrative as Literature*. New York: Paulist Press.

Keck, Leander. 1970–71. "The Spirit and the Dove." *New Testament Studies* 17:41–67.

Kee, Howard Clark. 1967–68. "The Terminology of Mark's Exorcism Stories." *New Testament Studies* 14:232–46.

Keener, Craig S. 2003. *The Gospel of John: A Commentary*. 2 vols. Peabody, MA: Hendrickson.

Kelhoffer, James A. 2000. *Miracle and Mission: The Authentication of Missionaries and Their Message in the Longer Ending of Mark*. Tübingen: Mohr Siebeck.

Kennedy, George A., ed. and trans. 2003. *Progymnasmata: Greek Textbooks of Prose Composition and Rhetoric*. Writings from the Greco-Roman World 10. Atlanta: Society of Biblical Literature.

Kilgallen, John J. 1985. "John the Baptist, the Sinful Woman, and the Pharisee." *Journal of Biblical Literature* 104:675–79.

Klassen, William. 1981. "'A Child of Peace' (Luke 10:6) in First Century Context." *New Testament Studies* 27:488–506.

Klein, Günter. 1964. "Lukas 1, 1–4 als Theologisches Programm." In *Zeit und Geschichte: Dankesgabe an Rudolf Bultmann zum 80. Geburtstag*, edited by Erich Dinkler, 193–216. Tübingen: Mohr.

Köppen, Klaus Peter. 1961. *Die Auslegung der Versuchungsgeschichte unter besonderer Berücksichtigung der Alten Kirche*. Tübingen: Mohr.

Krieger, Murray. 1992. *Ekphrasis: The Illusion of the Natural Sign*. Baltimore: Johns Hopkins University Press.

Kvalbein, Hans. 1998. "The Wonders of the End-Time: Metaphoric Language in 4Q521 and the Interpretation of Matthew 11.5 Par." *Journal for the Study of the Pseudepigrapha* 18:87–110.

Kwong, Ivan Shing Chung. 2005. *The Word Order of the Gospel of Luke: Its Foregrounded Messages*. Library of New Testament Studies 298. New York: T&T Clark.

Lambrecht, Jan. 1985. *The Sermon on the Mount: Proclamation and Exhortation*. Wilmington, DE: Glazier.

Landes, George M. 1996. "Jonah in Luke: The Hebrew Bible Background to the Interpretation of the 'Sign of Jonah' Pericope in Luke 11:29–32." In *Gift of God in Due Season*, edited by Richard D. Weis and David McLain Carr, 133–63. Sheffield: Sheffield Academic Press.

Laurentin, René. 1957. *Structure et théologie de Luc I–II*. Paris: Gabalda.

Leaney, A. R. C. 1961–62. "The Birth Narratives in St. Luke and St. Matthew." *New Testament Studies* 8:158–66.

Lee, Simon S. 2009. *Jesus' Transfiguration and the Believers' Transformation.* Wissenschaftliche Untersuchungen zum Neuen Testament 2/265. Tübingen: Mohr Siebeck.

Levinsohn, Stephen H. 1987. *Textual Connections in Acts.* Decatur, GA: Scholars Press.

———. 2000. *Discourse Features of New Testament Greek: A Coursebook on the Information Structure of New Testament Greek.* 2nd ed. Dallas: SIL.

Linnemann, Eta. 1970. *Studien zur Passionsgeschichte.* Göttingen: Vandenhoeck & Ruprecht.

Longenecker, Bruce W. 2008. "A Humorous Jesus? Orality, Structure and Characterisation in Luke 14:15–24, and Beyond." *Biblical Interpretation* 16:179–204.

———. 2009. "The Story of the Samaritan and the Innkeeper (Luke 10:30–35): A Study in Character Rehabilitation." *Biblical Interpretation* 17:422–47.

———. 2010. *Remember the Poor: Paul, Poverty, and the Greco-Roman World.* Grand Rapids: Eerdmans.

———. 2012. *Hearing the Silence: Jesus on the Edge and God in the Gap; Luke 4 in Narrative Perspective.* Eugene, OR: Wipf & Stock.

Lüdemann, Gerd. 1994. *The Resurrection of Jesus: History, Experience, Theology.* Translated by John Stephen Bowden. Minneapolis: Augsburg Fortress.

Luz, Ulrich. 2001–7. *Matthew: A Commentary.* Translated by James E. Crouch. 3 vols. Hermeneia. Minneapolis: Fortress.

Mack, Burton L., and Vernon K. Robbins. 1989. *Patterns of Persuasion in the Gospels.* Sonoma, CA: Polebridge.

Magness, Jodi. 2005. "Ossuaries and the Burials of Jesus and James." *Journal of Biblical Literature* 124:121–54.

Malherbe, Abraham J. 1996. "The Christianization of a *Topos* (Luke 12:13–34)." *Novum Testamentum* 38:123–35.

Malina, Bruce J. 1988. "Patron and Client: The Analogy behind Synoptic Theology." *Forum* 4:2–32.

Malina, Bruce J., and Jerome H. Neyrey. 1996. *Portraits of Paul: An Archaeology of Ancient Personality.* Louisville: Westminster John Knox.

Manson, Thomas Walter. 1949. *Sayings of Jesus.* London: SCM.

Marcus, Joel. 1995. "Jesus' Baptismal Vision." *New Testament Studies* 41:512–21.

———. 2006. "Crucifixion as Parodic Exaltation." *Journal of Biblical Literature* 125:73–87.

———. 2000–2009. *Mark.* 2 vols. Anchor Bible 27–27A. New Haven: Yale University Press.

Marcus, Ralph, trans. 1937. *Josephus: Jewish Antiquities, Books 9–11.* Loeb Classical Library 326. Cambridge, MA: Harvard University Press.

Marshall, I. Howard. 1978. *The Gospel of Luke: A Commentary on the Greek Text.* New International Greek Testament Commentary. Grand Rapids: Eerdmans.

———. 1993. "Acts and the 'Former Treatise.'" In *The Book of Acts in Its Ancient Literary Setting,* edited by Bruce W. Winter and Andrew D. Clarke, 163–82. Vol.

1 of *The Book of Acts in Its First Century Setting*. Edited by Bruce W. Winter. 5 vols. Grand Rapids: Eerdmans.

Martin, L. T., and D. Hurst, trans. 1990. *Bede the Venerable: Homilies on the Gospels*. 2 vols. Cistercian Studies 110–11. Kalamazoo, MI: Cistercian.

Martin, Michael W. 2005. "Defending the 'Western Non-Interpolations': The Case for Anti-Separationist Tendenz in the Longer Alexandrian Readings." *Journal of Biblical Literature* 124:269–94.

———. 2008. "Progymnastic Topic Lists: A Compositional Template for Luke and Other *Bioi*?" *New Testament Studies* 54:18–41.

Martini, Carlo Maria. 1999. "He Explained the Scripture to Us (Luke 24:32)." Translated by Henry Wansbrough. *SEDOS Bulletin* 31:112–17.

Maxwell, Kathy Reiko. 2010. *Hearing between the Lines: The Audience as Fellow-Workers in Luke-Acts and Its Literary Milieu*. New York: T&T Clark.

McCarthy, C., trans. and ed. 1993. *Saint Ephrem's Commentary on Tatian's Diatessaron: An English Translation of Chester Beatty Syriac MS 709*. Journal of Semitic Studies Supplement 2. Oxford: Oxford University Press.

McCown, Chester Charlton. 1939. "Luke's Translation of Semitic into Hellenistic Custom." *Journal of Biblical Literature* 58:213–20.

McIver, Robert K. 1994. "One Hundred-Fold Yield—Miraculous or Mundane? Matthew 13:8, 23; Mark 4:8, 20; Luke 8:8." *New Testament Studies* 40:606–8.

Meeks, Kenneth. 2000. *Driving While Black: Highways, Shopping Malls, Taxicabs, Sidewalks; How to Fight Back if You Are a Victim of Racial Profiling*. New York: Broadway Books.

Meier, John P. 1991–2009. *A Marginal Jew: Rethinking the Historical Jesus*. 4 vols. New York: Doubleday.

Mekkattukunnel, Andrews George. 2001. *The Priestly Blessing of the Risen Christ: An Exegetico-Theological Analysis of Luke 24,50–53*. New York: Peter Lang.

Menken, Martinus J. J. 1988. "The Position of *Splanchizesthai* and *Splanchna* in the Gospel of Luke." *Novum Testamentum* 30:107–14.

Metzger, Bruce Manning. 1980. *New Testament Studies, Philological, Versional, and Patristic*. Leiden: Brill.

———. 1994. *A Textual Commentary on the Greek New Testament*. 2nd ed. Stuttgart: Deutsche Bibelgesellschaft.

Meyer, Marvin, ed. 2007. *The Nag Hammadi Scriptures: The International Edition*. New York: HarperCollins.

Miller, David L. 1971. "Ἐμπαίζειν: Playing the Mock Game." *Journal of Biblical Literature* 90:309–13.

Mitchell, Alan C. 1990. "Zacchaeus Revisited: Luke 19:8 as a Defense." *Biblica* 71:153–76.

Moessner, David P. 1989. *Lord of the Banquet: The Literary and Theological Significance of the Lukan Travel Narrative*. Minneapolis: Augsburg Fortress.

———. 1996. "'Eyewitnesses,' 'Informed Contemporaries,' and 'Unknowing Inquirers': Josephus' Criteria for Authentic Historiography and the Meaning of παρακολουθέω." *Novum Testamentum* 38:105–22.

———. 1999a. "The Appeal and Power of Poetics (Luke 1:1–4): Luke's Superior Credentials (*Parēkolouthēkoti*), Narrative Sequence (*Kathexēs*), and Firmness of Understanding (*Hē Asphaleia*) for the Reader." In *Jesus and the Heritage of Israel: Luke's Narrative Claim upon Israel's Legacy*, edited by David P. Moessner, 84–123. Harrisburg, PA: Trinity.

———. 1999b. "The Lukan Prologues in the Light of Ancient Narrative Hermeneutics: *Parēkolouthēkoti* and the Credentialed Author." In *The Unity of Luke-Acts*, edited by Jozef Verheyden, 399–417. Louvain: Peeters.

———. 2008. "The Triadic Synergy of Hellenistic Poetics in the Narrative Epistemology of Dionysius of Halicarnassus and the Authorial Intent of the Evangelist Luke (Luke 1:1–4; Acts 1:1–8)." *Neotestamentica* 42:289–304.

Moessner, David P., Daniel Marguerat, Mikeal C. Parsons, and Michael Wolter, eds. 2012. *Paul and the Heritage of Israel: Paul's Claim upon Israel's Legacy in Luke and Acts in the Light of the Pauline Letters*. Library of New Testament Studies 452. New York: Continuum.

Moo, Douglas J. 1983. *The Old Testament in the Gospel Passion Narratives*. Sheffield: Almond.

Moore, Clifford H., and John Jackson, trans. 1931. *Tacitus: Histories, Books 4–5. Annals, Books 1–3*. Loeb Classical Library 249. London: Heinemann.

Morris, Leon. 1974. *The Gospel according to St. Luke*. Tyndale New Testament Commentaries. Grand Rapids: Eerdmans.

Muddiman, John B. 1992. "Fast, Fasting." In *The Anchor Bible Dictionary*, edited by David Noel Freedman, 2:773–76. 6 vols. New York: Doubleday.

Mullen, J. Patrick. 2004. *Dining with Pharisees*. Collegeville, MN: Liturgical Press.

Murray, A. T., trans. 1924. *Homer: Iliad, Books 1–12*. Loeb Classical Library 170. London: Heinemann.

Nave, Guy D., Jr. 2002. *The Role and Function of Repentance in Luke-Acts*. Atlanta: Society of Biblical Literature.

Neagoe, Alexandru. 2002. *The Trial of the Gospel: An Apologetic Reading of Luke's Trial Narratives*. Society for New Testament Studies Monograph Series 116. Cambridge: Cambridge University Press.

Neale, David A. 1991. *None but the Sinners: Religious Categories in the Gospel of Luke*. Sheffield: JSOT Press.

Nelson, Peter K. 1994. *Leadership and Discipleship: A Study of Luke 22:24–30*. Atlanta: Scholars Press.

Neyrey, Jerome H. 1980. "The Absence of Jesus' Emotions: The Lucan Redaction of Lk 22:39–46." *Biblica* 61:153–71.

———. 1985. *The Passion according to Luke: A Redaction Study of Luke's Soteriology*. New York: Paulist Press.

Nolland, John. 1989–93. *Luke*. 3 vols. Word Biblical Commentary. Dallas: Word.

Norton, Michael I., and Dan Ariely. 2011. "Building a Better America—One Wealth Quintile at a Time." *Perspectives on Psychological Science* 6:9–12.

Novakovic, Lidija. 2003. *Messiah, the Healer of the Sick: A Study of Jesus as the Son of David in the Gospel of Matthew*. Tübingen: Mohr Siebeck.

———. 2007. "4Q521: The Works of the Messiah or the Signs of the Messianic Time?" In *Qumran Studies: New Approaches, New Questions*, edited by Michael Thomas Davis and Brent A. Strawn, 208–31. Grand Rapids: Eerdmans.

O'Connor, Jerome Murphy. 1995. *Paul the Letter-Writer: His World, His Options, His Skills*. Collegeville, MN: Liturgical Press.

O'Day, Gail R. 2004. "'There the ? Will Gather Together' (Luke 17:37): Bird-Watching as an Exegetical Activity." In *Literary Encounters with the Reign of God*, edited by Sharon H. Ringe and H. C. Paul Kim, 288–303. New York: T&T Clark.

Oden, Thomas C., and Christopher A. Hall, eds. 1998. *Mark*. Ancient Christian Commentary on Scripture. Downers Grove, IL: InterVarsity.

O'Fearghail, Fearghus. 1991. *The Introduction to Luke-Acts: A Study of the Role of Lk 1,1–4,44 in the Composition of Luke's Two-Volume Work*. Analecta biblica 126. Rome: Pontifical Biblical Institute.

Omanson, Roger L. 2006. *A Textual Guide to the Greek New Testament: An Adaptation of Bruce Metzger's Textual Commentary for the Needs of Translators*. Stuttgart: Deutsche Bibelgesellschaft.

Orchard, R. K. 1937. "On the Composition of Luke 7,36–50." *Journal of Theological Studies* 38:243–45.

O'Toole, Robert F. 1987. "Luke's Message in Luke 9:1–50." *Catholic Biblical Quarterly* 49:74–89.

———. 1992. "Some Exegetical Reflections on Luke 13:10–17." *Biblica* 73:84–107.

Owen-Ball, David T. 1993. "Rabbinic Rhetoric and the Tribute Passage (Matt. 22:15–22; Mark 12:13–17; Luke 20:20–26)." *Novum Testamentum* 35:1–14.

Paffenroth, Kim. 1996. "The Testing of the Sage: 1 Kings 10:1–13 and Q 4:1–13 (Lk 4:1–13)." *Expository Times* 107:142–43.

Palmer, Darryl W. 1993. "Acts and the Ancient Historical Monograph." In *The Book of Acts in Its Ancient Literary Setting*, edited by Bruce W. Winter and Andrew D. Clarke, 1–29. Vol. 1 of *The Book of Acts in Its First Century Setting*. Edited by Bruce W. Winter. 5 vols. Grand Rapids: Eerdmans.

Parker, David C. 1997. *The Living Text of the Gospels*. Cambridge: Cambridge University Press.

Parsons, Mikeal C. 1986. "A Christological Tendency in $\mathfrak{P}^{75}$." *Journal of Biblical Literature* 105:463–79.

———. 1987. *The Departure of Jesus in Luke-Acts: The Ascension Narratives in Context*. Sheffield: JSOT Press.

———. 1990. "Reading a Beginning/Beginning a Reading: Tracing Literary Theory on Narrative Openings." *Semeia* 52:11–31.

———. 2005. "Mark 2:23–28." *Interpretation* 59:57–60.

———. 2007. *Luke: Storyteller, Interpreter, Evangelist*. Peabody, MA: Hendrickson.

———. 2008a. *Acts*. Paideia Commentaries on the New Testament. Grand Rapids: Baker Academic.

———. 2008b. "Exegesis 'By the Numbers': Numerology and the New Testament." *Perspectives in Religious Studies* 35:25–43.

———. 2009. "Hearing Acts as a Sequel to a Multiform Gospel: Historical and Hermeneutical Reflections on Acts, Luke, and the ΠΟΛΛΟΙ." In *Rethinking the Unity and Reception of Luke and Acts*, edited by Andrew F. Gregory and C. Kavin Rowe, 128–52. Columbia: University of South Carolina Press.

———. 2011. *Body and Character in Luke and Acts: The Subversion of Physiognomy in Early Christianity*. Waco: Baylor University Press.

Parsons, Mikeal C., and Richard I. Pervo. 1993. *Rethinking the Unity of Luke and Acts*. Minneapolis: Fortress.

Parsons, Mikeal C., and Jason Whitlark. 2006. "The 'Seven' Last Words: A Numerical Motivation for the Insertion of Luke 23:34a." *New Testament Studies* 52:188–204.

Paton, W. R., trans. 1925. *Polybius: The Histories, Books 9–15*. Loeb Classical Library 159. London: Heinemann.

Patillon, Michel, and Giancarlo Bolognesi, eds. and trans. 1997. *Aelius Theon: Progymnasmata*. Paris: Les Belles Lettres.

Payne, Philip B. 1978–79. "The Order of Sowing and Ploughing in the Parable of the Sower." *New Testament Studies* 25:123–29.

Penner, Todd C. 2003. "Reconfiguring the Rhetorical Study of Acts: Reflections on the Method in and Learning of a Progymnastic Poetics." *Perspectives in Religious Studies* 30:425–39.

Perry, Menakhem. 1979. "Literary Dynamics: How the Order of the Text Creates Its Meaning [with an Analysis of Faulkner's 'A Rose for Emily']." *Poetics Today* 1:35–64, 311–61.

Phillips, Jane E., trans. 2003. *Desiderius Erasmus: Paraphrase on Luke 11–24*. Toronto: University of Toronto Press.

Piper, John. 1979. *"Love Your Enemies": Jesus's Love Command in the Synoptic Gospels and in the Early Christian Paranesis; A History of the Tradition and Interpretation of Its Uses*. Society for New Testament Studies Monograph Series 38. Cambridge: Cambridge University Press.

Pitre, Brant James. 2001. "Blessing the Barren and Warning the Fecund: Jesus' Message for Women concerning Pregnancy and Childbirth." *Journal for the Study of the New Testament* 81:59–80.

Plummer, Alfred. 1903. *A Critical and Exegetical Commentary on the Gospel according to St. Luke*. 6th ed. International Critical Commentary. New York: Scribner's.

Porter, Stanley E. 1989. *Verbal Aspect in the Greek of the New Testament, with Reference to Tense and Mood*. Studies in Biblical Greek 1. New York: Peter Lang.

Powell, Mark Alan. 1990. "Types of Readers and Their Relevance for Biblical Hermeneutics." *Trinity Seminary Review* 12:67–76.

———. 2001. *Chasing the Eastern Star: Adventures in Biblical Reader-Response Criticism*. Louisville: Westminster John Knox.

Price, Robert M. 1997. *Widow Traditions in Luke-Acts*. Atlanta: Scholars Press.

Prince, Deborah Thompson. 2007. "The 'Ghost' of Jesus: Luke 24 in Light of Ancient Narratives of Post-Mortem Apparitions." *Journal for the Study of the New Testament* 29:287–301.

Rabinowitz, Peter J. 1987. *Before Reading: Narrative Conventions and the Politics of Interpretation*. Ithaca, NY: Cornell University Press.

Rackham, H., trans. 1935. *Aristotle: Athenian Constitution. Eudemian Ethics. Virtues and Vices*. Loeb Classical Library 285. Cambridge, MA: Harvard University Press.

Rau, Gottfried. 1965. "Das Volk in der lukanischen Passionsgeschichte: Eine Konjektur zu Lk 23:13." *Zeitschrift für die neutestamentliche Wissenschaft und die Kunde der älteren Kirche* 56:41–51.

Reardon, Bryan P., trans. 1989. "Chariton: *Chaereas and Callirhoe*." In *Collected Ancient Greek Novels*, edited by B. P. Reardon, 17–124. Berkeley: University of California Press.

Rehkopf, Friedrich. 1959. *Die lukanische Sonderquelle: Ihr Umfang und Sprachgebrauch*. Wissenschaftliche Untersuchungen zum Neuen Testament 5. Tübingen: Mohr.

Reich, Keith A. 2011. *Figuring Jesus: The Power of Rhetorical Figures of Speech in the Gospel of Luke*. Leiden: Brill.

Reicke, Bo Ivar. 1978. "Jesus, Simeon and Anna (Luke 2:21–40)." In *Saved by Hope: Essays in Honor of Richard C. Oudersluys*, edited by James I. Cook, 96–108. Grand Rapids: Eerdmans.

Reid, Barbara E. 1996. *Choosing the Better Part: Women in the Gospel of Luke*. Collegeville, MN: Liturgical Press.

Renan, Joseph Ernest. 1863. *La vie de Jésus*. Paris: Michel Levy Freres.

Rhoads, David, and Donald Michie. 1982. *Mark as Story: An Introduction to the Narrative of a Gospel*. Philadelphia: Fortress.

Richardson, Peter. 1996. *Herod: King of the Jews and Friend of the Romans*. Columbia: University of South Carolina Press.

Riesner, Rainer. 2007. "Wo lag das neutestamentliche Emmaus (Lukas 24,13)?" *Zeitschrift für antikes Christentum* 11:201–20.

Rimmon-Kenan, Shlomith. 2002. *Narrative Fiction: Contemporary Poetics*. London: Routledge.

Robbins, Vernon K. 1978. "By Land and by Sea: The We-Passages [in Acts] and Ancient Sea Voyages." In *Perspectives on Luke-Acts*, edited by Charles H. Talbert, 215–42. Danville, VA: Association of Baptist Professors of Religion.

Robinson, James McConkey, Paul Hoffmann, and John S. Kloppenborg, eds. 2000. *The Critical Edition of Q: A Synopsis including the Gospels of Matthew and Luke, Mark and Thomas with English, German, and French Translations of Q and Thomas*. Hermeneia. Minneapolis: Fortress.

Rohrbaugh, Richard L. 1991. "The Pre-Industrial City in Luke-Acts: Urban Social Relations." In *The Social World of Luke-Acts: Models for Interpretation*, edited by Jerome H. Neyrey, 125–49. Peabody, MA: Hendrickson.

Rolfe, J. C., trans. 1914. *Julius. Augustus. Tiberius. Gaius Caligula*. Vol. 1 of *Suetonius: Lives of the Caesars*. Loeb Classical Library 31. London: Heinemann.

Roth, S. John. 1997. *The Blind, the Lame, and the Poor: Character Types in Luke-Acts*. Sheffield: Sheffield Academic Press.

Rowe, C. Kavin. 2005. "History, Hermeneutics and the Unity of Luke-Acts." *Journal for the Study of the New Testament* 28:131–57.

———. 2006. *Early Narrative Christology: The Lord in the Gospel of Luke*. Berlin: de Gruyter.

———. 2007. "Literary Unity and Reception History: Reading Luke-Acts as Luke and Acts." *Journal for the Study of the New Testament* 29:449–57.

Russell, Donald A., trans. 2001. *Quintilian: The Orator's Education, Books 3–5*. Loeb Classical Library 125. Cambridge, MA: Harvard University Press.

Ruzer, Serge. 2002. "From 'Love Your Neighbor' to 'Love Your Enemy': Trajectories in Early Jewish Exegesis." *Revue biblique* 109:371–89.

Ryan, William Granger, trans. 1995. *Jacobus de Voragine*. Vol. 1 of *The Golden Legend: Readings on the Saints*. Princeton, NJ: Princeton University Press.

Safrai, Shemuel. 1999. "The Synagogue the Centurion Built." *Jerusalem Perspective* 55:12–14.

Said, Edward W. 1985. *Beginnings: Intention and Method*. Rev. ed. New York: Columbia University Press.

Saller, Richard. 2003. "Women, Slaves, and the Economy of the Roman Household." In *Early Christian Families in Context: An Interdisciplinary Dialogue*, edited by David L. Balch and Carolyn Osiek, 185–204. Grand Rapids: Eerdmans.

Sams, Ferrol. 1991. *When All the World Was Young*. Atlanta: Longstreet.

Sanders, E. P. 1993. *The Historical Figure of Jesus*. New York: Penguin.

Sawyer, Ronald D. 1949–50. "Was Peter the Companion of Cleopas on Easter Afternoon?" *Expository Times* 61:91–93.

Schneider, Gerhard. 1977. *Das Evangelium nach Lukas*. 2 vols. Ökumenischer Taschenbuch-Kommentar zum Neuen Testament. Würzburg: Echter Verlag.

Schottroff, Luise. 1995. *Lydia's Impatient Sisters: A Feminist Social History of Early Christianity*. Louisville: Westminster John Knox.

Schrage, Wolfgang. 1964. *Das Verhältnis des Thomas-Evangeliums zur synoptischen Tradition und zu den koptischen Evangelienübersetzungen*. Berlin: Töpelmann.

Schürmann, Heinz. 1963. "Das Thomasevangelium und das lukanische Sondergut." *Biblische Zeitschrift* 7:236–60.

———. 1982. *Kommentar zu Kap. 1,1–9,50*. Vol. 1 of *Das Lukasevangelium*. 2nd ed. Herders theologischer Kommentar zum Neuen Testament 3/1. Freiburg: Herder.

Scott, Bernard Brandon. 1989. *Hear Then the Parable: A Commentary on the Parables of Jesus*. Minneapolis: Augsburg Fortress.

Seim, Turid Karlsen. 1994. *The Double Message: Patterns of Gender in Luke and Acts*. Nashville: Abingdon.

———. 2001. "Abraham, Ancestor or Archetype? A Comparison of Abraham-Language in 4 Maccabees and Luke-Acts." In *Antiquity and Humanity: Essays on Ancient Religion and Philosophy, Presented to Hans Dieter Betz on His 70th Birthday*, edited by Adela Yarbro Collins and Margaret M. Mitchell, 27–42. Tübingen: Mohr Siebeck.

Sellew, Philip. 1992. "Interior Monologue as a Narrative Device in the Parables of Luke." *Journal of Biblical Literature* 111:239–53.

Senior, Donald. 1989. *The Passion of Jesus in the Gospel of Luke*. Passion Series 3. Wilmington, DE: Glazier.

Sheeley, Steven M. 1992. *Narrative Asides in Luke-Acts*. Journal for the Study of the New Testament Supplement Series 72. Sheffield: JSOT Press.

Shelton, Jo-Ann. 1998. *As the Romans Did: A Sourcebook in Roman Social History*. 2nd ed. Oxford: Oxford University Press.

Shiell, William David. 2004. *Reading Acts: The Lector and the Early Christian Audience*. Leiden: Brill.

Shiner, Whitney T. 2003. *Proclaiming the Gospel: First-Century Performance of Mark*. New York: Trinity.

Shuler, Philip L. 1975. "The Synoptic Gospels and the Problem of Genre." PhD diss., McMaster University.

———. 1982. *A Genre for the Gospels: The Biographical Character of Matthew*. Philadelphia: Fortress.

———. 1990. "The Genre(s) of the Gospels." In *Interrelations of the Gospels*, edited by David Laird Dungan, 459–83. Louvain: Leuven University Press.

Sider, Ronald J., Philip N. Olson, and Heidi Rolland Unruh. 2002. *Churches That Make a Difference: Reaching Your Community with Good News and Good Works*. Grand Rapids: Baker Books.

Siker, Jeffrey S. 1991. *Disinheriting the Jews: Abraham in Early Christian Controversy*. Louisville: Westminster John Knox.

Simon, Maurice, trans. 1983. "Song of Songs Rabbah." In *Esther. Song of Songs*, edited by H. Freedman and M. Simon, 1–327. Vol. 9 in *Midrash Rabbah*. 3rd ed. London: Soncino.

Smith, Dennis E., Michael E. Williams, Jo-Ann Elizabeth Jennings, Pam McGrath, and Mikeal C. Parsons. 2005. *Synoptic Stories about Jesus*. Vol. 9 of *Storyteller's Companion to the Bible*. Edited by Dennis E. Smith and Michael E. Williams. Nashville: Abingdon.

Smith, R. Payne, trans. 1983. *Saint Cyril of Alexandria: Commentary on the Gospel of Saint Luke*. Long Island, NY: Studion.

Snodgrass, Klyne. 1972. "Western Non-Interpolations." *Journal of Biblical Literature* 91:369–79.

———. 1997. "*Anaideia* and the Friend at Midnight (Luke 11:8)." *Journal of Biblical Literature* 116:505–13.

Soards, Marion L. 1987a. *The Passion according to Luke: The Special Material of Luke 22*. Sheffield: JSOT Press.

———. 1987b. "Tradition, Composition, and Theology in Jesus' Speech to the Daughters of Jerusalem." *Biblica* 68:221–44.

Spencer, Patrick E. 2007. "The Unity of Luke-Acts: A Four-Bolted Hermeneutical Hinge." *Currents in Biblical Research* 5:341–66.

Squires, John T. 1993. *The Plan of God in Luke-Acts*. Society for New Testament Studies Monograph Series 76. Cambridge: Cambridge University Press.

Stambaugh, John E., and David L. Balch. 1986. *The New Testament in Its Social Environment*. Philadelphia: Westminster.

Stanley, David M. 1980. *Jesus in Gethsemane*. New York: Paulist Press.

Stegman, Thomas D. 2007. "Reading Luke 12:13–34 as an Elaboration of a Chreia: How Hermogenes of Tarsus Sheds Light on Luke's Gospel." *Novum Testamentum* 49:328–52.

Stegner, William Richard. 1990. "The Temptation Narrative: A Study in the Use of Scripture by Early Jewish Christians." *Biblical Research* 35:5–17.

Steiner, M. 1962. *La tentation de Jésus dans l'interprétation patristique de Saint Justin à Origène*. Études bibliques. Paris: Gabalda.

Sterling, Gregory E. 2001. "*Mors Philosophi*: The Death of Jesus in Luke." *Harvard Theological Review* 94:383–402.

Sternberg, Meir. 1978. *Expositional Modes and Temporal Ordering in Fiction*. Baltimore: Johns Hopkins University Press.

Strauss, David Friedrich. 1835–36. *Das Leben Jesu kritisch bearbeitet*. Tübingen: Osiander.

Strauss, Mark L. 1995. *The Davidic Messiah in Luke-Acts: The Promise and Its Fulfillment in Lukan Christology*. Sheffield: Sheffield Academic Press.

Talbert, Charles H. 1977. *What Is a Gospel? The Genre of the Canonical Gospels*. Philadelphia: Fortress.

———. 1980. "Prophecies of Future Greatness: The Contributions of Greco-Roman Biographies to an Understanding of Luke 1:5–4:15." In *Divine Helmsman: Studies of God's Control of Human Events, Presented to Lou H. Silberman*, edited by James L. Crenshaw and Samuel Sandmel, 129–41. New York: Ktav.

———. 1982. *Reading Luke: A Literary and Theological Commentary on the Third Gospel*. Macon, GA: Smyth & Helwys.

———. 1991. *Learning through Suffering: The Educational Value of Suffering in the New Testament and Its Milieu*. Collegeville, MN: Liturgical Press.

———. 1998. "Conversion in the Acts of the Apostles: Ancient Auditors' Perceptions." In *Literary Studies in Luke-Acts: Essays in Honor of Joseph B. Tyson*, edited by Richard P. Thompson and Thomas E. Phillips, 141–53. Macon, GA: Mercer University Press.

———. 2002. *Reading Luke: A Literary and Theological Commentary on the Third Gospel*. Rev. ed. Macon, GA: Smyth & Helwys.

———. 2003. *Reading Luke-Acts in Its Mediterranean Milieu*. Supplements to Novum Testamentum 107. Leiden: Brill.

———. 2006. *Reading the Sermon on the Mount: Character Formation and Decision Making in Matthew 5–7*. Grand Rapids: Baker Academic.

Tannehill, Robert C. 1986–90. *The Narrative Unity of Luke-Acts: A Literary Interpretation*. 2 vols. Foundations and Facets. Minneapolis: Fortress.

———. 1994. "Should We Love Simon the Pharisee? Hermeneutical Reflections on the Pharisees in Luke." *Currents in Theology and Mission* 21:424–33.

———. 1996. *Luke*. Abingdon New Testament Commentaries. Nashville: Abingdon.

Taylor, Nicholas H. 2001. "The Temptation of Jesus on the Mountain: A Palestinian Christian Polemic against Agrippa I." *Journal for the Study of the New Testament* 83:27–49.

Taylor, Vincent. 1972. *The Passion Narrative of St. Luke: A Critical and Historical Investigation.* Cambridge: Cambridge University Press.

Thackeray, H. St. J., trans. 1927. *Josephus: The Jewish War, Books 1 and 2.* Loeb Classical Library 203. London: Heinemann.

———, trans. 1928. *Josephus: The Jewish War, Books 5–7.* Loeb Classical Library 210. London: Heinemann.

Thackeray, H. St. J., and Ralph Marcus, trans. 1930. *Josephus: Jewish Antiquities, Books 4–6.* Loeb Classical Library 490. London: Heinemann.

Thorley, John. 1979. "The Nativity Census: What Does Luke Actually Say?" *Greece & Rome*, 2nd series, 26:81–84.

Tiede, David L. 1980. *Prophecy and History in Luke-Acts.* Philadelphia: Fortress.

———. 1988. *Luke.* Augsburg Commentary on the New Testament. Minneapolis: Fortress.

Tolkien, J. R. R. 1957. *The Lord of the Rings: The Return of the King.* London: Allen & Unwin.

Tomkinson, T., trans. 1998. *St. Ambrose of Milan: Exposition of the Holy Gospel according to Saint Luke with Fragments on the Prophecy of Isaias.* Etna, CA: Center for Traditionalist Orthodox Studies.

Topel, L. John. 2001. *Children of a Compassionate God: A Theological Exegesis of Luke 6:20–49.* Collegeville, MN: Liturgical Press.

Trudinger, L. Paul. 1974–75. "Davidic Links with the Betrayal of Jesus: Some Observations." *Expository Times* 86:278–79.

Tucker, Jeffrey T. 1998. *Example Stories: Perspectives on Four Parables in the Gospel of Luke.* Sheffield: Sheffield Academic Press.

Tuckett, Christopher M. 1992. "The Temptation Narrative in Q." In *The Four Gospels 1992: Festschrift Frans Neirynck,* edited by Frans van Segbroek and C. M. Tuckett, 1:479–507. Bibliotheca ephemeridum theologicarum lovaniensium 100. Louvain: Peeters.

Udoh, Fabian E. 2005. *To Caesar What Is Caesar's: Tribute, Taxes, and Imperial Administration in Early Roman Palestine 63 B.C.E–70 C.E.* Brown Judaic Studies 343. Providence: Brown Judaic Studies.

Unnik, Willem Cornelis van. 1973. "Remarks on the Purpose of Luke's Historical Writing (Luke 1:1–4)." In *Sparsa Collecta: The Collected Essays of W. C. van Unnik,* 6–15. Supplements to Novum Testamentum 29. Leiden: Brill.

Vielhauer, Philipp Adam Christoph. 1963. "On the 'Paulinism' of Acts." *Perkins School of Theology Journal* 17:5–18.

Vince, J. H., trans. 1935. *Orations 21–26: Against Meidias. Against Androtion. Against Aristocrates. Against Timocrates. Against Aristogeiton 1 and 2.* Vol. 3 of *Demosthenes.* Loeb Classical Library 299. Cambridge, MA: Harvard University Press.

Vinson, Richard B. 2008. *Luke.* Smith & Helwys Bible Commentary. Macon, GA: Smith & Helwys.

Votaw, C. W. 1915. "The Gospels and Contemporary Biographies." *American Journal of Theology* 19:45–73, 217–49.

Wallace, Daniel B. 1996. *Greek Grammar beyond the Basics: An Exegetical Syntax of the New Testament*. Grand Rapids: Zondervan.

Weissenrieder, Annette. 2003. *Images of Illness in the Gospel of Luke: Insights of Ancient Medical Texts*. Wissenschaftliche Untersuchungen zum Neuen Testament 2/164. Tübingen: Mohr Siebeck.

Westcott, Brooke Foss, and Fenton John Anthony Hort. 1881. *The New Testament in the Original Greek*. New York: Harper.

White, K. D. 1964. "The Parable of the Sower." *Journal of Theological Studies* 15:300–307.

Wilkinson, John. 1980. *Health and Healing: Studies in New Testament Principles and Practice*. Edinburgh: Handsel.

Williams, Burma P., and Richard S. Williams. 1995. "Finger Numbers in the Roman World and the Early Middle Ages." *Isis* 86:587–608.

Wink, Walter. 1968. *John the Baptist in the Gospel Tradition*. Society for New Testament Studies Monograph Series 7. Cambridge: Cambridge University Press.

Witherington, Ben, III. 1984. *Women in the Ministry of Jesus*. Cambridge: Cambridge University Press.

Wolterstorff, Nicholas. 2008. *Justice: Rights and Wrongs*. Princeton, NJ: Princeton University Press.

Wood, Ralph C. 2003. *The Gospel according to Tolkien: Visions of the Kingdom in Middle-Earth*. Louisville: Westminster John Knox.

Woods, Edward. 2001. *The Finger of God and Pneumatology in Luke-Acts*. Journal for the Study of the New Testament: Supplement Series 205. Sheffield: Sheffield Academic Press.

Wright, N. T. 1996. *Jesus and the Victory of God*. Vol. 2 of *Christian Origins and the Question of God*. Minneapolis: Fortress.

———. 2003. *The Resurrection of the Son of God*. Vol. 3 of *Christian Origins and the Question of God*. Minneapolis: Fortress.

Wuellner, Wilhelm. 1967. *The Meaning of "Fishers of Men."* New Testament Library. Philadelphia: Westminster.

York, John O. 1991. *The Last Shall Be First: The Rhetoric of Reversal in Luke*. Journal for the Study of the New Testament: Supplement Series 46. Sheffield: JSOT Press.

Young, Robin Darling. 1991. "The 'Woman with the Soul of Abraham': Traditions about the Mother of the Maccabean Martyrs." In *"Women Like This": New Perspectives on Jewish Women in the Greco-Roman World*, edited by Amy-Jill Levine, 67–81. Atlanta: Scholars Press.

Zafiropoulos, Christos A. 2001. *Ethics in Aesop's Fables: The Augustana Collection*. Mnemosyne Supplements 216. Leiden: Brill.

Index of Subjects

Aaron, 23, 34, 156, 157, 191, 328
Abel, 198–99
Abijah, 23, 34
Abraham, 36–37, 39, 42–43, 47, 66, 69, 70, 168, 181, 190, 218, 219, 220, 223, 241, 250, 251, 280, 286, 296, 338, 339
abyss, 139–40
Acts of the Apostles
　date of, 19, 26
　relationship to the Gospel of Luke, 10–11
　as sequel to multiple Gospels, 12, 19
　text of, 112
　"we" passages, 5–6
Adam, 70, 71, 73, 74, 241
Ahab, 68, 328
alliteration, 134
almsgiving, 109, 196, 208
Ananias (husband of Sapphira), 203
anaphora, 174
Andrew, 87, 99
angels, 23, 35, 36, 37, 38, 39, 40, 43, 53, 54, 73, 83, 152, 154, 192, 202, 208, 212, 237, 250, 296, 304, 320, 348, 350. *See also* Gabriel
Anna, 54, 56, 264
Annas, 64
anti-family sayings, 229
Antioch, 6, 8
Antiochus IV Epiphanes, 138
antithesis (*contentio*), 200, 211, 270, 298
Apollos, 69
aposiopesis, 319
Aquila, 171
Archelaus, 53

Arimathea, 345, 346
ascension, 155, 156, 163, 318
Augustus, 34, 49–50, 53, 82, 266, 294
authorial audience 4, 11, 12–13, 16–19, 21, 26, 28, 31, 35, 50, 53, 54, 58, 59, 66, 68, 71, 81, 86, 87, 89, 90, 91, 92, 93, 94, 96, 98, 100, 103, 105, 117, 124, 128, 129, 132, 137, 138, 139, 140, 141, 143, 149, 150–51, 156, 164, 168, 172, 176, 182, 209, 210, 211, 215, 224, 226, 240, 245, 246, 248, 253, 265, 270, 277, 279, 280, 282, 299, 304, 305, 324, 325, 328, 329, 337, 341, 350, 352, 355, 357
autonomasia, 198

baptism, 15, 21, 28, 62–70, 75, 81, 126, 128, 152, 176, 211, 291–92
Barabbas, 332–33, 338
Barnabas, 8, 171
Bartholomew, 99
beatitude (makarism), 41, 125, 178, 189, 192, 209, 210, 225, 227, 283, 334
　in the Sermon on the Plain, 100–106
Beelzebul controversy, 190–92
Benedictus, 44, 45, 46–49, 55
benefaction, 108–10, 116–21, 122, 123, 186, 312–13
Bethany, 282, 355
Bethlehem, 23, 60
Bethphage, 282
Bethsaida, 149, 174–75
biography (*bios/bioi*), 13–15, 19, 21, 25, 27, 45, 64, 69, 86, 163, 204, 287, 307, 340, 344. *See also* encomium

Index of Subjects

blind beggar, 136, 257, 275–77, 280, 284
brevitas, 331

Cadbury, Henry J., 7
Caesar. *See* Augustus; Caligula; Julius Caesar; Tiberius; Vespasian
Caesarea Philippi, 151
Caiaphas, 64, 323
Cain, 241
Caligula, 202
Callirhoe, 130
Capernaum, 79, 82, 84–86, 90, 91, 117, 118, 175
census, 47, 49–50
centurion
 at the cross, 106, 212–13, 335, 340, 341
 with a sick slave, 108, 116–21, 123, 125
Cheltenham Canon, 10
chiasm, 41, 80–81, 116, 179, 349
chief priests. *See* priests
children, 36, 127, 159, 178, 186, 199, 252, 267–68, 271, 276, 284, 335
Chorazin, 174–75
chreia, 89, 93, 97, 171, 189, 203–7, 239
 of action, 148, 149, 150, 312, 351
 apocritic/responsive, 168–70, 175–80, 203, 204, 262
 mixed, 160
Christ. *See* Messiah
Cleopas, 350, 352, 357
Codex Bezae, 10, 352
Codex Claromontanus, 10
coins, Roman, 202, 294–95, 298
commonplace. *See* topos
commutatio, 153
comparison. *See* synkrisis
compassion, 106–7, 111, 116, 121, 122, 144, 180, 181, 182, 187, 202, 215, 239, 242, 263, 298, 314, 335
conduplicatio, 138, 182–83, 225, 314, 333
contentio. *See* antithesis
Cornelius, 29, 118, 152
correctio, 269
counting, on one's hands, 236–37
crowd (*ochlos/ochloi*), 321, 328, 340, 341–42. *See also* people (*laos*)
Crucifixion, the, 42, 133, 333–42
Cynics, 173, 226, 275

daughter of Abraham, 66, 218–20
daughters of Jerusalem, 335
David, 15, 23, 38, 39, 40, 46, 49, 53, 54, 68, 70, 96–97, 241, 276, 277, 283, 297, 318

demons, 81, 84, 85, 86, 127, 133, 136, 137, 138–40, 144, 146, 152, 158–59, 160, 176, 190–92, 193, 198, 218, 224, 269, 276, 313–14, 319. *See also* exorcisms
devil, the. *See* Satan
dialogue, 36, 38, 66–67, 93, 179, 189, 200, 268, 270, 271, 291, 299, 355
dikaios, 106, 213, 341, 346
disciples
 argue about who is the greatest, 159
 ask Jesus about parables, 134–36, 253
 ask Jesus to increase their faith, 252–53
 disbelieve the women's report, 349
 fail to cast out spirit of epilepsy, 158
 fail to understand passion predictions, 159
 female disciples, 132–34, 335, 340, 341, 342, 347, 348
 fishermen called, 87–89
 in Gethsemane, 321
 lack of faith of, 138
 Levi called, 87, 92–93, 133, 144, 354
 mission of the seventy(-two), 147, 167, 170–78
 mission of the Twelve, 145, 146–47, 170, 171
 participate in feeding of the five thousand, 149–51
 risen Jesus appears to, 353–56
 Satan's desire to sift them, 314–15
 scold people for bringing children to Jesus, 267–68
 at the Transfiguration, 154–57
 Twelve chosen, 99–100
discipleship sayings, 153–54
divorce, 249
dream-vision, 33–40, 53–54, 154–57

eagles, 262
education (*paideia*), 17–18, 91, 331
ekphrasis, 69, 155, 321. *See also* oracular demonstration
elaboration (*exergasia*), 89, 93, 150, 170, 175–78, 189, 203–8, 312. *See also chreia*
elders, 117–20, 152, 291, 322, 325, 326
Elijah, 36, 68, 83, 122–23, 124, 147–48, 151, 152, 155–57, 159, 163, 167, 168, 328
Elisha, 83, 117, 151, 170, 258
Elizabeth, 23, 33, 34, 36, 37, 38, 39, 42–43, 48, 73, 346
 gives birth to John the Baptist, 44–45
 visited by Mary, 40–42
Emmaus, 148, 150, 349–57

Index of Subjects

encomium, 13–15, 22, 44, 45, 67, 68, 123, 126, 176, 194, 197, 203, 204, 282, 307, 339, 340, 344, 346
enthymeme, 97, 170
entimos, 118
epanadiplosis, 138
epanaphora, 134, 146, 199
epecheirēsan, 27
Ephraim, 241
Esau, 241, 242
eschatological banquet, 102, 105, 209, 216, 223, 227–29, 272, 310, 319, 354
eschatological discourse, 299–305
Essenes, 315
eternal life, 164, 179, 248, 269, 271, 354
ethos, 17–18
eudokia(s), 54
Eve, 57, 74
exclamatio, 196, 323
exemplum, 179
exergasia. *See* elaboration
exodus (*exodos*), 71, 156, 163, 167, 230, 275, 308–9, 355
exorcisms, 86, 290
  of a boy with a spirit of epilepsy, 157–59
  of the Gerasene demoniac, 138–40
  of a man in the Capernaum synagogue, 84–85
  of Mary Magdalene, 133
  of a mute man, 190–92
  performed by one not following Jesus, 160
  performed by the seventy(-two), 176
eyewitnesses, 5, 6, 7, 26, 27, 28, 178
Ezekiel, 169

fable, 184, 185, 186, 239, 248
faith, 41, 42, 91, 92, 120, 121, 131, 136, 138, 141, 142, 143, 144, 160, 207, 219, 252–53, 258, 265, 269, 277, 314, 315, 319
Farrer hypothesis, 13, 325
fasting, 56, 75, 93–95, 266
Father, as title for God, 23, 59, 111, 154, 178, 183, 186, 207, 314, 319, 320, 337, 340, 355
Feasts
  of Dedication, 283
  of Tabernacles, 283
  of Unleavened Bread, 307, 308
  See also Passover; Pentecost
Festus, 329
forgiveness, 48, 65, 69, 75, 82, 92, 112, 130–32, 156, 191, 203, 251–52, 272, 315, 337, 339, 355
friendship, 118, 183–88, 330

Gabriel, 28, 37–39, 45, 72, 73, 139
Galilee, 23, 38, 56, 64, 77, 79, 80, 84, 87, 90, 104, 118, 133, 138, 173, 174, 256, 328, 329, 335, 340, 341, 342, 346, 347, 348
Gehenna, 201, 208
Gentiles, 5, 7, 8, 9, 18, 29, 49, 56, 83, 117, 120, 125, 136, 140, 147, 170, 171, 173, 175, 204, 207, 223, 224, 274, 286, 290, 302–3, 312, 330, 339
Gethsemane, 156, 307, 317–23
Gideon, 38–39
Gloria in Excelsis, 55
gnostics, 321
Golden Rule, 100, 110, 112
good Samaritan. *See* parables
great omission, 151
great reversal. *See* reversal
greed, 189, 196, 203–8, 226, 278

Hades, 175, 250–51
hair, women's, 129–30
Hannah, 38, 55, 338
healings
  of a bent woman, 216–20, 304
  of a blind beggar, 275–77
  of a boy with a spirit of epilepsy, 157–59
  of a centurion's servant, 108, 116–21, 123, 125
  of the high priest's servant, 322
  of a leper, 90, 257–58
  of a man with a withered hand, 97–99
  of a man with dropsy, 225–26
  of a paralytic, 90–92, 291
  of Peter's mother-in-law, 85–86
  of ten lepers, 121, 256–58, 275
  by the Twelve, 147
  of a woman with a hemorrhage, 141–42, 144
  See also exorcisms; resuscitations
Herod Agrippa II, 329
Herod Antipas, 64, 118, 133
  arrest/imprisonment of John the Baptist by, 46, 68
  beheading of John the Baptist by, 148, 329
  desire to kill Jesus, 148, 224–25, 329
  examination of Jesus by, 148, 190, 274, 324, 329–30, 331, 339, 341
  perplexity concerning Jesus's identity, 145, 147–48, 151, 152, 153, 157
Herodias, 68
Herod Philip, 64, 68, 149
Herod the Great, 34, 60, 329
Hobart, William K., 7

Index of Subjects

Holy Spirit, 6, 36, 40, 46, 49, 55, 57, 67, 80, 85, 105, 138, 152, 176, 178, 183, 186, 191, 203
   blasphemy against, 202–3
   and Jesus's baptism, 62–63, 68–69, 81
   and Jesus's conception, 23, 39, 60
   and Jesus's temptation, 74, 318
   at Pentecost, 211
hospitality, 51, 66, 86, 131, 146–47, 149, 150, 159, 168, 173, 182–83, 186–88, 223, 268, 279, 316
hyperbaton, 4, 97, 222
hyperbole, 196, 200, 229, 252, 270, 328
hypophora, 179, 292, 295

imago (simile), 197, 220
infancy narrative, 59–61
inflection (*polyptoton/klisis*), 35, 185, 239–41, 285
innocence, 330, 331, 338, 339, 341
interrogatio. See rhetorical question
intertextuality, 12–13, 17, 122, 151, 170, 282–84, 302
invective, 65, 67, 175, 189, 194, 197, 279, 282
Isaac, 42–43, 223, 241, 296
Ishmael, 241

Jacob, 15, 39, 223, 241, 242, 296, 320–21
Jairus, 136, 141–44
James (son of Alphaeus), 100
James (son of Zebedee), 87, 89, 93, 99, 100, 143, 154, 156, 168, 173, 181, 271, 309
Jannes and Jambres, 251
Jehoiakim, 263
Jehoshaphat, 263
Jehu, 283
Jeremiah, 155, 169, 338
Jericho, 180, 275, 277, 279, 280
Jerusalem 5, 6, 7, 15, 16, 23, 29, 54, 55, 56, 57, 58, 59, 73, 83–84, 90, 101, 103, 105, 150, 156, 163, 167, 168, 180, 201, 211, 213, 214, 215, 221, 224, 225, 227, 230, 256, 270, 273, 275, 281, 282, 283, 284, 289, 299, 300, 301, 302, 303, 309, 313, 318, 324, 329, 333, 335, 336, 349, 350, 352, 354, 355, 357
Jesus
   accused of being an agent of Beelzebul, 190–92
   action in the temple of, 289–91
   annunciation of birth of, 38–42
   anointing by a sinful woman of, 127–32
   arrest of, 321–23
   ascension of, 155, 355
   baptism of, 15, 21, 28, 62–64, 68–70, 75, 81, 176
   birth of, 49–54
   burial of, 345–48
   compared to John the Baptist, 21–24, 39, 62, 67–68
   crucifixion of, 42, 133, 333–42
   death of, 14, 15, 34, 230, 285, 334, 338, 340, 351, 354
   eschatological discourse of, 299–305
   genealogy of, 70
   Messianic identity of. *See* Messiah
   mockery of, 324–25
   nurture and training of, 57–59, 279
   parallels with Isaac of, 42–43
   passion predictions of, 152–53, 159, 259, 273, 274, 348
   post-resurrection appearances of, 148, 150, 287, 340, 345, 349–56
   predicts his betrayal, 312
   predicts Peter's denial, 315
   presentation in the temple of, 54–57
   resurrection of, 103, 105, 134, 154, 155, 156, 163, 176, 211, 222, 274, 285, 343–44, 348–49, 350, 351, 353, 356
   sermon in Nazareth synagogue of, 80–84, 122, 258
   Sermon on the Plain of, 100–115
   temptation of, 63–64, 68, 69, 70–75, 83, 95, 105, 190, 318–19, 320
   transfiguration of, 145, 152, 154–57, 158, 163, 167, 309
   trials of
      before Herod Antipas, 148, 190, 274, 324, 329–30, 331, 339, 341
      before the Jewish leaders, 323–27
      before Pilate, 274, 324, 327–33, 338, 341, 342
   "triumphal" entry of, 124, 273, 282–85, 346
   See also exorcisms; healings; miracles; parables; resuscitations
Joanna, 133, 134, 348
Job, 92, 296, 338
John (son of Zebedee), 87, 89, 93, 99, 100, 133, 143, 154, 156, 160, 168, 171, 173, 181, 271, 309, 310
John, Gospel of, 215, 354
John Mark, 171
John the Baptist, 61, 73, 116, 121, 128, 147, 148, 152, 183, 249, 279, 285, 291–92
   annunciation of birth, 33–38, 53, 61
   arrest and imprisonment, 68

Index of Subjects

baptizes Jesus, 28, 62–64, 68–70
beheaded by Herod, 148, 329
birth and upbringing of, 44–49, 61, 73, 190
compared to Jesus, 21–24, 33, 39, 62, 67–68, 123–27
as forerunner to the Messiah, 36, 46, 48, 126, 171, 191
Jesus's remarks concerning, 125–27
ministry of, 28, 64–68, 170, 214
sends disciples to question Jesus, 121, 123–25, 147, 276
Jonah, 193–95
Joseph (husband of Mary), 23, 38, 42–43, 60, 82, 104
and birth of Jesus, 49–54
and nurture/upbringing of Jesus, 56–59
presents Jesus in temple, 54–56
Joseph (son of Jacob), 241
Joseph of Arimathea, 34, 345–48
joy, 36, 41, 53, 73, 103, 105, 135, 176, 178, 236, 237, 248, 280, 283, 338, 353, 355
Judas (son of James), 100
Judas Iscariot, 75, 100, 135, 203, 211, 312, 314, 319
agrees to betray Jesus, 307–8
betrays Jesus in Gethsemane, 321–23, 342
Judea, 23, 34, 45, 49, 52, 64, 87, 90, 101, 104, 123, 147, 202, 214, 231, 252, 277, 278, 302, 327, 328
Julius Caesar, 67

katalyma, 51, 309
kathexēs, 29–30
kingdom of God, 8, 15, 39, 69, 79, 86–87, 102, 103, 105, 116, 123, 126, 132, 134, 135, 136, 146, 148, 149, 152, 154, 156, 169, 170, 173, 176, 183, 191, 192, 199, 207–8, 213, 220–21, 223, 227, 229, 233, 244, 249, 253, 256, 258–59, 265, 267–68, 270, 271, 272, 281, 283, 286, 304, 310, 312, 314, 319, 338, 345, 346, 354, 356
king of the Jews, 328, 337
klisis. *See* inflection
kyrios. *See* Lord

laos. *See* people
Last Supper, 15, 148, 150, 209, 262, 307, 309–17, 318, 351, 354
lawyers, 126, 163–64, 179–81, 189, 195, 197–99, 225, 243, 269
Lazarus (parable character), 165, 205, 244, 249–51, 252, 254–55, 354

lector, 3–4
Legion, 139–40
lepers, 90, 121, 123, 124, 256–58, 275
Levi, 87, 92–93, 133, 144, 354
Levite, 180
licentia (frank speech), 326
logos, 84
Lord, 10, 15, 23, 27, 28, 30, 34, 35, 36, 38, 39, 40, 44, 45, 46, 47, 48, 49, 51, 53, 54, 55, 56, 59, 65, 71, 73, 74, 81, 82, 85, 89, 90, 97, 98, 105, 114, 115, 119, 120, 121, 122, 123, 126, 137, 138, 144, 152, 156, 168, 169, 170, 171–72, 176, 178, 179, 182, 183, 196, 197, 208, 209, 210, 218, 221, 222, 223, 225, 249, 252, 253, 261, 262, 264, 276, 279, 282, 283, 295, 296, 297, 315, 316, 322, 324, 329, 345, 348, 352, 353, 357
Lord's Prayer, 179, 183, 319
Lot, 259–61
Lot's wife, 261
"Lukan community," 17, 19
Luke (author), 5–9
ethnic identity of, 7–8
literary artistry of, 8–9
as physician, 5–9, 322
"we" passages, 5–7
Luke, Gospel of
audience of, 12–13, 15–18
authorship of, 5–9
date of, 19
genre of, 13–15
"great omission," 151
infancy narrative, 59–61
passion narrative, 307–40
preface, 25–32
relationship to Acts, 10–11
relationship to other Gospels, 12–13, 26–30
structure of, 16
text of, 9–13
travel narrative, 156, 163–286
Lydia, 130

magi, 60–61
magicians, 60–61
Magnificat, 28, 41, 42–43, 45, 48, 49, 55, 106
Manasseh (son of Joseph), 241
Mark, Gospel of, 27–30
feeding of the four thousand in, 150
Jesus's calling of the disciples in, 87–88
Jesus's healing of a leper in, 90
John the Baptist's imprisonment in, 68
Martha, 135, 179, 182–83, 187, 354

389

Index of Subjects

Mary (mother of James), 348, 349
Mary (mother of Jesus), 23–24, 28, 33, 42–43, 48, 49, 54, 60, 86, 106, 136, 137, 139, 212, 316
  annunciation to, 38–40
  and birth of Jesus, 49–54
  and nurture/upbringing of Jesus, 56–59
  presents Jesus in temple, 54–56
  visits Elizabeth, 40–42
Mary Magdalene, 133–34, 348–49
Mary of Bethany, 133, 135, 179, 182–83, 187, 354
Master, as title for Jesus, 89, 137, 138, 142, 156, 160, 257
Matthew (author), 38
Matthew (disciple), 92, 99, 100
Matthew, Gospel of
  feeding of the four thousand in, 150
  genealogy of Jesus in, 70
  infancy narrative in, 59–61
  quotation formula in, 38
  temptation narrative in, 71–72
maxim, 110, 112, 114, 136, 208
mercy, 41, 42, 43, 45, 46, 47, 48, 108, 111, 117, 180–81, 215, 252, 257, 258, 271, 276, 336
Messiah (Christ), 15, 18, 23, 28, 36, 39, 42, 46, 49, 50, 53, 55, 59, 61, 66, 67, 69, 70, 72, 73, 74, 75, 77, 81, 82, 84, 86, 92, 97, 101, 115, 124, 125, 144, 145, 148, 152, 153, 154, 156, 160, 172, 176, 177, 179, 181, 182, 190, 220, 230, 231, 237, 238, 274, 276, 283, 284, 285, 286, 297, 300, 312, 326, 327, 328, 337, 341, 345, 351, 354, 355, 356, 357
Messianic Apocalypse, 125
metonymy, 36, 41, 47, 191, 207
millstones, 252
minor agreements, 325
minor characters, 136
miracles
  calming the storm, 137–38
  feeding of the five thousand, 148–51, 351, 354
  great catch of fish, 87–89
  See also exorcisms; healings; resuscitations
Moses, 15, 39, 54, 58, 60–61, 71, 90, 95, 151, 155–57, 163, 167, 244, 250, 251, 295, 296, 328, 344, 351, 355
Most High, 15, 39, 48, 100, 111, 139, 161, 221
Mount of Olives, 135, 282, 283, 300, 305, 315, 317, 318, 319, 333
Muratorian Canon, 7

Naaman, 83, 117–18, 258
Nain, 121–23
Nathan, 68

Nazareth, 19, 21, 23, 38, 56, 58, 59, 60, 79–84, 95, 104, 117, 122, 258
Nehemiah, 338
Nicanor, 155
Noah, 259–61
Nunc Dimittis, 55–56

Onias, 155
oracular demonstration, 154–55. See also *ekphrasis*

paideia. *See* education
parables
  of the barren fig tree, 189, 214–15, 271
  of the blind leading the blind, 113
  of the children in the marketplace, 127
  of counting the cost, 229–30
  of the faithful and wise steward, 209–11
  of the fig tree and the other trees, 289, 304
  of the friend at midnight, 179, 183–86, 187–88, 262, 271
  of the good Samaritan, 51, 53, 163–64, 179–82, 187–88, 243, 269, 270, 271–72, 306
  of the great banquet (big dinner), 135, 227–29, 272, 354
  of the laborers in the vineyard, 246
  of the lamp on a stand, 136
  of the leaven, 221
  of the lost coin, 165, 235, 271
  of the lost sheep, 165, 235, 271
  of the lowest seat at the banquet, 164, 226
  of the master and slave, 253
  of the minas (evil tyrant), 273, 280–82
  of the moneylender, 131
  of the mustard seed, 220–21
  of the old and new garments, 94–96
  of the old wine and new wineskins, 94–96
  of the persistent widow and the unjust judge, 258, 262–65, 271
  of the Pharisee and the tax collector, 164, 165, 179, 265–67, 272
  of the prodigal son (lost sons/loving father), 136, 180, 204, 235, 238–43, 267, 270, 271
  of the rich fool, 203, 205–6, 210
  of the rich man and Lazarus, 165, 205, 244, 249–51, 252, 254–55, 354
  of the sower, 134–36, 319
  of the talents, 246
  of the tenants, 246, 289, 292–93
  in the travel narrative, 163–65, 271–72
  of the unclean spirit, 192
  of the unrighteous steward, 165, 205, 244, 245–49

390

Index of Subjects

of the watchful master, 209
of the watchful servants, 209
of the wise and foolish builders, 114–15
paradise, 74, 338–39
paraphrasis (paraphrase), 48, 68, 81, 86, 99, 101, 126, 150, 275–77
parousia, 155, 209–10, 357
passion narrative, 307–42
passion predictions, 152–53, 159, 259, 273, 274, 275, 348
Passover, 58, 133, 208, 213, 283, 307–17, 329, 332
patronage, 121, 185–86, 313
Paul, 5–9, 27, 85, 103, 109, 115, 150, 171, 203, 219, 328, 329
penitent thief, 257, 267, 335, 336, 338, 341
Pentecost, 63, 147, 167, 211, 355
people (*laos*), 35, 37, 38, 40, 67, 68, 101, 117, 126, 127, 136, 142, 148, 159, 199, 217, 277, 283, 285, 289, 291, 292, 293, 295, 297, 305, 307, 325, 327, 328, 330, 331, 332, 335, 337, 338, 341–42, 350. *See also* crowd (*ochlos/ ochloi*)
performance criticism, 4
Peter, 10, 29, 30, 42, 90, 93, 99, 100, 129, 133, 142, 143, 171, 209, 210, 271, 309, 310, 322
  confession of Jesus as Messiah, 86, 145, 151–53, 327
  denial of Jesus, 135, 203, 323–24, 336
  Jesus's calling and commission of, 87–89, 267, 271
  Jesus's healing of his mother-in-law, 85–86, 88, 133
  Jesus's prediction of his denial, 315
  presence at the Transfiguration, 154–57
  risen Jesus's appearance to, 352, 353
  Satan's desire to sift, 135, 314–15, 319
Pharaoh, 190, 191, 275, 328
Pharisees, 90–92, 93–97, 126–27, 128, 130, 147, 164, 165, 179, 183, 189, 195–99, 200, 201, 224, 225, 226, 229, 236, 242, 244, 249, 258–59, 265–67, 284, 295, 306, 329, 354
philanthropy, 109, 168, 180, 186–88
Philip (the apostle), 99
Philip (the evangelist), 83, 85
physiognomy, 65–66, 172, 194–95, 217–20, 278–80, 285–86
plan of God, 127, 320, 338
pleonasm, 201
polyptoton. See inflection
Pontius Pilate, 34, 64, 213, 214, 215, 345, 346
  trial of Jesus before, 274, 324, 327–33, 338, 341, 342

poor, the, 52, 81, 83, 84, 102, 104, 105, 107, 122, 123, 124, 125, 136, 194, 196, 201, 227, 228, 244, 249–51, 252, 254–55, 263, 269, 270, 279–80, 285, 298, 299, 306
priests, 23, 34, 35, 40, 45, 54, 64, 90, 96, 135, 152, 155, 180, 195, 257, 258, 290, 291, 293, 307, 316, 322, 323, 325, 326, 327, 328, 330, 332, 338, 350, 355
Priscilla, 171
prodigal son. *See* parables
progymnasmata, 14, 17, 18, 21, 22, 123, 150, 175, 248, 344
Prologue to the Gospels (Anti-Marcionite Prologue), 7–8
Ptolemy I, 291–92

Q, 12–13, 325
Queen of Sheba, 193–94, 207
Quirinius, 47, 49

Rachel, 38
recency effect, 72
repentance, 63, 65, 66, 67, 69, 93, 126, 127, 128, 130, 132, 144, 156, 164, 174, 175, 193, 194, 213, 214, 223, 236, 237, 250, 251, 252, 267, 271, 277, 314, 336, 338, 339, 341, 342, 355
repetitio. See epanaphora
resurrection
  of the dead, 222, 227, 258, 295–97, 338
  of Jesus, 103, 105, 134, 154, 155, 156, 163, 176, 211, 222, 274, 285, 343–44, 348–49, 350, 351, 352–53, 356
resurrection narratives, 343–45
resuscitations
  of Jairus's daughter, 141, 143–44
  of the widow of Nain's son, 121–23, 148
Reuben, 241
reversal, 41, 106, 159–60, 164, 181, 224, 226, 249–51, 305–6
rhetoric, 4, 9, 16–19, 30, 98, 239–40, 344
rhetorical plausibility, 88
rhetorical question (*interrogatio*), 66, 92, 98, 106, 113, 153, 179, 190, 196, 204, 212, 226, 229, 258, 297, 313. *See also hypophora*
rich ruler, 136, 164, 179, 243, 265, 267, 268–71
Romans/Roman Empire, 17, 50, 53, 60, 61, 118–19, 140, 202, 212, 236, 262, 263, 267, 268, 273–74, 277, 278, 279, 283, 294, 302, 303, 316, 326, 327, 328, 332, 335, 336, 346, 350, 356
Rome (city), 54, 202, 303
Ruth, 263

391

Index of Subjects

Sabbath, 80, 84, 87, 96–99, 115, 144, 217–20, 225–26, 347–48
Sadducees, 289, 295–97
Salome, 349
salt, 230–31
Samaria, 256, 328
Samaritans, 51, 53, 121, 163, 167–69, 179–82, 187–88, 243, 257, 258, 269, 270, 272, 275, 286, 306
Samuel, 55, 57, 58
Sanhedrin, 324, 326, 328
Sapphira, 203
Satan (the devil), 63, 190, 191, 192, 218–19, 304
  desire to sift the disciples, 135, 314–15, 319
  enters Judas, 135, 203, 307–8, 319
  Jesus's vision of the fall of, 176–78, 190
  temptation of Jesus by, 70–73, 74–75, 83, 190, 318–19, 320, 329
Saul (king of Israel), 241
Saul of Tarsus. *See* Paul
scribes, 91–92, 93–96, 97–99, 127, 147, 153, 199, 236, 290, 291, 293, 297, 298, 307, 325, 326, 330
Sea of Galilee, 87, 137–38, 139
Sermon on the Plain, 79, 100–115, 117
Seth, 241
shepherds, 23–24, 38, 49, 53–54, 60–61, 235, 236–38, 271, 341
Sidon, 83, 101, 174–75
Silas, 171
Simeon, 28, 34, 54, 55, 56, 125, 152, 161, 212, 316, 345, 346
simile. *See imago*
similitudo, 313
Simon of Cyrene, 334–35, 341
Simon Peter. *See* Peter
Simon the Cananaean/Zealot, 100
Simon the Pharisee, 116, 127–32, 147, 183
sinners, 69, 93, 108, 110, 123, 127, 128, 144, 168, 196, 213, 214, 236, 277, 279, 306, 354
Skull, the, 336–38
slaves, 18, 81, 83, 104, 116, 117–20, 123, 125, 156, 208–10, 227–28, 230, 239, 245–47, 253, 281–82, 309, 322
Sodom, 173, 174, 260, 261
Solomon, 193–95, 203, 207
son of Abraham, 66, 280, 286, 339
Son of David, 276–77, 297
Son of God, 39, 40, 50, 63, 70, 85, 86, 106, 327, 341
Son of Man, 92, 97, 98, 103, 104, 108, 109, 115, 123, 127, 144, 152–53, 159, 169, 193, 202–3, 209, 258, 259, 260, 261, 265, 273, 274, 280, 303, 304, 305, 312, 316, 322, 326, 340, 348
Stephen, 84, 109
Suffering Servant, 316, 321, 329
Susanna, 133, 348
sword, 56–57, 212, 302, 315, 316–17, 322
symposium, 4, 129, 312, 354
synecdoche, 41, 103
synkrisis, 21–24, 33, 38, 39, 40, 48, 57, 62, 67–68, 122, 123, 126, 151, 175, 194, 197, 260, 282, 346
synonymy, 310

table fellowship, 173, 223, 354–55
Tamar, 263
tax collectors, 67, 69, 92–93, 100, 123, 126, 127, 133, 164, 165, 179, 236, 265–67, 268, 272, 277–80, 328, 354. *See also* Levi; Zacchaeus
taxes, paying to Caesar, 294–95, 328
Teacher, as title for Jesus, 114, 130, 143, 158, 163, 169, 179, 197, 203, 204, 269, 284, 294, 295, 297, 300, 309, 310
Tel Aviv School, 31
temple, 8, 42, 48, 198, 265, 267, 283, 287, 299, 300, 305, 323, 356
  disciples worshiping in, 348, 355
  Jesus's expelling of the moneychangers from, 289–90
  Jesus's prediction of the destruction of, 299–300
  Jesus's teaching in, 291–99, 305
  presentation of Jesus in, 49, 54–57, 152
  tearing of the curtain of, 339
  temptation of Jesus on pinnacle of, 72–74
  twelve-year-old Jesus in, 58–59
  Zechariah's vision in, 34–38
temptation. *See* Jesus, temptation of
testimony, 90, 119, 147, 161, 269, 301, 327, 350
  divine, 33, 120, 157
  human, 120, 204, 207
Thaddaeus, 100
Theophilus, 26, 31
Thomas, 99, 100
Tiberius, 34, 64, 202, 289, 294–95, 328
Tobias, 295
topos (commonplace), 183, 185, 280–81, 330
traductio, 193, 197
Transfiguration, the, 145, 152, 154–57, 158, 163, 167, 309
travel narrative, 156, 163–286
"triumphal" entry, 124, 273, 282–85, 346
triumphus, 283

Twelve, the. *See* disciples
Two Ways, 114–15
Tyre, 6, 101, 174–75

Vespasian, 119

"we" passages, 5–7
widows, 56, 83, 111, 116, 121–22, 123, 125, 133, 136, 148, 258, 262–65, 271, 289, 295, 297–99
wisdom, 36, 57, 59, 95, 102, 127, 193–94, 195, 198, 237, 279, 301

woes, 41, 100–102, 106, 174–75, 178, 189, 195, 196–99, 246, 251, 293, 302, 312

Zacchaeus, 136, 275, 277–80, 285–86, 339, 354
Zechariah (father of John the Baptist), 23, 42, 43, 44, 45, 65, 72, 355
  Benedictus of, 44, 45, 46–49, 122
  encounter with Gabriel, 33–40, 53, 54, 73, 190
Zechariah (son of Jehoiada), 198–99

Index of Modern Authors

Aker, Ben, 62
Alexander, Loveday, 25
Allison, Dale C., Jr., 64, 70, 71, 143, 168, 195, 198, 343, 344
Alsup, John, 344
André, Jacques, 66, 172
Annand, Rupert, 352
Ariely, Dan, 254
Arterbury, Andrew E., 131, 147, 168, 182, 183, 187

Babbitt, Frank Cole, 193
Bailey, Kenneth E., 51, 131, 245
Balch, David L., 95, 120, 188
Ball, David T., 294, 295
Barclay, John M. G., 343
Barr, Beth Allison, xiii
Barrett, C. K., 186, 290
Barth, Karl, 294
Bass, Kenneth, 351
Basser, H. W., 156, 157
Bauckham, Richard J., 17, 19, 180, 250, 251
Bauer, Johannes Baptist, 153
Beasley-Murray, George, 62, 69
Beavis, Mary Ann, 185, 245, 246
Berger, Klaus, 82
Betz, Hans Dieter, 111, 112, 113
Beutler, Christian, 100
Bird, Michael F., 10
Blomberg, Craig L., 205, 238
Bock, Darrell L., 3, 21, 35, 42, 48, 50, 54, 103, 109, 110, 111, 113, 126, 127, 128, 131, 145, 154, 171, 172, 173, 174, 176, 178, 222, 247, 252, 253, 262, 274, 276, 277, 314, 320, 325, 326, 327, 330
Bockmuehl, Markus, 10, 18, 169, 338

Bode, Edward Lynn, 343
Bonhoeffer, Dietrich, 231
Boring, M. Eugene, 82
Bornkamm, Günther, 306
Bosold, Iris, 172
Bovon, François, 3, 21, 73, 75, 134, 142, 143, 212, 236, 237, 238, 299, 308, 309, 324, 325, 326, 327, 329, 331, 332, 333, 338, 340
Braun, Willi, 226, 228
Brawley, Robert L., 42, 66, 70
Bridge, Steven L., 262
Brookins, Timothy A., 276, 277
Brown, Raymond E., 50, 57, 70, 87, 316, 317, 318, 319, 320, 321, 323, 324, 325, 327, 328, 329, 330, 332, 335, 339, 340, 341, 346, 347
Brueggemann, Walter, 241
Bultmann, Rudolph, 13, 63, 87, 88
Burridge, Richard, 13, 14, 15, 19
Butler, H. E., 29, 239, 319, 340

Cadbury, Henry J., 6, 7, 25, 29
Callan, Terrance, 25
Calvin, John, 75
Campbell, Constantine R., 98
Caplan, Harry, 36, 41, 138, 153, 199, 200, 292, 319, 333
Caragounis, Chrys C., 222
Carlson, Stephen C., 47
Carroll, John T., 3, 159, 222, 223, 252, 253, 256, 259, 263, 266, 267, 268, 269, 296, 298, 301, 302, 303, 304, 308, 309, 311, 312, 314, 325, 326, 328, 330
Carter, Warren, 16, 262
Cary, Earnest, 263
Clark, Ronald R., Jr., 268
Clivaz, Claire, 312, 320, 321

395

Index of Modern Authors

Cohen, A., 184
Cohen, Shaye J. D., 141, 142
Coleridge, Mark, 40
Collins, Adela Yarbro, 343
Colpe, Carsten, 82
Colson, F. H., 82, 230
Conyers, A. J., 188
Conzelmann, Hans, 307, 355
Cooper, John M., 269
Corley, Kathleen E., 128, 129
Cosgrove, Charles H., 129, 130
Cotter, Wendy J., 119, 122, 263
Couroyer, Bernard, 112
Craddock, Fred B., 231, 275
Crehan, Joseph H., 352
Cribiore, Raffaella, 17
Crossan, John Dominic, 245, 343, 356, 357
Crump, David, 315
Culpepper, R. Alan, 3, 21, 26, 35, 40, 45, 59, 88, 94, 97, 99, 101, 122, 123, 124, 128, 134, 135, 137, 146, 147, 148, 153, 154, 158, 160, 171, 176, 178, 182, 190, 191, 192, 194, 195, 201, 209, 210, 212, 213, 215, 221, 228, 230, 247, 252, 257, 258, 259, 262, 268, 282, 300, 301, 309, 310, 314, 315, 316, 317, 331, 332, 333, 341
Culy, Martin M., xiii, 4, 9, 41, 46, 54, 98, 113, 118, 126, 132, 146, 152, 198, 199, 200, 211, 214, 222, 256, 296, 301, 308, 310, 323, 328, 331, 333, 347

Dahl, Nils Alstrup, 42, 66, 221
Danby, Herbert, 112, 222, 277
Danker, Frederick W., 12, 98, 116, 118, 120, 133, 172, 173, 176, 192, 196, 197, 198, 200, 201, 207, 208, 210, 213, 221, 223, 229, 230, 291, 296, 298, 299, 302, 312, 329, 341
Darr, John A., 68, 225
Dean-Jones, Lesley Ann, 142
De Boer, Esther A., 133
De Lacy, Phillip H., 229
Derrett, J. Duncan M., 264, 294
Dibelius, Martin, 63
Dillon, Richard J., 207
Doble, Peter, 351
Dobson, Brian, 118
Dodd, C. H., 247
Dodson, Derek S., 33, 37, 38, 40, 154, 155
Donahue, John R., 67
Donald, Trevor, 196
Donaldson, Terence L., 72
Doran, Robert, 266, 267
Du Plessis, I. I., 25

Ehrman, Bart D., 30
Einarson, Benedict, 229
Eliot, T. S., 32
Ellis, E. Earle, 212
Emmrich, Martin, 193
Erickson, Richard J., 62
Eriksson, Anders, 94, 95, 96
Ernst, Josef, 21, 325
Esler, Philip Francis, 96
Evans, C. F., 343
Evans, Craig A., 167, 180, 346
Ewald, Marie Liguori, 51

Fee, Gordon D., 183
Fiore, Benjamin, 188
Fitzmyer, Joseph A., 3, 7, 8, 21, 35, 45, 46, 47, 50, 54, 58, 84, 85, 87, 88, 91, 94, 118, 122, 124, 128, 134, 137, 152, 153, 154, 158, 174, 175, 176, 178, 183, 190, 191, 193, 194, 195, 197, 198, 200, 201, 202, 204, 205, 206, 208, 209, 210, 211, 213, 214, 220, 221, 222, 224, 243, 247–48, 249, 253, 258, 259, 260, 261, 263, 264, 265, 266, 267, 268, 269, 270, 290, 291,292, 298, 304, 310, 311, 314, 315, 317, 323, 325, 327, 329, 330, 331, 332, 336, 340, 345, 346, 347
Flannery-Dailey, Frances, 155
Forbes, Greg, 96
Foster, Paul, 351
Fowler, Robert M., 15
Frye, Northrop, 241
Fuller, Reginald, 151, 343
Funk, Robert W., 181

Gamba, G. G., 320
Gamble, Harry Y., 4
García Martínez, Florentino, 125
Garland, David E., 3, 168, 172, 173, 178, 191, 196, 197, 198, 199, 200, 206, 211, 212, 213, 215, 222, 223, 224, 227, 228, 230, 261, 262, 263, 267, 268, 269, 270, 295, 296, 298, 302, 303, 304, 308, 310, 312, 313, 315, 316, 317, 324, 326, 327, 329, 332, 333, 339, 347, 353
Garland, Robert, 279
Garnsey, Peter, 188
Garrett, Susan R., 177, 195, 307, 308
Gathercole, Simon, 176, 177
Geldenhuys, Norval, 176
Glasson, Thomas Francis, 318
Gleason, Maud W., 18
González, Justo L., 267, 306
Goodacre, Mark, 13, 325

Index of Modern Authors

Goodman, Martin, 118
Gowler, David B, 117, 118, 120
Gray-Fow, Michael, 118
Green, Joel B., 3, 64, 66, 69, 80, 84, 85, 86, 87, 88, 91, 94, 95, 96, 116, 117, 118, 123, 124, 125, 126, 127, 128, 167, 207, 216, 228, 309, 317, 320, 321
Gregory, Andrew, 10
Gressmann, Hugo, 250
Grundmann, Walter, 88, 108, 219, 325
Gutwenger, Engelbert, 8

Hall, Christopher A., 28
Hamm, Dennis, 35, 267, 280, 355
Hanks, Tom, 118
Hanson, Ann Ellis, 142
Hanson, John, 33, 38
Harmon, A. M., 279
Hartman, Lars, 62
Hartsock, Chad, 124, 275
Hawkins, John C., 151
Hays, Christopher M., 196
Hays, Richard B., 351
Heil, John Paul, 131, 149
Helmbold, W. C., 291
Hemer, Colin J., 6
Hengel, Martin, 9
Hester, David C., 70
Hett, W. S., 194, 217, 218, 225, 278
Hicks, R. D., 150, 187
Hill, Edmund, 60, 74–75, 356
Hobart, William K., 7, 322
Hock, Ronald F., 14, 187, 188, 204
Hoehner, Harold W., 68
Hofer, Andrew, 351
Hoffmann, Paul, 72
Holmes, Michael W., 220, 311
Hooker, Morna D., 193
Hornik, Heidi J., xiii, 42, 352
Hornsby, Teresa J., 128
Hort, F. J. A., 10
Hubbard, Benjamin J., 88
Hubbell, H. M., 33, 120
Huffman, Norman A., 352
Humphrey, Edith M., 155, 156, 176
Humphrey, Hugh M., 70
Hurst, D., 75

Isaac, Benjamin, 118

Jackson, John, 119
Jeffrey, David Lyle, 265, 269, 295, 296, 328

Jeremias, Joachim, 35, 134, 248, 264, 310
Jervell, Jacob, 8, 219
Johnson, Luke T., 3, 10, 11, 17, 19, 21, 36, 47, 48, 49, 84, 86, 90, 93, 94, 114, 128, 146, 148, 153, 174, 175, 190, 191, 193, 196, 197, 199, 200, 201, 202, 209, 210, 213, 221, 222, 223, 229, 252, 253, 257, 258, 259, 265, 266, 268, 275, 276, 290, 291, 292, 300, 301, 302, 304, 305, 309, 310, 312, 313, 314, 315, 328, 329, 331, 339, 353
Juel, Donald, 274
Just, Arthur A., 52, 132, 150, 213, 221, 252, 326, 327, 328, 330

Kähler, Christoph, 70
Karris, Robert J., 52, 105, 150
Keck, Leander E., 63
Kee, Howard Clark, 85
Keener, Craig S., 85
Kelhoffer, James A., 12
Kennedy, George A., 17, 22, 28, 29, 30, 44, 45, 48, 57, 67, 88, 89, 149, 150, 155, 160, 168, 186, 204, 248, 275, 281, 344, 346
Kilgallen, John J., 128
Kittel, Gerhard, 60, 176
Klassen, William, 173
Klein, Günter, 25, 27
Kloppenborg, John S., 72
Köppen, Klaus Peter, 73
Krieger, Murray, 69
Kvalbein, Hans, 125
Kwong, Ivan Shing Chung, 314

Lambrecht, Jan, 100
Landes, George M., 193
Laurentin, René, 21
Leaney, A. R. C., 21
Lee, Simon S., 157
Leonard, Bill J., xiii
Levinsohn, Stephen H., 48, 151
Linnemann, Eta, 317
Longenecker, Bruce W., 83, 182, 228, 254
Lüdemann, Gerd, 343
Luz, Ulrich, 143

Mack, Burton L., 170
Magness, Jodi, 346
Malherbe, Abraham J., 203, 205
Malina, Bruce J., 186, 225
Manson, Thomas Walter, 126, 193, 197, 212, 222
Marcus, Joel, 96, 176, 325
Marcus, Ralph, 260, 263, 299

Index of Modern Authors

Marguerat, Daniel, xiii
Marshall, I. Howard, xiii, 25, 34, 35, 46, 47, 54, 66, 85, 98, 111, 112, 113, 118, 125, 126, 131, 151, 158, 160, 172, 173, 176, 190, 192, 193, 200, 209, 210, 211, 212, 213, 214, 223, 224, 230, 254, 278, 314, 339
Martin, L. T., 75
Martin, Michael W., 10, 14, 21, 22, 70, 123, 312, 344
Martini, Carlo Maria, 351
Maxwell, Kathy Reiko, 83
McCarthy, C., 74
McCown, Chester Charlton, 91
McIver, Robert K., 134
Meeks, Kenneth, 286
Meier, John P., 52, 104
Mekkattukunnel, Andrews George, 355
Menken, Martinus J. J., 180
Metzger, Bruce M., 11, 142, 352
Meyer, Marvin, 236
Michie, Donald, 136
Miller, David L., 324
Mitchell, Alan C., 279, 280
Moessner, David P., xiii, 6, 25, 29, 30, 145
Moo, Douglas J., 316
Moore, Clifford H., 119
Morris, Leon, 21
Muddiman, John B., 94
Mullen, J. Patrick, 129
Murray, A. T., 184

Nave, Guy D., Jr., 93
Neagoe, Alexandru, 327
Neale, David A., 93, 130, 277
Nelson, Peter K., 313, 314
Neyrey, Jerome H., 225, 320, 335
Nolland, John, 21, 26, 65, 67, 102, 103, 109, 132, 138, 147, 174, 175, 177, 178, 180, 186, 197, 208, 211, 213, 221, 249, 265, 270, 303, 309
Norton, Michael I., 254
Novakovic, Lidija, 125, 276

O'Connor, Jerome Murphy, 3
O'Day, Gail R., 261, 262
Oden, Thomas C. 28
O'Fearghail, Fearghus, 24
Olson, Philip N., 255
Omanson, Roger L., 171
Orchard, R. K., 129
Osiek, Carolyn, 120
O'Toole, Robert F., 145, 216, 219
Owen-Ball, David T., 294

Paffenroth, Kim, 70
Palmer, Darryl W., 25
Parker, David C., 310, 311
Parsons, Mikeal C., 3, 9, 10, 11, 12, 16, 18, 26, 27, 30, 31, 33, 34, 35, 41, 42, 46, 54, 59, 66, 69, 70, 72, 88, 95, 97, 98, 100, 106, 111, 113, 118, 126, 132, 146, 152, 163, 187, 194, 198, 199, 200, 211, 214, 217, 222, 225, 236, 256, 258, 279, 285, 296, 301, 308, 310, 311, 323, 328, 331, 333, 337, 347, 352, 355
Paton, W. R., 226
Payne, Philip B., 134
Penner, Todd C., 17
Perry, Menakhem, 31, 72
Pervo, Richard I., xiii, 10, 11
Phillips, Jane E., 292
Piper, John, 108
Pitre, Brant James, 335, 336
Plummer, Alfred, 21, 47, 54, 85, 87, 109, 129, 147, 168, 261
Porter, Stanley E., 98
Powell, Mark Alan, 15, 60
Price, Robert M., 122
Prince, Deborah Thompson, 353

Rabinowitz, Peter J., 16
Rackham, H., 278
Rau, Gottfried, 331
Reardon, Bryan P., 130
Rehkopf, Friedrich, 112
Reich, Keith A., 201, 269
Reicke, Bo Ivar, 55
Reid, Barbara E., 262, 263, 264
Renan, Joseph Ernest, 13
Rhoads, David, 136
Richardson, Peter, 68
Riesner, Rainer, 349
Rimmon-Kenan, Shlomith, 31
Robbins, Vernon K., 7, 170
Robinson, James McConkey, 72
Rohrbaugh, Richard L., 227, 228
Rolfe, J. C., 266
Roth, S. John, 227
Rowe, C. Kavin, 10, 122, 123, 172
Russell, Donald A., 14
Ruzer, Serge, 108
Ryan, William Granger, 9

Safrai, Shemuel, 118
Said, Edward W., 31
Saller, Richard, 188, 309
Sams, Ferrol, 160

Index of Modern Authors

Sanders, E. P., 63–64
Sawyer, Ronald D., 352
Schneider, Gerhard, 303
Schottroff, Luise, 264
Schrage, Wolfgang, 334
Schürmann, Heinz, 123, 124, 334
Scott, Bernard Brandon, 241, 242, 246, 248
Seim, Turid Karlsen, 66, 216, 219
Sellew, Philip, 205
Senior, Donald, 314, 335, 336
Sheeley, Steven M., 47, 126
Shelton, Jo-Ann, 185
Shiell, William David, 4
Shiner, Whitney T., 4
Shuler, Philip L., 13, 14, 340
Sider, Ronald J., 255
Siker, Jeffrey S., 66
Simon, Maurice, 238
Smith, Dennis E., 277
Smith, R. Payne, 74, 237, 278, 317
Snodgrass, Klyne, 186
Soards, Marion L., 317, 334
Spencer, Patrick E., 10
Squires, John T., 320
Stambaugh, John E., 188
Stanley, David M., 318, 319
Stegman, Thomas D., 203, 207, 208
Stegner, William Richard, 70
Steiner, M., 73
Sterling, Gregory E., 321
Sternberg, Meir, 31
Stigall, Joshua J., xiii, 9, 41, 46, 54, 98, 113, 118, 126, 132, 146, 152, 198, 199, 200, 211, 214, 222, 256, 296, 301, 308, 310, 323, 328, 331, 333, 347
Strauss, David Friedrich, 343
Strauss, Mark L., 15

Talbert, Charles H., 3, 13, 16, 21, 26, 40, 41, 54, 55, 57, 59, 62, 63, 85, 87, 88, 91, 100, 101, 102, 105, 110, 115, 128, 153, 171, 183, 189, 195, 197, 208, 211, 214, 253, 256, 267, 269, 270, 280, 292, 293, 296, 297, 308, 321, 335
Tannehill, Robert C., 29, 41, 61, 69, 128, 132, 189, 195, 201, 211, 213, 227, 229, 243
Taylor, Nicholas H., 70

Taylor, Vincent, 317
Thackeray, H. St. J., 53, 299, 300
Thorley, John, 47
Tiede, David L., 8, 94, 122, 199, 213
Tolkien, J. R. R., 305
Tomkinson, T., 74
Topel, L. John, 100, 101, 102, 103, 105, 106, 108, 109, 110, 111, 112, 113, 114
Trudinger, L. Paul, 318
Tucker, Jeffrey T., 181
Tuckett, Christopher M., 70, 72
Tyson, Joseph B., xiii

Udoh, Fabian E., 294
Unnik, Willem Cornelis van, 25
Unruh, Heidi Rolland, 255

Vielhauer, Philipp Adam Christoph, xiii, 6
Vince, J. H., 66
Vinson, Richard B., 3, 221, 222, 223, 228, 230, 252, 257, 264, 265, 266, 268, 282, 296, 297, 298, 313
Voragine, Jacobus de, 9
Votaw, C. W., 13

Wallace, Daniel B., 41, 98, 267
Weaver, C. Douglas, xiii
Weissenrieder, Annette, 141, 142, 158
Westcott, B. F., 10
White, K. D., 134
Whitlark, Jason A., 337
Wilkinson, John, 217
Williams, Burma P., 236, 237
Williams, Richard S., 236, 237
Wink, Walter, 67
Witherington, Ben, III, 129
Wolter, Michael, xiii
Wolterstorff, Nicholas, 107
Wood, Ralph C., 306
Woods, Edward, 191
Wright, N. T., 155, 343, 344, 356
Wuellner, Wilhelm, 89

York, John O., 164
Young, Robin Darling, 219

Zafiropoulos, Christos A., 184

Index of Scripture and Ancient Sources

OLD TESTAMENT

Genesis
1:2 138, 140
1:26 70, 294
2:8 LXX 221
3:14 177
3:15 57
4 198
4:10 198
6:1–4 296
10 171
13:13 173
14:14 220
14:18 111
17–18 38
17:12 45
17:17 37
18:1–16 187
18:4 195
18:12 36
19:1–23 174, 187
19:1–26 260
19:17 261
19:24 260
19:26 LXX 261
20:3–8 36
24:10–61 187
27:15 313
27:36 313
29:30–31 229
30:22–23 38
31:10–13 36
32 320
37:3 313
37:35 LXX 175
42:13 313
43:16–34 187
46:2–6 36
48:14 313
48:19 313
50:15–21 91

Exodus
1–2 60
2:11 34
2:15–22 187
3–4 89
5:4 LXX 328
6:30 36
7:3 275
8:15 275
8:19 191
12:6 LXX 308
12:11 208
12:21 LXX 308
13 55
13:2 55, 85
13:3 LXX 46
13:11–16 55
16 71, 151
16:3 71
17 71
17:2–3 71
19:4 262
20:12–16 269
22:22–24 263
23:4–5 108
23:12 96
23:20 126
24:1–9 155
24:9–10 53
24:15–18 155
27:20 208
30:7–8 35
30:19–21 195
31:18 191
32 71
33:21–23 351
34:6 LXX 264
34:21 96
34:28 94
34:29 155
40:12 195

Leviticus
4:1–2 59
5:17 59
10:9 36
11:15 206
12:1–8 55
12:3 45
13 257
13–14 90
13:45 257
15 141
15:26 141
16:10 193
17:11 92
18:16 68

19:14 LXX 252
19:18 108, 179
19:34 108
19:35–36 112
20:3 269
20:21 68
22:10–13 258
22:25 258
24:2 208
25 81
25:10 82
25:10 LXX 81
25:36 247

Numbers
5:2 257
6:3 35
11 151
11:6 71
14:18 LXX 264
15:27–30 211
15:38–40 143
18:15–16 55
19:16 197
21:6–9 177
27:1–11 204
28:1–10 34
28:2–8 265
36:7–9 204

Deuteronomy
5:12–15 98
5:14 96

401

Index of Scripture and Ancient Sources

5:16–20 269
6:5 179
6:5–8 294
8:15 177
10:18 263
10:19 108
11:21 296
14:14 206
14:22–29 266
18:15 156
19:15 331
21:15–17 229
21:22–23 346
21:23 347
22:1–4 108
24:17 263
25:5 295
25:13–16 111
29:23 260
32:5 127
32:8 111
32:10–12 262
32:20 127
32:43 LXX 320

Joshua
2:1–22 187
22:24 LXX 85

Judges
2:10 127
4:17–22 187
6 38, 89
6:12 39
6:15 36
6:23 172
11:12 LXX 85
13 38
13:2 34
13:4 36
13:22 36
14:6 229
19:1 34
19:20 172
19:21 195

Ruth
1:20–21 263

1 Samuel
1–2 55
1:19–20 38
7:6 94
17:14 313
21:1–6 96

2 Samuel
1:12 94
3:35–38 94
6:1–5 283
6:18 283
7:12–14 297
12:15–23 279
12:16 94
13:28 LXX 172
14:11 302
15 318
15:14 302
15:23 LXX 318
16:10 LXX 85
19:22 LXX 85
22:3 LXX 46
23:4 LXX 48–49

1 Kings
1:52 302
3:1–5 34
10:1–13 194
10:4–5 207
10:27 253
12:11 LXX 331
12:14 LXX 331
14:15 126
17 122
17:1–24 83
17:10 122
17:18 LXX 85
17:19–21 122
17:22 122
17:23 LXX 122
18:1 64
18:17 328
18:46 208
19:19–21 170

2 Kings
1:9–12 168
2:1–8:29 151
3:13 LXX 85
4:29 208
4:42–44 151
5 117, 122, 258
5:1–2 117
5:1–19 83
5:2–3 117
5:5–10 117
5:14 117
7:3 257
9:1 208
9:13 283

1 Chronicles
4:10 LXX 46
27:28 253

2 Chronicles
9:1–12 194
10:14 LXX 331
19:6–7 263
24:20–22 198
24:22 198

Nehemiah
5:19 338
9:17 LXX 264

Esther
5:8 227

Job
1:6–12 177
1:8–12 314
2:1–7 177
2:2–5 314
4:7 213
8:21 103
14:13 338
14:14 296
18:15 260
22:19 103
30:25 103
38:3 208
38:41 206

Psalms
1 114
1:1 102
2 273
2:2 329
6:5 LXX 175
6:9 LXX 223
7:12 LXX 264
8:3 191
9 241
11:6 260
13:1 LXX 205
14:1 196
16:4–5 312
17:3 LXX [18:2] 46
17:4 102
18:1–3 266
18:8 LXX 178
18:17 103
22:1 (21:2 LXX) 340
22:7 337
22:18 337
23 236, 271
24:1 205, 295
25:7 338
25:19 103
31:5 (30:6 LXX) 340
31:18 LXX 341
34:7–8 305
34:8 269
35:19 103
37:1–2 91
38:11 342
41:1 102
41:3–4 91
43 156
43:2 157
43:3 156, 157
44:23 271
44:23–24 184
52:6 103
58:4 177
65:7 140
68:22 LXX 252
69:21 337
74:9 LXX [75:8] 46
74:12–14 138
78:8 127
78:65 184, 271
82:6 111
85:15 LXX 264
88:1–3 264
88:8 342
88:13–14 264
88:18 LXX [89:17] 46
89:8–10 138
90:13 LXX 177
95:10 127
100:5 269
105:26 156, 157
106:1 269
107:1 269
107:17 91
110 297
110:1 297, 326
112 205
113–18 283
113:7 107
114:6 LXX 178
118 283
118:1 266
118:1–4 269
118:13 LXX 178
118:22–23 293
118:26 283
118:29 269
123:1 267
126:1–6 103
126:2 103

402

Index of Scripture and Ancient Sources

131:17 LXX [132:17] 46
136:1 269
137 356
137:1 103
140:3 177
141:2 35
144:8 LXX 264
147:9 206
148:14 LXX 46

Proverbs

3:11–12 91
6:12 196
12:13 305
14:21 102
19:12 223
22:9 194
23:24–25 192
30:7–9 270

Ecclesiastes

3:4 103
8:15 205

Song of Songs

2:15 LXX 225

Isaiah

1:11–17 98
1:17 263
3:9 173
3:14 196
4:1 156
5 293
6:1–4 88
6:1–10 88
6:5 88, 89
6:7–10 88
6:9 LXX 134
11:6 172
14:11–15 177
14:13 175
14:15 175
14:30 300
17:12 303
23 175
24:17–18 305
25:6 223
25:6–8 310
29:18–19 124
29:35–36 124
30:33 260
33:22–24 92
34:4 303
34:13–14 193
35:5–6 229
35:10 103
40:3 48
40:5 56
40:6–8 207
42:1 156, 157
42:6 56
42:18 124
43:5–6 223–24
43:8 124
46:13 56
49:6 56
49:9–10 102
50:6 LXX 274
51:9–10 139
51:19 300
52:9–10 56
53 273
53:2–12 91
53:7 329
53:8 332
53:12 316, 336
54:5–6 94
55:1–2 310
56:2 98
56:7 289, 290
57:17 91
58:10 LXX 48
58:16 81
60:2 LXX 48
60:20 103
61:1 81, 124
61:1–2 81
61:1–4 82
61:2 103
61:3 103
62:4–5 94
65:13 102
65:13–14 310
65:17–25 103
65:25 172
66:5 103

Jeremiah

1:1–3 34
1:2 64
1:5 36
1:13–19 177
1:17 208
2:2 94
7 305
7:11 290
7:29 127
7:29–34 201
15:15 338
16:4 302
16:5–9 169
16:9 94
16:16 89
20:7–8 103
23:5 341
23:5 LXX 49
23:14 173
25:22 175
31:13 103
31:25 LXX [48:25] 46
31:34 92
34:18–19 210
38:15 326
46:10 302
51:63 252

Lamentations

2:11–12 302
2:20 302
3:14 103

Ezekiel

1:3 64
2:9–10 177
4:13 LXX 46
13:4–5 LXX 225
13:10–16 115
16:48 173
16:56 173
17:22 221
17:23 221
21:2 167
21:26 267
24:16–24 169
33:13 265
34:2–6 236
34:11–16 236
34:29 102
36:29–30 300
44:2 LXX 46

Daniel

2:21 303
7 97
7:13 153, 326
7:13–14 304
8:13 302
9:3 94
9:24–27 303
12.2 269
12:12 102

Hosea

1:1 64
2:16–23 94
6:11 171
9:7 302
9:16 336
10:8 335

Joel

1:1 64
2:10 303, 339
2:31 339
3:4–8 175
3:13 171

Amos

1:1 34
1:9–10 175
1:13 302
2:7 107
4:2 89
4:4–5 200
5:18 339
8:1–3 177
8:9 339
8:11–12 300

Jonah

1:1 65

Micah

4:11–13 171
6:8 197
7:6 212

Nahum

2:1 208

Habakkuk

1:14–15 89
2:18–19 LXX 45

Zephaniah

1:15 339
3:11–12 274

Haggai

2:6 303
2:21 303

Zechariah

3:1–2 177
3:2 LXX 85
3:8 LXX 49
6:12 LXX 49
9:3 175

403

9:9 284, 341
12:3 302
14 318
14:5 300

Malachi
1:2–3 242
2:16 LXX 46
3:1 36, 48, 126
3:1–2 289
3:5 263
3:20 LXX 48
3:23 LXX 157
4:2 143
4:5 156
4:5–6 36
4:6 156

DEUTEROCANONICAL BOOKS

1 Esdras
4:30 109

2 Esdras (*4 Ezra*)
4:23–25 264
6:17 303
6:49–52 138
7:36 201
8:1–3 221
16:18–22 300

Judith
1:1 34
9:1 265

1 Maccabees
2:1–2 45
2:39–41 96
5:13 302
8:10 302

2 Maccabees
5:19 96
7:37–38 91
9:5 46
9:8 138
9:16 299
10:25 208
15:12–16 155

3 Maccabees
2:5 260
3:17 299
4:16 45

4 Maccabees
7:19 223, 296
13:14–15 201
13:17 223
14:20 219
15:28 219
16:25 296
17:6 219
18:20 219

Sirach
prol. 1 27
2:5–6 91
4:10 111
6:7 184
6:14–17 184
11:18–19 203
14:8–10 194–95
21:2 177
29:23–24 173
31:8 102
50 38
51:3 223

Susanna
55 210

Tobit
1:2 34
1:17 346
2:7 346
4:7–12 196
4:15 110
4:16 205
7:11 295
12:8 94
12:15 192
13:14 102
14:6 303

Wisdom of Solomon
2:10–11 263
2:18 337
3:4–6 91
6:6 211
10:4–8 259
15:1 264
17:1 91

NEW TESTAMENT

Matthew
1–2 59
1:1–17 70
1:18–19 57
1:22–23 38
2 60
2:15 38
2:17–18 38
2:23 38
3:1 65
3:4–5 98–99
3:8–9 66
3:14–15 63
3:17 63
4:1–13 63, 71
4:8 72
4:11 320
5:2–12 100, 101
5:4 103
5:6 102
5:26 202
5:39 322
5:39–40 100
5:40 109
5:43–44 100, 108
5:44 108
5:45 100
5:46 100
5:48 100
6:19–20 208
6:21 208
6:22–23 194
7:1 100
7:2 100, 112
7:3–5 101, 113
7:12 100
7:16–17 101, 114
7:21 101
7:23 223
7:24–27 101
7:26–27 115
7:28 117
8:1–4 90
8:5 117
8:5–13 117
8:12 223
8:18–22 168
8:23–27 137
9:9–13 92
9:11 93
9:37–38 170
10:1–2 99
10:2–4 99–100
10:5–6 171
10:7–16 170
10:13 173
10:24 101, 113
10:29 202
10:34 316
10:37 229
10:39 261
10:42 252
11:1–5 124
11:3 283
11:4–5 124
11:7–30 126
11:21 174
12:28 191
12:29–30 191
12:34–35 101
12:38–42 193
13:31 221
13:31–32 220
13:33 221
13:42 223
13:50 223
13:53–58 82
13:55 104
13:57 83
14:12 148
14:13–21 148
14:21 149
15:14 101, 113
15:36 150
16 152
16:5–6 200
16:13–20 151
16:16–19 152
16:17 332
17:1 154
17:3 155
17:9 154
17:18 159
17:19–21 251
18:1 312
18:2 159
18:6 252
18:6–7 251
18:10 252
18:14 252
18:15 251
18:22 252
19:22 243, 270
19:28 314
21:9 283
21:16 178
21:18–19 214
21:33 293
21:33–46 292
22:13 223
23 189, 200
23:4 197
23:5–7 197
23:13 199
23:15 173
23:23 196
23:25 196

Index of Scripture and Ancient Sources

23:27–28 197
23:29–32 198
23:34–36 198
23:39 283
24:3 300
24:28 262
24:43 209
24:51 223
25:1 208
25:11 138
25:14 281
25:14–30 280
25:30 223, 282
26:6–13 128
26:21–29 311
26:26 150
26:31 315
26:33 98
26:36–46 321
26:47 322
26:47–56 321
26:49 322
26:56 322
26:57 323
26:57–68 323
26:63 327
26:68 325
26:73 324
27:11 328
27:15 332
27:17 332
27:22 333
27:26 334
27:33 337
27:33–44 336
27:57 346
28:16–20 355
28:17 352

Mark

1:1 28
1:4 65
1:6 126
1:9–13 28
1:11 63
1:12–13 63, 71
1:13 320
1:16–18 89
1:16–20 30, 87
1:21 84
1:21–39 84
1:24 85
1:32–34 86
1:40–45 90
1:45 90
2:1 90, 104, 105
2:1–3:6 97

2:13–17 92
2:16 93
2:17 93
2:18 93–94
3:1 97
3:2 98
3:3 97
3:5–6 99
3:14 99
3:16–19 99–100
3:20–21 137
3:22 190
3:22–27 63
3:27 191
4 134
4:12 134
4:24 112
4:30–32 220
4:31 221
4:35 137
4:35–41 137
5 143
5:1–2 139
5:1–20 138
5:3–5 139
5:10 139
5:43 144
6:1–6 82
6:3 104
6:4 83
6:7 146
6:16 148
6:17–18 68
6:30–44 151
6:32–44 148
6:41 267
6:44 149
6:45–8:26 151
6:48 351
6:56 143
7:1–9 195
7:6 200
7:34 267
8 152
8:6 150
8:11–12 193
8:15 200
8:27–30 151
8:38 154
9:2 154
9:4 155
9:11–13 158
9:11–29 157
9:21–27 158
9:25–26 159
9:28–29 158, 251
9:36 159

9:42 251, 252
10:2–9 249
10:14 268
10:19 269
10:22 136, 243, 270
10:32–33 274
10:32–34 275
10:35–45 275
10:38 211
10:43–44 312
10:45 91
10:46 332
10:46–52 275
10:48 276
10:49 276
10:51 276
10:52 277
11:8 283
11:9 283
11:12–14 290
11:13–14 214
11:15 289
11:15–17 289
11:16 289
11:17 289
11:20–21 214
11:20–25 290
11:27–28 291
12:1–12 292
12:2 293
12:6 293
12:24 296
13:3 300, 305
13:14 4
13:27 304
13:28 304
13:32 210
14:3–9 128
14:12 308, 309
14:17 310
14:18 310
14:18–25 311
14:22 150
14:26–27 315
14:30 315
14:32–42 321
14:36 340
14:43 322
14:43–52 321
14:45 322
14:50 135, 322
14:53–65 323
14:55–59 327
14:61 327
14:62 326
14:65 274
15:2 328

15:6 332
15:14 333
15:15 332, 334
15:17–20 330
15:20 334, 336
15:22 337
15:22–32 336
15:34 340
15:43 345
15:44–45 345
15:46 345
15:47 347
16:1 347, 348
16:8 28
16:18 176

Luke

1 73
1–2 21, 28, 59, 62
1–4 48
1:1 12, 25, 26, 27, 30
1:1–2 26
1:1–4 5, 11, 25–32,
    34, 62, 72, 88, 137
1:1–4:13 21, 22
1:2 26, 28, 84, 178,
    355
1:3 26
1:3–4 26
1:4 26, 30
1:5 23, 34, 49, 64, 87
1:5–6 73
1:5–10 33–34
1:5–23 72, 73, 355
1:5–25 33–38, 53, 65,
    120, 154, 157
1:5–38 40
1:5–56 33–43
1:5–4:13 67
1:6 34, 45, 58, 346
1:7 34
1:8–9 34
1:10 35, 185, 239, 265
1:11 33, 35, 73
1:11–12 23
1:11–20 33, 35–37
1:12 35, 53
1:13 35, 36, 45
1:13–14 36
1:13–17 23
1:14 41, 45, 103, 176
1:15 36
1:16 36
1:16–17 65
1:17 35, 36, 41, 48,
    65, 126, 212
1:18 36, 73, 98

405

Index of Scripture and Ancient Sources

1:18–20 72
1:18–23 23
1:19 73
1:19–20 37
1:21 35, 265
1:21–24 37
1:21–25 33, 37–38
1:22 45, 190, 355
1:24–25 23
1:25 38
1:26 23
1:26–27 38
1:26–31 14
1:26–38 33, 38–40, 53
1:27 23
1:28 38
1:28–29 23
1:28–38 38–40
1:29 39, 54
1:30–33 39
1:30–37 23
1:31 54
1:32 48, 111, 139
1:32–33 15
1:34 39
1:34–35 183
1:35 23, 85, 86, 111
1:35–37 39
1:38 28, 40
1:38–45 23
1:39 40
1:39–40 40
1:39–41 40
1:39–56 33, 40–42
1:41 36, 40, 267
1:42 40
1:42–45 40–41
1:43 40
1:44 41, 267
1:45 41, 102
1:46 41, 103
1:46–55 40, 41–42, 55, 121
1:46–56 23
1:47–50 181
1:48 28, 41
1:48–50 41
1:49 41
1:50 41, 45, 48
1:51 41
1:51–53 41, 49, 102, 106, 159
1:51–55 41
1:52 41, 53
1:52–53 41, 81
1:53–55 164, 224
1:54 41, 45, 48, 181
1:54–55 42
1:55 42
1:56 40, 42
1:57 23, 45
1:57–58 45
1:57–63 44–45
1:57–66 39, 44–46
1:57–80 44–49
1:57–2:52 40, 44–61
1:58 23, 45, 48
1:59 45, 47, 58
1:60 45
1:61 45
1:62 45
1:63 45
1:64–65 44, 45
1:66 44, 46
1:67–68 46
1:67–75 46–48
1:67–79 55, 65
1:67–80 44, 46–49
1:68 35, 122
1:68–75 48
1:68–79 121
1:69 46, 47, 297
1:70 46–47
1:70–75 46
1:71 46, 47, 48, 108
1:72 45, 47, 181
1:73 42, 47
1:73–75 42
1:74 108
1:74–75 47
1:76 47, 48, 65, 111, 126
1:76–79 46, 48–49
1:77 48, 65, 68, 81, 275
1:77–79 49
1:78 45, 48, 94, 181
1:79 49, 56, 172
1:80 24, 39, 46, 49, 57, 64, 65, 171, 279
2 51, 60
2:1 34, 49, 339
2:1–7 23, 49–52, 327
2:1–21 49–54
2:1–39 14
2:1–52 44, 49–59
2:2 47, 49
2:3–7 50
2:4 23, 297
2:7 50, 150, 309, 353
2:8 53
2:8–13 23
2:8–20 23

2:8–21 49, 52–54
2:9 23, 53
2:10 41, 53, 103, 176
2:10–12 23
2:10–14 53–54
2:11 53, 59, 152, 339
2:12 23, 54, 267, 353
2:13 23
2:13–14 55
2:14 23, 53, 54, 172, 212
2:15–21 53, 54
2:15–27 39
2:16 267, 353
2:19 24, 54, 59, 136
2:20 341
2:21 24, 54, 58
2:22 54
2:22–24 54–55, 58
2:22–39 49, 54–57
2:23 54, 85
2:24 54
2:25 28, 34, 346
2:25–27 58
2:25–28 55
2:25–35 54, 55–56
2:25–39 24
2:26 152
2:26–35 152
2:27 55
2:29 172
2:29–30 28
2:29–32 55–56
2:32 35, 136
2:33 56
2:34 56, 126, 161, 212, 346
2:34–35 56, 211
2:34–40 39
2:35 212, 314
2:36–37 56, 94
2:36–38 54, 56, 58, 264
2:37 94
2:38 56, 124
2:39 54, 55, 56
2:40 46, 57
2:40–52 14, 24, 49, 56–59, 80
2:41–43 57, 58
2:41–51 55, 72
2:42 58
2:43 58
2:43–44 342
2:43–45 58
2:46–48 58
2:46–49 289

2:48–50 57, 72, 212
2:49 23, 59, 340
2:49–50 58, 59, 87
2:50 275
2:51 136
2:51–52 58, 59
2:52 57, 279
3 21
3:1 34, 49, 133, 327
3:1–2 64
3:1–6 64–65
3:1–9 125
3:1–20 62, 64–68, 69
3:1–4:13 62–75
3:2 64, 323
3:3 48, 65, 93
3:3–18 36
3:4 126
3:4–6 65
3:6 64
3:7 65, 66
3:7–17 64, 65–68
3:8 42, 66, 69, 93, 223, 285
3:8–9 66
3:9 66, 211, 214
3:10 66
3:11 67
3:12 66
3:13 67
3:14 66, 67
3:15 67, 148, 152, 327
3:16 191
3:16–17 67
3:17 124, 211, 314
3:18–20 64, 68
3:19 224, 329
3:19–20 64, 329
3:20 46
3:21 99, 101, 152
3:21–22 68–70, 292
3:21–23 24
3:21–28 14
3:21–38 23
3:21–4:13 62, 68–73
3:22 15, 63, 70, 81, 86, 157, 321, 327
3:23–31 297
3:23–38 68, 70
3:38 70, 73
4 81, 82, 89, 106, 118
4:1–2 94
4:1–13 14, 24, 63, 68, 70–73, 318
4:2 71, 102, 105, 190, 318

406

Index of Scripture and Ancient Sources

4:4 71
4:8 71
4:9 72
4:9–12 329
4:12 71
4:13 73, 308, 319, 320
4:14 85, 132
4:14–15 80
4:14–30 15, 80–84, 316
4:14–44 79–87
4:14–6:49 77, 79–115
4:14–9:50 15, 77, 80, 87
4:14–19:44 15
4:14–21:38 14
4:15 341
4:16 80, 81
4:16–20 80
4:16–21 80
4:16–22 80
4:16–30 73, 79, 80, 86, 88
4:16–43 80
4:17 81
4:18 48, 84, 86, 105, 124, 146, 149, 152, 176, 337
4:18–19 81, 102, 285
4:20 81
4:21 82, 94, 339
4:22 80, 82, 120
4:23 82, 112, 117, 175
4:23–27 80
4:23–29 80
4:24 82
4:25–27 83
4:26 122, 148
4:27 117, 258
4:28 83
4:28–29 80
4:29 83, 105
4:30 80, 83
4:31 84
4:31–37 84, 117, 175
4:31–43 79, 80, 86
4:31–44 84–87
4:31–5:11 87
4:32 84, 86
4:33 84, 85
4:33–34 85
4:33–37 117
4:34 86, 213
4:35 85
4:36 146
4:36–37 85
4:37 86

4:38 84, 85
4:38–39 30, 84, 87, 117, 133
4:39 85
4:40 84
4:40–41 86, 117, 176
4:40–44 84
4:41 15, 84, 85, 86, 152, 276, 327
4:42 84, 86
4:43 59, 87, 102, 132
4:43–44 149
4:44 80, 83, 87, 132
5 91, 121, 313, 354
5:1 84, 137
5:1–3 88
5:1–10 314
5:1–11 30, 84, 85, 87–89, 92
5:1–6:16 79, 87–100
5:4–7 88
5:5 89, 257
5:6 89
5:7 89
5:8 89, 90, 93, 129, 267
5:8–9 88
5:10 88, 89
5:10–11 87, 99, 100
5:11 89, 93, 271
5:12 90, 258
5:12–16 87, 90, 258
5:13 142
5:13–14 90
5:14 258
5:15 86, 90
5:16 63, 90, 99, 149, 152
5:17 90, 146
5:17–20 136
5:17–26 87, 90–92, 144, 189, 291
5:17–6:11 99
5:18 261
5:18–19 90
5:20 91, 323
5:20–21 48
5:21 91, 105, 147
5:22–23 92
5:23–24 48, 97, 337
5:24 92, 144, 153, 326
5:25 92
5:25–26 341
5:26 82, 92
5:27 265
5:27–28 87, 92–93
5:27–30 328

5:27–32 133, 144
5:29 93
5:29–39 87, 93–95
5:30 93, 128, 277, 354
5:31–32 93
5:32 144
5:33 94
5:33–35 22
5:33–39 96
5:34 94
5:35 94
5:36 112
5:36–39 94
5:39 95
6 108
6:1 96
6:1–5 87, 96–97, 115, 144
6:2 96
6:3 102
6:3–4 96, 98, 226
6:5 97, 98, 144, 153
6:6 97
6:6–11 73, 87, 95, 96, 97–99, 115
6:7 98, 259
6:8 97
6:9 98, 213, 222
6:10 98
6:11 97, 99, 105
6:12 63, 99, 152, 318
6:12–16 87, 99–101, 107, 132
6:13 99, 146
6:14 314, 315
6:14–16 99–100
6:17 87, 101, 108
6:17–19 101
6:17–49 79, 100–115
6:18 101
6:18–19 101
6:19 146
6:20 101, 105, 149
6:20–21 81
6:20–23 100, 101
6:20–26 41, 101–6, 114, 164, 189, 224
6:21 102, 103, 104, 354
6:22 103, 108, 109
6:22–23 106
6:23 103, 105, 111, 223
6:24 246, 277
6:24–25 106, 159
6:24–26 100, 101
6:25 103

6:26 106
6:27 101, 107, 108
6:27–28 100, 106, 108, 337
6:27–30 106
6:27–31 106
6:27–36 111
6:27–38 101, 106–12
6:29 109
6:29–30 100, 106, 109
6:30 109, 230
6:31 100, 106, 110
6:32 100, 110
6:32–34 106, 110
6:33 100
6:34 100, 110
6:35 100, 106, 110, 111
6:35–36 67, 106, 111, 114
6:36 100
6:37 100, 111
6:37–38 101, 106, 107, 111, 112
6:38 100, 112
6:39 101, 112, 113
6:39–42 111, 112
6:39–49 101, 106, 107, 112–15
6:40 101, 113
6:41–42 101, 111, 113, 270
6:43–44 101
6:43–45 114
6:45 101, 136
6:46–49 101, 114, 223
7 52, 116, 118, 122, 123, 125, 129, 130, 188, 265, 354
7:1 117
7:1–10 116–21, 122, 175
7:1–50 116–32
7:1–8:56 77, 116–44
7:2 116, 118
7:2–3 116, 117
7:3 116
7:3–5 117
7:4 117, 120
7:4–5 117
7:4–6 118
7:5 108
7:6 118, 120
7:6–8 119–20
7:6–9 117
7:9 120
7:10 116, 117, 121

407

Index of Scripture and Ancient Sources

7:11–12 121, 122
7:11–16 148
7:11–17 116, 121–23, 124, 298
7:12 122
7:13 103, 122, 171, 180
7:13–15 121
7:14 122
7:14–15 122
7:15 122, 151
7:16 122, 128, 148, 341
7:17 86, 87
7:18 123
7:18–19 123
7:18–23 123–25
7:18–33 22
7:18–35 116, 128, 194
7:19 147, 171, 283
7:20 65, 124, 276
7:21 81, 124, 176
7:21–23 123
7:22 81, 105, 122, 124, 190, 228
7:23 102, 125
7:24 125
7:24–25 125
7:24–27 123
7:24–35 123, 125–27
7:26 126, 128, 130
7:27 65, 126, 171
7:28 68, 123, 126, 170
7:29 127, 291
7:29–30 126, 128, 320
7:30 127, 128, 130, 291
7:31 127
7:32 103, 127
7:33 36, 123
7:33–34 127
7:34 93, 105, 123, 128, 153, 164, 277, 314, 326, 354
7:35 36, 127, 198, 237
7:36 128, 182, 195
7:36–46 182
7:36–50 93, 116, 121, 127–32, 183, 187, 189
7:37 128
7:37–38 128
7:38 103
7:39 128, 130, 195
7:40 130
7:41–42 130, 131
7:42 108, 132

7:43 81, 132
7:44–46 132
7:45 108
7:47 131, 132, 337
7:48 131, 132
7:48–49 48
7:49 131, 147
7:50 131
8 116, 137, 144
8:1 29, 132
8:1–3 86, 105, 116, 132–34, 149, 342
8:1–56 116, 132–44
8:2–3 347, 348
8:3 133, 348
8:4 134
8:4–8 221
8:4–15 134–36
8:4–21 116, 132, 134–37
8:5 134
8:5–8 134
8:6–8 134
8:8 134, 231
8:9 134
8:9–10 149
8:10 134, 154
8:11 84, 135
8:11–15 223
8:12 131, 135, 319
8:13 103, 183, 319
8:14 135
8:15 136, 183
8:16 136, 261
8:16–17 136, 201
8:16–18 134, 136–37
8:17 136
8:18 137
8:19 136
8:19–20 137
8:19–21 134, 137, 212, 229
8:21 137, 183, 192
8:22 137
8:22–25 137–38
8:22–56 116, 132, 137–44
8:23 137
8:24 137, 138, 257, 314
8:25 138, 140, 147
8:26–27 139
8:26–39 136, 137, 138–40, 144
8:27 139
8:28 84, 85, 111, 139
8:29 81, 139

8:30 139
8:31 139
8:32 140
8:33 140
8:34–35 140
8:36–37 140
8:37 140
8:38–39 140
8:39 144
8:40–42 121, 141
8:40–56 136, 137, 141–44
8:41 269
8:42 141
8:43 141, 142
8:43–48 121
8:44 142, 143
8:45 142, 257
8:46 142, 146
8:46–47 142
8:48 131, 142
8:49 130, 143
8:49–56 121
8:50 143
8:51 143
8:52 103, 143
8:53 143
8:54–55 144
8:55 144, 354
8:56 144
9 161, 321, 354
9–10 181
9–19 163
9:1 99, 146, 148, 171, 176
9:1–5 105, 149, 170
9:1–6 145, 146–47, 171
9:1–17 145–51
9:1–50 77, 145–61
9:2 146, 261
9:2–9 329
9:3 146, 172, 315
9:4 316
9:4–5 146–47
9:5 161
9:6 147, 148
9:7 64, 147, 148
9:7–8 147
9:7–9 22, 145, 147–48, 151, 329
9:7–20 22
9:8 152
9:9 64, 147, 148
9:10 146, 148, 149, 253

9:10–17 93, 102, 145, 148–51, 174, 351
9:11 149
9:12 149
9:12–17 223
9:13 149
9:14 149
9:14–15 133
9:15 149
9:16 149, 312, 351
9:17 102, 150
9:18 63, 99, 148, 151, 152, 154
9:18–27 145, 151–54
9:19 152, 153
9:20 86, 152, 153, 327
9:22 59, 105, 134, 153, 222, 274, 308, 316, 351
9:22–23 152–53
9:23 153, 334–35
9:23–24 229
9:24 153, 164, 224
9:24–25 213
9:25 153
9:26 153–54
9:26–27 304
9:27 154, 258
9:28 90, 154, 156, 318
9:28–29 63, 99
9:28–36 53, 145, 152, 154–57, 163
9:29 154
9:29–31 154
9:29–34 69
9:30 155, 348, 355
9:30–31 308
9:31 71, 156, 163, 167, 309
9:32 156
9:32–33 154
9:33 156, 257
9:34 157
9:34–36 154
9:35 327
9:35–36 157
9:36 154, 157
9:37–38 158
9:37–43 145, 157–59
9:38 130
9:39 158
9:40 158, 290
9:41 158
9:42 158, 159
9:43 159
9:43–44 159
9:43–50 145, 159–60

Index of Scripture and Ancient Sources

9:44 153, 274, 316, 340, 351
9:45 159
9:46 159, 312, 313
9:46–48 268
9:47 313
9:47–48 159, 160
9:48 159, 160, 313
9:49 160, 257, 290
9:50 160, 192
9:51 156, 163, 167, 211, 221
9:51–56 169, 181, 187
9:51–62 167–70
9:51–11:13 165, 167–88, 201
9:51–14:35 165, 181, 224, 227, 267, 271
9:51–19:44 15, 145, 163
9:52–53 168, 328
9:52–69 229
9:53 168
9:54 168, 173, 181, 211
9:55–56 168
9:56 153
9:57 170, 221
9:57–60 168–69
9:57–62 170, 171, 172
9:58 105, 153
9:59 170
9:61 169–70
9:62 170
10 8, 53, 161, 164, 179, 187, 269, 286, 354
10:1 171
10:1–2 105, 176
10:1–12 147, 171–74
10:1–24 167, 170–78
10:2 171, 176
10:3 172, 316
10:4 172, 315
10:5–6 172
10:6–8 316
10:7–8 171, 173
10:9 105, 173, 258
10:10–11 223
10:10–12 173
10:11 105, 258
10:13 174
10:13–16 174–75
10:13–24 174
10:14 175
10:15 175, 177
10:16 175

10:17 175, 176
10:17–18 190
10:17–20 176
10:17–24 175–78, 203
10:18 175, 176, 177, 321
10:19 176, 177
10:20 105, 176, 178
10:21 124, 176, 178, 340
10:21–22 105
10:22 176, 178
10:23 102, 149, 178
10:23–24 176
10:24 178, 229
10:25 66, 130, 164, 179, 221, 269
10:25–28 179
10:25–37 168, 179–82, 188, 243, 272
10:25–11:13 167, 179–86
10:26 179, 295
10:27 179, 197
10:28 179
10:29 179
10:29–37 179
10:29–11:13 179
10:30–35 180
10:34 51
10:36 180
10:37 180, 181
10:38 152, 182
10:38–40 182
10:38–42 93, 133, 135, 179, 182–83, 187, 188
10:39 171, 182
10:39–40 182
10:40 182
10:41 138, 171, 314
10:41–42 182, 314
10:42 188
11 52, 179, 265, 354
11:1 22, 63, 90, 99, 152, 318
11:1–4 179, 183
11:1–13 183, 186, 191
11:2 304, 320, 340
11:4 48, 191, 319, 337
11:5–7 183–84
11:5–8 183, 187, 188, 262
11:5–13 179, 183–86, 271
11:7 261
11:8 184, 185, 186

11:9–13 184, 185, 186, 271
11:10 222
11:11–12 177
11:11–13 186
11:13 183, 203
11:14 189, 190, 290
11:14–16 190
11:14–20 191
11:14–36 189, 190–95
11:14–13:9 165, 189–215
11:15 190, 221, 269, 290
11:15–16 189, 190
11:16 190, 191, 193, 329
11:17–18 190
11:17–26 189, 190–92
11:18 290
11:19 190, 191, 290
11:20 102, 105, 154, 191, 192, 197, 259, 290
11:21–22 191
11:23 192
11:24 193
11:24–26 133, 192
11:27 40, 192, 221, 334
11:27–28 102, 189, 192–93, 334
11:28 192, 193, 334
11:29 127, 193
11:29–36 189, 193–95
11:30 153, 193
11:31 198
11:31–32 193–94
11:33 136
11:33–36 194, 278
11:34–36 194, 195, 201
11:35 195
11:37 195
11:37–41 297
11:37–54 93, 128, 189, 195–99, 200
11:38 195
11:39 196, 199
11:39–41 195, 300
11:39–44 195
11:40 196
11:41 196, 208
11:42 195, 196, 197, 199, 266
11:43 195, 197, 199

11:44 195, 197, 199, 200, 321
11:45 130, 195, 197, 221
11:46 195, 197, 199
11:46–52 195
11:47 199
11:47–48 198
11:47–51 195
11:49 237
11:49–51 198
11:50 127
11:52 195, 199
11:53–54 195, 199
12:1 114, 200, 212, 221
12:1–12 189, 200–203, 213
12:1–59 213
12:1–13:9 189, 200–214
12:2 136
12:2–3 200
12:4 202, 262
12:4–5 201
12:5 208
12:6 201
12:6–7 201
12:7 302
12:8 153
12:8–9 202
12:9 208
12:10 153, 202
12:11 135
12:11–12 203
12:12 124
12:13 130, 204, 221
12:13–14 203
12:13–21 261
12:13–34 189, 203–8
12:14 204
12:15 153, 203, 204, 262
12:16 136, 205
12:16–21 203, 246, 277
12:17 205
12:18 205
12:18–19 260
12:19 205, 210, 260, 304
12:20 112, 196, 205
12:21 206
12:22 135, 206, 262
12:22–23 203
12:22–31 304
12:23 206, 262

409

Index of Scripture and Ancient Sources

12:24 206, 207
12:24–27 203
12:25 135, 279, 280
12:25–26 207
12:27 207
12:27–28 203
12:28 207
12:29 260
12:29–30 204, 207
12:30–32 204, 207
12:31–34 261
12:32–33 314
12:33 204, 208
12:33–34 204, 230
12:34 204, 208
12:35 208
12:35–40 253
12:35–48 189, 208–11
12:36–38 209
12:37 209
12:37–38 102
12:38 209
12:39 209
12:39–40 209
12:40 153, 209
12:41 209, 221
12:41–46 209
12:42 209–10
12:42–48 253
12:43 102
12:43–44 210
12:45 210, 260
12:46 210
12:47–48 211
12:48 112, 211
12:49 211
12:49–51 211
12:49–53 189, 211–12, 316
12:50 274
12:51–53 229
12:52–53 212
12:54–55 212
12:54–59 189, 212–13
12:56 114, 212
12:57 212
12:58 269
12:58–59 213
12:59 202
13 66, 165, 217, 285
13:1 64, 213, 221, 327, 330
13:1–7 271
13:1–9 99, 189, 213–14
13:2–3 213
13:3 213

13:4 214
13:5 214
13:6–9 66, 214
13:10–11 217, 278
13:10–13 217–18
13:10–17 73, 216–20, 275
13:10–14:35 165, 216–31
13:11 216, 304
13:11–13 216
13:12 323
13:12–13 216, 218
13:13 216, 341
13:14 216
13:14–15 218
13:14–17 216, 218–20
13:15 114
13:15–16 217
13:16 218, 219, 220
13:17 217, 220
13:18–19 220
13:18–21 222
13:18–35 216, 220–25
13:20–21 221
13:22 221
13:23 221, 222
13:23–24 296
13:24 222
13:25 222, 223
13:25–27 253
13:26 223, 353
13:27 223, 227
13:28 223
13:29 105, 209, 223, 310, 314
13:30 47, 224, 276
13:31 64, 124, 127, 133, 148, 213, 224, 329, 331
13:31–37 329
13:32 290
13:32–33 224, 274, 330
13:33 59, 84, 134, 308
13:34 199, 225, 285, 302, 314
13:34–35 335
13:35 225, 283
14 52, 165, 265, 354
14:1 195, 259, 267, 269
14:1–4 225
14:1–6 99, 225–26, 275
14:1–14 216, 225–27
14:1–24 93, 128

14:2–3 195
14:5–6 226
14:7 226
14:7–11 164, 197
14:7–14 226–27
14:8 118
14:8–10 226
14:11 120, 164, 226
14:12 229, 246, 277
14:12–14 227
14:13 93, 102, 105
14:13–14 228
14:14 102, 227, 338
14:15 102, 227, 229, 304
14:15–24 135, 216, 223, 227–29, 272, 310
14:16–17 227
14:16–24 189, 253
14:18 227
14:18–19 260
14:18–20 228
14:20 260
14:21 102, 105, 228
14:21–23 314
14:22 228
14:23 228
14:24 228
14:25 229
14:25–26 229
14:25–35 216, 229–31
14:27 229
14:28–30 229
14:31–32 230
14:33 230
14:34–35 230
14:35 231
15 204, 240, 242, 262
15:1 93, 236, 277
15:1–2 236, 242, 328
15:1–7 235, 236–37
15:1–32 233, 235–43
15:1–19:44 165
15:2 93, 265, 354
15:3–6 236
15:3–7 271
15:6 103, 236
15:7 93, 103, 236
15:8–10 235, 237–38, 271
15:9 103
15:10 103
15:11 240
15:11–24 238–41
15:11–32 235, 238–42, 252, 271, 313

15:12 204, 240
15:13 240
15:14 102
15:17 240
15:18 240, 267
15:19 240
15:20 180, 240
15:21 240
15:22 47, 240
15:24 240
15:25 240, 242
15:25–32 240–42
15:27 240
15:28 240
15:29 240
15:29–30 241
15:30 129, 136, 240
15:31 242
15:32 103
16 118, 354
16:1 136, 205
16:1–2 245
16:1–8 210, 245–47
16:1–13 244, 245–49, 253, 277
16:1–17:10 233, 244–55
16:3 275
16:3–7 247
16:8 173, 247, 248
16:8–9 248
16:8–13 247–49
16:9 112, 248
16:10 248
16:10–12 248
16:10–13 248
16:11 248
16:12 248
16:13 248, 269
16:13–14 265
16:14–15 197, 244
16:14–18 68, 244, 249
16:15 135, 196
16:16 22, 102, 105, 171
16:16–17 244
16:18 249
16:19 205, 330
16:19–25 244
16:19–26 249–50
16:19–31 136, 205, 246, 252, 261, 296
16:20 102, 105
16:20–21 102
16:22 102, 105
16:24 181
16:27–31 244, 250–51

Index of Scripture and Ancient Sources

16:31 244
17:1 282
17:1–3 251–52
17:1–10 244, 251–53
17:3 337, 338
17:3–4 251, 252
17:4 48
17:5 253
17:5–6 251
17:6 253
17:7–8 309
17:7–9 253
17:7–10 209, 251
17:10 253
17:11 221, 256, 273
17:11–19 121, 168, 256–58, 275
17:11–18:30 233, 256–72, 273
17:12 257
17:12–14 256
17:12–19 256
17:13 181, 257
17:14 257, 258
17:15 341
17:15–16 258
17:15–19 256
17:16–18 257
17:17–18 258
17:19 131, 258
17:20 258
17:20–21 258–59, 304
17:20–18:8 256, 258–65
17:21 102, 105, 259
17:22 153, 259
17:22–25 258, 259
17:23 259, 300
17:24 153, 259, 262, 305
17:25 105, 127, 259, 274, 308
17:26 153, 259
17:26–27 259
17:26–30 258, 259–60, 282
17:27 136
17:28 259, 260
17:28–30 260
17:29 260
17:30 153
17:31 260–61
17:31–33 260
17:31–37 258, 260–62
17:32 261
17:33 261
17:34–35 261

17:34–37 260
17:36 261
17:37 261, 262
18 164, 165, 243, 272
18:1 262
18:1–8 258, 262–65, 271, 298
18:2 262, 265
18:3 263
18:4 264, 265
18:4–5 263
18:5 264
18:8 153, 265
18:9 265
18:9–14 179, 265–67
18:9–30 256, 265–71
18:10 265
18:11 93, 265, 266, 277
18:12 266
18:13 266, 342
18:14 120, 164, 227, 267
18:15 267, 284
18:15–17 265, 267–68, 276
18:16 199, 268, 276
18:16–17 282
18:17 268
18:18 66, 130, 164, 179, 269
18:18–23 267, 268, 269–70
18:18–25 136
18:18–30 230, 265, 268–71
18:19 269
18:20 269
18:21 269
18:22 269
18:23 270
18:24 270
18:24–25 270
18:24–27 296
18:24–30 268, 270–71
18:25 246, 277
18:26 222
18:26–27 270
18:28 271
18:28–29 229
18:29 229
18:29–30 271
18:31 153, 273, 316
18:31–33 327
18:31–34 256, 273–75
18:31–19:44 233, 256, 273–86

18:32 325, 351
18:32–33 274
18:34 274–75, 276
18:35 81, 275
18:35–43 121, 124, 136, 275–77
18:35–19:10 256, 273, 275–80
18:36 277
18:36–38 276
18:36–39 277
18:38 257
18:38–39 181
18:39 276, 277, 284
18:40–41 276
18:41 276
18:42 131, 277
18:43 277, 280, 341
19 66, 67, 73, 282, 354
19:1 277
19:1–9 182
19:1–10 93, 136, 187, 275, 277–80, 285, 328
19:2 277
19:3 59, 278
19:4 279
19:5 82, 279
19:6 279
19:7 93, 279
19:8 105, 267, 279
19:9 42, 82, 280, 339
19:10 153, 280
19:11 281, 304
19:11–27 256, 273, 280–82
19:12 281
19:13 281
19:14 281
19:15 281
19:16–19 281
19:20–21 281
19:21 223
19:22–24 281–82
19:25 282
19:26 137, 282
19:27 282
19:28 221, 282
19:28–44 256, 273, 282–85
19:29–31 282
19:30 284, 346
19:32–35 282
19:36 283
19:37–38 283
19:38 124, 225

19:39 130, 284
19:40 284–85
19:41 84, 103, 105
19:41–42 285
19:41–44 225, 335
19:42 230, 285
19:42–44 302
19:43 108, 285
19:43–44 285
19:44 285, 300
19:45 260
19:45–46 290
19:45–48 72, 73, 289–91, 305
19:45–21:38 287
19:45–24:53 287
19:46 298
19:47 47, 72, 290, 291
19:47–48 293, 328, 330
19:47–20:1 291
19:48 291
20:1 291
20:1–2 291
20:1–8 22, 289, 291–92, 326
20:3–4 291
20:5–6 292, 294, 295
20:6 328, 330
20:7 292
20:8 292
20:9–16 292
20:9–19 289, 292–93
20:16 293
20:17–18 293
20:19 124, 293, 328, 330, 340
20:20 259, 294
20:20–26 289
20:21 130
20:21–22 294
20:22 64
20:23–24 294
20:25 64, 294, 328
20:26 295, 328
20:27–31 295
20:27–40 295–97
20:27–44 289, 295–97
20:28 130
20:32–33 295
20:34–36 296
20:35 260, 296
20:36 173
20:37–38 296
20:39 130
20:39–40 297
20:41 297

411

Index of Scripture and Ancient Sources

20:41–44 97, 178, 276, 297
20:42–43 297
20:43 108
20:44 97, 297
20:45 297, 330
20:45–47 297
20:45–21:4 289, 297–99
20:46–47 197
20:47 298
21:1 136, 298
21:1–4 133, 136, 246, 277, 299
21:2 102, 202, 298
21:2–3 105
21:3 102
21:3–4 298
21:5 299
21:5–6 299–300
21:5–28 289, 299–304
21:6 299
21:7 130, 299, 300, 302
21:7–11 300–301
21:7–28 299
21:8–9 300
21:8–11 299
21:10–11 299, 300
21:12–17 103, 301
21:12–19 301–2
21:12–27 177
21:16 229
21:18 177, 201
21:18–19 302
21:19 136
21:20 302
21:20–24 299, 300, 302
21:20–28 302–4
21:21–22 302
21:23 35, 302
21:23–24 335
21:24 302
21:25–26 303, 305
21:25–28 299, 301
21:27 153
21:27–28 303
21:28 302, 305–6
21:29–31 304
21:29–33 304
21:29–38 289, 304–5
21:32 127
21:32–33 304
21:34 210
21:34–35 135, 304
21:34–36 304–5

21:36 153, 305
21:37–38 305
21:38 328, 330
22 52, 148, 354
22:1–2 307
22:1–6 307–8
22:1–13 307–9
22:1–23:49 14, 15, 277, 287, 307–42
22:2 307, 328, 330, 342
22:3 135, 203, 314, 319
22:3–4 307
22:3–6 312
22:4–5 346
22:5 308
22:6 308, 342
22:7 308
22:7–13 133, 308–9
22:8 309, 310
22:9 309
22:10–12 309
22:11 51, 130, 309
22:13 309
22:14 309
22:14–23 309–12
22:14–30 223
22:14–38 93, 307, 308, 309–17
22:15–16 310
22:15–23 311
22:16 105, 229
22:17–18 310
22:18 229, 310
22:19 150, 262, 312, 351, 354
22:19–20 311, 312
22:21 325
22:21–23 312
22:22 153
22:23 312, 317
22:24 312, 317
22:24–27 133, 276, 309, 312
22:24–34 312–15
22:25 312
22:26 313, 354
22:27 209, 313
22:28 183, 313, 317
22:28–30 99, 209
22:29–30 314
22:30 105, 304, 319, 354
22:31 135, 314, 319, 321
22:32 63, 315, 324

22:33 135, 315, 317, 324
22:34 315, 323, 325
22:35 170, 315
22:35–38 315–17
22:36 316
22:37 229, 273, 308, 316, 325, 336
22:38 316, 317, 322
22:39 318
22:39–46 63, 156, 317–21
22:39–53 307, 317–23
22:40 135, 318
22:40–41 152
22:41 99, 320, 321
22:42 312, 319, 320, 333, 340
22:43 320
22:43–44 9, 320
22:44 152, 320
22:44–45 99
22:45 321
22:46 135, 152, 318, 321
22:47 127, 322, 342
22:47–48 312
22:47–53 321–23, 325
22:48 153, 322
22:49 222, 322
22:49–50 316
22:49–51 135
22:50 64, 322
22:51 322
22:52 316, 325, 327
22:52–53 322–23
22:53 124, 308, 310, 329, 339, 340
22:54 64, 105, 203, 323
22:54–55 323
22:54–62 135, 325
22:54–65 323–25
22:54–23:25 307, 323–33
22:56 323
22:57 323
22:58 315, 323
22:59 323
22:60 315, 323, 324
22:61–62 324
22:62 103, 336
22:63 274, 323, 324, 325, 326, 327
22:63–64 105
22:63–65 312
22:64 324, 325

22:65 325
22:66 325, 327
22:66–71 325–27, 346
22:67 326
22:67–68 326
22:69 153, 326
22:69–70 178
22:70 323, 327
22:70–71 328
22:71 327
23 337
23:1 64, 327
23:1–5 327–28
23:1–25 339
23:2 64, 327–28, 330, 331
23:3 64, 328
23:4 64, 328, 341, 342
23:5 87, 328, 330
23:6 64, 324
23:6–7 329
23:6–12 329–30, 341
23:7 329
23:7–8 64
23:8 190, 329, 339
23:9 329
23:10 330
23:11 274, 330
23:11–12 64
23:11–13 64
23:12 329, 330
23:13 269, 332, 338, 342
23:13–14 330
23:13–25 330–33
23:14 331, 341, 342
23:15 64, 148, 330, 331, 332, 341
23:16 331
23:17 331, 332
23:18 331, 332, 338, 346
23:19 332
23:20 64, 333
23:21 333, 338
23:22 274, 333, 341
23:23 333
23:24 64, 333
23:25 332, 333
23:26 334, 341
23:26–32 192, 333, 334–36
23:26–49 307, 333–40
23:27 335, 338, 341
23:28 103
23:28–30 335
23:29 102, 334

412

Index of Scripture and Ancient Sources

23:30 335
23:31 112, 336
23:32 336, 341
23:32–33 316
23:33 312, 336
23:33–39 336
23:33–43 109, 334, 336–39
23:34 48, 109, 337, 340
23:35 230, 269, 332, 337, 342
23:35–38 105
23:36 274
23:36–37 337
23:38 337
23:39 105, 337
23:39–43 296, 341
23:40 338
23:40–41 267
23:40–43 336, 338
23:41 338
23:42 257, 338
23:43 82, 105, 221, 339
23:44–45 339
23:44–49 334, 339–40
23:45 339
23:46 63, 99, 152, 274, 340
23:47 34, 106, 213, 341, 346
23:47–49 340, 341
23:48 267, 332, 342
23:49 133, 335, 341, 342, 346, 348
23:50 34
23:50–51 345
23:50–53 127
23:50–56 345
23:50–24:53 14, 15, 287
23:52 64
23:52–53 346
23:53 347
23:54 347
23:55 335, 346, 347, 348
23:56 347, 348
24 10, 52, 148, 321, 354
24:1 348
24:1–11 345
24:2–3 348
24:3 10, 262
24:4 155, 348
24:5 10, 348
24:6–7 155, 348
24:7 153, 308, 350
24:8 133
24:8–9 348
24:10 345, 347, 348
24:10–11 349
24:12 10, 349, 352
24:13 349
24:13–27 349
24:13–35 345
24:14 349
24:15 349
24:16 349
24:17 350
24:18 350
24:19 14, 15, 350
24:19–20 350
24:20 269
24:21 350
24:22–24 350
24:23 262, 348
24:25 351
24:26 105, 154, 308, 351
24:27 351
24:28 351
24:28–35 349
24:29 351
24:29–32 93
24:30 150, 351
24:31 83, 178, 351, 352
24:32 199, 352
24:33 124, 352
24:33–34 352
24:34 35, 203, 352
24:35 352
24:36 10, 83, 172, 352–53
24:36–49 351
24:36–53 345
24:37 353
24:38 35
24:38–39 353
24:40 10, 353
24:41 103, 105, 353
24:41–43 93
24:42 353
24:43 353
24:44 273, 308, 355
24:44–46 351
24:45–46 355
24:46 164, 273
24:47 93, 156, 170, 171, 303, 355
24:48 178, 355
24:48–49 147
24:49 49, 167, 340, 355

24:50 355
24:50–53 355
24:51 10, 355
24:52 10, 103, 176
24:52–53 355
24:53 73, 348

Q

3:8–9 66
4:1–13 71
4:5 72
6:20–23 100, 101
6:21 103
6:27 108
6:27–28 100, 108
6:29 100, 109
6:30 100
6:31 100
6:32 100
6:34 100
6:35 100
6:36 100
6:37–38 100
6:39 101
6:40 101, 113
6:41–42 101, 113
6:43–44 101
6:43–45 114
6:45 101
6:46–49 101, 115
7:1 117
7:3 117
7:6–9 117
7:18–19 124
7:22–23 124
7:24–30 126
9:57–60 168
10:2–12 170

John

1:11 51
1:12–13 111
1:31–34 63
2 354
3:35 178
4 309
4:8–9 181, 258
4:14 354
4:35 170, 171
4:46–54 117
5:14 91
6 354
6:1–15 148
6:35 354
6:51 354
6:54–56 354

7:29 178
9:2 213, 279
9:7 214
9:11 214
9:16 132
10 237
10:14–15 178
10:24–25 326
12:1–8 128
12:25 229, 261
12:27–33 177
13:1 310
13:1–17 209
13:3 178
13:16 113
13:37 315
15:20 113
17:2 178
17:12 173
17:25 178
18:1–11 321
18:10 322
18:13 323
18:33 328
18:39 332
19:38 346
20:24–29 353
21:1–11 87

Acts

1 135, 156
1:1 14
1:4–8 183
1:5 69
1:9 318
1:10 155
1:10–11 69
1:11 155
1:12 318
1:12–14 136
1:13 99–100
1:16–25 315
1:18 211
1:22 69
1:24 196
1:25 203, 211
2 211, 321, 355
2:1 167
2:1–3 63
2:1–5 69
2:3 35, 321
2:14–39 315
2:22–24 14
2:23 316, 320, 331, 333
2:34–35 297
2:37 66

413

2:42 357
2:42–47 208
2:44 188
2:46 357
3–4 285
3:6 176
3:13–14 331
3:14 34
3:15 335, 341
3:17 331
3:22 156
3:24 29
3:25 42
4:1 295
4:2 338
4:3 301, 315
4:8–13 315
4:10 176
4:17–18 176
4:25–26 273, 329
4:28 320
4:30 176
4:32–35 208
5:4 203
5:9 203
5:15 142
5:17 295
5:18 301
5:31 93, 335
5:38–39 320
5:39 203
5:40 176
6:1 210
6:1–6 299, 309
6:5 85
6:9 301
6:10 301
6:13–14 95
7 84
7:2 35
7:2–17 42
7:26 35
7:30 35
7:37 156
7:48 161
7:52 34, 198, 301, 341
7:58 85
7:59–60 301
7:60 109
8 285, 355
8:3 301
8:5–40 85
8:9 60
8:11 60
8:33 332
8:40 83
9:1–31 85

9:2 301
9:4 138, 314
9:4–5 301
9:11 187
9:17 35
9:27 176
9:29 27
9:36–43 121
9:40 262
9:43–11:3 182
10 29, 188
10–11 118, 173
10:2 196
10:22 182
10:23 182
10:36 172
10:37 69
10:38 109
11 29
11:4 29
11:16–18 69
11:18 93
12 177
12:1 301
12:2 301
12:3 315
12:3–5 301
12:4 301
12:12–17 323
13 161
13:2 94
13:6 60
13:6–12 301
13:8 60
13:8–12 301
13:22–23 297
13:24 93
13:24–25 69
13:31 35
13:33–37 297
13:36 320
13:44–51 301
13:48–52 147
13:50 47
14:3 161
14:15–17 214
14:23 94
15 222
15:8 196
15:13–15 201
15:14 330
16:4 26
16:9 35
16:10–17 5
16:11–15 187
16:19–24 301
16:30 66

17:1–5 301
17:4 47
17:5–7 187
17:26 70
17:32 338
18:2–3 187
18:9–10 301
18:12–17 301
18:23 29
18:24–26 69
18:24–28 69
19:1–7 69
19:4 93
19:8–10 301
19:12 142
19:13 27
19:13–14 190
20:5–15 5
20:7 357
20:7–12 121
20:11 357
20:19 183
20:21 93
20:27 320
20:28 7
21:1–18 5
21:2–4 5–6
21:3–6 182
21:7 182
21:7–16 187
21:8–16 182
21:20 200
21:27 301
21:27–36 301
22:4 301
22:7–8 301
22:10 66
22:14 34, 341
22:17–22 34
23:2–8 328
23:6 295
23:7 295
23:8 295
23:11 301
23:24–33 301
24:1 301
24:2 27
24:10 27, 301
25 329
25:2 47
25:13–26 301
26:2 301
26:11 301
26:12 200
26:14–15 301
26:16 35
26:20 93

26:27 301
26:30 301
27:1–28:16 5
27:3 187, 188
27:9 94
28 342
28:2 188
28:6–10 182
28:7 182
28:7–10 187
28:13–14 182
28:16 301
28:17 47

Romans
1:3 297
2:4–5 214
3:25 7
5:3–4 91, 302
8:14–15 111
8:25 302
8:32 42
9:13 242
9:29 174
11:25–27 303
12:14 109
12:15 103
13:9 269
13:13 304
16:20 177

1 Corinthians
1:24 198, 237
1:30 198
2:7 198
7 296
9:7 254
9:10 254
9:27 264
10:16 132
11 254, 311
11:2 26
11:23 26, 150
11:23–24 150
11:30 91
11:32 91
13:2 253
15:3 7

2 Corinthians
1:6 302
4:5–12 115
5:21 7
6:9 331
12:2 339
12:4 339

Galatians
1:3–4 91
2 173
4:5–6 111

Ephesians
1:18 195
2:3 173
2:14–21 340
6:14 208

Philippians
3:4–6 266
3:6 34
4:6–7 262

Colossians
1:11 302
1:24 91
2:3 198
2:15 177
3:12 48
4:10–11 8
4:14 7, 8

1 Thessalonians
1:3 302
5:2 209
5:6 305
5:6–7 210
5:7 304

2 Thessalonians
1:4 302
1:10 161
2:8 4

1 Timothy
1:15 267
4:13 4

2 Timothy
4:9–11 7

Philemon
24 7

Hebrews
1:1 27
5:8 320
6:14 222
11:4 198
11:17–18 42

11:37 210
12:5 190
12:24 198

James
1:2–3 91
2:2–3 330
2:7 103
4:9 103
5:6 341
5:16 91

1 Peter
1:13 208
2:7 293
2:22–25 329
3:18 341
4:7 305
5:13 190

2 Peter
2:5 259
2:6 174
2:17 193
3:3–4 209
3:4 210
3:8–10 209
3:9–10 214
3:10 209

1 John
2:1 341
3:12 198

Jude
7 174

Revelation
1:3 4
2:7 339
3:3 209, 210
3:20 209, 222
12:7–10 177
12:7–12 177
16:15 209
19:9 229
20:3 140
20:3–10 177
21:1 138

OLD TESTAMENT PSEUDEPIGRAPHA

Ahiqar
8.25 215

Apocalypse of Elijah
2.38 335

2 Baruch
5.1–10 296
10.13–16 335
29.4 138, 310
34.1–43.3 34

3 Baruch
1.2 264
16 210

1 Enoch
10.4–6 140
13.5 267
15.1–7 296
18.11–16 140
22 338
22.5–7 198
37.4 269
40.9 269
58.3 269
62.14 310
83.4 177
96:1–2 262
97.8–9 206
100.2 212
104.4 296

2 Enoch
29.3–6 176
61.1 110

Joseph and Aseneth
10.17 267

Jubilees
2.29–30 96
4.31 198
5.6 140
11.11 134
23.19 212
32.1–2 34

Letter of Aristeas
95 35
207 108, 110

Liber antiquitatum biblicarum (Pseudo-Philo)
16.2–3 198

Life of Adam and Eve
11–14 176

Odes of Solomon
9.68 46

Psalms of Solomon
3.12 269
17.21 297
17.32 341
17.50 102
18.4–5 91

Sibylline Oracles
1.100–103 201
2.283–312 201
3.796–807 177

Testament of Abraham
4.7 173
4.10 173
10 168
20.18–19 338

Testament of Benjamin
3.3 315
4.1–5.4 108

Testament of Gad
6.3–4 252

Testament of Judah
18–19 203
23.3 300–301

Testament of Levi
8.1–19 34
18.12 177

Testament of Moses
7 196, 199

Testament of Naphtali
1   110
3.4–5   259

Testament of Solomon
20.17   177

DEAD SEA SCROLLS

CD (Damascus Document)
5.19   251
6.15–16   290
8.8   211
10.3   211
B19.33b–35   222

1QapGen^{ar}
6.2   259
20.29   190

1QM (War Scroll)
15.14   208

1QpHab
9.1–7   290
15.34–35   266

1QS (Rule of the Community)
1.2–10   108
5.12   211
5.14–20   248
9.8–9   248

1QSa
2.12–21   310

4Q504 (frg. 6)
6–8   262

4Q521
2.2.6–14   125

4QSam^a
1.3   36

11QMelch
12–13   177
13   81

11QtgJob
30.1   208

NEW TESTAMENT APOCRYPHA

Acts of Philip
26–27   168

Acts of Pilate
12–17   346

Apostolic Constitutions and Canons
8.22   4

Gospel of Peter
2   346
6.21–24   347

Gospel of Thomas
10   211
14   170
20   220, 221
21   209
26   113
34   113
39.1–2   199
46   126
65   292
73   170, 171
76   208
79   192, 334
82   211
89.1   196
89.2   196
91   212
96   221
107   236

Infancy Gospel of Thomas
7.5–8   192
14   58
17.3   192

Narrative of Joseph of Arimathea
5   346

Protevangelium of James
5.10   192
6.10   192
19.16   192

RABBINIC WRITINGS

Mishnah
Baba Batra
8–9   204
8:1   263

Baba Qamma
8.6   322

Berakot
5.5   160
6.1   312

Ketubbot
4.4   143
11.1   263
12.3   263

Miqwa'ot
9.6   198

Pesaḥim
5   308

Qiddušin
4.3   181, 258

Šabbat
7.2   96
23.5   347

Sanhedrin
2.5   284
10.1   221–22

Šebi'it
9.1   196

Šeqalim
1.3   290
6.5   298

Soṭah
1.7   112

Tamid
5.1   265
5.4   35

Ṭehar
7.6   277

Yadayim
1.1   196

Yoma
8.6   98

Tosefta
Berakot
3.7   96
6.18   266
7.2   134

Babylonian Talmud
'Abodah Zarah
18a   339

Berakot
28b   266

Niddah
70b   295

Šabbat
31a   110
73b   134
101a   292
114a   198
119a   292

Sanhedrin
43a   328

Soṭah
48a   184, 271

Sukkah
49b   196

Ta'anit
20a   126

Yoma
85b   96

Index of Scripture and Ancient Sources

OTHER RABBINIC WRITINGS

'Abot de Rabbi Nathan
24   115
41   252

Esther Rabbah
3.6   293

Leviticus Rabbah
3.3   267
34.3   292
107a   299

Mekilta
109B (on Exodus 31:14)   96

Midrash to Psalms
9   241
43   156, 157

Ruth Rabbah
6.4   279

Song of Songs Rabbah
1.1.9   238

Tanḥuma Toledot
5   172

Targum to Song of Songs
4.16   35

APOSTOLIC FATHERS

Barnabas
9.7–9   220
9.8   220
12.11   297
18–21   114

1 Clement
11   261
13.2   112
36.2   195

2 Clement
5.2–4   172

Didache
1–6   114
1.4   109
1.5–6   109
8.1   266
9.1–3   311
16.1   208

Diognetus
56   268

Hermas, Similitudes
9.9.6   129
15.1–3   129
92.6   27

Ignatius, Magnesians
10.2   200

Papias, Fragments
3.15   30

Polycarp, Philippians
2.1   208
2.3   112

ANCIENT AUTHORS

Aelius Aristides
Hieroi logoi
4.17   321

Aeschylus
Eumenides
94–104   155

Ambrose
De Cain et Abel
1.8   42

Expositio Evangelii secundum Lucam
2.61   57
4.7.14   74
4.33–34   74
7.207–8   238

Aphthonius
Progymnasmata
8   175
18R–21R   281
22R   14
23   160, 275
24–25   207
31R   175
31R–32R   22, 68, 123
41   15
42   14

Apuleius
Florida
19   122

Metamorphoses
2.17   129
3.12   227

Archilochus
Carmina
67a   302

Aristophanes
Lysistrata
1308–13   129

Aristotle
Ethica eudemia
1233a.16–20   278

Ethica nichomachea
3.6   201
4.2.29   299
4.3.1123b.7   278
4.8.1128a.8–13   278
8.4.2–6   330
9.8.2   187

Historia animalium
1.1.488b.20   225

Rhetorica
1.4.12   30
1.5.3   30
2.23.4   186

Arrian
Epicteti dissertationes
1.3.7   172
1.3.7–9   225

Athenaeus
Deipnosophistae
13.590   129

Augustine
De civitate Dei
16.32   42

De consensu evangelistarum
2.6.18   28

Sermones
175.1   237
200   60
235.2   356
284.5   74–75

Bede
Exposition of the Gospel of Luke
1   52

Homilies on the Gospels
1.12   75

Caelius Aurelianus
Tardarum passionum
1.4.61   158

Celsus
De medicina
2.6.16–18   122

Chariton
De Chaerea et Callirhoe
2.5.4   187
3.5   188
5.97   187
8.8.15   130

Cicero
De amicitia
6.20   187

De divinatione
1.1–2   305
2.26.56   324
2.75   96

Index of Scripture and Ancient Sources

De inventione rhetorica
20.28 88

De oratore
2.60.245 279
3.221–23 194

Topica
20.76–77 33, 69
20.78 120
26.97 88

Clement of Alexandria

Stromata
9 220

Corpus Hippocraticum

De morbo sacro
7.10 158
7.12 158

Cyril of Alexandria

Commentarium in Lucam
Homily 12 74
Homily 106 237
Homily 127 278
Homily 145 317

Cyril of Jerusalem

Catechetical Lectures
19.8 261

Demetrius

De elocutione
25 134

Demosthenes

In Aristogitonem
1.25.52 66

Orationes
19.225 186

Dio Cassius

Historia Romana
65.7.2 277
65.8 119

Dio Chrysostom

Charidemus (Or. 30)
26 70

Orationes (Or. 32)
14–30 93
30 197

Venator (Or. 7)
7.21–22 187
7.45 187
7.56–58 187
7.57–58 187

Diodorus Siculus

Bibliotheca historica
1.9.6 259
1.25.6 122
1.25.27 122
1.27.3–4 122
1.28.1 259
5.31.3 259

Diogenes Laertius

Vitae philosophorum
3.19 329
3.98 186–87
6.39 150
9.15 329
10.14 57

Dionysius of Halicarnassus

Antiquitates romanae
10.10.7 263

De Thucydide
9 30

Ephrem the Syrian

Commentary on Tatian's Diatessaron
4.8B–C 74

Epictetus

Diatribai (Dissertationes)
1.19.8–9 201
1.26.6–7 211
2.22.19 208
2.23 292
3.10.12–20 201
3.15.10–13 230
3.22.9–15 114
3.22.85 196
3.22.89 275
3.23 93
3.30 93
4.1.91 58
4.10.23 196

Epiphanius

Panarion
51.110 8
78.11 57

Euripides

Alcestis
788–89 205

Danae
Frag. 327 299

Hippolytus
198–202 129

Eusebius

Historia ecclesiastica
3.4 6

Galen

On Prognosis
3.15 (618K) 142

Heliodorus

Aethiopica
1.2 129
2.22.2 187
3.4 129

Herodotus

Historiae
1.105 279
2.139 210

Hesiod

Opera et dies
1.235 279
1.349–51 112
1.443 170

Hippolytus

Traditio apostolica
1.12 4

Homer

Iliad
1.611 184
16.34–35 132
23 155, 344

Odyssey
1.311–18 187
5.188–89 110
9.266–71 187
18.339 210

Horace

Carmina
2.3.2 302
2.10.21–22 302

Epistulae
1.15.28 173

Satirae
2.6.107–9 209

Irenaeus

Adversus haereses
1.8.1 30
3.7.2 4
3.14.1 6
4.5 42
4.31.3 261

Isocrates

Nicocles (Or. 3)
49.1 110

Jerome

Commentariorum in Isaiam libri XVIII
3.6 8
73 176

Commentariorum in Matthaeum libri IV
Preface 6

Tractatus in Psalmos
44 51

Joannes Cassianus
Collationes
24.26.7 236

John Chrysostom
Homiliae in epistulam ad Galatas commentarius
1.3 278

Homiliae in epistulam ad Romanos
18.7 278

Homiliae in Matthaeum
10.1 278

Josephus
Against Apion
1.13 27
1.70 175
1.307 252
2.39 8
2.211 346

Antiquities of the Jews
1.204 261
4.254–55 295
5.348 57, 58
6.149 299
8.46 191
9.29 181, 258
10.283 263
11.140 260
11.326–28 34
14.204 67
14.309 339
14.392 67
14.406 67
18.16–17 295
18:55–59 213
18:60–62 213
18:86–87 213
18.109–19 68

Jewish War
1.110 265
1.288 67
1.398–400 330
2.60–62 53
2.124 316
2.129 195
2.164–65 295
2.169–77 213
2.587 58
4.326–33 302
5.222 300
5.420–38 302
5.512–18 302
6.201–22 302
6.285–87 300
6.288–300 303
6.300–309 300
6.303–4 332
6.420–26 309
7.132–57 283
7.218 277

The Life
40 27

Justin Martyr
Apologia i
16.1 109
65–67 311

Apologia ii
12 339

Dialogus cum Tryphone
105 340

Juvenal
Satirae
1.169–70 230
10.248–49 231

Livy
Historiae
13.12.3.4–5 263

Longus
Daphnis and Chloe
1.3.1–20 187
1.4 129
2.15.1 204
2.23 129

3.9 187
4.6 187

Lucian
Symposium
18 279

Melito
Fragments
9 42
10 42
11 42
15 42

Menander
Dyskolos
726.427–28 187

Nicolaus
Progymnasmata
4.18–19 239
17–24 149
20 160
51 14, 45
51–52 70
52 14, 46, 56–57
59–60 14, 45, 70
60 22, 123

Origen
Commentarii in evangelium Joannis
1.5.30 352
1.8.50 352

Commentarium in evangelium Matthaei
4 128

Contra Celsum
1.69 321
2.62 352
2.68 352

Exhortatio ad martyrium
29.32–37 320–21

Fragmenta in Lucam
36 352
96 74

Homiliae in Jeremiam
20 352

Homiliae in Lucam
17 57
34.9 181

Ovid
Metamorphoses
1.477 129
4.320–24 192
4.794–803 129
8.611–725 349
8.626–724 187
15.787 339

Pausanius
Graeciae descriptio
9.8.5 111
38.13 53

Petronius
Satyricon
45 130
94.1 192
111–12 346

Philo
De Abrahamo
105 230

De decalogo
51 269

In Flaccum
83–84 346

Legatio ad Gaium
145–49 82
299–305 330

Quis rerum divinarum heres
199 35

De sacrificiis Abelis et Caini
63 208

De specialibus legibus
3.155 108

419

Index of Scripture and Ancient Sources

De virtutibus
7 113

De vita Mosis
1.20–24 57
1.21 58
1.27 58
2.52–56 259
2.291 344

Philostratus

Vita Apollonii
1.2 305
4.34 33
8.31 344

Vita sophistarum
2.1 208
532 204

Photius

Lexicon
271 143

Plato

Apologia
39 339

Euthyphro
3d 186

Gorgias
486C 109
508C–D 109

Respublica
361e–362a 341
554b 113

Sophista
222A 89

Plautus

Miles gloriosus
203–4 237
790–93 129

Pliny the Elder

Naturalis historia
2.30 339
12.1 186

18.19.49 170
35.7.23 206

Plutarch

De adulatore et amico
49F 187
56 106
56–67 193
65A 187

Aemilius Paullus
39 186

Alcibiades
39.4a 344

De cohibenda ira
458A–B 291

Consolatio ad Apollonium
117–17 164

De cupiditate divitiarum
524D 205

De curiositate
518E 277

Eumenes
6.4 33

De facie in orbe lunae
921–22 264

De liberis educandis
2 279

Lucullus
12.1 33

Marcius Coriolanus
3.5–6 344

Quaestiones romanae et graecae
109 200

Romulus
27.6 339

Septum sapientium convivium
147E 227

De sera numinis vindicta
554A–B 229

Polemo

De physiognomia
11 217
172 172
174 225

Pollux

Onomasticon
9.123 324
9.129 324

Polybius

Historiae
2.10.5 341
2.37.4 27
13.2.2 226

Pseudo-Aristotle

Physiognomica
807b.1 194
807b.7 194
807b.19 194
807b.23 194
807b.29 194
807b.35 194
808a.1 194
808a.3 194
808a.8 194
808a.9 194
808a.12 194
808a.16 194
808a.28 194
808a.30 194, 278
808a.34 194
808b.6 194
809a 217
810b.10–12 217
810b.25–32 217
811a.28–29 218
811b.5–6 218
811b.6–7 218
811b.9–10 218
811b.21–22 218
811b.25–26 218
811b.30–31 218

811b.31–32 218
812a.7–8 218
812a.17 225
812b.8 194
813a.21 194
813a.31–32 218
813a.32–34 218
814b.3–4 194

Pseudo-Epiphanius

Testimony Book
7.30 143

Pseudo-Hermogenes

Progymnasmata
4 186
6–8 149
7–8 150, 175, 203
8 208
15 14, 45, 70
15–16 62
16 14, 28, 46, 57, 123, 339, 340
16–17 340, 344
17 346
19 14, 28, 46, 57, 67

Quintilian

Declamationes
268 186

Institutio oratoria
1.9.2 275
1.10.35 236
3.7.15 14
3.7.17 340
4.2 88
4.2.83 29
8.3.62 9
8.6.29–30 198
8.6.62–67 97, 222
9.1.34 35, 185, 239, 285
9.2.7 66, 92
9.2.54 319
9.3.27 239, 240
9.3.28 239
9.3.28–29 138, 310
9.3.30 174
9.3.37 239
9.3.45–46 201, 310
9.3.67 239
9.3.70–74 193, 197
9.3.81–86 200, 211, 270

Index of Scripture and Ancient Sources

Seneca
De beneficiis
2.1.1 110

De brevitate vitae
14.4 185

Epistulae morales
4 201
44.1 70
101.4 206

Ad Lucilium
8.3 186
119.16 186

Troades
290 96

Sextus Empiricus
Pyrrhoniae hypotyposes
1.136 208

Sophocles
Elektra
410–25 155

Stobaeus
Florilegium
4.5.76 186

Strabo
Geographica
4.6.6 58

Suetonius
Divus Augustus
76 266

De grammaticis
4 275

Vespasianus
7.2 119

Tacitus
Annales
1.17 202
1.26 202

6.29 346
11.15 186

Dialogus de oratoribus
28–29 192

Historiae
4.81 119

Tertullian
Adversus Marcionem
3.13 60
4.18 128

De idololatria
15 295

De praescriptione haereticorum
41 4

Theon
Progymnasmata
60.18 17
62 48, 275
71.6 17
72 248
74–75 35
74.24–35 239, 285
74.24–75.8 185
75 248
75–76 248
78 14, 28, 30, 307, 340
78.9 17
79 29
80 29, 30
81–82 268
83 99
83.15–19 137
84.19–24 88
85 35
85.29–31 185, 285
86–87 29
87 66
89 66–67, 270
96 89, 149, 168
98 168, 175, 204, 262
99 150, 170
101.10–103.2 239
103 89
106.1 281

107P 48, 68, 275
107P–108P 48, 275
109 44
110 14, 44, 46, 57
110P 89
111 59
112 22
118 69, 155

Varro
De lingua latina
7.44 129

Virgil
Aeneid
1.341–72 155
2.254–60 155
3.65 129
5.705–39 155
6 50, 327
8.152–69 187

Georgica
1.467 339

Xenophon
Hellenica
2.3.43 185

Memorabilia
1.2.49–55 230

Xenophon of Ephesus
An Ephesian Tale of Anthia and Habrocomes
1.2 129
3.5 129

ANONYMOUS ANCIENT WORKS
Homeric Hymns
2.176–78 129

Life of Aesop
3 246

Passion of Perpetua and Felicity
20 129

De physiognomonia (Anonymous Latin)
20 194
126 172
128 66

Res gestae divi Augusti
16 313

Rhetorica ad Alexandrum
1438a.28–31 29
1446b.36–38 110

Rhetorica ad Herennium
1.8.14 88
1.9.15 29
3.2.3 30
4.13.19 134, 146, 174, 199
4.14.21 193, 199
4.15.21 200, 211, 270, 298
4.15.22 66, 92, 98, 106, 153, 190, 196, 212, 226, 229, 258, 323
4.17.24 136
4.18.38 310
4.22.30–31 239
4.23.33–24.34 179, 292
4.26.36 269
4.28.38 138, 183, 225, 314, 333
4.28.39 153
4.30.41 319
4.32.43 36, 47
4.33.44 41, 103, 270, 328
4.36.48 326
4.39.51 9
4.42.54 201
4.43.56 203
4.45.59–48.61 313
4.49 179
4.49.62 197, 220
4.50.68 69
4.52.65 67, 270
4.54.68 137, 331
4.55.68 155